Macintosh Revelations

SECOND EDITION

KEN MAKI

WILEY COMPUTER PUBLISHING

John Wiley & Sons, Inc.

New York • Chichester • Weinheim • Brisbane • Singapore • Toronto

To Sara Eliana bet Avraham,
What a journey! Thank you for sharing it.
Baruch Hashem.
Akiva ben Avraham

Publisher: Robert Ipsen
Editor: Cary Sullivan
Assistant Editor: Kathryn Malm
Managing Editor: Angela Murphy
Electronic Products, Associate Editor: Mike Sosa
Text Design & Composition: Electric Ink, Ltd.

Designations used by companies to distinguish their products are often claimed as trademarks. In all instances where John Wiley & Sons, Inc. is aware of a claim, the product names appear in initial capital or all capital letters. Readers, however, should contact the appropriate companies for more complete information regarding trademarks and registration.

This text is printed on acid-free paper.

This publication is designed to provide accurate and authoritative information in regard to the subject matter covered. It is sold with the understanding that the publisher is not engaged in rendering professional service. If expert assistance is required, the services of a competent professional person should be sought.

Library of Congress Cataloging-in-Publication Data:

Maki, Ken.
    Macintosh revelations / Ken Maki, — 2nd ed.
        p.   cm.
    Includes index.
    ISBN 0-471-19563-4 (pbk./CD-ROM)
    1. Macintosh (Computer)   I. Title.
QA76.8.M3M3625   1998
004.165—dc21   97-37449

Printed in the United States of America
10 9 8 7 6 5 4 3 2 1

Acknowledgments

This is the Second Edition of Macintosh Revelations. I'm not sure I believe it is finally done. I always end up feeling that the book is one of those never ending projects. And this one was no exception.

There are so many people to thank, without whose help and support I wouldn't have been able to write this book: my family, wife, and friends, and lots of people in the Macintosh industry. Way too many to thank individually. So if I miss someone here I apologize now.

My wife, who has edited almost every page of this book, several times (she worked on the first edition too), while working a full time job of her own, deserves much of the credit for this book. Chris, without your help this book wouldn't have been done. Not only that, but I had to have been impossible to live with. "Thank you" doesn't even begin to say how I feel. I love you.

To my clients. There have been times that you didn't receive the service I felt you deserved because I was trying to juggle too many balls at the same time. Thank you for your patience and understanding. The book is done and it's back to my real job now.

To my editors, Cary Sullivan and Kathryn Malm, at John Wiley & Sons: You're both wonderful ladies. When I decided to take go to Haiti as my first deadline passed, I'm sure both of you were more than a little anxious. I've often wondered what "deadline" really means. I'm glad I didn't find out. You've been more than patient and, as always, encouraging and helpful. If not a little stern at times. Thank you many times over.

There are many people in the Macintosh community who've helped with software, hardware, advice, and support that I can't begin to name them all, so I'm going to thank everyone who helped in this blanket statement–you know who you are.

Additional thanks go to both BMUG and the Portland Macintosh Users Group (PMUG) for their support and help. BMUG was more than generous in putting together the CD-ROM included with this book, and my friends at PMUG who helped plug the holes I created when I couldn't fulfill all of my obligations because of my writing schedule.

And, of course, there is the production crew who physically made this a book: Angela Murphy was in charge of production and made sure the book got published, while Nancy Kruse Hannigan, the copy editor, made sure my grammar was not too atrocious. And, finally, Karl Barndt of Electric Ink did the typesetting and layout. Thank you all.

Finally, I want to thank my family again. Without their support and understanding, I'd still be writing the first chapter.

Contents

CHAPTER 5

Keeping Track of Your Data 107

PART II THE MACINTOSH SYSTEM

CHAPTER 6

Getting the Most from Your OS 143

CHAPTER 7

System Enhancements 195

CHAPTER 8

Customizing Your System 235

CHAPTER 9

Installing Your System and Software 253

PART III GETTING THE MOST FROM YOUR MAC'S DISK DRIVES

CHAPTER 10

Macintosh Disk Drives 279

CHAPTER 11

Essential File, Disk, and Data Information   327

PART IV   COMMUNICATIONS AND NETWORKING

CHAPTER 12

Reaching the Outside World   363

CHAPTER 13

Networking for the Beginner 395

CHAPTER 16

Common Macintosh Problems **503**

CHAPTER 17

Macintosh Hardware Problems **523**

CHAPTER 18

System and Application Troubleshooting   549

CHAPTER 19

Disk Crashes and Data Recovery   569

Introduction

I'm flabbergasted. A book that I wrote sold well enough the first time around to be turned into a second edition. It's a shame that computer books go out of date so quickly. But *Macintosh Revelations* lasted longer than some other books do. And this edition should be good for a couple of years, too. We have produced a second edition because Apple has released a new version of its operating system (the software that makes the Mac work), Mac OS 8. Enough changes had been made to the old version of the operating system that the first edition of *Revelations* was getting a bit moldy. Hence, the second edition of *Macintosh Revelations*.

In the Introduction to the first edition of *Revelations*, I talked about how amazed I was that I written the book. I guess I'm just as surprised at the second edition. If it weren't for computers and the Macintosh, I'd never have written a single book. But, I'm not so special.

I've written a book about the Mac. It is only because the Mac is an enabling tool that this book was written in the first place. And tools like the Mac should be used to their fullest. I guess this is the message or the purpose of this book. I want everyone to have the ability to do what they thought was impossible. Learning how to get the most from your Mac is one way that you can achieve some of your goals and maybe even fulfill a dream.

Macintosh Revelations is not your usual computer book. Most Macintosh books try to tell you everything there is to know about the Macintosh, its software, and everything to which it connects. You find copious amounts of information that you then have to decipher, and usually, only a small amount of the information in the book applies to you or your computing needs. In *Macintosh Revelations*, you won't find instructions for using every major program written for the Mac or charts of Macintosh models with their technical specifications. These mundane details about the Mac are helpful, but they miss a very important point. They don't teach you *how* to use your Mac; they only *tell* you about it.

This book is designed to teach you how your Mac works and how to use *any* Macintosh program. It begins with the assumption that you don't know anything about computers or the Macintosh, and it ends by providing you with the principles you need to correct problems you might encounter.

No magic is involved in learning to use a Mac; it is work. But if you take the time to learn what is in the second edition of *Macintosh Revelations*, you may never need to buy another Macintosh book. You'll have the knowledge you need to figure out how new software works, and you'll have what you need to get the most from your Mac.

This Book Is for

Anyone, both the beginner and experienced user, who is perplexed about his or her Macintosh. If you're tired of using just one or two programs and want to do more with your Mac, the second edition of *Macintosh Revelations* will help you. If you're new to computing and to Macintoshes, you are holding a book that explains and teaches you what you need to know. If you want to learn about your Mac from a more conceptual point of view, *Macintosh Revelations* can help. For the more advanced Mac user, the most valuable aspect of this book is the accompanying CD-ROM. This in itself is worth more than the cost of the book; you can read about the CD-ROM in Appendix B.

How to Use This Book

How you use *Macintosh Revelations* is up to you and your experience with computers or the Mac. The second edition of *Macintosh Revelations* progressively moves you from one level of knowledge to the next by giving you a solid understanding about all aspects of your Mac. This is not a technical reference—you won't find your Macintosh model in here. This is a book that begins by assuming you know nothing about computers, and it ends by showing you how to perform tasks for which most people hire consultants. It could put me out of a job.

Here is a brief summary for each chapter of the second edition of *Macintosh Revelations*:

Part I   Introducing the Macintosh

In this part of the second edition of *Macintosh Revelations*, you learn what a computer is, how to set it up, and how to use it.

Chapter 1   How Your Macintosh Computer Works—This chapter is about computers in general. You learn about the parts of a computer, what they are, and how they function. It is a technical description of your Macintosh in nontechnical terms.

Chapter 2   Macintosh Beginnings—Here you learn how to set up and turn on your Mac. This chapter familiarizes you with the actual computer.

Chapter 3   Using Your Macintosh—In this chapter you learn the basics for using your Mac. The first time someone turns on a Mac, he or she is confronted with an amazing number of issues. This chapter explains what you need to know to start using a Mac.

Chapter 4   Using Macintosh Software—All Macintosh programs use the same principles. This chapter uses a program that comes with every Macintosh to teach you those principles and lays the groundwork for using any other Macintosh program.

Chapter 5   Keeping Track of Your Data—Computers are used to create and store information. If you don't know where the information is, it is not much use. This chapter teaches you how to store your information so that you can easily find it when you need it.

Part II   The Macintosh System

In this part of *Macintosh Revelations*, you find out all about what makes your Macintosh work. Every computer has a system; this is your guide to the Macintosh's system.

Chapter 6   Getting the Most from Your OS—This chapter is an in-depth exploration of what makes your Mac work the way it does. By exploring the operating system (OS), you learn a lot about your Mac in general.

Chapter 7   System Enhancements—This chapter explains some of the new and more complex aspects of the Mac OS 8. You are introduced to Apple's new technologies and, at the same time, you learn more about your Mac's capabilities.

Chapter 8   Customizing Your System—Now you can begin to truly make your Mac your own. With the information in this chapter and the contents of the *Revelations* CD-ROM, you have the ability to customize every aspect of how your Mac works.

Chapter 9   Installing Your System and Software—If you know how to install your Mac's System software, you know how to install most programs you encounter. Knowing how to install the Mac OS is something you need to know if you ever have trouble with your Mac; it is like knowing how to change a tire on a car.

Part III   Getting the Most from Your Mac's Disk Drives

Once you've learned about how the Mac's software works, you might want to know more about the hardware. This part provides you with more technical information about the Mac itself. By understanding what is in these chapters, you can become a salesperson's nightmare.

Chapter 10   Macintosh Disk Drives—This chapter has everything you ever wanted to know about disk drives—and more. You learn what disk drives are and why they are important to you.

Chapter 11   Essential File, Disk, and Data Information—Your disk drives hold all your information. This chapter talks about your information and provides tips for keeping it safe.

Part IV   *Communications and Networking*

Connecting your Macintosh to other computers and the outside world is something that you will eventually want to do. This part of *Macintosh Revelations* provides you with the basic information you need to accomplish this task.

Chapter 12   Reaching the Outside World—This chapter is about using your Macintosh with a modem. It tells you how to set up your software so that you can communicate with other computers or information services.

Chapter 13   Networking for the Beginner—In the office, you might need to connect your Macintosh to other Macs to exchange information. This chapter explains how to do this.

Chapter 14   Surfing the Net—Do you want to get connected to the Internet? How do you make sense of the jargon? This chapter gets you connected and gives you your first surfing lesson. And if you are adventurous, you will get past the onramp and onto the Information Superhighway (that's what some call it, I prefer the Internet).

Part V   *Troubleshooting*

Troubleshooting is the process of determining what is wrong with your Macintosh. Yes, Macs do have problems from time to time. In this part of the book, you find the information you need to fix almost any Macintosh problem. Read this part before you need it.

Chapter 15   Avoiding Problems—This chapter talks about maintenance and how to avoid trouble, which means Macintosh problems. If you follow the guidelines in this chapter, you may never need the other four chapters in this part of the book.

Chapter 16   Common Macintosh Problems—It's fright night. If you want to know what can go wrong with your Mac, read this chapter. If something does go wrong with your Mac, read this chapter. Knowing the problem is the first step toward fixing it.

Chapter 17   Macintosh Hardware Problems—This chapter helps you decide if you have a software problem or a problem with the physical Macintosh. It also helps you determine what type of problem you have.

Chapter 18   System and Application Troubleshooting—When your Mac is misbehaving, you have to straighten it out. This chapter provides detailed steps for restoring your Macintosh to its proper operating conditions.

Chapter 19   Disk Crashes and Data Recovery—When things go wrong, you may need to know how to retrieve your information. This is the chapter you need if you ever must recover your data when it seems hopeless. Don't despair; all is not lost.

Appendix A   Finder Shortcuts—In Appendix A is a list of Macintosh shortcuts that help you use your Macintosh more efficiently, if you choose to use them. After you've read the first part of *Macintosh Revelations*, review these shortcuts and experiment with them.

Appendix B   BMUG's Macintosh Revelations CD-ROM—This appendix contains a brief description of the files and programs on the BMUG *Revelations* disc. This is really a remarkable collection of programs, utilities, and other types of files. This CD-ROM from the Berkeley Macintosh Users Group is a wonderful resource.

The BMUG Macintosh Revelations *CD-ROM*

This is a special CD-ROM prepared by the BMUG for inclusion with *Macintosh Revelations*. The CD-ROM contains more than 600 megabytes of programs, pictures, and utilities. The CD-ROM gives you the opportunity to customize and learn about your Mac without spending any extra money. Enjoy.

Contacting the Author

The author can be contacted at the following e-mail address:

Internet   kmaki@sysmc.com

How Your Macintosh Computer Works

Introduction

A lot of you will think I'm joking when I say that when you buy a Macintosh computer, you've purchased the most innovative and easy-to-use computer available. Every new Mac comes from the box ready to work for you—with a little bit of practice, you'll soon be creating letters, reports, and graphics; cruising the Internet; and doing almost everything else you want a Mac to do.

I did say "a little practice," didn't I? I don't mean to be discouraging, but the Macintosh is a powerful tool, and you have to learn how to work with it. At first, all kinds of things (icons and menus and other things) on the screen may not make sense to you. As you start to explore, things may happen that you don't understand. And even though you're convinced that you're the cause of these happenings, you're not quite sure *how* you caused them. You may even think that your Mac is living its own life and not really reacting to your instructions. Well, I'm here to tell you otherwise. Your Macintosh is actually behaving just as it should (in most cases), and you are not crazy.

If you've ever wondered how your Macintosh works (in a general sense), then this chapter is for you. If you are an experienced Mac user, you may be tempted to skip this chapter because you'll assume it is too elementary. You might want to reconsider. I recommend that you read this chapter unless you can answer the following questions:

❖ What is a computer?
❖ What are the two tasks that a computer does?
❖ What is binary code or representation?
❖ What are the two meanings of CPU?
❖ What is the difference between RAM, ROM, and disk space?
❖ And what is the difference between a bit, byte, kilobyte, and megabyte?

If you're new to the Mac, or if you don't know the answer to even one of the above questions, you should read this chapter. Now, you may be thinking, "Why do I have to know these things? All those technical terms are arcane and belong in computer voodoo land, not in my head. If I wanted to know this stuff, I would have a degree in computer science or electronic engineering." I know where you're coming from, but believe me, sooner or later you'll need to know this stuff. By learning it now, you'll be well on the road to using your Mac to its fullest potential.

Not knowing your Mac is like not knowing your car's capabilities. If you didn't know that you could drive your car thousands of miles, you would not use it to make a cross-country trip. To make that trip you also need to know about maintaining your car, getting the fuel it needs, reading a road map, and the rules of the road.

To take your Mac on a similar trip, you need to know the basics of how your Mac works. You won't get all of this information from this first chapter, but this chapter is the beginning of the journey. In this chapter, you learn about computers in general—what a computer is and how it works. The intention here is to make you comfortable with your Mac. If you know what the Mac is doing and how it is doing what it does, then you will be in control.

Just What, Exactly, Is a Computer?

Although you don't read books about your car in order to use it, if you think for a moment, you'll realize that you know quite a bit about your car, cars in general, the automobile industry, and the infrastructure that supports your car. Now you need to learn some comparable information about your Macintosh. The first place to start is not with the Macintosh, but with computers in general. After all, your Mac is just a computer.

All the cars on the road today have many similarities that you could easily name (they all have steering wheels, gas pedals and brakes, an engine that needs oil and gas, etc.). Likewise, every computer you see shares many similarities. The rest of this section discusses topics that apply to all computers. If you already know how a computer works, you may want to skip this section. If you're not sure, read on.

Whatever you may think of your Macintosh, it's just a tool. There is nothing mystical or supernatural about a Mac (or any computer), just as there is nothing magical about your car. The only thing that makes a car special is what it can do for you. Regardless of what you do with your Mac, remember that it is only a tool.

Computers are used to perform complex tasks that would take hours, months, days, and years to do by hand. But a computer can do only what it has been told to do and nothing else. Your car can't take off by itself and drive around the block; similarly, your Mac can't do anything it hasn't been told to do. Let's look at this tool and see how it really works.

Hardware versus Software

To understand your Macintosh, you have to know a little bit about its separate parts, how they work and interrelate. Your Mac is a combination of physical components and the instructions that tell the physical components what to do. The physical part of the computer is called *hardware*, and the instructions are its *software*.

Hardware   The physical components of your computer, including the monitor, keyboard, mouse, disk drives, and memory.

Software   Word processors, spreadsheets, games, Mac OS 8, and other sets of instructions that tell the computer's hardware what to do.

Everything a computer does is the direct result of its software (and you) telling it what to do. Software is written to work with specific hardware. Software written for the Macintosh will require Macintosh or Macintosh-compatible hardware, while software written for some other type of computer will not run on your Mac, unless your Macintosh has been specifically configured to use it. (See the note "Running Non-Macintosh Software on Your Mac.")

What makes software so difficult to understand is that you never see it. All you see are its results—what it makes your computer do. This is why people think computers are more than a tool. Software is like music on an LP, a CD, or a cassette tape. You never see the actual music, but you hear it when it is played on the appropriate device. Just as your CD player does not work without a CD, your computer will not work without software. Think of the software as the music and the computer as the stereo.

Understanding how your Mac uses software and hardware is the next step in the process of understanding your computer. Before you continue, however, familiarize yourself with Figure 1.1.

How a Macintosh Works

Because the basic function of your Macintosh, or any computer, is to process data, understanding how your Macintosh processes data is one of the most important computing fundamentals you can know. Knowing what your Mac is doing in a general sense can help you later on when you may start to think that there has to be an easier way to do something. All computers process data using the same principles. This section will look at how a computer processes this stuff called data.

Running Non-Macintosh Software on Your Mac

This may sound confusing, but you should know that the Macintosh does have the ability to run software made for other computers. Making the Macintosh act like some other type of computer is an advanced Macintosh topic, explained in Chapter 11, "Essential File, Disk, and Data Information."

Figure 1.1   *A basic Macintosh system.*

Some Really Technical Stuff

When a computer processes data it performs one of two actions: adding or comparing numbers. Everything your computer does is a result of these processes, regardless of how complicated the task. Your computer adds and compares so quickly that it can use the results to manipulate any data you put into it.

The best way to understand how you computer adds and compares is to look at a simple example that demonstrates the basic concept of multiplying numbers. When the command to multiply 10 by 12 is put into the computer, the computer stores the numbers 10, 0, and 0. The numbers are stored in registers, which are special temporary storage sections. One register is set to 10 and will not change, and the other two are set to 0 (see Figure 1.2).

The computer then puts 12 into register B and 1 into register C. The registers now read 10, 12, and 1. The computer then compares the registers with 10 (A) and 1(C) to see if they are equal. Because they are not equal, the computer adds 12 and 1

continues

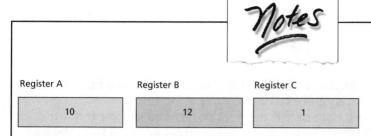

Figure 1.2 *The registers.*

to the two variable registers and performs the compare function again. This process is repeated until register C equals 10. Once register C equals 10, register B will equal 120. The computer has just multiplied 10 by 12. Figure 1.3 illustrates this process.

Every function of a computer is based on this principle. This is not to say that computers can't perform complex functions; it is just the process a computer uses,

continues

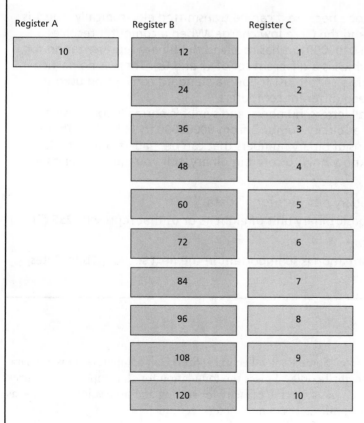

Figure 1.3 *The add and compare process.*

reduced to a simple explanation. Remembering this computing fact will help you later when the overall process gets more complex.

Your computer can process data only if the data possesses a specific format. Every time information is put into your computer, it is translated into a form the computer can use. This translation process occurs with all information or data put into a computer, even though you'll never see it happen. If the computer encounters a type of data that it cannot translate, the computer cannot process the data.

The computer turns all information into a series of 1s and 0s, *regardless of how the information looks to you*. These 1s and 0s are a code that can be used to represent all the letters of the alphabet and numbers. This method of representation is called *binary code*.

Binary   A numbering system with a base of two. All binary numbers are represented using two digits: 0 and 1.

Computers use binary code because it can be transmitted electronically. The 1 is a high charge of electricity, and the 0 is a low charge. When a computer receives a series of 1s and 0s that equal 01000001, it has received the binary representation for the letter "A" (not an "a," which is a different set of 1s and 0s). There is no particular reason why 01000001 equals "A"; it just follows a standard convention used to exchange information between different computers.

The computer equates all letters, numbers, and symbols normally found on a typewriter (plus a few more) as binary numbers from 00000000 to 11111111. There are 256 different combinations of binary numbers that can be made from eight 0s and 1s. You do not need to know how to count in binary, but you must understand the following:

❖ The computer uses binary numbers for all data.

❖ All computers use a basic binary unit of eight 1s or 0s that represent 256 different combinations.

You'll see why this information is so important in the next section, "Bits, Bytes, and More."

Bits, Bytes, and More

As discussed in the note "Some Really Technical Stuff," all computers translate data into binary units of eight 1s or 0s. This is the foundation for all computing measurements. Every computer has a specific capacity for storing and processing data. Just as we can measure space or distances in millimeters, centimeters, meters, and kilometers, specific terms are used for measuring the amount of space in a computer. These terms are bit, byte, kilobyte, megabyte, and gigabyte.

Bit   Abbreviation of binary digit, either a 1 or a 0

Byte   8 bits

Kilobyte   1024 bytes

Megabyte   1024 kilobytes

Gigabyte   1024 megabytes

The smallest possible data unit is a *bit* and equals one 1 or 0 (a single binary element). The next unit is a *byte*, which is eight 1s or 0s. The byte is the smallest binary unit because a byte can represent a letter, number, or symbol. With computing measurements, the next larger unit is always 1024 of the preceding unit. Following this rule, the next unit is a kilobyte, which is 1024 bytes. A megabyte is 1024 kilobytes, and a gigabyte is 1024 megabytes.

Hardware

Figure 1.4 shows basic computer hardware so that you can easily identify the different parts. The parts of the computer system shown in Figure 1.4 will be explained in the following sections.

Let's first discuss the internal parts of your computer:

❖ Logic board
❖ Processors
❖ Power supply
❖ Memory

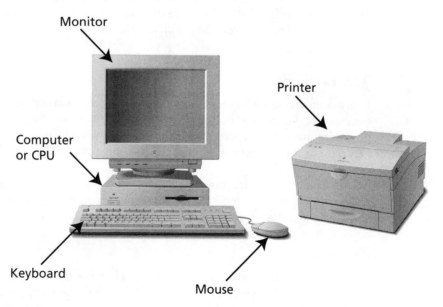

Figure 1.4   A typical computer.

Inside a Macintosh Quadra 900 or 950

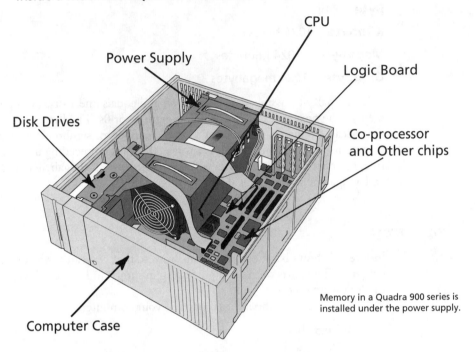

Figure 1.5   *The guts of a typical computer.*

Figure 1.5 shows the inside of a computer. Although computers now have disk drives inside the CPU, disk drives are discussed later in a section called "Storage Devices." Hold tight—everything will be covered.

The Logic Board

Every computer has a logic board (sometimes called a motherboard), which is a large circuit board inside your computer (see Figure 1.6). Your computer's memory, processor, and other important chips are plugged into the logic board. In fact, all the hardware in your computer either is directly plugged into the logic board or is connected to it by cables.

You won't need to deal directly with the logic board very often. What you really need to know are the computer's specifications (processor speed, memory size, and so on) and what they mean.

The Processors

Attached to the logic board are your computer's processors. Your computer can have a number of processors, but first we'll discuss the primary processor, called the Central Processing Unit (CPU). The CPU is the "engine" of your computer. It takes

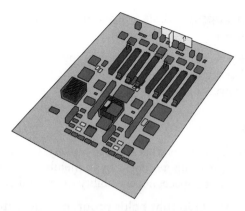

Figure 1.6 *A logic board.*

data, combines it with instructions from you and your software, and produces the results you want. The CPU organizes flow of information inside your computer; the faster your CPU, the faster your Macintosh will run. A CPU's speed is rated in megahertz (MHz)—the higher the MHz rating, the faster the CPU.

Megahertz   Millions of cycles per second, a rating used to identify the speed of many computer components. The higher the megahertz rating, the faster the component.

What makes a CPU powerful is the number of transistors it contains. The original CPU in the first Mac had about 68,000 transistors; the newest Macs produced today have CPUs with 2.8 million transistors. Currently, the number of transistors doubles from one generation of processor to the next, which occurs about once every two years. Doubling the number of transistors, however, results in computing power that is about four times that of the previous generation.

Although a processor doesn't do much more than add and compare numbers, as CPUs get more complicated this basic function is enhanced so that computers can perform complex processing operations, allowing the CPU to process data more efficiently and quickly. To explain in detail how the CPU works would require that you and I both have advanced degrees in electronic engineering—and even then it would be pretty tough. Just remember that a CPU works by juggling lots of numbers really quickly.

There are also several types of coprocessors, which are like turbo-chargers for an engine. Coprocessors help the CPU run faster by doing some of its work. Your Macintosh might have a math coprocessor (FPU), a paged memory management unit (PMMU), and a digital signal processor (DSP). Coprocessors are used to assist the CPU in performing certain functions.

Power Supply

Your Mac must convert the power it receives from the electrical outlet in the wall into power it can use. This task is done by the Mac's power supply.

Power Supply   A step-down transformer that reduces the voltage for the computer.

The power supply, which resides inside the CPU case, can be compared to your car's alternator or (in older cars) its generator. If something goes wrong with your Mac's power supply, your Mac will not work.

Memory

Every computer has what is called *memory*. Computer memory is not like human memory; the computer does not "remember" anything. Think of memory of as storage or working space, not the ability to remember and recall information.

Memory   Chip that holds programs and data either temporarily, Random Access Memory (RAM), or permanently, Read Only Memory (ROM). Many people confuse memory with hard drive space. Memory indicates how much software and data your computer can manipulate at one time while it is running. Hard disk space indicates how much software and data your computer can store permanently.

The two types of memory in your computer are Random Access Memory and Read Only Memory, called RAM and ROM. Although similar, each type of memory has a different function.

The best way to describe how memory works is to compare it to post office boxes. Post office boxes are arranged in rows, and each box can contain mail. Computer memory has a similar arrangement, only each slot, or individual post office box, holds an electronic charge. Each slot is one bit of computer data that the CPU checks to see if the bit is on or off.

The more memory you have in your computer, the more boxes you have to store bits. The average Macintosh today comes with 16 Megabytes (16MB) of RAM (and up to 8MB of ROM). This means that the computer will have 134,217,728 bits of RAM. Because it takes 8192 bits to equal one page of printed material, we're talking about 16,384 pages. This is a lot of space.

When your computer is working, it loads its system software and any programs you're using into RAM. The programs, in turn, load your data into RAM so that they can manipulate it. It is up to the CPU to keep track of where all this data (system software, programs, and the data manipulated by the programs) is in memory and to access it properly. It is a complex process.

One important thing you need to remember about RAM is that its contents are temporary. When the power to your Macintosh is turned off, anything in RAM is lost and gone forever. RAM needs the power supplied by your computer to operate. Also, any data at any place in RAM can be quickly changed.

ROM is structured just like RAM except that the data held in ROM is permanent and does not change. Your computer uses the data in ROM, which is actually part of the system software, to operate. (It is possible to put all the system software in ROM, but if that were done, using new system software when it is created would be impossible without changing the Mac's ROM. For this reason the ROM contains only some of the Macintosh's system software.)

All the data in memory can be accessed very quickly. Memory, however, is not the only means your computer has of storing data. Memory should not be considered as true storage: It is the space your Mac uses while it's doing its work, much as you use the top of your desk.

When you're working at your desk you place the things you'll be using—pens, paper, books—on your desk. Your tools are the same as the software and data your Mac loads into RAM. As you continue to work, you put more things on your desk. Eventually your desk gets so full that you can't continue to work without putting some of the material away, back into drawers, cupboards, and file cabinets.

The same thing happens with your computer. As RAM fills up, it becomes necessary to put away some of what is in RAM but is not being used. This data will be kept on a more permanent storage medium, and the computer will retrieve it from storage when it is needed. This entire process is called *memory management*.

The quantity of RAM you can put into your computer will depend on the model of Macintosh you have (this information can also be found in Chapter 11). The primary points you need to know about memory are these:

❖ Memory is a form of storage space.

❖ RAM is the space your computer uses to do its work.

❖ The contents of RAM disappear when your computer is turned off, and new data is put into RAM when it is turned on.

❖ ROM is permanent storage space for some of your Mac's system software.

Other particulars about memory will be discussed as the need arises throughout the rest of the book.

Peripherals

Any device that is connected to your computer is called a peripheral device. Peripheral devices are anything and everything except the cables used to connect the devices to the CPU. A peripheral device name usually describes its function.

Peripheral Device   Any hardware device that is connected to your Macintosh, other than the CPU.

The remainder of this section will talk about some of the peripheral devices you'll find attached to computers. I will first discuss storage devices, then input and output devices.

Storage Devices

The best way to understand computer data storage is to look at a little bit of computer history. The history lesson may have the added value of giving some perspective to this discussion of computers. Technical information about disk drives can be found in Part III, "Getting the Most from Your Mac's Disk Drives."

Regardless of how fast your CPU can process data, you first need a way to put the data into the computer quickly. To truly make it useful, you need a way to store the data so that you can reuse it. In the early days of computing, paper ticker tape and punch cards were used to input data into computers, and the output device was almost always a printer.

It didn't take long for users to realize that those punch cards and reams of printer paper were inadequate. First, hardware engineers developed tape drives and used them for both input and data storage. Using tapes, however, became inefficient as computers became faster. Tape drives could not access data fast enough. To meet new needs for speed, hardware engineers developed very large disk drives.

The first disk drives were the size of four metal desks, two with their ends placed together and the other two stacked on top. The disk was a very large drum that rotated at about 200 revolutions per minute (RPMs), and it looked like the disks from very early phonographs. The disk drive stored data on magnetic material, and its total capacity was about 20 megabytes.

In the 1960s, engineers found a way to reduce the size of the disk drive to that of a small filing cabinet. IBM developed the first drive of this type; it had a 30-megabyte fixed disk and a 30-megabyte removable disk. The fixed disk was used as the working drive, and the removable disk was for data backup. IBM called it a 30-30, and it became known as a Winchester, after the rifle. The name "Winchester" hence became the designation for any drive that used the same technology as the fixed disk in the IBM drive.

Having a large hard drive solved only half the problem. Users still needed a convenient means for inputting data. Punch cards just didn't make it. It was the late 1970s that produced a floppy disk drive that used a disk made of heavy mylar with a ferrous oxide coating, similar to the coating used on recording tape. It was eight inches in diameter and held about 80KB. The disk was flexible, looked like a large LP record, and was called a floppy disk.

The technology used in floppy disks and drives has advanced to the point where all Macintoshes use a 3.5-inch floppy drive. Over the years the capacity of the 3.5-inch floppy has gone from 400 kilobytes to 1.44 megabytes. Even though floppy drive technology has progressed a long way, it has not stopped. The next generation of floppies will hold over 2 megabytes of data.

Hard drive technology has also continued to evolve. The same era that gave birth to the floppy also witnessed the miniaturization of the hard drive. By the early 1980s, hard drives became small enough for use with the new personal computers. A 20MB drive was 5.5 inches cubed and considered to be large enough to meet any computing need. The optimism evident at the beginning of the PC age rapidly gave way to the realities of the technology: Access to data creates more data, and there may never be a storage medium large enough.

Even today, depending on the type of work you do, your hard drive will probably soon be too small. Moreover, a drive that holds a gigabyte of data, which, by the way, is the same physical size as the first 20MB drives, will soon be too small. And speaking of small, the smallest drives today are the size of a pack of cigarettes and hold a gigabyte of data.

For the time being, what you need to know is that your Mac has both a floppy and a hard disk drive. The floppy disk is the primary means for inputting programs and exchanging data with other Macs. Your hard drive is for storing your data permanently so it can be quickly accessed by your Mac. You will learn a lot more about your hard drive in Chapter 5, "Keeping Track of Your Data."

Input and Output

Any piece of hardware that is used to put data into your computer is called an *input device*. Any piece of hardware that displays, prints, or otherwise moves data out of your computer is called an *output device*. And some hardware devices used for both inputting and outputting data are called *input/output devices*. Everything connected to your computer, except the CPU and cables, is either an input or an output device.

Figure 1.7 shows a complete computer system including a printer. Each device is labeled according to its function.

The following is a list of the hardware you're likely to have with your Mac, with each item described according to its function.

Device	Function	Description
Keyboard	Input	The keyboard is used to put typed information into your computer.
Mouse	Input	The mouse is used to give commands to your Mac.
Monitor	Output	It is on the monitor that you will see the results of what you have told your computer to do.

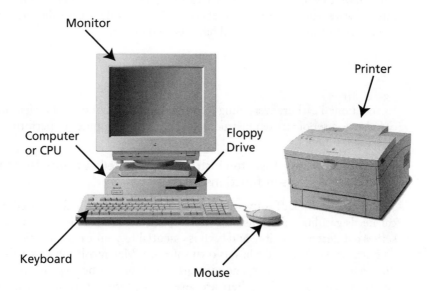

This computer does not have a CD-ROM drive and the hard drive is inside the CPU.

Figure 1.7 *A complete computer system.*

Device	Function	Description
Printer	Output	The printer delivers the results of your computer's work as printed information.
CD-ROM drive	Input	CD disks hold data that is read into your computer through the drive.
Modem	Input/output	A modem is used to connect your Mac to a telephone line, which the modem uses to send data from your computer to another one and to receive data from the other computer and place it into yours.
Hard and floppy disk drives	Input/output	The various types of disk drives are used to store data onto disks or read it from the disks that contain the data.

Although a few other devices can be used with a computer, this list covers the most important and frequently used input and output devices. Normally they are referred to by their names. The terms "input" and "output" are used to describe their basic function.

Driver   Software that allows a computer to access a peripheral device.

One very important thing you need to remember is that any device attached to your computer requires software before your Mac can receive data from or send data to the device. Usually this software is part of computer's system software, and so you won't have to worry about it. On occasion, though, you will be required to install this software. Any software that lets your Mac use a device is called a *driver*, and every input or output device will have its own driver.

Software

As mentioned earlier, everything a computer does is controlled by its software. *Software* is a set of written instructions that tells a computer to perform a function or a series of functions.

Software   A set of written instructions that tells a computer to perform a function or a series of functions.

You might think of software as being something like the fluids used in your car. A car needs gasoline, oil, transmission fluid, and hydraulic fluid. Each type of fluid serves a different function, and each is essential to your car's operation.

Each type of computer has its own software. Macintosh software will not run on a different type of computer, and software made for another type of computer will not run on a Macintosh. Next, there are several categories of software and several different types within each category. Although I will not discuss all the different types of software in this section, I will cover most of them in this book. The categories of software you need to know about right now are these:

❖ System software
❖ Application software
❖ Utility software

Something you should keep in mind when you think about software is that people write it. Computers do not tell themselves what to do—people tell computers what to do. No matter how complex and sophisticated the software may seem, it is still the result of human efforts.

System Software

Of all the software you possess, your system software is the most important. System software is what makes your computer work—like the oil in your car's engine.

System Software that controls the general operations of the computer. The Mac's system software is called the System.

The system software for any computer controls all the computer's basic functions and interacts with your application software. System software works in conjunction with the Mac's ROM at the time you start your Mac. The ROM contains the instructions that tell your Mac to start. After the Mac starts, it will go through a process called *loading the system*, during which time the software needed to operate all of the Macintosh's hardware is loaded into memory.

Once the System is loaded into memory, your Mac is a fully functioning computer, ready to run your application software. Figure 1.8 provides an example of how the Mac loads the System and application software.

The ROM is at the bottom of the chart with the System sitting on top of the ROM. The System is in RAM. After, or on top of, the System you will see the space in RAM where your applications fit into memory. When your application is loaded into RAM you can start doing work on your Mac.

6 Megabytes free

Free Memory for programs

2 Megabytes used for System Software

The Macintosh System Software

The ROMS

Figure 1.8   *How the System loads into memory.*

Part of the Mac's System is the software that provides you with the Mac's interface. The *interface* is what allows you to interact with the Macintosh; it serves the same function as the controls and instrument panel of your car.

Interface   The means by which you interact with a computer. Merriam Webster's dictionary defines interface as "the place at which independent and often unrelated systems meet and act on or communicate with each other."

Understanding your Mac's System and interface is critical to your success with the Macintosh. You will find that the System is a primary topic throughout this book. For the time being, however, what you really need to know is that your Mac system software allows the Mac to function and is needed to use any other program.

Application Software

The following list of major tasks represents most application software or programs you'll use. You may use software from several of these categories to do a project.

- ❖ Word processing
- ❖ Database
- ❖ Spreadsheets
- ❖ Communications
- ❖ Graphics
- ❖ Page layout
- ❖ Multimedia
- ❖ Other categories

Program   Software that you use to accomplish a task or tasks.

The rest of this section briefly describes each of these categories.

Word Processing

Word processing programs are used to create and modify written documents. Everything you do with a word processor has one goal: to make the creation of your written communications as easy and attractive as possible. Toward this end, most word processors check your spelling and grammar as well as provide tools for arranging or formatting the words you type. All the text for this book was written on a Macintosh using a word processing program.

Database

A database program allows you to keep collections of related data and easily organize and arrange the data for reports. A database program can be used for many things, such as keeping track of all your video cassettes, sales records, or employee information. Some database programs also let you create your own applications to meet special needs.

Databases are very powerful tools because they let you arrange your information in so many different ways. You view and manipulate selected samplings of data according to any specified criteria. For example, you could easily select all your customers from specific states or according to their purchasing histories. If you're using your Mac at home you can catalogue receipts, update auto records, or maintain a family mailing list.

Spreadsheets

Spreadsheet programs are used for any information that can be kept in rows and columns. If you have ever used columnar paper, you have used the equivalent of a spreadsheet. Spreadsheet programs do a lot more than let you store information in rows and columns (see Figure 1.9); you can add numbers across the rows and columns, make charts, and create reports with spreadsheets.

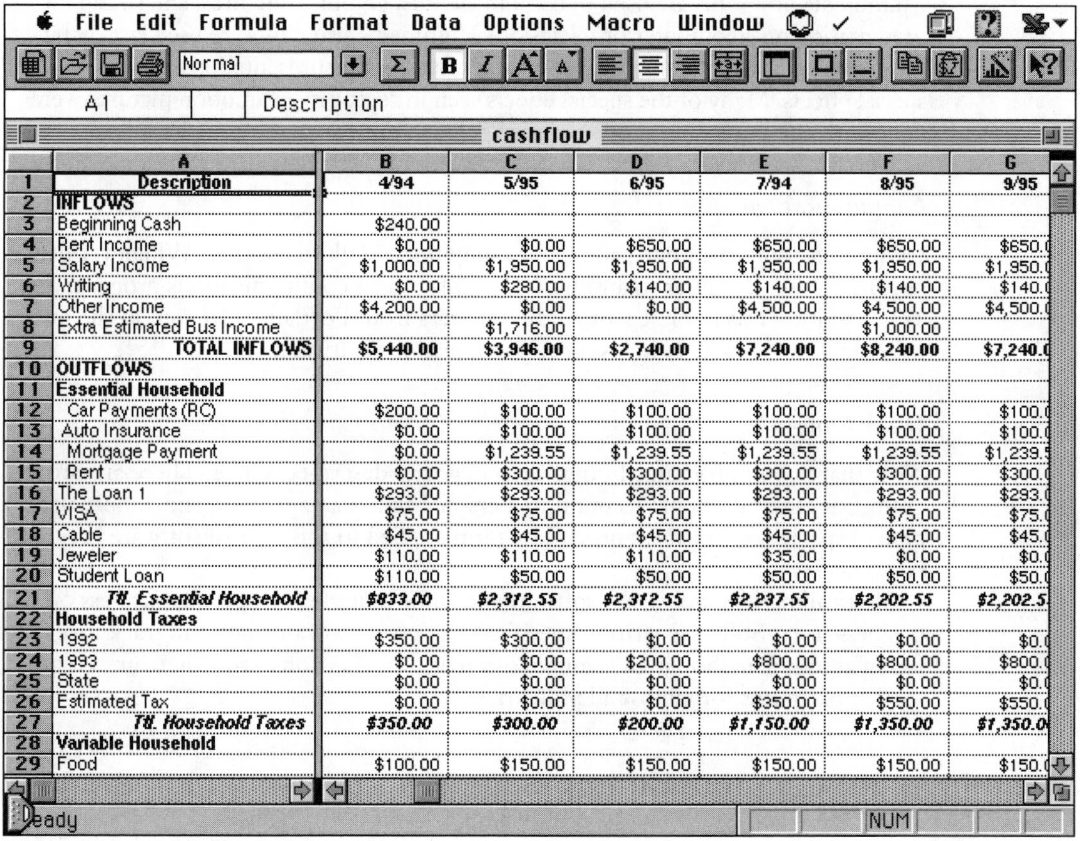

	A	B	C	D	E	F	G
	Description	**4/94**	**5/95**	**6/95**	**7/94**	**8/95**	**9/95**
2	**INFLOWS**						
3	Beginning Cash	$240.00					
4	Rent Income	$0.00	$0.00	$650.00	$650.00	$650.00	$650.0
5	Salary Income	$1,000.00	$1,950.00	$1,950.00	$1,950.00	$1,950.00	$1,950.0
6	Writing	$0.00	$280.00	$140.00	$140.00	$140.00	$140.0
7	Other Income	$4,200.00	$0.00	$0.00	$4,500.00	$4,500.00	$4,500.0
8	Extra Estimated Bus Income		$1,716.00			$1,000.00	
9	**TOTAL INFLOWS**	**$5,440.00**	**$3,946.00**	**$2,740.00**	**$7,240.00**	**$8,240.00**	**$7,240.0**
10	**OUTFLOWS**						
11	**Essential Household**						
12	Car Payments (RC)	$200.00	$100.00	$100.00	$100.00	$100.00	$100.0
13	Auto Insurance	$0.00	$100.00	$100.00	$100.00	$100.00	$100.0
14	Mortgage Payment	$0.00	$1,239.55	$1,239.55	$1,239.55	$1,239.55	$1,239.5
15	Rent	$0.00	$300.00	$300.00	$300.00	$300.00	$300.0
16	The Loan 1	$293.00	$293.00	$293.00	$293.00	$293.00	$293.0
17	VISA	$75.00	$75.00	$75.00	$75.00	$75.00	$75.0
18	Cable	$45.00	$45.00	$45.00	$45.00	$45.00	$45.0
19	Jeweler	$110.00	$110.00	$110.00	$35.00	$0.00	$0.0
20	Student Loan	$110.00	$50.00	$50.00	$50.00	$50.00	$50.0
21	**Ttl. Essential Household**	**$833.00**	**$2,312.55**	**$2,312.55**	**$2,237.55**	**$2,202.55**	**$2,202.5**
22	**Household Taxes**						
23	1992	$350.00	$300.00	$0.00	$0.00	$0.00	$0.0
24	1993	$0.00	$0.00	$200.00	$800.00	$800.00	$800.0
25	State	$0.00	$0.00	$0.00	$0.00	$0.00	$0.0
26	Estimated Tax	$0.00	$0.00	$0.00	$350.00	$550.00	$550.0
27	**Ttl. Household Taxes**	**$350.00**	**$300.00**	**$200.00**	**$1,150.00**	**$1,350.00**	**$1,350.0**
28	**Variable Household**						
29	Food	$100.00	$150.00	$150.00	$150.00	$150.00	$150.0

Figure 1.9 An example spreadsheet.

Graphics

Graphics programs are any software applications that let you create, manipulate, or view a picture of some type. These packages range from simple to very complex. Fifteen years ago almost every ad you saw was created by a graphic artist, working by hand. Now ads are created almost exclusively by computer. Even many of the graphics you'll see on the evening news were created with a computer. All the figures in this book were either created or modified using a graphics package.

Page Layout

Page layout programs are made specifically for combining what was done with a graphics program and a word processing program to make a single page, catalogue, or book. This way all of the document's parts (the text, notes, figures, and so on) can be easily and effectively combined to make a book. The pages for this book were created using a page layout package.

Multimedia

Multimedia programs are used to combine words, graphics, pictures, and sound for presentation on a computer or television. Multimedia programs are used largely by businesses, television, and movie companies for creating presentations, advertising, and special effects. Many of the special effects seen in recent major motion pictures were done with computers. A lot of animation is being done with multimedia software.

Communications

Communications programs allow one computer to talk to another. Whenever data is sent from one computer to another, it is sent using a communications program. While writing this book, I sent all the chapters from Portland, Oregon, to the publisher in New York City by using communications software.

Other Categories

Note that not all programs fit into the categories described above. There are programs for entertainment, accounting, personal time management, and almost any type of specialized business need. The term applied to this type of software is *vertical market software*.

Vertical market software is software made for a single and specific business or business need. Software written specifically to create work orders and track inventory for an auto repair shop is an example of vertical market software. There are vertical market programs for almost all industries.

Utility Software

Utility software can be equated to special-purpose fluids, such as hydraulic fluid, or the tools you would use to work on your car. Just like your car, your computer will require maintenance, inspections, and repairs. Often these tasks are done with software tools called *utility programs*.

Listing the different types of utility software would be like listing all the tools you could find in a garage. Rather than list or categorize utility software, I will discuss the various programs you'll need throughout the book where appropriate.

Summary

This chapter is intended as preparatory background information for using your Mac. You may have read this and decided that it is information you really don't need. Just reading it, though, may be enough to help you avoid some common pitfalls that computer users everywhere have encountered.

The most important things to remember are those stated at the beginning of the chapter:

1. A computer is stupid.
2. The computer cannot hurt you.
3. A computer does only what it has been told to do.
4. Unless you use a hammer on the computer, you cannot hurt it.
5. All computers are based on the same principles.

The second most important parts of the chapter are the sections about computer counting and data processing. If these concepts are still unclear, reread these sections. If you do not understand either of these concepts you will often find yourself confused as you work to figure out your Mac.

Macintosh Beginnings

Introduction

This chapter assumes that your experience with computers is minimal (none) and that you've just received your Mac. Even if this is not true and you really do have some experience with a Mac, you may want to read this chapter because it contains information that will make it easier for you to operate your Mac. You may even learn something you didn't know.

You must follow specific steps when setting up a Macintosh—these steps are outlined throughout the rest of this chapter. There are many ways to do the same tasks, and if you have experience with the Mac or with computers in general, you might find the steps presented here to be different from what you usually do. That's OK— what's important in this section is that you know everything you need to do to set up a Mac properly.

This chapter also has information that will help you fix many problems you may have with your Mac. You may think talking about problems is premature, but you'll find that most problems are easy to fix (and that you can actually avoid most problems) if you develop good Mac habits from the beginning.

Now, onward! Let's assume that you have a brand new Macintosh and you want to set it up and start using it.

Setting Up a Macintosh

It's a grand day when you bring home your first Macintosh. Some of us get excited even if it isn't our first Mac. Usually you would take the Mac out of its box, set it up, plug it in, and turn it on. Because this is your first Mac, you need to slow down and take your time while doing these steps. There is nothing confusing about what you're going to do, but there are some things you'll want to remember.

Where Will You Put It?

Before taking your Mac from the box, you need to have a place to put it; you probably thought about this before buying your Mac. In case your eagerness got the better of you, now is the time to consider the following points.

You'll want enough space to work comfortably. Just because your Mac will fit in a corner, it does not follow that you should necessarily put it there. You need to think about how much you will use the Mac and how many things you'll want close at hand (such as books and papers) while working on your Mac.

You'll need a three-prong (grounded) power outlet close to your Mac, but don't plug your Mac directly into the wall. Buy a surge protector and plug it into the wall, then plug your Mac into the surge protector. A surge protector is cheap insurance against lightning, electrical spikes, short circuits, and other hazards that can turn your Mac into a pile of smoking plastic.

Finally, you'll need at least a table and chair. If you can afford to do so, you might even consider getting a Macintosh computer workstation. If you do buy a

Leaving Your Mac On

Many people shudder at the idea of not turning off their computer, but there are good reasons for leaving it on 24 hours a day. The electrical components on the Mac's logic board and power supply expand as they get warm and contract as they get cold. The more often you turn your computer on and off, the more often the chips expand and contract, eventually wearing them out. Your hard drive is designed to be left on all the time (unless you are using a Macintosh Portable or PowerBook). Starting and stopping the hard drive every time you turn your Mac on and off is very hard on it.

Make sure you are using a very good surge protector. It should shut off if there is a brown-out (if your power drops below a predetermined voltage, all of the lights in a room or your house usually will dim when a brown-out occurs) and not come back on until you switch the power back on. Keep in mind that a power surge usually follows a brownout and that a power surge can really harm your Mac.

Many companies make good surge protectors. Look for one that comes with a guarantee to replace your computer equipment if it is damaged by a power surge. One company with this type of guarantee is PanaMax. DataShield also makes an excellent surge protector. but it does not offer a guarantee. Do not use an inexpensive power strip or surge protector; they are not up to the task of protecting thousands of dollars worth of Macintosh equipment.

computer workstation, make sure it will work with your Mac. Many workstations are made for IBM or IBM-compatible computers and do not work well with some Macs. Also, before you buy a workstation, read the section "Other Safety Considerations" later in this chapter.

Unpacking Your Mac

Once you know where you will put the Mac, all that's left is unpacking it. When you unpack your Mac, open each box by carefully cutting any tape on the flaps; you do not want to cut or mar the finish on your components. Take your time and when you're done, check to make sure that you didn't leave anything in the box. Also, don't throw the box away for awhile, just in case your Mac was damaged in shipping and needs to be returned. When you unpack your Mac, try to be organized and place similar items together. Keep all your manuals, disks, receipts, and packing slips together so that you will know where everything is when you need it.

Every Macintosh and peripheral has a packing list that details what should be in the box. Find this list and check off each item against what is in the box. If anything is missing, you will want to call the store where you purchased the equipment or the manufacturer.

Before you start to set up your Macintosh, unpack all the boxes, except for any software you might have purchased. With everything out of the box and organized, you can easily see how your Mac fits together.

A First Look at Your Mac

Now that you have made a mess of your space with boxes, hardware, manuals, and other sundry stuff, it is time to identify everything (if you haven't done so already). Figure 2.1 shows what most people get with the first Mac they buy.

Add ons

I mention some items here that I have not discussed, such as diskettes, microphones, and other items. Although these items are important, they require more than just a definition as an explanation. Over the course of the next three chapters, I will cover add-ons. Just be patient.

A Macintosh Quadra 840AV system.

Figure 2.1   *A complete Macintosh system.*

What Every Mac Should Have

When I discussed computers in general (Chapter 1), I said that you would need a CPU, monitor, and keyboard to have a functioning system. The same is true of your Mac. You should have the following components:

❖ Macintosh CPU, power cord, and mouse
❖ Monitor, power cord, and cable
❖ Keyboard and cable

If you do not have any of the above items, you cannot set up your Mac. If you purchased a printer, you should also have these components:

❖ The printer, power cord, and printer cable

You should make sure that any peripheral you purchase comes with the proper cable to connect it to your Mac and a power cord or adapter. Once you've confirmed that you have everything you need, you're ready to set everything up.

Because every Mac has the ability to record sound, it also comes with a microphone. The microphone is not required to make your Mac run, but you should find one in the box.

Putting Your Mac Together

By now, you might be thinking that you'll never get your Mac up and running. Hang in there; you're almost done. The next step is to put your Macintosh together but, before going through the actual setup, you should take a few minutes to become more familiar with your Mac. If you know what gets plugged in where before you start putting your Mac together, you'll find the setup process a lot easier.

The Macintosh's Ports

Whenever a peripheral device is connected to your Mac, it is plugged into a port. The first things to look for, therefore, are the ports on the back of your Macintosh.

Port   A socket on the Mac into which you plug other things (such as a mouse) so that they can communicate with your Mac.

Your Macintosh has several ports, usually located at the back of the Macintosh. Figure 2.2 shows all standard Macintosh ports. On some Macs, you'll find some of these ports duplicated, while others will have a single port that serves double duty.

Every Mac will have at least one of the ports described below. Each Macintosh port has a symbol associated with it, which is usually stamped on the CPU case above the port. The symbols are displayed next to each definition below. The number of ports will vary, depending on the model of Macintosh, but you can figure on at least one of each of the following (the only exceptions to this rule are all the Macintosh Duo computers).

The following are ports found on most Macintoshes:

⌨ *ADB (Apple Desktop Bus)   The connection used for keyboards, pointing devices (the mouse), and sometimes other devices, such as modems.

⇔ *SCSI or Small Computer System Interface (pronounced *SKUH-zee*) A standard interface that enables the Macintosh to connect a peripheral device, usually a hard disk drive.

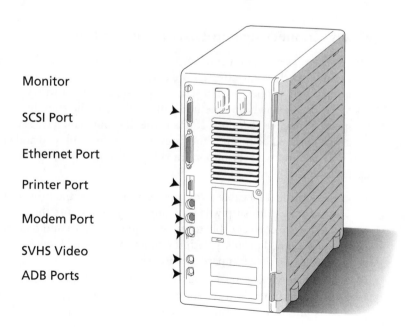

Monitor

SCSI Port

Ethernet Port

Printer Port

Modem Port

SVHS Video

ADB Ports

Figure 2.2   *The Macintosh's ports.*

✆ ***Serial**   A connector on the back of the Macintosh that enables the user to connect serial devices using a serial interface (also called a serial interface).

🖳 ***Printer/Apple Talk**   A serial port used for connecting the Macintosh to a network and/or a printer.

↔ **Ethernet**   An interface for connecting the Macintosh to other computers for the purpose of exchanging data (networking). Some printers can be connected to a Mac via the Ethernet port.

🎤 ***Sound In**   A connection for putting sound into a Mac from an external sound source, such as an external microphone.

◀» ***Sound Out**   A connector for attaching external speakers to a Mac. This port can also be used to send sound from the Macintosh to other devices that use sound input (such as a tape recorder).

▭ **Monitor**   The connector used to attach a monitor to a Macintosh.

▦ **Serial/Printer**   This port is found on only some Macintoshes, primarily PowerBooks, and is an AppleTalk or a serial port.

The ports marked with an asterisk (*) are standard on all Macintoshes, except for the Macintosh Duo. If your Mac does not have one of the ports listed above, it will be missing the Ethernet port or the monitor port if it has a built-in monitor or uses a PCI video card.

Safely Connecting and Disconnecting Devices

Simply stated, setting up your Mac is a matter of placing the hardware on a table or desk and properly connecting all the cords. Even the pros sometimes forget to connect everything properly when setting up systems. Don't worry if you make a mistake—just work slowly and methodically, following the steps in this section. There is no special sequence to follow. If this is the first time you have set up a system, use the sequence outlined below; it is the safest method for both you and your new equipment. There are two very important rules to follow whenever you connect peripheral cables to your Macintosh:

1. Never force a cable into a connection port. If the cable does not easily fit into the port, stop what you are doing. Make sure that you are trying to connect the correct cable to its corresponding port and that the pins in the cable are aligned properly with the holes in the port. Figure 2.2 shows the ports available on a standard Macintosh.

2. When connecting a cable between the CPU and a peripheral or between two peripherals, leave some slack in the cable. A taut cable that strains the connection port can damage the Mac, the peripheral, or both.

To set up your Macintosh:

1. Place the Macintosh CPU on the desk or table. It is possible to place some CPUs on the floor. If you place your Mac on the floor, next to or under your desk, you need to make sure that your cables can reach the CPU without being strained.
2. Attach the monitor, keyboard, and printer cables to the back of the CPU.
3. Position the Macintosh on the table so that you have room for the keyboard and mouse.
4. Attach the keyboard.
5. Attach the mouse to the keyboard. Some Macs have two ADB ports; in that case, you can use either port for the keyboard. You can also attach the keyboard in one port and the mouse in the other. Each ADB port will support up to five peripherals.
6. Place the monitor on top of the CPU or on your table (desk) top. If you place the monitor on the table, make sure the cable will reach from the CPU to the monitor.
7. Connect the cable to the monitor.
8. Attach the power cord to the monitor. Some monitor cords are designed to plug into the CPU, like the one shown in Figure 2.3. Also, some monitors

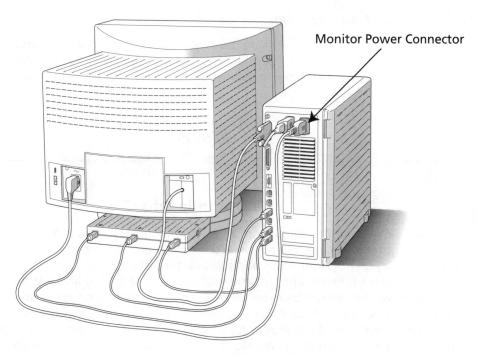

Monitor Power Connector

Figure 2.3   *A monitor power connector on a CPU.*

are designed to work the other way around—you plug the CPU's power cord into the monitor instead of plugging the monitor's power cord into the CPU.

9. Connect the monitor's power cable to the CPU if your CPU has the correct power connector. Otherwise, connect the monitor's power cable to your surge protector.

10. Attach the power cord to your printer.

11. Attach the power cord to your CPU.

12. Plug your surge protector into the wall; if it has an on/off switch, turn it off.

13. Plug the power cords from the CPU, printer, and monitor (if you're not plugging the monitor into the CPU) into the surge protector.

14. Turn on the surge protector.

15. Turn on the monitor's power switch. The power switch for each type of monitor is in a different location; examine your monitor to find the power switch and refer to its manual if necessary.

16. Turn on the power to the printer.

You're now ready to start your Macintosh. Before you do so, read the next section about safety considerations and the section entitled "Turning on Your Mac."

Other Safety Considerations

The table or desk you use for the Mac should be ergonomically correct. Figure 2.4 shows a person sitting in front of a computer in an ergonomically correct position. This consideration is a suggestion; you can work with your Mac in any position that

Ergonomic Info

Getting information about computer ergonomics is not easy. You'll find that every computer magazine will run an article about ergonomics a couple of times a year, but they do not offer much additional information.

Ergonomics is important, but you will find that designing and setting up an ergonomic workspace can be expensive. To find information on ergonomics, you should check with your local college, university, or public library. Computer manufacturers (including Apple) are increasingly aware of and are implementing ergonomic designs for their computers; if you do not use the computer to take advantage of its ergonomic design, however, the design will not help.

Figure 2.4 *An ergonomic workstation.*

is right for you. You do need to know about certain injuries, called repetitive stress injuries, caused by repeatedly performing the same movements. Computer usage has been associated with these types of injuries.

To prevent repetitive stress injuries, you should set up your Mac as shown in Figure 2.4.

You should be aware of the height of the keyboard and mouse in relation to your arms and hands. Your hands and forearms should be parallel to the ground as you work at the keyboard. If you are seated too high or low, you will begin to experience discomfort after working for only a short period of time. Figure 2.4 should be used for reference only; if you want more information about computer ergonomics, you should contact your local university or an ergonomics consultant.

Firing Up Your Mac for the First Time

Now it's time to start your Macintosh; this section is very important. You will learn some terms that are specific to the Macintosh and its operation. Anyone who uses a Mac without learning these terms will be at a serious disadvantage. He or she will not be able to talk to anyone technically about the Mac or what it is doing—making it difficult to get help over the phone or to understand manuals. I cannot stress enough how important it is to learn these basic terms.

Turning on Your Mac

Now, you should have your Mac set up with all of the cables connected. Everything should be plugged into the power source, and some of your devices should already be turned on. If you have any questions, repeat the steps in the section "Putting It All Together." Once everything is set up, all you have to determine is how your particular Mac is turned on.

Some Macintosh models can be turned on from the keyboard; others have to be turned on using the power switch. The best way to determine which type of Mac you have is to check the manual that came with it. You should find the instructions for turning it on somewhere near page 4 or 5 of your Macintosh manual.

If you wish to learn by experimentation, you can start by trying to turn on your Mac with the keyboard's power-on key. Every Macintosh keyboard, except for the PowerBooks, which cannot be turned on using the keyboard, has a power-on key. The keyboard's power-on key will have one of these two symbols (P or I) on it as well.

To start your Mac with the power-on key, just press the key. Depending on the type of keyboard you have, it could have a symbol like I or _ next to or on the power-on key. If pressing the power-on key does not turn on your Mac, your Mac may not support this feature or any of the following conditions may be present:

- ❖ The keyboard cord is not connected properly.
- ❖ The power cord is not plugged in.
- ❖ The surge protector is turned off.

If you are certain that the Mac should start with the power-on key, then you need to check the items listed above. Otherwise, you need to find your Mac's power switch. Wherever the power switch happens to be—on the front or the back of the CPU—it will have an I symbol next to or stamped on the switch. If you have any doubts, check your Macintosh manual; it will identify the exact location of your power switch.

Once you've found the power switch, just press it. As long as everything is connected properly, your Mac will start. When your Mac starts, you'll hear it start to whir, and the monitor will turn on. On the front panel of some Macintoshes, you might see a light come on as well.

As Your Mac Starts

As your Macintosh starts up, several things will happen on the screen. This sequence of events is called the *boot* process.

Boot   Another way to say *start up*. Starting up is often accomplished by first loading a small program that then reads a larger program into memory. The program is said to pull itself up by its own bootstraps—hence, the term *bootstrapping* or *booting*.

A complete and technical description of what the Mac does as it starts up can be found in Chapter 17. For now, all you need to know is that the Mac starts itself through a complicated process of checking its hardware and then loading the System into memory. Most of what takes place does so behind the scenes, but some visual indicators tell you that your Mac is starting up.

As your Mac starts, you see an image in the middle of the monitor. This image—and many others—are called *icons*. The icon you see as your Mac starts looks like this: ▣.

Icon   An image that graphically represents an object, a concept, or a message. Icons on the outside of the computer show you where to plug in cables, such as the disk drive icon on the back panel that marks the disk drive connector. Icons on the screen represent disks, documents, application programs, or other things.

The smiling Mac icon tells you that the Mac is starting up. The next image you'll see is a rectangle.

While the message "Welcome to Macintosh" is displayed on your screen, you may see more icons flash across the bottom of your screen, starting in the lower left corner. These icons represent software being loaded into your Mac's memory as it starts. Because all Macs come from the factory ready to run, you should have no problems starting your Mac.

If Things Go Wrong

Things can go wrong—your Mac may not start properly straight from the box. If this happens to you, read this entire section before you decide what to do.

Although rare, you might have problems immediately. If you do, you will have to decide whether to fix the problem yourself or take the Mac back to the store where you purchased it. If you are unfamiliar with computers and the Mac, you should probably box it up and take it back to the store. If this is not possible, you will have to figure out what is wrong and fix it. You could be in for quite a challenge at this point.

To attempt to get your Mac up and running:

1. Check all your cable connections.
2. Make sure the Mac is plugged in and that the outlet you're using has power. If you're unsure about the power outlet, plug a lamp into it to see if the outlet has power. Don't forget about any outlets that can be turned on by a wall switch.
3. Turn on the Mac again. If it starts, you're home free.
4. If it still doesn't start, call the store where you purchased the Mac to see if someone there can help.
5. If the store cannot help, call Apple's Technical Support at (800) SOS-APPL (767–2775). Apple Technical Support is open from 9:00 A.M. to 9:00 P.M. (Eastern Standard Time). The people who handle the calls are very good, but you might have to wait awhile to speak to a technician.

When a Mac does not start, it will often try to tell you why. The following list may help to determine what is wrong. This list is not a troubleshooting guide, but a quick list of what might be wrong, with some suggestions.

❖ If your Mac displays an icon that looks like ▣, call the store where you purchased the Mac. Tell the representative that you have a *Sad Mac icon* and make arrangements to take the computer back. Usually, this means that something is wrong with the computer itself.

❖ If your Mac displays the question mark icon (?), it means that your Mac cannot find a disk from which to start up. You will probably have to install the System software onto your hard drive before you can use the Mac. Instructions for doing this can be found in Chapter 6.

❖ An icon of a disk with an X through it means that the disk you are using to start up does not have the necessary software. (Usually, you will see this icon only when you try to start from a floppy disk that cannot start the Mac.) If you see this icon when first starting your Mac and if you are not trying to start from a floppy disk, call the store where you purchased the Mac and make arrangements to take it back and let the store fix the problem.

If you do not want to call Apple or if you want to try to fix the problem yourself, you can proceed to the last part of this book, "Troubleshooting," and work your way through those chapters. At this moment, though, unless you are an experienced Mac user, you should find someone to help you. Check out the options already listed and look at the manual that came with your Mac; be sure to check your cables again.

You probably will not encounter these circumstances, but every once in awhile, people have problems with a Mac straight out of the box. I just want to give you an idea of what to do if this happens.

Navigating the Macintosh Screen

Once the Mac starts, you will find yourself looking at a screen that has all kinds of icons, words, and strange boxes. If you are new to the Mac and computers, there is no reason why any of what you see should make sense. The remainder of this chapter is about using your Macintosh; it assumes that you've never used a Mac and that you've just taken it from the box and set it up.

At the beginning of each exercise, your Mac should display something similar to the accompanying figures in this book—if it does not, you should not do the exercise but read further. At some point, you will find the information you need to make your Mac show an image like the one in the corresponding example.

Shutting down and restarting your Mac will get you to a point that is close to the beginning point for the examples. You will then be able to make what your Mac is displaying look like the figures in this book.

Your Mouse

When you use your Mac, you will do 90 percent of your tasks with either the keyboard or the mouse. You use the keyboard to enter text-based information into your Mac; you use the mouse to perform many different types of operations. Of these two devices, the mouse will be the more perplexing. It is a unique device; on most Macs, it looks like the one shown in Figure 2.5.

You use the mouse to move the *pointer* (which looks like ▸) across the monitor's screen. It is a mechanical device that houses a ball that is rolled across a surface. As the ball in the mouse turns, it moves the pointer on the screen. You can move the mouse in any direction, and, as you do so, the pointer on the screen will move in the same direction as the mouse. When you hold and move your mouse, the cord that connects the mouse to the computer should face away from you.

Pointer   A small shape on the screen (▸) that follows the movement of the mouse or shows where your next action will take place. The pointer can be an arrow, an I-beam, a crosshair, or a wristwatch.

If you have a Macintosh PowerBook, you will not have a mouse. Instead, you'll have a trackball or a trackpad such as the ones shown in Figure 2.6. The trackball is

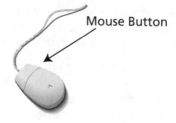

Mouse Button

Figure 2.5   *The mouse.*

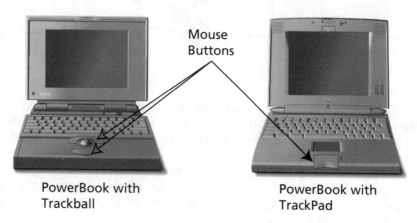

Mouse
Buttons

PowerBook with
Trackball

PowerBook with
TrackPad

Figure 2.6   *A PowerBook trackball and a PowerBook trackpad.*

an inverted mouse; rather than rolling the mouse across a surface, you'll roll the ball. As you move the ball, the pointer on the screen will also move.

The trackpad is a new device that does not use a ball, but the results of using it are the same as using a mouse. The trackpad is a pressure-sensitive flat pad; as you move your finger across the pad, the pointer on the screen moves in the same direction as your finger.

Regardless of what type of mouse your Mac has, using it might take some practice because it does more than just move the pointer around the screen. Each mouse has a button that, when depressed, activates the pointer, telling it to *select* whatever is under the pointer at the time. Everything you do with the mouse will be a combination of moving the pointer and pressing the button. In all, you can perform two basic actions with the mouse: clicking and dragging.

Click (v.)   To position the pointer on something and then press and quickly release the mouse button. (n.) The act of clicking.

Drag   To position the pointer on something, press and hold the mouse button, move the mouse, and release the mouse button. When you release the mouse button, you either confirm a selection or move an object to a new location.

Clicking is the act of placing the pointer over an icon and pressing and releasing the mouse button. Dragging is done by depressing the mouse button and then moving the pointer while you hold down the mouse button. In either case, pressing the mouse button causes the Macintosh to *select* something. The process of selecting something tells the Macintosh that you want to use or manipulate the object selected.

Select (v.)   To designate where the next action will take place. To select using a mouse, click on an icon or drag across screen information. In some applications, you can select items in menus by typing a letter or number at a prompt, by using a combination keypress, or by using arrow keys.

The Right Way

Every action you perform on your Mac can usually be done in several different ways. There is no *right* way; there are only ways that work. As we look at the things you can do with your Macintosh, I will cover any alternatives to standard ways for accomplishing a given task.

As you get more familiar with your Mac, you will need to experiment with the different ways of doing things. You may discover that you are more comfortable and can get more work done by using an alternate method. Do not be afraid to experiment; you will not hurt your Macintosh.

Using the mouse gets more complicated. Although all mouse actions are based on clicking and dragging, you can modify the meaning of your actions by the number of clicks you perform or by holding down a key on the keyboard while clicking the mouse to modify the meaning of a click or drag operation.

In the next chapter, we discuss the most common mouse actions you can perform. At this time, all you are going to do is move the pointer around the screen and get acquainted with the mouse. In the next section, you use the mouse to select different objects to get a feel for how they work.

The Finder

The Finder is your portal to the Macintosh. It is the place where you begin a journey that can take you around the world. It is the place from which you can create a world of your own, which is what you will do as you use your Macintosh. The Finder is the program that you see when you start your Macintosh, and it is from here that you will start your programs and perform many of your computer housekeeping functions.

Figure 2.7 shows the Macintosh's Finder, also known as the *desktop*. The terms "desktop" and "Finder" are often used interchangeably so that whenever someone

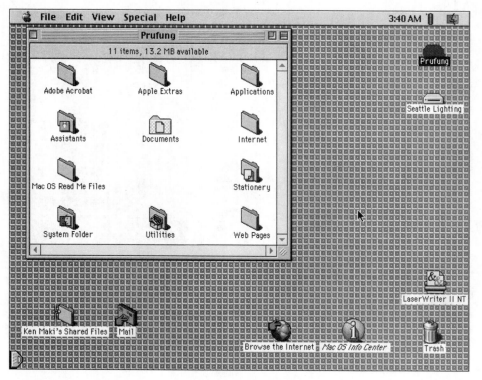

Figure 2.7 *The Macintosh Finder.*

talks about the desktop, he or she is talking about the Finder. The Finder is part of the Mac's system software; it is your entry point into the entire Macintosh system.

Finder The application that maintains the Macintosh desktop and starts up other programs at the user's request. You use the Finder to manage documents and applications and to get information to and from disks. You see the desktop upon starting up your computer.

From the Finder, you have access to all your documents and programs, and you do a lot of your housekeeping from the Finder. I'm getting ahead of myself, though. Before I should talk about what you can do, you need to know what everything is. Figure 2.8 is the same illustration as 2.7, only it shows the names assigned to each element of the Finder.

Everything you see in the Finder has a function or purpose; there is no wasted space. The primary function of the Finder is to create an association between what you see and what you might find in the real world. Those items are supposed to function just like their real world counterparts.

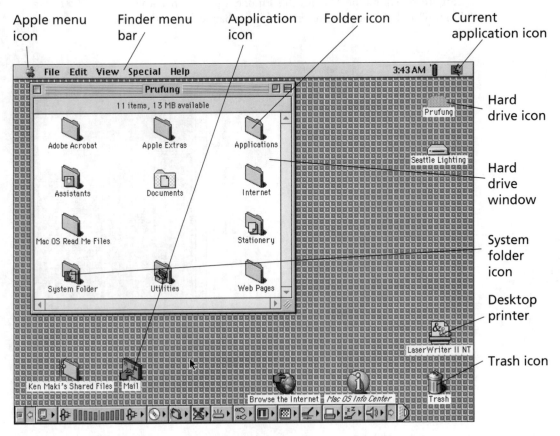

Figure 2.8 *The Finder.*

This association between what you see and the real world is called a *metaphor*. Metaphors are very important to the Macintosh; every icon inside the Macintosh is designed to look like something you might find in the real world to facilitate easy identification. An example of this is the trash can, the icon in the lower right corner of your screen (also shown in Figure 2.8). It is usually referred to as the *Trash*.

Trash   An icon on the desktop that you use to discard documents, folders, and applications.

The Trash is the Mac's counterpart to the trash can that (probably) sits next to your desk. The actual mechanics for trashing something are discussed in Chapter 5.

The Desktop and Icons

If you refer back to Figure 2.8, you see the area of the Finder called the desktop. Even though the terms "desktop" and "Finder" are often used interchangeably, the desktop is really the area indicated in Figure 2.8. The metaphor for the desktop is your real-world desk. Just like your home or office desk, the Macintosh desktop can become quite messy. Figure 2.9 is an example of a cluttered desktop.

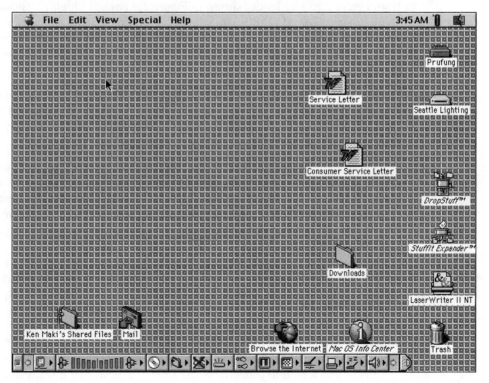

Figure 2.9   *A cluttered and customized desktop.*

Customizing Your Desktop

I know you're eager to start making your Mac your own. The ability to customize our machines is one of the reasons why we have Macintoshes. I'm afraid you'll just have to wait a bit before I tell you how to customize the desktop. Before you start playing around with your computer's appearance you need to understand how the Finder works.

If I tried to explain how to use and customize the Finder at the same time, I'd end up talking in circles (a problem that I sometimes have) and hopelessly confuse myself. If you really can't wait and have to start customizing your Finder now, go to Chapter 9. There you'll find all that you need to personalize your Mac. If you get confused after doing so, don't say I didn't warn you.

Note that Figure 2.9 looks a lot more complicated and in many ways different from Figure 2.8. The Finder shown in Figure 2.9 has been highly customized and shows what you can do and where you can go on this Macintosh journey. It is a glimpse into your future because you will learn how to modify and customize your Mac's Finder in Chapter 9. For the time being, let's look at an uncustomized desktop and Finder.

Desktop   The working environment on the Macintosh—the menu bar and the gray area on the screen. You can have a number of documents on the desktop at the same time. At the Finder level, the desktop displays the Trash and the icons (and windows) of disks that have been accessed.

Any icon you see on the desktop is a tool, document, or container. Tools are programs; documents are data files created by programs; and the containers are where the tools and documents are stored. The icons you see represent *real* items, and by manipulating icons, you actually perform some action on the object in your Macintosh's memory or on the hard drive represented by the icon. It is important that you understand this before you start using your Mac.

I said earlier that you cannot hurt the Mac by using it. You can lose data or information if you are not careful. Losing data is what most people fear, which is another reason why you need to understand thoroughly how your Mac works. By understanding what is happening from the beginning, you will be less likely to lose data; if you develop good work habits now, you'll probably never lose any data.

You must understand that anything represented by an icon seen on the desktop is real; it is like the paper, pencil, or other object on your physical desk. Just because it appears on the screen of your Macintosh does not mean that it really does not exist; it does.

What may give an icon a sense of unreality comes from the concept of an icon being a metaphor for the real world—and the fact that much of what we see on television screens is not real. As human beings, we tend to assume that unless something has physical attributes, it is not real. You must guard against this tendency. The objects you see on your Mac's screen do take up space and have form, and they obey laws of physics just like the items on our desk—only they do so completely within your Macintosh.

Menus and Windows

Across the top of your Macintosh's screen is a white bar with the words *File, Edit, View, Label,* and *Special;* on the right-hand side of the screen appear the time, a question mark icon, and an icon that looks like a Macintosh (see Figure 2.10). This white area is called a menu bar, and almost every program you'll use will have one.

Menu bar   The horizontal strip at the top of the screen that contains menu titles.

A menu is a basic computing concept, one not unique to the Macintosh. What is unique to the Macintosh is that Apple established standards for how programmers (the people who write computer programs) use menus. By understanding these standards, you will have the basic knowledge you need to begin using any Macintosh program.

You need to be aware of a certain method to the madness. Some menus will be the same regardless of the program you're using, and all programs will share similar or common attributes. In a way, understanding menus will be like learning a language. All languages have a basic set of rules that apply in almost all circumstances. Then, all of a sudden, a word comes along that does not follow the same rules as the other words. The wayward word is an exception to the rule.

You will encounter the same principle at work in your Macintosh and in how the rules Apple established for its operation apply. Most of the time, your Mac will operate according to Apple's standards, but, out of the blue, some program will offer an exception to the rule. These exceptions do not happen often, but you do need to know about them; I will make every effort to point them out as they occur.

The basic way menus work is always the same. Each word in the menu bar is the name of a menu. You can access menus by doing the following:

1. Place the very tip of the pointer on the word or icon in the menu bar.
2. Press the mouse button.

These actions will cause a menu to drop down. When you access the menu, you are offered a list of choices, commands that you can tell the Macintosh to perform. Figure 2.11 shows the contents of the File menu.

| File Edit View Special Help | 3:48 AM |

Figure 2.10   *The Finder's menu bar.*

Figure 2.11 *The Finder's File menu.*

Menu A list of choices presented by a program, from which you can select an action.

Menu item A choice in a menu, usually a command to the current application.

The File menu is an attribute shared by all programs. Every program with a menu bar will have at least a File and Edit menu. The File menu is used to access and print your data; the Edit menu is used for manipulating your document while you are working on it. You will learn more about menus as we go on. At the moment, let's get used to how the Mac works by learning how to use the mouse. The following steps take you through a simple procedure that requires you to use your mouse to select an icon and a menu to get some information from your Macintosh.

These steps illustrate how you use your mouse and demonstrate how a menu functions:

1. Position the pointer over the icon in the upper right corner of the desktop that has the name MacintoshHD (see Figure 2.12). This is the Macintosh's hard drive icon.

2. Click the mouse button. This action selects the hard drive icon. You will see the icon and its name change from (A), a light-colored or white icon with text in black on white, into an icon that is black or colored with text in white on black. Or (B), the icon and text were already black or colored with white text on a black background. You want the icon to look like Figure 2.13.

3. Move the pointer over the word *File* in the menu bar (Figure 2.14).

Figure 2.12　*The hard drive icon.*

Figure 2.13　*The selected hard drive icon.*

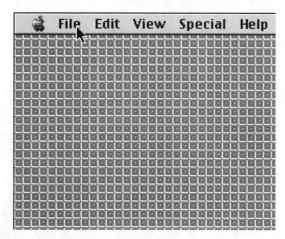

Figure 2.14　*The pointer on the File menu.*

4. Press and hold the mouse button. This action activates the File menu, causing it to drop down, as shown in Figure 2.15.

5. With the mouse button depressed, move the pointer over the words *Get Info*. Moving the mouse with the button depressed is called dragging. When

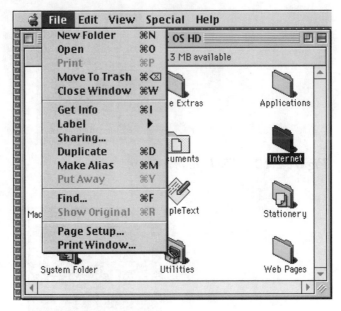

Figure 2.15   *The File menu.*

the Get Info menu item is selected, the words *Get Info* are white with a black band appearing across the menu, as shown in Figure 2.16.

6. Release the mouse button. This causes the menu item to flash as the menu disappears. Immediately, as the menu disappears, you see what is called a window appear in almost the same location as the File menu. Your screen should look like Figure 2.17.

Figure 2.16   *The selected Get Info menu item.*

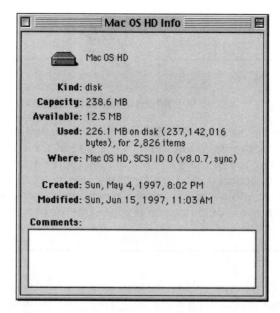

Figure 2.17   *The MacintoshHD Info window.*

By completing the above steps, you've just selected your hard drive and opened its Get Info window using the Get Info menu command. If I had been talking to you, I simply would have asked you to open the Get Info window for your hard drive. The entire procedure required six steps, but it is normally considered a single action. Not only that, but the same action can be done in three steps.

Before you can repeat the process, though, you'll have to close the drive's Get Info window.

To do this (assuming you've done nothing else since you opened the Get Info window), use the File menu again:

1. Select the File menu (by clicking and holding down the mouse button on the word File in the menu bar).
2. Drag the pointer to the word Close Window.

This will cause the Get Info window to disappear.

Close   To turn a window back into the icon that represents it by choosing the Close command or by clicking the close box on the left side of the window's title bar.

To open the Get Info window in three steps:

1. Position the pointer over the icon in the upper right corner of the desktop that has the name MacintoshHD.
2. Click the mouse button to select the hard drive.
3. Hold down the command key (⌘) and press the **I** key at the same time.

Mousing Around

Using the mouse is not easy for everyone. You will sometimes run out of space as you move your mouse, bumping into the side of the computer or sliding it off the edge of the table. When this happens, lift the mouse from the table surface and move it in the direction opposite to the one in which you want the pointer to move. When you set the mouse down, continue moving it in the direction that you want the pointer to move. You'll have to practice this movement, but it will soon become automatic.

The result should be the same as the one the six steps produced. Now you can close the Get Info window using a similar technique that will take only one step instead of three.

1. Hold down the command key (⌘) and press the **W** key at the same time.

The steps where you either open or close an item using the command key (⌘) are called command key equivalents and represent another way to access your menus. In Figure 2.15, you see in the Finder's File menu, next to some of the menu items, the ⌘ symbol plus a letter. Each of these is a keyboard equivalent that allows you to perform the menu command associated with the command key instead of accessing the menu item with your mouse. This is an example of performing the same steps using different techniques.

Windows

The discussion of menus also introduced an interface element that has not been discussed yet: the window. A *window* is a standard computer device for providing information, and it is also the primary element of most programs.

Window   The area that displays information on a desktop; you view a document through a window. You can open or close a window, move it around on the desktop, and sometimes change its size, scroll through it, and edit its contents.

You've seen one example of how a window works. The window in Figure 2.17, however, is only an information window. You can look at the information it gives you and open, close, or move the window, but you cannot change anything else in the window. Other windows are entry points into your Macintosh in which you view and do your work.

Windows are complex; you need to be fresh and ready to learn a bunch of new terms as well as the things you can do with a window. Perform the steps in the next section and then go on to Chapter 3.

Shutting Down the Mac

When you are finished using your Mac, you will probably want to turn it off. Remember that the Mac is not like your other tools; when you are finished using the Mac, you do not just pull the plug. When it is shut off, the Mac has to go through a series of steps to ensure that it shuts off properly. Although depressing the power switch (on some models) can shut the Mac off, doing so too many times will cause problems and may even lose your data.

There are two ways to shut down your Mac. The first method is to use the Shut Down command from the Special Menu in the Finder.

To do this:

1. Place the pointer over the Special menu in the menu bar and then click and hold the mouse button down. You will see a menu like the one in Figure 2.18.

2. Drag the pointer to the Shut Down menu item (see Figure 2.19).

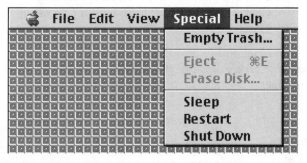

Figure 2.18   *The Special menu.*

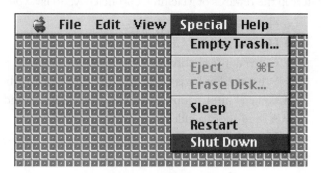

Figure 2.19   *Selecting the Shut Down menu item.*

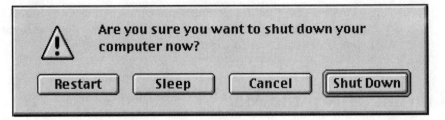

Figure 2.20 *The Shut Down dialog box.*

3. One of two things will happen: either your Macintosh will turn off, or a dialog box (a message) will appear that says it is safe to turn off your Macintosh. (Included with the message will be a button labeled Restart. Dialog boxes and buttons will be covered in Chapter 3.)

4. If you see the Shut Down dialog box, turn off your Macintosh.

The alternative method for shutting off your Macintosh is to press the Power-on key. This is the same key you pressed to turn on your Mac.

The steps for using the alternative shut down are:

1. Press the Power-on key. A dialog box like the one in Figure 2.20 will appear.

2. Your options are to Restart, Sleep, Cancel, or Shut Down your Macintosh. Clicking on the Shut Down button or pressing Return will shut down your Mac.

Your Macintosh is now shut down, and it is probably time to take a break. When you come back, follow the instructions listed at the beginning of this chapter to start your Mac.

Summary

If you are new to the Mac and to computers, you may be feeling a little overwhelmed by now. Learning to use your new tool is not an easy task, but, if you stick with it, you will reap the rewards of Macintosh proficiency. So far, you have learned the following:

❖ How to set up your Macintosh

❖ How to start up your Macintosh

❖ General information about your mouse and how to use it

❖ What the Finder is (there is a lot more to learn about the Finder)

❖ General information about the desktop, icons, and menus

❖ A little about windows

❖ How to shut down your Mac

This is quite a bit for a novice. If you're not comfortable with any of the topics covered so far, take the time to reread the appropriate sections of this chapter. On the other hand, if you have some experience with computers or the Mac, you may have learned something from this chapter that you didn't already know.

The next chapter covers how to run a program and what to do with it. My methods for teaching these things are somewhat unorthodox, but I have faith that you'll learn what you need to know.

CHAPTER 3

Using Your Macintosh

Introduction

In the last chapter, we looked at setting up, starting, and the beginning to use your Mac. Chapter 2 covered these topics:

❖ How to start up your Macintosh

❖ Your mouse and how to use it

❖ The Finder and metaphors

❖ The desktop, icons, and menus

❖ A little about windows

❖ How to shut down your Mac

This chapter continues to explore the Finder and windows, but its major emphasis is on how to use most Macintosh programs. You will learn the different types of programs you'll find in the Macintosh world and introductory steps for starting and using any Macintosh program.

By the time you finish this chapter, you should have the basic knowledge you need to use your Mac. Chapter 5, "Keeping Track of Your Data," is one of the most important chapters in the book. Until you've finished Chapter 5, you will not have all the knowledge you need to fully use your Mac.

The adventure continues.

More about the Finder

As you learned in Chapter 2, the Finder is the program you use to access and manage all the data you put into your Mac. In this chapter, we explore two primary elements of the Finder: windows and menus, the primary elements in all Macintosh programs. Part I gives you 65 to 75 percent of what you need to use any Macintosh program.

The Anatomy of a Window

Windows are your portals into the Macintosh. Almost all the information you'll receive from your Mac and any work you do will usually be done inside a window. The window you saw when we explored menus gave you information about your hard drive (see Figure 3.1).

Window The area that displays information on a desktop; you view a document through a window. You can open or close a window, move it around on the desktop, and sometimes change its size, scroll through it, and edit its contents.

The Get Info window has two elements that are common to all standard windows. One is the Close box; the other is the title bar; both are indicated in Figure 3.1. This window also has a Comments field where, by typing text on your keyboard, you could place a note or reference about the hard drive (or the item for which you were getting information).

We will play with a few windows to illustrate how they work and to give you some practice. Before you start this exercise, be sure that your Finder looks like Figure 3.2. If it does not, close all open windows using the Close Window command from the File menu (these steps are listed in Chapter 2). If the Close Window command is grayed out, move the pointer into the open window and click the mouse button (remember, clicking means pressing and releasing the mouse button once). This process activates the window. Now, use the ⌘+W keyboard option (or the Close Window menu command) to close the open window. Do this for any open windows.

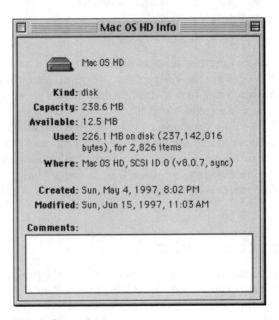

Figure 3.1 *The Get Info window.*

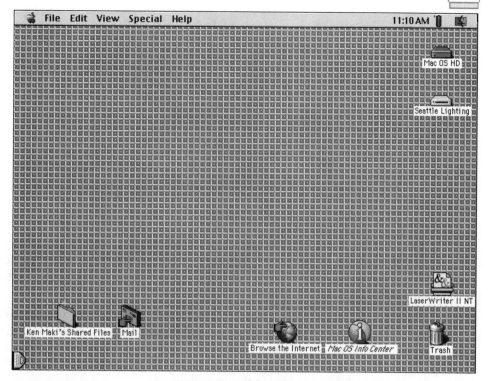

Figure 3.2 *The Finder with everything closed.*

Now, if your screen looks like Figure 3.2, you are ready to begin. In this first set of steps, you will open your hard disk, identify and describe the window's elements, and take a quick look at what is on your hard disk. You will use everything you've learned up to this point—and more—in this example. If you have difficulty with any of these steps, repeat this exercise until you can do it comfortably.

To view what's on your hard disk:

1. Move the pointer so that its tip is over your hard drive, as shown in Figure 3.3.

2. Open the hard drive by double-clicking the mouse, which means clicking the mouse button twice. Double-clicking the mouse on an icon is the same as using the Open command from the File menu or the ⌘+O keyboard option.

   As soon as you've clicked once, click again; remember, when the word "click" is used by itself it means pushing the mouse button down and then immediately releasing the button. Be sure you do not move the pointer when you double-click. Many people experience frustration at this point because they move the mouse while clicking the mouse button, which causes the pointer to move off the icon and nothing to be selected.

Figure 3.3 *Positioning the pointer.*

Double-click (v.)   To position the pointer where you want an action to take place, and then to press and release the mouse button twice in quick succession without moving the mouse.

3. You will see a window open on the desktop; it should look like Figure 3.4. This window displays the contents of your hard drive and is different from the Get Info window we looked at earlier. It has more components and displays something different. Each of the window's parts is marked in Figure 3.4 and defined in the list below.

Figure 3.4 shows the hard drive window and the names of the window's elements or controls. Some of these elements are informational only; others are used to manipulate the window itself. With your mouse (by clicking or dragging), you can move, change the size, view different areas of the window, or close the window.

Title bar   The horizontal bar at the top of a window that shows the name of the window's contents. You can move the window by dragging the title bar.

Zoom box   A small box with a smaller box enclosed in it found on the right side of the title bar of some windows. Clicking the zoom box expands the window to its maximum size; clicking it again returns the window to its original size.

Scroll bar   A rectangular bar that may be along the right side or bottom edge of a window. Clicking or dragging in the scroll bar causes your view of the document to change.

Scroll arrow   An arrow at either end of a scroll bar. Clicking a scroll arrow moves a document or directory one line. Pressing a scroll arrow moves a document continuously.

Grow region   A window region, usually within the content region, where dragging changes the size of an active window.

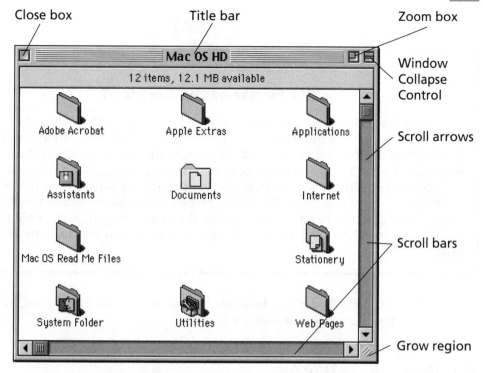

Close box   Title bar   Zoom box

Window Collapse Control

Scroll arrows

Scroll bars

Grow region

Figure 3.4   *The hard disk window.*

Go-away region   A region in a window frame. Clicking inside this region of the active window makes the window close or disappear.

Close box   The small box on the left side of the title bar of an active window. Clicking it closes the window.

Window Collapse Control   A small box with a bar in it found on the right side of the title bar of some windows. Clicking the Window Collapse control causes the window to disappear, displaying only the title bar; clicking it again restores the window to its original condition.

Scroll   (1) To move a document or directory in its window so that a different part of it is visible; (2) to move all the text on the screen upward or downward and, in some cases, sideways.

Inside the window in Figure 3.4, you see icons that represent the contents of a hard drive. When you look at your own Mac, you will see the contents of your hard drive. You will access, open, or otherwise manipulate what is on your hard drive with your mouse. The only times you'll use your keyboard while in the Finder will be to type names or to issue keyboard-equivalent commands.

However, before you work inside the window, you will learn how to manipulate the window itself. Actually, you will learn how to manipulate two windows that are

The Finder or the Desktop?

The phrase "in the Finder" refers to the Macintosh Desktop. The other phrases you'll hear are "on the Desktop," "in the Desktop," and other location references in which either the Desktop or the Finder is the subject. This terminology is usually very imprecise and can be confusing for both new and experienced Macintosh users.

Because the Finder is a program, the least confusing way to refer to what you are doing on the Mac is to say "I'm in the Finder." This communicates which program, in this case, the Finder, you are using. If you are using another program, you would say "I'm in [the program name]" to indicate that you are currently using that program.

open in the Finder. The following exercises step you through each of the basic operations that you can perform on a window.

Working with the Window

The window in Figure 3.4 is representative of a normal Macintosh window. It is has all the elements of the windows you will use when working with other applications, so the principles you'll learn here will, in most cases, apply to your other Macintosh programs.

Because you are learning principles, you will encounter programs that do not always follow the rules; you will have to think about what you're doing until these steps become automatic.

With the Mac, you need to become aware of a variety of indicators. This process is called *feedback*. If your Mac is not waiting for you to do something, it will provide you with indicators that let you know what it is doing and its status. Some of the things it will tell you are these:

❖ Which window is active

❖ What item(s) are selected

❖ When it is busy and unavailable

❖ If it is waiting for you to do something

As you work through the exercises, keep the concept of feedback in mind and look for similarities from one example to the next. Then, when you start working with programs, look for similarities between programs and how they work. You'll learn that, up to a point, all Macintosh programs have the same features and capabilities.

All documents you create using programs on your Macintosh will appear in a window. In this sense, the window is your document. But some programs, like the

Finder, do not produce documents. Instead, the Finder's window tells you what is inside your Mac and how your data is organized. Understanding this will make it possible for you to use a wide variety of Macintosh programs, even those you've never used before. Now, on to the exercises.

Inside the Window

In this section, you will do a series of exercises. These exercises have several goals in mind:

❖ To help make you familiar with using the Finder
❖ To demonstrate how window controls operate
❖ To provide a practice space for using your mouse
❖ To demonstrate the features of any standard window

Each exercise is based on the definitions given in the previous section, "The Anatomy of a Window," or on operations that can be performed from the Finder. The defined window objects are also the controls you will want to know how to use. The lessons in this section are these:

❖ Selecting, hiding, and moving a window
❖ Hiding the window
❖ Using the zoom box
❖ Using the grow region
❖ Scrolling the window contents
❖ Using multiple windows
❖ Viewing the contents of a window

Figure 3.5 is the same window we opened earlier, only it is shown as it would appear on your Desktop. Your Desktop should look similar to Figure 3.5. The steps for getting to this point are listed in the section, "The Anatomy of a Window."

If you have trouble performing one of the following exercises or one of the steps in an exercise, take the time to practice. Being able to perform the steps listed below is essential to using your Mac. If you find yourself getting frustrated, take a break.

Selecting and Moving a Window

First, you will move the window around. You can position a window anywhere on your Desktop.

To practice selecting and moving a window:

1. Select the window. You can have only one window selected at a time. When a window is selected, it will have six horizontal lines that fill the title bar on either side of the window's name, as in Figure 3.5.

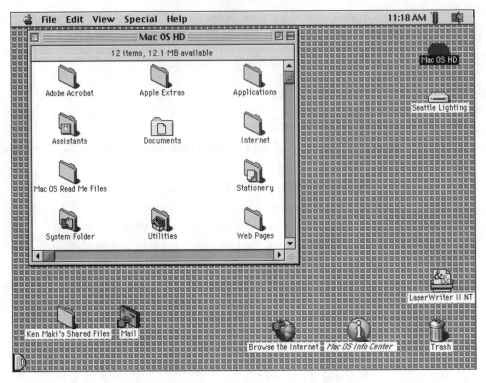

Figure 3.5   *The Desktop with an open window.*

The System Version

Although it is a little early to talk about what version of the Macintosh System your Mac is running, it is a question that will consistently come up. How your Mac behaves will depend on its System version. The examples in this book are based on the Macintosh System version 8, the latest version of the system.

To determine which version of the System you're running, follow these steps while in the Finder:

1. Select the Apple menu.

   The Apple menu is on the far left and is an icon that looks like an Apple. (See Figure 3.5.)

2. Select the menu item, *About This Computer...* .

3. A window like the one in Figure 3.6 will appear.

Figure 3.6 *The About This Computer window.*

4. After checking the system version, close the window by clicking in the Go-away box.

2. Click the desktop outside of the window. When you do this, the window is no longer selected and the horizontal lines in the title bar disappear (see Figure 3.7).

3. Click on the window to select it again; notice that the horizontal bars reappear in the title bar.

4. Move a window by dragging it by the title bar. Remember, dragging is the action of placing the pointer on the object (in this case, the title bar), depressing the mouse button, and then moving the mouse. As the pointer moves, the window will also move. You can then move the window to a new location. Drag the window from one side of your screen to the other.

5. Move the window back to its original position by following the above steps in reverse.

Hiding the Window

Hiding a window without closing it is a feature introduced in System 7.5. (See the note, "The System Version.") If, when you try this, the window does not function as

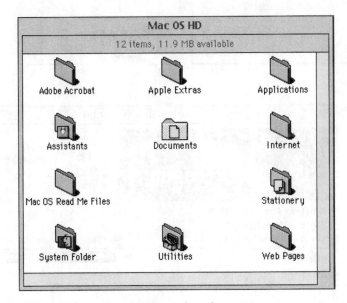

Figure 3.7   *The window when it is not selected.*

described in these steps, then you are probably using a version earlier than System 7.5 and should just go to the next lesson.

To hide a window:

1. Double-click on the title bar or click the Collapse control; the window will disappear, leaving only the title bar, as shown in Figure 3.8.
2. Double-click on the window's title bar or click the Collapse control again to make the window reappear.

This feature is useful when you use multiple windows and want to leave a window open but do not need it immediately. A window can be selected even though it is hidden, but you will have to check the title bar to determine the window's status. Hiding or displaying a window automatically selects the window.

Turning a Window into a Pop-up Window

Any Finder window can be displayed as a pop-up window, with a tab similar to a file folder's tab, as shown in Figure 3.9. This is a new feature of Mac OS 8.

Figure 3.8   *The window with only a title bar showing.*

Figure 3.9   *A window tab.*

To turn a window into a tab:

1. Grab the window by the title bar.
2. Drag it to the bottom of your screen.
3. When the window's outline turns into a tab release the mouse button.

Another way to turn a window into a pop-up window is to perform the following steps:

1. Select a window. (This process is also called "making a window active.")
2. Select the View menu.
3. Drag down to the *as Pop-up Window* menu item and release the mouse button.

To restore the window, reverse the steps listed above. If you select the second set of steps substitute "as Window" for step 3.

Once a window has been turned into a tab you can also access the window's contents by clicking on the tab, which will cause the window to pop up, as shown in Figure 3.10. Clicking on the tab a second time will cause the window to disappear, leaving just the tab visible.

Using the Zoom Box

The zoom box is used to expand a window so that it completely reveals the contents of a window or fills the Macintosh screen.

Your Comfort Level

There is almost always more than one way to accomplish any task when you use a computer. You will have to experiment to discover which method is most comfortable for you. There is no right or wrong way to accomplish these tasks. All that is important is that you are comfortable with how you perform these tasks.

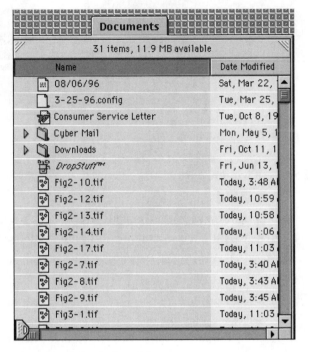

Figure 3.10 *An expanded window tab.*

To zoom a window:

1. Select the window.
2. Click in the zoom box, the small square within a square on the right side of the title bar.
3. The window will expand to display everything in the window or to fill the Mac's entire screen (see Figure 3.11).
4. Click in the zoom box again to return the window to its original position and size—or to its *default* position.

Default   A value, action, or setting that a computer system assumes, unless the user gives an explicit instruction to the contrary.

Defaults are settings that the computer automatically assumes. In this example, the original position of the window is considered to be a default, but it is a default that you have set. Some defaults are set by the Macintosh and are unchangeable.

Using the Grow Region

The grow region, often called the *grow box*, is the window control that you use to set the default size or visible area of a window. The grow box is located in the lower

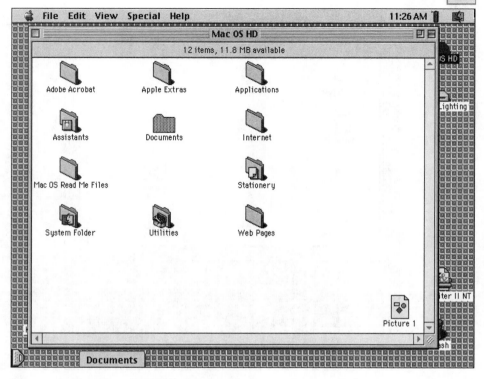

Figure 3.11 *An expanded window.*

right corner of the window. You use this function to change the size of a window and when you are working with multiple windows.

To change the size of the window:

1. Select the window.
2. To increase the visible area of a window, drag the grow box down and to the right. To decrease the visible area of a window, drag the grow box up and to the left. Figure 3.12 shows the window we've been working with after it has been enlarged.
3. Once you've changed a window's size, click on the zoom box.
4. Click on the zoom box again. Notice that the window returns to the new size and position that you've set. This is the new default setting for your window.

Some windows, in some programs, do not have a grow box. The grow box is an optional feature that a programmer can choose to omit. Usually, your program windows will have all the same features found in Finder windows, but not always. If you have a program that does not have all the window elements we're discussing, do not be alarmed; it is just a quirk of the program you're using.

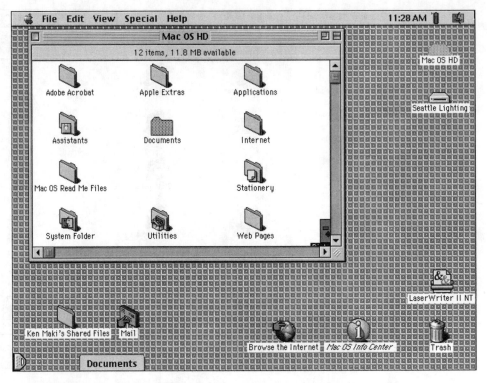

Figure 3.12 *An enlarged window.*

Viewing the Contents of a Window

There are several different ways to view the items in a window while in the Finder. The method you'll eventually select will depend purely on personal preference. You will probably use several different views for your windows, but you need to be aware of and know how to adjust your viewing method.

When you are in the Finder, you can use one of seven attributes for viewing the contents of a window or your files. These attributes are found in the View menu:

- ❖ As Icons—Displays all files using an icon.
- ❖ As List—Displays your files as a list.
- ❖ As Buttons—Displays your files as a button.

The default view is *as Icons* (see Figure 3.13). The *as Icons* view allows you to arrange your files in any order and to place them in any position. The *as Buttons* view turns the contents of a window into buttons, where clicking on a file button will open the file (you'll learn more about opening files in Chapter 4). And the *as List* view arranges all the window's contents as a list.

The *as List* view of a window displays the windows contents based on the file attributes of the items in the window, such as name. A file attribute is a property associated with a file. A file is the generic name for referring to the items you see inside a window while in the Finder. Files are discussed in detail in Chapter 5.

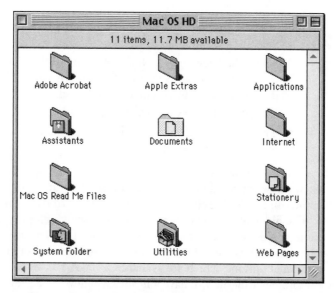

Figure 3.13 *A window viewed as Icons.*

In all the figures up to this point, the view has been set to *as Icon* mode. Figure 3.14 shows what a window looks like when its view is set to *as List*.

File   Any named, ordered collection of information stored on a disk. Application programs and operating systems on disks are examples of files. You make a file when you create text or graphics, give the material a name, and save it to disk. In this sense, *file* is synonymous with *document.*

Name	Date Modified
▷ ◻ Adobe Acrobat	Fri, Jun 13, 1997,
▷ ◻ Apple Extras	Fri, Jun 13, 1997,
▷ ◻ Applications	Today, 3:39 AM
▷ ◻ Assistants	Thu, Jun 12, 1997,
▷ ◻ Documents	Today, 11:31 AM
▷ ◻ Internet	Thu, Jun 12, 1997,
▷ ◻ Mac OS Read Me Files	Today, 3:38 AM
▷ ◻ Stationery	Thu, Jun 12, 1997,
▷ ◻ System Folder	Fri, Jun 13, 1997,
▷ ◻ Utilities	Thu, Jun 12, 1997,
▷ ◻ Web Pages	Thu, Jun 12, 1997,

Mac OS HD — 11 items, 11.6 MB available

Figure 3.14 *A window viewed as List.*

To change a window's view:

1. Select the window.
2. Select the View menu. Notice that one of the view options will have a check mark next to a view selection (see Figure 3.15). The check mark indicates the View mode that is currently selected.
3. Drag down to the view selection you wish to use and release the mouse button.
4. The window will change and display its contents according to the View mode you have selected.

Figure 3.14 shows the window after the *as List* View mode has been selected. In the window, notice that it now has a header line that indicates how the information in the window is viewed. In Figure 3.14, the word *Name* in the header is selected.

The file name is one of the attributes by which files can be viewed. In the View menu you'll see a menu item called *Arrange*. The *Arrange* menu item is a hierarchical menu that offers you additional choices when it is selected. Figure 3.16 shows the additional options, which are available.

A Finder window will have a header whenever it is viewed as a list. The selected word in the header will tell you how the information in the window is sorted. You can quickly change the sorting order of the information without using the *Arrange* menu by clicking on the header attribute name.

To demonstrate this, click on the word *Size* in your window's header, then click on the word *Name*. The information in the window will be sorted by size and then by name. Figure 3.17 shows the same window we've been using, with the files sorted by size.

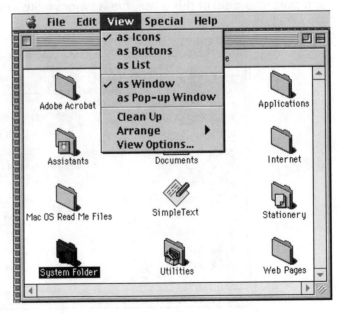

Figure 3.15   *The View menu.*

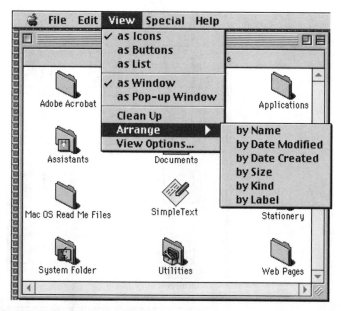

Figure 3.16   *The Arrange menu.*

The final View mode that we have to discuss is the view *as Buttons* option. Figure 3.18 shows the same window we've been using with the view *as Buttons* menu item selected. The view *as Buttons* mode is a special-purpose View mode that turns the file's icons into buttons. Compare Figure 3.18 with Figure 3.13; notice that the only difference is that the icons are now buttons. Clicking on one of the buttons will

Name	Date Modified	Size	Kind
▷ 🗂 System Folder	Fri, Jun 13, 1997, 2:50 PM	118.8 MB	folder
▷ 🗀 Applications	Today, 3:39 AM	63.5 MB	folder
▷ 🗀 Internet	Thu, Jun 12, 1997, 6:33 PM	18.5 MB	folder
▷ 🗀 Apple Extras	Fri, Jun 13, 1997, 12:37 AM	14 MB	folder
▷ 🗀 Adobe Acrobat	Fri, Jun 13, 1997, 12:37 AM	3.3 MB	folder
▷ 🗀 Documents	Today, 11:33 AM	2.9 MB	folder
▷ 🗀 Utilities	Thu, Jun 12, 1997, 7:17 PM	620K	folder
▷ 🗀 Assistants	Thu, Jun 12, 1997, 6:33 PM	440K	folder
▷ 🗀 Web Pages	Thu, Jun 12, 1997, 7:17 PM	336K	folder
▷ 🗀 Mac OS Read Me Files	Today, 3:38 AM	196K	folder
▷ 🗀 Stationery	Thu, Jun 12, 1997, 7:14 PM	108K	folder

Mac OS HD — 11 items, 11.5 MB available

Figure 3.17   *The window viewed by size.*

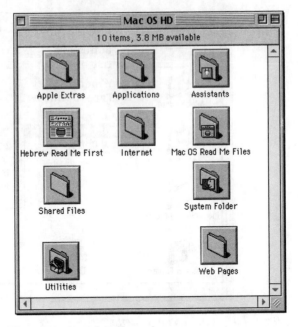

Figure 3.18   *The icons viewed as Buttons.*

cause the file or folder to open as if you had double-clicked on the same icon when it was being viewed in the *as Icon* mode.

Finally, you may have noticed at the bottom of the View menu a menu item such as *Icon View Options....* The name of this will change depending on the selected (check marked) View option. Selecting the *View Options* menu item will present you with a dialog box similar to the one in Figure 3.19.

In the dialog box you have several options that determine how your window appears. For a window viewed as icons you have the option of keeping your files arranged by name or by grid and whether to use a large or a small icon for the file. For each of the View modes you have options specific to the view in use.

Outline Views

You may have noticed the triangles in the margin of a window, next to folder names, when you view a window in a list mode. Clicking on a triangle will expand the folder and let you view its contents in an outline fashion. Many people prefer to open folders by clicking on the triangle rather than double-clicking on the icon. This is another option with which you should experiment.

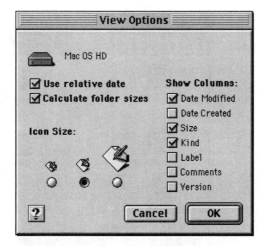

Figure 3.19 *Icon View Options dialog box.*

Before going on to the next section, experiment with your window by changing how its information is displayed. Using different View modes can be helpful when it comes time to look for a document and you've forgotten its name or where you've put it. There are other reasons why you want to use one of the available View options, but those will be discussed in later chapters.

Scrolling through a Window's Contents

A window can contain information that is not visible within the area of the window as it is displayed. You can see only a portion of what is contained in the window—it's like looking through a real window and being able to see only what the window frames. If you could move the window, you would be able to see another view, but you would still be constrained by the size of the window.

When there is more in a window than you can see due to the window's size, scroll bars will appear on the right and bottom of the window. Figure 3.20 shows a window that contains information that is not visible. Notice the scroll bars.

The process of moving the contents of a window to see what is not visible is called *scrolling*, hence the name "scroll bars." Think of the window and scroll bars as an ancient Roman scroll—as you read the scroll, you have to roll it on one end and unroll it at the other.

Scroll (1) To move a document or directory in its window so that a different part of it is visible; (2) to move all the text on the screen upward or downward and, in some cases, sideways.

Active scroll bars indicate that the window contains something you cannot see. An *active* scroll bar is one that is gray and has a scroll box and arrows. The term *active* means that a control can be used; all the window controls we're discussing are active if you can use them.

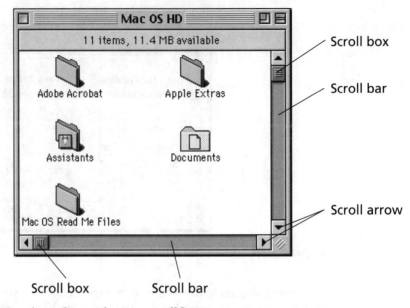

Figure 3.20 *A window with active scroll bars*

If the scroll bar is inactive, as in the window in Figure 3.21, you are viewing the window's entire contents.

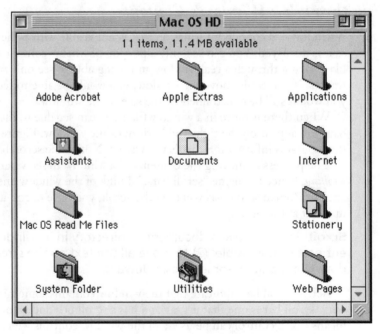

Figure 3.21 *A window with an inactive scroll bar.*

To see what is hidden in the window, you have to move the window's contents by manipulating the window controls, as indicated in Figure 3.20. Scroll controls are a consistent element for all Macintosh application windows; a set of rules governs how these controls work. To demonstrate how the scroll bars work, let's do an exercise that uses much of what you've learned in this chapter.

The following steps will demonstrate how scroll bars work:

1. Select your window.
2. Click in the window's zoom box so that the window expands to fill your screen. If the window does not fill the entire screen, use the window's grow box and expand the screen manually so that it fills or almost fills your entire screen.
3. From the File menu, select *New Folder*.
4. Select the new *untitled folder* that is created and drag it to the lower right corner of the window. Be careful that you don't drag the folder outside the window (see Figure 3.22).
5. Reduce the window's size by using the grow box. You should reduce the window so that you cannot see the folder you just created. Figure 3.23 shows how your window should look. Compare Figure 3.23 with Figure 3.22.

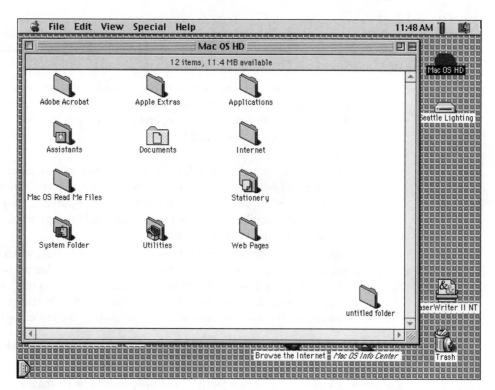

Figure 3.22 *The expanded window with an untitled folder.*

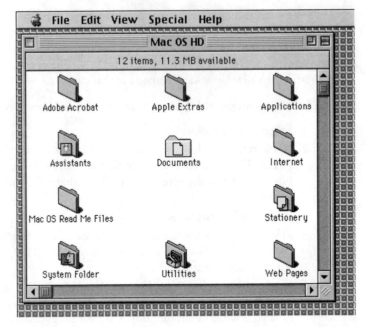

Figure 3.23　The reduced window.

Notice that your window has scroll bars across the bottom and on the right side of the window. Now, you can experiment with the scroll controls. In Figure 3.20, all the scroll controls are marked. The following list explains the use and function of each control:

❖ Scroll box—The scroll box serves two functions: First, it is an indicator that shows what portion of the window you are viewing. The indicator function is relative to the size of the window, and the scroll box shows the window's position relative to the top and bottom or the left and right of the window's contents.

Second, it is a manual control for moving the window's contents. By dragging the scroll box, you move the window's contents up and down or right and left, depending on which scroll box you're manipulating. In Figure 3.24, notice that the scroll boxes are to the far right and bottom of the window and that the untitled folder is visible.

❖ Scroll arrows—The scroll arrows are manual controls that, when clicked, move the window's contents one line in the direction indicated by the arrow. If you use the vertical scroll arrows, the window's contents will move one row up or down, depending on the arrow you use. The horizontal scroll arrows move the window's contents one column to the left or right.

Row A horizontal arrangement of character cells or graphics pixels on the screen.

Column A vertical arrangement of graphic points or character cells on the display screen.

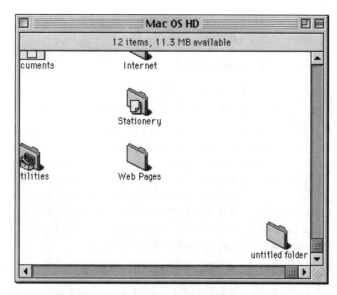

Figure 3.24 *The scroll boxes at the right and bottom.*

❖ Rows and columns are defined by the primary screen element of the program you're using. When you are in the Finder, a column or row is defined by the icons on the screen. A column is equivalent to the width of an icon, and a row equals an icon's height. A word processor uses letters and numbers (alphanumeric characters), so a row would be a row of letters like a line on a page, while a column will usually be defined by an arbitrary amount of space, such as a half inch. Each program will utilize the scroll arrows in its own fashion, and you'll have to experiment, but the basic rules described here will usually apply.

❖ Scroll bars—The scroll bars are the gray areas between the scroll arrows. In addition to indicating that the window contains additional information, they are also controls. When you click in a scroll bar you click between a scroll arrow and the scroll box. Clicking scrolls the window one screen height or width in the direction of the scroll arrow. Placing the pointer in the scroll bar and holding the mouse button down causes the window to scroll rapidly because the Mac interprets the continually depressed mouse button as rapid and continuous clicks.

Using Multiple Windows

One of the features of the Macintosh is that multiple windows can be open simultaneously. In addition to working with multiple windows, you can also run several programs simultaneously. Only one window can be active at a time.

To start with, you will open multiple windows while in the Finder. When you first get your Mac, you might have a couple of folder icons in your hard drive's window. If you don't, you should have at least two at this point: the untitled folder you created earlier and the System Folder.

To open the untitled folder:

1. Scroll to the untitled folder.
2. Double-click on the untitled folder.

When you open this folder, it appears as a window in front of your hard drive's window. Your screen should look something like Figure 3.25.

The things you should notice about this window are its header and the title bar. The header will tell you how many items are in the folder (in this case, it should say 0), how much disk space is used, and how much is available. The title bar will say *untitled folder*, and it will be the active window, signified by the lines in the title bar. The hard drive window will be open, but its title bar will be clean, without the horizontal lines, indicating that it is inactive.

If the untitled window fills up a large portion of your screen, do the following:

1. Shrink the size of the window with the grow box.
2. Move the window, dragging it by the title bar, so that you can see the hard drive window behind the untitled folder window.

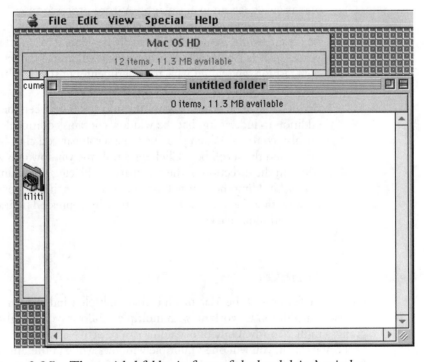

Figure 3.25   *The untitled folder in front of the hard drive's window.*

Clicking Too Much

One of the most common mistakes new Macintosh users make has to do with clicking the mouse. You need to be conscious of when you perform a single click versus a double click because you could run programs that you didn't want to run or open windows you did not want to open.

Once you can see the hard drive window, you can switch back and forth between the windows. You do this by positioning the pointer in the window you want to activate and clicking. When you click in a window that is not active, the window is brought to the front and activated.

Get used to using multiple windows; it can be confusing to have a half dozen windows open at the same time. Some programs have a window menu that lets you quickly move from one open window to another, but the Finder does not have this ability.

Toward this end, you might want to create a few more untitled folders. Each new untitled folder you create will be named *untitled folder*, with a sequence number, such as 2, 3, or 4, for each successive window you open. Thus, the second new folder you create will be named *untitled folder 2*.

Make a few folders and practice opening, closing, moving, and switching between them. If you spend half an hour now developing this skill, using your Mac will be easier later on.

A Few Comments about Using Windows

The art of utilizing your windows involves using all the controls listed in this section. On the surface, each of the manipulations you can perform is fairly basic. By practicing and using these controls together, you will soon be jumping from window to window, making your Mac do what you want it to do.

More about Menus

In this section, we look at the Finder's menus and learn how to use menus in general. Windows are used to view and work on your documents; menus are where you'll find the program's controls. You've used some of the Finder's menu functions in the last two chapters, but you haven't really learned about menus.

Menus are one of the ways you tell a program what you want it and, by extension, your Mac to do. To make using programs easier, Apple established some guidelines for programmers. The result is that program menus are similar for all Macintosh programs.

Menu Elements

All Macintosh programs have the same menu structure, which consists of a menu bar, menu titles, and menu items. Figure 3.26 shows the Finder's menu bar, a menu title, and the menu items from the File menu.

Menu title   A word, phrase, or icon in the menu bar that designates one menu. Pressing on the menu title causes the title to be highlighted and its menu to appear below it.

Menu item   A choice in a menu, usually a command to the current application.

In Figure 3.26, some of the menu items are black and others are gray. The black menu items can be used or are active, but the gray ones are inactive. A menu item is inactive because it requires a special condition to be active—usually, the selection of a specific object. When using the Finder, you usually need an icon or window selected. Once an icon is selected, other menu items become active, as shown in Figure 3.27.

Compare the items in Figure 3.27 with those in Figure 3.26, and you see the menu items that are now active because there is a folder selected in the open window. In general, this principle operates in all Macintosh programs, not just the Finder. A specific condition must exist for some of the menu items to be active; those that are active all the time will always affect your document.

As you worked through the exercises in the last section, you used several different menu commands, so you already know how to access and use menus. What you have

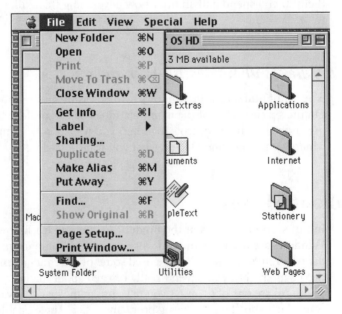

Figure 3.26   *The Finder's File menu.*

Figure 3.27 *Active menu items in the Finder's File menu.*

to learn is what the different menus and menu items do. Rather than read a list of all the menu items and their definitions here, you will learn what the menu items do as you work through the first part of this book. By the end of Chapter 5, you'll have a good grasp of how the Finder works, including the menu items and their functions. Also, in Appendix C, you'll find a list of shortcuts that apply to the Finder and some of the rules that govern how the Mac operates.

Summary

This chapter was about using the Finder. We talked about windows, menus, and other Finder elements. Although it is a short chapter it contains a lot of information, especially if you're new to the Mac. If you're confused or uncomfortable with the concepts covered in this chapter you should go back and read it again before going forward. Understanding how the Finder works is essential to efficiently using your Mac.

If you feel that you've got a good grasp of the material in this chapter, then you're ready to learn how to use an application. That is what the next chapter is about: using an application. Once you've finished the next two chapters you'll have the basic knowledge you need to use your Mac. Right now you're well on your way.

CHAPTER 4

Using Macintosh Software

The reason to have a Macintosh is to run your favorite software. Whatever software you use has specific characteristics—some characteristics are common to all Macintosh software, and others are unique to a particular piece of software (or program).

Chapter 3 discussed windows and menus. In this chapter, we look at using a program that comes with every new Macintosh—the SimpleText program. In addition to learning this program, you will learn about its features, which are common to all Macintosh programs.

Macintosh software is designed so that once you learn the basics of one program, you can immediately use other programs—all Mac programs share some features. You won't be an instant expert with every new program you pick up, but the amount of time you need to invest to become proficient will shrink.

As you progress through this book, the language becomes more technical and builds on the information presented in previous chapters. In this chapter, there are no instructions for scrolling through windows or for selecting menu items. Instead, you will be told to scroll the window or to select a specific menu. If you find that you're having trouble with these operations, review Chapters 2 and 3 before proceeding. Each successive chapter will make similar assumptions.

What Is a Program?

The only program we've looked at so far is the Finder, which is not a typical program because it is always running and so you do not have to start it. In a sense, the Finder is a program that lets you use all your other Macintosh applications, which makes it similar to the Macintosh's master program.

Program (n.) (1) A set of instructions describing actions for a computer to perform to accomplish some task, conforming to the rules and conventions of a particular programming language; (2) a file containing coded instructions to the computer.

Any other program you use on your Mac must be started, run, or booted. These terms all say the same thing: Somehow, you have to access to the program. Once the program is running, you can use it to create or modify your documents.

Document   Whatever you create with an application program—information you enter, modify, view, or save.

Most programs you use display the documents in a window, and you access the program's features through its menus (that is why they were discussed in the last chapter). Before you continue, if you are not familiar with either menus or windows, review Chapter 3.

Otherwise, let's continue; next we look at the basics for using programs. Keep in mind that even though we use a specific program as an example, every Macintosh program behaves in a manner similar to that of the one in our examples.

Starting a Program

Before you can use a program, it has to be started or run. Depending on the type of program you're using, it can be started in one of two ways. You can manipulate either the program's icon or the icon of a document created by the program.

Run   To start a program. When you run a program, you tell your computer to load the program from your hard disk into memory so that you can use it.

Figure 4.1 shows the Macintosh with an open window. In the window, you see an icon named SimpleText, a text processor, which is a program used to type documents, such as memos and letters. SimpleText is not a sophisticated program; hence, the name.

If you use an older Mac, the program is called TeachText, SimpleText's predecessor. Figure 4.1 assumes that you just opened and started your Mac; it shows what you see if your Mac is a new model. If you are somewhat familiar with your Mac or have been experimenting with it, your screen will probably not look like the one shown in Figure 4.1.

If your screen does not look like Figure 4.1 or if you cannot find the SimpleText program (from here on, read TeachText if you don't have SimpleText), you will have to search for it. If you need help finding SimpleText, jump ahead to Chapter 5 and read the section, "When Your File Is Not Where It Should Be."

To open SimpleText directly:

1. Double-click on the application's icon.
2. Select the application by clicking on it and selecting the Open command from the Finder's File menu.

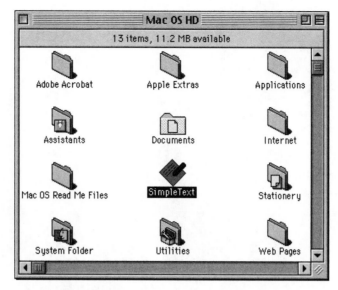

Figure 4.1 *The SimpleText icon.*

3. Select the application by clicking on its icon and use the keyboard equivalent (⌘+**O**) for the Open command from the Finder's File menu.

Performing any one of the above actions will cause SimpleText to start. When it starts, a rectangle zooms out from the program icon and your pointer icon turns into a watch icon.

Whenever your pointer turns into a watch icon or some other animated icon, it means that your Macintosh is busy performing a task. You cannot regain control until the Mac has finished its task. You will see examples of other animated cursors throughout the book. Once SimpleText has started, your screen looks like Figure 4.2.

Using a Program

Now that you have a program up and running, what do you do with it? Well, for starters, just type a few words on your keyboard. As you press each letter's key, that letter will appear in SimpleText's window. Now, type a paragraph, but do not press the Enter key when you reach the end of the line. Your typed words will be handled differently than they would be on a typewriter. (If you've used a computer before, you probably know what I'm talking about.) The program automatically starts a new line of text when the end of the previous line is reached. This feature of most text and word processors is called a *word wrap*.

By now, your screen looks something like Figure 4.3. The text you've entered will be different.

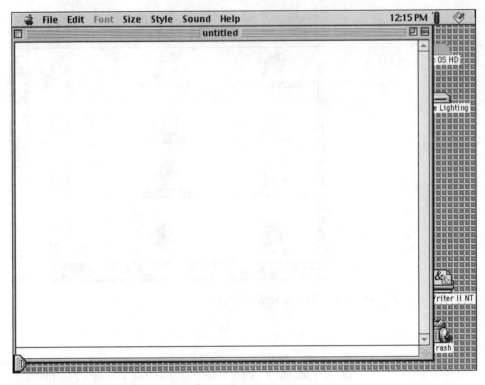

Figure 4.2   *SimpleText, up and running.*

Now, you should notice some specific things about how your Mac behaves. Each item listed below applies to all Macintosh programs, not just SimpleText:

❖ As you move the pointer across the screen, the pointer changes into an I-beam (I) as it enters SimpleText's window.

❖ When you type, you see a blinking indicator called the insertion point (I), which indicates where the letters and numbers will appear when you type.

❖ To change the position of the insertion point, place the I-beam where you want the new letters to appear, then click the mouse button.

❖ As soon as you move the pointer outside the window, it becomes the standard Macintosh pointer.

❖ Whenever the pointer is an I-beam, it has become a text manipulation tool.

❖ You can select letters, words, paragraphs, and entire documents so that you can manipulate the text.

❖ Any selected text can be copied or cut (removed) and subsequently pasted into the same document or another document.

Insertion point   The place in a document where something will be added, which is represented by a blinking vertical bar. You select the insertion point by clicking where you want to make the change in the document.

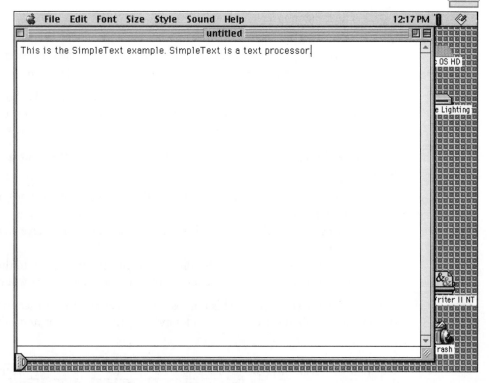

Figure 4.3 *SimpleText with some writing.*

I-beam A type of pointer shaped like the capital letter "I" and used in entering and editing text.

When you consider what you can do with just a simple text processor, you begin to see some of the advantages and complexity of any Macintosh program. For the remainder of this section, we look at these features.

Manipulating Text

In this section, we go through the steps you need to learn to manipulate what you've already typed. Each of the capabilities listed in the last section will be covered.

What you learn in this section is critical to using your Mac successfully. Every one of these functions is standard for every Macintosh program, including the Finder. Of course, there are always some exceptions to the rules, and any programs you might find that do not react as described are aberrant.

To insert text into your document:

1. Locate your insertion point (|).
2. Move your I-beam (I) to a different location other than where your insertion point is located.

3. Click the mouse.

4. Your insertion point will now be where you just clicked.

5. Start typing; your new text will begin where you placed the insertion point.

6. Do not do anything else; the next example starts at this point.

This is the standard technique for editing text. If you press your keyboard's Delete key, the text to the left of the insertion point is removed. Now that you've added some text, let's assume that you've made a mistake and want to remove the new text.

To remove the text, select the text you just entered and then cut it from the document:

1. Place the I-beam at the beginning or the end of the text you just entered.

2. Hold down the mouse button and drag the I-beam through the text you want to select. The text that is selected is displayed in reverse video, as shown in Figure 4.4.

3. Once the text is selected, use the Edit menu and drag down to the *Cut* menu item. When you release the mouse button, the selected text will disappear.

The text that just disappeared is not lost; it has been moved to a section of the Mac's memory called the Clipboard, a temporary storage area for items that are

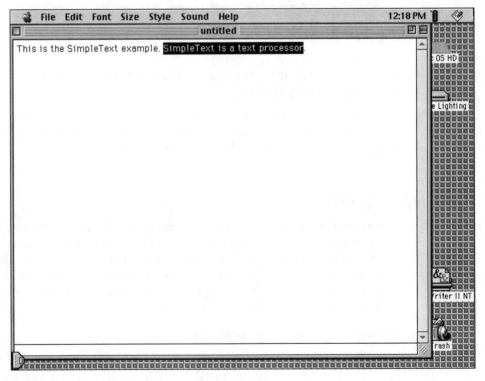

Figure 4.4 *Selected text.*

either copied or cut. The Clipboard will hold only the last item you copied or cut. You cannot store multiple items in the Clipboard.

Clipboard The holding place for what you last cut or copied; a buffer area in memory. Information on the Clipboard can be inserted (pasted) into documents.

To paste the text that you just cut back into your document:

1. Place the insertion point at a new location in your document.
2. Go to the Edit menu and select the *Paste* menu item.

The text you just cut will be placed where you put the insertion point. If you wanted to, you could paste the text again because it is still in the Clipboard. Text in the Clipboard remains there until you replace it by using the Cut or Copy command, which puts new material in the Clipboard.

The *Copy* menu item works just like the *Cut* menu item except that the text you select is not removed from the document. Repeat the above steps, this time using the Copy instead of the Cut command.

Now that you've selected text manually by dragging and using the menus to cut, copy, and paste, let's go over the shortcuts for performing these actions. First, we look at the different ways you can select text. The following list describes the different text selection methods:

❖ Double-clicking—Double-clicking on a word selects the entire word.

❖ Shift-clicking—Holding down the Shift key on the keyboard while clicking the mouse selects all the text between the insertion point and the I-beam.

❖ Shift-double-clicking—Holding down the Shift key on the keyboard while double-clicking the mouse selects all the text between the insertion point and the entire word under the I-beam.

❖ Select All—This menu item selects everything within your document. Select All can also be performed by using the ⌘+**A** keyboard-equivalent command.

These different methods will all work in SimpleText. Other selection methods that you can employ in other programs are presented in the section, "Additional Selection Methods and Other Commands."

The alternative methods for performing a cut, copy, or paste operation involve keyboard commands and function keys (if you use a keyboard that has them). Function keys are the F1, F2, F3, and other similarly labeled keys across the top of your keyboard or on the numeric keypad of an adjustable keyboard.

The following describes the various ways to perform a cut, copy, and paste operation:

❖ Cut—The command key option to cut selected text is ⌘+**X**. You can also execute a by pressing the F2 function key.

❖ Copy—The command key option to cut selected text is ⌘+**C**. You can also execute a cut by pressing the F3 function key.

❖ Paste—The command key option to cut selected text is ⌘+**V**. You can also execute a paste by pressing the F4 function key.

Once again, these commands work in any Macintosh program and are not just features of the SimpleText program. These steps are your foundation for working with the Macintosh. Repeat the steps in this section, using each of the different techniques for selecting and manipulating text. As you use your Mac, you will find that one of these techniques works better for you than the others; that technique will become your preferred method for performing these operations.

Changing Fonts in SimpleText

So far, the only menu we've used in SimpleText is the Edit menu. There are also the File, Font, Size, Style, and Sound menus. The File menu will be covered in the section, "Saving Your Work." In this section, we look at the Font, Size, Style, and Sound menus.

Most Macintosh programs let you modify how your text appears on the screen. TeachText does not have these features, but you should read this section anyway. Every word processing and almost all other Macintosh programs have these features.

When you use other programs, the features we're about to discuss do not always appear in separate menus. Sometimes they will be combined in a single menu or divided unequally in a couple of menus. Later in this chapter, we discuss how to experiment with other programs in the section, "How to Experiment with Software."

For the moment, however, we concentrate on SimpleText and how to change the text font, size, and style. After you learn basic text manipulation, which is a very quick process, spend some time experimenting with these features until you're comfortable with their implementation.

The first things to look at are the Fonts. You may choose the type of font (sometimes called "typeface") you use in your documents.

Font   A complete set of characters in one design, size, and style. In traditional typography usage, a *font* may be restricted to a particular size and style, or it may comprise multiple sizes and styles of a typeface design.

Before changing the font, check which font you're using:

1. To select the Font menu, hold down the mouse button. The active font, Geneva, has a check mark next to it (see Figure 4.5).
2. Drag down and select a font, say, Times, then release the mouse button.
3. Start typing. All the new text you enter is in the Times font.

You've just changed the font for all new text from Geneva to Times. This change, however, applies only to the new text you type, starting at the insertion point. If you use the I-beam and change the insertion point's location (outside of the new text typed in Times), the font will revert to Geneva. Similarly, if you move the insertion point to a location where you've used Times, the font changes to Times.

Try moving the insertion point to various sections of your document and then checking the Font menu. Also, try adding a few more font types and selecting different fonts. After you have four or five fonts, perform the check again. You need to be

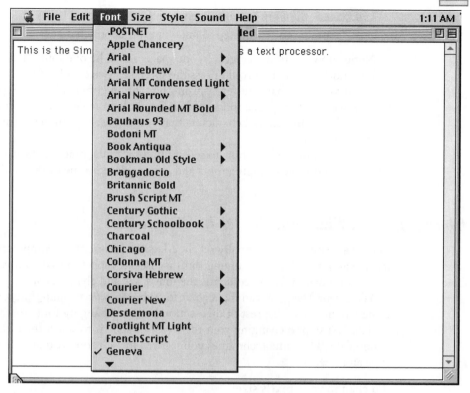

Figure 4.5   *SimpleText's Font menu.*

comfortable with using multiple fonts within a single document and changing the
font from one space or character to the next.

To understand how this works:

1. Place your insertion point where there is a change in fonts, as shown in
   Figure 4.6.
2. Check the Font menu to see which font is selected.
3. Use the cursor keys on the keyboard and move the insertion point by pressing the ⌘ key.

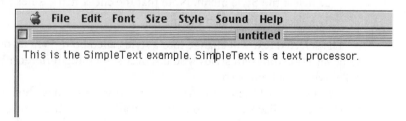

Figure 4.6   *The insertion point where the font changes.*

4. Check the Font menu to see which font is selected.

5. Continue to repeat steps 3 and 4 until the font changes.

Notice how the font changes. In one space, it will be one font; in the next space, it will be another font. You could press the space key twice and, between the two spaces, have a font that is different from the font on either side of the spaces. This feature makes using special fonts, such as Symbol, possible. The Symbol font is a font which contains special characters that you can use for emphasis and customizing your documents.

If you are unsure about how to select different fonts, practice the above steps until you are comfortable changing fonts and have explored some of the available fonts.

Changing Font Sizes and Styles in SimpleText

One Mac feature that originally set the Mac apart from other computers was its ability to manipulate fonts. Changing fonts is just one aspect of that ability. The other part of font manipulation concerns the font's size and characteristics.

With your Mac, you can make your fonts **bold**, *italic*, or underlined, and you can change their sizes. The rest of this section looks at changing font sizes and styles.

The first step to changing your text's size or style is to select the text you want to manipulate. The same techniques you learned for selecting text are used to change style and size.

To change your text's size:

1. Select the text you want to change.
2. Select the Size menu; notice that 12 is the default size. Now, drag down to size 18 and release the mouse button.
3. The size of the selected text increases.

Experiment with changing the size of your text in different areas so that you get used to how this feature works. Fonts are measured according to points; one point is $\frac{1}{72}$nd of an inch.

Changing the style of your text is much like changing its size.

To change your text's style:

1. Select the text you want to change.
2. Select the Style menu. Note that the check mark is next to Plain.
3. Select the Bold menu item.

The selected text will change into a style called bold. When you repeat the above steps selecting different styles, you discover something different: You can select multiple styles simultaneously.

If you select *Bold* and *Underlined*, your text will look like **this**. As you experiment more, you will discover that you can make all kinds of interesting combinations. And when you're tired of changing styles, you can change them back to normal by selecting the Style menu item *Normal*.

In the menus, notice the command key equivalents. Usually ⌘+**B**, ⌘+**U**, and ⌘+**I** will work in any program to change your selected text to bold, underlined, and italic text. In SimpleText, you can also use ⌘+**T** to change the text back to normal. The command keys for other styles and for reverting the text to normal will differ from program to program. Unfortunately, this is an inconvenience you'll have to accept.

Saving Your Work

At the moment, everything you typed into SimpleText is stored in your Mac's RAM. If you were to turn off the computer right now (don't do it), all of your typing would be lost. Now you need to move your typing from the Mac's memory onto its hard drive so that you can recall what you've typed. This process is called *saving* the file.

Save   To store information by transferring it from main memory to a disk. Work not saved disappears when you switch off the computer or when the power is interrupted.

The actual process of saving files is easy. What is complicated about this process, however, is placing the files where you can easily find them again. The topic of file location is discussed in Chapter 5. In this section, we demonstrate only how to save a file.

To save your SimpleText document to the Mac's Desktop:

1. Select the File menu.
2. Select the *Save As…* menu option.
3. A window called a Save As dialog box appears, which looks like Figure 4.7.
4. Click the Desktop button.
5. Click in the File Name field where it says *Untitled 1*.
6. Type a name, such as *Test Document*.
7. Click the OK button.

These actions will save your document with the name *Test Document* to your Desktop. The file is written to the Mac's hard drive and saved exactly as it appears on the screen.

Ellipsis in a Menu

Something you should notice about the Save As… menu item is the ellipsis, which means that your Mac will require more information before it can execute the command. A dialog box appears that requests this information.

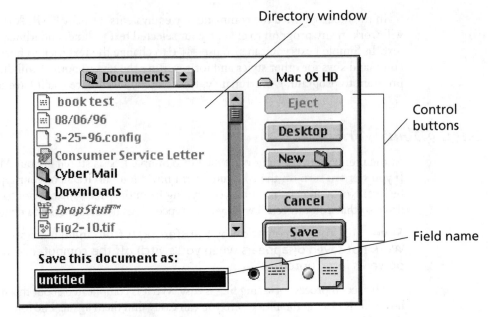

Directory window

Control buttons

Field name

Figure 4.7   *The Save As dialog box.*

In SimpleText, the first time you save a document you can select either the *Save* or *Save As...* menu item; the Save As dialog box then appears. Other programs have a grayed-out Save command; your only choice then is the *Save As...* menu item. If both the *Save* and *Save As...* menu items are available, you can perform your initial Save As by using the ⌘+**S** command key option.

Dialog Box   (1) A box that contains a message requesting more information. Sometimes, the message warns you that you're asking your computer to do something it can't do or that you're about to destroy some of your information. In these cases, the message is often accompanied by a beep; (2) a box that a Macintosh application displays to request information or to report that it is waiting for a process to complete.

Button   A push button-like image in dialog boxes, on which you click to designate, confirm, or cancel an action. (Compare to *mouse button*.)

To make some changes in your document:

1. Before you make any changes, select the File menu. Notice that the *Save* menu item is now gray. This means that it cannot be selected because there are no changes in your document to save.
2. Make some changes in your document.
3. Select the File menu. Notice that the *Save* menu item is now selectable. The program—in this case, SimpleText—makes the *Save* menu item available as soon as you make any changes in the document. The change can be as subtle as adding a single space.

Dialog Boxes

The Save As dialog box is a standard Macintosh convention found in every Macintosh program and is used to create data documents. Dialog boxes appear whenever your Mac needs extra information or is telling you something important about itself.

Whenever a dialog box appears, you have to address the issue at hand—namely, whatever the dialog box asks of you. In our example in this section, you must provide a name for your file and click the OK button. If you decide not to save your document, you can click the Cancel button; the dialog box will disappear and your document will not be saved.

Most dialog boxes will have, at minimum, an OK button and a Cancel button. Some, however, will have just an OK button. When a dialog box has only an OK button, you have no choice but to acknowledge the message and click the OK button. Any other action you try to perform, short of shutting off the Mac, will not work.

4. Select the *Save* menu item.

When you make changes to a document that has been saved, the changes are transferred to the saved document only when you execute a Save command. Changes made to a document are not saved until you tell the Mac to do so. Saving your document adds the changes you've made to the original document file. You can always tell which document you're working on by checking your window's title, which will usually be the file's name. In our example, the window name will be Test Document.

The easiest way to make sure your work is saved while you work is to periodically use the ⌘+S command key option. Saving your changes is something you should do regularly. All too often, people do not regularly save their changes and sometimes lose their hard work.

Save Your Work

Periodically save the changes you've made to your document. This way, if your Mac malfunctions (something that will occasionally happen), your work will still be saved.

Other File Menu Functions

In all Macintosh programs, functions for manipulating files and for printing are found in the File menu. At a minimum, you have the following options from the File menu. Each menu command is listed, with its command key equivalent and a brief description. If no command key equivalent is listed for a menu item, it does not have one.

New	⌘+N	Creates a new, blank document.
Open	⌘+O	Opens an existing document. This command is discussed in Chapter 5.
Close	⌘+W	Closes an open document.
Save	⌘+S	Saves changes in a document.
Save As...		Saves a document with a new name.
Print Setup...		Used to configure your printer.
Print	⌘+P	Prints your documents.
Quit	⌘+Q	Closes the program.

You are always asked to save your changes before the document closes or before you quit the program. The Quit command will be discussed in more detail later in the section, "Quitting and Restarting Your Program."

The *Print Setup...* and *Print* menu items tell your printer how you want your document printed and to print your documents. Printing your documents is not a complicated process; with the Mac OS 8, however, printing is more complicated and requires more discussion than you'll find here. A more detailed discussion about printing will be found in Chapter 8. Check that your printer is connected to your Macintosh and turned on.

To print your document:

1. Select *Page Setup...* from the File menu.
2. A Page Setup dialog box, similar to the one in Figure 4.8, appears.
3. Using the controls in the dialog box select how you want your document printed.
4. Click the OK button.
5. Select the *Print* menu item or use the command key equivalent.
6. A Print dialog box, similar to the one in Figure 4.9, appears.

In both the Print Setup and the Print dialog boxes, you can select among various options, which will depend on the printer you're using. The example we use here is for a LaserWriter, but you could use a different type of printer and so have different options. Because there are so many possibilities, you may have to refer to your printer manual for a full explanation of your options.

The following are the Page Setup dialog box options:

❖ Paper—With this option, you tell the Mac what type of paper you have in your printer.

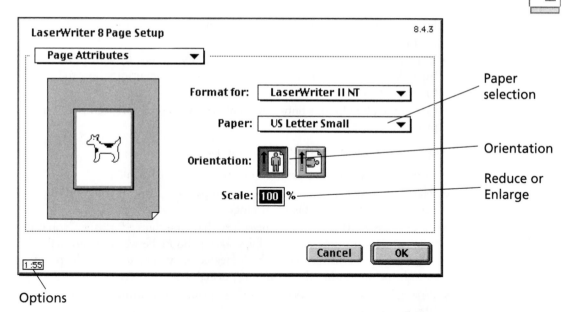

Options

Figure 4.8 *The Print Setup dialog box.*

❖ Reduce or Enlarge—You can choose to reduce or enlarge the size of the printed output. Usually, you use 100 percent, which means that you print at the normal size.

❖ Orientation—The icons tell it all. You can tell the printer to print your document in a normal position (portrait) or sideways (landscape). Regardless of

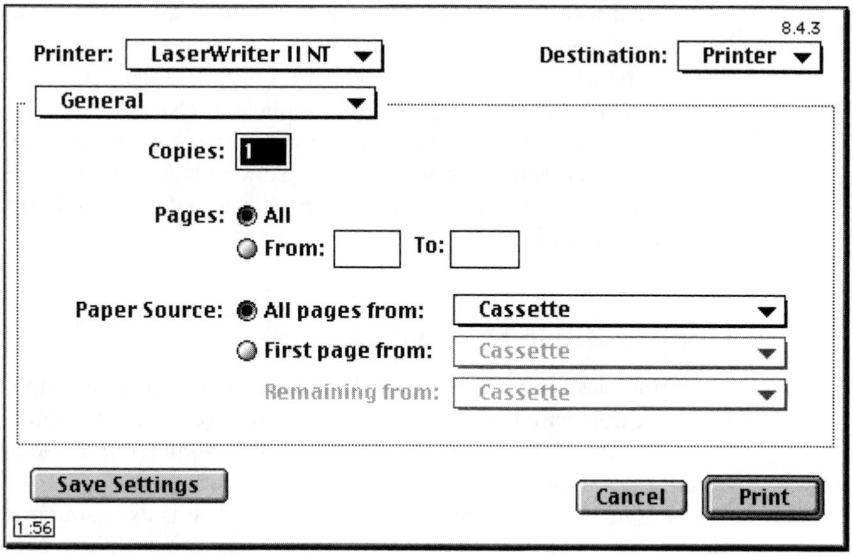

Figure 4.9 *The Print dialog box.*

how your paper goes into the printer, your printer can print the document in either orientation.

❖ Printer Effects—Printer effects are options determined by your printer's capabilities. For the LaserWriter, the options tell the printer how to handle fonts and graphic images.

❖ Options—The Options button presents you with settings specific to your printer and its capabilities.

The following are the Print dialog box options:

❖ Copies—This tells your printer how many copies to print.

❖ Pages—This option lets you select which pages to print. If you want to print page 5, enter 5 to 5 for the print range.

❖ Paper Source—If your printer has more than one source for paper, you can tell it which source to use. Usually, you can choose between the normal paper tray and a manual feed, which means that you hand-insert the paper into the printer rather than using its normal paper source.

❖ Destination—For LaserWriters you can print to the printer or to a PostScript file.

These instructions and explanations are the bare minimum you need to print. Printing is complex enough to require a series of explanations throughout the book. Before you can be proficient at printing, you must understand your printer; becoming familiar with your printer's manual as well will help.

Using Multiple Windows and Program Switching

Most Macintosh programs, SimpleText included, can open several documents at the same time. In addition to multiple documents open in one program, you can also have several programs running, each with multiple documents open at the same time—now you're operating a fairly complicated system.

Knowing how to manage your programs and documents is essential to mastering your Mac. This section discusses the fundamentals of using multiple documents and switching between multiple programs. First, we look at using multiple documents within an application.

Using Multiple Documents

The principles for using multiple documents within an application are very similar to using multiple windows in the Finder. If you haven't read Chapter 3, review the section, "The Anatomy of a Window." You'll find 90 percent of the information you need for using multiple documents in that section.

Using multiple documents in any Mac program is like using multiple windows in the Macintosh Finder. Some programs make using multiple documents easy by providing a Window menu that lists your open documents; others require you to move the document windows around. A quick look at SimpleText helps in this matter. Perform these steps using SimpleText (TeachText does not have the ability to open multiple documents).

To open multiple documents:

1. Open a New Window using the ⌘+N or the *New* menu item from the File menu.
2. Now, two windows are open, but the new document completely covers the other document.
3. Resize the new document using the grow box.
4. Once the document window is resized, click on your original window, which is behind the new document.
5. Select some text from your original window and copy it.
6. Resize the current window so that you can see the window behind it.
7. Click on the window that is behind and bring it forward.
8. Zoom the front document window and paste in the copied text.

Now, you have two document windows, each with text. If you want to switch quickly between the two windows, you need to configure both windows using the grow box. The secret here is to configure the two windows so that they can both be seen, regardless of which window is in front. Figure 4.10 shows one configuration that works. Now, with your windows configured, bring forward the window you want to use.

Another Text Editor

As you know, a CD-ROM is included with this book. If you have a CD-ROM drive, you can use all the programs on the CD-ROM (at the moment, you may not know how to access these programs, so this note may be premature). There is a program on the CD-ROM disk called SaintEdit that you can use instead of SimpleText or TeachText.

If you use TeachText instead of SimpleText, you have discovered that TeachText is very limited when compared to SimpleText. To get more out of this chapter, repeat the exercises in this chapter with SaintEdit.

Instructions for copying programs (moving a program or data file from one disk to another) are covered in Chapter 5. Once you've learned to do this, repeat these exercises using SaintEdit, which is found in the CD-ROM's Utilities folder. There are differences between SaintEdit and SimpleText—namely, the ability to use styles—but you learn more using SaintEdit than using TeachText.

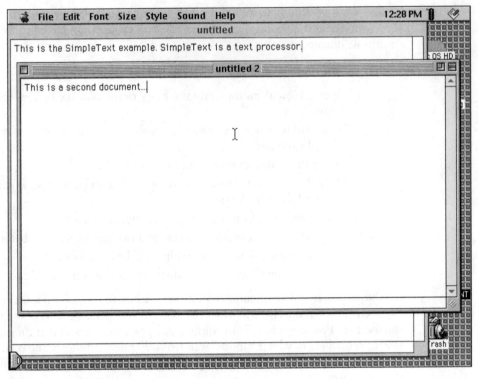

Figure 4.10 *Window configuration for using multiple documents.*

To quickly switch between the document windows:

1. Zoom the window to full size by clicking in the zoom box.
2. When you want to use the window in back, click in the zoom box again. The window will return to its original position.
3. Now you can select the other window.
4. Zoom it to work in it.
5. When you want to use the other window, repeat steps 2 and 3.

This technique works in any application where the document window has a zoom box. Practice using multiple windows now. Learning to use your Mac is a lot like learning any other new skill: You have to practice and be patient. Practicing now will pay off later when you have to work on multiple documents while under a deadline.

Using Multiple Programs

Using multiple programs is a lot like using multiple documents, only switching between programs is easier. To show you how to use multiple programs, we're not going to run another application; instead, you will switch between SimpleText and the Finder.

Layering or Tiling Elements

Bringing a window forward is the terminology used for selecting a window that may be behind another. The same terminology is used in programs that use objects, which are elements that can be layered within the same window. The programs that use objects are most often graphics programs.

When you encounter a program with objects, keep in mind that the objects will often behave like document windows or windows in the Finder. They can be layered, one object can hide another, or they can overlap.

This is an example of a principle that works in many different circumstances. Think of the things you learn about operating your Mac in terms of principles rather than as isolated steps that apply in only one situation. This approach is one of the keys to becoming a Macintosh master.

If you haven't noticed, there is an icon in the upper right corner of your screen. In SimpleText this icon is a smaller representation of the SimpleText icon that you double-clicked to start the program. This icon changes depending on the program you're currently using, so it indicates which program is running. The icon is also the Application menu (see Figure 4.11).

When you click on the Application menu, you see the following menu items:

❖ *Hide SimpleText*

❖ *Hide Others*

❖ *Show All*

❖ A list of all active applications

Each Application menu item is described below so that you can learn how it works. Each description explains what happens when the menu item is selected. Read all the descriptions before experimenting so that you understand how to navigate between your applications.

The *Hide [application name]* menu item   The *Hide [application name]* menu item hides the application you're using. Selecting *Hide SimpleText* will cause SimpleText to be suspended, hiding its windows and menu bar. The program still runs, but it is not visible. If you have more programs running than just SimpleText when you select the Hide menu item, you switch to the last program is use before you opened SimpleText. If you are returned to the Finder, it means that the Finder was the last program you used, probably to start SimpleText or the application you're now using.

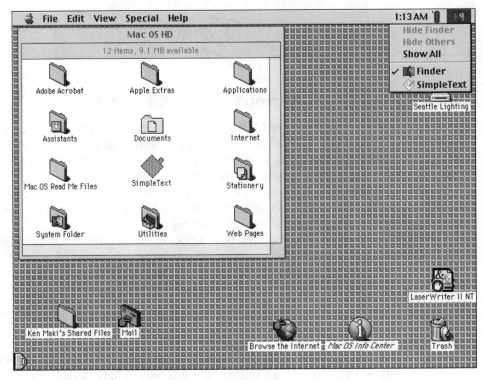

Figure 4.11 *Using the Application menu while running SimpleText.*

The *Hide Others* menu item   The *Hide Others* menu item hides all the applications you're running except the one you're using. This command causes the open windows and menus for all your other programs to be hidden. Using this command also grays out both the *Hide* and *Hide Others* menu items, which are unavailable if you're running two programs and one is hidden.

The *Show All* menu item   The *Show All* menu item is used to make all your hidden applications reappear.

The list of active applications   Any program running is included in the applications list. The active application has a check mark next to it. If a program is hidden, its icon is gray. You can switch from one program to another by selecting the program's name from the applications list.

There are two reasons for hiding the applications you're not using. One is to speed up your Mac; it doesn't have to do quite as much work when a program is hidden. The other reason is that your Mac's screen will be less cluttered.

You can also selectively hide programs by switching to the program and then hiding it. This can be advantageous when you're using several programs and need to switch between only two of them. There is another, convenient way to switch between two programs.

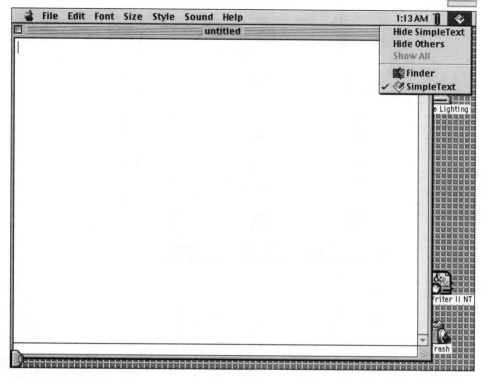

Figure 4.12 *SimpleText as the active application.*

When you have two active applications, you can switch between them by clicking a document window of either program. With our current example, you can witness this capability by switching between SimpleText and the Finder.

To switch between active applications:

1. SimpleText is the active application and your application menu looks like Figure 4.12.
2. Click outside of the SimpleText document window on the right side.
3. This switches you to the Finder. Now, your screen looks something like Figure 4.13. Notice that the SimpleText window is visible and that its title bar indicates it is inactive.
4. Now, click in the SimpleText document window that is in the background.
5. The SimpleText document is now the active window.
6. Repeat steps 2 and 3 while holding down the Option key.

If you repeat the exercise while holding down the Option key, you see that SimpleText was hidden when you switched to the Finder. Whenever you switch applications while holding down the Option key, the application you're switching from will be hidden, even when using the Application menu.

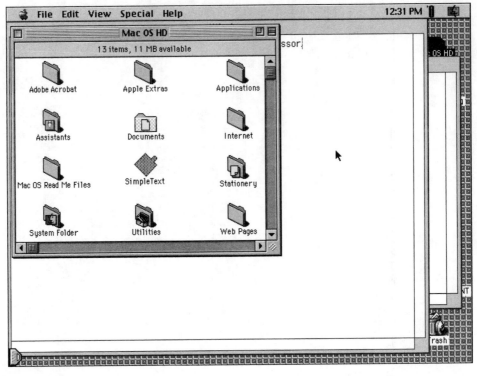

Figure 4.13 *After switching to the Finder.*

As with all the other operation techniques in this chapter, experiment with program switching. It is another of the basic skills you will need when you use your Mac.

Quitting and Restarting Your Program

Now, it is time to quit SimpleText: Select the *Quit* menu item from the File menu or use the ⌘+Q command key option. Either action will cause SimpleText to quit and return you to the Finder. If you are running multiple programs, you are returned to the last program that you were in when you quit your current program. Quitting works like program switching in this respect.

Once you've quit SimpleText, you can always restart it by double-clicking on the application. If you want to start a program and open a document at the same time, double-click on a document icon. Earlier, you saved a SimpleText document called *Test Document;* it should be on your Desktop. If you double-click on the document, SimpleText will start and the document will open at the same time.

Because this technique for starting a program also involves opening a file, this is all I'm going to say about it at the moment. You'll find more information about files in Chapter 5.

Checking the Clipboard

While you're switching back and forth between the Finder and SimpleText, check the contents of the Macintosh's Clipboard. To check the Clipboard's contents, you must be in the Finder, where a *Show Clipboard* menu item appears in the Edit menu.

Select the *Show Clipboard* menu item. A window appears, showing you what is in the Clipboard. You will also see the file type. (File types are discussed in Chapter 5.)

This concludes the instructional part of this chapter. The remainder covers other command functions found in most Macintosh programs, a section about Apple's online help system called AppleGuide, a description of software types, and some tips for learning more about software.

Additional Selection Methods and Other Commands

Some Macintosh features common in most programs are missing in SimpleText. This section looks at some of the features and functions you should know about. Remember this section so that you can practice what is listed here when you start using other programs.

The Undo Function

The Macintosh has a feature called *Undo*. This feature lets you reverse whatever you've done since your last mouse click or the last time you pressed the Enter key on your keyboard. The Undo command can be used to remove an edit you've made to a document, reverse an accidental cut, or remove something you just pasted into that document.

In a note earlier in this chapter, I mentioned a program on the CD-ROM called SaintEdit, a good program to use for the following steps. (You will have to come back to this chapter after you've installed SaintEdit.)

To perform the Undo function:

1. Open your program and type something into the document window.
2. Select the Edit menu and drag down to the *Undo* menu item.
3. An alternative to using the Menu command is to use the keyboard equivalent (⌘+Z).

Once you execute this command, the text you just entered disappears. If you want the text to return, repeat the Undo command. Undo is a toggle command, which means that each time you perform the command it switches back and forth between the last two commands, one of which is the Undo command itself. Undo is really an undo and a redo command.

4. Move the pointer and click the mouse somewhere within your document.

5. Now, execute the Undo command as described in steps 1 or 2 above.

Notice that the Undo command does not do anything because there is now nothing to undo. When you get the opportunity, practice this command. It is very useful; you will want it in your repertoire of skills.

Selection Techniques You Will Want to Know

Once again, the items in this section are techniques that do not work in SimpleText but are, nevertheless, standard Macintosh functions that work in almost every other program. Like the Undo command, these techniques do work in SaintEdit; once you've installed it, you should try these functions.

No steps are listed here because each of these techniques is a single command. Type a couple of paragraphs and try them out.

❖ **Triple-clicking**—This technique selects an entire paragraph.

❖ **Command (⌘) Click**—This technique selects an entire sentence (this does not work in SaintEdit; try it in other programs).

❖ **Using the Shift key**—When you press the Shift key in combination with another command, the Shift key becomes a modifier. There are several ways it can be used. One is to double-click on a word and then hold the Shift key down as you click on subsequent words. Each time you click on another word, it too becomes selected.

Another way is to use the Shift key in conjunction with the cursor keys. When you hold the Shift key down and press a cursor key, you select text as you move the insertion point. This selection technique can also be used to deselect text if you dragged through too much text.

These techniques are Macintosh standards that should be included in every program. Sometimes they get left out, so experiment with your programs to see if these techniques work. Appendix B lists the standard Macintosh command keys and keyboard shortcuts.

Using AppleGuide

AppleGuide is a feature of Mac OS 8. It is an online help system and Apple's new method for providing you with help—it is like having a program's manual available at all times. AppleGuide has not been mentioned until now because it is easier to use if you are familiar with windows, menus, and some basic Macintosh skills.

At the time of this writing, AppleGuide works only in the Finder and a few other programs. In the future, most commercial programs you purchase will use AppleGuide, which is accessible from the Help menu, the icon with the ? next to the Application menu.

If the program you're using supports AppleGuide, it has menu items following the *Show Balloons* menu item. Figure 4.14 shows the Help menu while in the Finder.

Notice that *Macintosh Guide*, *Shortcuts*, and *PowerTalk* are menu items that you can choose. The other menu options, *About Balloon Help...* and *Show Balloons*, are another available help system (see the note for more information about Balloon Help).

In this section, we look at the Macintosh Guide. Once you're familiar with it, you can go on and explore the other AppleGuides at your leisure. The most unique feature of AppleGuide is that it will walk you through the required steps for most Macintosh operations while providing a detailed description.

In the following, we'll look at just one example available in the Macintosh Guide:

1. From the Finder, select the Macintosh Guide menu item from the Help menu.
2. When the Macintosh Guide window opens, click on the Topics button (Figure 4.15).

   Notice that this window looks different from the ones we've used up to this point. Also, if you click outside the window, it does not disappear. AppleGuide takes control of your Mac and, even though you can switch programs and access your windows, it remains present and in front of anything else you try to do. This is a help system, not a normal application.

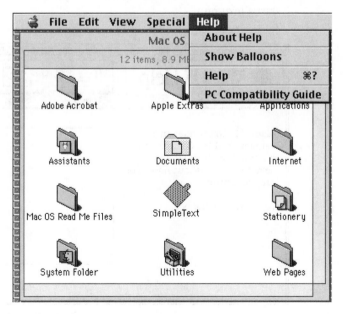

Figure 4.14 *The Help menu.*

Balloon Help

Balloon Help is a help system that causes balloons with explanations to appear as you move the pointer to different areas of the screen. The balloons, like those used in comic strips, provide only a brief description of the object.

Turn on Balloon Help by selecting the *Show Balloons* menu item; when the balloons are turned on, the menu item changes to *Hide Balloons*. This is an example of a toggling menu; some menus, when selected, change to indicate that something can be turned off or on.

Balloon Help is useful when you are unfamiliar with the elements in a program; the balloons identify different window parts and offer a brief description. Balloons will soon get in the way and be more of an annoyance than a help. As such, they are mentioned here so that you can use Balloon Help if you wish.

3. When the topics appear, click on Working with Programs.
4. A list of additional topics appears on the right side. Click on Open a Program.
5. Click the OK button.
6. A window like the one in Figure 4.16 appears with instructions on how to start a program.

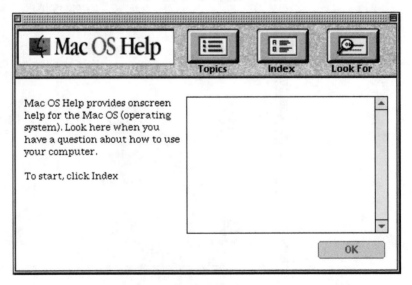

Figure 4.15   *The Macintosh Guide window.*

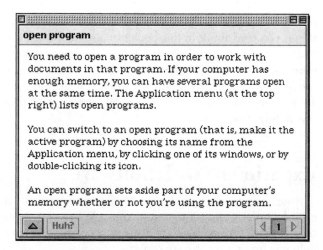

Figure 4.16   *The Starting a Program window.*

7. After reading the information in the window, click the Huh? button.
8. Another window titled *Definitions Tips for Finding Files* opens to give you additional help (see Figure 4.17).
9. Continue to play with various options from the Definitions Tips for Finding Files window.
10. When you are finished, click on the Close box to quit AppleGuide.

By using the controls shown in Figure 4.17, you can spend a lot of time exploring AppleGuide. What makes AppleGuide unique is its ability to open programs, mark

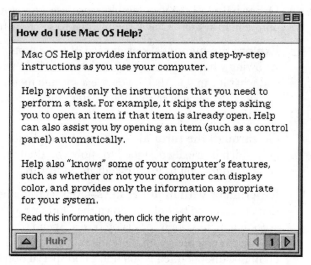

Figure 4.17   *The Definitions Tips for Finding Files window.*

the screen, and, in general, walk you through complicated procedures. Many of the things you read about in this book can also be found in AppleGuide.

Spend a few hours playing with AppleGuide as you read this book because it offers a unique way to explore your Macintosh's system safely. Just remember that the Macintosh operates according to a set of rules and that, many times, when you are told or shown steps, you are actually seeing principles that you can apply to other computing situations.

How to Experiment with Software

Throughout this chapter, I have urged you to experiment. Your exploration, though, must be orderly and somewhat planned. When you install new software, take some time to learn the program and its features. The following is a list of suggestions to help you become a software expert:

Review the manual—Become familiar with the manual's layout and any terms particular to the software. Look at the index; it is easier to find topics you need help with by looking there than in the table of contents.

Start the program—When you start the program, look at the screen for a few minutes before you do anything. Study the menu names, the window layout, and any elements that are new to you.

Turn on Balloon Help—With Balloon Help, you can identify any screen elements you don't recognize. Just move the pointer to those screen elements you don't know. Don't forget to turn off Balloon Help when you're finished.

Check for an AppleGuide—See if the program has an AppleGuide. If it does, explore the topics and index so that you can learn what type of help is available.

Other help—If the program does not use AppleGuide, see if there is another online help system. Check the manual to see how to access it.

Explore the menus—Look at each of the menus and their menu items. Knowing what menu options you have will help you understand the program and what it can do. Also, if you see a specific menu item referenced in the manual, you'll know where to find it. After you've looked at the menu items, try the ones that are unfamiliar.

Go through the tutorial—The more complicated programs often have a tutorial, which is usually designed to show you the basic features of the program and introduce you to its more advanced features.

Experiment with modifier keys—Many programs build in special functions that are accessed by holding down the Option, Command, or Control keys while accessing menus, tools, or dialog boxes. Spend some time trying the different modifier key options with these items. When you do this type of experimenting, do not be disappointed if you don't find special options. In the chapters on System software, you will see the results of this type of experimentation.

How the Mac's Graphical Interface Is Designed

Throughout this chapter, you've read about how the menus, windows, and other aspects of the Mac are consistent from one program to the next. It is this consistency that makes experimentation possible and profitable. But the consistency built into Macintosh programs did not happen by accident.

When Apple created the Macintosh, it was very concerned with how you would interact with your computer and so established a set of guidelines called the *Human Interface Guidelines*. These guidelines were established so that programmers would create programs that conformed to specific standards of operability in all areas—from how the programs ran to what they asked you, including how to store your data. In principle, Apple wants every program to conform to specific visual and operational standards, so that by learning how to use one program, you will already know the basics for using other programs, which, in turn, keeps your learning curve to a minimum, making you more productive.

These are the major areas covered by the *Guidelines*, as outlined in *Inside Macintosh, Volume VI* (Reading, MA: Addison-Wesley, 1991):

❖ Metaphors from the real world—Whenever possible, you should be able to relate what you see and do on your Macintosh to a similar event in the *real world*.

❖ Direct manipulation—Whenever you perform an action with your Mac, you should see an indication that you have done something. This is a reality check; if you throw a file into the trash, the trash can should bulge to verify that a file has been thrown away.

❖ See-and-point (not remember-and-type)—Apple does not want you to remember anything you do not need to remember. Thus, you have menus, buttons, a mouse, and icons. To use the Mac, all you have to do is figure out how to use the mouse.

❖ Consistency—By maintaining a specific function for menus, such as the File and Edit menus, the way the mouse operates, and, whenever possible, all the dialog boxes and messages, you will not have to learn a new vocabulary or set of commands for each program you use.

❖ WYSIWYG (what you see is what you get)—Whenever you work on a document, whether it is a picture, database report, or letter, what you see should be exactly what you get as a finished product.

❖ User control—You are in the driver's seat. Your Macintosh should never do anything without your expressed approval (although this is not reality, it is a great ideal).

❖ Feedback and dialog—Your Mac should always tell you what it is doing, dutiful servant that it is.

❖ Forgiveness—Apple wants you to be able to undo as many things as possible if you change your mind and to be notified of every action that is not reversible.

❖ Perceived stability—Your computing environment should be stable and should not change.

❖ Aesthetic integrity—Apple does not like ugly icons. The visual interface should not be distracting, and you should have control over your workspace (the Finder and Desktop).

This list represents the basis for everything your computer does. In a sense, the *Guidelines* are the key to the map that you need when using your Mac. By keeping these principles in mind, you can become a Macintosh master.

Summary

In this chapter, you have the basics for learning how to use your software. Even though the example used throughout the chapter is a simple program, it demonstrates many of the features you need for using other programs. Teaching you how to use SimpleText is actually a secondary goal; the primary goal is to demonstrate the features you find in most Mac programs and to provide you with the basic knowledge you need to use any Mac program.

The next chapter completes your basic Mac education. Once you read Chapter 5, you will have been exposed to all the basic skills and knowledge you need to start using your Mac. The rest of the book will build on the knowledge of these first five chapters and take you down the road of Macintosh self-sufficiency.

CHAPTER 5

Keeping Track of Your Data

Keeping your data safe, secure, and easily accessible takes some practice. Every time you turn on your Mac, you face the task of file management. Where are you going to put documents and graphics you've created? And once you've put them somewhere, how do you find them again? Do you need to keep your data secure or share it? And how do you keep your data safe?

The process of managing your data files is called *file management*, the topic of this chapter. All too often, people buy their Macs and start using them, doing an admirable job of teaching themselves the basics and becoming productive, only to find that they do not really know where on their hard drives their data is located. They can often find their data, but they have no idea how it ended up where it did or how to put it where they want it to be.

Part of their ignorance is justified. Certain files on your hard disk must remain in place for your Macintosh to run properly. Moving the wrong file from its proper location can cause your Mac to fail to start or a program to run improperly. If you do not know how to recognize the different types of files found on your Mac, it is not only reasonable but prudent that you do not move anything. This approach, however, is not the efficient way to use your Mac.

In this chapter, you will learn how to recognize different types of files, where they are stored, and how to move and copy your files. Other topics covered are finding files, keeping your data safe, and lots of details about how your Mac handles data. Read this entire chapter before trying any of the examples. The examples are designed to safeguard your data, but, if you make a mistake, you may lose some of your data or even render your Mac inoperable.

More about the Finder

In Chapters 2 and 3, you were introduced to the Finder and some of its functions. Now it is time to learn more about the Finder. All the functions related to file

107

management, with the exception of saving files within an application, are done from the Finder.

To use the Finder effectively, you need to learn several things:

❖ How to recognize icons

❖ How to create and name folders

❖ How files and folders are stored

What Are Those Icons?

By now, you know that icons are the graphic representations the Mac uses to identify various objects. These objects can be files, programs, devices, or even tools employed by applications. In addition to being a "metaphor from the real world," icons also represent functionality. Specific icons exemplify a particular capability, function, or purpose.

The main reason for knowing what different icons denote is to identify an icon's function. In Figure 5.1, you see a series of icons used in the Finder to represent files, drives, and devices.

The different types of icons in Figure 5.1 are as follows:

❖ **An application file**   Any icon that has a diamond, such as the SimpleText icon, represents a program that you can double-click on to start. According to Apple's specifications, all applications are supposed to use some form of a diamond for their icons. However, not all programs conform to this standard. Usually, an application's icon is distinctive and different from the other types of icons but they don't always look like a diamond.

❖ **An application data file**   All icons like the *document* icon in Figure 5.1 represent user-created data files. The icon is designed to look like a piece of paper with a folded corner. Some programs do not conform to this standard, which means that you may have to learn to recognize some additional document icons. Also, some programs create different icons for different types of data.

❖ **Disk icon**   Disk icons represent disk drives. When a disk icon is opened, it displays the files and folders on the disk. There are different types of disks, and their icons are different to denote their type. Figure 5.1 shows some of the different types of disk icons you will encounter. Hard disk icons will vary in their appearance; notice the two different icons in Figure 5.1 for the hard drives.

❖ **Folder icons**   The icon labeled Folder represents a manila file folder, just like the ones in your filing cabinet. The difference between a real-world folder and a Macintosh folder is that you can put folders within folders on the Macintosh, but in the physical universe, folders usually do not fit inside each other.

❖ **Special-purpose folder icons**   In addition to the generic folder icon, there are special-purpose folder icons. Although you should use these only to specify that the folder has a special purpose, as the Control Panels Folder that goes in the System Folder does, some software manufacturers do create

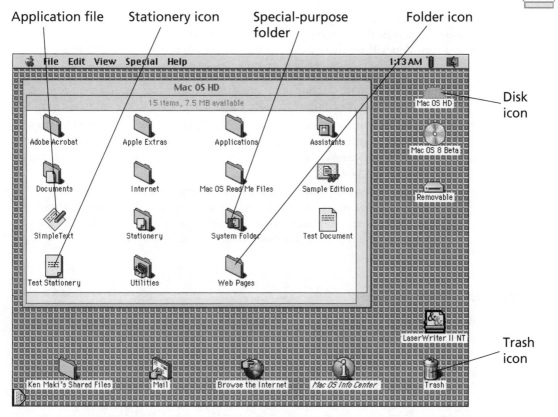

Figure 5.1 *The Macintosh Desktop.*

folders that appear to be special-purpose folders just so that they can distinguish their product (a subliminal form of advertising).

❖ **The Trash icon** The Trash icon, another special-purpose icon, symbolizes a real-world trash can; its function is similar. You put your unwanted files in the Trash icon.

❖ **Stationery icons** Stationery icons represent templates, which are user-created documents, actually forms, that you can use again and again. Rather than re-create your form each time you need it, double-click on the stationery icon to open a document that you can then customize and save as a new data document.

Template A predefined set of contents (numbers, text, and formulas) for a spreadsheet, designed for some specific purpose or task—for example, a budget template.

❖ **Edition icons** The Edition icon is a special-purpose icon created by a function called *Publish and Subscribe*, which will be discussed later in the section, "Manipulating Your Files."

Some of the icons in Figure 5.1 are not discussed in this chapter. They are special-purpose icons that represent devices and functions that require a more detailed discussion. You will see these icons as you explore your Macintosh, and you should be aware of them even though they are only being introduced in this section.

- ❖ **Catalog icons** Catalog icons are similar to drive icons, but they contain only certain types of information. Catalog icons are discussed in Chapter 8.
- ❖ **Desktop Printer icons** If you're using QuickDraw GX or the Desktop Printer extensions, component parts of Mac OS 8.0, your printers are represented as Desktop icons. Information about QuickDraw GX and Desktop Printers can be found in Chapter 8.
- ❖ **System icons** System icons are special-purpose icons that represent the files your Mac needs to run. There is a whole series of system icons, with each type of icon representing a different type of system element. These icons and the files they represent are discussed in Chapter 7.

More about Icons

As mentioned in Chapters 2 and 3, icons, even though they are graphic representations, are also real objects. When you manipulate an icon, you manipulate a file inside your Macintosh. Manipulating the file may result in the manipulation of a peripheral device connected to your Mac; operation of any part of your Mac is caused by one of the files in your Mac.

In a sense, I have oversimplified what happens when you use your Mac. For the moment, it is an adequate explanation because 98 percent of all the icons you see represent files, whether program, system, or data files. The other 2 percent of the icons you'll encounter represent devices, such as disk drives and printers, and offer a means to manipulate them. In those computers that use Microsoft Windows (we in the Mac world like to think of them as that other type of computer), icons always represent files. It is important to keep this distinction in mind.

Although the Mac is easy to use, exercise some caution when using it. Just moving the right file to the wrong location can cause your Mac to malfunction.

Getting Organized

This section is the final installment of information you need to use your Mac. You know how to start and use a program, save a file, and view the contents of a folder, and you are generally familiar with your Mac's Desktop. Now, you will learn how to organize your Mac so that you know where your data is stored and how to find it.

Some of the examples in this section display hard drives that are more complex and contain more information than you have on your system. Once more, the principles demonstrated are what's important. How you organize your Mac is entirely up to you.

Keeping your hard drive organized can be a constant battle; if you don't do it consistently, the mess can quickly crowd you off your disk.

Using Your Folders

In Chapter 3 you learned how to create folders, but how to use folders was covered only superficially. You will use everything you learned about using windows as you work with folders. In this section, we look at what folders are and how they work; the topics covered are as follows:

❖ More about your folders
❖ Nesting folders
❖ Naming folders

Folders are used to store your Mac's computer files. They are also used to group and categorize those same files. The Mac does some of the organization automatically, or rather the programs that install software onto your Mac do the work. For the moment, we are primarily concerned with the organization of the files you create.

Folder   A holder of documents, applications, and even other folders on the Desktop. Folders act as subdirectories, allowing you to organize information in any way you like.

To see how your Mac uses a folder let's look inside your System folder. **During this exercise, all you will do is look, which means you're going to open, look, and close the System folder:**

1. Make sure your hard drive is open.
2. Select the System folder; it is labeled *System Folder*.
3. Open the System folder (see Figure 5.2).
4. Now, look at the files using the various View menu items in the View menu.
5. Resize the window when necessary so that you can see the files.
6. When you are through looking, close the System Folder window.

This exercise is meant to show you only how a folder is used to hold files. You should have noticed the folders in the System folder. The System folder contains all the files that run your Mac. You'll have to wait until Chapter 7 for an explanation of these files.

A folder is sometimes called a directory because the folder's counterpart on other computers is called a directory.

Directory   A list of the contents of a disk or a specific folder. Some directories contain subdirectories. A directory is sometimes called a *catalog*.

Thus, the System folder is also called the System Directory. This terminology is not common when talking about the Mac, but it is used occasionally.

Nesting Your Folders

The folders contained in the System folder in Figure 5.2 are called *nested folders* or *subdirectories*. Remember that your Mac's folders are like their real-world counter-

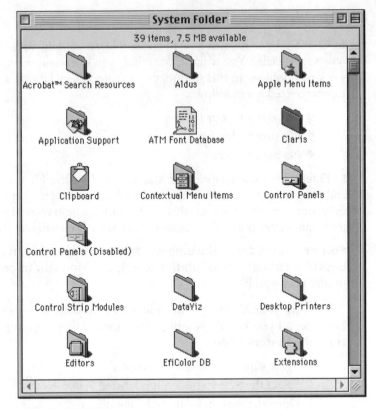

Figure 5.2   *The open System folder.*

parts, file folders. The process of placing folders inside of folders is called *nesting* and is the result of the Mac's hierarchical file system, which can be described in several ways. Think of the system as a tree: The hard drive is the trunk, each folder is a branch, and each nested folder is another branch coming from the main branch. Figure 5.3 shows this concept.

To demonstrate how this works on your Mac, let's work through an exercise in which we make folders and name them. Naming folders is easy; you will use some of the principles discussed in Chapter 4.

If you have worked your way through this book consecutively, starting with Chapter 1, you have created at least one folder in Chapter 3, when you learned how to work with windows.

Now, let's use the folder you created and play with it:

1. Find the folder called *untitled folder*.
2. Move your pointer over the folder's name and click once. A box appears around the folder's name, as shown in Figure 5.3.
3. Type in a new name.

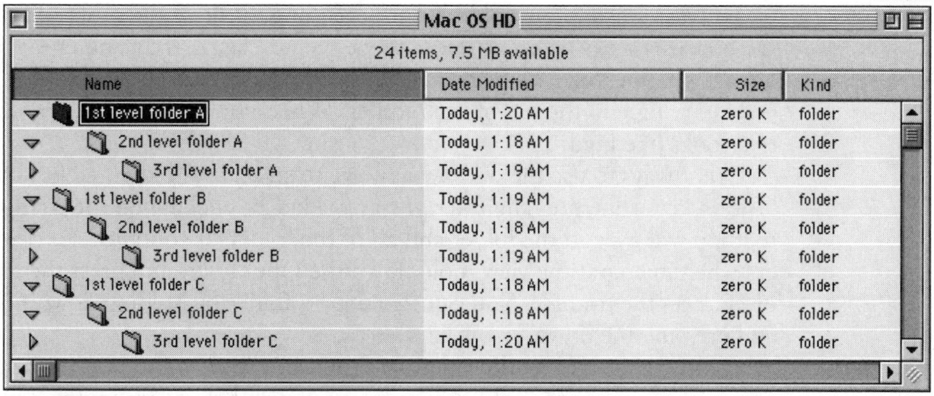

Name	Date Modified	Size	Kind
Mac OS HD — 24 items, 7.5 MB available			
▽ 📁 1st level folder A	Today, 1:20 AM	zero K	folder
▽ 📁 2nd level folder A	Today, 1:18 AM	zero K	folder
▷ 📁 3rd level folder A	Today, 1:19 AM	zero K	folder
▽ 📁 1st level folder B	Today, 1:19 AM	zero K	folder
▽ 📁 2nd level folder B	Today, 1:18 AM	zero K	folder
▷ 📁 3rd level folder B	Today, 1:19 AM	zero K	folder
▽ 📁 1st level folder C	Today, 1:18 AM	zero K	folder
▽ 📁 2nd level folder C	Today, 1:18 AM	zero K	folder
▷ 📁 3rd level folder C	Today, 1:20 AM	zero K	folder

Figure 5.3 *An untitled folder's name selected for editing.*

4. Deselect the folder to set the name. Press the Enter key or click in the window, but not on the new name.

5. Open your renamed folder.

6. Create a new folder inside the window that opens.

7. When the folder is created, just start typing to rename it. When you create a new folder, you don't have to select the folder's name to rename it.

8. Repeat steps 5 through 7, two more times.

9. Close all open windows except your hard drive. If you want to close all of your open windows with a single mouse click, hold down the Option key when you click in the Close box. This clicking technique will close every open window, including your hard drive's window.

Renaming Files

The steps for naming a folder also apply to renaming data files. In step 3, if you move the pointer over the folder's name, the pointer turns into an I-beam. Clicking the mouse when the pointer is over the folder's name places an insertion, just as if you were editing text. All the text editing techniques discussed in Chapter 4 apply to the Finder when editing file names, including using the cut, copy, and paste functions.

When editing file or folder names, you will encounter some limitations: The name cannot exceed 32 characters, nor can it contain a colon (:) or a carriage return (the invisible character that your Mac creates when you use the Enter key); otherwise, you can use any name you want.

You just created four folders, with each one inside of the other. The easiest way to see how this looks on your Mac is to view your hard drive using one of the list views: View by Name, Size, Date, or Kind. Then, expand each of your folders by clicking on the triangle to the left of each folder. When you've done this, you see something that looks like Figure 5.4.

Other ways to use the outline view are to select the folder and hold down the Option key while pressing the right-arrow key or clicking on the triangle. This method will expand the folder and all of the folders it contains. To close all the folders when in an outline view, hold down the Option key and press the left-arrow key or click on the triangle. You can also open a folder by holding down the Option key and pressing the down-arrow key.

Figure 5.4 uses an outline view to show your folders and how each folder contains others. The number of folders you can nest is, in theory, unlimited, but you will reach a practical limit before you reach the limit of folders the Mac can actually nest. In most cases, you will find that nesting folders deeper than two or three becomes awkward—but this is a personal opinion; you may want to build a labyrinth.

Take the time now to understand how nested folders work. Remember, each folder can contain data files as well as folders, and the number of items you can place in a folder can be unlimited (in theory)—but there is a practical limit. If you put several hundred files and folders into a single folder, you'll find that the Mac will take a long time to open that folder.

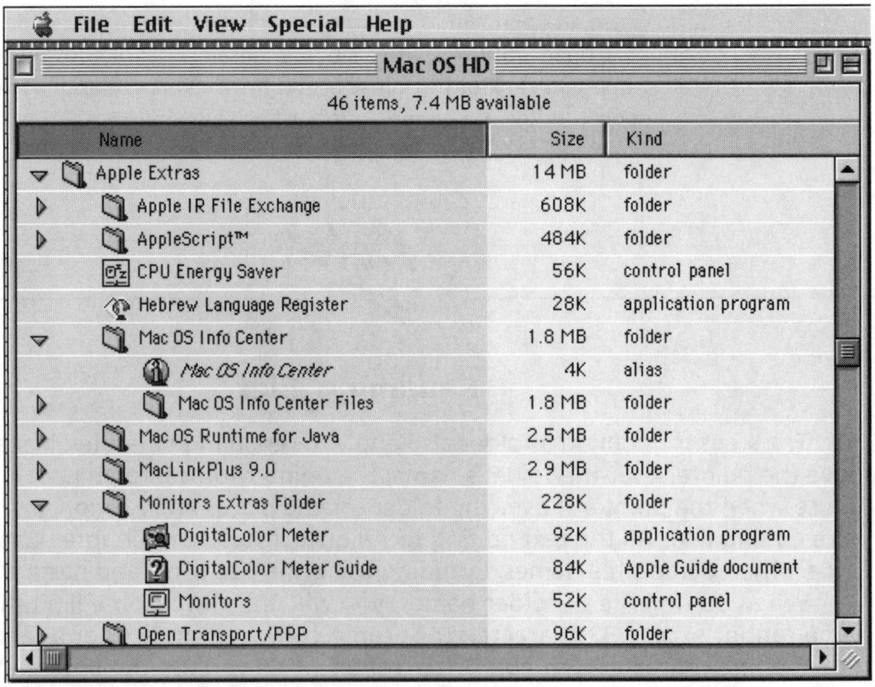

Name	Size	Kind
▽ 📁 Apple Extras	14 MB	folder
▷ 📁 Apple IR File Exchange	608K	folder
▷ 📁 AppleScript™	484K	folder
📄 CPU Energy Saver	56K	control panel
📄 Hebrew Language Register	28K	application program
▽ 📁 Mac OS Info Center	1.8 MB	folder
📄 *Mac OS Info Center*	4K	alias
▷ 📁 Mac OS Info Center Files	1.8 MB	folder
▷ 📁 Mac OS Runtime for Java	2.5 MB	folder
▷ 📁 MacLinkPlus 9.0	2.9 MB	folder
▽ 📁 Monitors Extras Folder	228K	folder
📄 DigitalColor Meter	92K	application program
📄 DigitalColor Meter Guide	84K	Apple Guide document
📄 Monitors	52K	control panel
▷ 📁 Open Transport/PPP	96K	folder

Mac OS HD — 46 items, 7.4 MB available

File　Edit　View　Special　Help

Figure 5.4　*The expanded folders.*

Setting Up a System for Your Folders

How you organize your data is a personal matter. If you have some secret code you want to use and can remember what it all means, then knock yourself out. Most people, though, will want to use folder names that reflect their work habits and make finding their data easy. The following is a suggestion to demonstrate how you can organize your data.

One method that works well is to set up your hard drive with a limited number of folders named by category. Using this method, you would have your System folder and Applications, Utilities, and Data folders. You can have more folders if necessary, but the more folders you have on the top level of your drive, the harder it will be to find one of those hundreds of files.

After you have your basic categories set up, you can subdivide the folders by putting folders inside each other. (You should put items in your System folder only when you know that they belong there.) After you install programs on your Mac, try dividing your Applications folder according to category by dividing it into Word Processing, Spreadsheets, Databases, Graphics, and so on. If you do not have multiple programs of a specific type, you can just put the application, such as Microsoft Excel, into the Applications folder without nesting it inside a spreadsheet folder. The idea is to group like programs with like programs, but only if necessary.

In Figure 5.5, three folders are set up in the fashion described. The most important folder to work on is your Data (or Documents) folder. Inside it, you may want to set up your subsidiary folders according to clients, projects, or a similar categorization that works for you. One possible way to set up the structure is by Customers, with a folder named for each customer and subdivided by letters, invoices, orders, and so on.

I hope that this structure seems self-evident. What makes it work is that you will be able to find your data easily—if you use this system conscientiously. All too often,

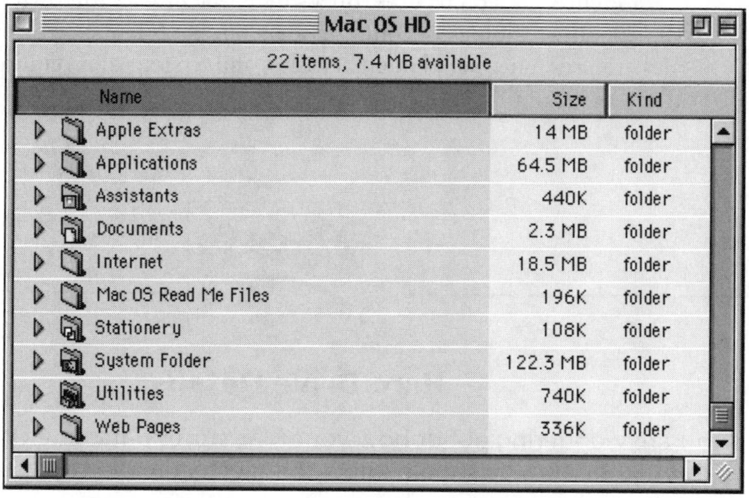

Mac OS HD		
22 items, 7.4 MB available		
Name	Size	Kind
▷ Apple Extras	14 MB	folder
▷ Applications	64.5 MB	folder
▷ Assistants	440K	folder
▷ Documents	2.3 MB	folder
▷ Internet	18.5 MB	folder
▷ Mac OS Read Me Files	196K	folder
▷ Stationery	108K	folder
▷ System Folder	122.3 MB	folder
▷ Utilities	740K	folder
▷ Web Pages	336K	folder

Figure 5.5 *An example for setting up your folder hierarchy.*

people create a folder on the fly without thinking about where to put it, stick a couple of files in the folder, and then repeat the process. This haphazard approach can result in hundreds of folders with just a few files in each, leaving you with no idea of where the document you want is located.

The other advantage to a system like this is that it prevents sensory overload. The average person can remember seven (plus or minus two) groups of information at a single time. So, if 20 folders are visible, you will spend more time looking for the one you want than if you have a system that groups your data into easily digestible chunks. If you can keep your hierarchy for your data folders so that you never look at more than seven folders at a time (and you do not stack your folders so deep that you forget what subcategory you are in), you will always be able to find a document.

Before you set up your folders, read the section, "Saving Your Work and Opening Files from within Programs." A feature of Mac OS 8 discussed in that section could affect how you set up your folders. If you are not using Mac OS 8, use whatever organizational method you wish.

How Bad Can It Get?

You may think that organizing your data is no big deal because you don't have any at the moment, but you need to remember that you're planning for the future. This section gives you an idea of how bad it can get. The amount of data that you create and acquire can be phenomenal.

Six or seven years ago, a 20-megabyte hard disk was considered huge. Today, huge is an 8GB (1 gigabyte equals 1024 megabytes) drive. In the days of old, the system software for a Macintosh fit on an 800KB floppy disk. Today, it comes on more than a dozen 1.44 MB floppies or, more often, a CD-ROM. As the Macintosh's system software and programs become more complex and powerful, they also take up more disk space and everything becomes more complex.

In Figure 5.6, you will see, on a single Macintosh, four drives with more than 10,000 individual files, accounting for 900MB of disk space. Granted, some of these files are programs, supplementary files, and System files required for the Mac's operation. Some of them are essential; others are not.

Hard Drive Details

If you are wondering about how your Mac stores data on a drive, that subject is covered in Chapter 10. You should know the mechanics of how your Mac stores data, but you don't need to know it now.

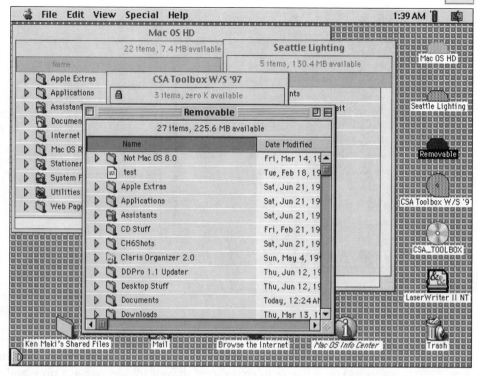

Figure 5.6   *Drives and files.*

As you can see, there is an awful lot of data on the machine in Figure 5.6; you may even predict that you'll never have anything close to what's shown. It is easy to underestimate how much data you'll collect. Even a 230MB hard drive can collect a lot of data; the one shown in Figure 5.7 has almost 5000 files.

If you had to find just one file out of the 5000 and if you didn't have a method for ordering your data, you could spend days looking for that single file. There are ways of finding your files that won't take days. If you forget the name of the file, you could be in trouble because most searching methods require that you know something about the file, such as its name. If you need to find a lost file, refer to the section, "When Your File Is Not Where It Should Be," later in this chapter.

Manipulating Your Files

This section is intended to serve two purposes: One is to teach you how to copy and move data; the other is to provide you with operational information that will make using your Mac easier. Some of the suggestions go beyond the basics and are geared for serious Mac work.

If you've been using your Mac for a while, you could have data scattered all over your drive. If this is the case, you may want to rearrange it. And even if you don't

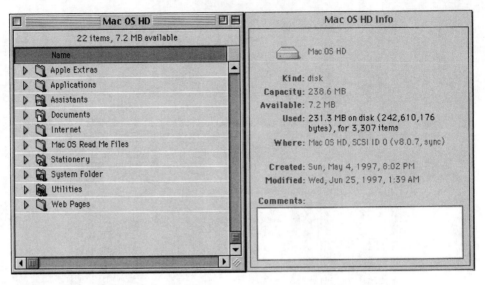

Figure 5.7 *A 230MB hard drive.*

want to rearrange your data, you may still need to know how to move and copy your files. If you're rearranging your data, you'll find this is the tedious part of the process: You will have to go through all your folders, one at a time, and move your data to its new folders.

There are some ways to make this process easier. First, you do not have to move your files one at a time. You can move or copy them in groups, thereby speeding up the process. If you want a specific file, it is easy to look for it if you remember all or part of its name.

For the beginner, the section "Moving Groups of Files" is good information for the future, but now you're more interested in basic file manipulations such as copying and moving. The next section, "Moving, Copying, and Deleting Files," looks at those basics first. The remaining sections cover those techniques and functions that can make accessing your files easier.

Moving, Copying, and Deleting Files

Now that you know about the Mac's hierarchical file structure and have some idea of where you will store your data, it's time to look at shuffling the data around. This section looks at the mechanics for performing each of these operations.

If you've been following the exercises, you've probably started to set up a system for your files and folders. And on your Desktop, you probably have one lonely file called *Test Document*. You will move this document around and then remove it from your hard drive. Once again, the steps you find here are more than just procedures for moving, copying, or deleting files. These procedures, especially those for moving files, are similar to functions in other programs.

Copying and Moving Files on the Same Disk

There are three different ways to copy files. One is to make a duplicate of a file; the second is to copy the file while it is being placed in a new location; and the third is to copy the file onto another disk. All of these methods make an exact copy of the file.

In Figure 5.8, you'll see the file *Test Document* on the Desktop.

To copy this document:

1. Select the document.

2. Select the *Duplicate* menu item from the File menu. You can also use the ⌘+D command key.

3. A new file called *Test Document copy* appears on your Desktop.

You've just created an exact copy of the *Test Document* file. If you double-click on the copy, your Mac will start SimpleText and open the file. Its contents will be the same as those of the original; the only difference is the document's name.

The second way to copy a file involves the same techniques you use when moving the file. First, we will move a file, which is nothing more than selecting the file's icon and dragging it to its new location. The new location can be a folder or an open window.

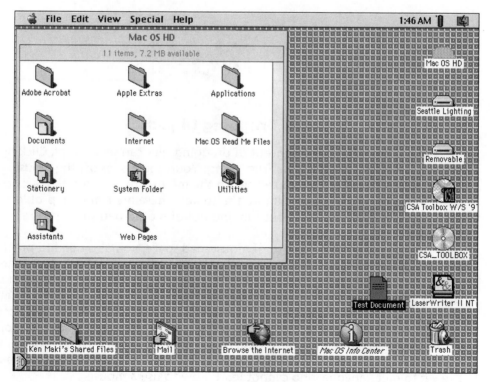

Figure 5.8   *The Desktop with the* Test Document.

To move the file "Test Document" into a folder on your hard drive:

1. Open your hard drive.
2. Create a new folder (this folder will be temporary).
3. Select either the *Test Document* or its copy.
4. Drag the file to the folder you just created. Remember, dragging means clicking and holding the mouse button down while selecting the file and then moving the file's icon to its destination. When you reach your destination and release the mouse button, the folder is highlighted.
5. When the folder highlights, stop moving the mouse and release the button. Your file disappears.
6. Open the folder onto which you just dragged the file. Inside is your file. It will be the only object in the folder because you just created the folder and it was empty until you moved the file into it.
7. If you had difficulty moving the file, move it back, close the folder, and try it again.
8. Repeat these steps as many times as needed.

Once you're comfortable with moving the file, you're ready to perform the next operation. If you're having trouble moving the file, you'll have trouble with this next exercise.

Dragging Objects

To the newcomer, the concept of dragging files can seem cruel. Clicking on and then dragging an object can be frustrating: Your finger slips off the mouse, you run out of mouse-pad space, or you let up on the mouse and the icon sits on top of the destination, not quite making it into the folder. These are common problems. The first and last require practice, but running out of mouse-pad space is cured in a different way.

Actually, when you run out of mouse-pad space, you also need to practice. In this case, you need to practice picking up the mouse while holding down the mouse button, and, while the mouse is in the air, moving it to the edge of the mouse pad. If you are moving the file to the left, you want to place the mouse on the right side of the mouse pad, and vice versa if you're moving the file in the other direction. Once you put the mouse back on the pad, resume moving the file to its destination. Writing this description is almost easier than doing the maneuver. If you're having this trouble, you'll just have to practice and practice and then practice some more. I've yet to meet anyone who cannot learn how to use a mouse.

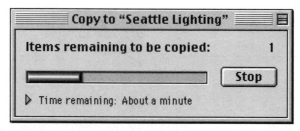

Figure 5.9   *The Copy dialog box.*

To make a copy of the file without moving the original:

1. Hold down the Option key on the keyboard.
2. Select the file *Test Document*.
3. Drag the file to the new folder created in the last exercise.
4. When you release the mouse button, a dialog box like the one in Figure 5.9 appears.
5. Open the folder.

Inside, you have two files: the one you moved in the last exercise and the copy you just made. Notice that the file you copied has the same name as the original and does not have the word *copy* appended to its name. Also, the original file is still on the Desktop.

Now, you need to know what happens when you try to copy or move a file into a location where a file with the same name already exists.

The following steps demonstrate what happens:

1. Close the folder.
2. Repeat steps 1 through 3 of the above sequence.
3. When you release the mouse button, a dialog box like the one in Figure 5.10 appears.
4. Click on the OK button.
5. Open the folder.

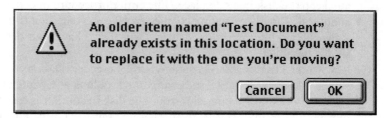

Figure 5.10   *The existing file dialog box.*

Default Button

The OK button in a dialog box, like the one in Figure 5.10, is called the *default* button. You can activate any button with a dark outline by pressing the Return or Enter key in addition to clicking on the button. Cancel, unless it is the default button, can be activated by pressing the Escape (Esc) key. Sometimes a program does not support the Escape key for cancel, and sometimes the Cancel button is the default button. Always look at dialog boxes when they are presented. It is all too easy to cause something you did not want to happen—such as erasing a few files—with the press of a key.

When you open the folder, two only files are in it because you replaced the file when you did the last copy. A rule of file storage is that you cannot have two files with the same name in the same location. When you copied a second copy of the *Test Document* file into the folder, you replaced the existing copy with the new copy of *Test Document*.

It is important to understand this concept because, if the first file in the folder is different from the second one, the first file is lost when you make the copy. The Mac will always warn you when you are about to replace a file with another that has the same name; ignoring or dismissing the warning is all too easy—you may realize only when it is too late that the file is gone.

Copying Files to Another Disk

One of the most common reasons for making a file copy is to put the file onto another disk for safe keeping. Just like paper documents, your computer documents may be valuable and fragile. If you trust the hard drive in your Macintosh as the sole repository of your data files, you will be disappointed.

At some time, you will have trouble with your hard drive, and you may face the possibility that all the data on it may be lost. Always copy your data to another disk and keep the disk in a safe place. The entire procedure of copying your data to another disk for safe keeping is called *backing up* your data. If the data is safely stored somewhere other than your Mac, you will always have your data—even if your Mac should be stolen.

Chapter 11 talks about keeping your data secure. Data security is a topic that you should take very seriously, so be sure to take a look at Chapter 11.

The process of copying files from one disk to another is easy because it is like moving files from one place to another on your hard disk. The difference is that when moving a file from one disk to another, you make a copy and your original files

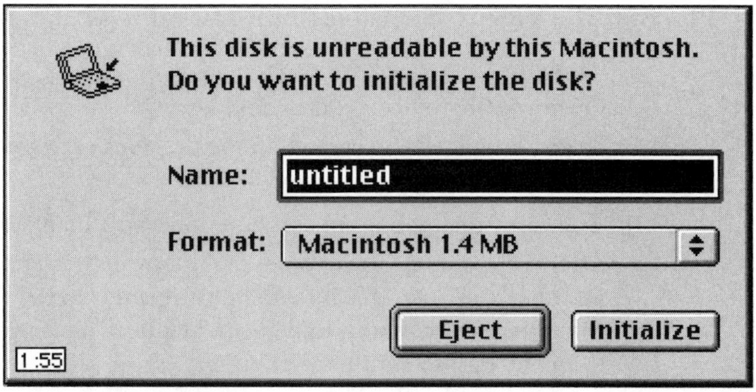

Figure 5.11 *This disk needs to be initialized.*

remain in place. To copy files onto another disk, you need to have a second hard disk drive or a floppy disk. Ideally for this exercise, you should use a floppy disk.

The following steps demonstrate the process of copying files:

1. Insert your floppy disk into the floppy disk drive.
2. If you see a message like the one in Figure 5.11, see the sidebar, "Formatting Floppy Disks."
3. The disk appears on your Desktop under your hard drive's icon.
4. Double-click on the floppy disk icon.
5. A window opens with disk's name in the title bar.
6. Select the *Test Document* file on the hard drive and drag it into the open window.
7. A dialog box like the one in Figure 5.12 appears.
8. The *Test Document* file appears in the window.

Moving the file into the window is the same as the moving it onto the disk's icon. If you repeat the above steps, dragging the file to the floppy disk's icon instead of the open window, the results are the same.

Figure 5.12 *The Copy dialog box.*

To copy the folder you created in the last exercise onto the other disk drive:

1. Close the floppy disk window.
2. Open your hard drive if it is closed.
3. Select the folder you created in the previous exercises.
4. Drag it onto the floppy icon.
5. The Copy dialog box appears and notes how many files are being copied.
6. After the files are copied, open the floppy disk; there you see your copied folder. If you open this folder and compare it to the original on the hard drive, you see that both folders are identical. You have just copied your data from one disk to another.

Copying data from one disk to the other is always done in the same manner. You can copy to an open window, a closed disk, or a folder icon. In this sense, copying data is just like the exercise for moving data, the one in which the file was moved to a folder. Some of the rules you need to keep in mind when copying and moving data are the following:

❖ Dragging a folder moves or copies the entire contents of the folder, including all subfolders.

❖ Dragging a disk icon onto another disk or folder icon copies the entire contents of the disk being dragged.

❖ If a drive has insufficient space to contain the files being copied, the Mac will display a dialog box like the one in Figure 5.13 and will not complete the operation.

❖ You will always be warned if you are about to overwrite (copy or move a file to a location that contains a file with the same name).

❖ A file with the same name as a folder cannot replace a folder and, vice versa, a folder with the same name as a file cannot replace the file.

Like everything else associated with computers and the Mac, some people find copying easy, others encounter difficulties. If you find these techniques hard, make more folders and practice moving and copying them.

Format To divide a disk into tracks and sectors where information can be stored. Blank disks must be formatted before you can save information on them for the first time; synonymous with *initialize.*

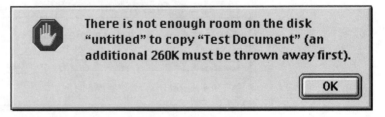

There is not enough room on the disk "untitled" to copy "Test Document" (an additional 260K must be thrown away first).

OK

Figure 5.13 Insufficient disk space.

Formatting Floppy Disks

Before any disk can be used on a Macintosh it has to be formatted. When your Mac can't read a disk, it will ask you if you want to initialize the disk. As long as you know that the disk is a new and blank disk, format it, telling the Mac OK when a dialog box like the one shown in Figure 5.11 appears.

If you know that the disk does contain data, do *not* initialize it. Initializing a floppy disk destroys any information it contains, and the data is irretrievably lost. A hard disk that is initialized as a result of the dialog box in Figure 5.11 can be retrieved, but doing so is difficult and not a recommended practice.

The term *initialize* is often used synonymously with *format*, but they have different meanings technically. You will find more information about formatting and initializing disks in Chapter 10.

Initialized disk   A disk that has been organized into tracks and sectors by the computer and is therefore ready to store information.

Deleting Files

If you've been doing the exercises in this chapter, you should have four copies of the *Test Document*. There is one on your Desktop, one in the folder on your hard drive, another on the floppy disk, and the fourth in the folder on the floppy. Now it is time to get rid of these files; the process of getting rid of files is technically called deleting the files. In Macintosh parlance, the files are *trashed*.

The process is called *trashing* because the files are dragged to the trash can icon in the lower right corner of the Desktop, called simply the Trash. The Trash icon is the metaphorical equivalent to the trash can next to your desk. When you move something into the trash, the Trash icon changes to show that it contains files that have not yet been deleted, as shown in Figure 5.14.

Figure 5.14   *The Trash icon when files need to be deleted.*

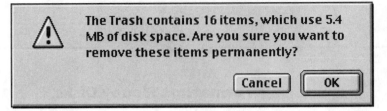

Figure 5.15 *The Trash warning.*

Moving files into the trash is the same as taking a piece of paper off your desk and throwing it into your trash can. The papers remain in the trash until you take out the trash to the garbage can. Likewise, your files remain in the Trash until you empty the Trash, which you do by selecting the *Empty Trash...* menu item from the Finder's Special menu. When you select the *Empty Trash...* menu item a dialog box like the one in Figure 5.15 appears.

Once you click on the OK button or press the Enter key, the Mac deletes all the files in the Trash, and they will be gone. GONE.

Because the files are not deleted until you select the *Empty Trash...* menu item, you can, as it were, dig through the Trash if you throw away a file accidentally. To dig through the Trash, all you have to do is open the Trash; you will see a window that shows all the files and folders you've put there. As you can in all other Finder windows, you can select how to view the files here as well. You cannot, though, open a file that is in the Trash.

If you want to check a file that is in the Trash before you chuck it out, you must move the file from the Trash and then open the file. If you try to open a file that is in the Trash, a dialog box like the one in Figure 5.16 appears.

You can perform two other actions on trashed items:

❖ Get Info
❖ Put Away

The Put Away command has not been discussed yet. It returns to their original locations files placed in the Trash or moved to the Desktop, which is wherever the file

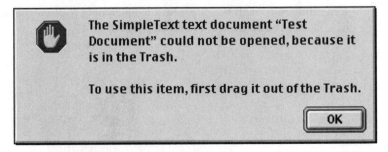

Figure 5.16   *The dialog box that appears when you try to open a file that is in the Trash.*

was located prior to being moved to the Trash or the Desktop. The *Put Away* menu item is found in the File menu and can be invoked with the ⌘+Y option key command.

To see how the Put Away function works:

1. Move the *Test Document* File on the Desktop to the Trash.
2. Open the Trash.
3. Select the *Test Document*.
4. Select the *Put Away* menu item or use the ⌘+Y option key command.
5. The *Test Document* file is automatically moved from the Trash back to the Desktop.

Once you've emptied the Trash, your files are gone. It is possible to retrieve a file that has been deleted, but it can be a lot of work. If you ever trash a file that you really need, you should turn off your Mac and read Chapter 18.

You should know about one more feature of the Trash. If you wish, you can turn off the warning when you select the *Empty Trash…* menu item by selecting the Trash and performing a Get Info… (⌘+I) command. The Trash's Get Info window looks like Figure 5.17.

In the Trash's Get Info window, there is a check box labeled *Warn before emptying*. When the check box is marked, your Mac warns you before it empties the Trash. When the box is not checked, the *Empty Trash…* menu item becomes *Empty Trash*, without the ellipsis. The ellipsis after a menu item indicates that you must provide more information or supply a confirmation before the command is executed.

Unmounting a Disk

When you formatted a floppy disk as described in the last section, "Copying Files to Another Disk," the disk, after being initialized, was *mounted* on the Desktop. Whenever you insert a disk into your Mac, it is mounted when it appears on the Desktop. When you are done with the disk, it must be unmounted.

Unmounting a disk is done in one of two ways: You can drag the disk's icon to the Trash, or you can use the *Put Away* menu item (or ⌘+Y) from the File menu. Both methods remove the disk's icon from the Desktop and eject the disk.

If you've been poking about, as you should, and if you have discovered the *Eject* menu item in the Special menu, you might wonder about its purpose. The *Eject* menu item is used to eject a disk without unmounting it. When a disk is ejected with the Eject (⌘+E) command, the Mac treats the disk as if it were still available. This command is useful for copying floppy disks or using two floppies at once. You'll find more information about how the Mac handles disks in Chapter 10.

Figure 5.17   The Trash's Get Info window.

Check box   A small box associated with an option in a dialog box. When you click the check box, you change the option or affect related options.

You now know almost everything there is to know about the Trash. Did you ever dream that the Trash could be so interesting?

Moving Groups of Files

At times you will want to clean up your drive. You might want to move Application folders to organize your programs or move data files to reorganize everything. Whatever your motives, you will move many files. This section assumes that you are organizing your hard drive as described in the "Getting Organized" section.

When you are ready to move your data and applications to new folders, you need to be methodical so that you don't miss any data and you put it all in the proper place. One way to accomplish this is to move your data through the hierarchy one step at a time.

If you have several Application folders on your drive that are not buried in other folders, open each Application folder to make sure you do not have data inside it. (It is easy to absentmindedly store a letter inside the same folder that contains your word processor.) The process might go something like this:

❖ Open your hard drive and view its contents by name. This will let you work with each folder in some type of order.

❖ Make sure your main folders are visible and accessible. You may want to put them on the Desktop under your Drive icons.

❖ Select your first folder and open it. If it contains folders and files, start with the files. Make a rough division of the files according to the main categories you have set up. Select the files for a specific category by clicking on the first

The Marquee

Another way to select groups of files is to use a Macintosh feature called a *marquee*. The marquee is a standard Macintosh selection tool that is invoked by dragging the pointer so that a rectangle is drawn around a group of objects. Figure 5.18 shows how the marquee appears when it is used to select a group of files.

You select all of these files by starting in one corner and dragging the pointer to the opposite corner. The marquee appears and selects all the objects enclosed in the rectangle created by dragging the pointer. The rectangle is the marquee because it can appear to be a series of moving dots on the screen, like the lights on a movie theater marquee.

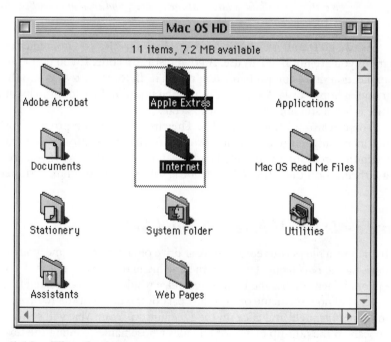

Figure 5.18 *The selection marquee.*

one you want, then selecting the rest by holding down the Shift key as you click on each additional file.

❖ Once you have all the files selected for the category, put the mouse over one of the selected files and drag it to the proper folder. All the selected files follow. If you want to copy files to the new folder rather than just move them, hold down the Option key before you click on the file to drag.

❖ Next, open the folder into which you just moved everything and continue to subdivide your files. If you want to process a couple of folders at a time, that's fine; just don't put so many individual files into a folder that you cannot easily move them to the next subcategory.

❖ As you clean all the data files from an application's folder, be sure to leave any files the application requires inside that folder. You can then simply move the application's folder to your new *Applications* folder. If you have any question about what files your application requires, check the manual. There is no reason to keep anything you do not need, unless you have disk space to spare (and if you do, count your blessings).

❖ Repeat this process for each folder until all of them have been emptied or moved. If you empty a folder, throw it into the Trash so that it will not be in your way. Trashing the folders and any files you no longer need as you go is a good way to measure your progress. *Do not empty the Trash until you are sure all of your data is safe in its new home, and then double-check the Trash to make sure you are not throwing away a file you need.*

As you go through the above process, look for files you no longer need or programs you are not likely to use. A good test is this one: If you don't know what an application does, you probably don't need it. Before you toss it into the Trash, copy it onto a floppy disk. Also, you can run the program before throwing it away to make sure it is not something you want to keep..

You can also trash *Read Me* files. They usually come on program disks and are pertinent only to the installation process, or they have information that you read when the program was installed and haven't looked at since. If you are not going to use them, trash them (the *Read Me* file is still on your program's Master Disk).

When Your File Is Not Where It Should Be

If you lose a file as you reorganize your drive or at any other time, you can search for it by using the *Find* menu item from the File menu or by using the ⌘+F command key option. When you use the Find command, a window that looks like Figure 5.19 appears.

If you know the name or even just part of the name of the file you want, type it into the *Find:* field and click on the *Find* button. Your Mac will scan the drive that appears in the pop-up menu for any files whose names contain the text you entered in the *Find:* field.

You can search specific disks or all mounted disks by using the pop-up menu, which lists each mounted disk and provides the option to search all disks.

Field   The place where you type information within a dialog box.

When an item is found that matches the search criteria, the folder or drive that contains the found file opens and the file is displayed in a window, as shown in Figure 5.20.

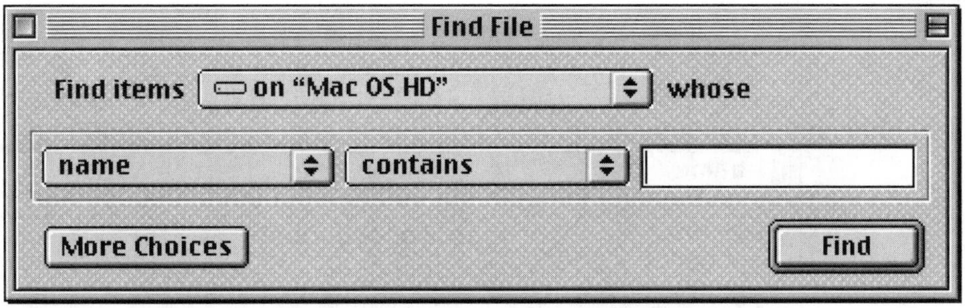

Figure 5.19 *The Find window.*

To narrow the search criteria, use the *More Choices* button. When you select this option, a window that looks like Figure 5.21 appears.

By using the extra choices and entering additional criteria, you can narrow your search considerably. Your choices consist of whether to use the name and/or some other file attribute, and whether it should match your criteria. The different combinations of choices are quite extensive; they are listed below. You have a total of 12 different attributes for performing your search.

❖ **Attribute criteria**   You can search for your file using its name, any normal file attributes, or specific comments placed in the file's comment box from

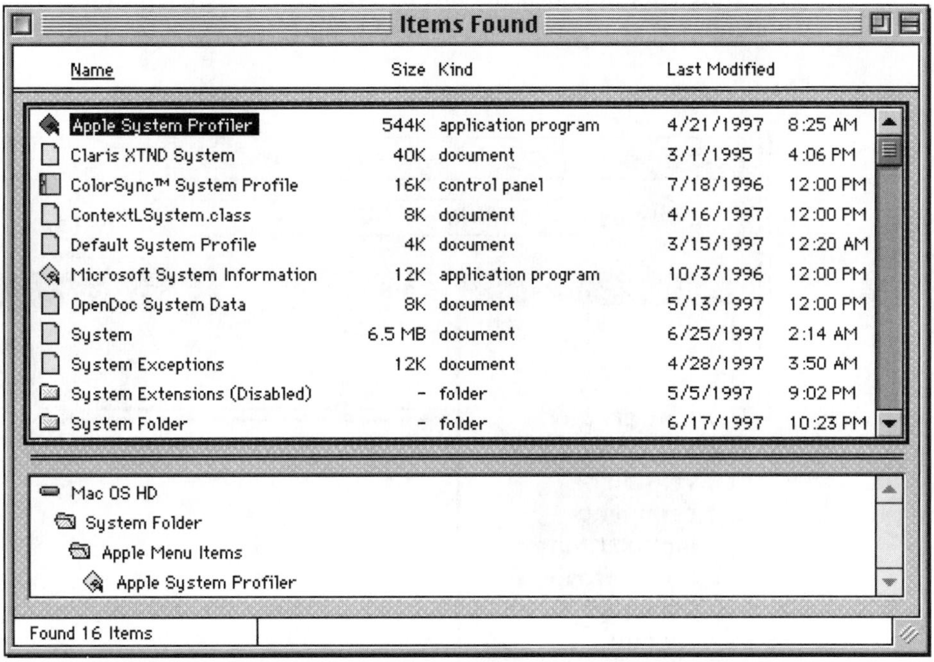

Figure 5.20 *The Items Found window.*

Figure 5.21   *The Find File window with search options.*

within its Info window. Figure 5.22 shows all the possible search criteria. Some of the items listed may not make any sense right now because they are topics not yet discussed. Advanced information about Macintosh files can be found in Chapter 11.

❖ **Conditional options**   Finally, you can specify search conditions, which are based on matching specific conditions with the attributes you choose for your search. Figure 5.23 shows the list of conditions applicable if you were conducting a search using the name of a file.

Different conditional options are available for each of the different attributes you might want to use. Spend a couple of minutes looking at the different options; you

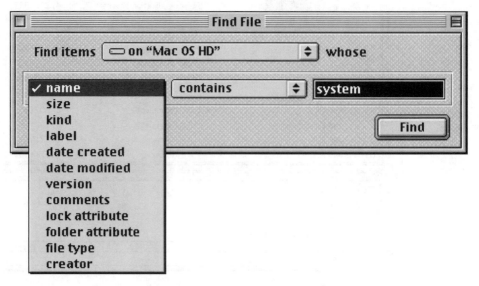

Figure 5.22   *The Find File window with attribute options.*

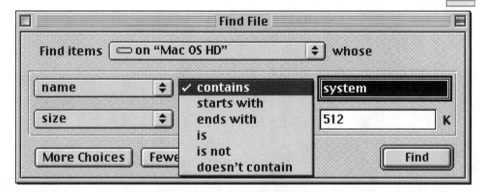

Figure 5.23 *The Find File window with condition options.*

might find some of them useful. Also, by clicking on the More Choices button you can use as many as 10 of the 12 file attributes simultaneously.

Versions of the Macintosh System, prior to 7.5, have Find functions that differ from those just described. If you use an earlier version of the System, experiment with the Find program or menu item to see how it differs.

Making and Using Aliases

Now that you have your data organized, it is time to make accessing it easier. One of the most useful functions in Mac OS 8 is the ability to make aliases. An *alias* is a small data file that stores the location of an original file, application, folder, or disk. When you double-click on an alias, it opens the file, folder, or disk that it represents.

To create an alias:

1. Select the item (a disk, folder, data file, or application).
2. Select the *Make Alias* menu item from the Special menu or use the ⌘+M command key option.
3. You see what looks like an exact duplicate of the item, except its title will be in *italics* and the name of the file is followed by the word *alias*.

Once you make an alias, you can move to any location on your hard drive. In Figure 5.24, a whole row of aliases appears toward the right of the Desktop. You can change the name of your aliases to anything that suits your fancy; doing so does not impair their function.

When you make an alias of an item and then move the original, double-clicking on the alias finds and opens the original file. Should you delete an item for which you have made an alias, the alias remains even though the original item no longer exists. This means your hard drive can become very cluttered with aliases that are no longer functional, so don't create confusion by forgetting to remove an alias you no longer need.

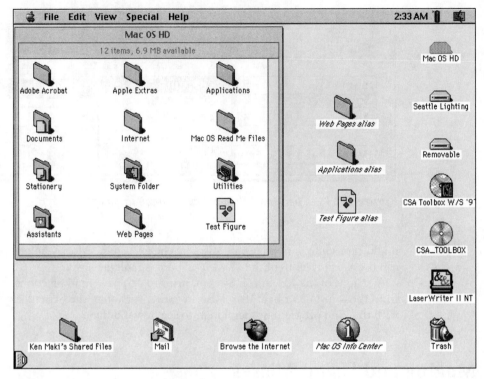

Figure 5.24   *Aliases on the Desktop.*

If you need to find out where the original of an alias resides, you can perform a Get Info... (⌘+I) on the alias to learn where the original item is supposed to be. In Figure 5.25, the original is located using the following nomenclature:

Dr. Who?:Utilities:SimpleText

This means of identifying the location of an item is called the *path* for the item and designates the hierarchy for the file. In this case, the path describes the program, SimpleText, as being on the hard drive, Dr. Who?, which contains a folder called Utilities that houses the SimpleText program. Figure 5.26 shows how the path translates to the actual hard disk location.

Pathname   The complete name of a document beginning with the name of the disk (also called the *volume name*), the name of the subdirectory it's in (if it's in one), and the name of the document. The pathname begins with a slash, and the parts of the pathname are separated by slashes. It's called a pathname because it describes the route to the document.

When you make an alias of a folder, it acts just like the regular folder. When you want to put something into a folder for which you have created an alias, just drag that item on top of the alias. Your Mac will move or copy the file to the folder as if you had dragged it on the original.

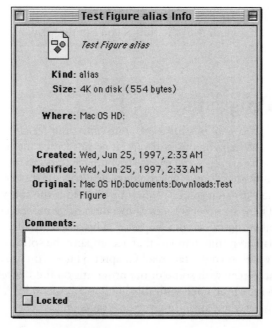

Figure 5.25 *Get Info on an alias.*

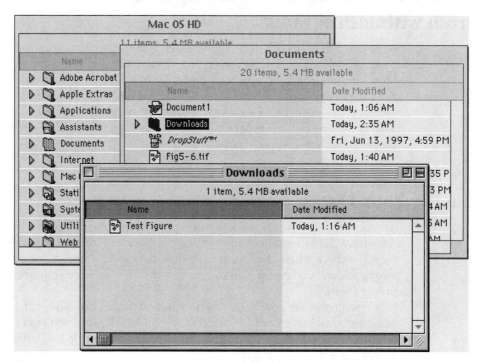

Figure 5.26 *The alias path shown via windows.*

Aliases are handy little items, and you'll find references to them throughout the book. Explaining all the things you can do with an alias would be premature at this point.

Installing Programs

The process of putting a program onto your Macintosh is called *installing* the program. When you buy software, it comes with a manual that tells you how to install the software. In some cases, all you have to do to install the software is copy the program from a floppy disk to your hard drive. If the software cannot be copied, it will come with an installer program that installs the software for you.

There are several types of installers. The most commonly used installer is Apple's installer, described in Chapter 6. The other installers you will encounter are explained in the manuals that accompany the software. If you are waiting to install software on your Mac, read Chapter 6 (after you finish this chapter, of course). If you want to play with some of the programs on the Berkeley Macintosh Users Group CD-ROM included with this book, read Appendix A for information about the CD-ROM disk and installing the programs on the disk.

Saving Your Work and Opening Files from within Programs

Now that you have your data organized, all you have to do is keep it that way. If you have no problems saving or finding your documents, you can skip this section. However, lots of people who have used their Macs for years have never really gotten the hang of navigating their way to the folder where they want, while using a program, to save their data. Likewise, they have the same problem when trying to open a data file from within a program. In this section, we look at both opening and saving files from within an application.

Saving Your Data

You need to know where you are storing your documents when you perform a Save As… from the File menu of any application. Even experienced Mac users sometimes forget to check where they are storing their data and, as a result, save a file in the wrong folder. It takes just a bit of care and attention to store your documents in their proper location.

To properly save your data, you have to understand how your hard disk is organized and how folders can be placed within folders. If, after you read this section, you are still confused by these topics, reread the section titled "Getting Organized" in this chapter.

Remember that your drive's organization is based on a hierarchy and that the entire structure of your drive and the series of nested folders is like a tree, as described earlier. If you go down the trunk of the tree (the top level of your drive), you can then climb back up the tree via the branch that contains the folder in which you want to store your document.

In Figure 5.27, the standard Save As dialog box for the SimpleText application is shown.

The first thing to note is where you currently are in your drive's hierarchy. At the top of the dialog box is an icon of an open folder titled Utilities, with a downward-pointing arrow. The arrow means that you are in a nested folder and that the entire structure (the folder icon and name) is a drop-down menu. Figure 5.27 shows the entire hierarchy for your current location when you click on the pop-up menu.

By dragging through the menu, you can select any folder between the one you are in and your hard drive, you can select the hard drive, or you can go to the Desktop to select a different disk drive. When you select the hard drive, you have access to any of the folders there, and you can then begin to navigate through a different chain of folders. Figure 5.28 shows the top level of the drive. Notice the drive icon and drive name in the drop-down menu.

Notice the black border around the window that contains the list of folders. The extra dark border means that the file selection window is selected. If you wish, you can navigate to a folder by typing the first letter of its name. Your Mac automatically selects the first folder that starts with the letter you type. When a folder is selected, the Save button in Figure 5.28 turns into an Open button, as shown in Figure 5.29.

Once the folder is highlighted and there is an Open button, pressing the Enter key opens the folder. To change the Open button to a Save button, press the Tab

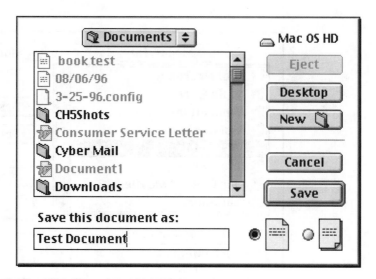

Figure 5.27 *The Save As... dialog box.*

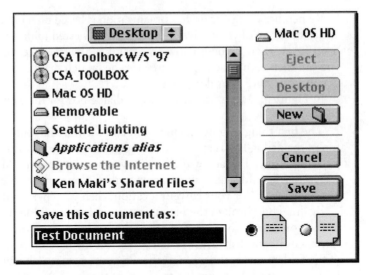

Figure 5.28   *The top level of the drive.*

key or place the pointer in the file name field and click. If you type in your file's name and press Enter, your file is saved in the folder or on the disk whose title appears in the pop-up menu.

If you want to create a new folder to store your document, just click on the button with the word *New* and the folder icon. A dialog box like the one in Figure 5.30 appears. The new folder you create is placed in the same location your file would be if you were saving a file; the new folder is for your document's new location.

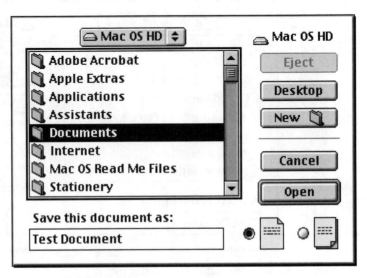

Figure 5.29   *The Open button.*

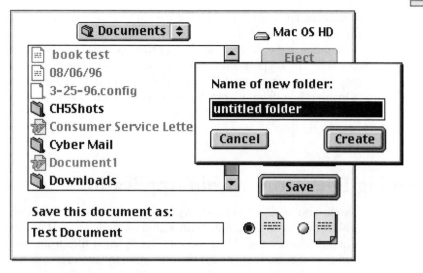

Figure 5.30 *Creating a folder from a Save As... dialog box.*

The dialog box used in these examples is the standard Macintosh Save As... dialog box. The Save As... dialog box is dynamic and can be altered by the program you're using. Figure 5.31 shows the Save As... dialog box created by Microsoft Word.

All of the functions described above are the same; the main difference is that there is an extra drop-down menu for selecting different file formats. Don't be surprised when you find variations on a theme as you save documents with different programs.

When you start any application, it will automatically save the documents you make in the same folder as the application or in the folder of the document you used

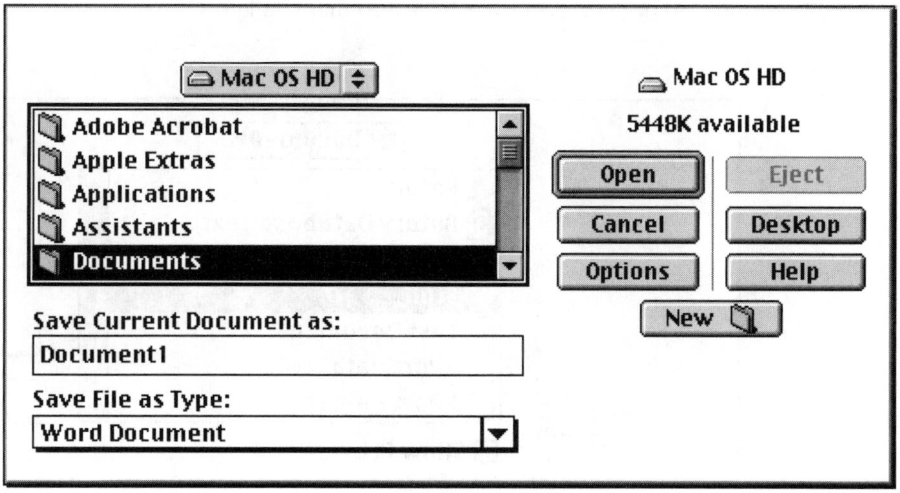

Figure 5.31 *Save As... dialog box in Microsoft Word.*

to start the application (by double-clicking on a document icon). If you want to save the document elsewhere, you have to navigate your way to it.

Another way to keep yourself organized is to use an alias of a folder or even of a disk drive. By keeping a few select aliases on your Desktop, you can access the folders they represent from any Save As… dialog box (discussed in the next section, "Opening Files from within Applications"). Simply click on the Desktop button from the dialog box, and you will have access to all your drives, any folder, and aliases on your Desktop.

Opening Files from within Applications

People who have problems saving files in the correct location will have the same problem when opening files from within an application: They won't know where to find their documents. The procedure for opening files from within an application is similar to that for saving your files. The dialog boxes are similar and vary only slightly, depending on the application. The major difference is that there are no fields into which you type anything.

To open a document from within an application, select the *Open* menu item from the File menu or use the ⌘+O command key. An Open dialog box similar to the one in Figure 5.32 appears.

As with the Save As dialog box, your location is that point where you last saved or opened a file. If you've organized your data and know where to find your document, you get the location in the same manner as described in an earlier section, "Saving Your Data." All you have to know is where you've saved your data.

This is the reason why you should be organized. If you do not make a conscious decision to save your data in a specific location, you'll forever be looking for that report or letter you wrote last week. Of course, you can always use the Find File program to locate those wayward files, but you'll waste a lot of time. A much better solution is to organize your hard drive so that you know where your data is stored.

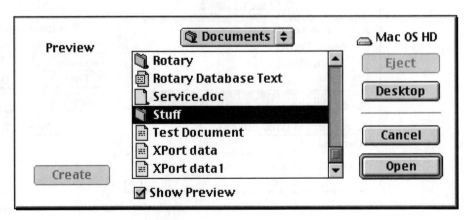

Figure 5.32   The Open dialog box.

Using the Documents Folder

One of the features of Mac OS 8 is an automatic default location for your documents. You can select for the default the folder where the program you're using is located or a special folder called *Documents*. You select either of these locations from a special configuration program, a Control Panel, called *General Controls*.

Mentioning this feature here is a bit premature because it involves some features and terms that haven't been introduced yet. But, because we're talking about data organization, you need to know about it. You will find more information about Control Panels in Chapter 7.

To access the General Controls Control Panel, select the *Control Panels* menu item in the Apple menu. From the *Control Panels* menu item, a list of items appears; drag your way to the *General Controls* menu item. This action presents you with a window, as shown in Figure 5.33.

In the lower right corner is a section called Documents. In this section, three radio buttons appear:

Radio button   A series of buttons for selecting an option when only one of the listed options can be chosen.

 ❖ Folder that contains the application
 ❖ Last folder used in the application
 ❖ Documents folder

These choices control the default location for saving or opening files from within an application. The default setting is the *last folder used in the application*. This setting

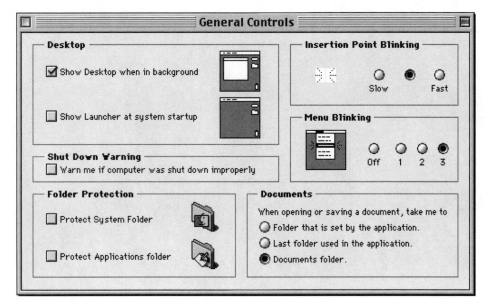

Figure 5.33   *The General Controls Control Panel.*

is the one used in the sections "Saving Your Data" and "Opening Files from within Applications." You can select the default location selection method you want to use. If you select *Documents folder*, your Mac creates a folder called Documents and places it on your Desktop. Then, every time you save or use the application's *Open* menu item, your location will default to the Documents folder. The *folder that contains the application* choice will default to the application's folder every time you save or use the application's *Open* menu item.

Summary

Phew! If you're not tired just from reading about all of this, I'd be surprised. There is a lot of information in this chapter, but now you have all the essential information you need to use your Mac.

You know about all the icons, how to use your folders and organize your data, and how to save your data from within an application. You have various techniques for using your Mac, and you are now on the road to Macintosh mastery.

Granted, there is a lot more to learn, but now you have all the basic information you need—not only to use your Mac, but also to understand most of the other chapters. From here, you can read the chapters as they appear in the book or you can jump around, selecting those chapters that interest you the most.

If, during your explorations, you encounter a topic or term that you don't understand, flip to the index to locate where the topic or term is first mentioned. Remember, learning the language associated with the Mac and computers will do more than anything else to make you an expert.

CHAPTER 6

Getting the Most from Your OS

Introduction

Τhis chapter will explore Mac OS 8. Although this chapter is called "Getting the Most from Your OS," it is really about understanding your operating system (OS) software. You cannot get the most from your Macintosh without a basic understanding of the operating system, so just sit back, have some fun, and learn as you go.

When the Macintosh computer was first made available as a commercial product, it rocked the computer world with its uniqueness. What made the Mac unique was its System software, or the System. You can use your Mac without learning about the OS. But, if you take the time to learn about the OS, you will have the knowledge you need to customize and fix your Mac. This is not just a chapter for computer nerds; it is for all Mac users who want to get more from their Mac.

You control your Mac through the contents of your Mac's System folder. You can control the sounds your Mac makes, how the Desktop looks, how it networks (as seen in Chapter 13), and how you customize it (as discussed in Chapter 8), to name just a few possibilities. In short, how your Mac functions, what it is capable of, and how it appears are all controlled through the System folder's contents.

This chapter is divided into the following sections:

❖ The Macintosh's OS history
❖ The System
❖ Inside the System folder
❖ Earlier versions of the System (Mac OS)

This chapter looks at each of the items you find in your System folder after a standard installation. The version of the Macintosh System covered in this chapter is Mac OS 8.

The Macintosh's OS History

The current incarnation of the Mac OS, formerly called the System, is Mac OS 8. Within each incarnation of the OS, there have been several incremental releases as the System evolves and changes. The last version of the previous System was System 7.6.1. And the version prior to System 7.6 was 7.5. System 7.5 went through a total of six incarnations, with the last one being 7.5.5. This same process will happen to Mac OS 8. Each incremental release fixes bugs, adds support for new Macintoshes, or adds features. Usually, each new release does all three.

Prior to System 7.5 there were versions 7.1 and 7.0 with their incarnations. And prior to System 7 there was version 6, with the last release of System 6 being 6.0.8. A version change usually means that there are substantial operating differences between the new system and the old, and the step up to System 7 from 6 had many operating differences. Advances in the Macintosh operating system software are part of an evolutionary process; each new System incorporates new capabilities as well as support for new, more powerful machines.

System 7 represented the long-promised and finally delivered System for the Macintosh. This is the version of the System that everyone waited for—for almost two years. Almost as soon as System 6.0 was introduced, System 7 was rumored. By the time the Macintosh SE/30, IIcx, and IIx were released, Macintosh power users were ready for an operating system that would take advantage of the new hardware features included in the new machines, such as the PMMU coprocessor. System 7 delivered on the promises. Although the jump from System 7 to 7.5 is not as dramatic as the jump from System 6 to 7, it was a major system upgrade.

Again, Apple has included major technological advancements with an OS upgrade. The first is the name, Mac OS 8, which is the new name for the System. The major enhancements that Apple has put into Mac OS 8 are:

❖ A multithreaded Finder
❖ OpenDoc
❖ Internet access
❖ Cyberdog
❖ Location Manager
❖ Mac OS Runtime for Java
❖ Personal Web sharing

These enhancements are discussed in Chapters 7 and 8. What is discussed in this chapter are the changes made to the Macintosh Finder. The changes to the Finder in Mac OS 8 are significant and include the following features:

❖ Menu enhancements
❖ Sticky menus
❖ View by button
❖ Spring-loaded folders
❖ Other folder enhancements

The features just listed are discussed in this chapter. The following items are discussed in Chapter 7:

- ❖ Multithreaded copying
- ❖ Background window updating status indicator
- ❖ Live window scrolling
- ❖ The Location Manager
- ❖ Improved color picker

Although this chapter focuses on Mac OS 8, you can use what you learn here with earlier versions of the Mac OS. Even if you do not have Mac OS 8, don't skip the rest of this chapter because you'll miss a lot of useful information.

The OS

Throughout the Mac's short history, the OS has gone through several incarnations, beginning with a System that came on one 400K floppy disk. Now, it comes on a CD-ROM, yet it has managed to keep those elements that originally made and con-

Should I Upgrade?

The enhancements in Mac OS 8 are the good news. The bad news is that Mac OS 8 requires a lot of memory to use all its enhancements. Whether you can use Mac OS 8 depends on your individual hardware system and your needs. Many people still are happily using System 7.X.

Upgrading your System software could mean upgrading your programs to take advantage of the new capabilities in Mac OS 8. This is especially true for utility programs that affect the Finder, the Finder's menu bar, and some disk utilities. If you run an older Mac, from the Mac Plus through the Mac IIcx, you will have to pass; Mac OS 8 will not run on your machine.

To run Mac OS 8, you really need a minimum of 16M of RAM and a 500MB hard drive. Ideally, you should have 32MB of RAM; 16MB will let you run a fully installed Mac OS 8 and you'll have about 2MB of RAM left for applications. The larger system requirements are just another aspect of software evolution. Every time Apple has enhanced the OS, it has required a more powerful Mac with more memory to run well.

If you are thinking about upgrading, read this chapter and Chapters 7 through 9. After you've read these chapters, you'll know what Mac OS 8 has to offer, and you can then make an educated decision.

tinue to denote the Mac as a unique computer. It is not the icons themselves but the way they operate that is unique. The Macintosh has a feel that has not been duplicated by any other computer, and this unique quality is possible only because of the OS.

Before any computer can be used, it must have software that will tell it how to work and what to do. The *operating system* is the term for this software. In the Macintosh, the operating system used to be called the System; now it called the Mac OS, or OS for short.

Operating system (1) A program that organizes the actions of the parts of the computer and its peripheral devices; (2) low-level software that controls a computer by performing basic tasks such as input/output, memory management, and interrupt handling. (See also *disk operating system.*)

When the term "OS" is used it refers to everything in the System folder. From here on out the System refers to the System file. For a Macintosh to work, it needs two things: a System file and one program.

The System file actually makes the Mac work, but without a program, the Macintosh cannot do anything. Normally, this program is the Finder, but there are times when you will use your Mac without the Finder. Usually, these occasions will occur when you are installing software; then, the Finder has been replaced with the Installer. Granted, you can't do much with your Mac when it doesn't have the Finder, but your Mac will still operate because it does have a System file.

Another aspect of the Mac OS is its ROM (Read Only Memory). The Macintosh's ROM contains part of the Mac's operating system. Although all computers have ROM of one type or another, very few computers have ROM like the Mac's, which contains much of the essential information your Mac needs to operate; the System works in tandem with the Mac's ROM.

But, even with the ROM, the Mac will not operate unless it starts (boots) from a disk that contains a System file. The disk that starts your Mac and contains the System that makes it operate is called a *system disk* or *startup disk*. You can always tell which disk is functioning as your startup disk because it is the disk that appears in the upper right corner of your screen (see Figure 6.1).

System disk A disk that contains the operating system and other system software needed to run applications.

Startup disk A disk with all the necessary program files—such as the Finder and System files contained in the System folder for the Macintosh—to set the computer into operation, sometimes called a *boot disk*.

Your Mac's startup disk controls all of the Mac's operations. You might have two or more hard drives, each with a System folder that is configured for a special purpose. Then, you would have different capabilities simply by restarting your Mac from the other disk. Controlling which disk you use to start your Mac is also a function of the Mac's System. Using different drives to start your Mac is discussed later in this chapter and in Chapter 10.

As you may have surmised, your System file can be found in your Mac's System folder. It is only one file of many, but it is the most essential file you have on your disk drive. Figure 6.2 shows the contents of the System folder and the System file.

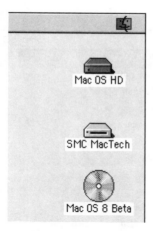

Figure 6.1 *The startup disk.*

You can do very little to nothing with the System file—it just is. You can even open your System file by double-clicking on it. Inside, you will see some items called *keyboard layouts* and *sounds*. Figure 6.3 shows an open System file.

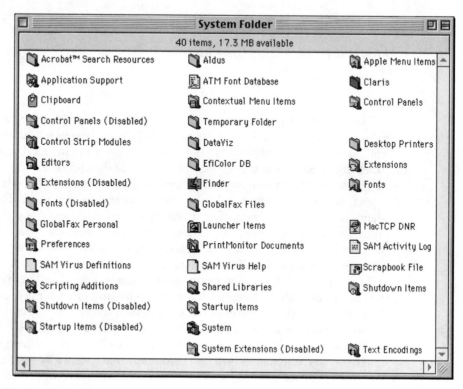

Figure 6.2 *The System folder.*

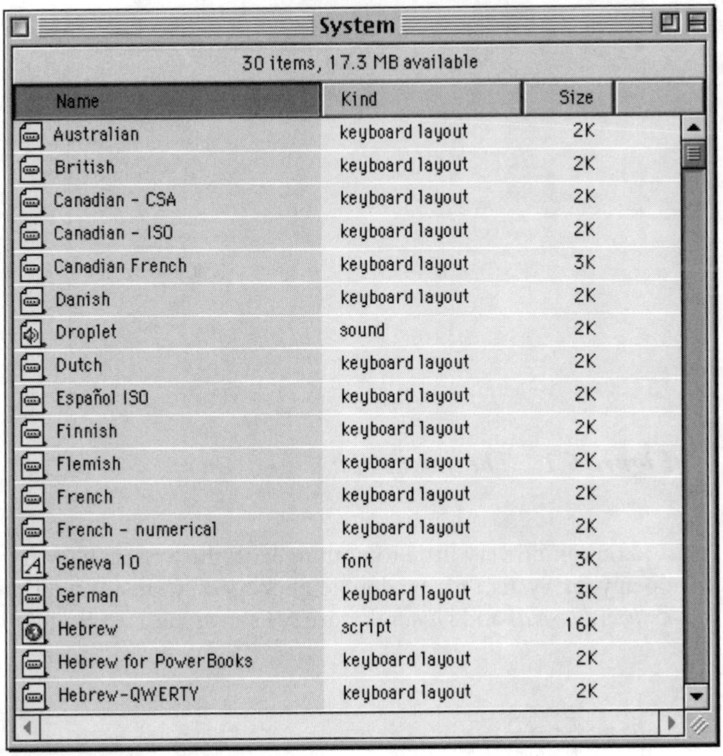

Figure 6.3 Inside the System file.

The keyboard layouts determine the characters your keyboard types when you press a letter. In Figure 6.3, you saw several keyboard layouts for different countries. You can select which keyboard layout your Mac uses from the Keyboard control panel, discussed later in the section, "The Control Panels Folder."

The sound files in your System file are the different sounds your Mac can make when it presents you with a dialog box and simultaneous alert noise. The Mac uses sounds to get your attention when it needs more information from you or wants to notify you about something. If you double-click on a sound file, your Mac will play the sound it contains. As with the keyboard layouts, you control what sounds your Mac makes from the Sounds control panel.

The only reason for opening your control panel is curiosity. There is really nothing you can do with the System file other than making sure your disk contains one. Whenever you look at your disk, if it has a System folder with an active System file, the folder will have an icon in it like the System folder in Figure 6.4.

You can have only one active System folder on a disk drive. Although it is possible to have several System files on a disk drive, only one of those Systems can control a Mac when the Mac is started with the disk. Actually, having more than one System on a disk can cause problems and is something to avoid.

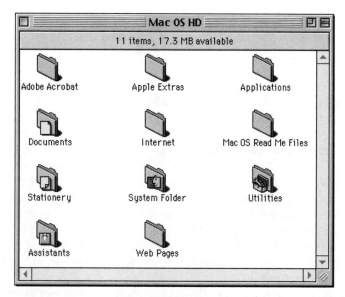

Figure 6.4 *A System folder.*

How It All Works

The Macintosh, or any computer, operates on a series of layers. The basic hardware, the first layer, provides the framework within which the software operates. The software that is built into the hardware is primarily contained in the ROM (Read Only Memory), which becomes the second layer.

The ROM is an extension of the computer's RAM and is accessed like RAM, except data cannot be written to it. When your Mac starts, it performs its hardware checks and goes through the boot-up sequence. Then, as it boots, it loads the System software that runs the Mac as the third layer.

The Finder then loads on top of the System software, which includes all of the Extensions and Control Panels, and becomes the fourth layer. After this, each program you run after the Finder starts and then layers itself in memory. This layering can lead to your Mac's memory becoming fragmented. If you run a program that requires a small amount of memory and one that requires a lot of memory, after you quit the small program, the memory it used is freed to be reused. Any program running that needs a chunk of memory larger than that freed by the small program you just quit can't utilize the newly freed memory. Nor can the newly freed memory

continues

become part of the block of memory above the large program that is running. So, you end up with a small chunk of memory, in the middle of occupied memory, that can't be used.

Figures 6.5 and 6.6 illustrate this process, using the *About This Macintosh...* command from the Apple menu. In Figure 6.5, SimpleText was started before Microsoft Word, and 7.9MB of memory is available for other programs.

In Figure 6.6, you can see that SimpleText is no longer running. Yet, the amount of available memory is the same as before. Something else you should notice is that the Mac OS's memory usage will fluctuate without releasing additional memory.

If you run a program that is smaller than the amount of memory that was freed, like the Key Caps program in Figure 6.7, it may run in the memory fragment freed by quitting SimpleText.

A small program will not always use memory that has been freed. Sometimes, it will load into the larger available contiguous block, reducing even further the amount of memory available. Also, each time you run a program, even if it loads into the fragmented memory, it still affects the larger block, reducing the available amount by a few kilobytes.

The layering of memory can be even more dramatic if you use programs that require a lot of memory. If you start and quit them often, you may find that, after awhile, you can no longer open all of them simultaneously. If you keep track of how you use memory, you will get more mileage from what you have. Most of us cannot

Figure 6.5 *Memory with SimpleText running.*

continues

Figure 6.6 *Memory without SimpleText running.*

afford huge quantities of memory, so maximizing your use of what you have could be advantageous.

Understanding these layers can help you optimize the number of programs you can run within a limited amount of memory. By first running the programs that you will use during your entire computing session and leaving them open, you increase the amount of memory you can use for other programs and lessen the fragmentation of your memory.

Figure 6.7 *Memory with the Key Caps program running.*

Inside the System Folder

In Figure 6.8, you see the insides of the Mac's System folder. It contains several folders and a few files. If you've been using your Mac for awhile and have installed software, your System folder could contain more folders and files than the one shown in Figure 6.8. Also, if you are not using Mac OS 8, you will see some differences between your System folder and the one in Figure 6.8.

There are four files in the System folder. The most important file is the System file, which we've already discussed. The other files are the Finder, Clipboard, and Scrapbook files. When a file is in the System folder and not contained within another folder, it is said to be loose in the System folder.

The Finder and System files are essential to your Mac's operation. If you move either file, your Mac will not start. The Clipboard and Scrapbook files are support files for other Macintosh functions. Whenever you perform a copy, cut, or paste command, either the information is put into the Clipboard file or it is copied from the Clipboard file into your application.

The Scrapbook file is a data file used by a desk accessory called the Scrapbook. If this file is moved, the Scrapbook desk accessory will not work because it looks for the Scrapbook file only in the top level of the System folder. The Scrapbook applications will be discussed later in the "Apple Menu Items" section.

The rest of this section looks at the folders you'll find in the System folder and the types of files they contain. Throughout this section, references are made to programs that may not be familiar or utility programs are mentioned that you don't have. Whenever possible, the examples will come from what you probably have as part of your System software or programs on the CD-ROM disk.

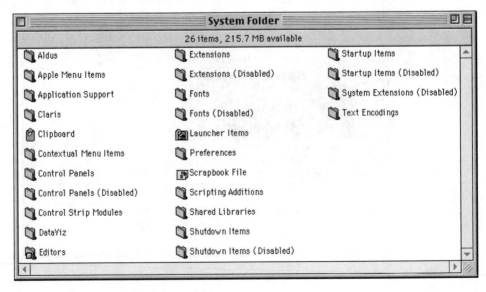

Figure 6.8   *Inside the System folder.*

Mac OS 8 Folders

Mac OS 8 will automatically create the following folders if they are missing at bootup:

- ❖ Apple Menu Items
- ❖ Control Panels
- ❖ Extensions
- ❖ Fonts
- ❖ Launcher Items
- ❖ Preferences
- ❖ Shutdown Items
- ❖ Startup Items

You should not remove these folders from your System folder; if you do, though, the next time you start your Mac, they will reappear. Other applications or System elements such as OpenDoc, AppleScript, or the Extensions Manager create the other folders shown in Figure 6.8.

The Finder

You've already read quite a bit about the Finder; by now, you know that it is what you're looking at after your Mac has started and that it creates and controls the Desktop. You can do a few more things with the Finder that have not been discussed yet. This section discusses the following features of the Mac OS 8 Finder:

- ❖ Drag-and-drop
- ❖ Stationery pads
- ❖ Customized icons
- ❖ Application's memory size
- ❖ Locking a file
- ❖ Additional Finder tricks

Drag-and-Drop

Drag-and-drop is a new feature of the Macintosh, introduced with System 7. It is the ability to select a document icon and drag it onto the icon of a program and release it (like moving a file to a folder), causing the application to start and open the file.

This procedure works only with applications that recognize the document's type resource (see Chapter 11 for more information on type resources). The type resource tells the Finder what type of file a document happens to be; for example, a text, a PICT, or a Text file.

If the application recognizes the file as one that it can open, it will highlight it and, when the mouse button is released, the application will start. This is useful for opening files that do not have a corresponding application but can be read by another program. This capability has also given rise to a family of utility programs. They operate on the drag-and-drop principle and do such things as automatically substitute applications, trash a file or group of files, or mount unmounted drives or network volumes.

Try dragging a Read Me file onto SimpleText. Notice that the SimpleText icon is selected, just as a folder is when a file is dragged onto the folder. When the mouse is released, SimpleText will start and open the file. Another thing to notice here is that the file being dragged was a SimpleText file, as indicated by the file's icon.

In Figure 6.9, the file being dragged to the Microsoft Word icon is a text file. As you can see, Microsoft Word can open it because Microsoft Word is selected. If you had double-clicked on the document icon being dragged, it would have started the program that created the file—in this case, AppleLink.

With System 7.5, the concept of drag-and-drop was expanded as an extension of copy-and-paste. Selecting text, sound, or a picture, in a System 7.5- or Mac OS 8- compatible program and dragging it to another application causes the selected text or picture to be moved as if you had performed a copy- and-paste. If you have System 7.5 or Mac OS 8, you can try this by moving text from a SimpleText document to a Sticky note (Sticky notes are discussed in the "Apple Menu Items" section).

Drag-and-drop can also be used to store selected text or a graphic to the Desktop, where it will stay as a text clipping. Drag the clippings file into another document. Figure 6.10 shows a closed and an open clipping file on the Mac's Desktop.

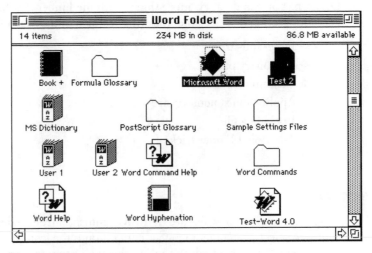

Figure 6.9 *Dragging and dropping a file onto a program other than the file's creator.*

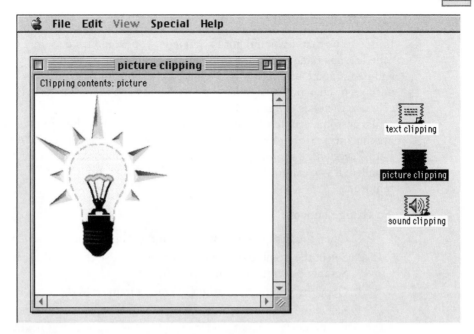

Figure 6.10   *Clipping files on the Desktop.*

Stationery Pads

A stationery pad is a file that, when opened, opens as an untitled document even though it contains information. An example is a file that has your company's logo, return address, salutation, and closing already completed, and that you use every time you write a letter. Rather than open your letterhead file, remembering to give it a new name every time, you can convert the file into stationery so that your Mac will always ask you to save the file with a new name. This is a handy tool for standardizing documents throughout an organization. You can also use stationery pads to create a core set of documents that are modified as needed. Stationery pads present another small way to increase your productivity. The first step in creating a stationery file is to make the base document and save it to your hard drive. After you've closed the new document, go to the Finder and locate your document.

Once you've found it, perform these steps:

1. Select the file.
2. Choose *Get Info* or (⌘+I) from the File menu.
3. In the bottom left corner of the Info window, check the box titled *Stationery pad*.

You can launch an application using a stationery pad by double-clicking on the stationery file. The document will open as an Untitled window within the program. When you are finished working on the file, save the file as a new document using the *Save As...* command from the File menu.

Customized Icons

It used to be that if you did not like an icon, you would have to drag out a utility called an *icon editor* to change it. Now you can change an icon using your Mac's copy and paste functions. Customized icons can be a means of identifying files for a special purpose or changing an application's icon you happen to think is ugly. The only rules are the ones you make.

To customize an icon, you need a graphic image. For this example, let's use a graphic image stored in your Mac's Scrapbook (as discussed in the "Apple Menu Items" section). This image was in your Mac's Scrapbook when your System was installed; if you cannot find the image used in this example, then it has been removed.

To change an icon:

1. Open the Scrapbook; it is found in the Apple menu.
2. Select the graphic shown in Figure 6.11. (Use the scroll bar in the Scrapbook window to find the graphic.)
3. Copy the graphic using the *Copy* menu item or ⌘+C.
4. Select the icon you want to change. You can change any icon displayed in the Finder.
5. Select the *Get Info* menu item (⌘+I) from the File menu.
6. Click on the icon in the Info window (a dark border appears around the icon) and use the keyboard paste command (⌘+P).

The graphic you copied replaces the original icon, as shown in Figure 6.12.

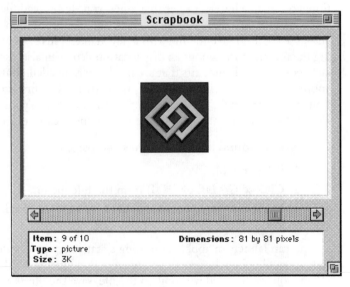

Figure 6.11   The graphic in the Scrapbook.

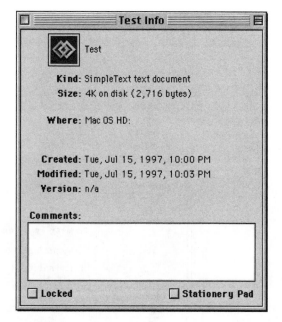

Figure 6.12 *The new icon.*

When you close, the icon on the Desktop will look like the graphic you pasted in. This works with large graphic files or small ones. The graphic will be reduced in size to replace the icon, but it will lose some or a lot of detail, depending on the graphic's size.

Application's Memory Size

The Finder not only controls the Macintosh interface, but it can also control some parts of the Mac's operating environment. For instance, it is from the Finder that you control how much memory an application will use when it runs. This function is also controlled from the Get Info window; Figure 6.13 shows the Get Info window from SimpleText.

In Figure 6.13, a box called Memory Requirements appears in the lower right corner. The suggested memory size for SimpleText is 512K, the minimum size is 192K, and the preferred memory (current) size is set to 512K. The minimum memory size is the least amount of memory an application can use and still work properly.

When your Mac is low on memory, it will look at the program's minimum memory size and, if the Mac has enough memory, it will open the program using the amount of memory in the minimum size setting. In some programs, you can tell them to use less than the minimum memory size by changing the setting, but the program may not work properly. It does not hurt to experiment if you do not have as much memory as you would like.

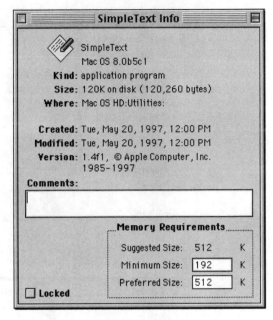

Figure 6.13 *The SimpleText Get Info window.*

To tell how much memory your Mac is using:

1. Switch to the Finder.
2. Select the *About This Macintosh* menu item from the Apple menu.
3. A window like the one in Figure 6.14 appears.

The window in Figure 6.14 shows how much memory your Mac has, how much is left for other programs, and how much each running program is using. The preferred size is the amount of memory your program will normally use, and the default setting for the preferred size is the same as the suggested size. At times a program may need more than the suggested amount of memory. An application usually requires enough memory to run, plus memory for each document that you open. If you have several documents open simultaneously or have very complicated documents, you might have to increase the application's memory size. You'll know to increase the preferred size if your application tells you that it is running out of memory.

Locking a File

Files can be locked at the Finder level if you want to protect them from being accidentally trashed. Locking a file will also make it function as if it were a stationery pad.

To lock a file:

1. Select the file.
2. Perform a *Get Info...* on the file.

Figure 6.14 *The About This Computer window.*

3. Click on the Lock check box to lock the file.

You can make the Finder delete a locked file by holding down the Option key as you select the *Empty Trash...* menu item from the Special menu. Under normal circumstances, however, locked files cannot be deleted.

Additional Finder Tricks

Apple has built some interesting tricks into the Finder, ones that we haven't discussed yet. All of these Finder Tricks are enhancements that Apple has made because either customers asked for the features or a programmer thought they would be a neat trick. The tricks I will discuss here are new to Mac OS 8 unless stated otherwise. Some of these features are the spring-opening folders, Sticky Menus, and others.

Spring-opening Folders

Spring-opening or spring-loaded folders are a strange little feature that you've probably seen by accident. I think some people may find it disconcerting to have a folder, or even several folders, automatically open. Which is exactly what happens if you drag a file onto a closed folder and you pause for a moment too long before you let go of the item you're dragging.

Another way to activate spring-loaded folders without dragging a file onto a folder is to perform one and a half clicks and move the magnifying glass that appears onto a folder. Holding the mouse button down after performing a full mouse click (up and down) equals one and a half mouse clicks.

The spring-open folders function is controlled by the Edit menu's *Preferences* menu item, shown in Figure 6.15. Your options are to turn on or off the spring-loaded folders and to adjust the speed with which they open.

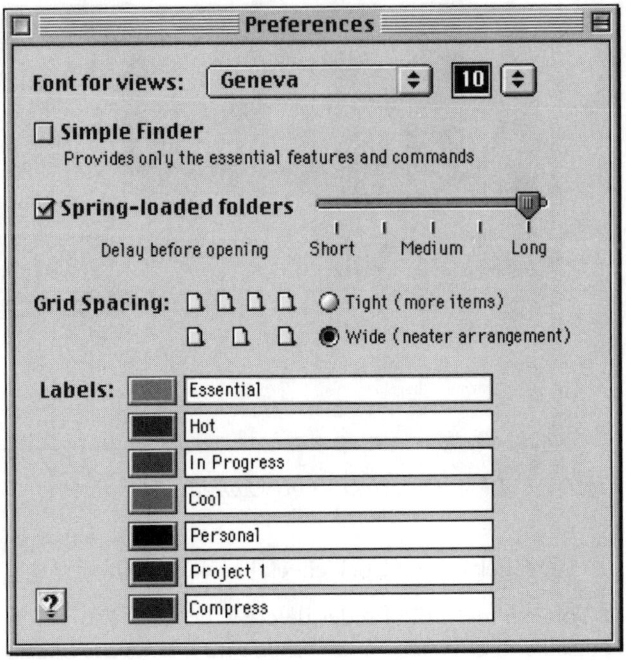

Figure 6.15   *The Finder's preferences.*

Sticky Menus

Your Mac can drop a menu when you drag your pointer over the menu. This feature, called Sticky menus, can be turned on or off by quickly clicking on any menu item. To activate Sticky menus, just place your pointer over any menu and quickly click the mouse. Remember, do not click and hold; just click quickly up and down on the mouse button. Once you've done this, any menu will automatically drop as the pointer moves over the menu. Sticky menus automatically turn off when you click the mouse. It doesn't matter if you select a menu item; you just have to click the mouse anywhere in the Finder.

Contextual Menus

A Contextual menu is a menu that modifies itself depending on the item selected. The Finder has a series of Contextual menus that can be activated by holding down the Control key when the pointer is on an icon. You will know that the Contextual menu feature has been activated because the pointer icon changes and a small menu appears next to the pointer.

The menu items change depending on the type of Finder icon the pointer is over. In general, the most frequently used menu items from the Help, Special, and File menus plus some Internet selections appear in Contextual menus. For more informa-tion about the Internet, see Chapter 14. Figure 6.16 shows what you see if you use

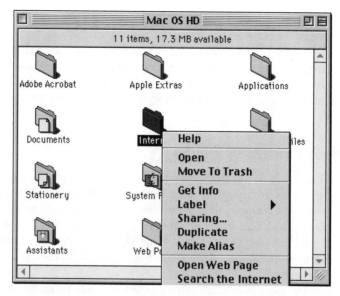

Figure 6.16 *The Contextual menu for a folder.*

the Contextual menu function when selecting a folder. Experiment with this feature on different types of icons. Also, most applications will most likely offer some type of Contextual menu in the near future.

Another function of the Finder (from System 7.X) that is easy to miss is the pop-up menu in a window's title bar. If you click on the name of a folder while holding down the x key, the path of the folder will be displayed as a pop-up menu. Figure 6.17 shows a pop-up menu; selecting one of the names will bring its window to the front.

If you want to move a window that is behind the one you are looking at, hold down the ⌘ key and click on the title bar of the window behind the selected one (the window with lines across its title bar is the selected window) and then move the window.

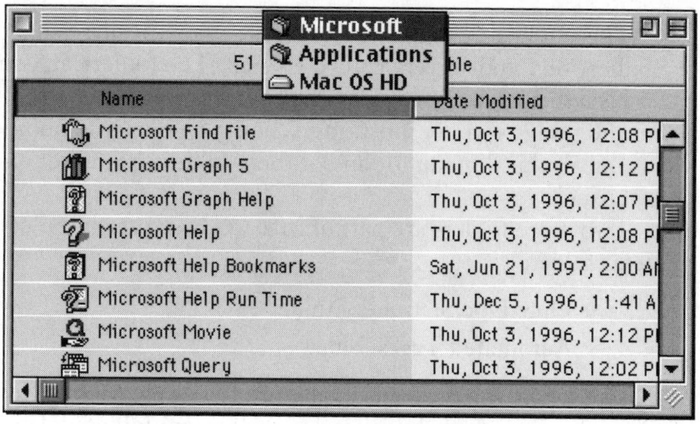

Figure 6.17 *The pop-up menu in the Finder window.*

This method is great for moving or copying a file to a folder that is in a window behind the one that contains the file you are moving.

In addition to documented Finder features, it seems that every time you turn around, someone is discovering something new about how it operates or a neat way to use its features to perform a new task. The best way to discover these tricks is to experiment. You can also pick up tricks and tips from *Mac User* and *MacWorld* magazines.

The Apple Menu Items Folder

The Apple Menu Items folder contains everything you see in the Apple menu. The programs in the Apple Menu Items folder are called desk accessories. Desk accessories are really small programs that can be run from any location on your hard drive. Desk accessories can be easily installed by dragging a desk accessory program onto the System folder icon. Your Mac automatically copies or moves the desk accessories to the Apple Menu Items folder, which makes the program available from the Apple menu.

The most important programs in the Apple menu are discussed in other sections and chapters of this book. You've already read about the Find File program in Chapter 5. Some folders in the Apple Menu Items folder, as well as some tricks you can perform with these folders, should be discussed here.

The contents of any folder placed in the Apple Menu Items folder can become a hierarchical menu. The Apple Menu Options control panel controls how the Apple menu behaves. This control panel turns on or off the hierarchical menus function for folders in the Apple menu. Figure 6.18 shows the Apple menu's hierarchical menu function.

The rest of this section looks at these folders and offers some suggestions for maximizing your use of the Apple Menu Items folder. These folders are as follows:

- ❖ Recent Applications folder
- ❖ Recent Documents folder
- ❖ Recent Servers folder

These folders, created by Mac OS 8, contain aliases for the last 10 documents, applications, and servers you've opened. The folders, in conjunction with the hierarchical menus, let you select these recent items from the Apple menu as a shortcut for the things you use most often. You can adjust the number of items that appear in a hierarchical menu for any of these folders from the Apple Menu Options control panel.

Two more folders are part of Mac OS 8 and are installed in the Apple Menu Items folder:

- ❖ OpenDoc Stationery folder
- ❖ Automated Tasks folder

The OpenDoc Stationery folder in the Apple Menu Items folder is an alias to the OpenDoc Stationery folder inside the System folder and available if you've installed OpenDoc. The Automated Tasks folder contains AppleScript files that can be used

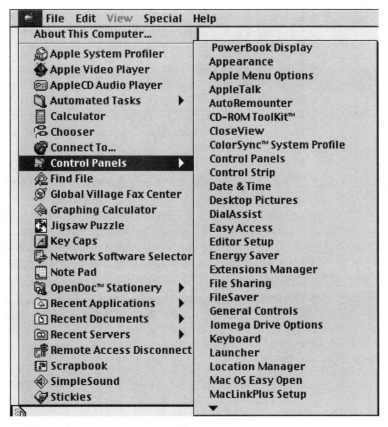

Figure 6.18 *An Apple menu's hierarchical menu.*

to perform quick configuration changes and other useful tasks. Both AppleScript and OpenDoc are discussed in Chapter 7.

You can also make your own hierarchical menus by placing folders or folder aliases in the Apple Menu Items folder. Some of the items you might consider placing there are folders that contain aliases of your stationery pads, utilities that you often use, or any other document that you may want to access quickly. You should experiment with the hierarchical menus and with placing aliases in the Apple Menu Items folder.

Apple Menu Items

The remainder of this section looks at each of the desk accessories that Apple distributes with Mac OS 8:

❖ AppleCD Audio Player—The AppleCD desk accessory is used to play Audio CDs on your Macintosh. It provides all the controls you find on your stereo, with the exception of a balance control.

❖ Calculator—The Calculator is just a quick-and-dirty DA that lets you perform quick calculations; it is quite handy. To clear the Calculator, hit the Escape or Clear key.

❖ Chooser—Of all of the desk accessories on your Mac, the Chooser is probably the most important. With it, you select what printer you are going to use; it also allows you to log onto an AppleShare network. You also use the Chooser to turn AppleTalk on or off. More information about file sharing and networks can be found in Chapter 13. Without this little piece of software, your Mac would lose over half its capabilities as a computing device. Figure 6.19 shows the Chooser.

There is very little to using the Chooser. To select a printer, its driver must be installed in the Extensions folder (discussed later in this chapter). If it is, its icon appears in the Chooser; just click on the icon to select the printer. If you are printing to a networked LaserWriter, AppleTalk must be on. Using the Chooser to log onto a network is discussed in Chapter 13.

❖ Find File—The Find File desk accessory was discussed in Chapter 5, "Keeping Track of Your Data." Find File is used to find those files you've misplaced.

❖ Graphing Calculator—The Graphing Calculator is a trigonometric calculator that graphs the results. Beyond this, I don't have a clue; play with it. Maybe you'll find it useful.

❖ Key Caps—Key Caps is the tool you use to find that elusive special character that you can never remember, such as trademark or copyright symbols. You can also use Key Caps to get foreign characters, such as the tilde or umlaut. Figure 6.20 shows Key Caps with an accented à and an ü.

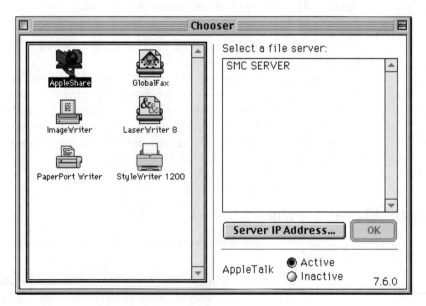

Figure 6.19 *The Chooser desk accessory.*

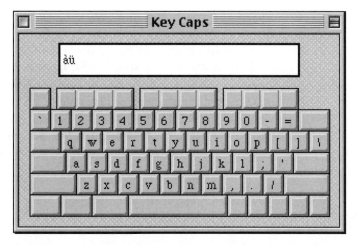

Figure 6.20 *Key Caps desk accessory.*

To use Key Caps, select the Font you are using in your document from the Key Caps menu. Once you see your font displayed on the simulated keyboard, you can see what special characters the font contains by pressing the Option, x, and Shift keys in various combinations. To create a foreign letter character, such as an umlauted Ü, you need to find the special character, which in this case is an option O. After you hold down the Option key and select the letter O, press the letter you want to combine with the special character—in this example, U. The letter you pressed will appear as the accented foreign character.

This process will work any time you type on the Mac, not just in Key Caps. If you create the character in Key Caps, however, you can copy or cut it from the Key Caps display and paste it into your document.

❖ Jigsaw Puzzle—Sit and play with it. When the puzzle is completed correctly, the world is put back together. To change the puzzle picture, copy a picture and paste it into the Jigsaw Puzzle.

❖ Network Software Selector—This utility is used to switch between classic networking and open transport. This utility is discussed in Chapter 13.

❖ Note Pad—Note Pad is a small program for keeping notes. It has eight pages, each of which can hold up to 32K of text; however, it has no file controls. You can use it to keep short notes, and it will work with the cut, copy, and paste commands. Using drag-and-drop, it can be handy for storing text.

❖ Scrapbook—The Scrapbook is where you can compile an eclectic collection of text, graphics, sounds, and even QuickTime movies (for the movies you'll need the QuickTime-compatible Scrapbook). To put something into the Scrapbook, just copy what you want to keep, open the Scrapbook, and paste it in. Later, when you want to reuse the item, open the Scrapbook, copy the item, and paste it into your document.

Whenever you copy something from the Scrapbook, you are stuck with the entire item. There is no way to use the Apple scrapbook to select a portion of a Scrapbook entry. The Scrapbook is drag-and-drop-compatible, so you can drag the items to and from the Scrapbook.

❖ SimpleSound—This small program can be used to select your Mac's alert sound, record a new sound, or play sounds.

❖ Stickies—The Stickies desk accessory lets you place electronic Post-it®-like notes on your screen. These are little text files you can use for reminders. Stickies are drag-and-drop-compatible. Figure 6.21 shows some Sticky notes.

The Control Panels Folder

A control panel is a special type of program whose function is to change system, machine, or interface preferences and configurations. Some examples of what you can control are your Mac's sounds, Desktop pattern, and the time and date. The whole idea behind control panels is that you can use them to control or set up user-configurable settings. They are a primary means for customizing your Macintosh and truly making it your machine.

Several control panels come as standard programs with Mac OS 8. Some of the best Macintosh utilities, though, also come as control panels. This section looks at the control panel functions, how they are installed, and the standard Apple control panels that come with Mac OS 8.

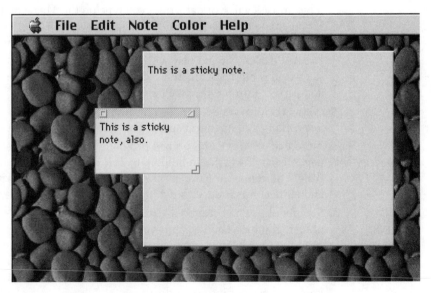

Figure 6.21 *Some Sticky notes.*

General Guidelines for Control Panels

A good example to illustrate control panels is the Sound control panel (see Figure 6.22). If the sound Control Panel was not installed with Mac OS 8 you'll find it in the Apple Extras folder. The Sound control panel allows you to change the types of sound and the volume of the sound your Mac makes. The Sound control panel also controls the playing of audio CDs and all sound functions on Power Macintoshes.

Your Mac's beep or alert sound is a system setting, one that comes from the System that controls your Macintosh. The volume, however, is stored in the PRAM and kept alive by the battery. If you set the volume and then boot from a disk other than the one you were using when you set the sound, the volume of your Mac's sound stays the same, but the sound itself could change—especially if the sound you used was not in the System on the second disk.

Another control panel, called General Controls, allows you to change how fast the insertion point blinks, how many times the menu item blinks when it is selected, and some Desktop controls. Some of these settings are stored in the System, and others are stored in the PRAM. (How many times a menu item blinks is stored in the PRAM.)

Control panels are normally accessed from the Control Panels folder in the Apple menu. Selecting the *Control Panels* menu item opens the Control Panels folder or lets you select a specific control panel through the Control Panels hierarchical menu. The *Control Panels* item in the Apple menu is an alias of the Control Panels folder inside your System folder. (See Chapter 5 for more on aliases.)

Installing control panels doesn't involve anything more than copying the control panel into the Control Panels folder. Mac OS 8 makes the installation process easy—all you have to do is drag the control panel onto your System folder icon. The Finder asks if you wish to move or copy the control panel into the Control Panels folder. When you see this message, clicking Yes will move or copy the control panel to the Control Panels folder. If a control panel should not be installed this way, special instructions accompany the control panel in either the manual or a Read Me file.

Understanding PRAM

You don't have to understand a lot of technical details about your Mac to use its control panels, but sometimes a little technical background helps. Your Mac stores settings from control panels in one of two places. Settings are stored on the Mac's startup drive or in special memory. This memory is called the *Parameter RAM* or *PRAM.* The settings stored in PRAM are maintained by your Mac's electric power, and when your Mac is turned off, a battery inside your Mac maintains these settings.

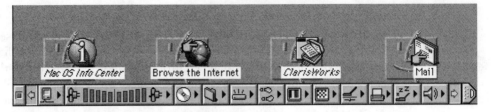

Figure 6.22   *The Sound control panel.*

As a rule, follow the instructions that come with any new control panel you purchase. Sometimes, installation may be complex enough to require an installer program (see Chapter 9). A control panel might require other files or modifications to the System file to function. One example is Mac OS 8's personal file sharing. It is implemented with several control panels, and the complicated installation process justifies the installation script.

Some of your control panels are memory-resident and loaded with your system at startup. Others are just programs that could be placed anywhere on your hard drive and still work. If you want to experiment with your control panels to find out which ones need to load with the System, you can do so by removing them from the Control Panels folder and the System folder and restarting your Mac.

After your Mac has restarted, double-click on the control panel you removed. If it works, then it is one that does not load into your Mac's System memory. You can place it anywhere on your hard drive and still use it. If you try to launch the control panel, though, and it does not work or you get a message saying that it needs to be installed (Figure 6.23) you will have to put it back into the Control Panels folder and restart your Mac before you can use it. If you decide to move some of your control panels, be careful. Test each one before moving it, and then keep it somewhere handy so that you can easily change whatever aspect of your Mac it controls.

If a control panel has been installed and you try to use it, only to receive a dialog box like the one shown in Figure 6.24, it means that you cannot use the control panel.

If you encounter this dialog box on your Macintosh when using a control panel, you can remove the control panel from the Control Panels folder and trash it. Usually, you will not have this problem; it occurs most often when you've installed

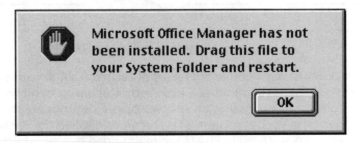

Figure 6.23   *The Control panel Microsoft Office Manager needs to be installed. Restart your Mac.*

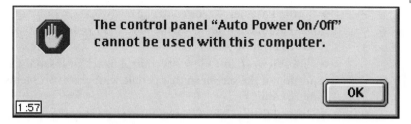

The control panel "Auto Power On/Off" cannot be used with this computer.

OK

1:57

Figure 6.24 *Control panel cannot be used with this Mac.*

your System so that it will work with any Macintosh rather than doing an install specifically for your model of Mac.

Mac OS 8's Control Panels

Several parts to Mac OS 8 are installed separately. As a result, the control panels and other system elements used by the other System functions, such as OpenDoc, Cyberdog, and MacLinkPlus, are discussed in other parts of the book. Otherwise, the following is a brief description of each control panel found in Mac OS 8. These descriptions are brief because most of these control panels are discussed in other parts of the book.

❖ PowerBook Display—When using a PowerBook that is able to use an external adapter, this control panel lets you configure the external monitor. You can use it as an extra monitor or to mirror the PowerBook's monitor (where what is on the PowerBook's monitor is displayed on the external monitor).

❖ Appearance—With the Appearance control panel, you can change the color of highlighted text and the color scheme for your window ornamentation. The Options button lets you set the title bar collapse option and your System font.

❖ Apple Menu Options—The Apple Menu Options control panel controls the Apple menu's hierarchical menus and how many items appear in the Recent folders.

❖ AppleTalk—The AppleTalk control panel is used to select the type of network you're going to use. This control panel is used only when OpenTransport is installed and active. Networking is discussed in Chapter 13.

❖ Auto Power On/Off—You can use the Power On/Off control panel to turn your Mac on and off at predetermined times. This can be useful for having your Mac perform automated tasks while you're away.

❖ AutoRemounter—AutoRemounter is a control panel used with PowerBooks when they are connected to an AppleTalk network. This control panel reconnects your PowerBook to the network when it starts automatically or when it is restarted.

❖ ColorSync System Profile—ColorSync is used to maintain consistent colors between your monitor and other output devices such as printers. Once it is set ColorSync works in the background.

❖ Button Disabler—This control panel works on only some Macs. It is used to prevent others from using the button on your Mac to adjust the sound or screen brightness.

❖ CloseView—CloseView is a control panel for disability access. It enlarges a portion of the screen so that people with vision problems can use the Mac more easily.

❖ Control Strip—The Control Strip is a utility that provides quick access to a number of Macintosh settings. Clicking on the icons in the Control Strip provides access to different functions from spinning the hard drive to turning on file sharing. Figure 6.25 shows the Control Strip on a PowerBook.

❖ Date & Time—The Date & Time control panel is used to set your computer's date, time, and time zone. This control panel is also used to set your Mac's default date and time formats. Also, you can configure the menu clock using this control panel.

❖ Desktop Pictures—This control panel lets you select your Mac's Desktop pattern or place a picture onto the Desktop. It has 103 different patterns from which to choose. If you don't find a pattern you like, you can use a third-party utility to set your Desktop pattern, or you can paste an image into the desktop picture's control panel. Notice that the screen shots

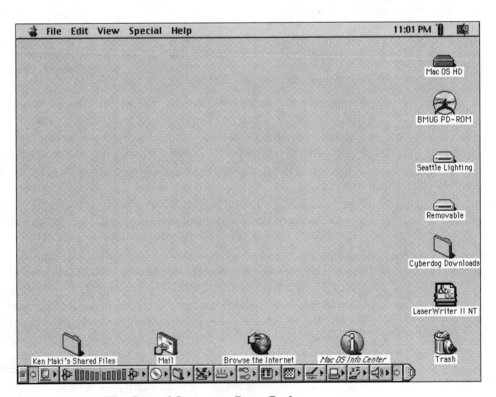

Figure 6.25 *The Control Strip on a PowerBook.*

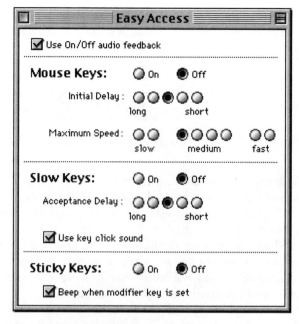

Figure 6.26   *Easy Access control panel.*

throughout the book have various Desktop patterns. These patterns were all changed with the Desktop Pictures Control panel.

❖ DialAssist—The DialAssist control panel stores the dialing settings for your location. These settings will then be used by telecommunications software when your modem dials the phone.

❖ Easy Access—Easy Access is one of those control panels that you either love or hate. Its intended users are people who have difficulty using a keyboard or a mouse (it will not improve your typing). Figure 6.26 shows the Easy Access control panel.

Easy Access has Mouse Keys, Slow Keys, and Sticky Keys as its features. Mouse Keys let you use the numeric keypad for moving the mouse cursor. You can activate it from the control panel or with the Command, Shift, and Clear (also the Num Lock key) x key option.

Sticky Keys is used to hold down a modifier key, such as the Option, x, Shift, and Control keys, while you press another key on the keyboard. It is activated by pressing the Shift key five times. When it is active, you will see a small icon appear on the right side of your menu bar (see Figure 6.27) and hear a little crescendo sound.

Figure 6.27   *The Sticky Keys indicator.*

Figure 6.28   *The modifier indicator in Sticky Keys.*

![11:23 PM indicator]

Figure 6.29   *Sticky Keys indicator after modifier has been pressed a second time.*

To deactivate it, press the Shift key five more times in succession. It will disappear and make a little de-crescendo sound as it shuts off.

After the indicator appears, if you press a modifier key, the indicator icon changes, as shown in Figure 6.28.

When you press the modifier a second time, the Modifier key is locked; you can then press the other key you want to use with it. Figure 6.29 shows the Sticky Keys indicator when the modifier key has been pressed a second time. Sticky Keys stays active until you are finished with it and put it away.

Sticky Keys has caused people to think that the supernatural is somehow trying to take over their Macintosh. Though it can be useful, if you happen to be tapping on your shift key as you try to form the thought that will change the world, your Mac might emit strange noises, and you'll think that you are losing your mind. It is easy to miss the association between the strange icon and the noise the Mac makes as it appears and disappears.

Slow Keys is used to set a delay before the key you pressed is activated. It can also be used in conjunction with Mouse Keys to give you more control over the cursor's movement. To turn Slow Keys on, hold the Enter key down for about eight seconds. When Slow Keys is activated, you will hear a little high-pitched dit, dit, dit (you really have to try it to hear the sound). You can turn it off the same way you turned it on.

❖ Extensions Manager—The Extensions Manager is an important control panel that controls which extensions will be loaded into memory as your Mac starts. You use this control panel for troubleshooting. To turn control panels on or off while starting your Mac, hold down the space bar to invoke the Extensions Manager.

❖ Energy Saver—The Energy Saver extension is used to set your Mac's green options. The green options are your Mac's energy saving capabilities. This control panel is used to tell your Mac when to put various components to sleep.

❖ File Sharing—The File Sharing control panel allows you to start or stop file sharing and program linking. It is also where you set your network name, the access password, and the name for your Macintosh (see Figure 6.30). The Macintosh name is the one that appears to others if you print to a networked LaserWriter at the same time others try to print to it. The File Sharing control panel also has an Activity Monitor section that allows you to watch who's using your Mac and how much of its processing power they are

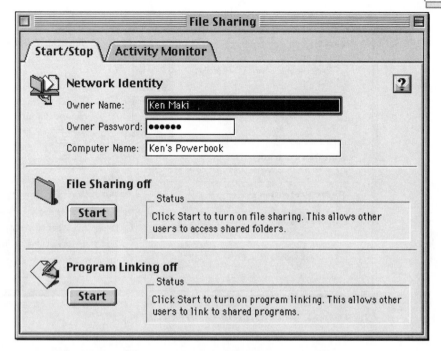

Figure 6.30 *The File Sharing control panel.*

consuming. You can disconnect users (if you are unhappy with how much of your CPU time they are consuming).

Networking is fairly complicated. The Setup Control panel is used in conjunction with the Network or AppleTalk control panel and the Users & Groups control panel; all three are used for personal file sharing. You can find more information on file sharing in Chapter 13.

❖ General Controls—The General Controls control panel (say that five times very rapidly) is used to set six different aspects of the Finder's interface (see Figure 6.31). It is used to set your Desktop preferences, the blinking rate of the insertion point, the number of times a selected menu item blinks, folder protection, default folder selections, and the Shut Down warning.

The following list briefly describes the General Controls options:

❖ With the Desktop controls, you can determine whether to show the Desktop while using other applications, and you can see whether you like the results.

❖ The Show Launcher option starts the Launcher control panel at startup.

❖ The *Warn me if computer was shut down improperly* option has your Mac tell whenever it starts if the Shut Down menu item (in the Special menu) or the Shut Down desk accessory was not used to shut down your Mac.

❖ Folder Protection locks the System Folder and/or your Applications folder if you do not want modifications made to either of these folders.

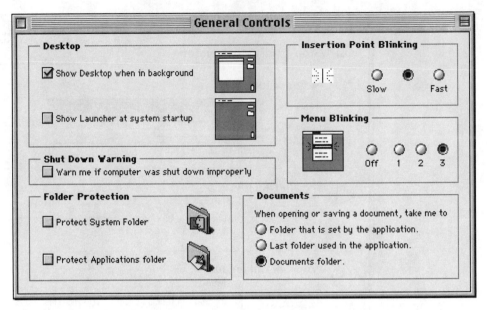

Figure 6.31   *The General Controls control panel.*

❖ The Insertion Point and Menu Blinking options control how rapidly your insertion point blinks and how many times your menu selections blink.

❖ The Documents section lets you select the default that is chosen when you perform a Save As... command. If you choose the Documents folder option, a folder called Documents is created on your Desktop, and all of your files will be saved inside the Documents folder.

❖ Keyboard—The Keyboard control panel lets you select the keyboard you want to use and set the delay time before a key starts repeating itself if held down. When you first install your System, this control panel is installed with only one keyboard option, the US keyboard. You can get foreign character and special keyboard layouts that you can install. One of the extra keyboard layouts you can install is the DVORAK keyboard layout from Nisus Software.

Figure 6.32 shows the Keyboard control panel with several foreign keyboard layouts. The U.S. keyboard layout is the selected one; however, you could select a keyboard layout for any of the countries listed in the control panel and type in Swiss French, German, or Dutch with this Macintosh. The keyboard layouts are listed alphabetically.

❖ Launcher—The Launcher is a control panel that you can use to open programs, control panels, and documents. The Launcher control panel uses a folder in the System folder called Launcher Items. The buttons that appear in the Launcher, as shown in Figure 6.33, are aliases in the Launcher Items folder. Dragging an icon from the Finder into the Launcher window creates a button and places an alias into the Launcher Items folder. To remove a

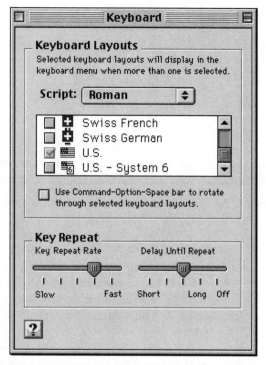

Figure 6.32 *The Keyboard control panel.*

Launcher button, hold down the Option key and drag the button from the Launcher window.

You can further customize the Launcher by putting folders inside the Launcher Items folder. The folder's name must have a • (option 8) in front of the folder's name, such as •Utilities. The folders become category buttons. When a category button is created, the items in the Launcher Items folder

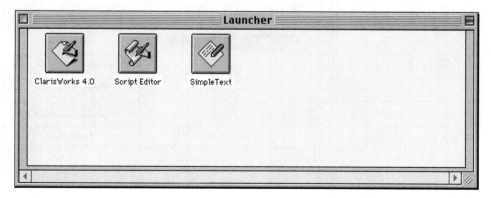

Figure 6.33 *The Launcher control panel.*

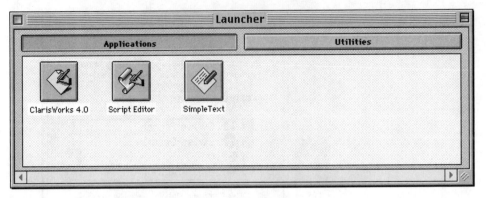

Figure 6.34   *A customized Launcher control panel.*

are categorized under an Applications button. Figure 6.34 shows a customized Launcher.

You can further customize the Launcher by changing the size of the buttons. You do this by holding down the Command key and the mouse button at the same time. A pop-up menu appears; you can select small, medium, or large buttons.

❖ Location Manager—The Location Manager lets you configure your Mac for different locations. You can configure your Mac to auto-open an application, use a specific Internet setup, startup with networking on or off, and adjust

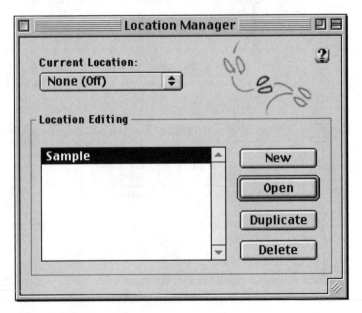

Figure 6.35   *The Location Manager.*

various other settings including specific extension sets. Figure 6.35 shows the Location Manager.

❖ Macintosh OS Easy Open—The Macintosh OS Easy Open control panel controls the Mac's built-in file translators. When you try to open a file for which you don't have the corresponding program, the Macintosh OS Easy Open control panel lets you control how your Mac behaves under such circumstances. The options are fairly self-explanatory; Figure 6.36 shows the Macintosh OS Easy Open control panel.

❖ MacTCP—MacTCP is a special networking control panel. The MacTCP control panel provides Internet Access by using classic networking. You can find out more about networking in Chapter 13 and the Internet in Chapter 14.

❖ Map—The Map control panel is used by your Mac's Internet software to properly date and time-stamp your e-mail. It also lets you determine the time anywhere in the world. You can also use it to find the longitude and latitude of any of the cities that have been entered, a handy feature if you are an astrology buff. Type *MID* into the text field and click Find or press *Enter* to learn where the *Middle of Nowhere* is really located. Now, who can live without knowing that?

Figure 6.37 shows the Map control panel. If you want to find out which cities are already entered into it, hold down the Command and Option keys while clicking on the Find button. By clicking on the Time Zone title, it will change to the Time Difference between two locations. Clicking on the *mi* (miles) label changes it to kilometers or a designation called *dg*, for degrees. This method will cycle you through each city, giving you the information you need.

❖ Memory—The Memory control panel allows you to set how much memory should be used for your RAM cache. On 68030 and 68040 Macs, it also allows you to configure your virtual memory and the addressing mode to either 32- or 24-bit. On PowerBooks and Macintosh Quadras, you can also set up a RAM disk with the Memory control panel. Figure 6.38 shows the Memory control panel with all the available options

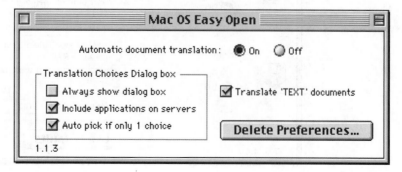

Figure 6.36 *Macintosh OS Easy Open control panel.*

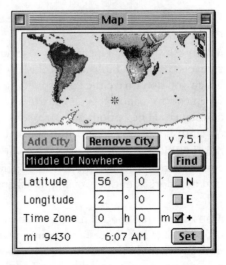

Figure 6.37   *The Map control panel.*

If you're using a PowerMac you have an option called the Modern Memory Manager; this selection should always be turned on. The Cache Size setting should be set at 96K for every 100MB of hard disk space on your startup volume. If you have a PowerMac you might try setting the Virtual Memory to 1M more than the amount of physical RAM in your Mac. With Virtual Memory turned on, PowerMac applications will use less memory.

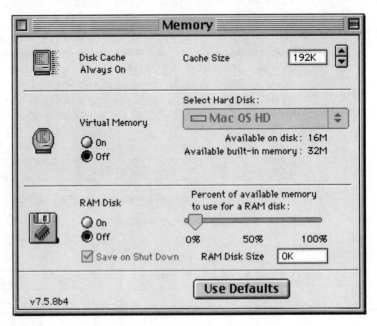

Figure 6.38   *The Memory control panel.*

❖ Modem—The Modem control panel is used to tell your Macintosh what type of modem you use and how it is connected to your Mac. This control panel is used by Mac OS 8's Internet software and telecommunications software designed to work with Mac OS 8.

❖ Monitors & Sound—The Monitors part of this control panel allows you to configure the setting for the number of grays or colors for your monitor. If you have multiple monitors, it will allow you to set the monitor on which the menu bar should appear and which monitor should be your startup monitor (the one on which the smiling Mac appears during the startup process). The startup monitor and the one on which the menu bar appears do not have to be the same monitor.

In Figure 6.39, you see two monitors. Monitor 1 is a gray-scale monitor attached to a PowerBook. It is capable of displaying 256 grays, and it is set to display the menu bar. The little smiling Mac (displayed by holding down the Option key) indicates that it is also the startup monitor. You can move the menu bar indicator and the smiling Mac indicator to either monitor by dragging them back and forth. These changes take effect the next time you start your Mac.

If you have installed a third-party monitor card, it can tap into the Monitor's control panel, and clicking on the Options button may give you additional configuration choices.

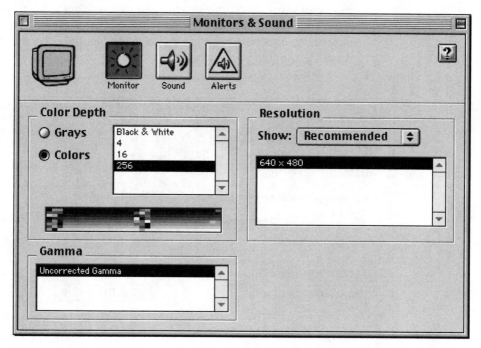

Figure 6.39 *The Monitors & Sound control panel.*

Depending on the monitor and card that you use, you may want to experiment with your monitor settings. Turning off the color or running in 256-color mode may provide you with a significant speed increase during screen refreshes (when the screen redraws itself). Also, utilities are available that automatically change the number of colors displayed based on what program you are currently running.

Use the sound portion of the Monitors & Sound control panel to select your System's sound and set its level. With the Alert section, you can create your own sound if you do not like those included with the System. Figure 6.40 shows the Sound control panel. On the left is a sliding control for setting the volume.

In the Alert section you can select the alert sound you want your Mac to use. When you select one of the Microphone options, you will be able to record a new sound by clicking on the Add button. This brings up a window with a set of controls similar to those you find on a tape recorder.

To create your own sound, press the Record button and then talk, play music, or make noise into your microphone. You can record 10 seconds of sound and then play back what you have recorded. If you don't like it, you can record a new sound; otherwise, save the sound by giving it a name. It will be stored in your System, and you can select it like any other sound. Just remember, 10 seconds of sound every time your Mac beeps could get old very quickly.

If you turn the sound off completely, your Mac still notifies you by making the menu bar flash. Normally, your Mac beeps to get your attention, like the alarm from the Alarm Clock. It also beeps when you try to perform a procedure that cannot be done, such as clicking the mouse outside of a dialog box that is demanding your attention. Primarily, it beeps because it is notifying

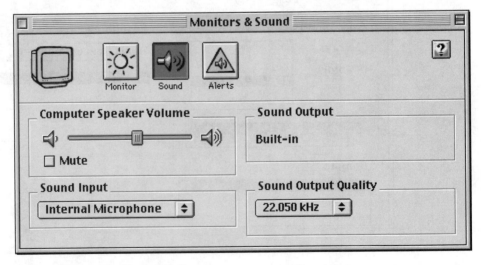

Figure 6.40   *The Sound section.*

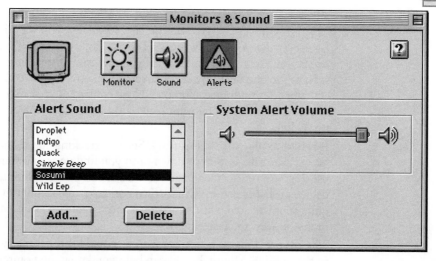

Figure 6.41　*The Alert section.*

you of some action you need to perform. Figure 6.41 shows the Alert section of the Monitors & Sound control panel.

❖ Mouse—The Mouse control panel is used to set the speed at which your mouse tracks and its double-click speed. When you set the double-click speed, the visual indicator on the mouse to the left (see Figure 6.42) represents the largest amount of time that may pass between two consecutive clicks for them to be recognized as a double-click. The double-click interval is another value stored in the parameter RAM.

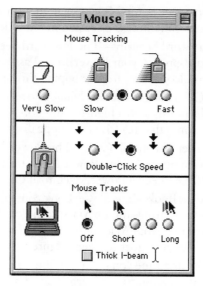

Figure 6.42　*The Mouse control panel.*

The setting for Mouse Tracking sets the ratio for mouse-to-screen representation. If you use a large monitor, say, 19 inches, you want it set to the fastest setting. You also want it set to the fastest setting if you want to get to where you are going in a hurry. If you are using a smaller monitor, however, such as the one on a PowerBook, setting the tracking speed too fast could actually be a hindrance. You could lose control of your mouse and end up selecting more than you want or moving your files to places where they do not belong.

It is best to play with this setting. Select a tracking speed and use it for a few hours, then adjust it up or down until you find your optimum setting. If you use a mouse replacement, such as a track ball or a graphics tablet, your device probably comes with its own control panel. Sometimes, these can get quite sophisticated, with built-in velocity enhancers, where the longer your mouse moves, the faster it goes.

The Mouse Tracks section is for PowerBooks. Sometimes you can lose track of the pointer. Mouse Tracks can help you know the pointer's location by displaying a trail.

❖ Network—The Network control panel allows you to select which network you'll use. The Network control panel appears only when you use Classic Networking. When you select it, it detects drivers for any network you have installed in your system. They can be the built-in LocalTalk, EtherTalk, AppleTalk Remote, or any other network driver you have installed. It is only one part of many required for using different networks. You can find more information on networking and network drivers in Chapter 13.

❖ Numbers—The Numbers control panel is used to set your Mac's default number format. You can choose the number format from a number of countries, as well as the currency symbol and the decimal and thousands separators.

❖ OpenDoc Setup—The OpenDoc control panel is used to set your OpenDoc environment. It is discussed in more detail in Chapter 7.

❖ Password Security—The Password Security control panel is used to password-protect your PowerBook. Password-protecting your PowerBook keeps unwelcome eyes from snooping through your data.

❖ PC Exchange—PC Exchange allows you to use MS-DOS disks on a Macintosh with a high-density floppy disk drive. The high-density drives are the ones that read 1.44M floppy disks.

❖ Power Macintosh Card—The Power Macintosh Card control panel is used to configure Apple's Power Macintosh Card. It is used to turn the Mac on or off. You need a Power Macintosh Card to use this control panel.

❖ PowerBook—The PowerBook control panel is used to configure the power-saving settings on the Macintosh Portable and all PowerBooks. You can set how long your Mac should wait before the hard drive spins down, the screen dims, and it goes to sleep. Figure 6.43 shows the PowerBook control panel.

The first time you open the PowerBook control panel, it shows only the Better Conservation/Performance part of the control panel, the Easy setup

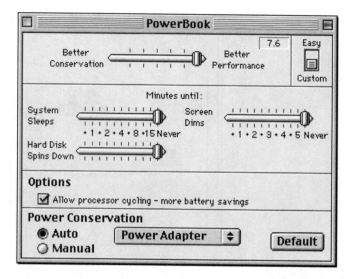

Figure 6.43   *The PowerBook control panel.*

configuration. When you click on the Easy/Custom switch, you have access
to the custom configuration shown in Figure 6.43.

Holding down the Option key when clicking on the Easy/Custom setup button lets you turn off processor cycling. Processor cycling sets the Mac's
CPU to run at half speed when the Mac is not busy.

❖ PowerBook Setup—The PowerBook setup is used to configure three aspects
of the Mac. It is used to select the internal or external modem, choose the
SCSI disk mode, and assign an automatic wake-up time. The available
options depend on your PowerBook's hardware.

❖ PPP—The PPP control panel is used to connect to the Internet with a
modem. It is an Open Transport component, discussed in Chapter 14.

❖ Startup Disk—The Startup Disk control panel lets you set the disk from
which your Mac will boot when you have more than one hard drive
attached. Clicking on one of the available volumes sets this preference. In
Figure 6.44, the disk set to start up the Mac is called "To Go." A more
detailed explanation of startup disks and switching between them can be
found in Chapter 10.

❖ TCP/IP—The TCP/IP control panel is another Open Transport component that enables your Mac to work on the Internet. The instructions for
configuring the TCP/IP control panel are explained in Chapter 14.

❖ Text—The Text control panel is used to set up how your Macintosh handles
text. You can choose the language script and the language your Mac uses.
The script controls the character set. English and most European languages
use the Roman script or character set.

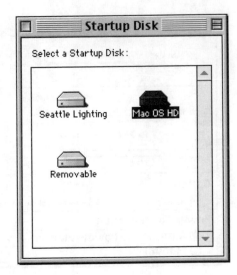

Figure 6.44   *The Startup Disk control panel.*

❖ Token Ring—The Token Ring control panel is used for Macintoshes that have a Token Ring network adapter. This control panel is part of Classic Networking.

❖ Trackpad—The Trackpad control panel is specifically for PowerBooks. It is similar to the Mouse control panel; it controls the tracking and clicking speed for the trackpad.

❖ Users & Groups—The Users & Groups control panel is part of file sharing. It allows you to specify those people who should have access to your Mac when you turn on file sharing and whether they will be able to use program linking.

Its other function is to let you put those individuals into groups so that it is easier to assign access privileges when you do decide to share a folder. A simple strategy for file access is to create two groups, *Minimal Access* and *Trustworthy* (you might want to use more tact in naming your groups). Everyone who belongs to the Minimal Access group is allowed read-only access to a folder, while your more computer-literate colleagues (theoretically, more trustworthy) are allowed to access more folders and write data as well as read it.

Figure 6.45 shows the setup for a single user. Once again, see Chapter 13 for more details on networking.

❖ Web Sharing—The Web Sharing control panel is used to configure your Mac as a personal Web Server. Web Sharing, new to the Mac OS, lets others access World Wide Web pages or files on your Macintosh using the same networking technology as the Internet. Web Sharing is discussed in Chapter 14, "Surfing the Net."

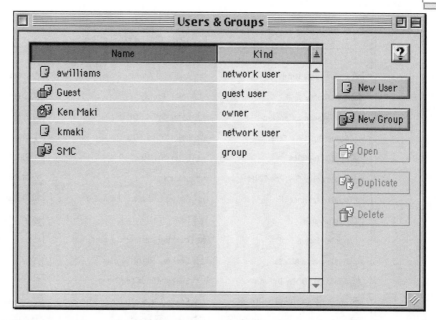

Figure 6.45 *The Users & Groups control panel.*

Your Extensions Folder

When Apple made the Mac OS capable of using extensions, the OS became extensible. An extension is a small program that loads into your Mac's memory as your Mac starts up. These small programs are one of the primary means for adding functionality to your Mac; the other method is the use of control panels.

With System 6.0.X, Apple made the System extensible through the use of small software programs called Inits. In System 7, the Inits became extensions, and they are now stored in the Extensions folder. Because of the extension's history you may hear old Mac hands call extensions Inits. In Figure 6.46, you can see some of the extensions and other files in the Extensions folder when you install Mac OS 8.

The icons you see flash across the bottom of your screen as your Mac boots are either extensions or control panels. As they flash across the screen they are loading into your Mac's memory. When an extension or control panel is loaded, it becomes part of the OS and operates at the same level as the System. Extensions that load at startup are called System extensions. Another type of extension is called a Chooser extension.

Chooser extensions are device drivers that are loaded only when your Mac needs them. Usually, these are printer drivers, but there are also Chooser extensions for networking. The other files that will find their way to the Extensions folder, such as AppleGuide files, are needed by the OS or programs installed on your Mac. The rest of this section discusses the extensions and other files in the Extensions folder that are standard with Mac OS 8. A brief description of each extension or file is given so that you can know what it does. The Extensions are discussed in the following order:

❖ System extensions

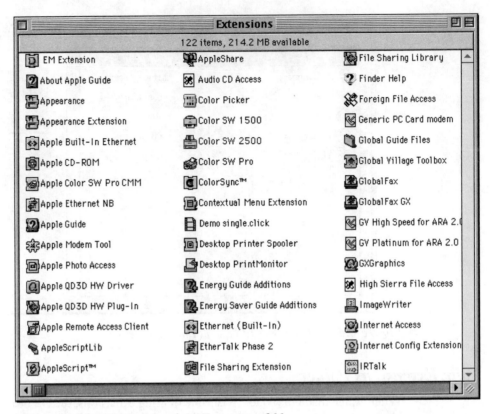

Figure 6.46   *The insides of the Extensions folder.*

- ❖ Chooser extensions
- ❖ Other files

System Extensions

System extensions are the extensions that enhance your System's capabilities. Fifty-four system extensions are installed on any Macintosh; we look at each of them. Some extensions work together, even though they have different names. All of the extensions that work together are discussed as a group.

- ❖ EM Extension—The EM Extension is the Extensions Manager control panel's companion. Without this extension, the Extensions Manager will not work. The EM has a space before its name, so it will appear and load first when your Mac starts up.
- ❖ Apple CD-ROM, Apple Photo Access, Audio CD Access, Foreign File Access, High Sierra File Access, and ISO 9660 File Access—All of these extensions are used when you have an Apple CD-ROM drive connected to your Macintosh. If you have a non-Apple CD-ROM drive, the Apple CD-

ROM extension will not work, but you do need all the other extensions. Instead of the Apple CD-ROM extension you'll need a third-party CD-ROM extension like FWB's CD-ROM Toolkit.

❖ AppleGuide and the associated guide documents—This extension makes AppleGuide work. AppleGuide is discussed in Chapter 7.

❖ AppleScript—AppleScript is Apple's system-level scripting language. A scripting language is a programming language that lets you automate Macintosh functions. AppleScript is covered in Chapter 7.

❖ Color Picker—The Color Picker is a tool that your Mac uses to select colors. The Color Picker extension adds options to the standard Macintosh color picker and works in conjunction with the Monitors and ColorSync extensions. Apple created a new Color Picker for Mac OS 8. It is easier to work with applications that allow you to select colors.

❖ ColorSync and Apple Color SW Pro CMM —The ColorSync extension works with and enables the ColorSync control panel. The Apple Color SW Pro CMM is the color management software used by ColorSync and the Apple StyleWriter Pro printer.

❖ Contextual Menu Extension—This extension enables the Finder's contextual menus.

❖ Desktop Printer Spooler—The Desktop Printer Spooler is the extension that enables print spooling with the Desktop printers.

❖ Ethernet (Built-In) and EtherTalk Phase 2—These extensions are the Ethernet extensions that enable Ethernet networking. An interesting bit of information you may want to remember is that the icon for the EtherTalk Phase 2 driver is distinguished from the Phase 1 driver by a set of double arrows.

❖ File Sharing Extension—The File Sharing extension is the integral part of Apple's personal file sharing.

❖ Find File Extension—This extension enables the Find File desk accessory.

❖ GXGraphics—GXGraphics works with the QuickDraw GX extension. QuickDraw GX is discussed in Chapter 7.

❖ Internet Config Extension—The Internet Config Extension maintains settings for your e-mail, Web browser, and other Internet applications.

❖ IRTalk—The IRTalk extension is used by Macs that have an infrared port to communicate with other devices with infrared capabilities, such as the Apple Message Pad 2000.

❖ MacTCP Token Ring Extension, Token Talk Phase 2, Token Talk Prep, and A/Rose—These are all Token Talk drivers used with Classic Networking. Unless you are connected to a Token Ring network, you do not need these extensions.

❖ MacinTalk and Speech Extensions—The Speech Manager, MacinTalk 3, and MacinTalk Pro extensions give your Mac the ability to talk, such as when you use SimpleText to speak the text.

❖ MacLinkPlus of Easy Open—This extension lets the Easy Open control panel work with the MacLinkPlus document translators.

❖ Network Extension—This is the software heart for the Mac's Classic Networking capabilities. This extension, in conjunction with the others, makes networking available. If the Network extension is not present, you are not able to access the Sharing Setup control panel. If you use Open Transport, the Networking extension is not present.

❖ Open Transport Extensions—A series of extensions has names that start with Open Transport Library. All of these extensions are used by Open Transport networking. If you use Open Transport, none of these should be removed.

❖ PC Card Modem Extension—This is the extension that enables a PCMCIA or PC Card modem to work with a PowerBook.

❖ DOS Card Extensions—PC Clipboard Translators, PC Network Extensions, PC Print Spooler, and the PC Setup Control panel all work together with an Apple or Reply DOS card to provide your Mac with PC (you know that other computer) capabilities.

❖ Power PC Monitors Extension and the QuickTime PowerPlug—All of the PowerPC extensions are special extensions that either enable or accelerate other extensions when they are used on a Power Macintosh.

❖ Printer Share—The Printer Share extension works with some of the Mac's printer drives (Chooser extensions) to allow a non-AppleTalk printer to be shared over a network.

❖ QuickDraw 3D—QuickDraw is Apple's graphics engine; it is built into the Mac's ROM. The 3D extension adds three-dimensional capabilities to QuickDraw.

❖ QuickTime Extensions—QuickTime, QuickTime MPEG Extension, QuickTime Musical Instruments, and QuickTime VR are all part of Apple's multimedia software. Each of these extensions provides additional multimedia capabilities to your Macintosh or any application that supports QuickTime. The MPEG extension lets a Mac play MPEG movies (the standard for the Microsoft Windows world). QuickTime instruments enhance the QuickTime's musical capabilities, and the VR extension enables QuickTime VR. Graphics and multimedia-capable applications, as well as Internet applications, use these extensions.

❖ Serial (Built-in)—The serial extension enhances the capabilities of the Mac's built-in serial ports.

❖ SystemAV—This extension enables the AV subsystems on Macs that have video capabilities.

❖ AppleVision—The AppleVision extension enables your Mac to use AppleVision monitors.

Chooser Extensions

Any type of device listed in the Chooser is made available by an extension stored in the Extensions folder. These include all the printer drivers, fax drivers, and

AppleShare drivers. None of these, with the exception of AppleShare, is memory-resident and only loads when you select them from the Chooser.

If you install software for any Apple Printer and do not need all of those extra drivers, taking up disk space and cluttering up your Chooser when you access it, throw the bums out. If you happen to get a printer later that needs a driver you have removed, you can always reinstall it.

In Figure 6.47, you see all of the Chooser extensions that are installed when you install your System software for any Macintosh printer, as well as the AppleShare extension. As Apple makes new printers, it will release new printer drivers.

Other Files

The Extensions folder is fairly straightforward when it is first installed. As you add software features to your Macintosh, though, the Extensions folder starts to take on a life of its own. It seems to become a living organism that has the capacity to hold any number of different types of files. Figure 6.48 shows an Extensions folder for a Mac that has been modestly set up with a few system software features. The rest of this section looks at some of the files and file types that can find their way to the Extensions folder.

❖ AppleGuide Documents—These are the data files that AppleGuide uses. Sometimes you find an AppleGuide document in the same folder as an application. Many will be placed in the Extensions folder.

❖ Communications Tools—If you are using a package that accesses the Communications Toolbox, the individual communications tools are stored

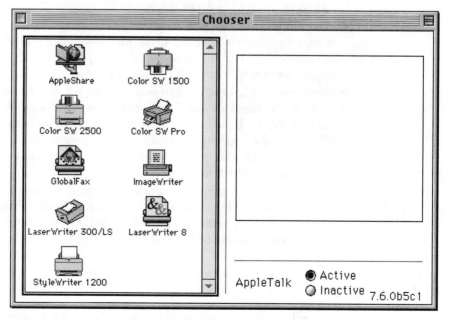

Figure 6.47 *The Chooser extensions.*

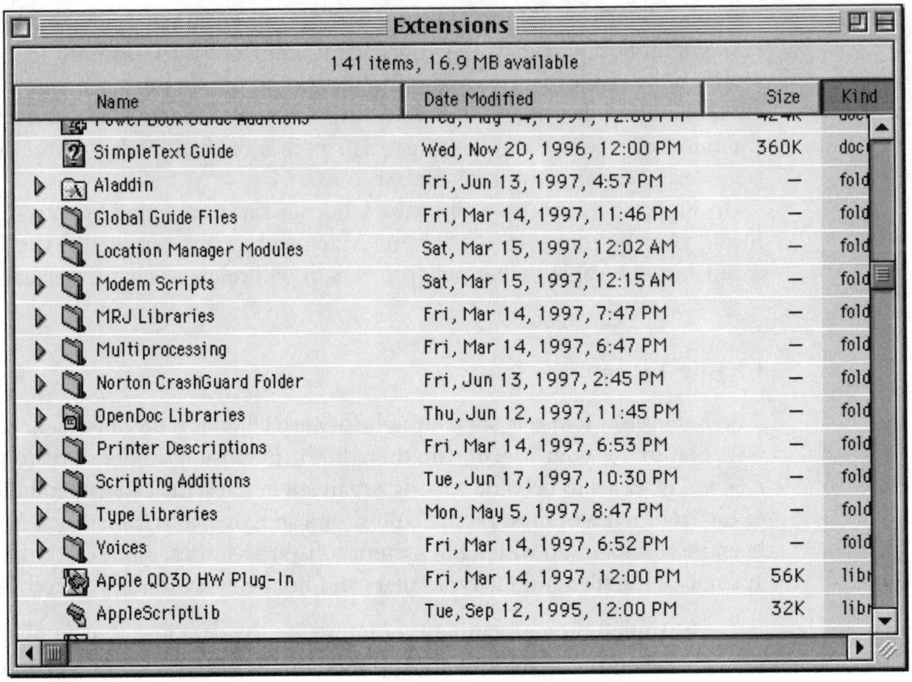

Figure 6.48 *Other folders in the Extensions folder.*

in the Extensions folder. The Communications Toolbox and data communications are covered in depth in Chapter 12.

❖ Print Monitor (background-only files)—The Print Monitor is one of the few applications that can be in the Extensions folder. It is primarily a background-only application. Background-only applications are the only programs that should be in the Extensions folder.

❖ Miscellaneous files—In the Extensions folder, you will find that the Finder Help file has found a home. In Figure 6.48, you will see folders named Aladdin, Printer Descriptions, and Scripting Additions in the Extensions folder. These are folders required by various programs and utilities installed on this particular Mac. And although you may not expect to see folders in the Extensions folder, this is where they live. You shouldn't move them.

In most cases, if a file can be in the Extensions folder, it can also be loose in the System folder. If it is put into the Extensions folder, though, when you drag the file's icon to the System Folder icon, or the application's installer puts it there, it should be left alone.

The Fonts Folder

Although fonts have not been discussed yet, other than as a selection that you can make while using a program, you need to know where they reside on your Macintosh.

All of your Mac's fonts are installed inside the Fonts folder, which is in the System folder. The only time an exception to this rule occurs is when you use a Font utility, such as SuitCase or Master Juggler. Fonts are a complicated subject, covered in more detail in Chapter 7.

The Preferences Folder

The Preferences folder is where all programs are supposed to store their preference files. A preference file is usually created by a program and contains the program's configuration settings. The Preferences folder also has a tendency to become the receptacle for any miscellaneous files. Figure 6.49 shows the Preferences folder of a fully configured system. The files you see were all put there by the individual programs either after they had been run the first time or during the installation process.

You should play in this folder only if you are installing software and the instructions call for installing a file (which they should not) or if you are trying to fix a problem. Apple recommends to its developers that a program should still operate even if its preferences file is deleted from the Preferences folder. This means that you can experiment, but if you do, do so very carefully.

You should delete a preferences file if the settings are wrong, if you can't reset them, or if you want to revert to the program's default settings. Rather than deleting the file, just move it out of the Preferences folder, save it somewhere, and run the program. The program creates a new preferences file when it can't find its old one.

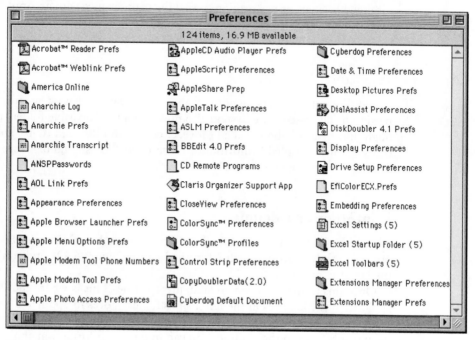

Figure 6.49 *A mature Preferences folder.*

(The exception to this might occur if the program installs a preferences file when one is already installed. This would not be in keeping with Apple's guidelines, but that doesn't mean that it doesn't happen.)

If the program does not work or if you did not get the result you expected, you can always restore the old preferences file. (You did save it, didn't you?) Chances are, you will not need to do this, but sometimes a preferences file can become corrupted. An example is personal file sharing. Sometimes the Users & Groups data file can become corrupted, and file sharing will not work as a result. If this should happen, the only thing to do is trash the old file and re-create your groups and users. Other programs can have similar problems, so if your application is misbehaving, you might want to try moving the preferences file so that the program will be forced to create a new one. If that solves the problem, throw away the old file.

The Startup and Shutdown Folders

Startup Items is the folder in which you place any file, program, or alias to a program that you want to run every time you start your Mac. The best way to use this folder is to put an alias for the program you want started in the Startup Items folder. The most important thing to remember about this folder is that it is used by the Finder. When the Finder starts, so do the applications in the Startup Items folder.

The Shutdown Items folder works in a similar manner. The programs or aliases in the Shutdown Items folder are run after you've selected the Shutdown menu item from the Special menu but before your Mac is shut down. This folder can be useful for doing backups or performing special file maintenance with an AppleScript prior to shutting down your Mac.

Other Folders Your Mac Uses

In addition to the folders mentioned above, your System has a few more folders that need to be discussed. The System also uses a couple of invisible folders that you might like to know about, called Move&Rename and Rescued Items, and one folder that you can see, called PrintMonitor Documents. You should be aware of these folders, even though you'll rarely use them.

PrintMonitor Documents

This folder is created the first time you print using a LaserWriter or StyleWriter printer, with Background Printing turned on (see Figure 6.50), and you're not using the Desktop printers.

Once this folder has been created, just let it be. This is where the Print Monitor application (which lives in the Extensions folder) stores its spooled documents while your Mac waits for the printer to finish what it is printing so that the next document can be sent to the printer. You can find more information about printing in Chapter 7.

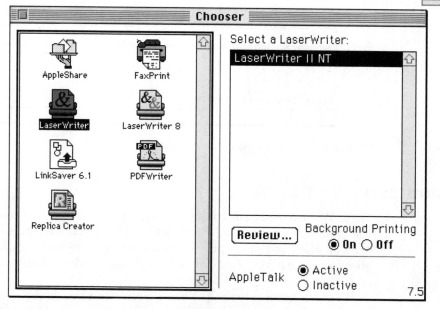

Figure 6.50 *Background Printing selection in the Chooser.*

Rescued Items from (Volume Name)

This is a folder that sometimes appears in your Trashcan after a system crash. A crash has occurred when your Mac stops functioning because of a software problem. When it restarts, the OS checks your System folder for temporary files, and it also checks an invisible folder on the top level of your hard drive, called Temporary Items, for temporary files. If it finds any files in the Temporary Items folder or temporary files in your System folder, it puts the temporary files into a folder called Rescued Items from (your drive's name), which is inside the Trash (see Figure 6.51).

Because many programs make temporary files when they run, this feature is an attempt to recover any data lost during a crash. Although most software publishers do not use this feature yet, we can hope that will become more common.

If your system crashes while you are working on an important document and your Mac creates this folder and places a temporary file in it, there is a possibility, albeit slim, that the software publisher can help you recover data that you may have lost. It might be worth a try. Even if the publisher can't help you get the data back, it might be worthwhile to start requesting this as a feature that they put into their next version.

Move&Rename Folder

The Move&Rename folder, created and used by System 7 File Sharing, is an invisible folder. Where you will see it is in some Save As... and Open dialog boxes or with a disk utility program, such as DiskTop, or with FileTools. Leave this folder alone. If you delete it, your Mac will just re-create it.

Figure 6.51   *The Rescued Items folder.*

Summary

Phew! We've covered a lot in this chapter. You now know almost everything about what your Mac's System folder contains. You know that it is extensible and what items go where and why. This information will help you when you have to talk to others about your Mac. And if all of this information did not sink in, you have the book as a reference.

We're not slowing down. The next chapter walks you through the steps for installing your System, a very important subject if you ever have to perform maintenance on your Mac. By the time you finish this part of the book, you'll be a Macintosh System expert.

System Enhancements

Introduction

In the previous chapters, we discussed only the operating system part of Mac OS 8. Mac OS 8 has more elements that are technically part of the OS, yet they are actually additions to the System. They are not required to make your Mac operate. These additions are software technologies that enhance and add functionality to the Macintosh. Some of these technologies have been around for a while, and others are new, but it is in Mac OS 8 that they've all been brought together.

These additions are as follows:

❖ AppleScript

❖ QuickDraw 3D

❖ Internet capabilities

❖ Java

❖ A new networking system

❖ The Location Manager

❖ The Color Picker

❖ Dead technologies

❖ QuickDraw GX

❖ OpenDoc

Because you have a choice regarding which parts of the Macintosh System you want to use, you should read this chapter before deciding whether you need or want the capabilities offered above. Each has its advantages and maybe some drawbacks. And there are some additions I recommend that you don't install.

Although the above list is impressive, I'm afraid you'll be disappointed by what I have to say. Most of these items do not require long explanations, and there isn't much for you to do other than know they are available. The Internet-related items are discussed in Chapter 14, and networking topics can be found in Chapter 13. Each of these technologies or OS additions is briefly discussed. After the discussion of each technology are instructions that use AppleScript and the Location Manager.

The next section of this chapter continues the discussion of Finder enhancements that was started in Chapter 6. These enhancements are as follows:

- ❖ Multithreaded copying
- ❖ Background window updating status indicator
- ❖ Live window scrolling

The last section in this chapter is about printing. This is the only place in the book where printers and printing are discussed other than the brief instructions found in Chapter 5 and the section about printer troubleshooting in Chapter 17.

I admit that this chapter is a hodgepodge. By the time you're finished you will have an overview of how the Mac operates, and you will know all the basics of the Mac OS. The remaining chapters go into greater detail about Macintosh operations and maintenance.

Brief Descriptions

Unless you already know about the items listed above, I'm sure you're wondering what I've been babbling about. New technologies, enhancements, and integral System components can sound an awful lot like a marketing specialist's sales pitch. So, just what are these system additions, and what do they do?

Well, that's what this section is about. Let's get rid of the smoke and mirrors and get down to business. In this section, you find out what each of these System components/technologies is and why you might want to use it.

AppleScript

AppleScript is a System-level scripting technology. Now, that does not say a lot unless you are a computer jock, and if you are, you can skip the rest of this section—you know about AppleScript. For the rest of you, a System-level scripting technology is simply a means of automating computing tasks that would otherwise require a number of steps or be very repetitive and time-consuming.

Before Apple released System 7.1, if you wanted to automate menu selections and such processes as logging into a file server, or if you wanted to control a program's actions automatically without using the keyboard or mouse, you had to use a macro utility.

Macro　(1) A user-defined command that tells an application to carry out a series of commands when you type the macro; (2) a recorded sequence of characters and commands identified by a name and possibly triggered by a keystroke. Using a macro utility, you can call upon a macro to play while you're working in an application. (See also Script); (3) a single keystroke or command that a program replaces with several keystrokes or commands.

The Other Scripting Language

Prior to AppleScript, one program that was not a macro utility, but a system-level scripting language, was available. The program, published by UserLand, is called Frontier and is discussed in the section, "Using AppleScript."

Macro utilities are great tools, but they can go only so far to accomplish a task. They cannot be used to control the System from the System software level. Macro utilities may be used only within a specific program and, even though they are very sophisticated, all they do is make the Mac mimic commands that you would normally do manually. A macro utility can select menu commands, automatically type in text, switch windows, and execute other similar functions. What it cannot do is send a message directly to another program or exchange data with another program without your help or intervention.

In contrast, AppleScript actually lets the OS communicate directly with other programs. It can perform many of the tasks previously done by macro utility programs, but it goes beyond and is different from a macro utility because AppleScript interacts directly with a program, sending it commands rather than mimicking commands you would perform manually.

The difference between a macro utility and AppleScript is best illustrated by an example. You can have a script that will open your spreadsheet program, perform some calculations and even enter data, and then transfer the data to your word-processing program. When the script opens your word processor, it takes the data from the spreadsheet, puts it into a document, formats the document, prints it, and then saves it in a special folder. Performing these steps with a macro utility is very difficult, if not almost impossible. With AppleScript all of this can be done automatically without your intervention, as long as the programs you're using are AppleScript-aware, or scriptable.

One of the best and most immediate examples of AppleScript you can have is the AppleGuide program mentioned in Chapter 8. AppleGuide can operate properly only because of AppleScript; it is AppleScript that performs the automated tasks that AppleGuide walks you through as you make an inquiry.

Although Apple started including AppleScript with System 7.1, the Finder in System 7.1 was not *scriptable*, thereby limiting AppleScript's capabilities. When an application, including the Finder, is scriptable, it receives commands sent by AppleScript and performs those commands. With System 7.5 the Finder became scriptable and easily automated.

There is another designation for a program that is AppleScript-compatible. A program is recordable if you can record an AppleScript script from within the program. A program can be scriptable, and thus AppleScript-compatible, even if it is not record-able. Similarly, a program that is not scriptable is not recordable.

The instructions for using AppleScript are found later in this chapter.

Internet Capabilities

It may sound silly to say that the Macintosh OS now has Internet capabilities because, in a sense, it has always had them. What I mean by Internet capabilities is that the ability to connect to the Internet is now built into Mac OS 8. Apple now provides you with all the tools needed to connect to and use the Internet. In the past, you got just the basic software you needed to connect to the Internet if your Mac was on a network and that network was connected to the Internet.

If you don't know what the Internet is or how to use it, or if you're just confused about the Internet, don't worry. You're not alone. Marketing hype surrounds the factual information about the Internet. Most of the hype implies that if you're not connected, you're not alive. But you already know that isn't true.

So just what is the Internet? The Internet is a huge network of computers. A net-work is two or more computers that are connected together so that they can share information, resources, and services. Resources are computing capabilities such as printers, hard disk space, and other peripherals. Services are usually information-sharing capabilities like electronic mail, discussion groups, group scheduling, plus other, more esoteric capabilities.

When you put your computer onto the Internet you join a worldwide community of computer networks that, when taken as a whole, are called the Internet. Although the Internet is the subject of Chapter 14, it is also the subject of entire books. Even worse, there are books about small parts of the Internet. Keep in mind that there is no way this book or Chapter 14 can adequately cover the subject.

With Mac OS 8, you now have all the basic software you need to connect to and use the Internet. If you think this is something you might want to do, read Chapter 14, "The Internet." There you'll find a more detailed description of the Internet, instructions on how to connect, and instructions on how to use the Internet tools included with Mac OS 8.

Java

Java usually means coffee—except in the computer world. In the computing world, Java is a programming language. The name Java was one of five possible names for the language. In this sense, Java is just the name used to describe a new technology. Its source is Sun Microsystems, Inc., the parent company of the company that created Java.

Java was first envisioned as a means for enhancing the capabilities of World Wide Web (WWW) pages, which are found on the Internet. Java has expanded beyond the Internet, and describing it today is not easy.

Java is a programming language that can create programs that run on any computer or in a WWW browser (the tool used to access the WWW). This means that someone can write a program using Java and it will run on any computer so long as the computer is able to run Java programs. Now I know that this sounds like a Catch-22—and it is, or it would be, except that soon no computers will be sold that are not able to run Java applications. All a computer needs to run a Java application is software that creates Virtual Java Machine, which runs with the computer's OS.

Apple calls this software the Mac OS Runtime for Java (MRJ). The MRJ creates a virtual Java computer that runs Java applications on the Macintosh. Right now (in my opinion), the MRJ is more interesting than practical. But, in the very near future Java could become the computer equalizer. Software developers could write their programs with Java just so they won't have to worry about what type of computer you have. If Java does become the primary language for creating applications, then you won't have to worry about whether a program will run on your Mac.

This is important right now because the Macintosh is losing ground in the software development world. Programmers write software for the Windows environment before they write programs for the Mac. The result is that the Mac is not always the computer of choice because the software for the job won't run on a Mac. Java could change this. Only time will tell.

Although Java is important, I do not provide instructions for using Java in this book because Java is not yet mission-critical. It is not essential to businesses, and very little can be done with Java right now. By the time Java takes off, a new Macintosh OS will probably be available. It has been rumored that Corel is writing a Java version of its Corel Office product.

If you want to play with Java, install the MRJ software, which is an optional Mac OS 8 installation; see Chapter 9 for instructions on installing Mac OS software. Read the "About MRJ" file after you install the software.

A New Networking System

Apple has spent several years redesigning its networking software. With Mac OS 7.5.3 it released its new networking software, now part of the Mac OS. The new networking technology is called Open Transport, or OT. Open Transport is shipped with all PCI Macintosh computers, and the old networking software, now called "Classic Networking," will not work with PCI Power Macintosh computers.

Apple recreated its networking system so that it could add more networking services and more easily enhance Macintosh networking by adding new features. One of the new features is called AppleTalk IP. AppleTalk IP is the implementation of AppleTalk (the standard Macintosh networking protocol—see Chapter 13) using the TCP/IP networking protocol. This new implementation of AppleTalk is faster—you won't even know that you're using it.

The major difference between Classic Networking and Open Transport is the networking control panels. Otherwise, using a networked Macintosh is the same. Macintosh networking is discussed in Chapter 13.

QuickDraw 3D

QuickDraw 3D is an extension of the Macintosh's graphics engine, called QuickDraw. The Mac uses a system called QuickDraw to display and print all the information you see on your Mac. QuickDraw 3D enables the Macintosh to display three-dimensional graphics.

To use QuickDraw 3D you need an application that has been written to take advantage of QuickDraw 3D, a PowerPC Macintosh, and 16MB of RAM. In a folder on the Mac OS 8 CD called QuickDraw 3D extras are some QuickDraw 3D utilities and demos. Install QuickDraw 3D if you want to view QuickDraw 3D-enabled WWW sites.

Other than running applications that take advantage of QuickDraw 3D, there is little you can do with it. QuickDraw 3D is a System-level technology. It is installed as an optional Mac OS 8 component. For more information about installing Mac OS software, see Chapter 9.

The Location Manager

The Location Manager is a new and optional component of Mac OS 8. Although it sounds like a PowerBook utility, it can be useful on a desktop Mac, too. The Location Manager allows you to configure your Mac with different tasks by letting you assign extension sets, mount specific network drives, and change system settings when your Mac starts up.

You might want to use this utility if you need specific system settings for playing games and another set of specifications for doing work. You can create a location called Games and another one called Work. Then, when you start your Mac, it will ask you which location you want to use. You could also use the Location Manager if you need to connect to different Internet sites that require you to change your Internet settings. You could create locations that are preconfigured for each of the different Internet networks.

Like most of the OS additions discussed in this chapter, the Location Manager requires a separate installation and has its own installer. Instructions for installing software are found in Chapter 9.

The New Color Picker

The new Color Picker is automatically installed with Mac OS 8. The Color Picker is the software device that lets you choose a color in any program that allows you to select or modify an item's color. The most accessible example is found in the Finder.

When you want to change the label color of an icon displayed in the Finder you use the Color Picker. To see the new Color Picker, perform the following steps:

1.   Select the Finder's Edit Menu.

2. Select the *Preferences* menu item. A window like the one in Figure 7.1 appears.

3. Double-click on one of the boxes to the left of the label fields.

4. The Color Picker appears in a window like the one in Figure 7.2.

In Figure 7.2 you see that different types of pickers are listed in a window on the left. Each of these pickers has a special purpose and allows you to set color attributes according to your needs. For example, Figure 7.2 shows the Crayon Picker. This picker is used to select one of the predefined colors (sorry, showing colors in black and white figures is difficult). The color you pick would then be assigned to the label you double-clicked.

The Color Picker was designed to make life easier for everyone. If you're a graphic artist, you will recognize that the Color Pickers is made specifically for printing, allowing you to select colors using the CYMK standard (Cyan, Yellow, Magenta, and Black) for color selection. If you use your Mac to edit and produce videos, you might want to use the RGB (Red, Green, and Blue) selection method with the RGB Picker. The final example is the HTML Picker. If you are a Web page designer, the HTML Picker lets you select colors and displays the color's hex value. These selection methods allow you to duplicate colors without remembering arcane numbers that have no clear relation to the color selection method you're using.

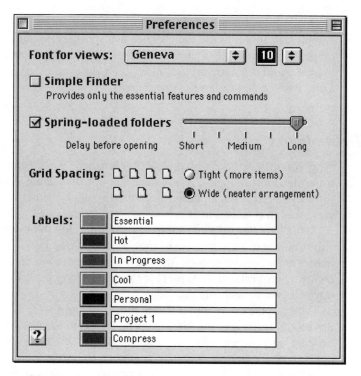

Figure 7.1 *The Finder's Preferences window.*

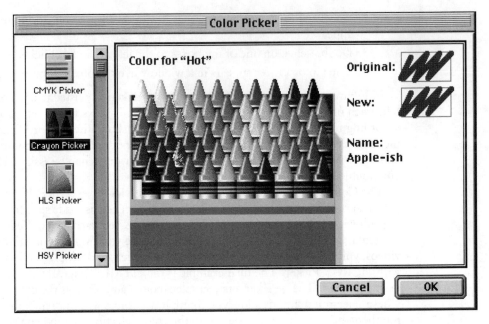

Figure 7.2 *The Color Picker.*

Depending on your needs, color selection will either be fairly simple or quite complex. I cannot do the topic justice in a short section like this one. I am not a graphic artist, and I have very little knowledge about color. If you need more information about color, invest in a book about the graphic arts or one about color. Otherwise you'll just have to experiment.

Dead Technologies

Now you may wonder why this section is called "dead technologies." This designation, "dead technologies," is my own. I doubt that Apple would appreciate my calling some of its technologies dead, but, I use this appellation for a reason: The technologies listed in this section are no longer being developed.

Apple has stopped all development on both OpenDoc and QuickDraw GX. Apple will continue to support both of these technologies, but do not expect to see any enhancements or new tools. Although OpenDoc has been taken over by another company (not related to Apple) for further development, I don't think the technology will ever be mainstream.

When Apple or any other major company says that it will stop development on a product, it is really saying that the product has been consigned to the trash bin. The product is too expensive to maintain, and there was not enough support from developers or the computing industry in general to justify continued development. Thus, even though the technology is supported, meaning that the technology will remain as an option and Apple will answer technical questions related to it, that technology is dead.

I do not endorse the use of dead technologies. If you have to use one, at some time you will be forced to switch to another solution. The computing industry moves too fast for you to become dependent on a discontinued product. It is better if you don't use the technology at all.

One example is OpenDoc. If you create documents with OpenDoc and you want to share them with other computer users, you have to convert your OpenDoc documents into a format that the other computer users can read. No software company will spend time or money to make its software capable of reading OpenDoc documents now that Apple has said it is abandoning the technology.

Why should you use it? As I said, you shouldn't. Just because it is available does not mean you need it. And if, for some reason, you do need it, you will know and disregard what I've said.

QuickDraw GX

QuickDraw GX was Apple's hope for a new Macintosh imaging system, introduced with System 7.5. It is a complex software addition that affects every aspect of your Macintosh; except for the improved printing features QuickDraw GX offers, you might never know it is there. Yet, QuickDraw GX radically changes how your Macintosh can handle fonts and images, and how it displays color.

QuickDraw GX requires its own installation and is not automatically installed when you install Mac OS 8. The Desktop Printer is used to monitor, control, and modify any of your printing jobs just like Mac OS 8 Desktop printers (discussed later in this chapter).

QuickDraw GX provides for additional document manipulation through the use of extensions, and a QuickDraw GX font can hold 65,000 different characters, rather than the 256 characters in non-QuickDraw GX fonts. The entire character set for a language, such as Chinese or Japanese, can be included in a single QuickDraw GX font, or the font can contain special information that controls how the font is printed by including special kerning, leading, and other typographical information.

For graphic artists, QuickDraw GX automates and simplifies much of their current work in font manipulation. Also, with a program that properly displays QuickDraw GX fonts, you have increased control and special-effects capabilities previously available only with special utilities. Programs that take full advantage of QuickDraw GX are able to rotate, manipulate, and otherwise perform special effects with fonts.

Finally, another feature of QuickDraw GX is the ability to maintain color consistency between various Macintosh monitor models. The blue font you used in a document appears on someone else's Mac, maintaining the same shade of blue that you created even though the other person uses a different monitor. QuickDraw GX works with the ColorSync control panel to maintain color-corrected images.

Apple says the following about QuickDraw GX in the "About QuickDraw GX" document on the Mac OS 8 CD-ROM:

"Beginning with Mac OS 8 and QuickDraw GX 1.1.6, Apple will provide a unified operating system printing architecture, standardizing on classic (non-GX) QuickDraw printing and printer drivers. With the unified printing architecture, QuickDraw GS printer drivers and QuickDraw GX printing extensions will not be supported in Mac OS 8 and future Mac OS releases."

Because the technology is no longer supported there really isn't any reason to say more about it. If you want to experiment, go ahead. Just remember that QuickDraw GX is a dead technology.

OpenDoc

OpenDoc is a new type of document that allows you to create custom documents by embedding small, special-purpose programs in the document. The document you create actually contains the program you used to create the document. Apple describes this process as "dropping parts into the document."

Thus, an OpenDoc document can contain a word processor and a spreadsheet as part of the same document. The best example of OpenDoc included with Mac OS 8 is Cyberdog. Cyberdog is an Internet program that lets you perform every major Internet function using OpenDoc. You can have a Cyberdog document that has a few FTP (File Transfer Protocol) sites, WWW sites, and a newsgroup or two all related to a single subject.

I think Cyberdog is too cool. Unfortunately, it too is in the dust bin with OpenDoc (see the "Dead Technologies" introduction). Cyberdog, however, is one reason why you might want to install OpenDoc. Be forewarned, though: As World Wide Web technology develops and new capabilities are added to the Web, they will not work with Cyberdog. If I knew that Cyberdog would continue to be developed, I'd use it without reservation. But I've used too many computers and software tools, only to have them disappear, to get hooked on something I know is not being improved and enhanced

Although Apple does not say that OpenDoc has been axed on the Mac OS 8 CD-ROM, it did say the following on its WWW site:

"We are moving more of our resources for component technology toward Java-based technology, which we believe is becoming the industry standard. OpenDoc and Cyberdog will ship in Mac OS 8, but we are not planning any major updates."*

As such, I'm not going to say any more about OpenDoc or Cyberdog. If you're interested, install them and play. Cyberdog uses all the principles about the Internet discussed in Chapter 14.

Using AppleScript

AppleScript is automatically installed as part of Mac OS 8, and it is a basic part of the Mac OS. How you use AppleScript depends on how much time you want to spend

---

*About OpenDoc. OpenDoc, Cyberdog, and CI Labs FAQ:, Source: http://opendoc.apple.com/dev/faq.4.97.htm.

learning and experimenting with it. This section looks briefly at installing AppleScript and the system elements you need. Then, we look at using AppleScript. This section concludes with a discussion about macro utilities and UserLand's Frontier.

Installation

Before you dive into AppleScript, check out the following definitions. These definitions are prerequisite to understanding what AppleScript does and are even fundamental to its use. They are the terms used when talking about AppleScript or its capabilities.

Script   A file that contains instructions that cause the Macintosh to perform a set of specific actions.

Dictionary   A set of commands contained within a program, which can be used by AppleScript.

Recordable   A program is recordable when you can perform a series of actions that can be stored in a script by AppleScript's Script Editor and repeated or played back.

Scriptable   A program that has a dictionary and/or is recordable.

When using Systems 7.1, 7.1.1, 7.1.2, and 7.5, AppleScript is automatically installed when you install your System. For Systems 7.0 and 7.0.1, you have to install AppleScript using the Apple Installer that comes with the AppleScript Scripter's Kit. When AppleScript is installed, several files are installed in various places on your hard drive. The primary components are the AppleScript system extension and the Script Editor. Table 7.1 describes AppleScript's files and their locations.

Although you can manually install AppleScript, always use the Mac OS 8.0 Installer. There are enough components to justify using the installer, and if you make a mistake as you manually install AppleScript, it will not work. AppleScript is installed when you perform an Easy Installation of Mac OS 8.0. For more information about installing software, see Chapter 9.

How AppleScript Works

Although AppleScript can be quite complex, you do not have to be a programmer or a *power user* to take advantage of its capabilities. There are several ways to use AppleScript, which vary in complexity. The simplest way to use AppleScript is to run a script that someone else has written; the next level of use is to record your own script; the third is to modify a script you've recorded or one written by someone else; and the fourth is to write your own script. Each of these levels of use is described in the next section.

AppleScript is actually a programming language, but you don't have to be a programmer to use it. AppleScript works by sending messages using a System technol-

Table 7.1   AppleScript Files

FILENAME	LOCATION	DESCRIPTION
AppleScript	Extensions Folder	AppleScript's primary element
Script Editor	AppleScript Folder	The program used to create a script
AppleScriptLib	Extensions Folder	A file required only by Power Macintosh computers
ObjectSupportLib	Extensions Folder	A file required only by Power Macintosh computers
FinderLib	AppleScript Folder	This file comes with Apple's Scripter's Kit and is used to write scripts that interact with pre-System 7.5 Finders
Scriptable Editor	AppleScript Folder	A recordable text editor included with Apple's Scripter's Kit
AppleScript Guide	AppleScript Folder	A text file which contains instructions for using AppleScript
Automated Tasks Folder	AppleScript Folder with an alias in the Apple Menu Items Folder	A set of scripts installed with Mac OS 8
More Automated Tasks Folder	AppleScript Folder	Additional scripts installed with Mac OS 8

ogy called AOEC, which stands for Apple Open Events Collaboration, to Macintosh programs.

Apple Open Events Collaboration (AOEC)   A technology developed by Apple to facilitate interapplication communications. With AOEC, a program can send commands to another program.

The program responds to the message by performing some actions and then sends a message back to AppleScript saying that the command has been executed. Then, AppleScript sends its next message to either the same program or another program, depending on what you want the Mac to do.

All Macintosh programs are supposed to have a dictionary that contains a set of commands with which AOEC can communicate. The dictionary is divided into *suites*, and every program should have a Required Suite and a Standard Suite. The Required Suite contains the commands *open*, *quit*, *print*, and *run*. These basic commands correspond to the *Open*, *Print*, and *Quit* menu items in the File menu, and *run* is the equivalent of double-clicking on the program from within the Finder.

The Standard Suite contains a more complex set of commands that AppleScript can use, but they are not as generic as those in the Required Suite. In addition to the Required and Standard Suites, a program that is truly AppleScript-compliant has an additional Suite named after the program itself. This additional Suite contains commands that are specific to the application and not general commands, such as those contained in the Required or Standard Suites.

By using the commands in the suites, you can operate a program by remote control. AppleScript is the controller we're talking about right now, but a program can control other programs using AOEC without using AppleScript. Apple developed the AOEC technology specifically to let programs communicate with each other: AOEC is not limited to AppleScript. AppleScript is just one implementation of AOEC.

Using Scripts

As previously mentioned, you employ AppleScript at one of four levels: You can run, record, modify, or write a script. In one sense, you always use the first level even if you write your own scripts because a script is pointless unless it is used. If you learn to write your own scripts, you can have a phenomenal amount of control over your Mac.

Even if you don't write your own scripts, you will find, as time goes on, scripts written by others that you might want to use. Apple has included a number of useful scripts with Mac OS 8 that simplify many routine functions, and if you subscribe to an online service or a users group, or if you explore electronic bulletin board systems (BBS), you will find other scripts you can use. Another good place to look for scripts is the World Wide Web (see Chapter 14).

Online service   An electronic information service that you access using a computer and a modem, which usually requires special software and charges a fee.

User group   A computer club in which computer users exchange tips and information, usually about a particular brand of computer.

Electronic bulletin board system (BBS)   A computerized version of the bulletin boards frequently found in grocery stores—places to leave messages and to advertise things you want to buy or sell. One thing you get from a computerized bulletin board that you can't get from a cork board is free software.

Regardless of how you choose to use AppleScript, you probably want to use it at one of the levels described in this section. There is no right or wrong way to use AppleScript; it is a tool that you can use to make your computing life easier.

Predefined Scripts

Predefined Scripts are data files created by the Script Editor that you run on your Macintosh. When a script is run, it sends commands to one or more programs, causing them to perform the tasks defined in the script. A number of scripts are included

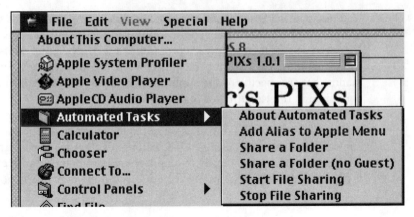

Figure 7.3   *The Automated Tasks menu.*

with System 7.5 that can be found in the AppleScript folder. You also find a selection in the Apple menu called Automated Tasks, which is an alias for one of the folders in the AppleScript folder. Figure 7.3 shows the Automated Tasks menu.

How a script operates depends on the person who wrote it. You will find that scripts do not have the same consistency as applications and they may even contain some surprises, so experimentation is the order of the day when you play with scripts. Scripts are run in one of two ways: Either you will execute a script as you would a program by double-clicking on it, or you will use drag-and-drop and drop a file or group of files onto a script.

In Figure 7.4, you see scripts with two types of icons. The scripts with the arrow in their icons are actually small applications that can run without accessing the Script

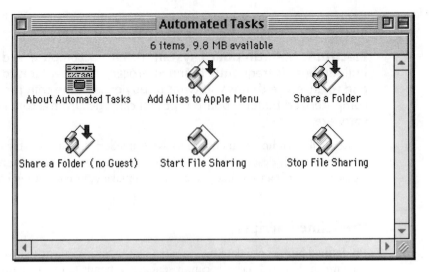

Figure 7.4   *The Automated Tasks folder.*

Editor. The other scripts are called compiled scripts, but when they run, they have to start the Script Editor before they can complete their assigned task.

Compile   To convert a program written in a high-level programming language (source code) into a file of commands in a lower-level language (object code) for later execution. To turn source code into an executable application.

Usually, when a script runs, you won't see much happen. Most scripts run as background tasks and have no interface. Some scripts are more complex; they have an interface and may even act more like utility programs. At the moment, however, these types of scripts are rare.

Background   A relatively inconspicuous place. A program operates *in the background* if it continues to function automatically while you use another program.

Using a script is done by either double-clicking on the script or selecting a file(s) and dragging and dropping the file(s) onto the script. The name of the script should tell you what it does. For the scripts shown in Figure 7.4, each script name describes the script's function. All of the application scripts, when executed from the Apple menu, can be used as files that are selected in the Finder. If you use the application scripts from the Automated Tasks folder, you must execute them using drag-and-drop.

The compiled scripts, when you double-click on them, start, perform their task, and quit. In some cases, you are alerted with a dialog box that tells you what has just happened. Whether you are notified depends on how the script was written.

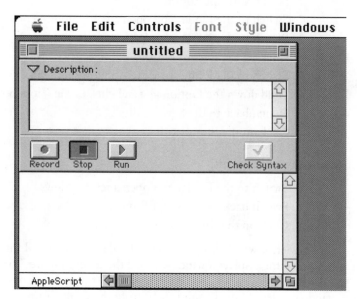

Figure 7.5   The Script Editor.

To get used to how scripts operate, experiment with the scripts in the More Automated Tasks folder. Start with the Hide/Show Folder Sizes script. Just double-click on the script. Other than experimenting with a script to see what it does, there is nothing else you need to do to use AppleScript.

Recording Scripts

Once you've used a few compiled or application scripts, you might want to create your own. The easiest way to create your own script is to record one. Scripts are recorded using the Script Editor application. Figure 7.5 shows the Script Editor as it appears when it is first started.

Notice that an untitled document window is open. In the Description part of the window, you can write a description of what the script does and instructions for using the script. Your script is automatically placed in the window below the control buttons as you record the script.

Before you record a script, you must know what you want to accomplish. Are you going to write a script that opens multiple programs? One that closes all the windows in the Finder? One that places all the files in a specific folder into another folder? Or one that does some other task that is generic in nature and does not rely on file names that will change?

Your major limitation with recorded scripts concerns variable values. To use variable values in a script you must write part of the script after it has been recorded. Modifying a script is discussed in the next section.

To record a script that will close all the open windows in the Finder:

1. Start the Script Editor.
2. Switch to the Finder and open a few windows.
3. Switch back to the Script Editor.
4. Click on the Record button.
5. Switch to the Finder (use the Application menu).
6. Hold down the Option key and click in the Close box of an open window.
7. Switch back to the Script Editor.
8. Click on the Stop button.

Now test your script:

1. Switch to the Finder and open a few windows.
2. Switch back to the Script Editor.
3. Click on the Run button.

The Script will run, switch to the Finder, and close all the open windows; the Script Editor displays a window called the *Result*. Figure 7.6 shows what the Script Editor looks like after you test your script. If your Mac does not show the Result window, select Show Result (⌘+L) from the Controls menu.

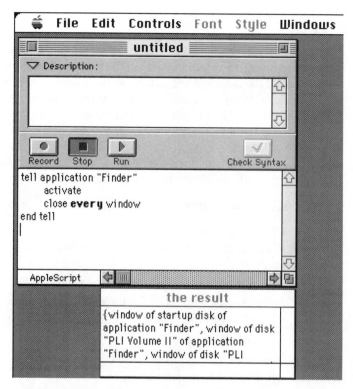

Figure 7.6 *The Script Editor after running the script.*

Now, you can save this script if you wish. If you do, save it as Text; if you save with any other option, you'll be disappointed. This script does not run as an application or a compiled script. This means that the script has to be modified before it runs from the Finder and works. (A discussion about saving scripts appears later in this chapter in the section, "Saving Scripts.") This modification is the subject of the next section.

Modifying Scripts

If you've been adventurous and have tried saving the script, as an application or a compiled script, from the last section, you have discovered that it does not work. The script works when run from the Script Editor but not when saved as an application. Why? Well, I really don't know; I can only speculate. When the program was run, the folder window containing it was no longer selected so that when the script activated (switched back to) the Finder, no windows were selected and the Close All command was ignored. Here, I could be wrong—I'm not a programmer.

I did figure out how to modify the script so that it would work the way I intended. To make my modification, I had to experiment a little, but I was able to make a modification that works. I'm babbling about this because you'll find yourself in similar predicaments when you start to create scripts.

There is no way to avoid this type of problem, and the only solution is speculation and experimentation. If you're not up to or don't care about experimenting with AppleScript, just use scripts written by other people. Using AppleScript, any other type of scripting, or macro utilities can become time-consuming. If you're not willing to spend the time to learn how these tools work, you'll never master them.

Now, let's get down to the business of making this script work. Right now, your script should read like the one shown in Figure 7.7.

Assuming that my theory about a window not being selected is correct, the next step is to tell the script to select a window before closing everything. There are two ways to do this: You can open a window, which automatically selects the window, or you can try to tell the Finder to select a specific window.

To do this simply, perform the following steps:

1. Open your script.
2. Place the insertion point after the last line in your script, which should be
   end tell
3. Switch to the Finder and open some windows.
4. Switch back to the Script Editor and click on the Record button.
5. Switch back to the Finder and select a window that is not active.
6. Move the window.
7. Switch back to the Script Editor.
8. Click on the Stop button.

Now, your script looks like the one shown in Figure 7.8. You had to move the window in step 6 because AppleScript does not consider selecting a nonactive window to be significant and, therefore, the Script Editor will not record by just selecting a window. You have to move it before the Script Editor records your actions.

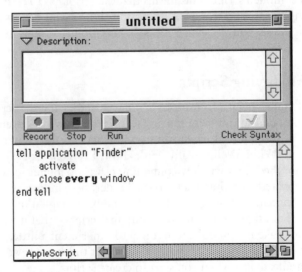

Figure 7.7 *Your script that won't work.*

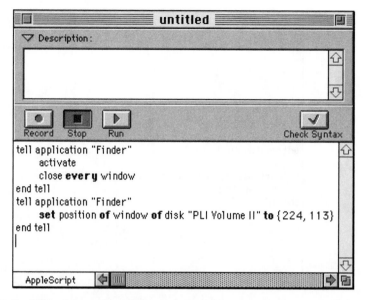

Figure 7.8 *The script, after the second recording session.*

The next steps are as follows:

1. Copy the line that starts with "**set** position **of** window. . . . "
2. Paste that line above the line that reads "close **every** window." When you've done this, the script looks like the one shown in Figure 7.9.

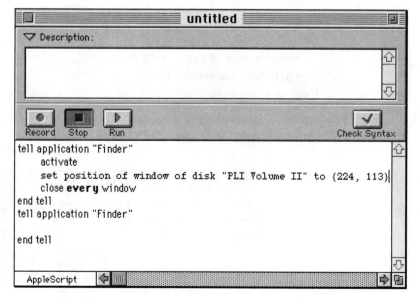

Figure 7.9 *The first modification.*

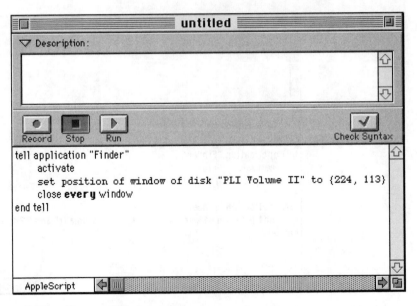

Figure 7.10   Your modified script.

3. Select the text in the script that was added after the first **"end tell"** statement.
4. Press the backspace or Delete key to remove the selected text.

Now, your script looks like the one shown in Figure 7.10, and you're ready to run the script. Click on the Run button. The script works fine.

To experiment some more:

1. Switch to the Finder.
2. Open some windows, but do not open the window you moved when you recorded the second part of your script.
3. Switch back to the Script Editor.
4. Click on the Run button.

This time, an error message like the one shown in Figure 7.11 appears. The window that you told AppleScript to select and move was not open, so the script failed.

Figure 7.11   The error message.

Now, you have to think of a different way to make the script work. Rather than selecting a window, how about opening a window? Whenever a window is opened, it is automatically selected. This should make our script work, but to know for sure, we have to try it.

To make the change in your script:

1. Switch to the Script Editor.
2. Select the line "**set** position **of** window. . . . "
3. Delete the line.
4. Place the insertion point after the last line in your script, which should be **end tell.**
5. Click on the Record button.
6. Switch to the Finder and open your startup drive by double-clicking on it.
7. Switch back to the Script Editor.
8. Click on the Stop button.

Your revised script looks like the one shown in Figure 7.12. Now, repeat the steps you just performed when you copied the "**set** position **of** window . . . " line and pasted it into the top portion of your script, substituting the line "open startup disk" for two lines that read "select startup disk" and "open selection." Once you've done that, your script looks like the one shown in Figure 7.13. Instead of the "select . . . " and "open selection" statements, you may have only one that says "open startup disk."

Now, this script works. To try it, open a few windows—even your startup disk's window—and run the script. Run the script without opening any windows; it still

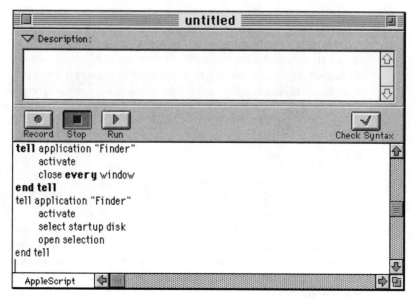

Figure 7.12   The revised script.

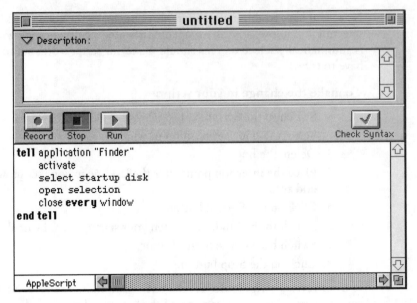

Figure 7.13 *The new and improved script.*

works. Now you have a script that works regardless of which windows are open, and you can save the script and use it.

If you're wondering what you can do with this script, you can do several things with it. One, you can place it in the Automated Tasks folder so that you can access it anytime you want. If you want your Mac, every time it starts, to start with all the Finder's windows closed, place the script or its alias in the Shutdown Items folder. This causes your Mac to close all open windows before it shuts down, thereby ensuring that your Mac will always look the same when you start it up.

Although these may sound like frivolous suggestions, they're not. This is the type of task that AppleScript was made to perform. Although it does not take advantage of all AppleScript's capabilities, this is something you can do to put your signature on your Mac, making it truly yours. Little tasks like this lead you to use AppleScript to accomplish more sophisticated results. Now, let's go on and save your script.

Saving Scripts

How you save a script depends on how you want to use it. If you look in the Script Editor's File menu, you see two *Save As...* menu items: One is the standard *Save As...* menu item; the other is a *Save As Run-Only...* menu item.

If you want to reopen the script and either edit it or view its contents, you must use the standard Save As... command. The Run-Only option saves the script so that the script commands cannot be read. You would use this option to protect your scripting efforts from prying eyes or if you planned to distribute your script as a commercial product.

Combining Scripts

The process of using a script from within another script is called *calling a script*. You can call both compiled and application scripts. (Calling a compiled or application script is an advanced scripting topic that is not covered in this book.)

AppleScript is a very powerful and complex tool. If you want to learn more about scripting and have access to Apple's reference materials, purchase the AppleScript Scripter's Kit from an authorized Apple dealer.

Other than making a script unreadable but executable, the Run-Only option has the same options as the standard Save As... command. The only option available in the standard *Save As...* menu item that is not in the Run-Only option is the ability to save a script as a text file. I guess it wouldn't make much sense to save a script as text if you didn't want anyone to read it.

When you select the *Save As...* menu item, the Save As dialog box shown in Figure 7.14 appears. Notice the pop-up menu, where you select the type of file you are saving.

You have three format choices for saving your scripts:

❖ Compiled script
❖ Application script
❖ Text script

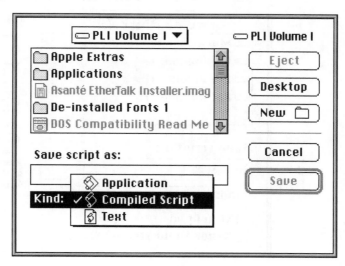

Figure 7.14 *The Script Editor's Save As dialog box.*

If you save a script as a compiled script, every time you run the script, it launches the Script Editor and you need to complete the command using the Script Editor's run command. Use the compiled script option if you want to perform more work on the script or if you want to use the script from another script (see the previous Note).

When you select the Application option, you tell AppleScript to save your script as a double-clickable application. When you run the script, it runs like any other program, without starting the Script Editor. Selecting the Application option causes the Save As dialog box to change, and you'll have two more options. Figure 7.15 shows the additional options.

The two additional options you have are Stay Open and Never Show Startup Screen. The Stay Open command is for scripts that perform tasks in the background. (Writing a script that stays open is an advanced scripting topic that is not covered in this book.)

The Never Show Startup Screen option prevents your script from displaying what is in the Script Editor's description box and asking if you want to run the script. Figure 7.16 shows a Startup Screen for the script we just wrote. If you want your script to run without requiring human acknowledgment, check the Never Show Startup Screen check box.

The final option you have is to save the script as a text file. Use this option if you want to work on your script with a text editor, such as SimpleText, instead of the Script Editor. Sometimes, programming editors, such as BBEdit (which is on the CD-ROM), are better suited than the Script Editor for writing a program. This is purely a matter of personal choice.

Chances are that you will use only the Save As Application option unless you will be doing some advanced scripting. But, who knows? Maybe you're the next AppleScript wizard.

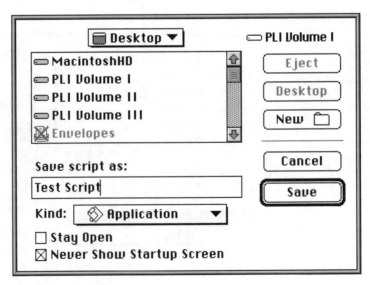

Figure 7.15 *Saving your script as an application.*

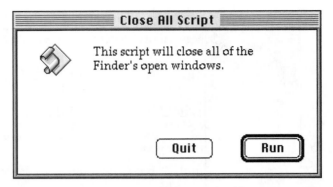

Figure 7.16 *A script's Startup Screen.*

Writing Scripts

As you've probably surmised, you can write a script and record one, or, in other words, you can perform a combination of both recording and writing. Writing a script lets you perform tasks that cannot be recorded, such as extracting data from a database program and placing it into a page layout or word processing program to create a catalog.

Every scriptable program has script commands that can be accessed only by writing a script. You can view these commands and get an idea of what they are by using the Script Editor's *Open Dictionary* menu item from the File menu. A program's dictionary shows all the additional AppleScript terms that program employs. Figure 7.17 shows the dictionary for the Finder in Mac OS 8.

AppleScript is also a programming language. If you have any inclination for programming, take a closer look at what you can do with AppleScript. The nice thing about AppleScript as a programming language is that it is more accessible than some of the other programming languages you could use on a Mac.

AppleScript was written to use English commands and syntax. This doesn't mean it is easy for everyone to use AppleScript, but it is easier than using a traditional programming language. To see what a more complex script looks like, open one of the scripts in the Automated Tasks folder. You'll immediately see what I'm talking about. Figure 7.18 shows the Share a Folder script.

Code   The statements or instructions that make up a program.

Syntax   The rules governing the structure of statements or instructions in a programming language.

You must exercise real time and patience when writing scripts. Whether you write programs using a traditional programming language or AppleScript, you have embarked on an endeavor that requires additional study, experimentation, and the perseverance to see the job through. Writing scripts is not for everyone, but everyone who has a Mac should know about AppleScript and what it can do.

By having an idea of what can be done with AppleScript, even if you don't write the scripts, you can look for scripts that do what you want or even hire someone to

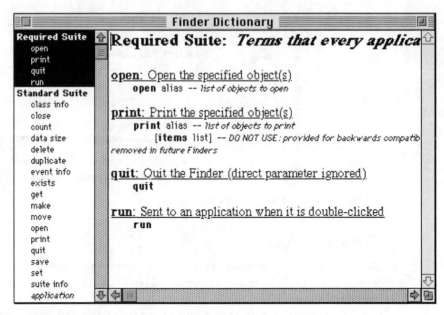

Figure 7.17 *The Finder's dictionary.*

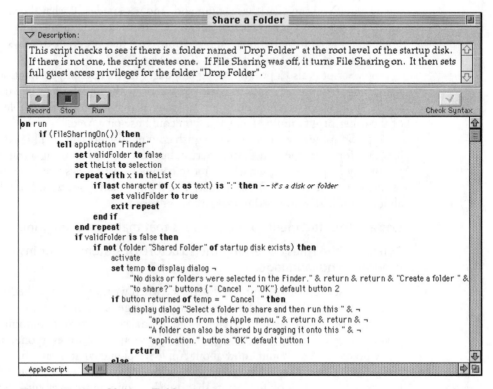

Figure 7.18 *Share a Folder script.*

write a script. If you're a member of a Macintosh users group, you might find some-one in the club who likes writing scripts for the heck of it.

As more programs become scriptable, writing scripts that automate more of your work will be possible. One of the goals driving AppleScript was not to make a scripting language to perform simple maintenance tasks, but to create a system that lets you control other programs and even programs on other machines over a network.

AppleScript is not a programming environment. AppleScript can be used to write useful utilities that allow you to automate tasks, allow programs to interact, and otherwise do useful things. It is not a tool with which to write a word processor, database, or some other application. For those jobs, you need a programming package. Some of the programming tools available for the Mac are mentioned in Chapter 9.

Other Scripting and Macro Utilities

This section covers three programs. Actually, it is about these programs and using them to enhance your Macintosh operations. Automating your Mac is only part of what this section covers.

With the tools mentioned in this section, you can do such things as change your type face by pressing a few keys, perform most Finder functions automatically, back up your data folder to a file server, and much more.

Although I will cite some examples, this section is more an informative introduction to these programs than a tutorial for their use; each of them would require a book to do it justice. Two of the programs are macro generators: One is called QuickKeys, and the other is Tempo. The third program is a System-level scripting language called Frontier that is similar to AppleScript.

All of these applications support Apple events, which means that you can use them to command other programs that also support Apple events. An Apple Event is the basis for AOEC, which is another name for the same technology used by AppleScript to interact with other programs.

These utilities can also interact with each other. If you have a clear idea about what you want to accomplish and are willing to take the time to make any of them work for you, you can make your Mac do amazing things. And if you are not concerned about making it do amazing things, you can still use QuickKeys and Tempo to perform basic functions automatically, thus saving time, which is money. This section looks first at QuickKeys, then Tempo, and, finally, Frontier.

Macro Utilities

Macro utilities are programs that can automate your work environment with or without AppleScript. They started out as a means for assigning keyboard commands to menu items and for recording mouse movements. Now, macro utilities are used to interact with and customize any program you might use, even those that are not AppleScript-compatible.

An example is the use of a PowerBook at work. You connect it to the network and, with a keystroke or menu selection, you can log onto the server and mount the

AppleShare volume(s), get your mail, and start all the applications you will use throughout the day. When it is time to go home, another command can quit your programs, log you off the server, and put your Mac to sleep. All you have to do is unplug it from the network and go home.

The intent behind these programs is to take the drudgery out of routine and time-consuming tasks that you constantly do. You can even use the full-featured macro utilities to automate tasks at a specific time. Maybe you want your Mac to call an online service every night and get your e-mail messages while you're snug in your bed. When you're ready to sit down in front of your Mac, all of your e-mail is waiting for your reply.

With any of these utilities, your imagination is the limit. What you have to remember is that none of this is magic. Making macros requires time and patience on your part; any of the macro utilities will be as useful as you make it. The hard part might be to keep from being overwhelmed by everything you can do with a macro.

The following sections will briefly discuss two macro utilities.

QuickKeys

QuickKeys, published by CE Software, is a keyboard macro program. It lets you assign keyboard commands to a macro that you create that performs some action, such as changing the font you are using, or changing your page layout from portrait to landscape and printing the document—all with one keyboard command.

It can be used to mount your networked volume or automatically save your work. In a sense, QuickKeys is like a command construction kit. You can use it to make enhancements to any program you use, not just the Finder. With QuickKeys, you have a powerful utility for creating a custom work environment. The possibilities with QuickKeys are endless. Should you be motivated, you can put together a macro that could almost be a program.

Tempo

Tempo comes in two flavors. You can get Tempo II Plus or Tempo•EZ. Tempo•EZ is a scaled-down version of Tempo II Plus for those who don't wish to become macro wizards but still want to create a few macros to automate menu selections, automatically enter text, or build more complex macros that record mouse movements and clicks.

Tempo II Plus is EZ's big brother. It is more like QuickKeys in its overall capabilities and can be used to create more complex macros. The macros created with Tempo II Plus can check for specific conditions, such as a graphic, before continuing, and can batch-process files.

Batch processing occurs when you select a group of files and perform the same action on all the selected files. You could move them from one folder to another or copy them to another drive for backup. Batch processing is handy for environments where lots of files are created and keeping track of what belongs where is difficult.

Buying Software

Whenever you purchase software, which package to choose when competing products are available can be a real dilemma. If you don't subscribe to either *MacWorld* or *Mac User* magazine, go to the local library or your users group and check back issues for product reviews and comparisons. Go to your local computer store and look at the different programs to see which one you feel most comfortable with. Finally, when you do buy, make sure that you can take the software back within 30 days for a full refund.

When you reserve the right to return software, some vendors have requirements about the package's condition; they may want a blank registration card and undamaged packaging returned before issuing you a refund. Find out the company's conditions for returning software before you purchase, and don't fill out or send in the software's registration card until you're sure you're going to keep the software.

UserLand's Frontier

UserLand named its scripting package Frontier because it brought capabilities to the Macintosh that are truly new. UserLand introduced its system-level scripting system more than a year before Apple put AppleScript into the System. On all other computing platforms, there is a system-level scripting language that can be used to write small programs to perform file maintenance, automatic processing, or batch processing functions. the Mac did not have these capabilities prior to AppleScript.

Frontier, as already stated, is a system-level scripting language—actually, it is a programming language. But, forget that for a minute. If you think too hard about it as a programming language, you might get scared and disregard what the package can do out of hand.

First of all, if you do not think that you want to write scripts, there are a lot of people who do and some scripts are available to the public. So, you can get scripts to perform such tasks as reconciling two folders on separate drives, making sure they both contain the same files. Most needs for batch processing are common. How do you find duplicate files, locked files, or aliases without associated files? These are just some of the things you can do with Frontier. One feature Frontier does nicely is adding menus to the Finder. These menus add searching, backup, and other file maintenance capabilities to your Finder. Frontier can also be used to set up to-do lists, launch multiple applications, search your hard drive for specific documents that it then places in a specific folder, or control applications via Apple events.

Because Frontier is a programming language, it is not easy to get into. The possibilities for creating system-level utilities, however, make it worthy of consideration.

Even if you're using AppleScript, you might consider using Frontier as well. Frontier offers some features you won't find in AppleScript, such as a database and a scripting language, that are really more powerful (have more capabilities) than AppleScript.

If you want to try it out, UserLand has a Frontier runtime package as shareware. Using the runtime, you can run scripts that others have made to see if they are useful, or you can distribute scripts you might write. The runtime is on the CD-ROM that comes with this book, and you can also find it on CompuServe (an online service) in the UserLand Forum; you can also find scripts there that have been released for public distribution. If you think that you might benefit from Frontier's capabilities, you should look into it.

Additional Finder Enhancements

In addition to the Finder's bells and whistles discussed in Chapter 6, Apple improved the Finder by adding the following capabilities.

❖ Multithreaded copying
❖ Background window updating status indicator
❖ Live window scrolling

The most exciting of these features is multithreaded copying, which means that you can copy more than one file or group of files at a time and continue to work while copying. In the past, anytime you copied a file or group of files you had to wait for the Mac to finish copying before you could do anything else. In short, having a multithreaded Finder means that the Finder can perform several tasks at the same time.

The "background window updating status indicator" is a small set of circular arrows that appear in the upper left corner of a window when a Finder window display is updating. The arrows, which usually appear when a window is opened, mean that the window is being updated and that you should wait before trying to do anything with the window's contents.

The third new item is called "live window scrolling." Live window scrolling is a fancy name that means that as you move a scroll bar the contents of the window move. Are you excited? I mention this only because Apple claimed that it was a new and exciting part of Mac OS 8.

Macintosh Printing

Now it is time to get serious. Although printing is usually a straightforward proposition, it is complex enough that a discussion about printing is needed. Also, with Mac OS 7.5.5, Apple introduced some new printing features that you may want to use. Apple calls its printing architecture "classic QuickDraw" printing. The only reason it uses this name is because of the fiasco with QuickDraw GX.

To fully understand Macintosh printing, you need to understand the following topics:

❖ System printing components
❖ QuickDraw, printers, and resolution
❖ Fonts
❖ Selecting and creating desktop printers
❖ Using Desktop printers

Let's just dive in. If you don't want to know all the details of printing, read the section "System Printing Components" and then jump to the section "Using Desktop Printers."

System Printing Components

Before your Mac can print it needs software that enables your Mac to communicate with the printer. If you upgraded your OS, the software for your printer was automatically installed if you use an Apple printer. If you do not use an Apple printer, chances are that your printer will work, but if it doesn't, you need to get new software from the printer manufacturer.

Driver   (1) A program, usually in a System folder, that lets a peripheral device and a computer send and receive files. Printer drivers control printers; a hard disk driver controls exchanges between a hard disk and a computer; (2) synonymous with resource.

The software that enables your Mac and printer to communicate with each other is called a *driver*. All Macintosh printer drivers are kept in the Extensions folder, which is inside your System folder. There is usually a different printer driver for each type of printer that Apple sells, and in some cases, specific printers have their own drivers. Thus, a LaserWriter uses the LaserWriter 8.4 printer driver, and an ImageWriter uses its own driver.

When you upgrade to Mac OS 8, the installer looks at your hard drive and installs drivers for the printers currently on your hard drive. If you install onto an empty hard drive or if you do a clean install and do not customize the installation, the installer installs a driver for every printer that Apple still supports. This means that you could have about a half-dozen printer drivers on your Mac.

To see how many printer drivers you have installed (as long as they are not shut off with the Extensions Manager control panel), open the Chooser desk accessory. Figure 7.19 shows the Chooser with several printer drivers.

The Chooser is the software component used by Macs for networking and selecting printers. The other system printing components used by the Macintosh are as follows:

❖ The Desktop Printer Spooler extension
❖ The Desktop PrintMonitor extension

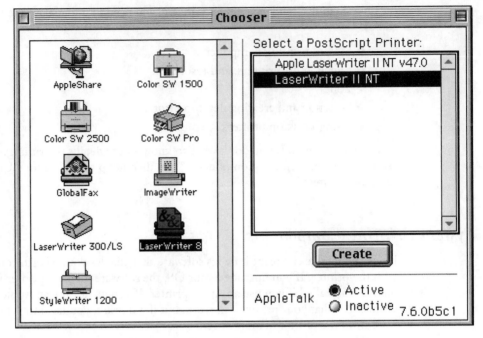

Figure 7.19   *The Chooser with several printer drivers.*

- ❖ The Printer Share extension
- ❖ The PrintingLib extension
- ❖ The PrintMonitor

All the extensions containing the name Desktop are required if you want to use Desktop printers. Desktop printers are printers that appear on the Finder's desktop. Desktop printers offer you more control over the Mac's printing functions. If you don't want to use Desktop printers or if Desktop printers cause problems with some of your applications, you can turn them off with the Extensions Manager. Should you turn off Desktop printing you'll need the remaining extensions listed previously. The only extension you can safely turn off is the Printer Share extension—and only if you don't wish to share your printer with another Macintosh.

QuickDraw, Printers, and Resolution

When your Mac prints a document it has to translate what you see on the screen and send the information to your printer. Said this way, it sounds easy. A lot of things have to happen before your Mac actually prints. Here is a brief description of what happens.

Whatever you view on your screen is created by the Mac's graphic subsystem, called QuickDraw. QuickDraw is built into your Mac; it is the software that converts all information into dots so your computer can display the information. This process is called rasterizing. When you see an image on your screen you view an image that is composed of dots. The number of dots that you see is described by the number of dots per inch that your monitor can display; this is referred to as dots per inch or DPI. Most monitors have a DPI of 72 to 96 dots (pixels) per inch. To confuse matters just a bit more, most monitors are described by the total number of dots they can display. This can range from 640 by 480 to 1600 by 1200 pixels.

The number of dots that a monitor can display is controlled by the Mac's hardware. It is the combination of the video card and monitor that determines your Mac's display capabilities. For example, if you use a 15-inch monitor and have at least two megabytes of video RAM, your monitor can easily display 800 by 600 pixels.

By now, you are probably wondering what this has to do with printing. Hold on, we're getting there. The term used as a general description for your monitor's display capability is *resolution*. The 15-inch monitor we just mentioned has a resolution of 800 by 600 pixels. The number of dots per inch depends on the monitor's dot pitch, which can vary from .25 to .28 mm. At .28 dot pitch, the approximate DPI is 96. The smaller the dot pitch, the sharper the picture.

Just what does the monitor's resolution have to do with printing? In one sense, nothing, and in another sense, everything. Just as a monitor displays everything you see, the same terms describe printers and the same technology is used to print. One of the terms used to describe the sharpness of the printer's output is DPI.

The basic laser printer has a resolution from 300 to 600 DPI, and ink jet printers can print from 320 to 760 DPI. Here is the problem. If your Mac displays an image at 96 DPI, how is it possible to print the same image at 300 or 600 DPI? The number of pixels per inch used by the printer far exceeds the number of pixels per inch displayed on the monitor. Somehow the Mac must perform a conversion of some type.

If the Mac sent just the number of dots displayed on the screen to the printer, the resulting image would be too small to read. Because this is not the case, the Mac finds more dots to send to the printer so that the image or document produced by the printer looks like what you've been viewing on the screen. This conversion process is accomplished by QuickDraw. QuickDraw communicates with the printer driver and determines the printer's DPI. Then QuickDraw generates the number of dots needed by the printer and sends this information to the printer. And the printer then prints the document.

If your computer displayed the number of dots used by the printer, what you would see on the screen would be so large that you could see only a small portion of the document. What QuickTime does is generate an image from the information in the document's data file. Usually this information is numeric, and QuickTime, in conjunction with the printer driver, calculates the number of dots that the printer driver then sends to the printer. If you use a PostScript printer, like an Apple LaserWriter, the process changes a bit.

PostScript printers are computers in their own right. They use a program language called PostScript, which tells the printer how to print each document. When you print to a PostScript printer, QuickDraw and the printer driver convert the data in your document into the PostScript programming code, and the programming code is sent to the printer. The computer in the printer then generates the dots and prints the page. In the end, the result is the same; what is different is how the data from the computer is processed.

If the document you are trying to print is not numeric data (a vector graphic), it then consists of dots. Photo imaging software uses documents composed of dots. Usually when you look at images composed of dots, you'll know. Because the document has a specific number of dots, how it prints is determined by the resolution of the document. All QuickDraw does is send the dots contained in the document to the printer driver. With documents that do not have enough dots the printed result can be less than satisfactory, or the image may print smaller than you expected. In situations like this, you have to re-create the document or see if you can get an image with a higher resolution.

This whole business about resolution can get quite complicated. I hope this discussion has given you enough information for a basic understanding of what your computer does when it prints. If you need more information about resolution and printing, check out some books about graphics and printing.

Fonts

In the last section, we talked about resolution and how QuickDraw converts computer data into dots so that you can see the data on your monitor and print what you see. Any discussion about fonts assumes that you have some understanding about resolution. True, it is not necessary to understand resolution to use fonts, just as it is not necessary to understand resolution to use your computer or print. But, you might find it useful to have a basic understanding of fonts so that you can troubleshoot any font problems you might encounter.

Fonts are computer graphic documents that your Mac uses to generate any text you see on the screen. All fonts are stored inside your System folder in a folder called Fonts. When you open the Fonts folder you see two or three types of documents. Figure 7.20 shows the contents of the Fonts folder. You see two document types: a suitcase and a PostScript font.

The suitcase is a container document. When you double-click on a suitcase, it opens. Inside are the fonts, the files that QuickDraw uses to generate the text on the screen. There are two types of fonts. Figure 7.21 shows an open suitcase that contains the two different types of fonts. You can always tell a TrueType font from a bitmapped font by the number of A's in the font's icon. TrueType fonts have three A's, and bitmapped fonts only have one.

One type of font is called a bitmapped font; the other is a TrueType font. The bitmapped font is created by specifying the number of dots needed to display a font of a specific size. It is an image created entirely of dots. This is why bitmapped fonts are usually named with the typeface name and a number to designate the size of the font.

TrueType fonts are created by using a mathematical formula that describes the shape of the font. A TrueType font can be any size you want it to be. QuickDraw uses the font's mathematical formula to create the correct number of dots needed to display the font on the screen. Similarly, when a TrueType font is printed, QuickDraw recalculates the number of dots needed and sends them to the printer.

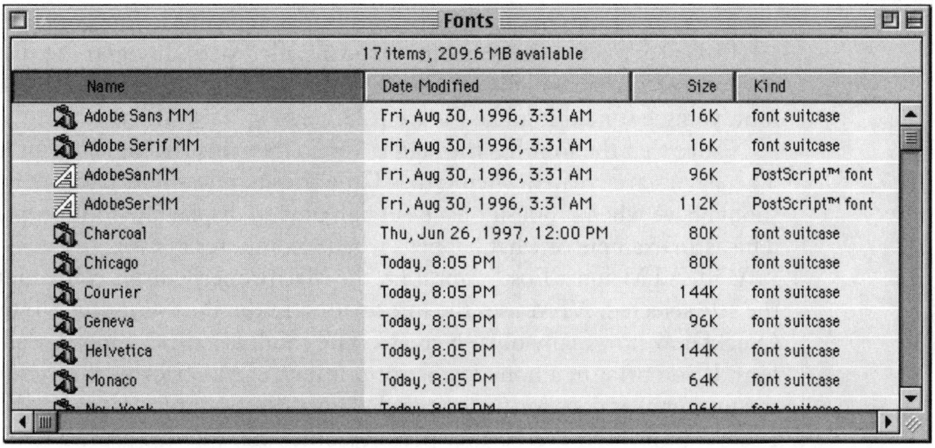

Figure 7.20   *Inside the Fonts folder.*

The bitmapped fonts represent technology that is older than TrueType fonts. They are still used because of PostScript printers. In some circumstances, a graphic artist may remove all the TrueType fonts from the system and use just the bitmapped fonts. The graphic artist does not use the bitmapped fonts alone; he or she also uses the PostScript font mentioned above and a control panel called ATM (Adobe Type Manager).

The bitmapped font by itself can be accurately displayed only at its created size. You might have font sizes of 10, 12, 14, 18, and 24 points inside a suitcase. Without

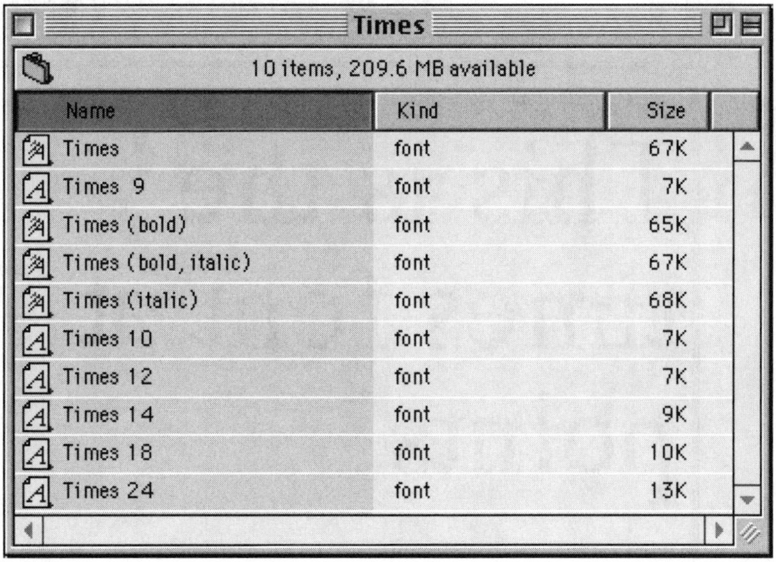

Figure 7.21   *The fonts inside a suitcase.*

the fonts corresponding to the PostScript font and ATM, you would be able to accurately display the font in only one of the installed sizes. If you try to display the font in a size other than what is installed without ATM and the corresponding PostScript font, you see something like Figure 7.22.

Notice that the font has the jaggies (of course, this is a highly technical term). The jaggies are created when QuickTime tries to guess how many dots the font should have when it doesn't have enough dots to display the font properly. It's ugly. This is an example of what happens when a computer guesses.

With ATM and a PostScript font, the Mac properly displays the font regardless of the size selected. ATM uses the information in the PostScript font to tell QuickDraw how many dots to create. The result is a nice, smooth, well-behaved font. If you print to a non-PostScript printer, ATM performs the same function for the printer as it does for the screen. When a PostScript font is printed on a PostScript printer, the PostScript font (sometimes called a printer font) is sent to the printer so that it will know how to print the font.

ATM is automatically installed with Mac OS 8. If ATM is properly installed you shouldn't ever have to worry about how your fonts are displayed. If you start to see jaggy fonts or if they are not printing properly, you'll know that something is wrong. The bitmapped font and the printer font are always located in the same folder, which is usually the Fonts folder.

Graphic artists and people who use a large number of fonts use a couple of font utilities that allow you to store fonts in folders other than the Fonts folder. Even

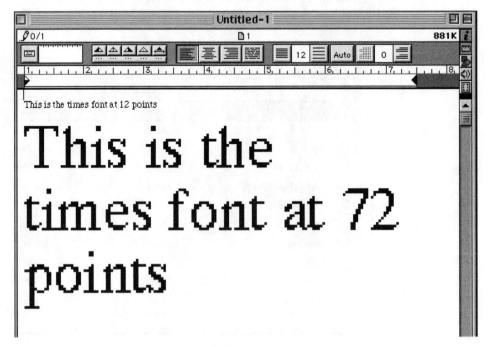

Figure 7.22 *A font displayed at 72 points.*

when you use one of these utilities, the bitmapped font and the printer font still reside in the same folder.

The font utilities that allow you to store fonts in different folders are called Suitcase (the most popular one) and Master Juggler. Suitcase is published by Symantec; Master Juggler Pro comes from Alsoft. You will know if you need either of these utilities because you'll have way too many fonts in your Fonts folder, selecting a font will become a chore, and your font life will be miserable.

Selecting and Creating Desktop Printers

Now we're ready to get down to the business of printing—almost. One of the innovations in Macintosh OS technology is the Desktop printer. It used to be that you selected your printer from the Chooser, and that was it. There was nothing more to do except select *Print* from the File menu and enjoy the results. People aren't happy if things are too simple, so now we have Desktop printers.

If you hanker for the simpler life and don't want to use Desktop printers, all you have to do is turn off any extension that has the name Desktop with some combination of Print. Then you, too, can return to the simple life and forget about the rest of this section. Otherwise, you need to read on.

The Desktop printer is more than an icon that appears on your desktop, as shown in Figure 7.23. The Desktop printer is a print spooler, which means that your Mac prints to your hard drive and then, when the Mac isn't busy, the print spooler sends the document to the printer. It seems as if you're working and printing at the same time, but in truth, you very rarely keep your computer busy enough to keep it from printing or doing some other task in the background.

Figure 7.23 *A Desktop printer on the desktop.*

You can create multiple Desktop printers for the same printer, or you could have Desktop printers for different printers, or both. The practical limit is seven Desktop printers. If you have more than seven, think about getting rid of a few. Desktop printers are like other Finder icons in that they can be selected, opened, and thrown into the trash. If you place your only Desktop printer into the trash, a new one is automatically created. You must have at least one Desktop printer.

Creating a Desktop printer is easy. Follow these four steps:

1. Open the Chooser (selected from the Finder's Apple menu).
2. Select the printer you want to use by clicking on the printer's icon.
3. Click the Create button.
4. A new Desktop printer appears on your desktop.

The only time you might run into trouble during the process of creating Desktop printer is if you select the wrong printer port or the wrong networked printer. If you make a mistake when creating a Desktop printer, throw away the Desktop printer icon and create a new Desktop printer.

Using Desktop Printers

Now that you have a Desktop printer you might want to know what you can do with it and how it works. In Figure 7.23, notice the dark border around the Desktop printer named LaserWriter II NT. This dark border means that the printer is the default printer. Whenever you print, the printer with the dark border is the one your Mac automatically selects.

When you select a Desktop printer, a Printing menu appears in the Finder. Figure 7.24 shows the contents of the Printing menu. The commands you can give

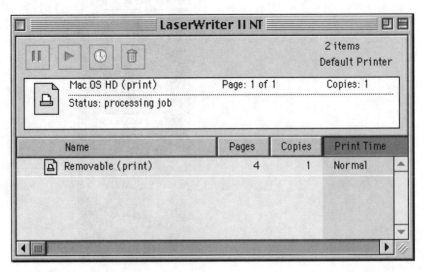

Figure 7.24 The Printing menu.

to a printer depend on the printer's capabilities. The options you have for a basic LaserWriter are as follows:

❖ Start Print Queue—If the Print Queue has been stopped, selecting this command causes the printer to resume printing.

❖ Stop Print Queue—Selecting this option causes the computer to store anything you print until you start the print queue. This option is useful for PowerBook owners who may want to print a document while away from the office. When they return, they can reconnect the computer to the printer and print all the queued documents.

❖ Get Printer Configuration—This command shows you information about your Laser printer and its installed fonts.

❖ Change Setup…—If you can modify your printer's setup you will use this command.

❖ Show Manual Feed Alert—The manual feed alert is a dialog box that tells you when to put paper into the printer if you selected Manual Feed when the document was printed.

❖ Set Default Printer—This command makes the printer your default printer.

Double-clicking on a Desktop printer icon opens a window like the one in Figure 7.25.

The window shown in Figure 7.25 is a Finder window. The Finder's menu commands that are available can be used on documents that appear in the window. Also, the contextual menu feature works with spooled documents. The buttons at the top of the Printer window can be used to pause a document that is printing, resume printing a paused document, schedule when a document will print, and delete (trash) a printer document. You can drag documents to change their printing order and

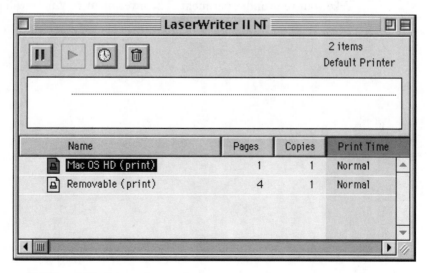

Figure 7.25 *A Desktop printer window.*

move them from one printer to another as long as the same printer driver is used to create the destination Desktop printer.

What I've presented here are just the printing basics. A lot more could be said, but then you would not have anything to discover for yourself. Spend some time printing documents and playing with the Desktop printers. Try stopping and starting the queue. Make a second Desktop printer and see what happens when you change the printer's settings. Drag the documents around and play with the buttons in the Printer window. A good way to start is by printing your hard drive's window. You may be surprised by what you learn.

Summary

You have covered a lot of ground in this chapter, and rather uneven ground. Going from Mac OS 8 technologies to Finder enhancements to printing is a bit disjointed. I'm not going to say the presentation is logical. Rather, this chapter tied up some loose ends.

This chapter does not contain everything there is to know about Mac OS 8's enhancements or printing, but you do have a good start. Use this chapter as a starting point for exploring the power of your Mac. The more you learn about how your Mac works, the more productive you'll be in the long run.

Keep in mind that setting up your Mac and learning how to use it is a time-consuming process, but the more time you invest now, the more you'll save later. For example, if you spend a few hours with AppleScript, you will find ways of using it to enhance how your Mac operates and you will develop or find some scripts that will save you time. Understanding how your Mac prints can help you be more productive and make your documents look more professional—not to mention making the printing process easier and more controllable.

Take your time and experiment. The investment you make will pay off in the long run.

CHAPTER 8

Customizing Your System

Introduction

Now that you know all the different System elements and tools that Apple provides, you are ready to make your Mac jump, dance, and sing. The reason to have a computer is to make your life easier, your business more productive, and/or maybe just to have fun. Whatever your reasons, you want to get the most from your Mac. The question is: What does it mean to get the most from your Mac? For some, it means learning everything they can without becoming a programmer. For others, it is finding the most expedient way to get a particular job done, while still others look to squeeze the maximum efficiency from their system. Usually, the answer is a combination of these responses.

One thing is sure: The answer to this question is different for each Macintosh owner. Therefore, there is no way to meet everybody's expectations or answer everybody's questions. I can, however, give you an idea of your Mac's potential. I'm sure you will find ways in which you can do make your Mac more than a glorified calculator or a very sophisticated typewriter.

This chapter explains some of the advanced features of Mac OS 8. In addition, it looks at software utilities for enhancing how you interact with your Mac.

Figure 8.1 is a picture of the Finder, but it is not the picture you are used to seeing. This version includes additional menus and a couple of indicators not found on the standard menu bar. The figure here is an example of what can be done; it is up to you to decide if you want to expand your Mac's native abilities. One thing to consider as you read this chapter is that a lot of the topics discussed require a time commitment. It is one thing to install a utility that allows you to customize your working environment; that will take only a few minutes. Making the utility really work for you, however, will take more time, experimentation, and a certain amount of dedication. Most of what is discussed in this chapter demands a commitment. Don't expect to install some of these utilities and experience a magical

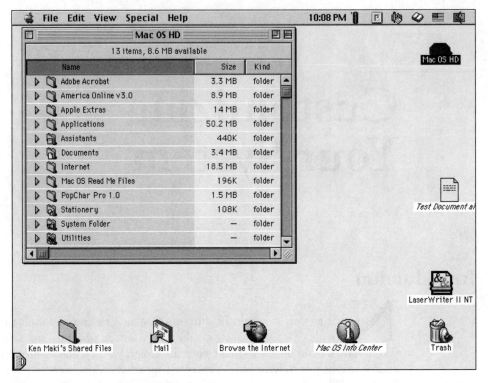

Figure 8.1 *An enhanced Finder.*

transformation of your Macintosh; the technology is not yet advanced enough for that to happen. Your Macintosh is *still just a computer*, which means that no matter how advanced the operating system may be, it will do only what you tell it to do. Sometimes, the telling takes time, but once your Mac has been told how to do something, it will not forget.

To determine if the amount of time it takes to customize your system is worth the effort, weigh the time spent teaching your Mac its new tricks against the time the customization saves. Unfortunately, this is also a Catch-22. You won't know how much time you'll save until you've installed the utility.

The topics of this chapter are as follows:

❖ Advanced Mac OS 8.0 features

❖ System utilities

❖ Programming options

Don't let these topics scare you; there is nothing here that you cannot master. Even programming can be simpler than you might think. If you can make your Mac do something you really need but can't find off-the-shelf, then you have accomplished something.

Advanced Mac OS 8 Features

Mac OS 8 is another incarnation of the Macintosh operating system that continues to demonstrate that the Mac stands head and shoulders over any other personal computing platform. A Macintosh is easier to use, enhance, and maintain than that other popular machine, which we won't mention. Suffice it to say that I'm actually conversant (in computer terms) with both platforms and the Mac is my computer of choice.

The Mac is more customizable; you can enhance how the Finder looks and operates. The Mac makes working in a workgroup environment, where several people work on a project simultaneously, very easy. And, for graphics applications, the Mac always has been a superior platform due to products like QuickTime. The following is a list of the advanced features in Mac OS 8:

- ❖ Publish and Subscribe
- ❖ QuickTime
- ❖ Apple Events and scripting
- ❖ Making your Mac talk to you

These are not all new features in Mac OS 8; most of them were present in Systems 7.5 and 7.6. They are the features that you can use to make your life easier or to have fun.

Subscribe and Publish

Mac OS 8 has a feature called Subscribe and Publish, which is similar to the Copy and Paste commands. Rather than being a one-time Copy and Paste, Subscribe and Publish creates a live link between what you copy and the document into which you paste the information. When you change the original, its counterpart in the other document changes automatically.

You use Subscribe and Publish by selecting part of a document and creating an *Edition*. Creating an Edition is called *Publishing*. The Edition is then placed into another document, created by a different program, by *Subscribing* to the Edition. Subscribing is similar to pasting the data from another file into your document, except that you won't be able to edit the information contained in the Edition. Information in an Edition can be edited only within the Edition's original document.

To edit the information from a subscription, open the original document from which the edition was created, edit the file, and save it. When you save the file the Edition is automatically updated, which, in turn, updates any document that contains the Edition as a subscription. This feature works over a network (see Chapter 13 for more information about networking), so if several people work on a project, such as a newsletter, one person can be working on the graphics, another on the page layout, and a third on the copy. Because all the information comes together in the Page Layout process, each of the different elements can be sent to the layout person via an Edition. Then, when revisions need to be made, the people responsible update their files, which, in turn, automatically update the newsletter.

Editions are useful for any document or process that uses data from various programs and is updated frequently. An example is a quarterly report, where the spreadsheet file needs to be changed every quarter but the word processing document in
which it is placed remains the same. You would update your spreadsheet file and
print the word processing document to complete your report. This can save time if
you have several reports that use the same data or a standard report in which the
information is frequently updated. Editions are useful if you have several publications that share graphics. If you Subscribe to Editions of the graphics rather than
placing them individually into each manual, when you update a graphic, it is updated
automatically in all the manuals.

The following steps graphically represent this process:

1. Select the text or graphic you want to publish and select the *Create
   Publisher...* item from the Edit menu (Figure 8.2).
2. In the Save dialog box that appears, save your Edition file.

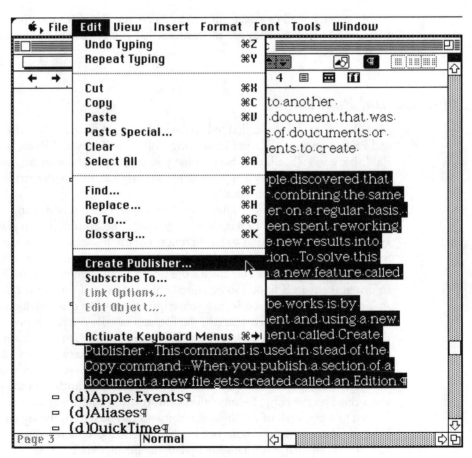

Figure 8.2   *Creating a Publisher in Microsoft Word.*

3. Open the other program you're going to use.

4. Choose the *Subscribe...* item from the Edit menu.

5. In the Open dialog box that appears, find and open the Edition file you just created.

6. The contents of the Edition file are placed into your document.

When you've published an Edition, the text or graphic is marked so you know that it is used in another file. Figure 8.3 shows the text and markers after an Edition has been published. When you subscribe to an Edition, the section of your document is also marked. Remember that you can't change the contents of an Edition from the Subscribing program. Figure 8.4 shows how a subscribed Edition appears in your document.

As always, you are constrained only by the limits of your imagination when using Subscribe and Publish. You can use it with databases, spreadsheets, word processing, and any other program that is fully System 7-compatible, which translates to any new program purchased today. Some older programs do not support Subscribe and Publish.

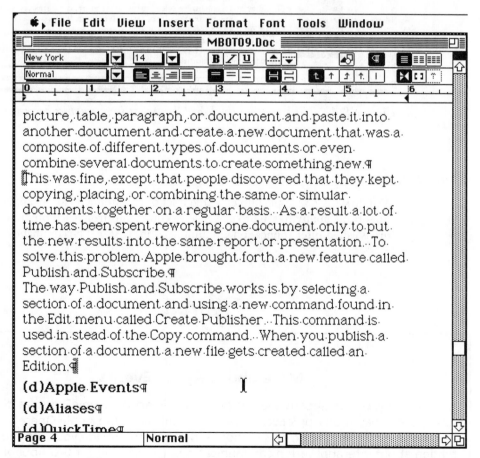

Figure 8.3　*The text used in the Edition and its markers.*

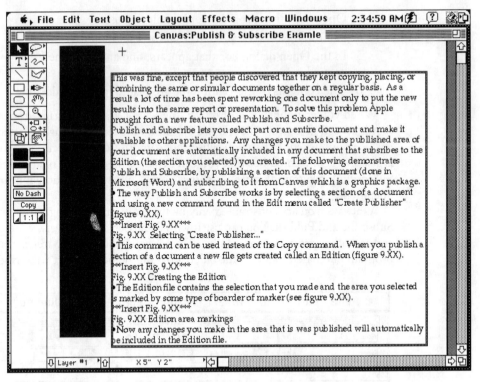

Figure 8.4   The text from the Word document in a graphics document (the graphics program is Canvas).

Apple Events

With System 7.5, Apple implemented a set of requirements for all applications to support the ability to send to and receive commands from each other. This new feature is called InterApplication Communications (IAC). The commands that are sent

More about Apple Events

Actually, you've already seen Apple Events in action. AppleScript, as discussed in Chapter 7, is based on AppleEvents, which is a subset of the Apple Open Collaboration Environment. This section is intended to provide you with more information about interapplication communications. (How's that for technobabble?)

Figure 8.5   Apple Events example.

from one program to another are called Apple Events, and every application is supposed to be able to respond to at least the following four commands:

- ❖ Open Application
- ❖ Open Documents
- ❖ Print Documents
- ❖ Quit Application

You can see a good example of how Apple Events work. Start up as many applications as your Mac can handle, then try to open one more. If you get a message like the one shown in Figure 8.5, you are witnessing an Apple Event in action.

In the previous example, the Finder requests permission to send an Apple Event command to the Finder. It is going to tell Finder to restart so the program will have enough memory to run. Apple has published a complete set of standard Apple Events and wants all applications to support a suite of Apple Events called Core Apple Events. In theory, it is possible for one application to control another almost completely.

You should know about Apple Events and interapplication communication because an increasing number of utilities allow you to perform all kinds of automated actions using Apple Events. A number of them are on the CD-ROM that comes with this book.

QuickTime

Previously, QuickTime was not part of the System proper but a product that you had to purchase and add. Since System 7.5, QuickTime has been included and considered a basic part of the Mac OS. QuickTime has several component parts as well: QuickTime VR, QuickTime MPEG, and QuickTime Musical Instruments. QuickTime and its components are installed when you install Apple's multimedia software while performing a custom install.

What is QuickTime? QuickTime is Apple's multimedia engine that enables your applications to use full-motion video, graphics, and sound as integral parts of their functions. It has built-in data compression, so a QuickTime or MPEG movie takes up as little space as possible. The uses for QuickTime are numerous: It can be used to include a slide show with verbal commentary in a word processing or spreadsheet document. You can put a full-motion video, complete with sound, into the quarterly report. The whole idea is based on the concept that a picture is worth a thousand words, and several pictures, especially if they are motion pictures, are worth a few million. And with QuickTime VR you can provide a panoramic view of an object, showing all sides of the object, a walkthrough of a building (even one that doesn't exist), or a prototype of your newest invention in action. QuickTime and QuickTime VR represent the next stage in the evolution of business, personal, and Internet computing.

What you need to view, or to include, QuickTime in your documents is the QuickTime system extension. It requires about 400K of system memory to work, and you need to be able to use 32-bit QuickDraw. In other words, you need a Macintosh with a 68020 or higher processor. QuickTime will not work on a Macintosh Plus, SE, Portable, PowerBook 100, or Classic. In computer years these are old, old machines; if you've never heard of them, don't be alarmed. The last one in this list was made almost five years ago. Most uses of QuickTime occur in the business world, where QuickTime is an essential component for desktop presentations, and in video animation and production. You will also find many World Wide Web sites that contain QuickTime and QuickTime VR presentations.

QuickTime VR was the first of several substantial upgrades to QuickTime; VR stands for Virtual Reality. QuickTime VR will move Apple's multimedia software into three-dimensional imaging and video movies. Where this technology will end up is anyone's guess, but, for the time being, you can use QuickTime to make and play movies on your Mac. Because QuickTime is as complex as some of Apple's

QuickTime's Usefulness

QuickTime is not yet used as an everyday tool. QuickTime files require too much disk space and inflate the size of a document dramatically. They are too big to effectively send over a network or a modem, and they cannot be printed. Until we reach the day when paper is no longer the primary medium for business and personal communications and data networks can handle the increased traffic load created by the large data files that QuickTime demands, it will remain a tool for specialists who work with video, desktop presentations, and other areas where moving images are needed. In the next few years, as video conferencing replaces physical conferences, we will begin to see a real need for QuickTime.

other technologies, you will have to find more information about QuickTime from other sources. Just for fun, some QuickTime tools and movies are included on the CD-ROM that comes with this book.

Making Your Mac Talk to You

If you perform a full install of Mac OS 8, one of the components installed on your Macintosh is the Text to Speech function. This function is controlled by the Speech Manager extension.

The Text to Speech installation will place files into your System folder that let your Mac talk to you; it will even read to you. It is sometimes fun and useful to have your Mac read what you've written. Most of the text editors, including SimpleText, and word-processing programs have the ability to read back part or all of the text in a document. One quick way to see if the Text to Speech software is installed on your Mac is to run SimpleText. If the Text to Speech software is installed, SimpleText will have an additional menu item called Sound (Figure 8.6). By selecting text, you can have it read to you in a variety of voices.

Those of you who have a Quadra AV or Power Macintosh can also issue voice commands to your Mac. To issue voice commands, you need the full installation of PlainTalk. Although the voice recognition features of PlainTalk are mediocre, this feature is still fun to explore. I'm not sure I would trust the technology to be a productivity tool yet. PlainTalk, however, does represent the future: that day when we will talk to our computers rather than use a mouse and keyboard. It will be several years before the technology is perfected to the point that you'll have a Voice Macintosh. If you have the equipment and practice, you should be able to make your Mac do some tasks vocally. It is fun to talk to your Mac—it will drive those around you nuts.

System Utilities

There are more utilities for enhancing your System and work environment than you can shake a stick at. When you consider all the shareware, freeware, and commercial programs available, you find that you have many choices regarding what packages to use.

You should consider using several different types of utilities. Many of the packages are discussed in other parts of this book, and some of them are even included on the CD-ROM that comes with it. Rather than providing in-depth tutorials for each type of utility, this section discusses the utilities available and briefly outlines their features.

Figure 8.6 *SimpleText's Sound menu.*

The different types of utilities listed are as follows:

- ❖ Finder enhancements and file tools
- ❖ System utilities
- ❖ Memory management
- ❖ Adding control panels
- ❖ Adding extensions

Although this section does not cover all available programs, it does give you a good idea of the types of enhancements you can make to your Macintosh operating environment. If you want a different way to access your applications and files, or if you're tired of the Desktop pattern and want something different, you can have what you want. Someone is always coming up with a new feature for your Mac, so if you don't see anything you like here, read the topical magazines.

Finder Enhancements and File Tools

A Finder enhancement utility is one that replaces the Finder or changes how the Finder operates. The programs discussed here are not single-function utilities; they have multiple features that change or replace the Finder interface or that can act as a Finder replacement for the purpose of file management. The Finder neither displays all the information about a file nor lets you change file attributes. Because there are

Utilities from the CD-ROM

Explore the BMUG CD-ROM that comes with this book. In the Utilities folder are several folders, one of which is called System Enhancements. In here are a variety of programs, control panels, extensions, and resources—far too many to list here— for enhancing how your Finder looks and operates. Play with some of these items to see if you find them useful. There are utilities that change the look of the Finder, enhance the editing keys on your keyboard, or control how your Mac behaves as it shuts down.

My only word of warning is that you should be careful when using shareware or freeware utilities like those included with this book. Many of these utilities were written before Mac OS 8 was released. Any utility that substantially modifies the Finder is apt to cause problems, especially those that play with the menu bar. Should you find that a utility is causing a problem, look at the Read Me file that comes with most utilities. In the Read Me or another info file, you'll probably find an e-mail or Web site address where you can get an updated version of the program.

times when you may want to view your files in a different format or get more information about a file, you may want to use one of the utilities listed in this section.

These programs are representative of what you can find in computer stores and from mail-order houses. It is not a market survey but an example of what is available.

At Ease

At Ease is an Apple product that replaces the Finder. It allows you to limit access to your hard disk and the programs someone else (such as your children or coworkers) may use. If you wish to have the Finder available to you, you can password-protect it. While At Ease is running, your desk accessories and any other folder aliases in your Apple Startup Items folder are not available without a password.

The real advantage to this program is that your hard drive is protected, and once you have arranged all your files, you are the only one who can change them. If you wish, you can force the person using your machine to save all of his or her work onto floppy disks. For a quick means of protecting your Macintosh from prying eyes and safeguarding your data, you would be hard-pressed to do better. Figure 8.7 shows the At Ease application. Remember that you determine what applications are available.

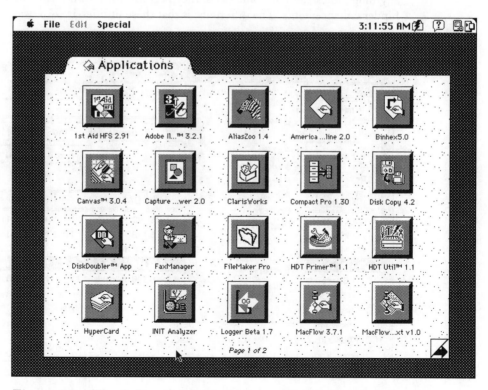

Figure 8.7 *The At Ease Desktop.*

DiskTop

DiskTop, published by CE Software, is a mini-Finder for use in other applications. With DiskTop, you can perform the most essential Finder functions without returning to the Finder. You may want to use DiskTop instead of the Finder; it is faster at many of its operations because it does not display icons. Using it to find that lost file, retrieve a folder on the fly, move a file or folder, and so on is faster than using the equivalent Finder function. Figure 8.8 shows DiskTop and its menu. When you double-click on a drive, a list of its folders and files appears. You can even use DiskTop for launching applications, as you would in the Finder.

DiskTop allows you to change the attributes of files, find files, and perform most Finder functions without going to the Finder. DiskTop comes with another program called Gopher, a program that searches for text strings in all the documents it can read. If you have forgotten the name of a file but know a name or a phrase in the document, you can find it using Gopher. It is a handy utility to use when you have hundreds of documents and need only one that contains a specific reference.

System Utilities

System utilities enhance or modify how your Macintosh operates. They do not do anything radical, and, in some cases, they perform some of the same functions as the Finder enhancements. The difference is that these utilities are extensions that

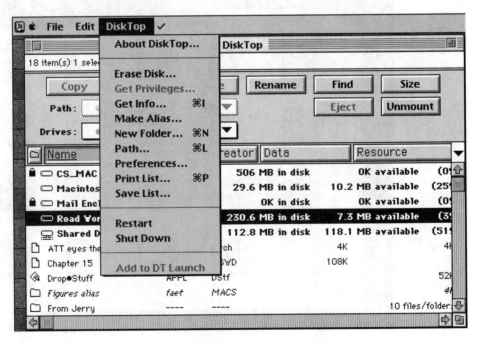

Figure 8.8   DiskTop with its menu.

directly modify the Finder. Hence, they work at a System level, not as an application running on top of the Finder.

The idea behind any set of utilities is to increase your productivity, save you time, and make using your Mac easier. When you purchase a set of utilities, you get a set of software tools that a company has put together because it thinks their tools are what the computer user needs. What you need in a set of utilities is highly individual; what one person finds to be useful, another may consider an annoyance. Carefully evaluate any set of utilities before you purchase.

This section looks at three utility sets; some single utilities are briefly listed as well. These programs have been selected so that you can see the wide variety of tools and get an idea of what you can do to customize your Mac.

Now Utilities

Even though some of the features of Now Utilities are mentioned in other areas of this book, they are all described here. Now Utilities is a collection of utilities that can be used selectively or all together. Now Utilities has one of the most popular utility suites available for the Mac. The various tools included in this package are listed here:

- ❖ NowMenus—NowMenus turns all of the folders or their aliases in your Apple Menu Items folder into a hierarchical menu. It works with subfolders as well. NowMenus also let you make custom menus for launching programs and selecting documents.

- ❖ NowSave—NowSave remembers to save your work for you. You set the interval between saves in keystrokes, minutes, or mouse clicks. NowSave also protects your work by recording your keystrokes. At least you can recover your text.

- ❖ Profiler—Profiler searches out all the details of your system. It looks at the hardware, your applications, control panels, and extensions, then generates a report that can be very useful for troubleshooting.

- ❖ Startup Manager—Startup Manager is an extension and Control panel manager. It lets you turn on or shut off any of your extensions and Control panels. Startup Manager can also help you isolate an extension or control panel that is causing problems.

- ❖ Super Boomerang—This extension modifies all your Open or Save dialog boxes so that you can quickly perform some Finder functions, such as finding and creating new folders. It also lets you quickly select folders you access often, among other tricks.

- ❖ Now FolderMenus—This extension can turn any menu into a hierarchical menu. This is a nice implementation of a useful utility.

- ❖ Now QuickFiler—This extension replaces the standard Find utility. You have more options and a faster search through your hard drive.

- ❖ WYSIWYG Menus—The final utility in this package enhances the Font menu in any of your applications. It combines font families, lets you reorder how they appear, and shows you the font in its typeface.

Other Utilities

In the remainder of this section, we look at a few other utilities. These utilities are single-purpose tools, utilities that have only one function rather than several. Often, the single-purpose utility does a better job than a Swiss Army Knife-type of tool because the single-purpose tool is developed with more care and focus. Usually, they have more features for their dedicated task and are better throughout. Make sure that you do not buy a suite of utilities just to get one specific function. Chances are that you can find a single-purpose utility that does a better job.

Once again, the utilities in this section are listed to represent what is available. This is by no means a market survey or tutorial on using these tools.

❖ KaBoom (Nova Development)—A sound utility that you can use to create, edit, and otherwise modify sound files. It controls which sounds play when certain events take place, and it provides a good editor for making your own sounds.

❖ MultiClip (Olduvai)—A utility that provides an (almost) unlimited number of clipboards and acts as a Scrapbook replacement. With MultiClip, you can retrieve that item you cut from your document 45 minutes ago and thought you had lost. It can also be used as a graphics catalog.

❖ Screenscapes (Kiwi Software)—A Desktop Pattern control panel replacement. With Screenscapes, you can place patterns and pictures on your desktop and even have them change while you're working on your Mac. Having a series of pictures or patterns, rather than just one, can be interesting.

❖ Chameleon (Logical Solutions)—Another Desktop Pattern control panel replacement that is quite different from Screenscapes. Chameleon has a built-in editor so that you can change your images. It also comes with its own variety of Desktop patterns.

❖ PopupFolder (Inline Software)—A utility like the Apple Menu Options control panel, only it goes a bit further. PopupFolder makes the contents of any folder and your hard drives available as a pop-up menu. Just click and hold down the mouse button while the pointer is on a folder; its contents pop up like a menu and are selectable.

❖ Icon-It! (Olduvai)—Replacement utility for Apple's Launcher control panel. It places a palette of icons on your Desktop that can be used to execute macros as well as launch programs. You can also use it to perform menu commands by clicking on a button rather than selecting the menu. Icon-It! can be used with any program to convert menus to icon buttons.

❖ ClickChange (Dubl-Click Software)—A utility that lets you customize your Mac's display elements. You can customize windows, scroll bars, pointers, and buttons, just to name a few. If you work hard enough, you can make your Mac look like it's not a Mac at all.

From the utilities listed you should have a better idea of how you can modify your Mac's interface. Utilities are being developed and revised all the time, and only some of the utility companies are represented in this chapter. Before you dive into installing a bunch of utilities, read the section "Adding Control Panels and

Extensions." If you neglect to read this section, you might find that you've bitten off more than you can chew, especially if things don't work right.

Memory Management Tools

Memory management is always a topic of concern for Mac users. No matter how much RAM you have, you never have enough. And if you have enough now, it won't be long until you don't. Anything you can do to make your use of RAM more efficient helps you make more efficient use of your Mac.

This section is about memory management utilities. After you read it you'll have a better idea of how your Mac uses memory and some of the tools that you can get to make it even more efficient.

RAM Disks

Besides using your RAM more efficiently, there are some utilities that let you use your RAM as a disk drive. Using RAM as a disk drive can dramatically increase the speed at which your Mac operates, especially when you put your System and programs onto the RAM disk.

Taking some of your memory and making your Mac recognize that memory as a disk drive creates a RAM disk. A RAM disk can be created on any Macintosh that has enough memory. The advantage of a RAM disk is speed. Using a RAM disk, you can run any applications and access any files on it at the same speed that your Mac processes anything in memory. The only limitation is the speed of your CPU and the minimum amount of time it takes to process the instructions or launch the program. Using a RAM disk, your Mac runs at its absolute fastest.

The disadvantage of a RAM disk is that it is volatile. If you crash, anything in the RAM disk could be lost and unrecoverable. Although Maxima saves your data by copying it to your hard drive when you shut down or restart, if you crash and restart, you could lose everything. This means that you must make sure that you periodically save a copy to your hard drive or to a floppy. Do this at comfortable intervals and points at which it will be easy to resume work, should you have to start over. If you have a RAM disk and you have used it without a problem for some time, becoming complacent and not make copies is all too easy—but you will probably make that mistake only once.

If you use a PowerBook, Quadra, or a PowerMac, the Memory control panel lets you create a RAM disk. There is an additional advantage in using a RAM disk with a PowerBook: Your Mac does not start, run, and stop your hard drive if you place the application you're using onto the RAM disk. By keeping hard disk access to a minimum you gain extra usage time when operating from batteries.

Following are a couple of utilities that you might want to use if you are using a RAM disk:

❖ Maxima (Connectix)—A RAM disk utility that saves the contents of your RAM disk to your hard drive when you restart or shut down your Mac. The people at Connectix know almost as much about the Mac's memory as the folks at Apple.

❖ RAM Disk Saver (Atticus Software)—The biggest danger you face when using a RAM disk is that if your Mac crashes, you lose the contents of your RAM disk. RAM Disk Saver can minimize this danger because it copies the contents of your RAM disk to your hard disk while you work. This happens automatically so that you don't have to think about the process once you've installed RAM Disk Saver. This utility is a must-have if you use a RAM disk.

Memory Management Utilities

As previously mentioned, memory management will become a concern to you at some time. The problem you will face is that you just won't have enough memory. This happens to everyone regardless of how much RAM they have installed—it is the way of the computer world. When you consider that the first Macintosh had 128KB of RAM 12 years ago and that now you can't buy a new Mac with less than 16MB, soon to be 32MB, of RAM, you see what I mean. RAM and hard disk space are the two things you'll never have enough of. It is like not having enough time in a day—except that you can buy more RAM or another hard disk.

We discuss two utilities that just might help you with your RAM problems (maybe you don't need to buy that RAM just yet):

❖ RamDoubler (Connectix)—This program makes your Mac think it has twice as much RAM as it really has. Good trick, no? RamDoubler works by using a combination of technologies. It compresses your RAM, uses virtual disk space, and takes advantage of RAM that is not being used by other programs. If you have a Mac that can have only 8MB of RAM, such as one of the earlier PowerBooks, RamDoubler was made for you.

There are some things to consider when using RamDoubler: One, you do not really have any more RAM. RamDoubler makes your Mac think it has more RAM and performs technical tricks to conserve RAM, but if you have only 8MB of RAM and want to run a full Mac OS 8.0, including QuickDraw GX and OpenDoc, RamDoubler will not help you. You must have enough RAM to start your Mac without RamDoubler.

Another concern can be performance. If you use all of your RAM, RamDoubler uses virtual memory (a process in which your hard drive is used as RAM), which can slow down your Mac. Also, any program that uses virtual memory, such as PhotoShop, does not work well with RamDoubler. Finally, if you have a lot of RAM, say, 64MB, and install RamDoubler, some functions, especially starting programs and switching programs, slow down. Even with these caveats, RamDoubler is a great utility for those Macs that do not have enough of the right stuff.

❖ OptiMem (Jump Software)—OptiMem does not make your Mac think it has more RAM; it just makes more efficient use of the RAM you have. When OptiMem is installed, you can open almost twice the number of applications that you can right now. OptiMem works by using the memory that a program might reserve for itself but does not use. Remember one of our earlier discussions, where we covered setting the preferred memory size for an application in a program's Get Info window? Well, OptiMem starts a program using its minimum memory requirements and then gives it more RAM if it needs it. The RAM not used by the program is then made available to other programs.

Some programs don't like what OptiMem does, but OptiMem deals with that by letting you tell it which programs to leave alone and from which ones to steal memory. Although OptiMem does not free as much memory as RamDoubler, you do get better performance.

Adding Control Panels and Extensions

Any program or utility that you add to your Mac's system will come with an installer or you will have to install it manually. If you install the utility with an installer, everything is placed where it belongs. Should you have to install the utility manually, it is still an easy process that takes only a couple of steps. Before you install any control panel or system extension to your System, however, read the documentation that comes with the utility and any Read Me files on the disk. The utilities we've been discussing are control panels and system extensions that get loaded into your Mac's memory as it starts up. Another term for these types of programs is *memory-resident*. When a memory-resident program is loaded, it becomes part of your Mac's System and is always available for use.

Part and parcel of being memory-resident is the possibility for one extension or control panel to conflict with another. This happens when two memory-resident utilities want to occupy the same location in your Mac's RAM. Quite often, manufacturers know about other programs that conflict with theirs and put this information in either their manual or the Read Me file. You need to read everything before you perform your installation. If you don't read the documentation, you will learn about possible problems the hard way—when your Mac crashes.

Now that you have the technical information you need, let's perform a manual installation. To manually install any item that belongs in your System folder, just drag the item to your System folder icon; your Mac automatically places the file in its proper folder. Control panels go in the Control Panels folder; extensions find their way to the Extensions folder. The same thing happens with fonts and sounds. When you drag an item on to the System folder, a message like the one shown in Figure 8.9 appears. After you've installed a new extension or control panel, you need to restart your Mac.

As you start to install utilities, keep a few things in mind. If you install a utility that has the same function as one already installed, there is a good chance that the new utility will conflict with the one that's installed. An example is installing a hierarchical menu utility while the Apple Menu Options control panel is active. If you don't remove or turn off the Apple Menu Options, the next time you select one of the hierarchical menus in the Apple menu, your Mac might crash. This is another reason to understand what your Mac's utilities do. If you install a utility that somehow

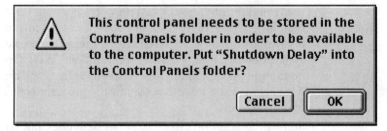

Figure 8.9 *The dialog box asking you if it is OK to install a system element.*

interacts with the Mac's Trash and then you install another one that also affects the Trash, you'll probably have a problem; this becomes a matter of experimentation. You won't know that you have a problem until you try to use one of the utilities; if you don't know that one or both of your utilities affect the Trash, you could search a long time for the problem caused by this conflict.

Try to learn what your system extensions and control panels do, in a general sense, and watch what you install. If you do have problems, read Chapter 18, "System and Application Troubleshooting," where specific steps for fixing these types of problems are discussed.

Remember the following points when installing memory-resident utilities:

1. Read the documentation.
2. Know what the new utility does.
3. Remove any utilities that have similar functions.
4. Install only one utility at a time.
5. Restart your Mac after you install each utility.
6. Use your Mac for awhile before you install another utility.
7. Repeat these steps for any memory-resident utility you install.

Summary

This chapter is, at best, a brief overview of some of the ways you can modify your Mac. Modifying your Mac is one way to make it your own, infusing your Mac with your personality. How you modify your Mac depends on how you view your computer. If using your Mac is a full-time occupation, you'll find yourself making changes and looking for ways to improve your performance. If your Mac is just a tool to accomplish a specific task, you won't want to take much time to play with it.

Don't let anyone tell you that you're using your Mac incorrectly unless you've asked for advice. I've seen too many instances in which a good-hearted person has tricked out someone's Mac and then left the country, so to speak, only to have the object of their good will misbehave. I hope this chapter has given you some insight into the possibilities and provided you with the knowledge you need to intelligently appropriate your Macintosh and make it your own.

Installing Your System and Software

S everal System versions ago, Apple introduced a program called the *Installer*. Its purpose was to automate and simplify what might otherwise be a complex and tedious process of installing your Macintosh's System software. Now you cannot properly install your System without the Installer, so the Installer is a primary topic of this chapter. Chapter 6 covers what the System actually does and how to use it.

This chapter shows you how to deal with the Installer, outlines some the different types of installations you can perform, and explains how you can upgrade to or install Mac OS 8. What you learn about the Installer in this chapter is not limited to installing Mac OS 8. About 60 percent or more of the software that you will install onto your Mac uses Apple's Installer. All the features covered in this chapter apply to the Apple Installer, whether you're installing Mac OS 8, applications, or utilities. Even though the primary focus of this chapter is installing System software, remember the principles involved so that you can use them when installing other software.

The following topics are covered in this chapter:

❖ The Apple Installer
❖ Using software updates
❖ Other types of installers

Do not be fooled by this short list of topics. The Apple Installer section contains a lot of technical information. In addition to learning about the Installer, you learn more about the System and your Macintosh. You learn technical details that might seem boring, but when the time comes for you to use this information, you'll know what you're doing and why.

At some point you will need the information in this chapter. You will eventually use this information for maintenance or troubleshooting. Possibly it will be late at night when you're working on a report that is due in the morning and things go wrong. (That's when things usually go wrong.) And if they do, this chapter, next to the troubleshooting chapters, could be the most important one in the book.

The Apple Installer

When you first got your Mac, it probably came with Mac OS 8 already installed. As you use your Mac or as new versions of the System are released, you will have to install or re-install your System, and you'll have to use the *Installer*. The Installer is a small program located on your Mac OS 8 CD. (Very few programs come on a floppy disk anymore; most are shipped on CD-ROMs.)

The installation process is no longer quick and simple. Although Apple has done everything possible to keep the process clean, its simplicity is actually an illusion. If you've read the manuals that came with your Mac or your Mac OS 8, you might wonder what the fuss is all about—the instructions in Apple's manuals are very straightforward. Apple has a nasty habit of not telling you everything, thinking that you don't need to know what your computer is doing or why things are done the way they are.

If you want to know what is happening and why, this section tells you as it looks at the following:

❖ What the Installer does

❖ Preparing for an upgrade or installation

❖ The installation

❖ After you upgrade

❖ Using the Installer to remove software

There is an order to the madness. You learn what the Installer does and the process of performing an installation. Before you install or re-install your Mac OS 8, read this whole section so that you know what to expect and what to do if something goes wrong.

If you started to install your System only to get a message that said something was wrong, you could spend the next hour trying to figure out the problem. Knowing what might happen before you start, as well as the precautions to take before you install your System, will save you time and possible heartache.

What the Installer Does

A very long time ago in computer years, with System 6.0.X, the Installer became an essential component for upgrading or installing the Macintosh System. The Installer consists of the Installer application and an Installer script. The Installer is a very flexible application that depends on the Installer script to perform its magic. Even though it is the script that controls the Installer, when we're talking about the installation process, we refer to the Installer instead of the Installer script.

What the Installer does is quite complicated, especially when you perform an Easy Install. It checks your Macintosh hardware to determine what model of Mac you use. It determines what type of disk drive onto which you are installing the System and checks the boot blocks of the drive for any necessary modifications. In addition to this, it checks your operating environment to determine what System software has previously been installed.

Boot block (1) An area on a formatted disk that signals the computer that the disk contains an application to be started up; (2) the first block of a file system or the first two logical blocks of a volume. The boot block contains the system's startup instructions.

The Installer is so important because the Installer script contains more than just instructions for installing the System. It also contains resources, bits of programming code, that can be essential for your Macintosh.

If you were to copy the System file, found in the System folder on the CD, onto your drive, you would not get the resources contained in the Installer script, and your new System would be unstable and prone to crashes. Even though the System on the Mac OS 8 CD will boot any Macintosh, it is not safe to run your Mac with this System. You need to install Mac OS 8 with the Installer.

Another reason for using the Installer is that the ROMs found on two different Macs, even if they are the same model, are not always identical. ROM in a Mac that was made in July may incorporate bug fixes or improvements that ROM in March Macs does not contain. The programmers responsible for the ROM and the operating system know this information and take it into consideration when writing Installer scripts. The Installer can determine what ROM your Mac has and make modifications to the System to compensate for differences in the ROM when it installs your System. This can mean the difference between smooth, trouble-free operation and irritating, random system errors.

System error (1) A crash that is accompanied by an alert box that has either a number code or phrase that identifies the source of the problem; (2) a generic term used for a *crash* or *hang*.

You should take several steps to make sure your installation is successful. Some of them are good maintenance steps that you should periodically perform, even when you are not installing or re-installing your System. Also, re-installing your System is some-

Technical Terms

Because of what the Installer does, some technical terms are thrown about freely in this chapter. Each of these terms is defined; you'll be referred to other chapters where more information regarding each term appears. The first of these terms is *boot block*.

Boot blocks are an area on every disk where information is stored that tells your Macintosh where to find the System file and other vital information about the disk drive. If there is a problem with a drive's boot blocks, your Macintosh cannot operate properly. More information about boot blocks can be found in Chapters 10 and 11.

thing that you should do occasionally, even when everything works properly. Re-installing the System can prevent and detect problems before they become disasters.

Preparing for an Upgrade or Installation

Unless you install the System onto a hard drive that has just been formatted, you need to take several steps before installing or re-installing your System. This section assumes that you have been using System 7.X. If you've been using System 6.0.X, think twice about installing Mac OS 8. You probably will not be too happy with the performance if Mac OS 8 even runs on your machine. If your Mac is a Mac II ci or later you can run Mac OS 8. You want to run Mac OS 8 on a Mac with a 68040 processor and preferably a PowerPC.

If you install your System onto a freshly formatted hard drive, you need to make sure your hard-drive driver is compatible with Mac OS 8; this is discussed in the coming section, "Update Your Hard-Disk Driver." All the essential information for updating a hard-drive driver is included in that section. From there, you can skip to the section, "Performing an Easy Install" or "Customizing Your Installation."

For the rest of you who are upgrading a System or re-installing your System, you need to read each of the following sections. Skipping any one of them could lead to an unsuccessful installation.

Back Up Your Hard Drive

Before you ever do anything radical with your Macintosh, always back up your hard drive. Even though installing the System may not seem like a radical procedure, it is. The first step to perform before upgrading or re-installing your System is to back up all your data.

Backup   A copy of a disk or of a file on a disk. It's a good idea to make backups of all your important disks and to use the copies for everyday work, keeping the originals in a safe place.

Information about backing up your hard drive appears in Chapter 11. Basically, to back up your hard drive, you need another hard drive, some type of storage backup mechanism, such as a tape drive, or a mess of floppy disks and a backup program. Unfortunately, Apple does not supply a backup program with its System software.

If you do not back up your entire hard drive, you need to back up your data files—you know, those files that you can't live without. If you would panic because a particular file got destroyed while you installed the System, copy that file onto a floppy disk. If it won't fit onto a floppy disk, read Chapter 11; do not install the System until the file is backed up.

Fixing Your Hard-Disk Directory

Every hard drive has a file that you can't see called the *volume directory*. This file tells your Mac where all the files on the hard drive are located. If something is wrong with the volume directory or your hard disk's directory, your Mac does not function properly. The Installer checks for this problem before it installs Mac OS 8. If the Installer detects a problem with your disk's directory, it does not complete the installation.

Volume directory   The main directory file of a volume (a hard drive can have several volumes). It contains the names and locations of the files on the volume, any of which may themselves be directory files (called subdirectories). The name of the volume directory is the name of the volume. The path name of every file on the volume starts with the volume directory name. (See also *directory file, subdirectory.*)

Directory file   Another name for the folders that appear on the top level of your Mac's hard drive. Although these appear to be the first set of folders on your Mac, they are the second to the volume directory. The folders contained by these folders or any other folder you see on your Mac are called subdirectories.

Subdirectory   Any folder which is inside of or contained by another folder.

The Mac has a very complex hard-disk structure, one that can easily be damaged. Also, a number of System software bugs have resulted in directory problems. Apple has spent a lot of time finding and correcting these bugs and none are super-critical, but re-installing your System is the perfect time to make sure your hard drive is fine. Perform this maintenance step even if you think it is redundant. If you try to install the System and there is a problem with your hard drive, the installation fails. It takes less time to check your hard drive and fix any problems than it does to start to install your System only to find out that you have problems. Play it safe from the very beginning.

To check your hard drive's directory, run Disk First Aid, found on your Disk Tools disk or in the Disk Tools folder on the Mac OS 8 CD. Disk First Aid fixes any directory damage caused by bugs in earlier System versions and checks for other disk-drive problems.

Running Disk First Aid is a simple task that takes just a few minutes. You cannot fix your startup disk or the disk that contains Disk First Aid with Disk First Aid. You have to boot your Macintosh from a drive other than the one you're fixing, from the Disk Tools disk or from the Mac OS 8 CD.

Follow these steps:

1. Boot your Mac with the Disk Tools disk. To boot from the CD, put the CD into your Mac; when you hear the start-up chime hold down the C key.
2. Start the Disk First Aid program. When it starts, a window like that shown in Figure 9.1 appears.
3. Select the drive you want to check by clicking on it.
4. Click on the Verify button. Verify checks the disk and tells you if it needs to be repaired.
5. If the disk needs to be repaired, click on the Repair button. After a disk has been repaired, a message that says the repair was successful appears.

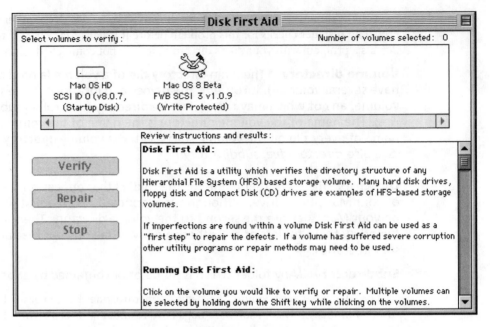

Figure 9.1 *The Disk First Aid window.*

6. Repeat steps 3 through 5 for any additional disks you wish to check.

7. Quit Disk First Aid.

If you were unable to repair a disk, the disk needs to be reformatted before you continue. Trying to install a System onto a damaged disk will only cause more problems, and a hard disk with a problem is a disaster waiting to happen. Chapter 10 tells you how to format your hard drive. Once you're sure your hard disk is healthy, go on to the next step, upgrading your hard disk's driver.

Update Your Hard-Disk Driver

The Mac has software called the SCSI Manager built into its ROM. The SCSI Manager tells the Mac how to communicate with SCSI peripherals, primarily hard drives. The SCSI Manager, when working with hard disks, uses what is called a *hard-disk driver*, stored on the hard drive and loaded into the Mac's memory as it boots. This means that the hard-disk driver and the SCSI Manager have to be compatible; if they are not, you have problems with your hard disk.

SCSI Manager   The part of the Macintosh Operating System that controls the exchange of information between a Macintosh and peripheral devices connected through the Small Computer Standard Interface (SCSI).

The next step is to make sure your hard-disk driver is compatible with Mac OS 8. If you use an Apple hard drive, you'll have no problems because you can update your hard disk's driver as part of the Mac OS 8 installation. If you do not use an Apple hard drive, check with the drive's manufacturer to make sure your drive is Mac OS 8-compatible. If you have to update your hard disk's driver and it is not an Apple drive, follow the manufacturer's instructions when you get your updated driver. You can find more information about hard-disk drivers in Chapters 10 and 11.

This completes the second step you need to perform before you install your System. Do not forget to do this; it's essential to upgrading your System.

Are Your Applications Compatible?

After you have checked and/or upgraded your drive, you're ready to go—or are you? You need to think about the programs you use. In most instances, if your program works with System 7.5, it will work with Mac OS 8. The programs that have problems are utility programs that alter the appearance of the Finder. It is always a good idea to upgrade all your important programs before you upgrade the operating system. Call the software's publisher or check its World Wide Web site for any applications that have to work after the upgrade (see Chapter 14 for information about the World Wide Web).

You also need to consider hardware upgrades, such as accelerators, third-party video displays, some scanners, and any piece of hardware you have had installed in your Mac. If the hardware was made before 1989, chances are very good that it is not Mac OS 8-compatible. If the hardware was manufactured before May 1991, it may or may not be compatible; you will have to check it out. All hardware that was System 7.0- or 7.5-compatible should be Mac OS 8-compatible.

If you have two hard drives, upgrade only one of them to Mac OS 8. Leave the other with your current System. This way, if you do run into problems, you can boot from the other drive and not suffer the pain of de-installing, then re-installing System software.

The Installation

Now that you know the prerequisites for installing your System, start planning your installation. As you can see, installing the System is a little more complicated that just running the Installer. Read this section, then make a plan.

Think about everything you will have to do and estimate how much time it will take; an Easy Install takes about an hour on a PowerMac 7200. Once you have your time estimate, double it. It often takes more time than you'd expect. If you're not sure that you'll have enough time, wait until you do. Although an installation is supposed to be fairly simple, if things don't go right, you could be in for a long session, or you could lose data, both.

This section describes three different types of Mac OS 8 installations. One is called an Easy Install. The next is a Custom Install, and the third type is a Maintenance Install. The Maintenance Install is the type of installation you do to upgrade or to remedy System problems.

Performing an Easy Install

An Easy Install is just that—an installation in which you don't make any decisions other than to install the System software. The Installer script is programmed to determine what you need and to install it. In many cases, an Easy Install will be fine, but on some occasions you will want to have more control over what is or is not installed. If you want more control over how your System is configured, do *not* use the Easy Install option.

The installation process starts in one of three ways. You can boot your Mac with the Disk Tools disk, the Mac OS 8 CD-ROM, or another hard drive and install from the Mac OS 8 CD-ROM. To start the installation process, double-click on the Install Mac OS icon.

To perform an Easy Install:

1. The first thing you see after launching the Installer is a Welcome window. It provides information about the steps to perform before installing Mac OS 8 and a Continue button (see Figure 9.2). Clicking the Continue button or pressing Return navigates you through the steps.

2. The next step is to select the hard drive where you will install Mac OS 8. Click on the pop-up menu, which shows Mac OS HD, in Figure 9.3. This window provides information about your selected hard drive, the current Mac OS, and the opportunity to perform a Clean Installation. If you want to perform a Clean Installation, check the "Perform Clean Installation"

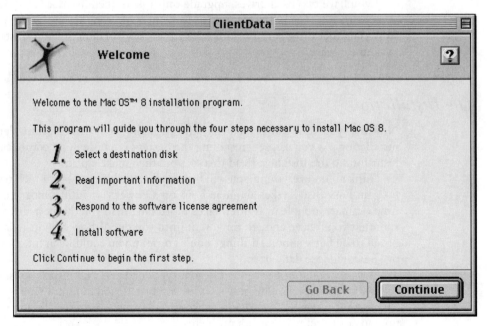

Figure 9.2   *The Installer's Welcome screen.*

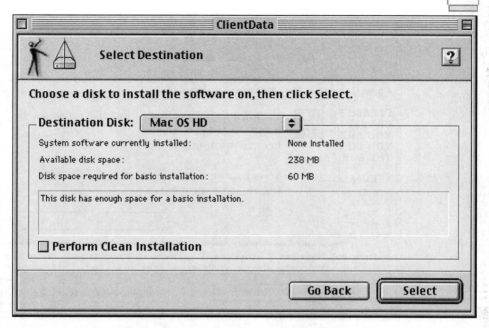

Figure 9.3 *The Installer's Select Destination window.*

Option. Figure 9.3 shows the Select Destination window. Click on the Select button to move to the next window.

3. The next window is an information window that contains copyright notices and late-breaking information about Mac OS 8. To get to the next window click on the Continue button.

4. After the information window, the Software License Agreement window appears. This window contains the Software License you must agree to before you can use Mac OS 8. The Continue button causes an agreement notice to appear (Figure 9.4). You must agree to the notice to install Mac OS 8.

5. After you click on the Agree button, the Install Software window appears. In this window, select the components of Mac OS 8 to install. If you are installing on a disk that does not have a System, a basic Mac OS 8 System with QuickDraw 3D, Internet Access, Cyberdog, and MacLinkPlus is automatically selected for installation. See Figure 9.5.

At this point you have several options. You can select additional software installations, as shown in Figure 9.6. Most of the software listed in Figure 9.6 is discussed in Chapter 7; some of it is discussed in Chapters 12 and 14.

The default software selection can be called an Easy Install because the Installer makes all your choices, performing a default Mac OS 8 installation. The Easy Install does not tell you what is being installed, only that *all of the recommended System software* for your Macintosh will be installed. If you're upgrading to Mac OS 8 the *installation includes all of the updated System software* for your Macintosh.

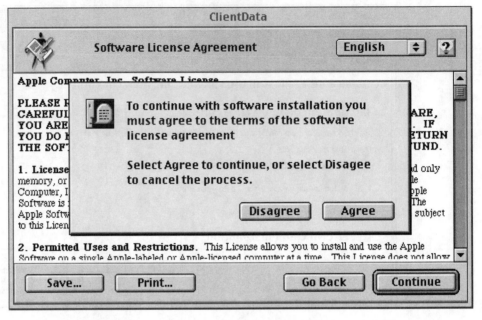

Figure 9.4 *The Software License Agreement dialog box.*

Figure 9.5 *The Install Software window.*

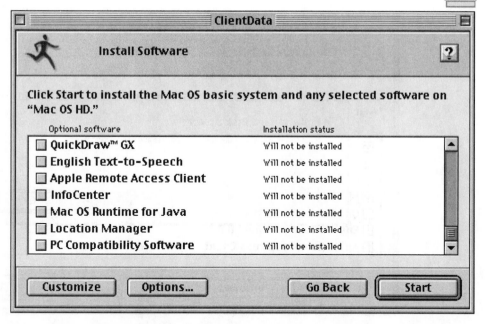

Figure 9.6 *Additional software options.*

The first time you perform an installation, I recommend that you do an Easy Install; a Custom Install is discussed later. Clicking the Start button starts the Easy Install. From this point on, the installation process is automatic. Once you are more familiar with the process you can experiment with customized installations. If there is System software (a System folder on the top level of your hard drive) on your hard drive, the Installer updates only the software already on your Mac.

The final choice you have to make before performing an Easy Install is whether to upgrade your hard-disk driver. Clicking on the Options... button presents the dialog box shown in Figure 9.7. The choice to update the drivers for all Apple hard disks is automatically selected. If you don't have any Apple hard drives, un-check this selection

6. The final step is to click on the Install button.

   The Installer first checks the hard drive, updates the driver, and starts the installation process. The Installer goes through a series of steps to determine exactly what it will install. Then, the Installer displays a window showing the folder(s) it uses from the CD-ROM, as shown in Figure 9.8.

7. When the install is done, you can continue with more installations or quit. If you're done, quit the Installer by clicking on the Quit button. If you click on the Continue button, you can install the System onto another disk by repeating steps 1–6. When you Quit after installing from a CD-ROM, restart using the *Restart* item from the Finder's Special menu. When your Mac restarts, your new System is running.

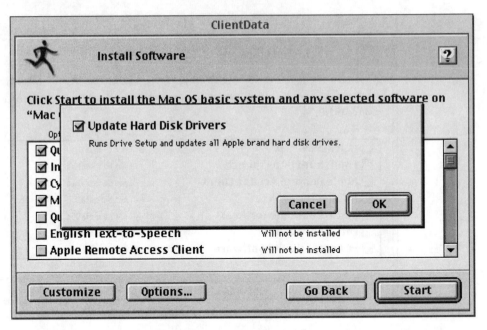

Figure 9.7 *The hard-disk driver update option.*

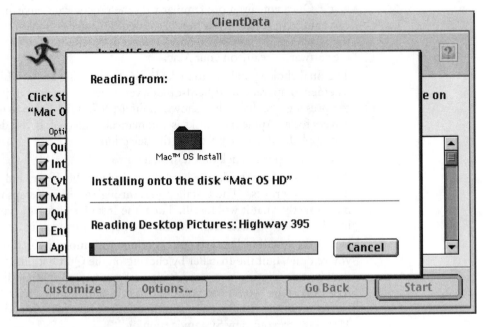

Figure 9.8 *The installation in progress.*

Doing a Clean Install

A Clean Install is an installation of Mac OS 8 that replaces your existing System folder with a new Mac OS 8 System folder. There is no need to perform a Clean Install if you are installing Mac OS 8 onto a newly formatted hard drive; a clean install is done automatically. The Clean Install places a new Mac OS 8 folder onto your hard drive while preserving your existing System folder. After the installation your old System folder does not work.

Customizing Your Installation

The basic instructions for using Apple's Installer are in the previous section, "Performing an Easy Install." I will not repeat the instructions for using the Installer here. If you skipped "Performing an Easy Install," glance through it now to familiarize yourself with those steps. This section discusses the Installer only in terms of a customized installation.

Ideally, you should perform a customized install because you can install the System elements you need or want. To perform a customized installation, click on the Customize button in the Install Software window shown in Figure 9.5. The Install Software window changes to the Custom Installation and Removal window, as shown in Figure 9.9.

The software selection is the same as that described earlier. The other steps that the installer goes through, such as checking the hard drive, are also the same. The

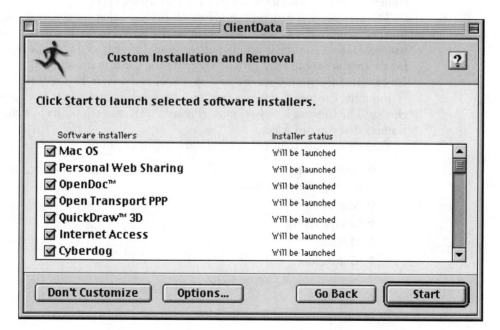

Figure 9.9   The Custom Installation and Removal window.

Figure 9.10   *The Mac OS 8.0 install dialog box.*

difference is that you have an opportunity to customize each software installation as the Mac OS Install program launches the individual installers. As each installer launches, a dialog box like the one in Figure 9.10 appears.

The next window that appears (Figure 9.11) is another version of Apple's installation program. Each of the software programs checked in the Install System Software window launches a similar installer application. In Figure 9.11, the default selection for the installer is the Easy Install. To get to the Custom Install window, select the Custom Install option from the pop-up menu, as shown in Figure 9.12.

From the Custom Install window, you can select as many or as few options as you choose. The Custom Install window (Figure 9.13) lists each of the System's software features that you can select.

Your choices are to install System software for any of the following:

- ❖ System Software—You can install software for just your Mac, any Mac, or a Core (minimal) System.
- ❖ Assistance
- ❖ Compatibility
- ❖ Mobility
- ❖ Multimedia
- ❖ Networking & Connectivity
- ❖ Printing
- ❖ Utility
- ❖ International

Figure 9.11 *The Installer window.*

Figure 9.12 *Installer's pop-up menu.*

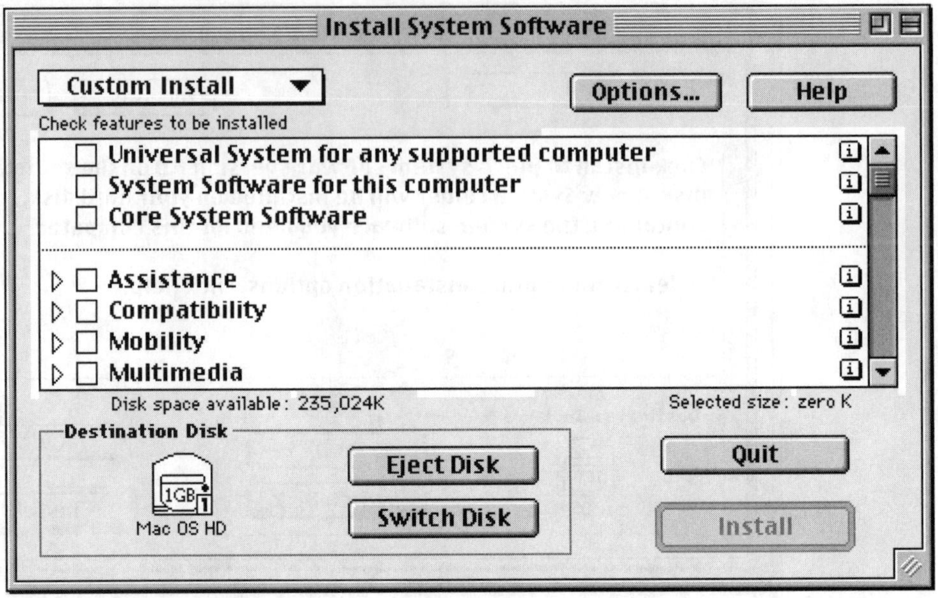

Figure 9.13 *The Custom Install window.*

In addition to the System software listed here, you can individually install any of the following system elements:

❖ Apple menu items

❖ Control panels

❖ Extensions

❖ Fonts

Next to each of these selections is an arrow. By clicking on the arrow, the category selection expands to list the items that you can install. Figure 9.14 shows the available Assistance selections.

If you install the System onto an external hard drive that you use on different machines, select the *Universal System for any supported computer* option. If you install the system onto your internal hard drive, select *System for this computer*. Which options you choose are entirely up to you. The *International* option installs keyboard layouts for several different countries.

Should you have any questions about an option, click on the information button to the right of most options. Clicking on the button displays a window that tells you about the option. Also, read Chapter 7 before attempting a custom installation. All of the control panels and most of the other options, some of which are extensions, are briefly explained.

Once you've gone through the list and selected the options you want, perform the installation using the steps described in the earlier section, "Performing an Easy Install." Besides customizing your System to meet your needs, there is one more reason for performing a Custom Install: to add capabilities that you did not install origi-

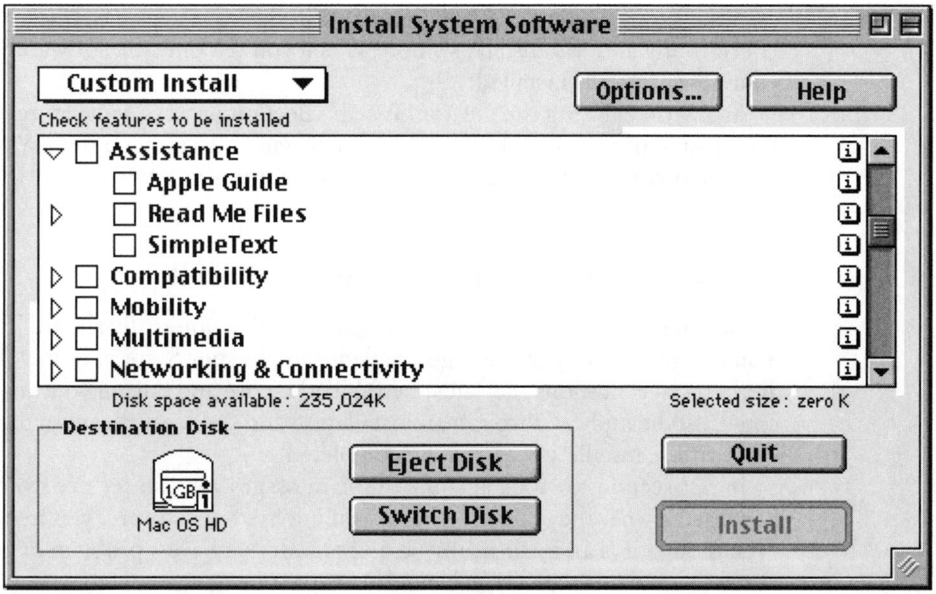

Figure 9.14 *The Assistance options.*

nally. Let's say you just got a LaserWriter (lucky you). In order for it to work with your Mac, you need to install the printer's driver. The easiest way to do this is via a Custom Install, in which you select just the LaserWriter, as shown in Figure 9.15.

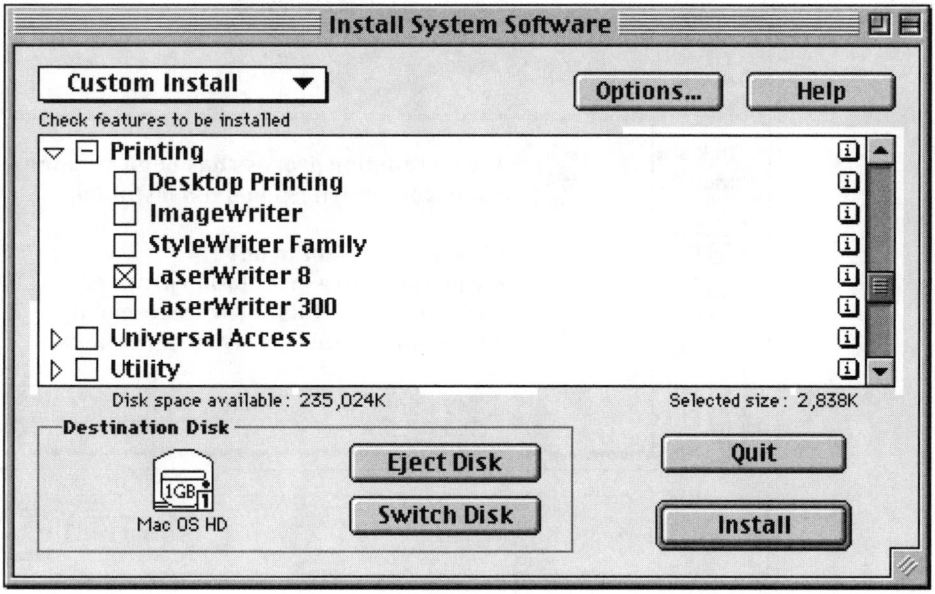

Figure 9.15 *Selecting a single element for installation.*

After selecting your LaserWriter driver, follow the steps described in the "Performing an Easy Install" section. When you're done, the software you need for your new printer is installed.

At any time during the Custom Install selection process, you can revert to the Easy Install process by selecting the Easy Install pop-up menu item. You can also quit the process without installing anything by pressing Quit.

Things That Can Happen during an Install

Some things can happen during an installation that you really should know about. You can get a variety of messages while installing your System. Some of the messages alert you to conditions that must be fulfilled before and during your installation. You could also be midway through an installation and suddenly receive a message telling you that the installation cannot be completed.

In this section, we look at some of the messages you can receive from the Installer and discuss what they mean. When installing System software, you need to stay alert even though it is an intrinsically boring task. If you have a problem or respond incorrectly to an inquiry, you may have to start over.

If you cancel an installation, whether anything is installed on your hard drive depends on timing—did you cancel during the first installer or latter ones? If you cancel an installation and one or more installers have finished, the software they install will be on your hard drive. Figure 9.16 shows the dialog box that you get when you cancel.

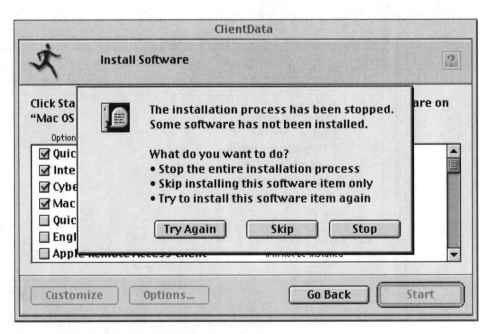

Figure 9.16 After canceling the installation.

Replacing Files during an Install

If you replace a file that was updated by some other software installation, you could have problems with the other software, and you might have to re-install an application. The challenge is determining which application needs to be re-installed. Should one of your programs break after an installation in which you replaced existing files, try re-installing the misbehaving application.

When you cancel an installation you always have a choice to resume, skip, or cancel the installation. If you continue, everything proceeds as if you had done nothing. If you stop, however, you may not be able to use the System on your hard drive. If the System should work, it will not be stable. In other words, do not use a hard drive with a System from an interrupted install. When stopping the install, the Installer performs some cleanup. You get a warning message after you have stopped the install process. Remember that the disk is no longer reliable as a startup disk.

While doing an install, if you are upgrading or re-installing your System software over an existing System folder, you could receive a dialog box like the one shown in Figure 9.17. This dialog box appears when the creation date of an item being replaced is newer than its replacement. If you receive this dialog box while installing Mac OS 8 you should think twice about whether you want to replace the file.

When upgrading an existing System folder, the Installer removes drivers, extensions, control panels, and resources from the System file and System folder prior to installing new elements. Before the Installer removes these items, it checks their dates and compares them with the dates of their replacements. If you are re-installing your

Figure 9.17 Replacing a newer file.

System, you are probably having problems, so you might as well replace all the items the Installer asks you about.

Another event that can occur during an installation is an error that causes the installation to abort. Virus checkers that haven't been turned off can cause an error or a problem with a file or your hard disk. When an error aborts the installation process, a message like the one shown n Figure 9.18 appears.

As you can see, you have three choices when an error occurs. Usually the Try Again choice fails. If you know the cause of the error, stop, fix the error, and then re-install Mac OS 8. The one message you should be very concerned about is a disk-error message. A disk-error message appears if the Installer has a hard time reading or writing to your disk or if it detects problems with the disk's structure. This message means one of two things: Either you didn't check your disk with Disk First Aid, or there is a problem with your disk that Disk First Aid could not detect or fix.

First, acknowledge the message and quit the Installer. After you've quit, run Disk First Aid. If Disk First Aid detects no problems, try installing the Mac OS 8 again. If the second install attempt is unsuccessful, you have only a couple of options:

- ❖ Your hard drive is seriously sick.
- ❖ Your Mac OS 8 CD is damaged and needs to be replaced.

It is more likely that your hard drive is seriously ill; CDs usually don't go bad. Whatever you do, don't boot from the hard drive until you've determined what is wrong. Your System could be seriously damaged due to an incomplete install. And, if your drive is damaged, booting from it could make matters worse.

To determine what is wrong:

1. Try to install the System again.
2. If the install fails, you probably have a hard-drive problem; read Chapters 10 and 18.

Figure 9.18   The abort dialog box.

Chances are, you have to back up your data (if you haven't already done so) and reformat your hard drive. A disk repair program, such as Norton Disk Doctor, published by Symantec, may be able to solve your problems. Read about disk drives and hard-disk troubleshooting before proceeding. What you learn has a definite bearing on what you do.

If you find yourself at this point and you still can't install your System, consider your data to be in imminent peril. If you haven't made a backup, make one now, even if you spend the entire night swapping floppy disks because you have to boot from your System Tools disk.

If you don't back up your data, at least turn off your Mac until you can read the necessary chapters or get help from a professional. If you do have a backup, the worst that can happen is that you have to reformat your hard drive and restore your data from the backup.

This information covers most of the contingencies that can occur while installing your new System. Remember that it is always better to err on the side of caution. If you are ever in doubt about what is happening during an installation, quit, read some more, contact a local users group for help, or call a professional consultant. Without a System, your Mac will not work and your data is useless.

Installing over a Network

When you have several Macs to upgrade, doing a network install is the easiest approach. The advantages of installing from a file server are speed and convenience.

This section provides instructions for installing your System software over a network. This procedure works with any software that uses the Apple Installer, version 3.2 or later. If you need instructions for using your network or setting it up, read Chapter 13.

It used to be that you had to copy all kinds of folders and arrange them just so on the network server before you could perform the installation. Now, all you have to do

Software License

If you do a network install, you are required by law to have a license agreement that allows you to install your software onto several machines. All software is copyrighted and protected by law for use with a specific number of computers. When you buy software at the computer store, you usually purchase software for use on a single computer. To install the software on more than one computer can be a violation of the license, and, if you are caught using it on more than one machine, you could be prosecuted.

is put the Mac OS 8 CD into the server and share the CD. Then mount the CD on the machine you're upgrading and run the Installer. This is just too simple, isn't it?

Doing a Minimum Install

A Minimum Install installs just the files needed to run your Mac. This special-purpose installation should be done only on a drive that you use for a special purpose and to conserve memory. Don't perform a Minimum Install (Core Installation) unless you know why.

Ready to Go

Now, it's time to get down to business. First of all, check to see that you have all of these items ready:

❖ Mac OS 8 CD

❖ A Mac OS 8 Disk Tools disk, or a Mac OS 8-compatible formatter for your hard drive

❖ A backup of your hard drive (If something should go wrong, you do not want to have to read the five chapters of Part V, "Troubleshooting," to fix it.)

❖ Your favorite nonalcoholic beverage and maybe a book

❖ Enough time to complete the task (the installation of Mac OS 8 could take more than an hour)

Now you are ready to begin. Installing the Mac OS 8 is not a fun task, but a necessary one. It is like changing the oil in your car: The task takes time, it is an inconvenience, and it can be messy. Not only that, but it is sometimes just the beginning. If you have to re-install software after installing the System, you're in for a few hours of work. Sometimes having the TV close by can help.

After You Upgrade

Now that you have installed your System, you may need to perform a few more tasks. If you upgraded over an existing version 7.X System, you're done. Test your Mac to make sure everything works as it should.

Run a few programs, play with your control panels, and spend a few minutes doing what you normally would do with your Mac—write a letter, create a report, or fiddle with your database. If everything works, you're home free.

If you've just done a Clean Install you have more work to do. It is time to put everything back where it belongs—another tedious process. As you restore your extensions, control panels, and preference files, you need to test your System frequently to make sure everything works properly.

The rest of this section explains how to restore parts of your System that were not installed by Apple's installer. Once all your software tools and toys have been restored and everything works, you are done.

Now all you have to do is re-install your fonts, desk accessories, and extensions. All of these should have been preserved if you did not throw away your old System folder and kept the ones you removed from your System before you trashed it.

Re-installing System Elements

This section tells you how to re-install your fonts, desk accessories, extensions, control panels, and preference files from your old System folder. *Ideally, you should re-install any of your commercial utilities, including fonts, from their original disks.* Some utilities must be restored from their master disks. You may not know which files can be manually installed and which ones have to be re-installed from their original disks. Not knowing which files are compatible can make the process described in this section a bit touchy.

So, if any of your software patches the System during installation and if you re-install the part of the utility that is an extension or control panel, it won't work. It could even cause your Mac to crash. For this reason, you need to test your Mac frequently when you manually install your extensions and control panels.

If you manually re-install your extensions and control panels, you need to restore everything in the manner presented. These instructions are brief but sufficient to get you up and running. Although this is a fairly simple process, be careful not to replace any devices installed by the Installer. Be forewarned: The simplicity can be deceiving.

Review Chapter 6 if you are unsure about where things belong. Having folders for everything is great for keeping order within the System folder, but should any of these devices not be Mac OS 8-compatible, they will not work properly when they are installed in their new homes. Repeat the following steps for each type of System element you restore. In the steps, the word *element* means extensions, control panels, preference, or font, depending on the type of System file you are moving.

To move your extensions after upgrading:
If you are re-installing Mac OS 8 or upgrading from an earlier version of System 7.X, follow these steps:

1. Open your old System folder.
2. Open your new System folder.
3. View the contents of both System folders By Name.
4. Open the *element* folder in your old System folder.
5. Open the *element* folder in your new System folder.
6. View both *element* folders by Name.
7. Arrange your Desktop so that you can see both of the *element* folders.
8. Move two *elements* from the old System folder to the *element* folder in the new System folder. Move only those *elements* that do not have a duplicate in your new System folder.
9. Restart your Mac after moving two *elements*. Make sure you remember the *elements'* names.
10. If your Mac crashes, boot it with your Disk Tools disk and remove one of the last two *elements* you moved.

11. Restart your Mac again.

12. If your Mac crashes, remove the other *element* and restart.

13. Your Mac should start. Repeat steps 8–10 using the *element* you removed in step 10.

14. If your Mac crashes, both of the *elements* are incompatible and should not be used. If it starts, the *element* removed in step 12 is incompatible and should not be used.

If you have a system *element* that is incompatible, contact the software publisher and get a new, updated version that is Mac OS 8-compatible.

During this process, be very careful not to replace one of your new System files with an old one. If you do, you will have to re-install the System to recover the lost file because your Mac will not run properly.

When moving fonts and desk accessories, take a couple more precautions. After you install a couple of desk accessories, run the desk accessory. Desk accessories do not load into memory when your Mac starts, so that the Mac did not crash does not mean the desk accessory is compatible. The only test is to run the desk accessory. If your Mac survives and doesn't crash, then the DA is compatible.

Fonts are another story. Be careful not to install duplicate fonts. Even though a suitcase does not have a duplicate name, you may still install a duplicate font. The fonts are inside the suitcase, so you could have one suitcase named *Chicago* and another named *New York* yet still have duplicate fonts. The only way to avoid duplicate fonts is to open the suitcases and compare their contents.

Fonts are tricky, so you should install them from their original disks rather than move them from the old System folder to the new.

The final part of this process is moving folders and files that do not belong in one of the other folders; I call them extras. When upgrading from System 7.X to Mac OS 8, this is a fairly easy process. Again, this is another argument for re-installing your software rather that trying to reconstruct your System folder.

Moving the extras should be done last. For System 6.0.X, after you've moved everything, all you have left can be moved from the old System folder to the new System folder. Move these files and the folder one or two at a time, testing your Mac frequently. Moving the extras from an old System 7.X folder to a new Mac OS 8 folder is fairly quick. Just follow the guidelines I set out here; don't move anything that already exists in the new System folder, and test frequently.

If you're lucky, when you've finished your Mac runs just fine. If you're not lucky, you have problems. At this point, if you have problems, you can either do a new Clean Install, re-install your software from your original disks, or read Part V of this book, which contains five chapters related to troubleshooting your Mac.

Doing a Maintenance Install

I've been calling the procedure described in this section a "clean install" for several years. Apple has built a feature into its Installer that is also called a "Clean Install" so

I now call this type of installation a Maintenance Install. The Maintenance Install in this section replaces the System, Finder, and other System elements. Whenever I re-install or upgrade a Mac I do a Maintenance Install.

To perform a Maintenance Install, throw away your System file and Finder. This is also the only way to guarantee that you get a clean System install and keep your existing configuration. If you install over your old System, the old System may be missing or may have damaged resources that the Installer does not re-install. This is especially true if you re-install because you have some type of problem.

The only time you should not trash your old System file is when you perform the upgrade over a network. Removing your System file when installing over the net-work makes doing the installation impossible. And when you trash your System and Finder you can no longer boot from your hard drive unless you successfully re-install Mac OS 8.

Trashing the System:

1. Open the Extensions Manager control panel and save your current exten-sion set.
2. Select the Mac OS 8 All set of extensions.
3. Restart your Mac and double check your extensions set.
4. Boot your Mac from the Disk Tools disk, as second hard drive, or your Mac OS 8 CD.
5. Open the System folder on your hard drive.
6. Select the System and the Finder (shift-click on them).
7. Drag them to the Trash.
8. Install Mac OS 8.
9. Reboot your Mac.
10. Empty the Trash using the *Empty Trash* command from the Special menu.
11. Select your original extension set from the Extensions Manager and reboot.

Once again, the only time trashing the System does not work is when you do an over-the-network install. If, after you install the System, you still have problems, you probably need to perform a Clean Install. Your Mac's problems might not be caused by System problems.

Using the Installer to Remove Software

You can also use the Installer to remove your System software. Say, for instance, you want to remove the ImageWriter drivers from your System because you got that LaserWriter and no longer use an ImageWriter. To do this, click on the Customize button from the Install Software window. Then select the Custom Remove pop-up menu item in the Installer window and follow the instructions for a Custom Install. Just remember that you are *removing* software rather than installing it.

Using Software Updates

Apple is committed to releasing quarterly updates for the Mac OS. These updates are enhancements and bug fixes. The feature enhancements are released as updates, and every once in a while they are released as major revisions of the Mac OS. You can find any updates at Apple's World Wide Web (WWW) site or your Authorized Apple Dealer. The updates all use an installer like the one described in this chapter.

Bug fix   A bug fix is a correction for a software problem. Usually these problems are small and rarely noticed.

Other Types of Installers and Installing Applications

Most software comes with an installer. Not all software, though, comes with Apple's Installer. Several companies make installers; you are likely to see some of them as you use your Mac.

Although these other installers have their own features, they all share one feature: They install all parts of a program in their proper place. Also, all software comes with installation instructions, which tell you how to use the installers; if the manual is very good, it tells you where a program's files are placed as well.

Whenever you install software, take a few minutes to see what files were installed. Check your System, Preferences, Control Panels, and Extensions folders. Also look in the folder the application creates for itself. The more you know about where the files are stored, the easier it will be if you have to rebuild your System or troubleshoot a problem with the application.

Summary

There you have it. Now you know all the various ways to install the Mac's System software and, by extension, other software. Although very little was said about software installations or using earlier versions of Apple's Installer, the principles for using the current versions of the Installer apply to both software installations and earlier versions of Installer.

As you go through this book, remember that you can always apply the examples and information presented in other computing situations. Such things as patching the System are discussed again. The structure of the System folder and the elements it contains are discussed again as well. In a sense, everything about the Mac can be circular, where one subject leads to another and eventually back to itself. After installing the System, we will go back and explore more of its capabilities.

Macintosh Disk Drives

Introduction

I f one aspect of your Mac is more important than all of the others, it is probably your Mac's disk drives. Knowing about your hard drive is almost as important as knowing how to use your computer because your hard drive holds all your work. In a sense, the drive is your Mac's heart. If your drive develops problems, all your data is at risk. Thus, learning about your drives is an important subject. You need to be able to detect problems early and perform minor maintenance so that you can know your data is safe.

In this chapter, you learn how your disk drives work, how to use them, and how to get the most from your Macintosh drives. In addition to learning about your floppy and hard-disk drives, this chapter looks at other storage media, including Optical Disk drives, CD-ROMs, and tape drives. By the time you finish reading this chapter, you will have a working knowledge of Macintosh storage systems.

The sections in this chapter are as follows:

❖ "The Macintosh Floppy Disk Drive." Here you find a detailed guide for your Macintosh floppy drive, including information on floppy disks, the drive mechanism, and how your drive reads and writes data. In addition, this section has information regarding disk formatting and more material on using, taking care of, and troubleshooting your floppy drives.

❖ "You and Your Hard Drives." This section covers everything you need to know about your hard drive(s). The subjects covered include the difference between floppy and hard-drive formats, the SCSI bus, and tips for getting the most from your drives. Some discussions are technical, but they are interspersed with many practical tips.

❖ "Your Storage Options." Just what are your options when it comes to data storage? If you want to know about optical drives, CD-ROM disks, tape drives, or other data storage options, you just have to read this section.

Your Macintosh Floppy Disk Drive

To fully understand your disk drive, you need to know what a floppy disk is and how it works. You will gain a working knowledge to help you avoid making mistakes with your floppy disks that could cause you to lose data or ruin your drive. You will also gain some basic skills to help you troubleshoot your system if and when something goes wrong.

Why Call It a Floppy Disk?

When you look at the floppy disk used in your Macintosh, you see a 3.5-inch square piece of plastic with a movable trapdoor on one side. You can identify the bottom of the disk by the quarter-sized spindle; the top's indent occupies about half the total space of the disk where you place the label (see Figure 10.1).

If you hold the disk so that the trapdoor faces you and the disk is right side up, you see a small, square hole in the upper right corner of the disk—the disk's write-lock indicator. On the opposite side of the disk is a movable tab. When the tab is moved so that it blocks the hole, the disk is unlocked, or write-enabled, which means your computer can write data to the disk. When you move the tab and expose a hole through the disk, your disk is write-disabled, or locked. Your Mac can read a locked disk, but it cannot write or put information onto a locked disk.

When you insert a disk into your Mac, the drive mechanism automatically opens the trapdoor so that it can access the disk. You can do this yourself by moving the door to the right if the trapdoor faces you. What you see is the disk itself; the plastic surrounding the disk and protecting it is called the *housing*. **Caution:** Be careful not

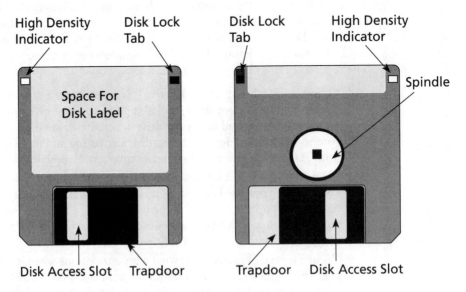

Figure 10.1 *Floppy disk, top and bottom view.*

to touch the actual disk. It is visible in the vertical slot revealed when you move the trapdoor.

Floppy disks are made of Mylar, a plastic material similar to that used for recording tape, and coated on both sides with a ferrous material so that they can hold a magnetic charge. Data is stored on this ferrous material similar to the way the grooves in a phonograph record hold the sound that a record player reproduces. The data consists of little pieces of magnetic material (usually iron or cobalt) being charged (on) or uncharged (off); each piece of material represents a bit, 8 bits become a byte, and all of this is recognizable to the computer.

High Density and Double Density

Disk size is determined not by the physical size of the drive, but by how much data it holds. A disk's data capacity is directly related to its density, which is determined by how much magnetic material is on a disk. The very first Macintoshes used a single-sided 3.5-inch disk drive that was 400 kilobytes in size. Some of these disks are still in use, and any Macintosh floppy drive can read them, but if you have a Mac running System 7.X or greater, you can't format or write to one of these early disks.

The next generation of Macs used a double-sided, double-density disk, or an 800-kilobyte disk. The Macs that have an 800K disk drive are the Mac 512KE, Plus, SE, and II. This size increase occurred because these drives could read both sides of a floppy disk; hence, the designation *double sided*. All new Macs produced since the SE/30 and the Mac IIcx have a high-density floppy drive (HDFD), also called a SuperDrive. The designation *high-density* versus double-density (the 800K floppy) describes an increase in the number of magnetic particles on a diskette. A high-density floppy disk holds 1.44 MB of data; you can differentiate it from an 800K floppy by the small, square hole in the upper left corner of the disk (see Figure 10.1).

How a Floppy Drive Works

At its simplest, a floppy disk drive can be compared to a phonograph. Instead of reproducing sound stored on the record, it reads data stored on the disk. It can also record (or write) to the same record. This section describes how a floppy drive works.

Every floppy drive consists of a spindle motor, an actuator arm, a read head, and a write head (see Figure 10.2). The spindle motor, which acts like the motor in a record player that turns the platter, turns the disk. The actuator arm contains the read and write heads in the same way the arm of a record player holds the needle. The actuator arm moves the drive's heads with an in-and-out motion over the surface of the floppy disk as it spins.

The disk drive has two actuator arms, one for each side of the disk. The actuator motor moves both arms simultaneously, positioning them in the same spot on opposite sides of the disk. A logic board on the drive controls the movement of the actuator arms and heads, which, in turn, is controlled by the logic board on the computer.

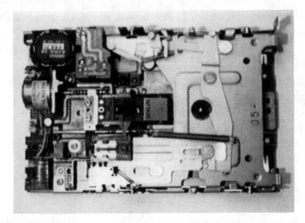

Figure 10.2 *Diagram of a floppy-disk drive.*

When you insert a floppy disk into your Mac, the trapdoor opens as the disk drops down onto the spindle and starts to spin. When the heads of the drive move, they rest on the floppy disk—actually, the floppy disk is pinched between the heads. At this point, your floppy disk is spinning at about 300 rpm while the actuator arms are moving in and out along the vertical slot in the disk's housing as they read or write data to the disk.

Reading and Writing Data

Very small electronic coils of a ferrous material in the heads are turned into small electromagnets when electricity is passed through them. Your Mac records (writes) data to the floppy disk by charging (turning on) the electromagnet, which, in turn, charges a small particle in the magnetic coating on the disk. As a result, each particle is either on or off. When the drive reads a disk, it senses a disruption or lack of disruption in the magnetic field of the disk and can tell if a particle is on or off. The on and off charges are binary signals that the computer then interprets and turns into meaningful output.

Formatting Your Diskettes

Usually, when you buy new floppy disks, they are unformatted. Your Mac cannot read a floppy disk until it has prepared it for use. The preparation process is called *formatting* or *initializing* the disk. When you format or initialize a disk, your Mac writes tracks and sectors to it and then adds boot blocks, a file directory, and the Desktop file.

If a disk has never been formatted, when you put it into your Mac, your Mac automatically detects this and asks if you want to initialize the disk. A dialog box like the one shown in Figure 10.3 appears. If you are sure the disk you inserted is blank, then click on the Initialize button; otherwise, click on the Cancel button.

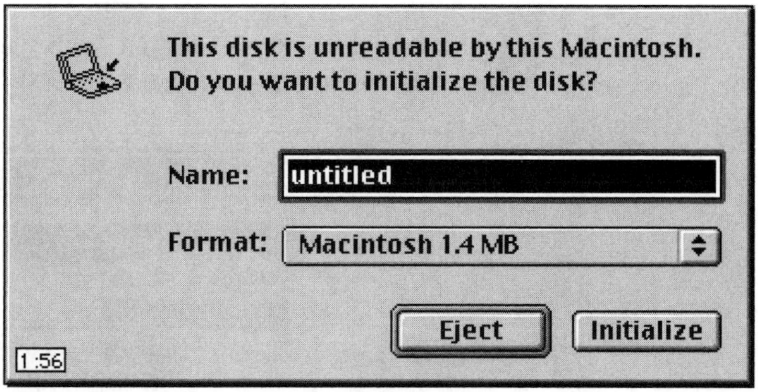

Figure 10.3 *The Disk initialization dialog box.*

The dialog box in Figure 10.3 automatically appears whenever your Mac cannot read a disk. If you have a disk that you know contains data, but you get this message, clicking on the Initialize button destroys all data on the disk. There are times when you want to erase all the data on a disk and restore it to a blank or empty condition.

To erase a disk:

1. Insert the disk into your Mac.
2. Select the disk.
3. Select the *Erase Disk* menu item from the Special menu. A dialog box like the one shown in Figure 10.4 appears.
4. Type the disk's name into the Name: field. You can give it a name that is up to 32 characters long.
5. Select the type of disk format you want to use. Figure 10.5 shows the available formatting options.

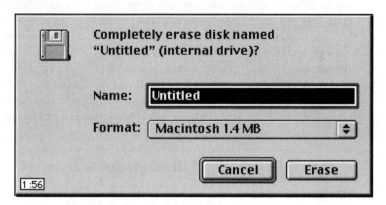

Figure 10.4 *The Erase Disk dialog box.*

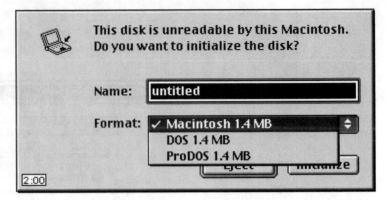

Figure 10.5   *The formatting options.*

6. Click on the Erase button. (Be careful—if your disk contains data you might want to save, the data will be destroyed. You don't get a second chance.) **Caution**: Always stop and think before you click the Initialize button; once you start formatting a disk, there is no way to stop the process, and recovering the data from a formatted floppy is impossible.

7. As your Mac formats the disk, a message that says "Initializing disk" appears. After a minute or so, it changes to "Verifying format," and then it says "Creating directories." You cannot interrupt the formatting process.

8. After the Mac finishes the formatting process, your newly formatted disk appears as an icon on your Desktop.

What Formatting Does

Although some of this information is academic, it introduces you to data structures and lays the groundwork for recovering data on your disks. Even though the disk recovery programs you will use do not require this knowledge, it is good information to have. You will have a better idea about what the recovery program is doing if it tells you that there is problem with the directory, a sector, or one of your files.

The topics in this section include discussions about tracks and sectors, boot blocks, and directory information. This is basic information; all of it, except where noted, is applicable to hard drives. If you have ever been working hard on your project at 2:00 A.M. to meet a deadline and you suddenly have a problem with your disk, you will appreciate this section—especially when you combine it with the recovery procedures discussed in Chapter 19, "Disk Crashes and Data Recovery."

Around the Track and through the Sectors

Formatting does several things to a disk. First, the Mac creates tracks, which are concentric rings placed on the disk. After it has placed tracks on your disk, the Mac

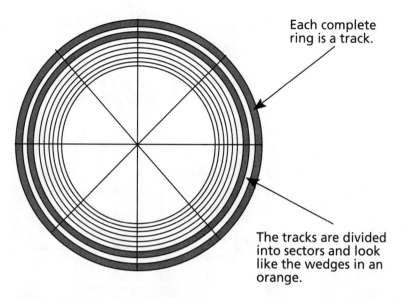

Each complete ring is a track.

The tracks are divided into sectors and look like the wedges in an orange.

Figure 10.6 *Tracks and sectors on a disk.*

divides each track into sectors (see Figure 10.6). A sector is a section of a track that is at least 512 bytes long. Each sector is then given a data storage area, a formatting mark, a CRC block, and a sector tag.

All the data stored on your disk occurs within the sectors. Most files are larger than 512 bytes, though, so a file usually occupies two or more sectors. Thus, a file that is 1,888 bytes occupies four sectors and uses a total of 2 KB of disk space. This means that you never really use all the space on a disk; there will always be some free space in sectors holding file fragments. In Figure 10.7, note that the file occupies 2K on the disk but is really 1,888 bytes in size.

Tracks A series of concentric circles that are magnetically drawn on the recording surface of a disk when it is formatted. Tracks are further divided into 8 to 12 consecutive *sectors.* A track corresponds to one ring of a constant radius around the disk.

Sector (1) Part of a track on a disk—when a disk is formatted, its recording surface is divided into tracks and sectors; (2) disk space composed of 512 consecutive bytes of standard information and 12 bytes of file tags.

Tip To look at the size of one of your files and to see how much space it takes up, select a file from your disk window by clicking on it. After selecting the file, go to the File menu and select the *Get Info* menu option. The result is a window similar to the one shown in Figure 10.7.

Your Mac uses the additional information in a sector to keep track of where your data is stored. The formatting mark is a sector identifier; it contains the number of the individual sector. The sector tag occurs only on floppy disks and stores file

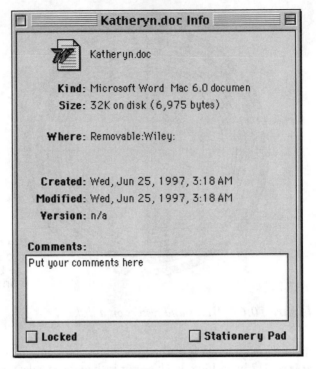

Figure 10.7   Get Info window for a file.

identification information that can be used in some data recovery processes. Your Mac uses the CRC block, which stands for Cyclical Redundancy Check, to check your data's integrity by storing a number in the sector CRC block. This number, calculated from the number of bytes in the sector, is called a *checksum*. Every time your Mac reads a sector, it recalculates this number. If the recalculated number does not match the number stored in the CRC block, your Mac tells you that you have a damaged file that it can't read. (You'll learn how to deal with this problem in Chapter 19.)

When a disk is formatted, in addition to tracks and sectors, your Mac puts system startup information, a volume information block, a file allocation table, and the Desktop file onto your disk. The following information is not 100 percent accurate in a technical sense. It is correct from an informational point of view in that it accurately describes the structure of a Macintosh disk. If you want more specific technical information, read *Inside Macintosh: Files*, published by Apple Computer, Inc.

System Startup Information

Every disk must have what are called *boot blocks*, which appear in the first two sectors (also called blocks) of the disk. This part of a disk contains the information your Macintosh needs to use the disk as a startup disk. A startup disk is capable of running your Macintosh. In order to do that, however, the disk must have a System file and a Finder (or other application) file on the disk. If the disk is not a startup disk, there is no data in the boot blocks. Regardless of the disk's ability to start your Macintosh, the boot blocks are still there.

Volume Information Block

The next set of blocks that your Mac puts on a formatted disk are called *volume information blocks*. These blocks contain critical information about your disk, including its name, size, creation date and time, modification date, the number of files on the disk, plus other information necessary for the Mac to use the disk.

Volume information block (VIB)   A nonrelocatable block that contains volume-specific information.

Volume Directory (Volume Bitmap)

The next file created is the volume bitmap, which contains a one-bit record for each block or sector on the disk. If the bit for a specific sector is turned on, the sector is in use and not available for data. If the bit for a sector is turned off, then the sector is free and available for data. Sometimes, the sector indicator in the volume bitmap does not get turned off after deleting a file. When this happens, some of the space you freed by deleting the file is not available for new data. It is not a serious problem, however, for floppy disks.

File Allocation Table

The file allocation table is where the Mac keeps track of all the data on your disk. It consists of two files called the *extents tree file* and the *catalog tree file*. The extents tree file, working in conjunction with the catalog tree, keeps track of your files. It uses a database structure called a *bee tree* to keep track of the files on your disk. This is a complicated process because a single file usually spans several sectors, and because these sectors do not need to be side by side (contiguous) and are often scattered all over the disk. This method for keeping track of your files is the HFS, or Hierarchical File System; it provides for the nested folder structure on your disks.

Desktop File

The Desktop file is a resource file that the Finder uses. It links your applications with their data files and keeps track of all your icons and the Finder's window positions. The Desktop file performs other functions, but they are not important at the moment.

The Macintosh cannot use a disk that does not have a Desktop file. Because the Desktop file is constantly being modified, there will be times when a disk will not work as expected and you will get an error message that says, "This disk is damaged. Do you wish to repair it?" If you get this message, click OK. When your Mac rebuilds the Desktop file, everything is fine and the disk works normally. If your Mac cannot rebuild the Desktop file, you get a message stating so, and the disk is ejected from your Mac.

When a Desktop file cannot be rebuilt, the only thing you can do with the disk is attempt to recover the data by using a file recovery utility (described in Chapter 19, "Disk Crashes and Data Recovery"). Even if you are able to rescue your data, your only hope of ever using the floppy disk again is to have someone with a DOS machine (definitely not a Macintosh) format the disk. When you get your disk back, try formatting it again. If it still doesn't format, give it back to the person with the DOS machine or throw it away. (If your Mac has the PC Exchange control panel installed, you can try to format the floppy as an MS-DOS disk.)

Care and Feeding of the Floppy Drive

When used and maintained properly, your floppy drive will probably never give you any grief. It is easy to make a mistake without knowing you've done something improperly and so cause damage to a disk, your drive, or both. This section is about taking care of your drives and your disks. It covers such mishaps as spilling liquids on your disks, unreadable disks, and general drive maintenance.

Formatting Different Size Disks

I previously discussed the three different types of Macintosh floppy drives. With the introduction of each new drive, Apple increased its drives' data capacity. Also, each new drive could read and write to a disk formatted by one of its predecessors. There is no forward compatibility, though. A 400K drive can't read an 800K disk. Likewise, a 400K or an 800K drive cannot read a 1.44M disk. The SuperDrive can format a 400K (only if you use System 6.0.X), an 800K, or a 1.44M disk. An 800K drive can also format a 400K disk (when you use System 6.0.X).

With an 800K DSDD (double-sided, double-density) disk drive, make sure that you do not use a high-density disk. An 800K drive will format a high-density disk as an 800K disk. If this should happen, the high-density disk is readable by other 800K drives, but a SuperDrive cannot read the disk and will want to initialize it. The SuperDrive detects the presence of high-density (HD) disks by the little hole opposite the write-protect tab and automatically tries to read it as a 1.44M disk. If you formatted the disk as an 800K disk, the SuperDrive will not recognize it.

The other problem you could encounter by using high-density disks in an 800K drive is data instability. Because the high-density disks use a denser magnetic material than 800K disks, a HD disk could lose its format when formatted in an 800K drive. Although this rarely happens, when it does you could lose important data. It is better to avoid this potential problem by using disks made for your drive.

How to Protect Your Floppy Drive during Transport

Whenever you move your Macintosh, protect your floppy drive by putting an expendable floppy disk into the drive after turning off the Mac. Apple used to ship all its Macs with 800K drives with a yellow, hard-plastic drive protector. These protectors work on the 800K drives, but they destroy a SuperDrive. The other danger posed by the plastic protector is in inserting it upside down. To do so requires that you force it into the drive, which destroys an 800K drive. Even though it has "This Side Up" boldly printed on the top, accidents do happen. Rather than risk an accident that could destroy your floppy drive, I recommend that you use an inexpensive floppy disk instead.

Apple no longer ships its drives with a protector because all the new drives are SuperDrives. Even with your SuperDrive, it's a good idea to use a floppy disk when transporting your Mac. This will prevent any damage to the drive if your Mac is jarred while it is being transported.

X Rays Cannot Hurt Your Disks

Before you send your Mac down that airport conveyer belt, make sure the security scanner is not a magnetic scanner and that it uses X rays, which are nothing more than a form of light and cannot harm your Mac or your disks. You actually stand a greater danger of damaging your disks by walking through the metal detector that uses magnetic fields to detect metal objects. Because some of the new scanners are magnetic you need to exercise some caution but, if it's an X-ray scanner, your Mac is in no danger. You might even save a few minutes because the security guard will not ask you to power up your computer to make sure it doesn't contain explosives.

Don't Force That Disk In

One of the biggest mistakes you can make while using your Macintosh floppy drive involves removing or inserting disks. On older Macintoshes, the drive automatically accepts and ejects its disks. If, when inserting a disk, you force it in, you can cause irreparable damage to your floppy drive. As you put the disk into the drive, there is a point at which some resistance begins. At this point, the drive starts opening the trapdoor on the disk. Immediately after the resistance begins, the disk drive grabs the disk and pulls it into the drive. If, for some reason, the drive does not accept the disk, *do not force it into the drive!* Forcing a disk into your drive can damage the drive, probably requiring a replacement.

With newer SuperDrives, you have to insert the floppy all the way into the drive before the Mac accepts the disk, so you don't have to worry about the Mac grabbing the disk. You should still be cautious and never force a disk into your Mac, regardless of the type of drive. When inserting a disk, if you encounter resistance, remove the disk. After you remove the disk, check the trapdoor by sliding it open. If the trapdoor opens smoothly, try to insert the disk into the drive again. If the drive still refuses to accept the disk, remove the disk and try another. If the same thing happens with another disk, you may have a damaged floppy drive. Take your Macintosh to an Apple Authorized Service Center and have it checked out.

Don't Pull Your Disk Out

Another way you can get into trouble with your floppy disks occurs when they do not eject properly and you try to force the disk out of the drive. When you unmount a disk by dragging your floppy disk icon to the Trash and the disk does not pop out all the way, do not grab the disk and try to pull it out. Sometimes the Mac reinserts the disk, and at other times it stays partly out but the Mac still has hold of it. If you grab the disk and it does not freely slide out of the Mac, gently push it in—90 percent of the time, the Mac reinserts the disk. If the disk does not reinsert, turn off your Macintosh and take it to an Apple Authorized Service Center.

Another occasional problem is that the Mac goes through the motions of ejecting your disk, but the disk never comes out of the drive. This problem is similar to the one just described. Turn off your Mac and take it to a Service Center.

Manually Ejecting Diskettes

If your floppy disk is stuck and you feel brave (I'm not recommending you try this), there is one more trick you can try. There is a very small hole to the right of the slot where you insert your floppy disks. Behind this hole is a manual eject lever that you can push with a straightened paper clip or a jeweler's screwdriver. If you choose to try this, do so with great caution. There could be a problem with the disk or the drive, and you could irreparably damage both the disk and the drive.

To manually eject the disk, insert your device of choice into the hole. As soon as you feel it press against the eject lever, gently begin to apply pressure. As the lever goes back, the disk begins to rise from its seated position and starts to pop out, just as it does when being ejected in a normal manner. If the disk pops out only partway when you've pushed the lever as far as it will go and then jumps back into the drive, *stop*. The drive needs professional attention. If, however, the disk pops all the way out, turn your Mac back on and insert a different disk after you check the trapdoor. If this disk works properly, erase it using the Special menu. You can be sure that the disk drive is OK only after you have formatted and copied data to and from the floppy disk. Once you manually eject the stuck floppy, throw the disk away. If the disk has data you need, try using it—but with great caution. Remember, *never* force a disk into your drive.

Using MS-DOS Disks

One of the SuperDrive's advantages (for some people) is that it can format, read, and write disks formatted from an MS-DOS or Windows computer. The Control Panel PC Exchange is what allows your Mac to read MS-DOS disks. If you use any System version prior to 7.5, you need a utility called Apple File Exchange. Apple File Exchange was originally on one of your System Tools disks.

Inserting Damaged Disks

At some time, you will probably insert a disk into your Mac and the dialog box shown in Figure 10.8 will appear. This dialog box signals that your disk is damaged. If you format the disk, you lose all your data.

If you want to salvage your data:

1. Click on the Cancel button. The Mac ejects the disk.
2. Insert the disk again.

If you get the same dialog box, proceed to Chapter 19, "Disk Crashes and Data Recovery," and read about recovering disks. If you click on the Initialize button, you will erase your disk.

Trying to Read a Wet Floppy

It is unavoidable: Some day, you will spill something on a floppy disk. When this happens, first, wipe the disk dry, then set it aside and let it thoroughly dry overnight. After your disk has dried, make sure the trapdoor is not stuck by sliding it open—be sure not to touch the disk. If the trapdoor sticks, carefully rip the door off. All the trapdoor does is protect the floppy inside the housing; a disk without a trapdoor will work just fine in your Mac.

Next, turn the spindle on the bottom of the disk—it should turn easily. If the spindle does not turn, do not put the disk into your Mac—the disk is probably ruined. Set the disk aside for another 24 hours to make sure it is completely dry, then try to turn the spindle again. If the spindle still doesn't move, pray that you have a backup.

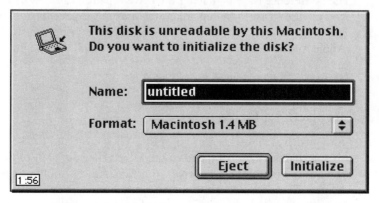

Figure 10.8   *A damaged disk's dialog box.*

If the spindle does turn, hold the trapdoor open (be careful not to touch the disk) and turn the spindle. As the disk turns inside its housing, visually check the disk for moisture and watermarks. If the disk still has moisture on it, set it aside and let it dry fully. If it has watermarks, the disk is probably ruined and you should just throw it away.

The critical issue in all of this is what you spilled on the disk. If it was a sticky liquid, such as soda or coffee with cream and sugar, and if your disk has watermarks, your disk is probably sticky. If you put this disk into your Mac, there is a very good chance that the residue on the disk will get on your drive's heads. If you just spilled water or black coffee on the disk and it is completely dry, you can try reading it. If you try to read the disk and *anything* unusual happens, eject the disk immediately.

If you spilled a sticky liquid on your disk and the data on it is critical, there is one more thing you might try. Using cold water, rinse off the disk, with the trapdoor open, then set it aside to dry. After the disk has dried, go through these steps again.

If your disk fails after trying all of this, it is probably dead—there is no guarantee that these steps will work. *Just putting a disk that has had something spilled on it into your Mac could ruin the floppy drive.* Try this only if you are desperate and willing to pay for a new disk drive.

Head Alignment

Sometimes, a floppy drive malfunctions for no apparent reason. One cause is that the heads are out of alignment. When this happens, the heads do not align properly on the floppy disk, and the drive cannot recognize the tracks or the data on a disk. A very clear indicator of this problem is being able to read a disk that you formatted in your machine but the same disk is unreadable in a different Mac, and vice versa.

If this happens to your drive, you have two choices: One is to take your Mac to an Authorized Apple Service Center and have the drive replaced. Apple Service Centers do not realign the heads on Macintosh disk drives. Your other option is to find someone who will do this type of repair. There are usually several technicians in any metropolitan area who work on Macs, even though they are not Apple-authorized. The difference is cost—having the drive repaired can cost half that of a new drive. If you choose to use an independent technician for your repairs, make sure you check his or her references. The only people trained by Apple to work on your Mac are Apple Authorized Service Providers and, as I said, they do not perform this type of repair. *Caveat Emptor.*

Replacing a Drive

Floppy drives die—this is a fact of life. They wear out, the heads get knocked loose, the mechanisms get bent, and so on. When they do, your only choice is to replace the drive. To replace your drive, your first choice should be the Apple Authorized Service Center. If you want to save a little money, you could buy a reconditioned drive at about half the cost of a new drive from Apple.

Once again, there are usually people who recondition Macintosh drives in any large metropolitan area. Sometimes they are not easy to find, but if you are persistent and look in the independent computer newspaper published in your area, you might find one of these ambitious service people advertising. These drives should have a 90-day warranty.

If you use your Mac only occasionally, be careful when buying anything with a 90-day warranty. You may not use it enough within 90 days to give the component or peripheral a good workout. If this picture reflects your Macintosh usage, make sure you buy accessories and peripherals with a one-year warranty.

Avoiding Magnets

Remember: All the data on your floppy disk consists of magnetically charged particles being in very exact positions, so you should be very careful not to expose your floppies to magnets. A lot of people have magnetic paper-clip holders on their desk. This type of device has a twofold danger: First, the holder has a magnet that does not need to come in direct contact with the floppy to destroy the data on it. Just knocking the holder over or placing a floppy too close to it could damage the disk. The other danger is in the paper clips themselves: While they sit in the holder, the paper clips can become magnetized. Although the possibility is remote, a magnetized paper clip could damage a floppy.

People often forget other magnetized devices, such as screwdrivers and other tools. Small appliances, such as Dustbusters, electric pencil sharpeners, or shredders, can all produce a magnetic charge strong enough to damage a disk. The list of devices that can cause magnetic damage is really quite long, so I won't list all of them. One more source of potential danger is your telephone. There is a speaker in the handset of your telephone, and although the chances of its damaging a floppy disk may be slim, remember that all speakers have a magnet. Also, the effects of a magnet need not be immediate; you might keep a floppy disk near a device with a magnet for a day and nothing happens, but, if the disk is left there for a week, it could be damaged.

The moral here is to find a safe place to keep your disk, preferably a special storage box in a location away from magnets and electrical appliances. If you are careful, you will have very few problems. If your desk is as messy as mine is, on occasion you'll lose a floppy either because you can't find it or because your paper-clip holder fell on it.

Placement of Your Mac

Where you place your Macintosh can affect both the machine and your floppy drives. First of all, never place your Macintosh in direct sunlight—heat is not your computer's friend. This also means that you should not position the Mac too close to heating vents. Because your floppies are actually thin Mylar disks, extreme heat can warp them and make them unusable, even though they are enclosed in plastic. Keep your disks out of direct sunlight, and away from heating vents, too.

Another potential source of floppy disk trouble can be your Mac Plus, SE, SE/30, or Mac Classic. All these models have a power supply on the left-hand side (when viewed from the front). The power supply is a step-down transformer that converts your household current to a lower voltage that works with your Mac. One of the by-products of this process is a magnetic field. If you keep your disks on the left-hand side of one of these computers, beware. Some of the disks could become unreadable, especially over a long period of time. The best thing to do is find another place for your disks.

One more placement issue pertains to the Macintosh IIcx, IIci, and Quadra 700. Each of these models has a fan that sits directly behind the floppy drive. The fan draws a lot of dust that gets into your machine through the floppy drive. In these Macs, I've seen hair, dust balls, and other large particles of dirt entangled in their drive mechanisms. The danger of getting a foreign particle in your drive increases if, to save desk space, you place the CPU near or on the floor. If you have one of these Macs, take it into a Service Center for cleaning at least once a year—once every six months would be even better. If your drive should fail, chances are very good that dust is the cause. Do not let an unscrupulous technician sell you a new drive until you are sure the old one is not just dirty.

Dirt and Your Floppy

Your floppy drive has enemies—dust, more dust, and smoke. Actually, these are computer enemies in general. As a rule, the Macintosh floppy disk does a good job of cleaning itself, but the drive does not. It is a good idea to take your Mac to a Service Center about once a year to have it cleaned, which will increase its overall life and make the floppy drive much more reliable. If too much dust builds up in your floppy

More Dust Dangers

Every Mac made since the Mac Plus (except PowerBooks) has a fan to cool the components inside the machine. This fan draws air—and dust—into and through the Mac. The dust also settles on your logic board and the Mac's other internal components.

As the dust buildup gets thicker, the dust acts as an insulator that increases the heat of your logic board's components. As the heat increases, it shortens the life of your Mac's components and, at some time, one of them will fail. If the failed component is on the logic board, your Apple Service Center will automatically want to exchange it.

drive, bad things happen: Your drive can act as if its heads are damaged and can fail to read and/or write; the eject mechanism can jam; or your drive could behave erratically. Also, the spindle motor might be unable to maintain a consistent speed because of dust buildup. Usually, when one of these problems occurs, the drive does not work. It is also possible for a drive to get so dirty that the only cure is replacement. To prevent this problem, have your Mac professionally cleaned once a year. Think of it as getting the oil in your car changed every 3000 miles.

Smoke is an enemy of your disk drive, and I do not recommend that you smoke around your Mac. Particles of smoke can be large enough to cause a problem if smoke should get between the heads and the disk; if you smoke, smoke with care.

Your Hard Drive(s) and You

This section is about your Mac's hard drive(s). As stated in the chapter's introduction, your hard drive is like your Mac's heart. If your drive works properly, your Mac works properly. If your drive has problems, your Mac has problems. You owe it to yourself to learn about your hard disk so that you can take care of it properly.

To get the most from this section, read the previous section on floppy drives. It contains information about disks in general that is not repeated here. In this section, we discuss how your hard drive works, the different types of hard drives, how to set up your Mac with its internal hard drive, and how to attach multiple hard drives to your Macintosh. We also discuss basic information about how data is stored on your disk and give you some tips on how to use your hard drives more effectively.

Note: If you are having trouble with your hard drive, read this section and then go to Part V, "Troubleshooting," for more detailed information about hard disk problems.

Dire Warning

It is probably not good form to begin a new section with a dire warning, but, when talking about hard drives, it is unavoidable. Your hard drive is the weakest link, the most fragile device, the least dependable peripheral attached to your Macintosh. If something is going to go wrong, it will be with your hard drive, so you should always be ready for your hard drive to die. Period.

If you always back up your data (as discussed in Chapter 11), you need not be so paranoid. If you don't back up your data, you should learn disk recovery because, when your drive crashes (malfunctions), it is too late to start learning about backing up your drive. Consider yourself warned.

SCSI (Small Computer Standard Interface)

All Macintosh hard drives use the Small Computer Standard Interface (SCSI), called a *scuzzy* interface, bus, or chain. This is Apple's chosen means to connect the Macintosh to external peripheral devices. The SCSI bus connects hard drives, scanners, printers, and other peripheral devices to your Mac. It can even connect other computers to your Macintosh.

The SCSI bus is fairly simple, but if it is not set up properly, your Mac will not work. In the following sections, we concentrate on setting up your hard drives using the SCSI bus. Any additional devices that use the SCSI bus are mentioned in their appropriate sections. In this section, however, we talk about all the ins and outs of the SCSI bus.

You should follow some basic rules when using any SCSI device and connecting it to your Mac (and to all *basic* rules there are always exceptions). The first rule is that any device attached to the bus has a number and that no two devices can have the same number. Second, the first and last devices on the bus need a terminator. A third rule is that there should be no more than 18 inches between SCSI devices. And the final rule is that the entire SCSI chain should be no longer than 15 feet in total.

Sometimes all the rules go out the window. In most cases, though, you can depend on these four rules. Later in this section, I discuss the exceptions.

Number of SCSI Devices

Let's begin with the number of devices you can attach to the Macintosh SCSI bus. You can connect seven additional SCSI devices to your Macintosh. If you have an internal hard drive and it is a SCSI drive, you already have one SCSI device and can attach only six more. All new Macs have a SCSI CD-ROM drive so, in most cases, you'll only be able to add five more devices.

SCSI ID Numbering

Next, each SCSI device has a SCSI ID number. You can use the numbers 0 to 6. The Macintosh always uses 7 as its ID number. When you attach several devices to the SCSI bus, the entire system is called a SCSI chain. Why call it a chain? All the connected peripherals are in serial, with one device being connected to another in a daisy chain. Figure 10.9 shows how several devices are connected to a Macintosh.

SCSI chain   A group of SCSI devices linked to each other through SCSI peripheral interface cables and linked to the SCSI port on the computer through a SCSI system cable.

If you have an Apple hard drive installed in your computer, the ID number of the internal hard drive should always be 0.

To check the SCSI ID number by using the *Get Info* command:

1. Highlight your hard drive icon.

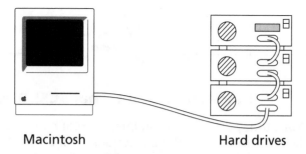

Macintosh   Hard drives

Figure 10.9 *Diagram of a SCSI chain.*

2. Go to the File menu and select the *Get Info* command.
3. An information window opens that looks like the one shown in Figure 10.10.

In Figure 10.11, you see the name of your hard drive next to its icon. Next to "Kind," you see the word "disk," under which is the disk's size information. What you are interested in right now, however, is the "Where" description, where you will find the name of the hard drive, the type of driver (usually the drive's manufacturer), and the drive's SCSI number. There are two windows in Figure 10.10. The one that says "Mac OS HD, SCSI ID 0" identifies the drive as number 0, and the one that

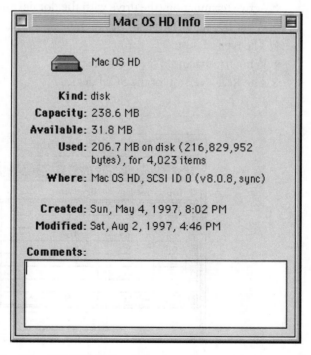

Figure 10.10 *Mac OS HD Info window.*

Macs without Internal SCSI Drives

Many Macs today do not have an internal SCSI hard drive. Instead, they use a standard called IDE, Integrated Drive Electronics. All these Macs use the standard SCSI bus for connecting external devices; therefore, all the information in this section about SCSI does apply. The only exception is that their internal hard drives do not use a SCSI ID number.

says "Dev.CD Feb 97 TC, FWB SCSI 3 v1.09" identifies the CD-ROM as SCSI number 3.

Sometimes, a drive's Info window does not identify its SCSI number. When this happens, it is best to use your formatting software or a good shareware utility, such as SCSIProbe, written by Robert Polic, to determine your drive's SCSI ID number. SCSIProbe (which is on the CD-ROM included with this book) gives you good information about the SCSI devices attached to your Mac. It tells you the following:

❖ Active termination (the drive with the dot next to the SCSI ID number)

❖ What ID numbers are in use

❖ The type of device

❖ Who manufactured the mechanism

❖ The ROM version of the SCSI device

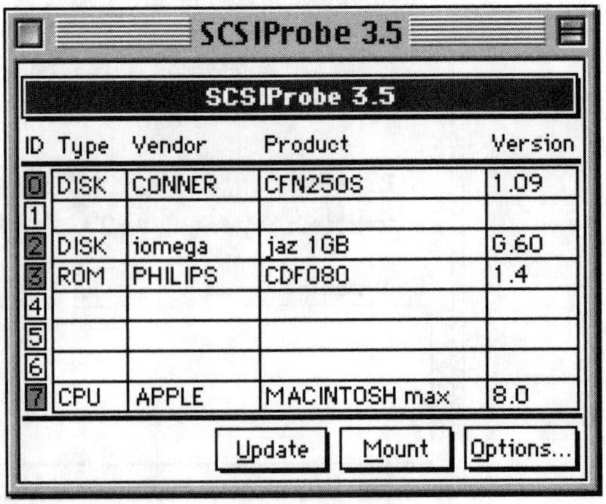

SCSIProbe 3.5

ID	Type	Vendor	Product	Version
0	DISK	CONNER	CFN250S	1.09
1				
2	DISK	iomega	jaz 1GB	G.60
3	ROM	PHILIPS	CDF080	1.4
4				
5				
6				
7	CPU	APPLE	MACINTOSH max	8.0

[Update] [Mount] [Options...]

Figure 10.11   *Drives viewed with SCSIProbe.*

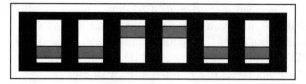

Figure 10.12 *A drawing of a dip switch.*

In Figure 10.11, you can see that three devices are in use with ID numbers 0, 1, 3, and 7—SCSI ID 7 is the Macintosh. SCSIProbe also shows that there are four free SCSI numbers that other devices can use.

Once you have figured out which ID numbers are in use, you will know what numbers to assign to other devices. How you assign ID numbers depends on the device itself. Most hard drives have a switch of some type that allows you to change the ID number. Your options for setting the ID for any SCSI device are as follows:

- ❖ No option—The ID number is preset at the factory and cannot be changed except by a technician.
- ❖ Dip switches (see Figure 10.12)—Consult the manual to configure.
- ❖ Rotary Switch (see Figure 10.13)—Change the ID number by pushing a button.
- ❖ Your SCSI ID number is set by your formatting software.

Figure 10.13 *A drawing of a rotary switch.*

Whatever method your SCSI device uses to set the SCSI ID number, rest assured that as soon as you have a new drive, scanner, or other SCSI device to attach, you will have a SCSI ID conflict. This is a derivative of Murphy's Law that states, "Whatever your existing SCSI ID numbers might be, any new SCSI device you purchase will be set to a number already in use."

What happens when you have two devices trying to use the same number is very simple. No SCSI device on the chain will operate, and usually your Mac won't start. Some Macs display the blinking disk icon, indicating they cannot find a startup disk, and others just freeze. There is no way to determine how any specific Mac will react to an ID conflict. Whatever the Mac does, it won't work properly. Always check your SCSI ID numbers when adding a new SCSI peripheral.

Never change a SCSI ID number while the drive or device is turned on. If you do, the ID for the device does not change. The ID numbers change only when the power to the device is turned off. Whenever you add or remove a SCSI device, turn your Mac off. If you don't, you could cause a short circuit that will damage both the SCSI device and your Macintosh.

Multiple SCSI Buses

Several of the high-end Macs produced over the last few years have multiple SCSI buses. When a Mac has multiple SCSI buses, it can use twice as many SCSI devices. Usually the high-end Macs have a single external SCSI bus and an internal SCSI bus, with all the internal drives connected to the internal bus.

Termination

Termination is the placement of a set of electronic resistors either on the logic board of the SCSI device or in an external device called a *terminator* (see Figure 10.14). A terminator stops the electric signals as they travel down the cables, preventing signal echoes and amplifying the power of the signal at the same time. The rule of thumb is that the first and last devices in a SCSI chain must be terminated.

Termination   The placement of impedance-matching circuits on a bus to maintain signal integrity.

Terminator   A device used in a SCSI chain to maintain the integrity of the signals passing along the SCSI chain. A SCSI chain should never have more than two terminators, one at each end of the chain. Also called a *cable terminator.*

Another rule associated with termination is that there should be no more than two terminators on any Macintosh SCSI chain. If you place a third terminator on the SCSI bus, you stand an excellent chance of damaging your Mac or your drive. Some drives are more sensitive to excessive termination than others. It is possible to damage your Macintosh with too many terminators. If you do, you may need a logic board replacement.

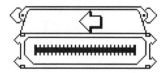

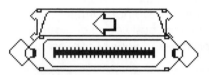

Figure 10.14 *External SCSI terminator.*

Your internal hard drive is terminated and counts as the first terminated device on your SCSI bus. Any additional devices you add to your Mac need to be unterminated, except the last device, which should be terminated. In almost all instances, termination is straightforward. If you have questions about how your Macintosh is terminated, look in your manual or consult a Macintosh technician.

If you need a terminator, go to your local computer store and pick up a standard external terminator. If you are still confused about termination, here is a list of the rules:

❖ There should be no more than two terminators on a SCSI chain.

❖ The first and last devices need to be terminated.

❖ Do not put more than two terminators on your SCSI chain, except as noted in the "SCSI Cables" section.

SCSI Cables

All that connects your Macintosh and its SCSI peripherals are the cables. And, just as the strength of a chain is determined by its weakest link, the quality and condition of your cables determine the integrity of your SCSI chain. Unfortunately, all cables are not alike—nor are the SCSI connectors on the different devices.

Cables come in lengths of 1 to 15 feet; they also come in different thicknesses and can be shielded or unshielded. All these factors affect how well your drives and other SCSI devices operate. Cable quality can be determined by two factors: First, your SCSI cable should always be shielded. A shielded cable has a metal foil wrapped around the insulation inside the cable. You cannot see the shielding when you purchase a SCSI cable, so request a shielded cable. Also, a shielded cable can usually be identified by its thickness. An unshielded cable is about a quarter of an inch thick; a shielded cable is about half an inch.

Second, using the same manufacturer's cables to connect all of your SCSI devices is a good idea. If that is not possible, then the next best thing is to have cables of the same type—that is, shielded. Mixing different types of cables can cause problems

SCSI Connector Caution

Even though this connector looks like the parallel connector on a DOS or Windows machine, it is not. Do not connect a parallel printer cable to this Macintosh port; if you do, you will seriously damage your Mac—especially by connecting the cable to a parallel printer and your Macintosh.

---

with signal strength. Different types of cables have different resistance ratings, also causing signal inconsistency. Most SCSI peripheral manufacturers ship their devices with unshielded cables to save money. If you purchase a SCSI peripheral and it comes with an unshielded cable, buy a new shielded cable.

The process of connecting SCSI peripherals to your Mac is fairly straightforward—you use a cable that connects your Mac's SCSI port to the SCSI peripheral. All Macs have a SCSI port. Desktop Macs have a 25-pin SCSI port, but the PowerBooks have a special 30-pin SCSI port that is distinguished by a symbol. Before you can connect a PowerBook to a SCSI device, you need a special cable called an HDI 30 SCSI Disk Adapter. This cable is inserted into your PowerBook's 30-pin SCSI port; it ends with a 25-pin connector port that is the same as the 25-pin SCSI port found on all other Macs.

Most SCSI peripherals you can buy have two SCSI ports—one for an incoming cable and the other to connect the device to another SCSI device. Figure 10.15 shows how SCSI devices are daisy chained using their ports.

External SCSI devices can have SCSI ports that are different from your Mac's. The most common port is a standard 50-pin SCSI port, but some devices have a 25-pin port like the one found on your Mac. A third type of port, called a SCSI II port, has a 50-pin port that is smaller than the current standard.

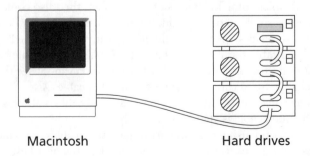

Macintosh   Hard drives

Figure 10.15 *A SCSI daisy chain.*

When you buy a SCSI peripheral, be sure you have the proper cables. You need a cable to connect the device to your Mac and any other SCSI devices you own. Because there are different types of SCSI ports, make sure you have the proper cables. The different combinations you could end up using are as follows:

❖ 25-pin to 50-pin
❖ 50-pin to 50-pin
❖ 25-pin to SCSI II
❖ 25-pin to 25-pin
❖ SCSI II to 50-pin
❖ SCSI II to SCSI II

If you have a Mac and two external hard drives, where one drive has SCSI II ports and the other has 50-pin ports, you need these two cables:

❖ A cable to connect your Mac to one drive
❖ A cable to connect the two drives

It does not matter how you position the drives or which SCSI drive ports you use, as long as each is connected as shown in Figure 10.15. You could use a 25-pin-to SCSI II cable to connect the Mac to the SCSI II drive, and a SCSI II-to-50-pin cable to connect the SCSI II drive to the 50-pin drive. Or, you could reverse the order, using a 25-pin to a 50-pin cable and a SCSI II to a 50-pin cable, to achieve the same results. What's important here is that each device connects to the next.

Some SCSI devices have only one SCSI port. If you happen to get one, it must be the last device in your SCSI chain, which means that you can use only one device (other than your Mac) that has a single SCSI port. Just be careful. Know how many

More SCSI Connectors

SCSI standards are constantly being developed. You can now purchase drives that use a 68-pin SCSI connector. The standard for these drives is called Fast and Wide. If you encounter a Fast and Wide SCSI drive you will usually have a Fast and Wide SCSI card installed in your Mac. If you don't have a special SCSI card you will need a 68-to-50-pin adapter to use the drive internally. When Fast and Wide SCSI drives are placed in external drive enclosures, the adapter is already installed, and you can use a standard 50-pin SCSI cable. Should the enclosure have a 68-pin external connector, you will need to have a special 68-to-50-pin cable made before you can use the drive. Usually Fast and Wide drives are used in arrays, discussed later in this chapter. A drive array is usually used on high-end graphic workstations and file servers.

and what types of ports your SCSI devices have so that you can plan to expand your computer system. If you don't know how your devices are configured, you'll end up making more than one trip to the computer store for cables.

The next concern is the length of your SCSI chain. It should not be longer than 15 feet in total, with a maximum distance of 1.5 feet between devices. These are Apple's recommended guidelines, and very good guidelines they are. But, as always, you must deal with exceptions and the real world. Quite often, it is not possible or desirable to place all your SCSI devices within 18 inches of your CPU. The considerations involved with positioning SCSI devices are numerous: The CPU is on the floor, the shelf to hold the scanner is 5 feet away, the hard drive is too noisy, *ad infinitum*. There are as many reasons as there are people for wanting to place the SCSI devices somewhere else.

Real-world configurations usually involve the use of 3- to 6-foot cables, and quite often the 18-foot length limit is exceeded. If your SCSI chain is longer than 18 feet, see if you can shorten it. Remember that the length is not the actual physical distance, but the length of the cables connecting the devices. You can stack three drives on top of each other and still exceed the length limit because the cables between each of your devices are 6 feet long.

If you have problems with your SCSI devices and your SCSI devices exceed the 18-foot limit, the best advice is to shorten your SCSI chain. You might try adding a third SCSI terminator. Because the terminator can also act as an amplifier, it can sometimes cure the problems. You should try this only in desperation—and with caution. The warnings in the section on termination are real—you could short out your system. If you try this, be careful. If anything (your Mac or your drives) acts strangely, shut down the system and remove the extra terminator, then shorten your SCSI chain. *If you must try this, do so with full knowledge that you could need a new drive(s) and/or a logic board before you are finished.*

The final note about SCSI cables pertains to the Macintosh PowerBook, which requires a special cable connector for connecting with external SCSI devices. Most of the PowerBooks can be used as an external hard disk (all except the 140, 160, and

Hard Drive Questions

Two questions that always come up are these: "What port on my hard drive should I use?" and "Does the SCSI ID number indicate where the device should be in the SCSI chain?" Neither of these questions matters. You can connect your SCSI cable to either port on the SCSI peripheral, and the ID number of the device has no relation to its position in the SCSI chain. There is no correct port—they are equal—and any number can be anywhere on the chain.

170), but this approach also requires a special cable. For any of the cables needed for a PowerBook, contact your Authorized Apple Dealer.

Your Macintosh Hard Drive

Currently, it is almost impossible to use a Macintosh without a hard disk drive, especially if you run Mac OS 8. Your hard disk is an electromechanical device designed to hold and very quickly access large quantities of computer data. Although most of the principles that apply to floppy disks also apply to hard disks, there are some major differences. The similarities are that hard drives have disks coated with a magnetic material to hold your data, just as floppy disks do. The differences begin with the hard drive disk's being constructed of metal or glass *platters*. A hard disk can have one or more platters, depending on the data capacity of the drive.

A hard disk also has read and write heads, but they do not rest on the platters as the heads on a floppy disk do. (Never touch them while the Macintosh is running.) Instead, the platters spin at a minimum speed of 3600 rpm, with newer disks spinning at 7200 rpm. The spinning platters create a cushion of air strong enough to float the heads just above the surface of the platters. The distance between the platter and the head is between 10 and 20 millionths of an inch, and the heads never touch the platters except when the power to the Macintosh and/or drive is turned off. When your drive loses power, its heads will automatically move to a landing zone and, after the platters stop spinning, come to rest.

The heads are attached to the end of an actuator arm just like a floppy drive's, and a stepper motor moves the actuator arm in short, rapid, concise strokes for accurate positioning. The specially designed motor moves the heads based on predetermined lengths, which makes it easier for the drive and computer to access your data rapidly. The heads keep their position because of special encoded tracks called *servos*, or servo encoding.

On a standard hard drive, an airtight metal case encloses the entire mechanism. It is airtight so that no air from the outside can get into the drive and interfere with the heads or the platters. The average piece of dust is several times larger than the space between the heads and the platter, and if one should get into the drive assembly, it could cause disastrous results. (Some hard drives have removable platters with exposed drive assemblies. The section "Optional Storage Devices," on removable media hard drives, describes these drives.)

Each hard drive, like its floppy counterpart, has a logic board that enables it and the computer to communicate. If the drive is external to the Macintosh, it has its own box and power supply; an internal hard drive uses the same power supply as the Macintosh. All drives that use this technology are Winchester drives. Almost every drive used on a Macintosh is a Winchester-type drive. The only exceptions are a removable media drive (manufactured by Bernoulli) and optical drives.

How Fast Is Fast?

As with every component of the Macintosh, your hard drive has a speed rating. Every manufacturer assigns a rating, measured in milliseconds (ms), to its drives.

These ratings are called *access time* and *seek time*. *Access time* is the speed with which the drive can reposition its heads from track to track, and *seek time* is the length of time it takes the drive to find a file. Current average access time for most Macintosh drives is from 10ms to 19ms; most Quantum drives operate at this speed. As a rule of thumb, the larger the drive's capacity, the faster the drive. Some of the fastest drives have an access time of 4ms or 5ms, which exceeds the capacity of most Macs.

In addition to the access and seek times, each drive also has a *data transfer rate* measured in megabits per second. However, these numbers are misleading. They represent an ideal data transfer rate, which is determined by sending data to and from the drive at the fastest possible rate without concern for error checking or other factors that affect the drive's overall speed. Even the high-end Macs, such as the PowerMac, cannot take advantage of a fast drive's optimum speed capacities.

These numbers represent the drive's speed as an independent subsystem operating under optimum conditions. The numbers are useful for making comparisons between different drives. As a rule, the faster the seek, access, and data transfer times, the faster the drive works with your Mac. Because the transfer of data requires communication between the devices involved, your data transfers at the lowest common denominator within your system. You can copy data from a slow drive to a fast drive, and the entire system operate at the speed of the slow drive. On the other hand, if you use a Quadra, a slow drive, and a fast drive, but you use the slow drive only to back up your data, the slow drive does not interfere and slow down the process.

Unless you have a PowerMac, you can easily purchase a hard drive that can run faster than your Mac's. When you look at a drive's capabilities, both the access time and the data transfer rate are important. The faster the access time, the quicker the drive operates; the same principle applies to the data transfer rate. If two drives have equal data transfer rates, the one with the faster access time operates more quickly on your Mac.

Today's hard-disk technology is getting so good that you don't have to be as concerned about drive speeds as you might have been a couple of years ago, but it never hurts to check these numbers and do some comparison shopping.

Form Factors

One of the terms that pop up when you look for drives is the term *form factor*, which refers to the physical size of the drive. Currently, there are five form factors or physical sizes for hard drives. Table 10.1 lists these different sizes.

These descriptions are only approximations; drive specifics vary slightly from one manufacturer to the next. The capacity of each of these different sizes changes constantly. An example is the 5.25 HH form factor. There are thousands of 5.25 HH hard drives in use, but I haven't found a manufacturer that is making new ones. This form factor is now used primarily for removable media and CD-ROM drives.

The numbers in the table provide a range for determining the capacity of drives with different form factors. A drive's form factor determines whether a drive will fit in your Mac or how much desk space it will require. Today, all new Macintoshes come with a 3.5 HH or LP drive, except PowerBooks, which have a 2.5 LP IDE drive (SCSI 2.5" drives are not being made anymore). Although some Macs can hold

Table 10.1 Physical Size of the Hard Drive

SIZE	DESCRIPTION	CAPACITY
5.25 FH (Full Height)	5.25" wide by 8 to 10" deep by 5" high	500M to 23GB
5.25 HH (Half Height)	5.25" wide by 8 to 10" deep by 1.75" high	80M to 9GB
3.5 HH (Half Height)	3.5" wide by 6" deep by 1.75" high	20M to 9.1GB
3.5 LP (Low Profile)	3.5" wide by 6" deep by 1" high	20M to 6.4GB
2.5 LP (Low Profile)	2.5" wide by 4" deep by .75" high	20M to 1.2GB

a 5.25 FH drive, you're better served to purchase an external drive if you need a drive this large. Using an external drive—although it requires additional desk space—is a better option.

Some of the high-capacity 3.5 HH or LP drives should be used externally with their own enclosure because of the amount of heat they generate. Mounting them internally in any Mac can result in the drive's premature demise. If you have purchased a raw drive (a plain drive without an external enclosure or an internal mounting kit), check with the drive's manufacturer to see if you can safely install it as an internal drive. This warning primarily applies to the high-capacity (4G and above) 3.5 HH drives.

Warranties

Every hard drive has an original manufacturer's warranty. Usually, the manufacturer—the company that puts the drive in an external case and supplies the formatting software when it sells you the drive—passes the original equipment manufacturer's (OEM) warranty on to you. Before you purchase a new drive, perform the following checks:

❖ Find out the type and length of the drive's warranty offered by the reseller.

❖ Ask the reseller about the manufacturer and type of drive mechanism in the unit you plan to purchase.

❖ Contact the mechanism's manufacturer and ask about the drive's warranty.

❖ If the manufacturer's warranty is different from the reseller's warranty, ask the reseller to give you the same warranty that it receives from the manufacturer.

Often the manufacturer of a drive gives the manufacturer that purchases a drive an extended warranty, but they do not allow you, the final purchaser, to take advantage of the warranty given to the manufacturer. If the vendor does not pass the full warranty on to you, find another vendor that will. There is not enough difference between drive vendors and their products to preclude your getting the full warranty. Besides, you pay for that warranty indirectly.

I've made so much about this issue because your hard drive is more likely to fail than any other component in your computer and because the warranty is a critical part of your investment. Unfortunately, when you buy a new computer you do not get an extended warranty on the hard drive. All computer manufacturers, including Apple, offer a one-year warranty on your system, including the hard drive. My advice can be applied only to third-party hard-drive manufacturers.

If you purchase a new system or a hard drive that does not have a warranty that exceeds one year, you can buy an extended warranty. For Macintosh computers, any Apple Dealer can sell you an AppleCare warranty that covers all the Apple components in your system, including Apple hard drives and memory.

Before you purchase an extended warranty, keep in mind that prices generally decrease. You could pay more for a two-year extended warranty than you would pay to replace your hard drive a year after you purchase it. Table 10.2 offers some insight regarding the cost of hard drives and how the price changes over time (all of these prices are from *Mac Week*, a weekly publication for Macintosh professionals).

As you can see from Table 10.2, prices drop dramatically after a year. You won't always see this dramatic price drop, but it is indicative of how prices change in the computer industry. Also, each year hard-drive manufacturers revamp their product line, often eliminating older models, thereby making it difficult to compare the cost of the same drive from year to year. In Table 10.2 the first two drives are the same, but the third drive is similar. Regardless of the inability to compare the same drive from one year to the next, you should still compare the cost of a long-term warranty with the cost of replacing the drive after the warranty has expired—especially if the warranty is for three years, one that would cover the last drive in listed in Table 10.2.

Starting Up

The discussion up to this point has been about your drive and its physical attributes, and how to purchase a drive, but I have not said much about using it with your Mac. To start your Mac, you need a System Startup disk. Apple assumes that you will be using a hard-disk drive with any Macintosh you purchase. (The days of running your computer on floppy disks are over.) You cannot be productive on a Macintosh without a hard-disk drive and that drive must be properly formatted and contain a System Folder. Chapter 9, "Installing Your System and Software," covers the process of installing your system. As long as you have a System and a properly attached drive, your Mac should start up and run without a problem.

Table 10.2 A Historic View of External Hard Drive Costs

DATE	DRIVE SIZE	TYPE AND SPEED	COST
October 10, 1995	2047 MB	Quantum 5400 RPM	$999.95
May 6, 1996	2047 MB	Quantum 5400 RPM	$699.95
May 5, 1997	2014 MB	Quantum 4500 RPM	$379.00

When more than one drive is attached, you need to make sure that any internally terminated drive is turned on; if it is not, your Mac does not recognize any of your drives. [Termination was discussed in the earlier section, "SCSI (Small Computer Standard Interface)."] When your Mac starts, notice a drive icon in the upper right corner of the Desktop. This icon represents the hard-disk drive that contains the System that is running the Mac. Even if all the other drives have System folders, only one System folder at a time controls the Mac.

There are several reasons why you might have multiple drives. Because any drive with a System folder can boot your Mac, you can configure your additional drives for different purposes. You can set up one System folder to run with the minimum amount of memory and another that allows you to use specific memory-intensive utilities.

Setting the Default Drive

The drive that starts your Mac is called the *default drive*. This section describes how to set your default drive.

To select your startup drive:

1. From the Apple menu, select *Control Panels*.
2. From the Control Panels menu, select the *Startup Disk* control panel. A window opens that displays the drives currently on your Desktop (see Figure 10.16).
3. Select the drive you want to use to run your Mac, then close the window.
4. Restart the computer.

The selected drive becomes the *default drive* or *default startup drive*.

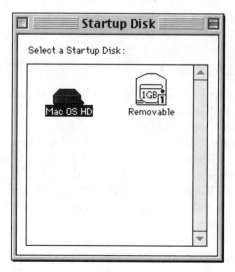

Figure 10.16 *The Startup Disk window.*

Bootable Disks

Even if a drive appears in the Startup Disk window and you select it, the drive still may not be a bootable disk. To be bootable, it must have a System file installed on it. If the Mac does not boot from your selected drive, refer to Chapters 16 and 17 for troubleshooting tips.

Desktop Files

The section on floppy disks explained the different data structures added to a floppy disk during formatting. With Mac OS 8, your hard drive has two additional files. These files are created by the System and serve the same function as (therefore, replace) the Desktop file in System 6.0.X.

The Desktop file under System 6.0.X could keep track of only 6000 files and often failed when the number of files reached 3500 to 4000. A disk with a large capacity and a lot of small files could soon have trouble under System 6.0.X. You could use the Desktop Manager from AppleShare, Apple's file server software, to solve this problem. But, because the Desktop Manager is licensed and can be used only with AppleShare, using it to manage your Desktop file could be yet another problem.

System 7.0 added two files—Desktop DB and Desktop DF—to the hard drive. These files enable your Mac to keep more than 6000 files without causing your hard-disk drive to crash. You can see all these files if you use a utility that displays invisible files (see Figure 10.17).

Hard Drive Sectors

The format on a hard drive is the same as that on a floppy drive, with a couple of exceptions. One difference is that the sectors do not contain sector tags. The main difference, however, is that the sector size of a hard disk can vary; it is usually about 16K on a 1.2GB hard drive, but it can be as large as 32K. The sector size on your hard drive depends on the size of the drive. The larger the drive capacity, the larger the sector size. Figure 10.18 shows the same file, except that the drive on the right is on a 250MB hard drive that uses 8K sectors, and the drive on the left uses 32K sectors and is 1GB. Files sizes are not measured by their actual size but by how many sectors they occupy.

Sector size can be a big problem, especially if you consistently use small files on a large hard drive. You could lose a lot of hard-disk space because of your disk's sector size. If you have this problem, you can partition your hard drive. *Partitioning* is a

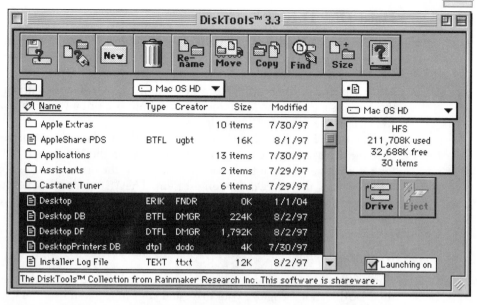

Figure 10.17 *The Desktop DB and Desktop DF files.*

procedure that makes two or more smaller drives, called *logical partitions*, out of a large disk drive. The procedures for partitioning a drive are detailed in the later section, "Formatting a Hard-Disk Drive."

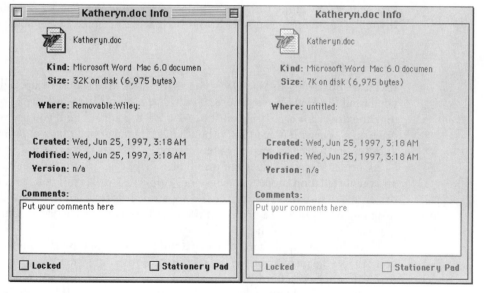

Figure 10.18 *File size and sector size comparison.*

Hard-Disk Drivers

All disk drives and other computer peripherals require a means of sending data to, and receiving data from, the CPU. This peripheral communication is accomplished via a *driver*, a program that tells the computer how to interact with the peripheral. Any peripheral device attached to your computer requires its own driver, even when the driver is a part of the Macintosh System Software or built into the Macintosh ROM, as is the driver for floppy drives.

The driver for a hard disk always resides on the hard drive. The driver is installed onto the drive during the formatting process. When the Macintosh starts up, it looks for a hard drive. When it finds one, the Mac reads the driver into memory and keeps it there during the entire computing session. The Mac can then access its hard drive whenever it needs to. If you have multiple hard drives attached to your Macintosh, the Mac stores the driver for each drive in memory when it starts up.

Driver Corruption

You might start up your computer—with the hard-disk drive attached—and find that the Mac does not recognize your drive and your Mac doesn't start. This situation could result from a cabling problem, a SCSI ID conflict, or a corrupted driver. (For more information about this problem and other possible solutions, see Chapters 15 and 18.) The driver is software and, like other software, it can become corrupted due to a system error, a bad sector, a power loss, or any of several other factors.

Another indicator that your driver has failed is the appearance of a Sad Mac icon when you turn on the computer (see Figure 10.19). The Sad Mac icon is a substitute for the Smiling Mac icon that appears when your Mac boots. The Sad Mac appears when your Mac has either hardware or software difficulty during the startup process. Procedures for dealing with the Sad Mac can be found in Part V, "Troubleshooting." If you're sure the problem is with your hard drive, Chapter 18 can help you.

Driver Compatibility

If you are upgrading to Mac OS 8, your hard disk's driver must be upgraded before you install the Mac OS 8 software. If you have multiple hard-disk drives on your system, the driver for each drive must be Mac OS 8-compatible. If you use your hard drive on a Mac with Mac OS 8 without updating the driver, you will probably experience strange behavior, such as system freezes, hard-disk drive crashes, and disk errors.

As a rule, Mac OS 8 does not install on a drive that has an incompatible driver, and the installation process updates your Apple disk drivers. If you use a third-party driver, make sure that your driver is compatible before you install Mac OS 8; installing Mac OS 8 on a drive that does not have compatible drivers can cause a crash and a total loss of data.

If you have an Apple hard-disk drive and the Drive Setup program from Apple, you can use the instructions in the section "Re-installing the Driver" to upgrade the driver. If you have a third-party hard-disk drive or driver, contact the manufacturer to determine whether your driver is Mac OS 8-compatible. If your driver is not compatible, either have the manufacturer send a compatible driver or purchase a third-

Figure 10.19   The Sad Mac icon.

party driver that is Mac OS 8-compatible. If your driver is compatible, install Mac OS 8 and then follow the instructions for running Disk First Aid in the following section.

Re-installing the Driver

You might need or want to re-install or upgrade the hard-disk driver for several reasons. Two of these reasons are to fix a corrupted driver or to upgrade your System version. Always upgrade your driver when updating or upgrading your System version; failure to do so can cause serious problems.

If you are using an Apple drive (Drive Setup works only on an Apple drive), follow these steps to upgrade the driver:

1. Boot the Mac by using the System Tools (System 6.0.X), Disk Tools (System 7.X or better) disk, or from your bootable System CD.

2. After the system boots, find the Drive Setup program on the disk and double-click on the Drive Setup icon.

3. The Drive Setup program displays a message saying it is searching for hard drives. Then Drive Setup displays all of your Mac's drives in the upper window (see Figure 10.20).

4. Select the drive you wish to use by clicking on its name. Make sure the drive you select has the correct SCSI ID. You find the SCSI ID on the right side of the drives displayed in Figure 10.21. The SCSI ID column is labeled ID.

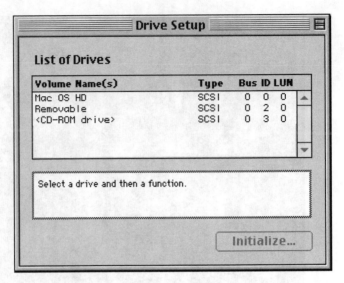

Figure 10.20   *The Apple Drive Setup window.*

Drive Setup displays the drive's name and SCSI ID. If you do not know the name or SCSI ID of the drive on which you want to work, stop everything. Either disconnect all external drives (if you are trying to work on your internal drive) or use one of the techniques described in the next section to determine your drive's number.

5. After you select the correct drive, select the *Update Driver* menu item from the Functions menu. The Installer updates the driver and tells you that the new driver will not be available until your Mac is restarted..

6. Click on the Quit button, then restart your Mac.

Driver Updating Cautions

Whenever you run your formatting software, be careful not to format your drive accidentally. If you format your drive, you lose all your data, and nothing on earth can return it except restoring it from a backup. Make sure that you have a backup, and never try any hard-drive maintenance when you are tired or distracted. One click of a button or an accidental menu selection can send all your data to Never-Never Land.

To update your driver on a third-party drive, refer to the reference manual for your hard-disk drive. There are as many formatters (formatting software) as there are hard-disk drive manufacturers, and each has its own method for updating the driver. With some formatters, such as Hard Disk ToolKit from FWB and Drive 7 from Casa Blanca Works, you can *sometimes* upgrade your driver, even if your drive is for-matted with and has a driver from a different hard-drive manufacturer. If you try to do so, use caution. There is no guarantee that either of these packages will upgrade your drive's driver, so back up your data. Read each message that appears on-screen; if the program asks to initialize your hard disk, cancel the procedure. All formatting software gives you an option to cancel prior to initializing or formatting a hard drive.

After you upgrade your hard-disk drive driver, use Disk First Aid, which is located on your Mac OS 8 CD-ROM or your Disk Tools disk. Earlier versions of the System software contained bugs in the extents and catalog tree files. These bugs caused minor problems, such as the inability to trash empty folders. These errors, which occurred only occasionally, were corrected in System 7 and later versions of the System. Unless you run Disk First Aid after you upgrade your driver, the prob-lems will persist.

To run Disk First Aid:

1. Boot your Mac using the Disk Tools disk, then locate and double-click on the Disk First Aid icon.

2. In the window that appears, select your hard drive (see Figure 10.21).

3. Click on the Repair button.

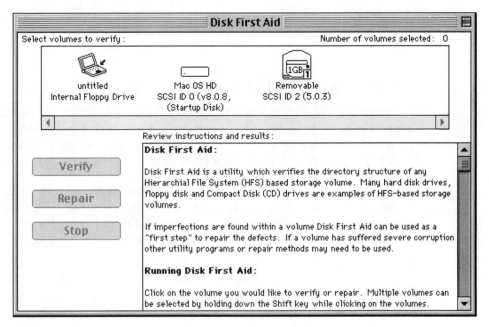

Figure 10.21   *The Disk First Aid window.*

Damaged Drives

Disk First Aid is the first tool to reach for when your hard drive misbehaves. It does more than correct problems left over by System 6.0.X—it can fix a hard drive that is malfunctioning. It will not *always* fix your drive's problems, but it will work about 80 percent of the time. If Disk First Aid is unable to repair your hard-disk drive, it will tell you. If so, you have serious problems. Back up all critical data (if you haven't done so yet), and format your hard drive. Although you might be able to repair your hard disk with a utility, such as Norton Utilities from Symantec or Disk Tools from Central Point Software, you should not just repair your drive and continue to work. (Using Norton Utilities is discussed in Part V, "Troubleshooting.") If Disk First Aid does not completely fix your drive, you will continue to have hard-disk problems, and all of your data is at risk.

Disk First Aid checks and verifies your drive's directory. If your hard-disk drive requires repairs, the program then informs you either that it was unable to repair the drive or that the repairs are complete.

The previous procedure uses the Disk First Aid utility that comes with System 7.5 and later. If you use an earlier version of Disk First Aid, get Norton Utilities for the Macintosh.

Formatting a Hard-Disk Drive

Every hard-disk drive comes with formatting software. In fact, what distinguishes one Macintosh hard-disk drive manufacturer from another is the formatting software and the case of the hard-disk drive. It is not uncommon to find several manufacturers using the same drive mechanism—and even the same case—and yet using different formatting software.

In addition to installing the driver, the formatter also formats your hard disk for use with the Mac. In this sense, it performs the same functions as the initialization process for a floppy disk (refer to the section, "How to Format Floppy Disks," earlier in this chapter). In addition, the formatter also sets up the following:

❖ The interleave—The interleave setting directly affects the speed of your hard-disk drive by determining how the drive stores data.

❖ The size of the drive's allocation block—Each disk partition has an allocation block size, and the size of the allocation block can affect the performance of the hard-disk drive.

❖ The size and number of partitions—The size of the bitmap partition determines the overall size of the hard-disk drive. If your formatting software predetermines this size, you may not be getting the maximum available space on your drive.

❖ Initializing your drive—After your drive has been formatted and partitioned, it needs to be initialized. The initialization process creates the hard drive's directory.

Selecting the Interleave Settings

The interleave setting determines how hard your hard-disk drive has to work, and it directly affects the drive's access time. Because the platters in your hard-disk drive rotate at speeds from 3600 to 10,000 rpm, the heads must be able to determine when they need to read and write data. The actuator arm performs part of this process by moving back and forth at predetermined intervals controlled by either a voice coil actuator or a stepper motor. The logic board on the drive performs the rest of the process.

Setting the Allocation Block Size

The allocation block size affects how much disk space your files use. If you use a large allocation block size on a small drive, for example, you might waste some hard-disk space. The type of data files you use should dictate the size of your drive's allo-

Voice Coil Actuators

The voice coil actuator is a small motor that operates on the same principles as sound used in your stereo speakers. The strength of the electric current passing through an electromagnet pulls the actuator arm or armature backward, thus positioning the heads. Some drives now have actuators positioned opposite each other, so that there are two heads; the result is that you can access data twice as fast.

There are three standard interleave settings: 1:1, 2:1, and 3:1. These ratios determine where data is written on your drive. Each track is divided into sectors where your drive must write and read its data as the sectors pass underneath the drive's heads. If the Mac is not fast enough to read data written in contiguous sectors (1:1), it has to wait while the platter spins an extra revolution before it can read the next sector. If your Mac is not fast enough to use a 1:1 interleave, it can't use Mac OS 8 either. The last version of the Macintosh System that will work on older Macs (of the Plus, SE, and Mac II variety) is System 7.5.5.

cation blocks. If you have large database files, use larger allocation blocks, which are read more quickly. If you keep only small word-processed files, use smaller allocation blocks so that you do not waste disk space. Regardless of the type of data you store, the ultimate factor for allocation block size is the size of the hard-disk partition. The larger the partition, the larger the allocation block size. As a rule of thumb, each gigabyte of hard-disk space requires a 16K allocation block; thus, a 2GB drive needs a 32K allocation block, and a 4GB drive needs a 96K allocation block. These are general guidelines that can vary depending on the type of drive you use.

The setting for your allocation block size is usually a transparent function of your formatter, and most formatters do not let you change it. To change the allocation block size, you must use a formatter such as Hard Disk ToolKit from FWB or Drive 7 from Casa Blanca, which are third-party formatters that allow you to customize your drive's format. Most formatters, even third-party formatters, do not give you the type of control you can get from Hard Disk ToolKit.

Setting Up Partitions

Some formatters enable you to partition your hard drive. When you partition your drive, the formatting software creates two or more bitmap partitions on your disk and tells the Mac that you have two drives instead of one. Because you do not have two physical drives, the partitions are called *logical partitions* or *logical drives*.

In addition to creating logical drives, a partition can have security features as well. You can generally password-protect a partition so that it will not mount without the correct password. Some formatters and partitioners can also encrypt the data in the partition, so that someone else cannot see the contents of the drive without knowing the correct password. On the downside, password-protecting a drive or a partition (regardless of the encryption factor) makes it very difficult, but not impossible, to access that drive without the password. If it is just password-protected and not encrypted, you can use a disk-recovery package to access all the data. If your partition is encrypted and you forget your password, it will be very difficult, if not impossible, to recover your hard drive.

Partitioning your disk drive can also increase speed. To create a partition, you must have contiguous disk space available. Because the space is contiguous and occupies a specific physical section of your hard drive, the heads have a shorter distance to travel to locate data. Each partition is positioned at a separate logical drive. The primary partition is the first partition created; it contains the physical track numbered 0. The Mac looks to this track for startup information when it boots from a disk.

Another reason for partitioning your hard drive is so that you can use it both on a Mac and on another type of computer, such as a PC. You can do this by partitioning your drive when you format it, leaving part of your drive free and unused. When you hook it up to another computer, that computer recognizes the partitioned part of the drive, and the other computer's formatter recognizes the remainder that is free. You can then partition the remaining space on the drive for the *other* computer. Creating this type of partition is an esoteric use for a Mac's hard drive. If you really want to do something like this, you will have to experiment.

Hard Disk Flaws

Over time, every hard drive has or can develop flaws in its magnetic media so that parts of the media cannot hold a charge. When you format your drive, the software finds these flawed sections by testing the drive after it has divided it into tracks and sectors. Whenever it finds a bad sector, it maps it out or makes it unavailable for use.

A bad sector table tracks the locations of the bad sectors; unfortunately, this table has a limited amount of space for storing the addresses of the bad sectors. If your drive suffers a head crash (where the heads strike or come in contact with the media) or—through normal wear and tear—develops too many bad sectors, your drive will not format. You then must purchase a new drive.

Low-Level Formatting

When you use formatting software to format your drive, you perform a low-level format. This process creates the tracks and allocation blocks on the drive, installs the driver, and writes the other necessary files to the hard disk. The formatter also checks the disk for actual physical defects and maps out any problematic allocation blocks, which prevents data from being stored in these sectors. Most formatters automatically map out bad sectors; however, some formatters ask you to perform the dirty deed.

A low-level format clears the disk and erases any data that the disk contains. Rather than perform a low-level format, you can initialize your drive, which is a high-level format. A high-level format erases and recreates the directory but does not erase the data on the disk. Therefore, although the Mac does not recognize the data, the data is recoverable. This same process occurs when you erase a single file: The directory reference for that file is deleted, but the file data is not actually erased until the space that the file contains is needed for another file.

To initialize a hard disk:

1. On the Desktop, select the icon of the hard disk you want to format. You cannot erase your Startup disk.
2. From the Special menu, choose *Erase Disk*.
3. In less than a minute, your drive is wiped clean and appears on the Desktop as an empty drive.

If you want to reformat your drive because you are having trouble, do not initialize it. You cannot fix a problem with your driver or the boot blocks by erasing the disk. You must reformat the disk to repair problems on this level. Trouble can be anything from system errors that will not go away even after you have reinstalled

Accidental Initialization

If you accidentally initialize a disk that contains data you need, turn off the computer and read the section on disk recovery in Chapter 19. Do not save, copy, or write any data to your hard disk until you have recovered the files.

your system (covered in Chapter 6), to frequent read and write errors. Before formatting your drive, be sure to read the chapters on troubleshooting.

Purchasing a New Formatter

Because your formatting software is responsible for the performance of your drive, you might want to purchase a new formatter. Apple's formatting software is fine, but it does not give you the control over your hard-disk drive that other formatters offer. Drive manufacturers often do not write the software that accompanies their drives; instead, a company might license formatting software from a vendor that sells different versions—with only minor interface modifications—to several different manufacturers. To get the most from your hard drive, consider purchasing new formatting software.

Several companies publish hard-drive formatters; they are listed in Table 10.3. That a publisher is included in the table does not constitute a recommendation.

Almost all the software publishers listed in Table 10.3 make several other hard-disk enhancement products in addition to their formatters.

Table 10.3   Hard Disk Formatters

PUBLISHER	PRODUCT NAME
CharisMac Engineering	1-Anubis
Bering Technology	Disk Café
Ontrack Computer Systems, Inc.	Disk Manager Mac 3.0
Golden Triangle Computer, Inc.	DiskMaker
Casa Blanca Works, Inc.	Drive 7
Software Architects, Inc.	FormatterOne
FWB, Inc.	Hard Disk ToolKit
Surf City Software	Lido 7
Peripheral Land, Inc.	PLI Formatter

Optional Storage Devices

Several different types of drive technologies are available for the Macintosh. To select the correct drive for your needs, you must know the pros and cons for each of the different technologies. The following sections look at the different technologies and their strengths and weaknesses.

SCSI Standards

The computer industry is a moving target. As soon as you think you have all the standards figured out, someone invents a new standard. So it is with SCSI standards. You should be aware of the SCSI standards you're likely to encounter. These standards are as follows:

- ❖ SCSI I—The original SCSI Standard.
- ❖ SCSI II—A standard that improves the SCSI I standard by providing faster and more reliable data throughput.
- ❖ SCSI II Fast—An addition to the SCSI II standard that requires a 50-pin cable to double the data throughput.
- ❖ SCSI II Wide—An option to the SCSI II standard that allows for increasing the data path from 8 to 16 or 32 bits. The implementation of SCSI II Wide requires a 68-pin cable.
- ❖ SCSI II Fast and Wide—A combination of both the SCSI II Fast and SCSI II Wide standards.
- ❖ UltraSCSI —UltraSCSI is the newest standard. It offers data throughputs that can double the speed of SCSI II Fast and Wide through a combination of increased drive speeds and improved electronics on the drive. UltraSCSI is also called SCSI III Fast and Wide. UltraSCSI uses the same cabling as SCSI II Fast and Wide.

For a Macintosh to take advantage of any of the SCSI Standards beyond Fast SCSI II, you must buy a third-party SCSI controller card. Unless you are creating a file server, high-end graphics workstation, or an Internet Web Server, you won't need the increased speeds of the newer SCSI standards. All SCSI Standards are backward compatible to SCSI I, but it doesn't make sense to buy an UltraSCSI drive to be used with a SCSI I or SCSI II Fast interface. You won't be able to take advantage of the extra speed for which you've paid.

RAID Systems

As the need for more hard-disk capacity, faster drives, and data security becomes more common, these needs are being met by a technology call RAID, or Redundant Array of Independent Drives. A RAID is a series of drives that are connected so that they can act as a single device; depending on the RAID configuration, a drive that fails can be reconstructed simply by installing a new drive.

There are six RAID categories called Levels. Each RAID level and its attributes are described here.

❖ Level Zero—A Level Zero RAID system consists of two or more drives connected in parallel so that data is written to both drives simultaneously through a process called *data striping*. Although you use two drives they appear to be a single drive. By writing to two or more drives at the same time, data throughput can be twice as fast. With Level Zero RAID there is no data redundancy. If one of the drives fails, all the data on both (or more) drives is lost.

❖ Level One—With a Level One RAID system you get increased data security, but you do not have the speed increase achieved by a Level Zero RAID system. Level One RAID consists of two, four, or more drives installed in pairs where data is written to two drives simultaneously, with the second drive being a copy of the first. This process is called *disk mirroring*. The advantage of a Level One RAID system is data security. If the primary drive fails it can be removed and the secondary drive can be used immediately.

❖ Levels Two, Three, and Four are not normally used with Macintosh systems.

❖ Level Five—A Level Five RAID system is called an *independent disk array*. It offers the highest level of data security, and although not the fastest of the RAIDs, it is very fast and adequate for most needs. The Level Five RAID operates by distributing data across several drives (usually three or more) and by storing parity data on all drives. This means that one drive can fail, but the data from the failed drive can be reconstructed by replacing the failed drive. The reconstruction takes place by using the parity stored on the other drives. In very high-end RAID systems (with prices starting around $14,000) you can have a hot-swappable RAID, which means you can replace a failed drive without turning off the system.

RAIDs usually require Fast and Wide or Ultra SCSI drives. For best results, you also need a special SCSI II Fast and Wide or Ultra SCSI controller card. If you need data redundancy and the ability to recover from a disaster quickly, you will want to explore RAID options in more detail.

Winchester Drives

The Winchester drive is the most popular drive used in any computer system, including the Macintosh. Winchester drives are very fast and, as a whole, reliable. The fastest drives have access times of about 3 milliseconds, and they have capacities from 20MB to 23GB.

Iomega

Iomega is one of the more innovative drive manufacturers in today's market. In the last two years it has brought two revolutionary drives to the market place. One is called the Zip drive; the other is called a Jaz drive.

The Zip drive is a 100MB floppy disk. Some of the Macintosh-compatible manufacturers include a Zip drive as a standard system component. Zip drives are inexpensive, rugged, and transportable. A Zip drive, however, should not be considered a hard-drive replacement. The drives are not fast, but they are very reliable. A Zip drive weights about a pound, and the disks are the same size as a floppy disk, only twice as thick. All of these features have made the Zip drive a favorite for backing up critical data, sending files to service bureaus, and exchanging files with friends.

Iomega's Jaz drive, on the other hand, is a 1GB removable hard drive. The Jaz drive uses Winchester technology and is moderately fast. The disk is four inches square, and the Jaz mechanism is a 3.5 HH drive. The Jaz drive is excellent for creating CD-ROM masters and for storing and transporting large graphics projects; it can even be used as a primary hard drive. The cost for a Jaz drive is also attractive, about $400 for a drive with one disk. Finally, a Jaz drive is relatively light and easily transported from one location to another.

SyQuest

SyQuest, a company in Fremont, California, developed a removable media drive based on Winchester technology. The first drive it produced had a capacity of 10MB, but it was not available for the Mac. When the company developed a 45MB drive several years ago, it became a popular storage medium because it was fast (25ms average access time), and the total data storage capacity was unlimited. If you need more disk space, you just buy a new disk.

SyQuest is currently selling a 135MB, a 194MB, and a 255MB 3.5-inch HH removable media drives that operate like their 5.25-inch siblings. The smaller drives are nice, compact drives that are highly portable. The SyQuest drive is a primary means for easily moving large data files from Mac to Mac, and it is a popular method with graphic artists for transporting large projects to prepress shops. SyQuest also makes an excellent backup and archive device.

The biggest drawback to the SyQuest technology is in the disks, which tend to fail more often than a regular Winchester disk. A SyQuest disk that is used constantly will last only about two years and, even though SyQuest drives come with a two-year warranty, the disks have only a one-year warranty. The other drawback is that a SyQuest drive is easy to damage through improper usage—trying to force a disk out before the disk has stopped spinning or while it is still on, for example. One of the nicest features of the SyQuest disk, however, is that it lets you change disks without restarting your Mac.

SyQuest does not market its drives to the public. You can get a SyQuest-based drive only through hard-drive vendors that market a disk drive based on the SyQuest mechanism under their own name and label. Because a large number of vendors offer these drives, the market and prices are competitive. Almost every major and minor Macintosh hard-disk vendor sells a model based on the SyQuest mechanism. These devices are a little more expensive than a fixed disk drive, but they offer unlimited storage capacity. If you want to back up a 1.2-gigabyte drive, do not use SyQuest disks—there are better backup strategies for high-capacity drives.

Optical Media Devices

Optical media devices all use a technology similar to that found in an audio compact disk player. All optical media devices are variations on a single theme: Optical media data is encoded in such a way that a laser can read the disk. The different types of drives and disks are as follows:

❖ Compact Disc-Read Only Media (CD-ROM)—A CD-ROM drive reads only prepared CD-ROM discs; it will not write data.

❖ Erasable Optical Drives—These drives read and write data to an optical disk similar to the CD-ROM disk.

❖ CDR (Recordable CD-ROM)—These devices are a CD-ROM drive with which you can record your own CD-ROM disks. They also double as CD-ROM readers.

The following sections provide a more detailed discussion of each of these drive types.

CD-ROM

CD-ROM drives are slow when compared to hard drives, but they have been speeding up over the last two years. Now the fastest drives have an access time around 30ms. The disks can, however, disseminate large amounts of data. Each CD-ROM can hold more than 600MB of data, making them perfect for providing large amounts of data to any number of users.

Currently, you can obtain large collections of shareware and public-domain programs from user groups on CD-ROMs, such as the one included with this book. Apple uses CD-ROMs to keep its dealers and developers up to date regarding the changes in its machines and technical information. And the Macintosh System is now distributed on CD-ROM. Both Adobe and Microsoft distribute programs and fonts on CD-ROMs, and other companies distribute mailing lists, collections of books, encyclopedias, and databases of all types, to name a few, on CD-ROM. A CD-ROM drive is now a business necessity—and a necessity for any Macintosh. More and more software is distributed on CD-ROMs. Also, every Macintosh available today automatically comes with a CD-ROM drive installed.

Erasable Optical Drives

Erasable optical drives are the future for data storage. These devices use a disk similar to the CD-ROM, except that they use a magnet to write data. The process works by using a laser to heat a section of the disk where a piece of magnetic material is embedded. When the temperature is high enough to free the magnetic particle, an electromagnet charges the particle, causing the particle to change position. The plastic material around the particle cools and freezes the particle in its place. Then, the drive uses a laser to read the reflected light off the disk, which is refracted at different angles, depending on the position of the particle. The different angles are the bits of data, similar to charged magnetic particles on a hard disk.

The advantage of this medium is that it is sensitive to magnetic fields only when it is hot or heated by the laser. As a result, the data is more stable than data on a hard disk. Manufacturers of erasable optical disks claim that the disks have a 10-year life, although the disks could last for 100 years. Because the disks are removable, they act like floppies, and you can use multiple disks.

Finally, the disks have high capacities. A 5.25-inch disk holds from 600MB to 2.4GB of data. Large corporations with huge databases use erasable optical drives attached to a juke box that can hold several hundred disks, providing online access to hundreds of gigabytes of data. In addition to the 5.25-inch drives, 3.5-inch drives became available at the end of 1991, each with a capacity of 120MB to 230MB. These disks are the same size as the standard Mac floppies, except that they are twice as thick.

Erasable optical disk drives are slow, although not as slow as CD-ROM drives. The basic drives are capable of access times in the 30ms to 120ms range, which makes them anywhere from 3 to 10 times slower than a Winchester hard drive. Currently, then, the erasable optical disk drives are best used for archiving data because their slow speed makes them difficult to use in real-world situations.

As this technology develops, speeds will increase. The first Winchester hard drives used on the Mac had access times in the 50ms range—and this was only five and a half years ago. In addition to the speed increasing, the erasable optical drives also will soon be able to read CD-ROMs—eliminating the need for a CD-ROM drive and an erasable optical disk. These disks and drives are the technology of the future.

CDR Drives

CDR drives are CD-ROM drives that can also write to recordable CD-ROM disks. Data gets written to the disks just once, then it can be read as many times as you wish. The disks have the same qualities as CD-ROM disks.

CDR drives make it possible for you to archive your data, to create your own music CDs, and to store large quantities of data inexpensively. The biggest drawback to a CDR drive is that you can't mount it on the Desktop and drag files and data onto the disk. You have to use a special program to write to the CD. It won't be long until a CDR is a necessity in most graphic shops and many businesses.

Tape Drives

A tape drive is another storage medium. These devices are good for backing up hard drives and archiving critical company information. Several types of drives are available, but one type is taking over the tape drive market in the Macintosh world: the DAT, or Digital Audio Tape, drive.

When compared to a DAT drive, all other tape drives pale. The DAT drive, like the CD-ROM drive, originated in the music industry, then moved into the computer world. The DAT is capable of very high speeds, and a single tape can hold from 1.2

to 24 gigabytes of data. Although DAT drives cost from $600 to $1800, these drives pay for themselves in time saving sand reduced media costs. A cartridge costs $20 to $30 and holds approximately 10 times the data of other devices.

If you need more than a single tape to back up your data, drives are available with loaders that allow you to stack several DAT tapes. When one tape is full, the loader makes another tape available to the drive. This way you can always have a full backup of all your data.

Even if you use a RAID configuration, you should also use an alternative backup method such as a DAT drive. The primary reason for having an alternative backup is so that you can take a backup off-site. This way, if anything happens to your system, such as fire or theft, you have a copy of your data and can restore your data and get back to work as soon as possible. Re-creating data is not fun.

SCSI RAM Disks

A couple of companies make large-capacity external RAM disks that connect to the Mac via the SCSI port. A SCSI RAM drive uses memory chips instead of a hard-drive mechanism. These disks are very expensive but very fast. They are usually 20MB to 512MB in size, and their primary advantage is that they are not mechanical—access times are 0 when tested with hard-disk testers.

The main disadvantage of this type of storage medium is its instability. If you experience a serious crash, you cannot recover your data. Although these disks usually have a battery backup in case of power failures, if the battery does not function, your data disappears and cannot be recovered. Justifying the cost of one of these systems is difficult, but if you use large programs, such as CAD/CAM, rendering programs, or very large graphics files, and if screen refresh rates and overall speed are critical, you might consider purchasing one of these drives.

Summary

This chapter covered most of the operating and technical aspects of your Macintosh drive subsystems. You should now know how both a floppy disk and a hard drive are formatted and how they operate. You also have learned how to prevent and remedy some of the more common disk-drive problems. In addition to an increased knowledge of your drives, you are now a more informed shopper, able to get the most for your money. And, perhaps more importantly, you are able to decide what type of drive you need.

And, if you should have problems with your hard-disk drive, you have the first building blocks for correcting the problem and saving your data. If you run into trouble with your hard drive, remember that, in most cases, all is not lost. Relax, review this chapter, and think before you do anything. If you panic, the situation will only get worse.

Essential File, Disk, and Data Information

I n the last chapter, we talked about your Mac's disk drives. Now, it is time to look at what is stored on your drives: all of your files and programs. This chapter is not about where your files are located, configuring your hard disk, or using the files. It is about the structure of your files and how to keep your data safe. Knowing about the structure and attributes of your files is an esoteric subject—even though it is fundamental to how your Mac works. The information in this chapter about file formats and attributes helps you use files that come from other types of computers, created by programs you don't have. Having this information is like knowing that you can take other streets when the one you normally use has a traffic jam.

The other part of this chapter, which discusses keeping your data safe, gives you a lot of information about backing up your data and safely storing it, plus strategies for making this task as painless as possible. Your work is valuable. If you don't safeguard it, no one else will.

Finally, at the end of this chapter is an off-topic discussion about using your Mac as a PC. The only reason I've put this brief discussion here is because it doesn't fit anywhere, but the information is valuable to some people. The only connecting thread is that I talk about using PC disks in a Mac and that does, in a strange way, open the door to the topic of using your Mac as a DOS/Windows machine.

Document Formats (or The Anatomy of Macintosh Files)

In Chapter 6, "Getting the Most from Your OS," several different types of files were mentioned; each file had its own icon representing the data files function. In addition to a function, each file also has a format. A file's format is how the program that created the file writes the data to the disk.

When you use a word processor, your data files contain more than just the words you write—it also contains all the data necessary to format your document. If you used **boldface** characters, underlined some of your text, or emphasized a point with *italics*, the program must somehow restore those attributes to your document so that it looks just as it did the last time you worked on it. To accomplish this, each program creates files that use different formats. As of yet, there is no universal document format. Some programs can interpret the formats of files created by other programs, but none can read all the different types of files.

Another aspect of a Macintosh file is that, as you view it in the Finder, you see a single file, but it could really be a collection of files. Complex data created by page layout, spreadsheet, and some database programs fall into this category.

If you ever have to recover one of these files, as described in Chapter 19, the file's complexity can make your recovery attempt more difficult. Often the recovery of complex files is not successful. Finally, complex files are more fragile; the more complex the file, the greater the likelihood of its becoming corrupted. By the time you finish this section, you will have a better understanding of how complex a Mac file really is.

This section looks at how files are constructed and where they obtain their attributes. The topics covered are as follows:

❖ Data and Resource forks
❖ Creators and types
❖ Missing applications
❖ How to use different formats
❖ Changing type and creator codes
❖ Other attributes

Data and Resource Forks

All Macintosh files can have a Data fork and a Resource fork. A *Resource fork* is the part of a file that contains machine code or data that is composed of program-like information. You cannot access the data in a Resource fork, but the file's program can use it. Most applications have only a Resource fork. The information contained in a Resource fork is there to make your Macintosh perform a specific function.

The *Data fork* is the part of a file that contains raw data. The file's program or another program that can read the file's format uses the data in the Data fork. One example occurs when one word processing program (for example, Microsoft Word) is able to read a file created by another word processing program (for example, MacWrite). Both of these programs store their data in different formats, and it is only because the format information is shared between the two software publishers (Microsoft and Claris) that each program can read files created by the other.

In Figure 11.1, you see a series of files as viewed through DiskTools (a disk utility discussed later in this chapter and included on the book's CD-ROM). With DiskTools, you can see the size of a file's Data and Resource forks. As you can see, all the data files have only Data forks, but the Microsoft Word application has a large

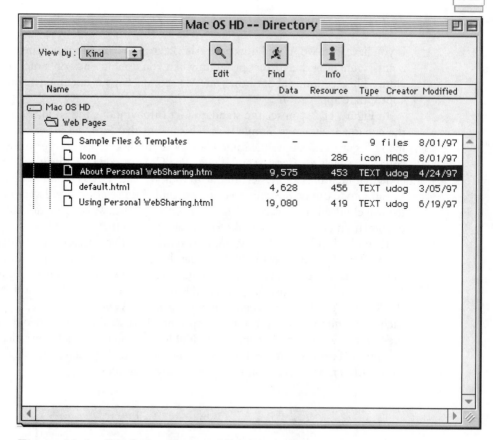

Figure 11.1 *Displaying Data and Resource information.*

Resource fork and a small Data fork. The importance of the Data and Resource forks to you, a Macintosh user, is probably nominal. You should be aware that they exist and that the Resource fork contains the data necessary to make a program run whereas the Data fork contains the actual data that a program uses and presents to you for processing.

The resources contained in a program's file are actually separate files all contained within a larger file that is the program itself. When your Mac runs a program, it uses the resources in the Resource fork by loading them into memory. Resources let your Mac load part of a program into memory, rather than the whole file. If the Mac needs a part of the program that is not in its memory, it goes to the disk drive and gets the resource it needs.

The Power Macintosh has brought some changes to the structure of Macintosh programs and how they run. Because the Power Mac uses a different type of CPU, it does not handle programs—if they are native Power Mac programs—in the same way. You still see a Resource fork in a Power Macintosh program, but when a Power Mac runs a program, it loads all the program's code into memory. This means that a Power Mac needs more RAM than the 680X0-based Macs when they run the same programs.

Creators and Types

If you have ever wondered how your Mac keeps track of different types of documents, launching the correct program when you double-click on a file, you are not alone. This section is about how your Mac connects your documents with their appropriate applications.

In Figure 11.2, you see the standard Get Info window; the Kind designation for the document shown is SimpleText. This means that SimpleText created the document. Figure 11.3 shows the same file viewed in DiskTools. There you see two codes, one each for Creator and Type. The Creator code for this file is "ttxt," the code that identifies all files created with SimpleText. The association made by the Creator code can be described as a parent and child relationship: Every parent knows its own children, and every child recognizes its parent. When you double-click on a document, it automatically looks for the application that created it.

If you look at Figure 11.3 again, notice that the Type designation for this file is "ttro." The Type code is the file's format designator, what any application looks for to see if it can open a particular file. Figure 11.4 shows an Open dialog box from Microsoft Word that displays all the files that Microsoft Word can read. Notice that the SimpleText file we've been looking at is listed. Word looks at the Type code for each of the files to see if it can read a specific file type; if it can, it then displays all the file types it can read and open. If you double-click on the SimpleText file, it launches the SimpleText program and opens the file; you can also open a SimpleText file from within most Macintosh word processing programs.

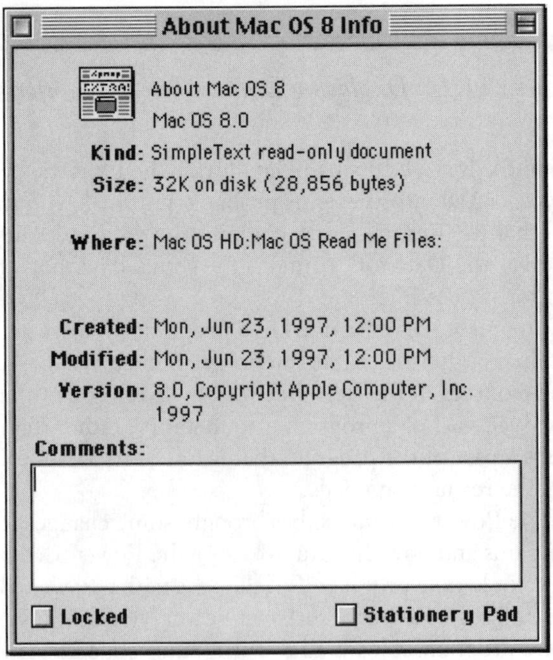

Figure 11.2 *A Get Info window displaying file kind.*

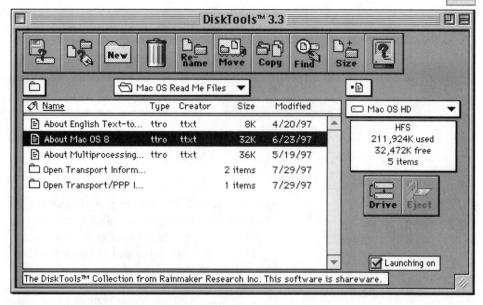

Figure 11.3 *Viewing a file's Creator and Type.*

Missing Applications

If you have not run across the dialog box in Figure 11.5 yet, you will. This is the dialog box you get when you double-click on an orphaned document that doesn't have a corresponding application. If you try to open a document that does not have a corresponding application that SimpleText can open, a dialog box appears that asks you if

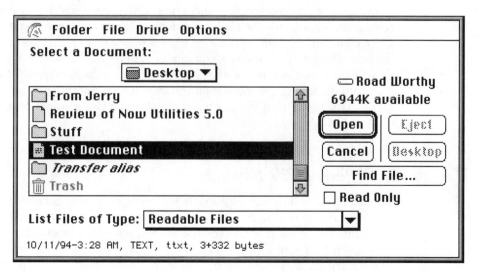

Figure 11.4 *Files viewed in Microsoft Word's Open dialog box.*

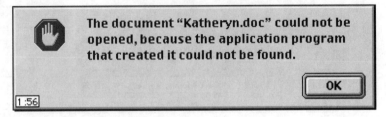

Figure 11.5 *Missing application dialog box.*

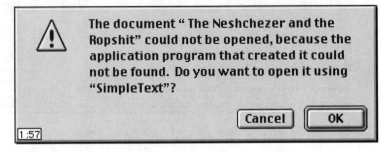

Figure 11.6 *Open with SimpleText dialog box.*

you want to use SimpleText to open it, as shown in Figure 11.6. SimpleText will open text and graphics files that are in the PICT format. (File formats are discussed in the next section, "How to Use Different Formats.")

Either (or both) of these dialog boxes can be annoying when it appears. In many cases, you want your PICT files to be opened by your graphics package, such as PhotoShop or Canvas. And, for other types of files, you may have a program that will open them but, because the file has a different creator code, you have to use the Open command from the application instead of just double-clicking on the data file. To help eliminate this nuisance, you can do a couple of things. One way to open these obnoxious files is to use what is called drag-and-drop, dragging the document's icon onto the icon of the application you want to use. Another way is to use the File menu's Open command from within the application you're using. Also, you can change the file's creator code.

How to Use Different File Formats

Because so many different file formats are in use, you could get a file from a friend and be unable to read it, even though most programs can open a variety of formats. Unfortunately, if the program you use will not open the document, you will either have to get the file in a format that your program can read or purchase the program that created the document. Both of these are time-consuming and possibly expensive options.

General Concepts

This section discusses some general file format concepts and some various file formats you will probably encounter. Some Macintosh standard formats can be used with a wide number of Macintosh programs. The following is a set of guidelines for working with various formats, but you will have to experiment with your applications and files to see which procedures work for you.

Opening Files Created in Other Formats—To determine if a program you use can open a file created in another format, follow this procedure. These are general steps that may not work with every program; if the steps do not work, experimentation is the order of the day. If you take time to experiment, when you need to translate that file, you'll be ready.

1. Open the program you want to use.
2. Select the *Open* or *Import* menu item from the File menu.
3. From the Open dialog box, select the file you want to open. Some Open dialog boxes have an Options button or a pop-up menu you can use to select the file format with which you want to work.
4. Open the file.

If the file you want to open is not listed in the Open dialog box, it means that your program can't open the file. In this case, you need to get a file format translator or a new copy of the file in a different format. If you plan to send a file to someone and you're not sure what format to use, use one of the formats listed in the next few sections.

To save a file in a format other than the program's native format, follow the preceding steps, substituting the *Save As...* or *Export* menu item for the *Open* or *Import* menu item. In either instance, whether exporting or importing foreign file formats, you may have to check your program's manual. If you do, look in the manual's index for the Importing or Exporting topics.

Word Processing Formats—Most word processing programs can open files created by other word processors, but when your word processor can't open the other word processing document, request that the file's creator save the document as an RTF file. RTF stands for Rich Text Format; RTF files work with every word processor I know.

Another format that is popular and can be opened by most programs is the MacWrite file format. MacWrite was the first word processing program made for the Macintosh. If there is a program format universal to the Macintosh, other than RTF, it is MacWrite.

One other word processing format almost as universal as MacWrite is Microsoft Word, the most popular word processor used on the Mac. Word's popularity has forced the publishers of other word processors to provide format compatibility.

The biggest problem you encounter with files created by MacWrite or Microsoft Word is the program's version. MacWrite is now called MacWrite Pro, and

Microsoft Word is at version 6.0. The files created by the latest versions of these programs probably create files that are not compatible with other word processors until those programs are updated. In the meantime, the file versions most compatible for these programs are files in MacWrite II format and Microsoft Word 4.0 or 5.0.

Graphics Formats—Three graphics file formats are popular on the Mac. Each can be used by almost all Mac programs, even those that are not graphics programs. These formats are as follows:

❖ PICT—The PICTure file format is a high-resolution image format used by high-end photo editing programs. The PICT format is used with color images.

❖ TIFF (Tagged Image File Format)—The TIFF format is a cross-platform format that can be used on all types of computers, as long as they have the right software. It is primarily a black-and-white format, but it can be used with color images. It is as close to a universal graphics format as you'll find.

❖ MacPaint (A bitmapped graphics file format)—MacPaint was the first graphics package created for the Mac. It uses what is called a *bitmapped file image* and is a Macintosh standard. It is not used very often, however, because MacPaint images do not produce the high-quality images you can get from TIFF or PICT images.

❖ EPS (Encapsulated PostScript)—The EPS format is a standard created by Adobe Systems that uses the PostScript page description language to create images. EPS is a Macintosh standard that many Mac programs can access. EPS is usually used by graphic artists and for high-end graphics production work.

Every graphics program—unless it is an EPS graphics program—uses one or all of these formats. Although graphics files and their formats are a fairly complex subject, you should have no problem using any of these formats. SimpleText will open PICT files if you don't have another program that uses the PICT format, but you can't edit the image.

Spreadsheet Programs—Although a discussion about spreadsheet formats is almost academic, spreadsheets do need to be mentioned. The discussion is academic because Microsoft Excel is the dominant Macintosh spreadsheet program; no other program even begins to compete. If you receive files from someone who has a PC running DOS or Windows, you have to deal with format translations. One format is universal to spreadsheets on almost all computing platforms: SYLK, which stands for Symbolic Link format. If you have problems with a spreadsheet file from another program, get a copy of the file saved in the SYLK format; it will work when all others fail. Although Excel reads Lotus 1-2-3 and some other file formats, the SYLK format always works.

Mac OS Easy Open

To make data translations easier, in Mac OS 8 Apple includes a utility called Mac OS Easy Open. This utility is a control panel that lists any application that can open the file when you attempt to open an orphaned document. The dialog box in Figure 11.7 shows the Mac OS Easy Open at work.

A Mac OS 8 Easy Install automatically installs Mac OS Easy Open onto your Macintosh. To configure Mac OS Easy Open, open the Mac OS Easy Open control panel. Your choices are these:

❖ Turn Easy Open on or off
❖ Always show the dialog box in Figure 11.7
❖ Search file servers for compatible applications
❖ Auto-pick the application if there is only one
❖ Translate TEXT documents

You'll have to experiment with some of these settings. When you have multiple applications that can open a particular file type, Mac OS Easy Open can be irritating when working with a lot of orphaned files—especially with the DataVIZ translators installed. Every time you open an orphaned file, even from a program's Open dialog box, Mac OS Easy Open presents you with its translation choices. If you use a utility that maps—that is, assigns specific document types to applications—Mac OS Easy Open becomes less irritating and more useful.

Included on the Mac OS 8 CD-ROM are an additional set of translators that work with Mac OS Easy Open from DataVIZ. These translators are primarily for translating MS-DOS and Microsoft Windows documents into Macintosh formats. More information about translating documents from other platforms into Macintosh documents appears in the next section.

MacLink Plus

Another option that helps you deal with files from other programs is to use a program that translates one file format into another. The most popular program for per-

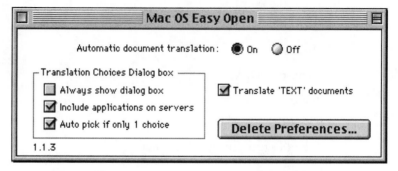

Figure 11.7   *Mac OS Easy Open.*

forming this task is called MacLink Plus from DataVIZ. This program, with its included file translators, enables you to convert a variety of Macintosh formats into other Mac formats; you can also convert Mac documents into MS-DOS files, and vice versa.

The Claris XTND System

Apple, through its subsidiary Claris, is trying to establish a system for translating documents with different or foreign formats by instituting a translation standard called Claris XTND. Whenever you purchase a Claris product, you get the basic system plus several translators as part of the software. In addition, several manufacturers are adopting this system as a means of providing file translations for their customers as well.

If you use MacWrite, Claris Works, or other Claris products, you can also add to your file translation capabilities by using MacLink translators. You can install all the MacLink translators so that they are available for use with your Claris- or XTND-compatible programs.

The following is a list of the available Claris translators (this list does not include the MacLink translators):

Acta 3.0

AppleWorks

EPSF PLFT (Encapsulated Postscript File)

MacDraw II 1.1

MacPaint

MacPaint 2.0

MacWrite

MacWrite 5.0

MacWrite II

Microsoft Word 3.0

Microsoft Word 4.0

Microsoft Word PC 4.0–5.0

Microsoft Works

Microsoft Works DB

PICT

RTF (Rich Text Format)

TIFF (Tagged Image File Format)

WordPerfect

WordPerfect PC 4.2

WordPerfect PC 5.0

WriteNow

All these translators work with any program that supports the use of XTND translators, such as Nisus's word processors, Nisus and Nisus Compact.

Apple File Exchange

On the Tidbits disk from an old set of System Disks (7.0.1) is a folder called Apple File Exchange. The Apple File Exchange is a program for converting files from Apple Pro-DOS and MS-DOS formats to Macintosh formats; it is also a program that allows you to read floppy disks of both types mentioned earlier (you must have a SuperDrive to read disks formatted on non-Mac machines). There is nothing exceptional about the Apple File Exchange, except that it also works with translators from MacLink. This is an old program; I mention it here just in case you work with an older Mac.

Changing Type and Creator Codes

Before you set out to change a Creator or Type code, you need to know what you are going to change and why. Otherwise, you will tell your Macintosh something completely erroneous, possibly resulting in problems. You also need a program that lets you change the Creator or Type codes. DiskTools, on the book's CD-ROM, by Evan Gross, is an excellent program for doing this and other file maintenance procedures. If you want to change only the Creator and Type codes, try using FileTyper 5.0.1, also on the CD-ROM.

To find out what Creator and Type you want to use, save a file from the program that you plan to use and check its codes with your file utility. Make sure you save the file you are going to use as a reference, using options that match the file you are changing. If you are changing a SimpleText file to a Word file, be sure you know the Creator and Type for a Word text file. Otherwise, things will not work as you expect.

For the following example, DiskTools is used, but the procedure is basically the same with any utility that can change these codes.

To change the Type and Creator codes:

1. Open DiskTools.
2. Select the file you want to change (in this case, the Read Me file).
3. Select the *Get Info* menu item from the DiskTools menu.
4. A dialog box like the one shown in Figure 11.8 appears.
5. In the dialog box, the Type and Creator codes are clearly marked in the upper right corner.
6. Enter the new Creator and Type codes into their respective boxes.

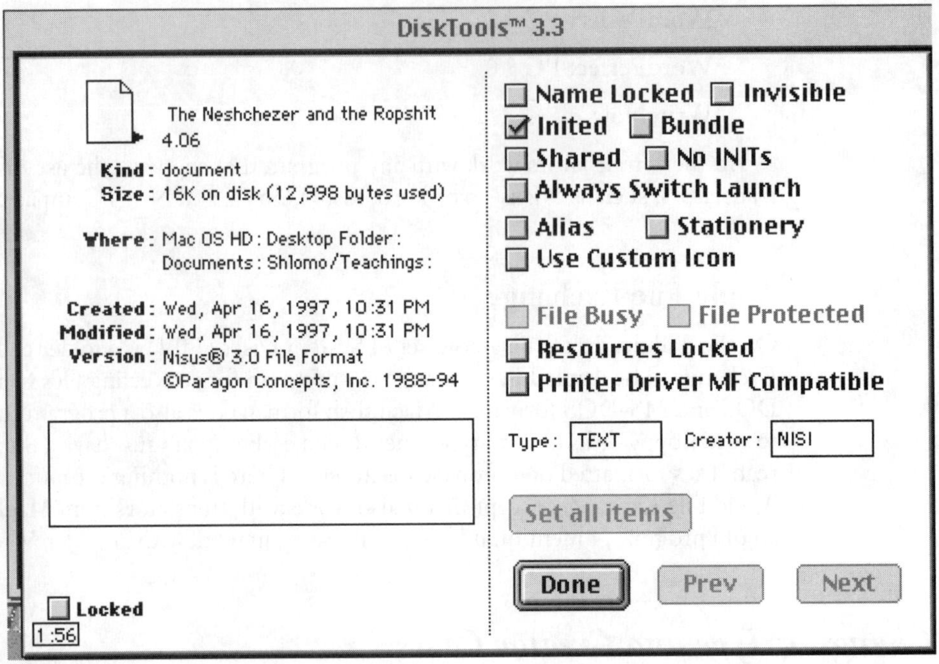

Figure 11.8   *DiskTools Get Info window.*

Figure 11.9 shows the same file with the Type and Creator changed to "TEXT" and "MSWD," respectively. The Type change designates the file as a text file; the Creator change tells your Mac that the file is a Microsoft Word file. After you make your changes, be sure to click the Change button.

After the Creator has been changed, the file appears as a Microsoft Word document on your Desktop. Figure 11.10 shows the Read Me file as a Microsoft Word document, and it opens in Word by double-clicking on it.

These basic procedures work with any Macintosh file. All the programs that let you change file attributes have a similar interface, and you should have no problem using them. You will have trouble if you use an incorrect code; doing so could cause the wrong application to open or the file to lose its association with all programs. Remember that changing a file's Type and/or Creator code does not change a file's contents, only which program it is associated with and the file-type identification. If you change a text file into a PICT file, your graphics programs recognize the file as a graphics file and may crash if you attempt to open the file.

Other Attributes

The Type and Creator codes are not the only attributes of a file. A file can also be locked so that it cannot be trashed, and it can be invisible. If you refer to Figure 11.8 or Figure 11.9, you see a list of attributes associated with the file. Even though several attributes are listed, I will discuss only the Locked and Invisible attributes. The

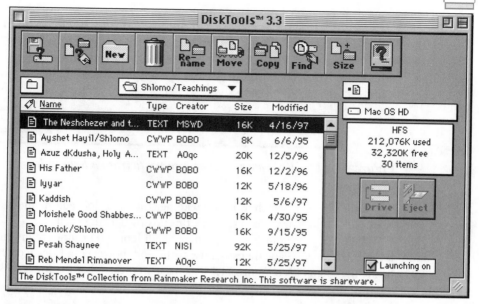

Figure 11.9   *After the change.*

rest of the attributes are system-related; if you do not know what you are doing, do not change them.

Locking or Unlocking Your Files

Sometimes, you copy a file onto your disk and, when you try to trash it, find out that it is locked. When this happens, a dialog box like the one shown in Figure 11.11 appears. If you want to trash the file without unlocking it, just hold down the Option key as you select the *Empty Trash* menu item. The Trash empties, erasing the file— regardless of its status.

You will want to lock a file so that changes cannot be made to it, but the warning shown in Figure 11.11 will appear if you try to trash it. You can lock a file by using DiskTools or a similar utility, or you can lock it by performing a Get Info on the file from the Finder. When you look at the Info window, notice the check box in the

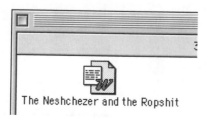

The Neshchezer and the Ropshit

Figure 11.10   *The Read Me File icon after the change.*

The Trash cannot be emptied, because all of the items in it (other than folders) are locked. To delete locked items, hold down the Option key while you choose Empty Trash.
OK
1:56

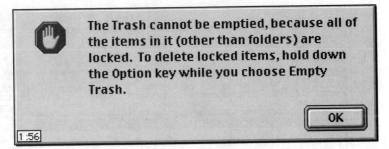

Figure 11.11 *What appears when you try to trash a locked file.*

bottom left corner, which indicates whether the file is locked; the file in Figure 11.12 is locked. To lock any file, just check this box by clicking on it.

When you view your files by Icon or Small Icon, you cannot tell if they are locked. When you view them as a list at the end, however, a Lock icon appears next to the file's name (see Figure 11.13). This icon means that the file is locked.

Invisible Files

Invisible files are just that: files that you cannot see from the Desktop. Usually, invisible files are system files to which you do not need access. One of the least expensive

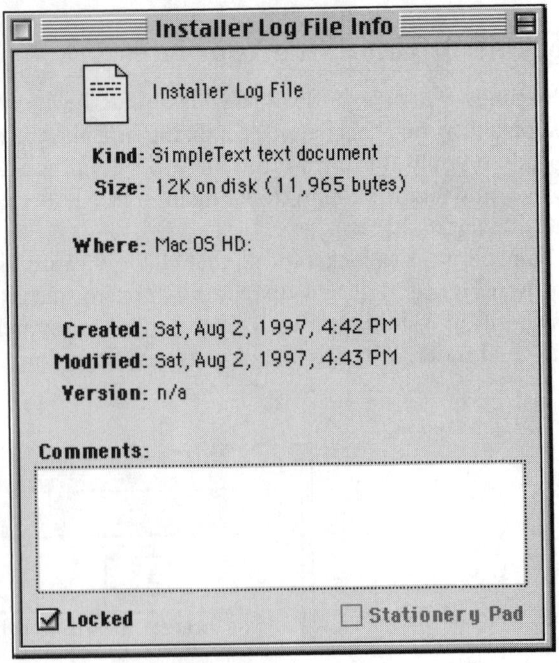

Installer Log File Info
Installer Log File
Kind: SimpleText text document
Size: 12K on disk (11,965 bytes)
Where: Mac OS HD:
Created: Sat, Aug 2, 1997, 4:42 PM
Modified: Sat, Aug 2, 1997, 4:43 PM
Version: n/a
Comments:
Locked
Stationery Pad

Figure 11.12 *A locked file.*

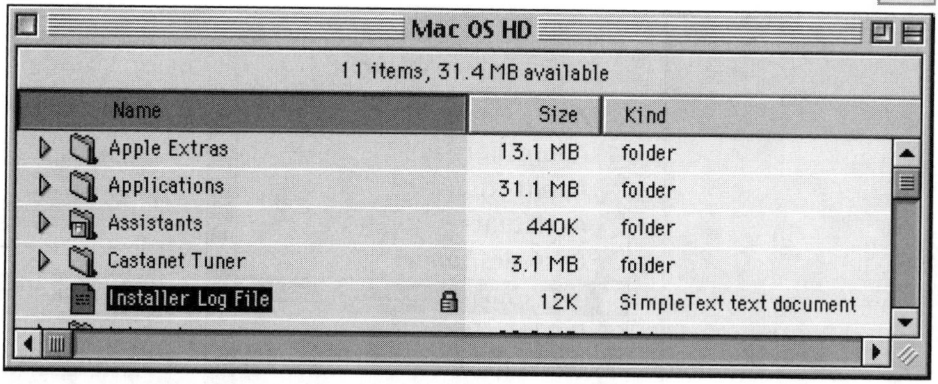

Figure 11.13 *A locked file in a Finder's list view.*

forms of data security is to make invisible a file you want to keep secure. If you do, just remember where it is. If you trash a folder with an invisible file in it, you lose the file.

To make a file invisible, you need a utility, such as DiskTools. Follow the same steps as you would to change a file's Creator or Type code, only check the Invisible box, as shown in Figure 11.14, instead of changing the codes. Once you click OK, the file is no longer be visible in the Finder.

With some programs, you are able to see invisible files from the program's Open file dialog box. Figure 11.15 shows an Open dialog box where the invisible file can be

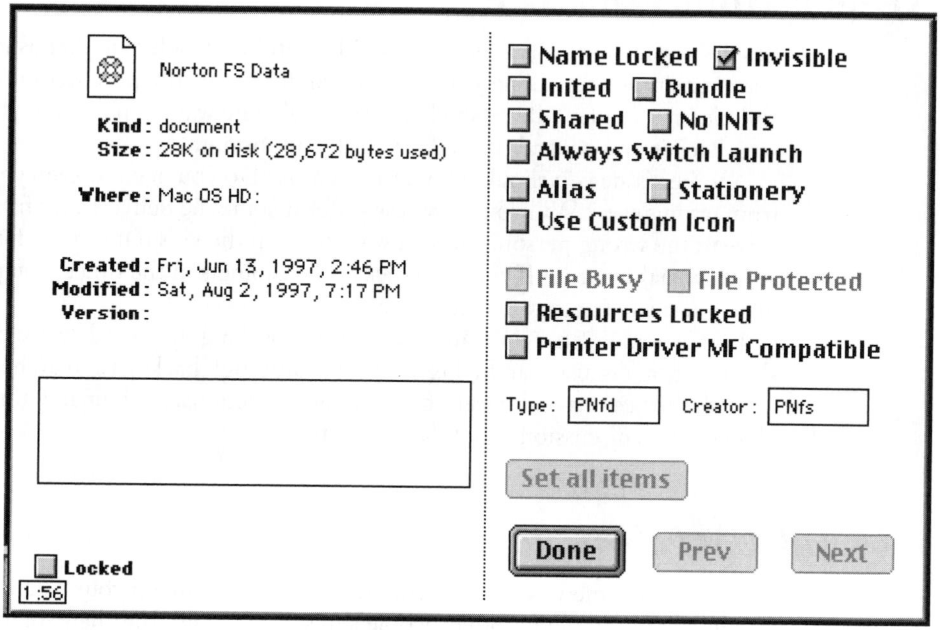

Figure 11.14 *An invisible file seen in DiskTools.*

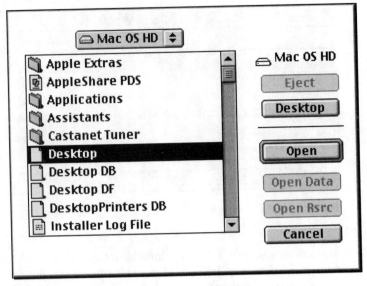

Figure 11.15   *Open dialog box with an invisible file.*

seen. If the file can be seen in an Open dialog box, it can be opened—but you have to know where to look.

Keeping Your Data Safe

Besides organizing your files, you should carefully consider another aspect of file management: safeguarding your data. Hard drives die, floppies become corrupted, and files are accidentally trashed. There is only one way to make sure your data is safe: Back it up—several times if it is really important.

Another issue you should ponder is security. Do you need to keep your data away from prying eyes? Will your business suffer if someone delivers files from your hard drive to the wrong person? Do you want to keep the kids out of your family's letters and financial records? If you have locked file cabinets in the office, you probably need a security strategy of some type.

In this section, strategies and methods for backing up your data are explored. A short section discusses archiving your data; although backups and archives are related, they can have different purposes and functions. And, finally, this section concludes with a discussion about data security.

Why Back Up? Paranoia!

If there were some way to scare you into always backing up your data, besides telling you horror stories about other people's misery, I would. But that wouldn't work. If you do not care about backing up your data so that you can survive the day when your hard drive crashes and all your files become scrambled bits and bytes, go straight to Chapter 19, "Disk Crashes and Data Recovery." Recovering your data can be expensive in time, potential data loss, and even dollars if you hire someone to do it. This, of course, assumes that your data is retrievable; sometimes, it isn't.

If you have to recover your data, you need to completely reconfigure your hard drive and reinstall all your applications and data. You may have to sort through thousands of files to determine what they contain before you can use them. If the situation is very bad, it could take you a year to find out if you really recovered all your data. Regarding data backups, there should be no decision to make—except how you will back up your data and how often.

Backup Decisions

Your first decision has been made: You *will* back up your hard drive. Now, you have to decide what medium to use, whether to back up the entire drive or just selected data, how many backups to make, and how often to back up your data.

The Medium—To back up your drive, you can use another hard drive, a removable media drive, a tape drive, or floppy disks. Of all your choices, using a hard drive is the easiest, most convenient, and most expensive. It is convenient and easy because all you have to do is make a Finder copy of your data. It is expensive because you lose the use of an expensive piece of hardware. And it is basically inadequate because you have only one backup.

Removable media hard drives are a much better solution. The removable disks are inexpensive, and you can make multiple backups and have an extra drive to boot (no pun intended). Some of the drives that use removable media are described in Chapter 10, "Macintosh Disk Drives." Any of the removable drives would work for backup purposes. However, the Rewritable Optical drives provide the best data security because of the longevity of the media—you can keep an optical backup for years. An alternative to a Rewritable Optical is a CDR CD-ROM backup.

Using a tape drive can be a two-edged sword: The media is inexpensive and easy to use. Tapes can fail, though, and they can easily be corrupted. To *know* that your data is secure, you have to restore some of the data from your backup because you can't look at the files. If you have lots of data to back up, such as a 4-gigabyte drive, or if you want the most reliable tape drive possible, use a DAT drive. It is very fast and can hold a lot of data (up to 24 gigabytes), and DAT tapes are reliable. Their disadvantage is price—a good DAT drive costs from $700 to $2500, depending on capacity. With a DAT drive, check your backups to make sure you can restore your data and then make multiple backups.

Finally, if you do not have massive amounts of data to back up and you do not want to incur the expense of additional hardware, your floppy drive is the way to go. Backing up to floppies can be tedious, especially the first time you back up your drive. Yet, it is still one of the most reliable methods available. Regardless of which media you choose, backing up and verifying your data are easy.

What to Back Up—If you have spent hours and hours configuring your hard drive, making Aliases, and meticulously arranging your data, you will want to back up your entire drive. If you have just a couple of applications and a fairly stock System folder, you may want to back up only your data. The criteria for this decision is based on how long it will take you to restore your drive and data. Usually, just backing up the whole drive is easiest. If you are concerned only about the data and are willing to take the time to reinstall your System and applications from scratch, then back up only your data. All good backup programs allow you to perform a selective backup.

You may want to do two backups—one of your System folder plus your applications, and another of your data. This way, you have to back up only your data once you have a stable working environment—meaning you are not adding new applications and changing your System configuration. This strategy offers you a means for first restoring your System and applications and then your data. You will not have to back up your applications and System files when you do incremental backups, yet everything will still be as you configured it so that you do not lose your working system environment.

How Many Backups Should You Make? —There is always the possibility that your backup could be corrupted. Scary thought, huh? Your drive has the ill grace to let you down, and then your backup turns out to be sour. You are not having a good day. And, as we all know, just because you're paranoid, it doesn't mean that they're not out to get you. So it is with your data. Make two backups. Then put one off-site in a safe place. Should your work place suffer from a fire, earthquake, tornado, or theft, and if you have an off-site backup, at least your data will be secure. Equipment can be replaced; your data cannot.

The moral here is to make at least two backups. This task is not as bad as it sounds, and, in the next section, some different ways of backing up your data are discussed.

Keeping Your Backups Current

After you make your initial, complete backups, your backup software lets you do incremental backups. If you use a tape drive, you can schedule your backups to take place when you are not working on your system. If you have to supervise your backup program, set aside some time for the chore.

The way to determine how often you perform an incremental back up depends on how much data you can afford to lose. If losing more than a day's work is unacceptable, then you need to back up each day before you are finished. Should re-creating a week's worth of work be a risk you are willing to live with, then you can back up once a week. The key here is how much data do you lose if you do not back up regularly, and how much will it cost to re-create it?

All backup software can tell if a file has been backed up and if the file has been modified since it was last backed up. This is accomplished by making the backup date for each file the date on which it is backed up. When you perform an incremental backup, the backup program compares the file's date modified with the backup date; if the backup date is equal to or older than the date modified, the file is not backed up. Thus, if you maintain two backup sets and you want them both to be incremental, make sure that one of your incremental backups does not modify the backup date; otherwise, your backup sets will not contain the same data.

The only way to do this is if the software package you use offers an option called a *differential* backup. The differential backup option backs up all data that has changed since the last backup, but it does not change the file's backup date. So, if you perform a differential backup and then do an incremental backup, maintaining two or more incremental backup sets becomes easier. This capability also allows you to make a separate backup of specific files, using your backup software, without skipping them when you do an incremental backup. It effectively allows you to have two or more backup sets of your critical files while maintaining a complete and up-to-date backup. If your software does not allow for this type of backup, you cannot keep two incremental backups that are in sync. Instead, you will have to use the software's archive or full-copy capabilities to make your second backup.

Most software packages, when performing an incremental backup, build on the full backup you've already made. The incremental backup backs up only the data that has changed. And so it is for each subsequent, incremental backup. After a while you will have a large number of incremental backup sets. Therefore, you'll want to make, a new, full backup on a regular basis (I like weekly); otherwise, you will have so many additional data sets that it will be difficult to keep track of them or to restore your data, should the need arise.

Off-Site Backups

Once you have determined what is an acceptable data loss, then decide how often you want to cycle your off-site backups. You may want to perform a weekly backup and, at the end of a month, take the last weekly backup home, returning with the old off-site backup to use for your next set of weekly backups. With such a cycle, you would not lose more than a month's worth of data in a worst-case scenario. For this process to work, when you recycle your off-site backup, you must do a full backup to reset the backup date on all of your files. If you perform an incremental backup, you back up only those files that have changed since you last performed an incremental backup. After a while, your two data sets could contain a variety of files that exist on only one of the two sets.

Only you can determine the frequency of your backup schedule. If you follow a procedure similar to the one just discussed, your data will be as safe as possible.

Backup Software

Efficient backups require some type of utility software that makes your backups for you. Without one of these utilities, you would have to copy your files to a hard disk or floppies as groups of files. Unless you use a hard drive to make periodic copies of your existing hard drive, you will never have a complete backup, and using a hard drive has the disadvantages noted earlier.

Before you purchase a backup program, be sure it has some features that make your life easier:

❖ Device compatibility—Decide what type of backup device you want to use, and then make sure the program you use supports it. Most backup programs support any of the devices previously mentioned, but it is best to check first.

❖ File selection—Selecting the files you want to back up should be easy. The more options you have for file selection, the better. You should be able to select the files by file type, date, kind, or any other attribute you want to use.

❖ Unattended and scheduled backups—If you want your data to be backed up while you are at home, then make sure you can schedule such a backup. If this feature is not important to you or if you are going to use floppies, you can waive this particular feature.

❖ Data compression and verification—Compressing your data can save a lot of space on your backup volume, especially if you use floppies or have several drives to back up. Good data compression can enable you to put twice as much data on your backup volume. Whenever you do a backup of critical data and/or compress it, it is a good idea to ensure the data's integrity by using the backup program's data verification option.

Verification can double the time it takes to perform the backup, but it is better to be safe than sorry. When you use data verification, the program double-checks each file and the backup medium, making sure the original file matches the backup. Always use the data verification option. The only other way to verify your backup is to restore some random files and manually verify your data—something you should do from time to time anyway.

❖ Network-compatible—Most backup software lets you back up a file server, but not all packages remotely back up other Macs on a network to a single storage device. If you need to back up several Macs over a network, look for software that is made specifically for backing up networked Macs.

❖ Data encryption—If you have high security needs, then your backup software should also be able to encrypt your data as it backs it up. Once again, if you use an option like this, you must always perform a selective restore of your data to verify it. Encrypted backups require extra steps to restore the data, and you can't forget the password. Always perform a limited restore of data you've encrypted.

❖ Selective restores—There will be occasions when you might want to restore only one or two files from your backup. Your backup software should allow you to perform selective restores to your hard drive.

The following is a list of some of the backup programs available on the market:

DiskFit Pro—This is one of the oldest backup utilities made for the Mac. Made by Dantz Development, it has been around for several years and is a tried and proven backup utility. If you have only one Mac to back up and plan to use floppy disks, it is probably the best backup utility you can get. It does not have all the features of some other programs, but, for a home office or personal Mac, it gives you all the data security you need.

DiskFit Pro also offers a few additional features that make it unique: One, it lets you perform incremental backups between two different backup sets, yet it keeps all your files on both sets complete, avoiding the problems previously mentioned. Two, it allows you to add disks to your backup set and resolve file differences without creating new incremental backup sets. This means that you have only one backup data set. Finally, it creates Finder-readable files, rather than a single backup file, that may be divided across tens of floppies or several backup volumes.

FastBack II—This is another long-standing backup program, made by Symantec. It offers most of the capabilities previously listed, with the notable exception of backing up networked Macs to a single device. One unique feature it does offer is the ability to restore files backed up from an MS-DOS machine to a Macintosh, and vice versa. If you have this need, you will find FastBack II invaluable.

MacTools Deluxe—One of the utilities included in MacTools, made by Central Point Software, is this backup utility. It is a complete and useful backup utility with a full set of basic features. If you select MacTools as your basic disk utility package, check out the backup program to see if it meets your needs before purchasing a different backup utility.

Norton Utilities—Like MacTools, Norton Utilities by Symantec also includes a backup utility. All the comments made about MacTools apply to Norton's program. Each of these utilities can perform differential and scheduled backups, recognize various backup devices, and perform selective restores. Both packages also include data compression and verification.

Retrospect and Retrospect Remote—Retrospect is also made by Dantz Development. What it provides that the other packages do not is the ability to back up remote devices over a network. It is not dependent on a file server, and it has most of the features previously listed, plus some extra capabilities. One feature is its ability to put files that have not been modified over a certain period of time onto your backup device and then delete them from your hard disk.

Special Tricks

When it comes to protecting your data, the more weapons you have in your arsenal, the more secure your data will be. As such, here are some suggestions that might make your data more secure.

Backing Up to a Server—One way to back up several Macintoshes on a network is to have your backup software perform the backups to a file server. Because the networking capabilities of the Macintosh are so flexible, you could even have one drive dedicated to the task of holding backups from ten other Macs on a network, without using an AppleShare file server. After all the Macs are backed up, you could then back up the drive that contains all the data from the other machines to a tape or another hard drive.

Because all the software previously listed performs scheduled backups, most of your backup requirements can be performed automatically. This type of system works well if you just back up the data from the other Macs, ignoring their system and application files. It is one way to reduce the headache of system backups for anyone with limited time for network administration.

Disk Mirroring—If you always need your data to be available, regardless of circumstances, consider using a second hard drive and a process called *disk mirroring*. Disk mirroring occurs when your data is backed up to another hard drive as you perform your work so that you can immediately have access to your data if your primary hard drive should fail. Sophisticated disk mirroring systems can even automatically switch to the backup drive, preventing any interruption in the computing process.

Almost all hard-drive manufacturers have devices and software specifically for this purpose. Disk mirroring is expensive, but if going offline (not being able to use your computer for any period of time) means a substantial loss of business or could result in some type of liability, you will want to check out this technology.

Data Synchronization—The PowerBook's popularity has created some new problems in data management. Quite often, people who have PowerBooks also have desktop Macs. The problem these people face is making sure the data on each of their Macs is the same. If you are in this position, you want to synchronize the data on your PowerBook with that on your desktop Mac. Several commercial programs can do this, or you can use Apple's File Assistant program that comes with Mac OS 8. All of these programs compare the contents or a folder of one disk drive with another folder or disk drive, and then reconcile the two folders or drives. The reconciliation process creates two identical drives or folders. Some sets of PowerBook utilities come with synchronization utilities.

Archives

Under certain circumstances, you may want to archive your data rather than just back it up. Usually, this is done when you are running low on disk space, need to provide an audit trail, or want an additional copy of all your data for security purposes.

Whatever your reasons, you can use any of the preceding backup programs to create your archive. It should be done on some type of removable media so that it is easy to store, easy to access, and easy to make multiple archives. If you need to keep a copy of your data for legal or tax purposes, consider using a CDR (Recordable CD-ROM) drive; a CD-ROM of your data maybe be accepted by the IRS and the courts as a permanent record of your data transactions. Don't take my word for this, check with your attorney.

If you decide to archive your data, keep at least two archives. If you make only one copy and something happens to it, well, you've been warned.

When you make an archive, if you use backup software, use the Full Copy option if it is supported. This option works like a differential backup. After you have made your archives, treat them as your backups. Keep copies in different locations; if all your data copies are in one place and something happens, you won't be happy.

Security Is Peace of Mind

Data security can come in many flavors. Your needs dictate the security measures you must take. Simple security can be password-protecting your screen saver so that no one can look at your screen while you go to lunch, while high-level security software encrypts your data and your archives.

This section look at the different levels and types of security you can employ and the software you can use. One of the strongest arguments for using some of the following security methods is this question: If your Mac were stolen, would you want whoever swiped it to be able to access your data? Your answer is probably "No."

Different Types and Levels of Security

Your security needs determine the type of security options you might want to employ. The U.S. government has procedures for disposing of sensitive materials that include the destruction of actual documents. When computers create documents, and when the computers used in sensitive areas are replaced, the disk drives from the computers are physically removed and dismantled, and the platters are then destroyed.

Erasing and even formatting a drive does not make getting the data or part of the data back impossible. It just depends on how badly someone wants the data and what resources are available to him or her. For most of your needs, however, one or a combination of the following methods is more than adequate to protect your data from prying eyes or industrial espionage.

Locking the Screen—If all you want to do is keep someone from looking at your work in progress while you're away from your Mac, a screen saver that can be password-protected is more than adequate. This approach prevents anyone who does not know the password from taking a casual look at your work. If someone really wants to see what's on your Mac, however, all he or she has to do is turn it off and then turn it back on. If you really want to keep your work private, you should also use one of the following methods.

File Security—The most basic form of file security is locking a file from the Get Info dialog box. This protects the document from being accidentally trashed and prevents it from being changed. The next step might be to make the file invisible, as previously mentioned. This will make the file invisible from the Desktop and some Open dialog boxes. If you can see the Desktop DB and DF files from an Open dialog box, however, then all of your invisible files are visible.

The next step is to use a data-encryption utility, such as the ones included with Norton Utilities or MacTools. These utilities allow you to encrypt a file or folder so that it cannot be read without the proper password. Encryption scrambles the data in a file and works just like a key. The key you supply is your password, which the program uses to compute how it will scramble your data. If you forget your password, you will never get the file unscrambled. Usually, a program that has encryption capabilities offers two types of encryption: a quick encryption scheme of some type and a U.S. government standard called DES that offers the most secure method of encryption used by most programs.

Encryption Security—Given a large enough computer, such as a supercomputer, and enough time, any encrypted file can be opened. For most people's needs, though, the encryption software currently on the market is more than adequate. If you are a spy trading in national secrets, however, none of the data security software on the market is good enough. This is what security really means. As long as you do not give out your password, no one can access your data without the help of the National Security Agency.

There is only one possible exception to this: One program on the market *may* offer unbreakable encryption. I say "may" because I don't think anyone knows for sure. All reports say that data encrypted with this program is impossible to access, but I'm not willing to say that the NSA cannot break the encryption scheme. The program is called MacPGP from ViaCrypt, and it is a difficult program to use effectively. To use MacPGP, you create a private or secret key that you have to keep secure; then, you make a public key that you distribute to others who use MacPGP.

By exchanging public keys with someone, you can encrypt a file designated specifically for someone else, using that person's public key. Once you've encrypted the file, the only people who can access the file are you and the person whose public key you've used. No one else can use the file. Even if someone should discover your private key, they'll need your password to access the file. It is said that even the NSA cannot access data encrypted in this manner—and maybe it is true. Regardless of the NSA's capabilities, MacPGP is the most secure data encryption program you can use.

Another aspect of MacPGP is its key-verification technology. MacPGP uses a verification method called a digital signature. People personally verify the authenticity of someone else's key before the key is distributed to other people. If I gave you my public key and you knew me personally, then you could vouch for my key with someone you might know. By passing a public key to other person whom you know you build a chain of trust. Although this is not the same as having an agency authenticate a key, it can be quite trustworthy.

Partition Security—If you have more data than just a folder to secure, you can create a partition on your hard drive and encrypt the data in the partition. You do not want to encrypt a huge folder because it will take half the morning to decrypt. If you use a password-protected partition, you can prevent others from mounting your drive—unless they have the password.

There are different ways to encrypt a partition. Some formatting utilities, such as FWB's Hard Disk ToolKit, offer the option of password protecting and/or encrypting a partition. La Cie's Silverlining offers partition password protection but no partition encryption. The difference between encrypting and password-protecting a partition is that the data on a password-protected volume is not encrypted and it is possible to recover the volume to get the data. On an encrypted volume, even if the volume is recovered, the data is scrambled and unusable.

Remember to safeguard your data with a backup. If you encrypt a partition and it crashes, it is gone. *The chances of recovering encrypted data from a crashed volume are almost nonexistent.*

Hard-Drive Security—Partition security is actually part of hard-drive security, and the same methods can be employed for an entire hard drive as for a partition. Some security utilities go a step further, preventing someone from even starting your Mac unless he or she has a special startup floppy that contains the key to unlock the drive and allow it to boot.

The main utility of this type is The NightWatch by Kent Marsh Ltd. Using its method it is not possible to access a drive—even with a recovery program. Without the magic floppy, the drive is completely inaccessible. If you run across a drive that has been locked in this manner and you want to use it, without the key, all you can do is reformat it.

File Deletion and Security Erasing—When you trash a file, it is still accessible. Anyone with a recovery utility or a disk editor (a utility that actually looks at the sectors of a drive) can access the file or the data it contains. If you want the deleted file to be truly erased and inaccessible, you need a utility that not only deletes the file, but also overwrites it.

Norton Utilities and other security utilities include programs that perform this task. These programs or their aliases can be put on the Desktop so that you can drag-and-drop a file or folder on top of them to activate the program and overwrite the file with nonsense characters. They usually provide a couple of levels of wiping security that determine how many times the space occupied by the file is overwritten; the more times a file is overwritten, the harder it becomes to get it back. For most mortals, having a file overwritten once is sufficient.

Don't think that you can really get back any file that has been overwritten—you can't. As mentioned at the beginning of this section, the government can. Your hard drive holds a ghost image of data that has previously been written to it and, with the right type of equipment, reading the ghost images and retrieving the data are possible.

The Risks of Encrypting Your Data

Using data encryption utilities poses some risks that you need to weigh against the benefit of keeping your information private. If you encrypt data and then forget your password, it is the same as losing the data forever. Unless your utility has a master password to unlock anything your program encrypts, your data is gone. At the same time, the master password makes the encrypted data less secure: Anyone who knows the master password for your program, or someone who has another copy of the program with his or her own master password, stands a chance of breaking in.

Keep an unencrypted backup of the data in a secure place, such as a safety deposit box. If the data is too sensitive to keep unless it is encrypted, then keep an encrypted copy using a password that you will not forget, and make sure you do not write the password anywhere.

In your work environment, change your password from time to time. Also, do not use words that can easily be guessed, such as derivatives of your name, birth date, social security number, and so on. These are the first passwords a data thief will try.

Security Software

When you get ready to shop for your security software, first decide what level of security you want. The range of products varies from encrypting files and folders to locking and encrypting your hard disk. If you just want something to keep casual eyes from getting into your private files, then all you need are the utilities that come with Norton Utilities or the MacTools package. But if your needs are heavy-duty, then consider the Kent Marsh line of products—they are the Macintosh security experts. Cassidy and Greene have a package called AIM that provides excellent security as well. And, for your most sensitive data, you can always use MacPGP.

Accessing DOS Files and Disks on the Mac

The previous section represents the school of hard conversion. If you are lucky, you will never have to use these conversion techniques. Most of your data conversion needs will be met by the software you use. The major software packages that create cross-platform-compatible files are discussed in the last section of this chapter.

Before we get to that, though, there are additional ways to get data from a Mac into a DOS system, and vice versa. This section looks at software that you can use in conjunction with Mac's floppy drive to transfer data. Some of the hardware available for cross-platform work is discussed as well. We also look at a couple of ways to turn your Mac into an IBM clone. This section is about getting the data into your Mac. The subsections cover software and using your Mac as a clone.

Software

Every Macintosh in recent history was shipped with a SuperDrive, which is a floppy drive able to read Macintosh HFS and MFS formats, DOS 760K and 1.44 Mg disks, and Apple ProDOS disks (the Apple IIe and GS). With this built-in ability, your Mac can read all 3.5-inch floppy disks. The focus of this section is on using your Mac drive to read disks from a DOS machine. Its subsections cover the Apple File Exchange Utility and PC Exchange.

Apple File Exchange (AFE) Utility

First of all, you do not need to purchase any additional software to read a DOS-formatted disk. All you need came with your System software in the form of the Apple File Exchange utility, which is on your Tidbits disk. With this utility, you can perform the following functions:

❖ Initialize disks in DOS, Macintosh, or Pro DOS formats

❖ Transfer data from your Mac to 3.5-inch disks within the preceding formats

❖ Perform data translation using either MacLink Plus or the built-in binary, text, or DCA/RFT formats

The basic operation of AFE is fairly straightforward. You run the program and get a window with two lists. When you insert an MS-DOS floppy, you get a window like the one shown in Figure 11.16. If you put a DOS disk into your Mac before running AFE, your Mac does not recognize the disk and wants to initialize it. The next step is to select the file you want to transfer by highlighting it. If the file is one you are going to use without translation, select the Default Translation mode from the MS-DOS to Mac menu (see Figure 11.17).

The types of files to use with the Default Translation are any files that you would use directly in other programs, such as Microsoft Word or Excel documents. If you are going to transfer a text file, use the Text translation capabilities of AFE to strip out the linefeeds. Figure 11.18 shows the different options available when you select Text translation.

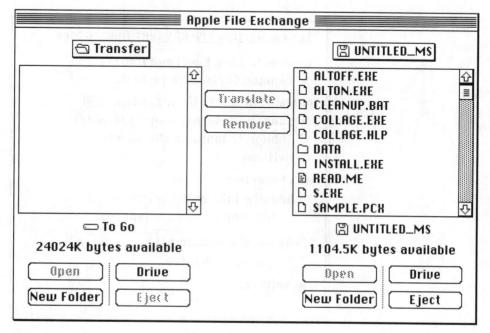

Figure 11.16 AFE after a DOS disk is inserted.

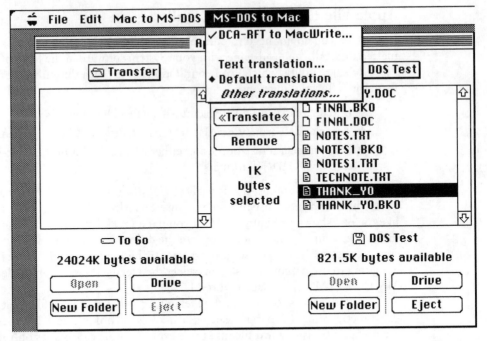

Figure 11.17 *The MS-DOS to Mac menu.*

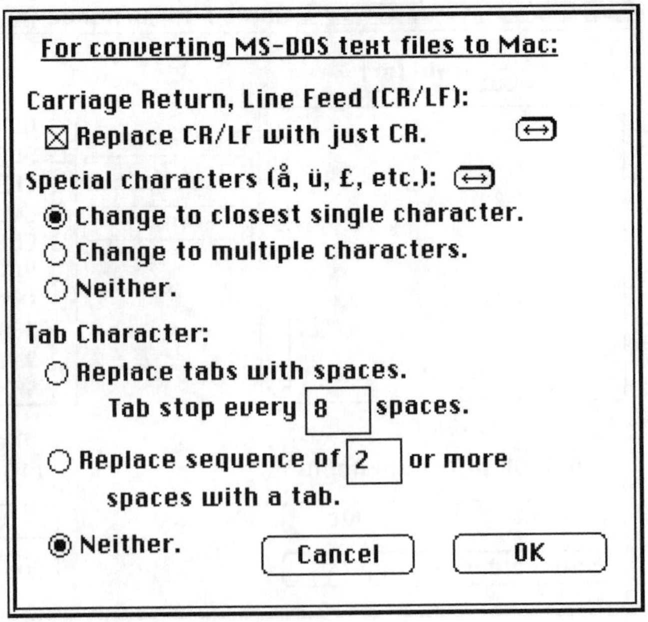

For converting MS-DOS text files to Mac:

Carriage Return, Line Feed (CR/LF):
☒ Replace CR/LF with just CR. ⟷

Special characters (å, ü, £, etc.): ⟷
◉ Change to closest single character.
○ Change to multiple characters.
○ Neither.

Tab Character:
○ Replace tabs with spaces.
    Tab stop every ⬚8⬚ spaces.

○ Replace sequence of ⬚2⬚ or more
    spaces with a tab.

◉ Neither. [Cancel] [OK]

Figure 11.18 *The Text translation options.*

Your main concern is replacing carriage returns and linefeeds with carriage returns. Your other options include changing special characters with diacritical marks. The options are limited, and changing them to their closest single character is probably the best selection.

With the last selection, you can replace tab characters with spaces, spaces with tabs, or leave all the spaces and tabs alone. Use the last selection if you want to change the formatting to use the text data in a spreadsheet or database. To get a feel for how this setting works, play with it. Using AFE to translate text files goes only halfway. If you want to use the document with a word processor, you still have to do the translation procedure in the last section.

The other available option is the DCA-RFT to MacWrite menu selection, but this is almost useless. You can use it only if you save the document you are going to transfer in the DCA-RFT format, which is specific to some word processors. You are better off using a Word-for-DOS format or an RTF format, and then performing a binary translation. Both of these formats retain formatting and every Macintosh word processor can read them.

Finally, you can use the MacLink translators with AFE. But if you have MacLink Plus, you are better off using the DOS Mounter that comes with it and the MacLink program directly. If you do decide to use the translators with AFE, make sure the translators are in the same folder as AFE. It takes AFE much longer to start up with the translators.

PC Exchange

PC Exchange is a new Apple Control Panel that mounts a DOS disk onto the Desktop just as if it were a Mac disk. It also lets you format DOS disks from the Desktop. Figure 11.19 shows a DOS disk mounted on the Desktop using PC Exchange. The best part of using PC Exchange is its ability to automatically assign an application to specific Mac programs. Figure 11.20 shows how to assign Microsoft Word to the .DOC extension. In Figure 11.21, you can see the extensions that have been assigned to PC Exchange.

Once you have made assignments for the DOS extensions and you open the disk, you see the files in a window with the appropriate icons for the assignments you have made. If you double-click on a file that you have assigned to an application, it launches that application and open the file at the same time. Figure 11.22 shows the same disk used in the AFE example with all .DOC and .TXT files assigned; you can see the different icons for the assigned files. If your disk has icons with a "PC" the files are unassigned.

Again, you have the problem described in the previous section on translating text files. DOS text files retain the carriage returns and linefeeds when you open them with PC Exchange. Figure 11.23 shows the text file used in the previous example. It is the same one that was moved from the Mac to the PC after formatting it for the PC. To use the file with a Mac word processor, you will have to perform a translation.

There is one problem with the version of PC Exchange that ships with Mac OS 8. It does not read Windows 95 long file names. This is a problem because a Windows

Figure 11.19 *A DOS disk on the Desktop using PC Exchange.*

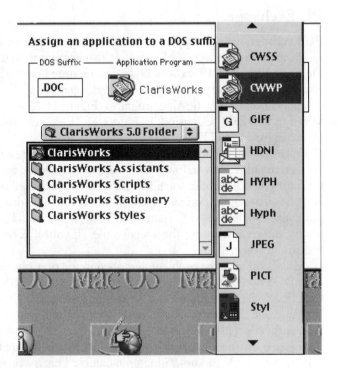

Figure 11.20 *Selecting the extension type.*

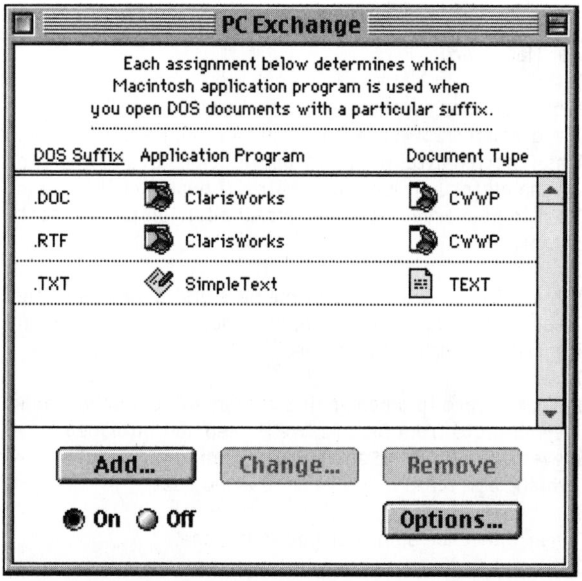

Figure 11.21 shown here.

Figure 11.21 *The assigned extensions in PC Exchange.*

95 file can have 256 characters in its name. When you mount one of these disks on your Mac, the names will be truncated into what is called an 8.3 format. This means that the file name will be eight characters long with a three-character extension. I hope that Apple fixes this problem in the very near future.

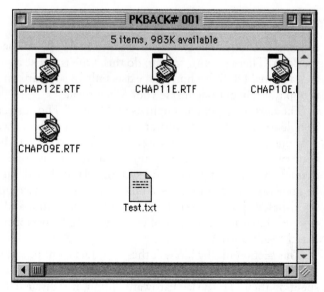

Figure 11.22 *File icons on a DOS disk with their appropriate assignments.*

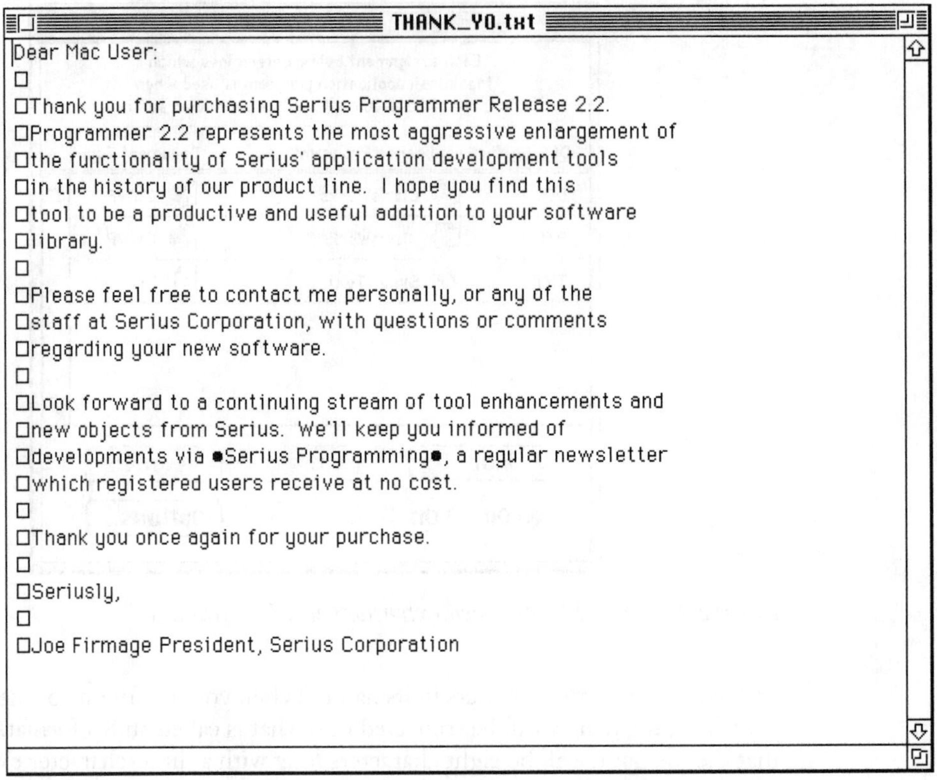

```
┌────────────────────────── THANK_YO.txt ──────────────────────────┐
│Dear Mac User:                                                      │⬆
│☐                                                                   │
│☐Thank you for purchasing Serius Programmer Release 2.2.            │
│☐Programmer 2.2 represents the most aggressive enlargement of       │
│☐the functionality of Serius' application development tools         │
│☐in the history of our product line.  I hope you find this          │
│☐tool to be a productive and useful addition to your software       │
│☐library.                                                           │
│☐                                                                   │
│☐Please feel free to contact me personally, or any of the          │
│☐staff at Serius Corporation, with questions or comments            │
│☐regarding your new software.                                       │
│☐                                                                   │
│☐Look forward to a continuing stream of tool enhancements and       │
│☐new objects from Serius.  We'll keep you informed of               │
│☐developments via ●Serius Programming●, a regular newsletter        │
│☐which registered users receive at no cost.                         │
│☐                                                                   │
│☐Thank you once again for your purchase.                            │
│☐                                                                   │
│☐Seriusly,                                                          │
│☐                                                                   │
│☐Joe Firmage President, Serius Corporation                          │
│                                                                    │⬇
└────────────────────────────────────────────────────────────────────┘
```

Figure 11.23   *An MS-DOS text file.*

Using Your Mac as a Clone (Ugh!)

It is possible to turn your Macintosh into an MS-DOS machine, in a manner of speaking. There are two ways to do this: One is to use a software emulator that creates a virtual DOS machine that exists only in software on your Mac. The other way is to physically put one inside your Macintosh.

The next question you might ask is "Why?" The answer is really quite simple: to be able to run MS-DOS software for some facet of your work. If you have to run only one or two DOS applications for your work, but a Mac performs the rest of your tasks without a problem, you might want to use one of these solutions. An example would be if your e-mail system is DOS-based, but all of your other work can be done on a Mac. Another example could be if your company has a proprietary DOS-based application that will never be turned into a Mac application. Except for this one application, the rest of your work can be performed more quickly and with better results on a Mac.

This section briefly looks at these products, but most of the section covers the software emulator rather than the hardware products. Because not much time is spent on the PC in a Mac hardware option, it is discussed first; then this section looks at the virtual PC.

The Mac versus Windows

The differences between using a Mac and a DOS-based machine are profound, even if the DOS-based machine is running Windows 95, Windows 97, or whatever they're calling it in Redmond. I use Macs and PCs, and after having done so for years, I can tell you that the Mac overall is a better platform than Windows 95.

I have a client whose shop is cross-platform; that is, they use both Macs and PCs. Over the course of the past year they spent ten times as much for maintenance on their PCs than they have for their Macs. To be fair to the other platform, more software is available for Windows machines than for Macs. But, if you can live without the software, the Mac costs less in the long run, and it is truly easier to use.

To really contrast the differences, think of a machine with Windows as an economy compact car that has been customized and turned into a sports car. The body is removed and replaced with a fiberglass custom body. The engine is reengineered to be really powerful and it is all put together with the best parts available. The new car looks great, sounds great, and is very fast. But when you drive it down the road, the ride is rough because the frame and suspension is still that of a cheap compact.

The Macintosh, on the other hand, is more like a luxury car designed with the driver in mind. It is given a powerful engine so that it can easily move its custom-designed body and interior. It was designed with the suspension as the starting point. No matter how fast or bumpy the road, the ride will always be smooth. The Mac is constructed with total computing vision in mind, while machines running Windows represent what happens when a screwdriver is used as a hammer.

PCs in a Mac

If you need a PC hardware solution, two companies make DOS or PC cards that you can put into your Mac. The companies are Radius, which just bought Reply, and Orange Micro. There are subtle differences between the products of these two companies, and I recommend that you shop carefully before you buy.

These products are PCI cards that contain a PC. You put them into your Mac and install the driver software; you now have a PC in your Mac. I have two problems with these products. One, if you compare costs between the PC card solution and a midrange Pentium computer, complete with monitor, you will spend the same amount of money. And the cards will run about 20 percent slower than an equivalent standalone PC.

The speed loss occurs because the cards have to share some of the Mac's subsystems. Orange Micro has a better solution insofar as its card is more complete, with full I/O except hard drives. The Radius solution, on the other hand, uses the Mac's I/O. If you have to have a PC card, do shop and read reviews before you buy.

PC Emulators

If you really have to run MS-DOS or Windows 95 software on your Mac, look at Insignia Solution's products. It makes two different emulators for the Macintosh, making it possible to turn any Power Mac into a PC clone. This interesting feat is done with software only, which creates a virtual PC machine that runs on your Mac.

If your company uses DOS or Windows software for which there is no Macintosh counterpart, or if you wish to explore the world of DOS, then you need to look at this software. Two companies ship products that emulate PCs on your Mac. One is Insignia Solutions and the other is Connectix. Insignia's product is called SoftWindows, and Connectix's product is called Virtual PC.

SoftWindows

All of Insignia's products are 100 percent 486/Pentium-compatible, except that SoftWindows will run only DOS and Windows 3.11 or Windows 95. The only time it will not work properly is if the DOS application makes a specific hardware call, where it interrogates a real PC for some specific hardware function in order to run. This is not a common occurrence, and you will probably not have a problem.

SoftWindows is designed to run on any Power Macintosh and comes in two flavors. One emulates a 486, and the other emulates a Pentium. Insignia has one trick over Virtual PC, which we'll look at in a minute, and that is that it has worked very closely with Microsoft. I have heard (but could not swear to this in court) that Insignia has received source code from Microsoft and tweaked its emulator to run more quickly with Microsoft programs. SoftWindows has a speed edge over Virtual PC.

Any of the Insignia products works just like a standard PC. It recognizes your SuperDrive as an IBM floppy drive and creates an MS-DOS hard-drive partition on your hard drive. You can also assign a Macintosh hard drive, a folder, or a networked volume as an additional drive. This can be helpful for transferring files between your virtual MS-DOS system and your Mac.

Virtual PC

Virtual PC is also a software emulator that runs on the Macintosh. It is different from SoftWindows in that it does not emulate a DOS machine; it actually emulates a PC's hardware. This difference between Virtual PC and SoftWindows is significant. It means that you can run any OS on the Virtual PC that will run on Pentium computer. So, do you want to run NT instead of Windows 95? With Virtual PC you can. Or how about Linux, up for a bit of UNIX? With Virtual PC you can.

Now for the down side. You need a very fast Power PC. Insignia recommends that you use a 240Mhz 604 PowerPC. That is a smoking machine. But if you've the hardware I do believe that Virtual PC is the better solution over SoftWindows. And as time goes on Connectix will improve its product. It just released version 1.0—it is new, but it works.

Basically, if you have an occasional need for access to an MS-DOS machine, you can have it with your Macintosh. If you do a lot of work in MS-DOS or Windows, you will probably want to get a real PC instead. If you're really serious about getting a PC, just a word to the wise: Get Windows NT, not Windows 95. NT is much nicer and way more powerful.

Summary

Although this chapter is steeped in paranoia, you should think about some of the issues it raised. Is your data safe? If you rely on your equipment and you do not make backups—don't! While writing the first edition of this book, I had a 300MB hard drive stop working in the middle of the afternoon. It stopped dead, and all of the data on it was lost.

Another incident that happened to me, also while writing the first edition of this book, was the loss of a PowerBook. This loss was more serious because it contained my communications software and all my passwords for my online services. Once again, the data was lost, and someone else could have accessed my accounts, received my mail, and sent messages in my name. (Use the Password Security Control panel on your PowerBook.)

I usually have two or three copies of my data. The loss of a machine or hard drive can happen to anyone—don't lose all your data as well because you didn't make a copy.

On the lighter side, you now know how your Mac links files with programs and how to change those links. If you need to share files with someone who doesn't have the same programs that you do, you now know what to do. It may take a little experimentation, but you know the basics that will see you through your task.

Whatever you do with your data, back it up!

Reaching the Outside World

Introduction

I t is now possible to pay your bills without writing a check, to obtain marketing demographics for a project, to purchase airline tickets, and to communicate with people around the globe, all with your computer. Data communications enable you to reach a rich and diverse realm of information. Would you like to read the news before it reaches your newspaper? Do you want to send memos to salespeople on the road? Would you like to acquire software without leaving your home or office?

These are just a few of the things that are possible, and more possibilities are discussed in this chapter. Entering the world of data communications, though, is not always easy. This chapter gives you the information you need to get your Mac and modem working. In it, the following topics are discussed:

❖ Data communications basics
❖ Communications hardware
❖ Quick guide for data communications
❖ Online services

Data Communications Basics

Most people are aware of the potential for using their computer to communicate with other computers and, by extension, with other people. The process of doing so is often awkward. Because most of the computers you will contact are not Macintoshes, venturing into data communications is like visiting a foreign land. It is getting better, but the data comm world is still more alien than the average Macintosh user would like.

To connect with computers that are not Macintoshes requires a device that acts as an equalizer that makes computer-to-computer communications possible. This section covers with these equalizers, which consist of hardware devices and software. This discussion is a basic primer on data communications. More advanced capabilities are mentioned, but they are left for you to explore on your own. This section covers the following topics:

- ❖ The equalizer
- ❖ Basic communications terminology
- ❖ The Macintosh communications toolbox

The Equalizer

All computers can communicate because they have a common language. No matter what differences you may see on the screens of dissimilar machines, there is always a way to exchange data. The easiest means for doing this is with a hardware device called a *modem*. The word "modem" is actually an acronym for *mo*dulation and *dem*odulation. It has become a common name for a hardware device that converts the digital data from your Macintosh (or other computer) into sound signals (*modulates*) that are then sent over regular telephone lines. It also converts these sound signals back into digital data (*demodulates*) for the receiving computer to use.

Connecting your Macintosh to other computers via your telephone line requires a modem. (There is more information about these devices in the upcoming section.) Just as your Mac does not work without a System folder, your modem needs software as well. The software that enables a computer and modem to work together and connect to another computer-modem combination is called *communications software*.

Basic Communications Terminology

The concepts that form the basis of data communications are really the same for all computers. If you are not familiar with data communications, many of the terms used here may seem confusing. Even if you have some experience with data communications, some of the terms will be new to you. This section attempts to make sense of them.

Although a thorough understanding of these terms is not a prerequisite to using your Mac with a modem, if you take the time to become familiar with these concepts, your explorations will be easier and more enjoyable.

Data Speed

There are two different measures of how fast data is transferred from one computer to another. One is BPS, or bits per second; the other is Baud rate, which is a measure of the signal speed. BPS and Baud rate are not always equivalent. BPS means that a specific number of bits per second, usually ranging from 300 to 56,000, are being transmitted from one computer to another. At 300 BPS, you send 37.5 bytes per second, or 2250 bytes per minute. This is equivalent to about two pages of text in a minute. At 19,200 BPS you send 2400 bytes per second, or 144,000 kilobytes per minute. This is usually the maximum speed at which two computers connected with a serial cable can communicate.

Baud rate is the signal speed that modems use to communicate. It is the number of signals sent per second. This means that a 300-Baud modem sends 300 signals per second, a 9600-Baud modem sends 9600. How much data is actually sent depends on how many bits are sent per signal. With older modems, the Baud rate and the BPS are usually the same. Most modems, however, can send multiple bits with each signal, which means that a 2400 BPS modem may operate at 600 Baud and send four bits with each signal.

The confusion between these two terms occurs because they are used interchangeably. Every communications package you use will ask you to set the Baud rate at which you want to communicate and never mention BPS, while all of the modems are actually rated at BPS and do not talk about their Baud rates. It gets worse: You can use a 9600 BPS modem that has error correction and data compression protocols that enable you to set your communications software's Baud rate at 57,600. It's no wonder that Macintosh users get confused and frustrated by all of this

Synchronous and Asynchronous Communications

This concept pertains to how your data is sent. *Synchronous transmission* means that every byte is sent immediately after the other, with a regular and scheduled interval between each byte. *Asynchronous transmissions* occur when the bytes sent can have a delay between them, although not every byte sent may have a delay between it and the following one.

Asynchronous communication is easier to perform and is the method used by older, less expensive modems. It is also slower than synchronous communications. Synchronous data transmissions are faster but require special hardware. Many of the newer modems are capable of synchronous communications. To achieve the highest data transmission rates possible, your modem must be capable of synchronous data communications.

Parity

Parity is a simple method of error detection. There are several different types of parity, which are listed here:

❖ Even—Even parity is a method for maintaining the number of 1s in a byte to be even. Remember, every byte is composed of 0s and 1s. If the number of 1s in a byte is odd, the parity bit is set to 1; if they are even, the parity bit is set to 0.

❖ Odd—This is the exact opposite of even parity. Instead of keeping the number of 1s even, they are kept to an odd number.

❖ Mark—This error-checking method always sets the parity bit to 1.

❖ Space—Space parity is the opposite of mark parity; the parity bit is always set to 0.

❖ None—In this case, no parity bit is set and more effective means of error detection are used.

With error correction and data correction built into modems, the use of a parity bit will someday disappear; but for the time being, it is still necessary. The parity setting for your software and the computer or modem you are connecting to must be the same.

The other significance regarding parity is that the number of bits per character is determined by whether you use a parity bit. If you use a parity bit, you must use seven bits per character; if not, you can use an eight-bit character.

Duplex Modems

There are two types of duplex modems: full and half. A full-duplex modem can receive and send data simultaneously; a half-duplex modem can send data and receive data—but not at the same time. With a full-duplex connection, your modem sends any characters you type back to your computer so that you can see what you are doing. If you have it set to half-duplex, you do not see what you are typing unless you specifically instruct your computer to display the characters as you type them. The software displays the characters through a feature called a *local echo*.

Stop Bits

A stop bit is a bit that is added after a byte has been sent. The number of stop bits can be 1, 1.5, 2, or auto. This is another communications parameter that you need to set in your software. If your software is intelligent enough, it will use the auto setting and you do not have to set the stop bit. Some software cannot detect the number of stop bits, so you have to know what they are in order to connect successfully to another computer.

Flow Control, Pacing, or Handshaking

Every device—modems and computers—has a buffer that can hold a specific amount of data. If the devices could not tell each other when their buffers are full, data sent after the buffer is filled would be lost. The method of communicating this information is called *flow control*, *pacing*, or *handshaking*. There are three types of flow control: hardware, software, or none.

Software flow control is also called XON/XOFF. Using software flow control, you can type ⌘+S to signal the other computer to stop sending data. By typing ⌘+Q, you can restart the transmission. Typing ⌘+C momentarily breaks the connection.

Hardware flow control sends an electronic signal between the devices to indicate whether they are ready to receive data. Even though it is always the receiving device that controls how the data flows, the flow control settings must be the same for both computers. Any new modem that you purchase today uses hardware flow control. If the modem does not come with a cable, make sure that the modem cable you purchase is a hardware flow control cable.

Hayes-Compatible

Modems that are Hayes-compatible are called smart modems and use what is called the *AT* command set developed by Hayes Microcomputer. These modems have features that you control by using AT commands. Because the AT command set is standard, most communications packages take care of it transparently.

You can use commands to make your modem automatically answer or dial the phone. They are also used to reset the modem, set the flow control, and for other features. The most important feature of Hayes-compatibility, however, is what Hayes calls an Improved Escape Sequence with Guard Time. The escape sequence is the set of commands that allows a modem to be placed in a command mode so that it can be configured. What makes the Hayes escape sequence unique is that the modem cannot be accidentally placed into its command mode. Other modems can unexpectedly be placed into their command modes by the data being transmitted through them.

The other major escape sequence is called Time Independent Escape Sequence. This is a different escape technology and does not necessarily offer the same security as the Hayes standard.

The concept of Hayes-compatibility has been confused with the AT command set for configuring your modem. Other AT command languages and software designed for a Hayes modem will work with a compatible modem if the AT command language is the same.

Communications Toolbox

Apple introduced the Communications Toolbox as an add-on for System 6.0.X and built it into System 7.X; it is now part of Mac OS 8. The Communications Toolbox is a set of standardized communications tools and procedures that Apple established to bring consistency to Macintosh communications.

Even though you may be using Mac OS 8, you will not be able to use the Communications Toolbox unless you have the special communications tools installed in your Extensions folder. These tools include the following:

❖ Apple Modem Tool—This is the tool that controls the modem. It recognizes an Apple, Hayes, or Hayes-compatible modem and uses the built-in serial ports of the Macintosh. The Modem Tool provides for configuring all your data communications parameters.

❖ AppleTalk ADSP Connection Tool—This tool is used for making AppleTalk connections using the AppleTalk Data Stream Protocol. This is actually a network tool even though it uses the Communications Toolbox. It lets two Macs on the same network connect using terminal emulation packages if both packages support the Communications Toolbox.

❖ Serial Connection Tool—The Serial Connection Tool is for establishing computer-to-computer connections. Like the Apple Modem Tool, it also provides for all configuration parameters.

❖ Text File Transfer Tool—The Text File Transfer Tool is used to control how text files are transferred from the computer to which you are connected. A text file is a file that contains only text with no formatting or font definitions. TeachText creates text-only files.

❖ TTY Tool—TTY stands for TeleType. This tool is used to configure your terminal, which controls how the data you receive from another computer appears on your monitor.

❖ VT102 Tool—The VT102 is another terminal emulation tool. It is made specifically for controlling the connection to DEC (Digital Equipment Corporation) VAX computers, which have special requirements regarding keyboard mapping and commands; the VT102 is required if you are going to log onto a DEC system and actually use that VAX computer with your Macintosh functioning as a terminal.

❖ XMODEM File Transfer Tool—This tool controls how binary (applications and compressed files) transfers are made between your Mac and another computer. If you are downloading (receiving) a file from another computer and it is not a text file, you have to use a file transfer protocol, such as XMODEM.

❖ Third-Party Tools—Manufacturers of modems and other computers can make Communications Toolbox tools to meet any special requirements their hardware might have. These tools could be special terminal emulators or a special connection tool. An example is the Hayes Modem Tool that was written by Hayes for use with the Communications Toolbox.

Programs that require the Communications Toolbox usually supply the communications tools necessary for their applications to work. Almost all communications software either use or offer the option of using the Communications Toolbox, largely because the Toolbox makes writing programs that have communications capabilities a lot easier.

Communications Hardware

The essential hardware component for data communications, other than your Mac, is your modem. Modems have changed dramatically over the last few years. They have gone from speeds of 1200 bps to 33,600 bps in the last nine years. They may soon run even faster, but 33.6K is getting close to the maximum capacity that standard phone lines can handle.

A wide variety of modems are available, each with different features. This section looks at these features and helps you determine your requirements for data communications needs.

56Kbs Modems

Several companies offer 56Kbs (kilobytes per second) modems. At the moment, two caveats limit the full use of 56Kbs modems: They only work with other modems made by the same manufacturer, and they require a digital line at both ends. A 56Kbs modems could work on a standard phone line, but I haven't yet heard of one that does. With the current rate of technology change, though, it is possible that 56Kbs modems will work on standard phone lines by the time this book is published.

What Is a Modem and What Can It Do?

The modem works by connecting to your telephone lines and to your Macintosh. It is a hardware bridge between your Mac and the rest of the world. In the simplest fashion, you can use a modem to connect to another computer. Each user can type, and whatever is typed is sent to the terminal of the connected computer.

More complex operations include transferring text and binary files. Transferring binary data is quite sophisticated and requires special protocols. Binary files can consist of any type of computer file that has been compressed to save space and transmit faster.

Some of the most advanced operations involve using a modem to take control of another Macintosh remotely or connecting to a remote network. In addition, modems and software are available that can turn your Mac into a fax machine, an answering machine, or a complete voice mail system.

Then we have the goodies that the online services and bulletin board services (BBSs) provide. Through these, you can have an e-mail account so that others can send you information, obtain shareware and freeware programs, have ongoing discussions with people who have similar interests, or get information on almost any subject.

Hardware and software manufacturers often maintain BBSs so that their customers can get technical support, software upgrades, and utility programs or just to make it easier to exchange information with their customers and vendors. Other people run BBSs as a hobby, using the BBS to bring together people with similar interests who might not otherwise communicate. Large companies may have a BBS for their employees and use it as a means of keeping everyone informed about company matters.

The Internet, however, is quickly replacing BBSs (see Chapter 14). Most companies now are using the World Wide Web and e-mail instead of BBSs. BBSs, though, are still used by user groups and special interest groups. The most popular Macintosh BBS is called First Class.

Let's not overlook one more important use for modems: They can and are used to connect physical networks that are in two different locations. Sometimes, it is a matter of dialing into a network to get e-mail; other uses include keeping an open line between two locations so that the two networks can appear to be one. Where there is a need to communicate and the users are not in immediate physical proximity, a modem can be the tool that keeps everyone in touch.

Protocols

Making modems work together has been achieved only by the establishment of standards. Each time using a higher BPS rate becomes possible, an industry-wide consensus must be reached before the modems are released to the public; otherwise, you have to use modems from the same manufacturer. The standards make it possible to use the same type of modem on any computer, which is what makes the modem an equalizer.

The established protocols and standards determine everything about the modem's functionality. Where differences may occur is in how the modem interacts with the computer at a software level. Even the commands that the modem can accept have a basic standard that can, and will, deviate somewhat from manufacturer to manufacturer.

Standards also apply to error correction and data compression. Some of the new high-speed modems have these capabilities; others do not. Because the same types of designations are used to describe a modem's various capabilities, you need to be very clear regarding what you want. The rest of this section covers the following topics:

- ❖ Modem standards
- ❖ Data compression protocols
- ❖ Modem speed

Modem Standards

The first set of standards establishes that all modems have the same characteristics for operating at different speeds. One of the most important characteristics is the frequency speed. The ability to recognize different frequency speeds determines the operating speed of the modem. Table 12.1 lists the various standards that most modems use. (If a modem does not use these standards, it probably does not work with those that do.)

Table 12.1 familiarizes you with the terminology used to describe modems. When you open your modem's manual, you will find several pages about the standards and their associated attributes for each of your modem's operating speeds. It is easy with the high-end (faster) modems to get confused between V.42 and V.42 bis. If you really want a V.42 bis modem and get one that is only V.42, you will be disappointed.

Currently, a new standard is emerging for 56,000 BPS modems. Although these modems are available and the standards have been set, they have not been ratified and proclaimed as standard. Perhaps, by the time you read this, the standards for 56,000 BPS modems will be in effect.

Table 12.1 Modem Standards

STANDARD AND SPEED	DESCRIPTION
Bell 103 (300 BPS)	The first standard used in the early stages of modem development.
CCITT V.21 (300 BPS)	The international standard for 300 BPS data communications. This standard was established after the fact for compatibility purposes.
The 212 Standard (1200 BPS)	Established to accommodate 1200 BPS transmissions; has backward compatibility to the Bell 103 standard.
The Bell 212a Standard (1200 BPS)	Uses a different frequency than the 212 standard; usually has the ability to connect with a modem that uses the 212 standard.
The 224 Standard (2400 BPS)	International standard (Europe and the United States). All modems designed in accordance have the ability to drop back to 1200 BPS. This is also called the CCITT* V.22 bis in Europe and the United States.
CCITT* V.32 (9600 BPS)	An international standard for full-duplex synchronous or asynchronous communication that uses a two-wire dial-up or leased-line environment. Also includes automatic drop back to 2400 BPS.
CCITT* V.32 bis (14,400 BPS)	This is similar to V.32 but defines the standards for data communications up to speeds of 14,400 BPS with a fall back to 12,000 BPS.

*CCITT stands for the Comit Consulatif International Tlgraphique et Tlphonique (International Consultative Committee on Telegraph and Telephone). This is an international organization for the establishment of protocols and standards for telephone and communications related industries.

Data-Compression and Error-Correction Protocols

Some modems have built-in data-compression capabilities. The ability to compress data as it is sent can increase both the Baud rate and bits-per-second speed of your modem. Because it is the modem that performs the data compression, the modem receiving the data and the one sending it must use the same protocols to achieve this task.

Another task that your modem automatically performs is error correction. There are several standards for error correction, and some of the error-correction protocols also provide data compression. Although you could probably live the rest of your life without ever knowing these things, knowing about them may demystify one of the most arcane areas of Macintosh operations.

Table 12.2 lists the different error-correction and data-compression protocols used in modems today.

Modem Speed

Modems have continuously evolved, with each stage resulting in a device capable of sending data at increasingly faster speeds. The lower-speed modems (2400 BPS) are full-duplex asynchronous devices, and the high-speed modems (9600, 14,400, and 28,800 BPS) are full-duplex synchronous or asynchronous devices. Speed becomes

Table 12.2 Error Correction and Data Compression

PROTOCOL	DESCRIPTION
MNP* Class 1	Error correction for asynchronous half-duplex communications.
MNP* Class 2	Error correction for asynchronous full-duplex communications.
MNP* Class 3	Error correction used to convert data into a synchronous protocol even though the actual data link is asynchronous. This protocol increases data transmission speeds because it eliminates the need for stop bits.
MNP* Class 4	Error correction that is basically the same as MNP 3, except that it has the added capability to negotiate the size of the data packet** sent.
MNP* Class 5	This is the first data compression standard established. It enables a modem to achieve a 2:1 rate of data compression. You should not use this protocol if you are transferring files that have been compressed by software.
CCITT V.42	This is another international standard; however, this one is for error correction. It provides better error correction than MNP 4 and works better over poor-quality phone lines. If V.42 cannot be used, the modem will automatically try MNP 4. If that fails, it will not use any error correction.
CCITT V.42 bis	This is a data compression protocol that is referred to as LAP-M***. It is also compatible with MNP 5 so that your modem will try to use MNP 5 if it cannot use V.42 bis. The difference is that V.42 bis is much more effective (compression rates of 4:1) than MNP 5; it can automatically detect files that have been compressed by software and will not try to compresses them again.

*MNP is the Microcom Networking Protocol.
**A data packet is a predefined number of bits or bytes all sent as a group.
***LAP-M is the Link Access Procedure for Modems.

an issue when your modem has V.42 bis or MNP 5 capabilities. With V.42 bis and MNP 5, you can, if your software sets up your modem properly, double the effective speed of a 2400 BPS modem to 4800 BPS; the same applies to 9,600 BPS modems.

Using a 9600 BPS modem with V.42 bis, your data rate can jump to 38,400 BPS (this provides a theoretical speed of 2,250K per minute), and your Baud rate can be as high as 57,600. Remember that Baud is not the same as BPS; Baud is the rate of the frequency signal you use to connect. There is a correlation between Baud and data rates: The higher the Baud, the faster the data transfers.

To obtain the maximum data rate possible for your modem, consider a few other factors: One is the condition of the phone lines. If the phone lines are not *clean*, meaning that there are fluctuations in the signal strength, or that there is static or noise (such as hearing another conversation while you're talking to someone else), your modem does not operate at its best. The error correction kicks into effect and ultimately reduces your overall speed.

If you are connecting to the Internet with a 56K modem, your Internet service provider must use digital lines and 56Kbs modems. Even though you might use an analog phone line, these modems can realize data receiving transfer rates up to 53Kbs and transmitting rates at 33.6Kbs. You can't obtain a full 56Kbs transfer rate because the FCC limits the power output for an ISP's modems. With error correction, the transfer rate at 53Kbs can be 115.2Kbs.

Next, your computer must be able to keep up with the data transfer rates. If you run your communications program in the background and work with a CPU-intensive application while receiving a file, your data transfer rate decreases because it cannot process the data it is receiving at its optimum rate. Also, if you use virtual memory or if your terminal package has a small data buffer, you impede the speed at which your Mac can process the data it is receiving, thus slowing down the modem.

Also, if you have a choice, use the modem port rather than the printer port. The modem port, present on all Macs since the SE, supports synchronous data transmissions; however, the printer port does not. If you do have to use the printer port, make sure AppleTalk is turned off in the Chooser. AppleTalk may interfere with data transfers because the AppleTalk driver takes control of the entire Mac.

The AT Command Set

Throughout the industry, a standard set of commands called the AT command is used to configure a modem. With the command set, you tell your modem whether to automatically dial, what error-correction and data-compression protocols to use, and specify other modem-controlled aspects of the data-communications process. The command set is in the public domain. It is available for any manufacturer to use and should not be confused with Hayes-compatibility. Hayes uses the Hayes Standard AT Command Set, and only those modems that use the same AT command language as Hayes are compatible. If a modem manufacturer claims to be Hayes-compatible, it must also use the Hayes patented escape sequence. There is a lot of confusion in the industry about this point.

If you have a modem that does not use the standard AT command language, you will probably have problems with it. Most software is written to take advantage of a full AT command language, rather than a subset of it. The set of AT commands your modem uses is found in your modem manual. Usually, your software takes care of all your configuration issues. If your communications software requires special drivers to work, make sure it has a driver that works with your modem.

The AT command set is not going to be listed here. It can differ in subtle ways from one manufacturer to another, and a list with an explanation of how each works would take its own book to describe.

Status Lights

Most modems have *status lights*, which tell you at what speed the modem is operating, if it is set to auto-answer, whether it is sending and receiving data, and so on. These lights are useful for keeping you informed and for troubleshooting. The problem is that there are no standards. Each manufacturer makes up its own combination of lights and assigns its own meanings to them. You will have to read your manual to figure out what they mean.

If the modem you are thinking about buying does not have status lights, think twice about purchasing it. Unless you feel comfortable with your data-communications skills, you could find yourself unable to determine what is going wrong. You might not want status lights only if you have an internal modem on a Macintosh Portable or PowerBook, or if you use a battery-powered modem with a portable Mac. In this case, the lights are another drain on your battery.

Fax

In the last few years, sending and receiving faxes became possible using your Macintosh. If you send documents that originated inside your computer, using your Mac as a fax machine can be a real time-saver. If you do not generate most of the faxes you send to others on your Mac, you may be better off using a standard fax machine. The time it takes to scan a document, not considering the cost of the scanner, may add up to a poor decision. Also, if you need paper copies of any faxes you receive, factor in the amount of time it takes to print a fax. If these issues are not a problem for you, the technology is great. You can get hardware and software that let you network your fax/modem so that several people on your network can use it. If you have a small business, a fax/modem can enable you to fax documents without leaving your desk to send or receive them.

All fax/modems serve double duty as data modems. The newest breed of fax/data modems operates at 14,400 or 28,800 BPS and can send faxes at the same rate. They are usually group 1 and group 3 fax-compatible devices, which means that they can communicate with all standard standalone fax machines—and operating one is as easy as using the Print command from within any application.

The only applications that do not work well with a fax/data modem are those that require a PostScript printer. Sometimes, setting up the software for your fax/modem can be a bit confusing, but exercising some patience pays off. Each software package usually consists of an extension that sets up the fax/data modem to automatically receive, a Chooser extension that lets you print a fax from almost any application, and a fax manager to set up phone books and view and print the faxes you receive. You can also convert graphics (PICT, TIFF, and MacPaint) into faxes, and vice versa. In addition, your fax/data modem probably has a control panel device for monitoring and notifying you of incoming faxes. Setting everything up usually takes some time, but once it is done, you won't have to fuss with your setup.

The one big drawback to most fax/modems is, that some modems, when set to receive faxes, cannot receive data—and vice versa. If you want a system that can receive faxes while using the same modem to let someone call in and have access to your network, you may need two modems—using one with the serial port and the other with the printer port. You also need a line-switching device of some sort. The line-switching device then routes incoming faxes to the fax/modem and data calls to your data modem. Some modems can have full data, fax, and voice capabilities.

The final drawback with a fax/modem is disk space. If you need to keep copies of your faxes for legal or other purposes, and especially if you receive a lot of them, you will find that they use a fair amount of disk space. You will either have to plan for this or be prepared to store old faxes on floppy disks.

Quick Guide for Data Communications

This section covers the following areas and tries to simplify your software options:

❖ General discussion of communications software
❖ Your data communications guide
❖ Macintosh data communications software
❖ Data communication utilities

General Discussion of Communications Software

You have to use your software to set up the Baud rate, configure your modem, and make the data connection. So, you need software that you are comfortable with, which could easily be none of the packages available. (In that case, you should choose the one that is the least uncomfortable.)

Three parts are absolutely necessary for a communications package to work. One part is setting up the communications parameters for your modem; another is configuring your terminal display; and the third is the terminal itself. Now, if you're new to data communications, I use some terms here that will be new to you.

All the basic terminology, as it relates to modems, has been covered. What you need now are those terms used in conjunction with communications software.

Software Terms and Protocols

Table 12.3 lists the terms you need to understand to set up your communications software and make it do what you want it to do.

Your Data Communications Guide

This section guides you through a simple terminal session for logging on to a local bulletin board. Because using BBSs or commercial services are probably the primary activity you will perform with your modem, this discussion might take some of the pain out of the process. This section goes through the steps of configuring your software, automatically and manually dialing into the BBS, logging in, and logging off. It also demonstrates the same procedures using the Macintosh Communications Toolbox. The topics are as follows:

❖ Your communications configuration
❖ Your terminal configuration

Table 12.3   Data Communication Terms

THE WORD	THE MEANING
8th Bit	When communicating in modes that do not ignore the size of the byte, meaning that they use stop bits, you want to strip the 8th bit from every character you send. This makes it easier for different error-correction protocols to process your data, and it is usually a default setting.
ASCII	ASCII stands for the American Standard Code for Information Interchange, and it is used as the acronym for the representation of numbers, characters, and control characters used in data or digital communications. There are 128 characters in the ASCII standard set and 256 in the extended set. Your modem manual or your software manual should include a chart of the ASCII set. There is a direct relationship between the 128 characters and the number of bits per byte your modem and communications package use . The number of bits per byte can be represented as 128, equal to 2^7, which is the maximum number of character representations for a 7-bit byte, while 256 equals 2^8, or the total possible for an 8-bit byte.
Auto Wrap	Auto Wrap is an available option when receiving text that exceeds the number of columns you have set for your terminal. Your options include whether to have a line feed and carriage return placed at the end of each line as it is wrapped.
Binary	Binary is the standard format (for the non-Macintosh world) when transferring data. It is in contra-distinction to MacBinary.
Capture	Capturing saves the data that you receive on your terminal to a text file as you receive it. You can open the capture file and read it at your leisure.
Carriage Return	This term is a holdover from the days of typewriters. (Remember them?) It now refers to the ASCII character that tells your terminal or word processor to start at the beginning of the next line when combined with a line feed. If you use a carriage return by itself, your terminal will just move the cursor back to the beginning of the line it is on and will not start a new one.
Columns	In data communications, a column is the space used by a single character. The standard column setting is 80, meaning that your terminal displays 80 characters across. You often have to tell the host how many columns you want displayed. If you capture data that you want to move to a spreadsheet or database, you may need to use a column width of 132 to 180.
Control Character	A control character is an ASCII number that represents a nontyping control code, such as a carriage return or a tab. The ASCII number for a carriage return is 013, and the number for a tab is 009.
CRC	Cycle Redundancy Check or checksum. This method adds the number of bytes in a data string. The receiving computer performs the same calculation

Table 12.3   Data Communication Terms

THE WORD	THE MEANING
	and checks the results against the number transmitted. If the numbers are not the same, an error has occurred. This is the fundamental procedure for all error detection and correction protocols.
Display Buffer	This is an area where data that has scrolled off the terminal's screen is kept. You can usually define the size of your display buffer, which enables you to go back and look at messages that have come and gone. Using a display buffer can save time because you will not have to ask for data to be retransmitted.
Echo	Setting the echo on for your terminal means that it displays each character as you type it. If you use a full-duplex modem, it usually echoes the characters you type so that you do not have to set the *local* echo. If you have a synchronous connection, however, you need the local echo turned on to see what you are typing and sending to the host computer. Most asynchronous connections echo what you type so that the local echo can be turned off.
	Echo is also the term used when you have data that you receive sent directly to your printer and printed as you are receiving it; this is called a printer echo.
Host	The host is the computer with which you hold the communications session. You are the remote computer if you initiated the contact.
IBM PC/ANSI	Terminal configuration that uses the ANSI standard for displaying text and graphics.
Kermit	This is a special file transfer protocol to send 8-bit data while using a 7-bit environment. It is used primarily in government and universities. It has error correction and the ability to send multiple files.
MacBinary	This is a special binary protocol that allows a Macintosh file to be transferred so that it retains all its file information, such as Creator and Type. It also keeps the Data and Resource forks separate. If you receive files that are not in MacBinary format you have to convert them to MacBinary format to use them on your Mac. Similarly, if you use an MS-DOS machine to receive Macintosh files, the files you receive are not in MacBinary format.
Packet	A packet is a group of bits or bytes that are looked at as a complete unit. Data transfer protocols use packets of varying sizes up to 1024 bytes to speed up data transmissions.
Remote	The remote computer is the computer that initiates the contact.
Row	A row is a line of text as it is displayed on your terminal. You can set how many rows of data you want displayed, and you can tell the host computer how many rows to send before it waits for you to tell it to send another set. Each set of rows is often referred to as a screen.

(continues)

Table 12.3 Data Communication Terms *(continued)*

THE WORD	THE MEANING
Scripts	A script is a macro that can be used to automate the login process. Some packages let you automate your entire communications session by using scripts. If the package you use has a powerful scripting language, you can actually use it to create your own special-purpose communications application.
Terminal	Generic term for the window that displays what you type or any text you receive during a communications session. Your terminal can be set up to interact with other computers, which also means that your keyboard will be remapped to conform to whatever the host computer requires.
TTY	Abbreviation for TeleType. This is the term used to describe a basic terminal configuration.
VT 52 through VT 320	These are designations for different terminal emulation configurations. They are primarily used with DEC (Digital Equipment Corporation) computers, also known as VAX computers.
XMODEM	A data transfer protocol for sending either text or binary files. It was one of the first protocols to include automatic error checking and correction during data transfer.
YMODEM	An extension of XMODEM. Its added abilities include sending multiple files, as well as the files' names and sizes.
YMODEM-G	This is a variation on the YMODEM protocol that sends files in rapid bursts without error correction. If an error occurs, the transfer is terminated, making it suitable only for error-free connections.
ZMODEM	ZMODEM is the latest in data transfer protocols. It works like YMODEM-G, except that it can retransmit data that has an error. If the transmission is interrupted, it can resume where it left off. This is the protocol to use with the V.42 bis modem.

❖ Logging in and signing on

❖ Logging off and hanging up

Your Communications Configuration

Before you can begin, you need to tell your Macintosh what type of modem you are using, its speed, where it is connected (serial or printer port), and all of the other information shown in Figure 12.1. Figure 12.2 shows the settings using the Macintosh Communications Toolbox (MCT). In both figures, you see that the Baud Rate, Data Bits, Parity, Stop Bits, and Flow Control are set here. Each allows for the specific modem selections—in this case, a Hayes modem—even though the modem in use is a Maxlite 96-144 pocket modem made by Macronix, Inc. This model is Hayes-compatible and works with this configuration.

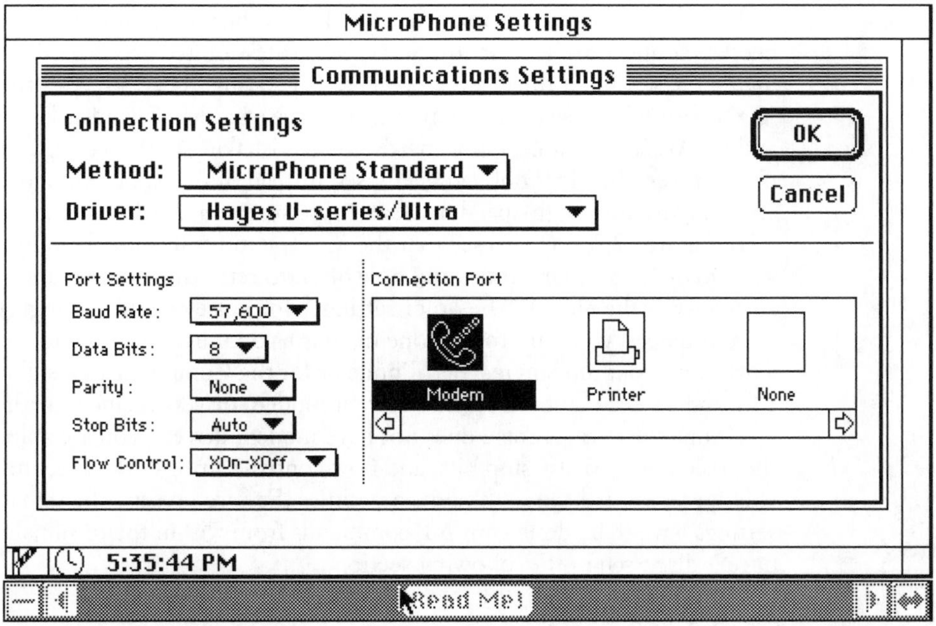

Figure 12.1   *Communications settings in MicroPhone II.*

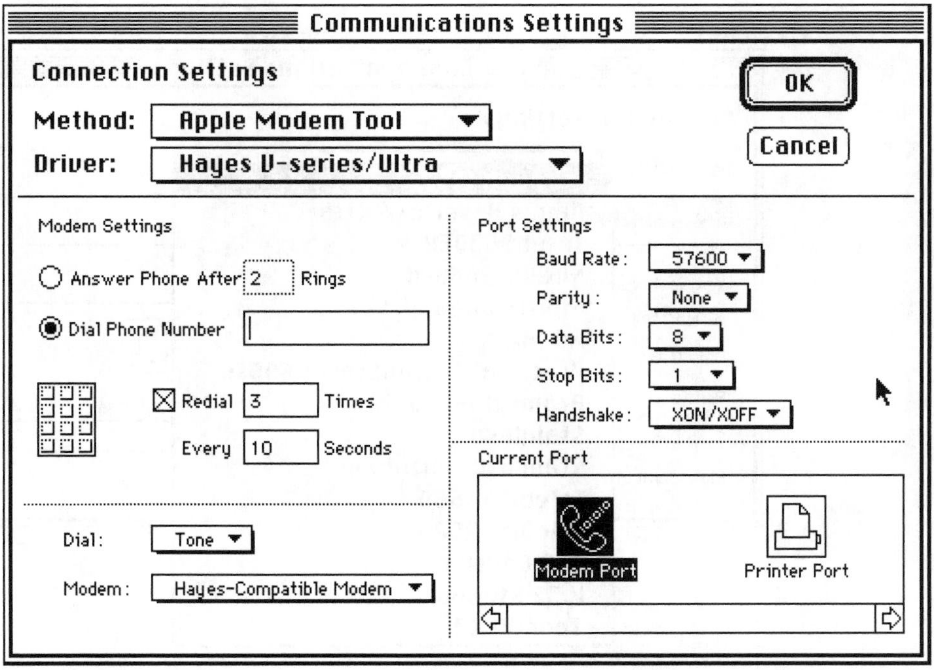

Figure 12.2   *Communications settings in the Communications Toolbox.*

Before you start, determine what Baud and other communications settings you need to connect to the host computer. Regardless of what your modem, you must match the setting of the terminal you are contacting. The Flow Control is set to XON/XOFF because the modem does not have a hardware handshaking cable attached and the MCT does not support hardware handshaking in this configuration. (It would if the Hayes Modem Tool had been used instead of the Apple Modem Tool.) If you are going to use a high-speed modem, make sure you use the modem port.

In Figure 12.2, you also see that the MCT settings include the phone number you want to dial, how many times and how often to retry the number, and whether to auto-answer the phone. The other setting is for pulse or tone dialing. (Under most circumstances, you want to use tone dialing.) You must select the modem driver that works with your modem in MicroPhone or for the Communications Toolbox. Figures 12.3 and 12.4 show some of the different modem drivers included with both setups.

If your software package does not have modem drivers, you are able to set only the basic Baud, parity, stop bits, and flow control settings. Most communications packages allow for this, although sometimes they are preset. The remainder of your settings have to be done with AT commands from within the terminal. This procedure is discussed in the following section.

Your Terminal Configuration

Figures 12.5 and 12.6 show the terminal options with both MicroPhone and the Communications Toolbox. Under most circumstances, you want to use the TTY

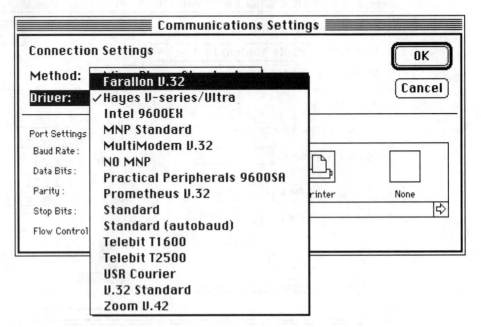

Figure 12.3   *Modem selections for MicroPhone.*

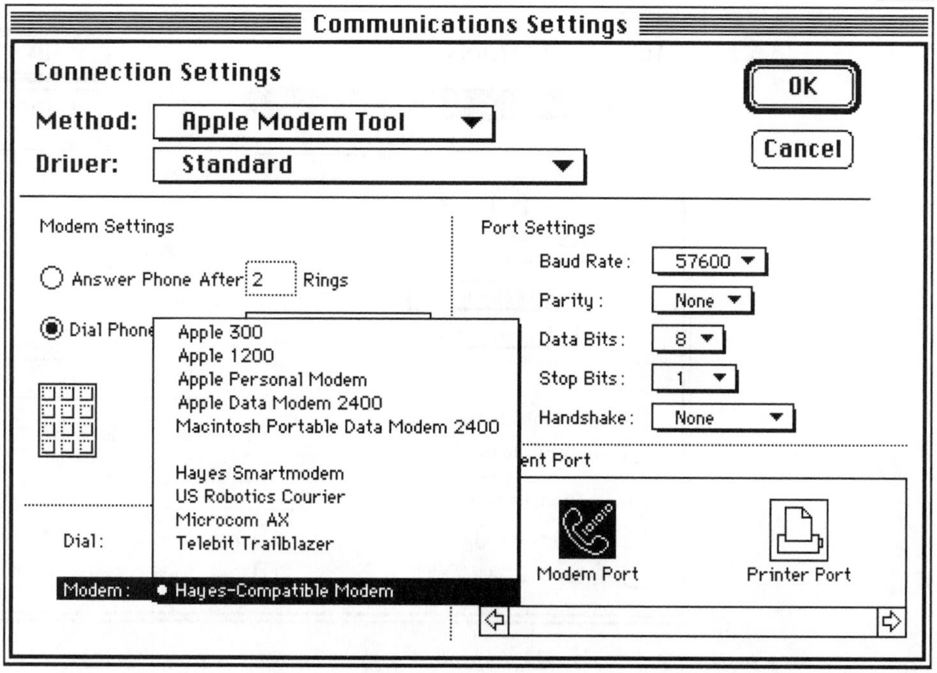

Figure 12.4 *Modem selections for the Apple Modem Tool.*

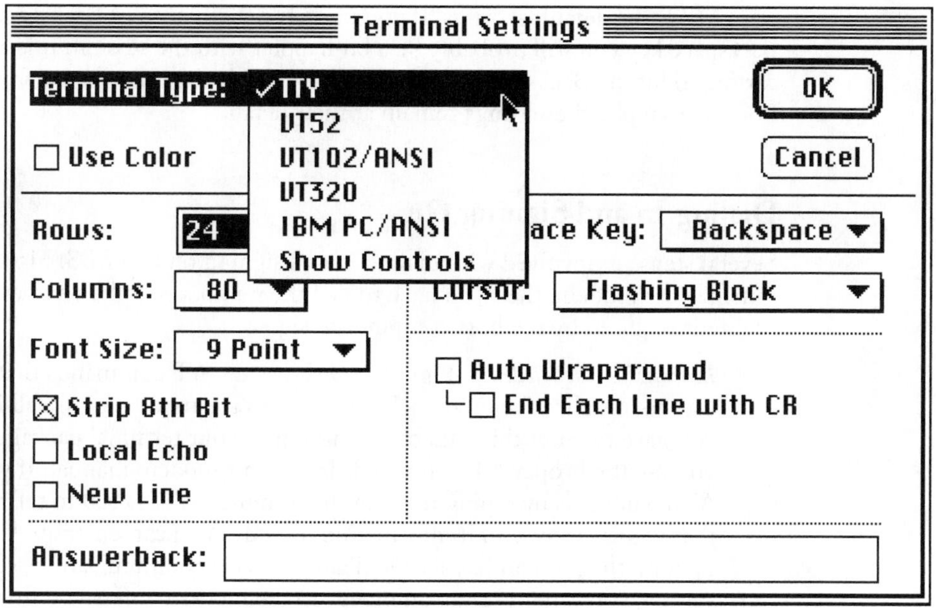

Figure 12.5 *Terminal options in MicroPhone.*

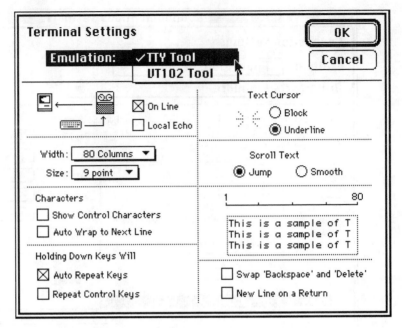

Figure 12.6 *Terminal options in the Communications Toolbox.*

setting. The terminal options you select control how the data you see in the terminal is displayed. Figures 12.7 and 12.8 show your basic options.

Most of the options are self-explanatory. For basic communications sessions, you want to use the default settings. If you press Delete instead of Backspace for the Backspace key you will probably be a bit happier with the session. It is always disconcerting to hit the Backspace key and not have finished before the cursor disappears. For the example, the settings remain at their defaults.

Dialing In and Signing On

Several steps are involved with dialing in and signing on to a BBS. First, you must initialize the modem; then you have to dial the number; finally, you have to perform the steps required by the host computer to sign on.

Initializing the Modem—Figure 12.9 shows the AT commands that MicroPhone uses to initialize the modem. This prepares the modem to use all its features. If you have to enter this data by typing it into your terminal package, make sure you use the proper AT commands from your modem manual. If you enter the AT commands by typing them in the terminal, AT is used to tell the modem that you want to send it information directly. You can enter an AT command up until the modem has started dialing; once a communications session has started, you cannot send commands to the modem unless you first send it the escape sequence. This will most likely end the session as well.

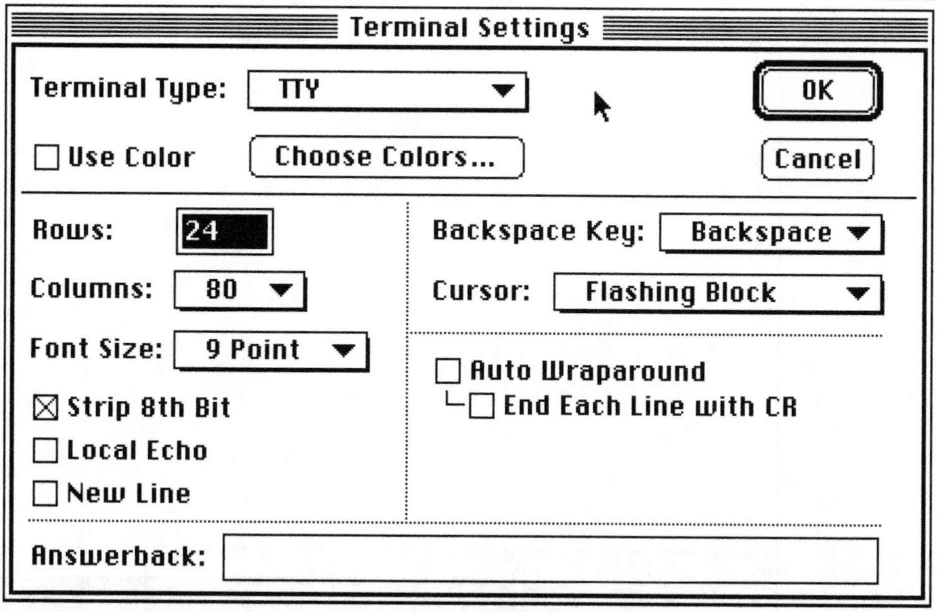

Figure 12.7 *Terminal settings in MicroPhone.*

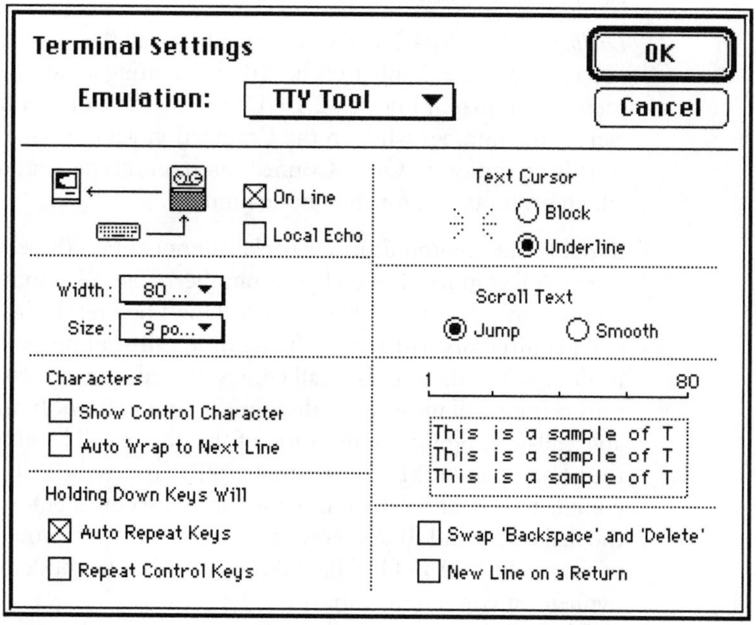

Figure 12.8 *Terminal settings in the Communications Toolbox.*

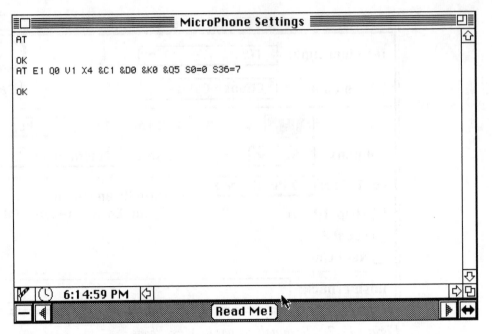

Figure 12.9   *Initializing the modem.*

The Communications Toolbox initializes the modem automatically as it dials your number. You cannot send any special AT commands with the communications toolbox other than those entered into the modem initialization field.

Dialing the Number—Now, you are ready to call the BBS. If you use MicroPhone, you can enter the number of the BBS by creating a New Service from the Phone menu, as shown in Figure 12.10. If you use the Communications Toolbox, you can set the number while in the Connection window (see Figure 12.2). There is usually an option to Open Connection in programs that use the Toolbox, which prompts you for the phone number.

Should your communications package not contain these niceties, you have to use an AT command to dial your number. The AT command to dial a number is commonly ATDT 18005551212. (Don't be literal with this number, or you will get directory assistance.) If you have call-waiting service on your line, turn it off before dialing in. If a call comes in while you are connected to the host, call-waiting will most likely disconnect your session. In most areas, you can disable call-waiting for the duration of the phone call by entering "*70," before the phone number. In this example, *70 disables the call-waiting, and the comma tells your modem to pause for two seconds before executing the rest of the dial command. If you enter the commands from your terminal, your command might be ATDT *70, 1800-555-1212. The modem ignores all spaces and hyphens in your command. If you have to dial 9 to get an outside line, enter "9," before the phone number. If you have several numbers to dial, enter those and put a comma after any number that would cause you to wait before contin-

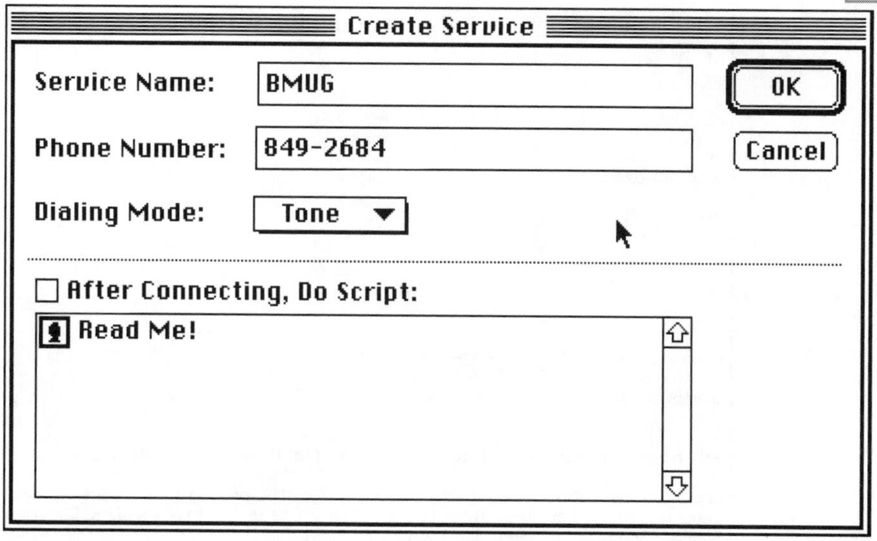

```
╔══════════════════ Create Service ══════════════════╗
║                                                      ║
║  Service Name:   [ BMUG                    ]  ( OK )║
║                                                      ║
║  Phone Number:   [ 849-2684                ] (Cancel)║
║                                                      ║
║  Dialing Mode:   [ Tone      ▼ ]                     ║
║ .................................................... ║
║  ☐ After Connecting, Do Script:                      ║
║  [⬆ Read Me!                              ⇧]         ║
║  [                                         ]         ║
║  [                                         ]         ║
║  [                                        ⇩]         ║
╚══════════════════════════════════════════════════════╝
```

Figure 12.10   *Creating a service in MicroPhone.*

uing if the wait is longer than two seconds; use as many commas as you need to make the connection. The AT command is executed when you press the Return or Enter keys if you are doing it by hand. In MicroPhone, just select the service you want from the Phone menu.

Logging On—Unless you turned off the speaker, your modem makes a racket once you dial the number. To begin with, you should probably leave the speaker turned on, even though it is annoying, so that you can tell if everything is going according to plan. You hear the modem dial, hear the other phone answer, and then you hear the *negation process,* where the two modems shriek at each other until their shrieks merge and a connection is made. Then, the modems shut up. Be sure you have the correct number. If you don't, you might dial a wrong number early in the morning and hear a sleepy voice answer the phone as your modem screams computer obscenities at the poor soul.

Connected—After the host's modem answers your modem, your modem displays the connection speed for the session, and you have to log in. Figures 12.11 and 12.12 show the connection and the login process. You have to give your name and whatever other personal information the service asks for; then you are asked to enter a password.

On most BBSs, you have to be validated, meaning that your membership may be checked, the information you provided during the initial login process may be scrutinized, or the Sysop (System Operator) may want to validate you. If nothing else, validation is a process in which you are given access to certain areas of the BBS. Once you are on, messages and miscellaneous information appear, and then you are able to go to the areas of interest to you. You might want to read the messages, check your mail, or download files. This is where your fun begins.

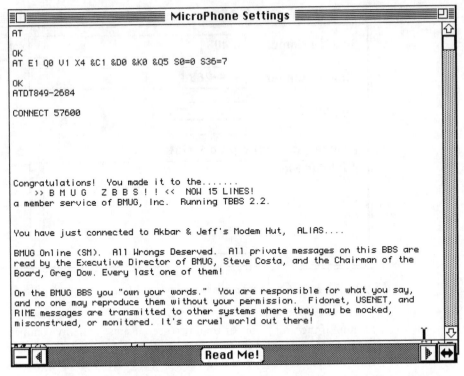

Figure 12.11   The initial login.

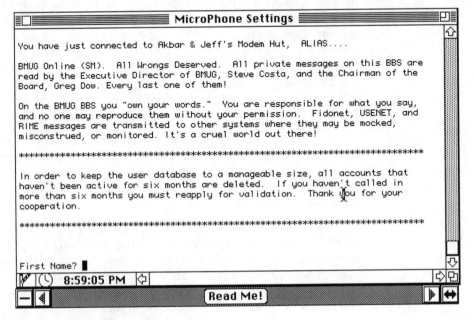

Figure 12.12   Signing on.

Playing Around, Logging Off, and Hanging Up

Now that you are connected, you can explore the BBS; there is no telling what you might find. If it is a special-interest BBS, you may want to talk to the people who use it, leave messages, or enter into ongoing debates. This is the land where you meet new and interesting people; what you do with it is up to you.

One of the things you probably want to do is download files. In addition to showing you how to log off and hang up your phone, this section briefly covers downloading files.

Downloading Files—This is a wonderful way to get shareware, freeware, or demo software. First, find your way to the file area and browse. Once you have found a file you want to download, select the protocol you want to use. If you have a halfway decent communications package, you have some choices. If not, you may have to use XMODEM or, preferably, ZMODEM.

When using ZMODEM, MicroPhone automatically receives the file. When using the Communications Toolbox, you can use XMODEM only for your file transfers. Figure 12.13 shows the status window that appears when you perform a download. Any communications package gives you a status window of some type. If possible, the amount of time required for the download is displayed so that you know if you have time to take a break before the process is completed. Once you have your file, you can go about your business.

Logging Off—When you are finished, you need to log off the host computer and hang up your modem. Logging off the host computer is easy: Just enter the

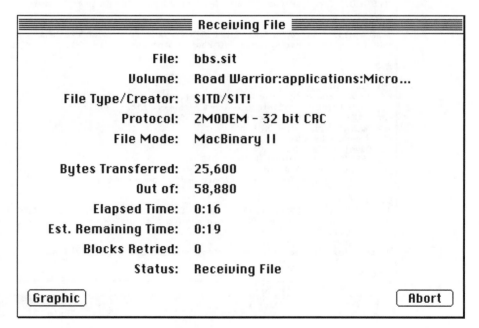

Figure 12.13   A download status file.

appropriate command. Figure 12.14 shows the final logoff from the sample session. After you have left the host system, your modem tells you that the connection is broken, as shown in Figure 12.15.

Now, all that is left to do is hang up your phone. Most software has a menu selection that hangs up your phone, but if you have to do it manually, type in the escape sequence to regain control of your modem. The standard escape command is +++. After you type the escape command, type ATH0, which hangs up your phone. Figure 12.16 shows what your terminal looks like after hanging up.

Courtesies and Suggestions

When you participate on BBSs or use online services, follow some courtesies and implied rules that have developed over the years. One rule is to be sure you don't type with your Caps Lock key depressed. WHEN YOU DO THIS, IT GIVES PEOPLE THE IMPRESSION THAT YOU ARE SHOUTING AT THEM. If you are joking but want to make sure the other person understands, the following

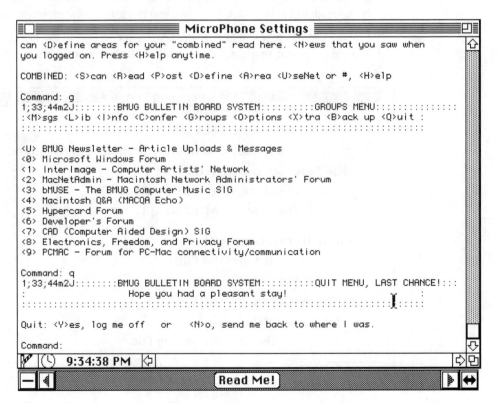

Figure 12.14   Logging off.

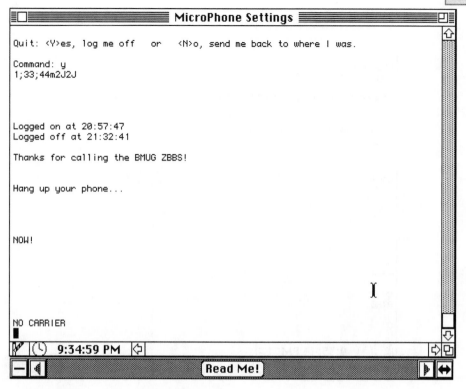

Figure 12.15   Your session is finished.

notation is often used :). It's supposed to represent a sideways smiley-face. You can also use ;) to indicate a wink. You can, of course, use the standard punctuation marks as well.

Going online and exploring can be like entering a foreign land or joining a club where everyone uses a secret handshake that you have to figure out. Take notice of what others do; think of it as watching the host or hostess at a formal dinner and following his or her lead.

Compression Utilities

Only a few data compression utilities are widely popular: Stuffit, Stuffit Deluxe, and Compactor. Although they all perform the same basic function, they do it in different ways and are not necessarily compatible.

Archived files usually have an extension added to the file name. Compactor files have .cpt as an extension, and Stuffit files usually have the extension .sit. Some Stuffit files can have another extension, .sea, which stands for self-extracting archive. These archives are programs that you double-click to extract, so you do not need to run the utility program. Using extensions help identify what type of archive you are using.

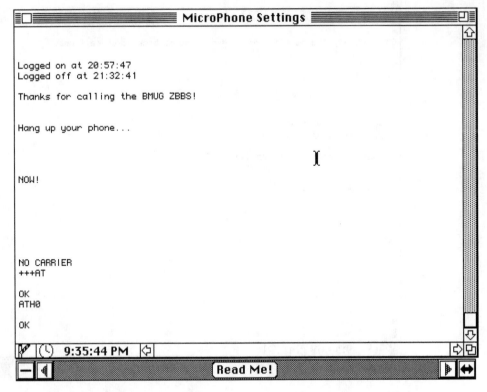

Figure 12.16   After hanging up.

Stuffit Deluxe—This is the most comprehensive of all available compression utilities. The original author of Stuffit, Ray Lau, wrote the program while in high school. He distributed it as shareware, and it is one of the shareware success stories. For several years, Stuffit was the only standard for data compression.

Stuffit Deluxe is the latest incarnation of the original Stuffit. It is Mac OS 8-compatible and decompresses a variety of different archive formats, including those for MS-DOS machines and UNIX formats. Figure 12.17 shows the basic working window for Stuffit Deluxe.

Stuffit Deluxe also comes with a useful utility called SpaceSaver, which automatically compresses files that have not been used for a predetermined amount of time (see Figure 12.18). It works in the background and is an excellent utility.

Stuffit Lite 3.5—This is the latest version of the shareware version of Stuffit. It is Mac OS 8-compatible and can be accessed via Apple Events, so it can be used with Frontier or QuickKeys (Deluxe is also Apple Events-aware). Stuffit Lite can be found on the CD-ROM included with this book. Figure 12.19 shows the file downloaded in the example above ready to be extracted by Stuffit Lite. Stuffit Deluxe and Stuffit Lite are published by Aladdin Systems, Inc.

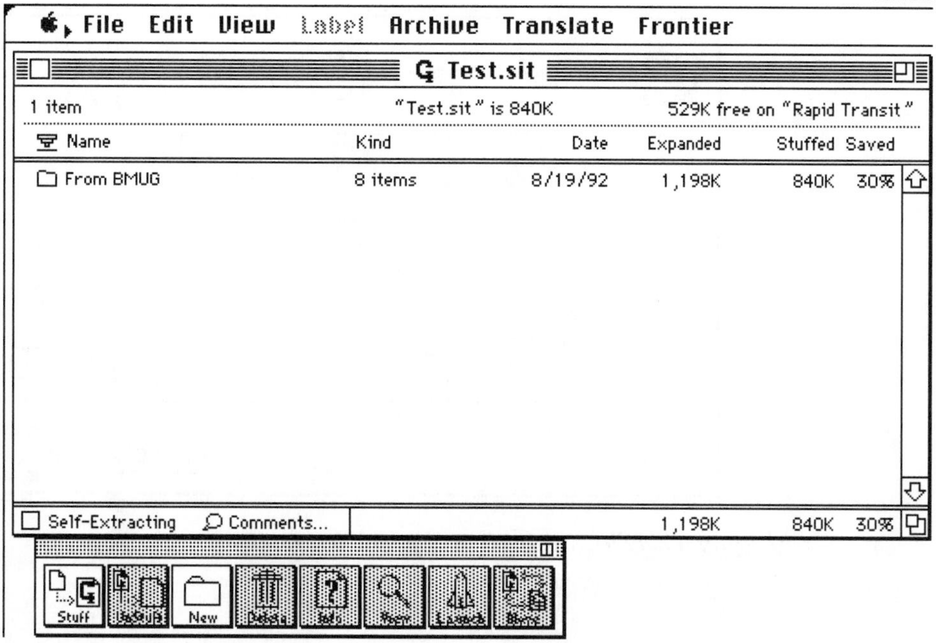

Figure 12.17 *Stuffit Deluxe's main window.*

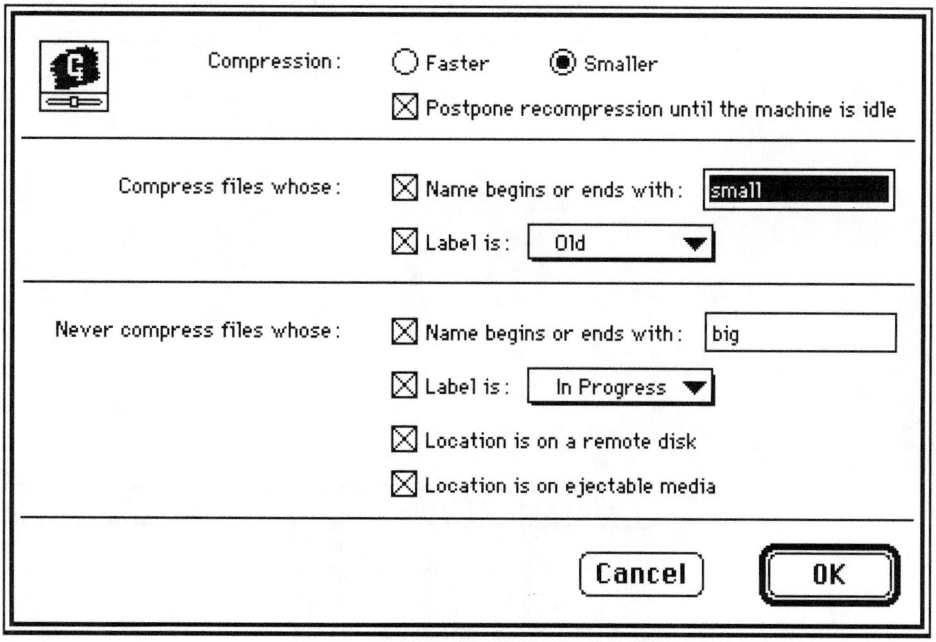

Figure 12.18a *Stuffit SpaceSaver's control panel.*

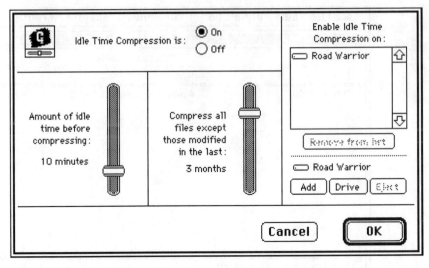

Figure 12.18b *Stuffit SpaceSaver's control panel.*

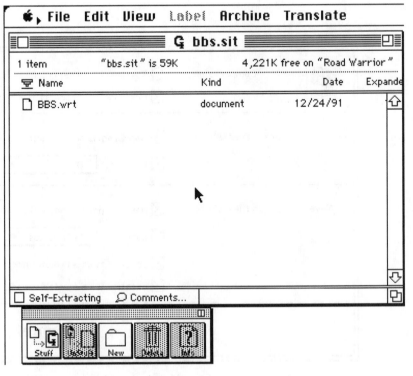

Figure 12.19 *Stuffit Lite's main window.*

Stuffit Expander—Stuffit Expander is discussed in Chapter 14, "Surfing the Net." Stuffit Expander is a utility on the CD-ROM included with this book. It is also included with Stuffit Deluxe. This is a drag-and-drop utility that can be used to decode and decompress downloaded data files.

Compactor—Published by Bill Goodman, Compactor is emerging as a new standard for data compression and is extremely easy to use. It is distributed as shareware and available on most BBSs and online services. Compactor is also on the CD-ROM included with this book.

Online Services

An online service is similar to a BBS except that it offers more content and often provides access to the Internet. There are two primary online services: America Online and CompuServe. Both of these services charge a monthly subscription fee and provide you with e-mail, access to news wire services, support sections from computer and software vendors, games, and many other services.

An online service is often attractive to new users because it offers an easy way to get online. Each service provides you with its own software, and navigating through the many service offerings is usually quick and easy. Although the online services provide similar services, they are indeed different. To decide which service is the right one for you, you may want to subscribe to each of them for one month and explore. Then, when you've decided on which service you want to use, cancel the other subscription.

On many occasions I've recommended that people try using one of the online services rather than going directly to the Internet. Setting up an account with an online service is easier than configuring your computer for Internet access, and you get all the same capabilities. The primary drawback is that information can be censored and Internet access is usually slower via an online service than when you connect to the Internet directly.

Although I usually use the Internet for most of my online work I keep a CompuServe account for those times when I'm traveling. Recently I went to Haiti on business. For the trip I opened an account with America Online because it had a local access number in Port au Prince. While in Haiti I had all my e-mail forwarded to my AOL account. This way I could stay in contact with my office while out of the country. It was easier to set up the AOL account than devising some method for accessing the Internet directly. There are many other ways to use online services. This is just one; you may find others.

Summary

You should now have enough information to participate in the world of data communications. In a sense, it is a step into virtual reality. You can get to know people and discuss with them anything under the sun—without ever seeing or actually speaking to them.

Communicating in this manner means that prejudices and visual impressions do not apply. You will experience a new way of communicating that may take a while to get used to, but you will soon become more adept at expressing yourself without hand movements and facial expressions.

CHAPTER 13

Networking for the Beginner

Introduction

Unless you have more than one Macintosh or work in an office environment where there are other Macs, you will be tempted to skip this chapter. Don't. This chapter is about connecting your Macintosh to other Macs, but it also contains information about your Mac that you'll need later on. Besides, networking is a subject with which you should be familiar because, at some point in the future, you will want to connect your Mac to other Macs.

Connecting your Mac to other Macintosh computers can be a central part of using your Mac. Networking is one of the easiest ways to share data with other Mac users. This chapter covers the basic information about connecting and using your Mac to other computers. You'll find the practical information you need to connect your Mac to other Macs to share data—without learning an entire lexicon of esoteric terms. The topics are as follows:

- ❖ What is a network?
- ❖ Connecting your Macs
- ❖ Using the network
- ❖ Using personal web sharing

What Is a Network?

A network, in the simplest sense, connects two computing devices together. The term really means more than just establishing a simple connection. A network involves connecting a few computers to many so that they can share peripheral devices and data and can exchange information. All things shared by networked computers are called *shared resources*.

395

Network   A collection of interconnected, individually controlled computers, together with the hardware and software used to connect them. A network allows users to share data and peripheral devices, such as printers and
storage media, to exchange electronic mail, data files, and more.

The simplest Macintosh network is one that connects your Mac to a PostScript
LaserWriter. As soon as you have done that, you have created a network. If several
people in your office have Macs, and if their Macs are connected a LaserWriter, your
office has a network. Once you have connected a Mac and a PostScript LaserWriter,
you have a *LAN* or a *local area network*. (The term LAN usually means more than just
one Mac and the LaserWriter, but, technically, you have a LAN with just your Mac
and these devices connected.) Figure 13.1 shows a basic network.

Local area network (LAN)   A group of computers connected so as to
share resources. The computers on a local area network are typically joined
by a single transmission cable and are located within a small area, such as a
single building or section of a building.

LAN is the acronym used to describe a single network and all the devices it contains for one, *local* physical location. The connection of all these different devices so
that they can send data between the different machines or share common *network services* or *resources* makes it a LAN. If , for instance, your office has several
Macintoshes, a couple of LaserWriters, and one very stubborn person who refused
to give up a beloved DOS machine all connected, you have a LAN.

To have a network, you need three basic components—the physical connection
between the computers (cabling), hardware in the computers to utilize the connection,
and software that makes the connection operate. Your Mac has networking software
and hardware built into its ROM and System. All you need to provide is the cabling.

In environments where users have networked their Macs, they usually are not
concerned with network terminology and couldn't care less that the network is called
an AppleTalk network. This apathy springs from the ease of networking Macs—
users do not need to know the technical nomenclature. All Macs, when networked,

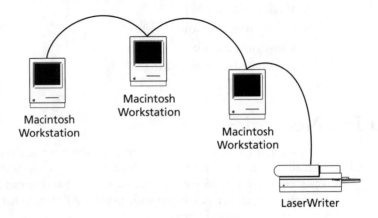

Figure 13.1   *Diagram of a basic network.*

constitute an AppleTalk network; AppleTalk is the name of the networking protocol employed by all Macs.

Protocol   Short for *communications protocol;* a formal set of rules for sending and receiving data on a communication line. For example, binary synchronous communications (BSC) is a protocol.

"Protocol" is a word that's used at different times, one that you should know if only to impress your friends. When referring to networks, "protocol" simply defines the software the computers use to communicate with each other. Because Macs use only one software protocol, most people never learn this term. Usually, in the Macintosh world, users define their network by the cabling standard used rather than the software standard.

You should also know about AppleTalk so that you can determine whether a device will work on your network. Several peripherals in addition to printers can be connected to your network, including modems, scanners, and serial port sharing devices. All the network devices are collectively referred to as AppleTalk-compatible or AppleTalk devices.

Connecting Your Macs

Apple has made all its Macintoshes to support a concept called *Plug and Play,* which means that, for most connections—networks included, all you have to do is plug in the cables and play the Mac; it is ready to go. Now, it's not really that simple, but almost.

Introduction to Network Cabling

Every Macintosh ever built can be networked via its printer port. In addition to the printer port, most of the newer Power Macs have a special network port called an Ethernet port. The physical network consists of the connectors and cabling that connects the Macs and the LaserWriter. Three cabling standards are commonly used for this task:

LocalTalk

PhoneNET

Ethernet

LocalTalk, the oldest cabling standard used for Mac networks, is no longer sold. It consists of an AppleTalk connector and round cabling, about the width of a pencil, that links each of the Macintoshes and the printer together. PhoneNET is a very close cousin to LocalTalk. PhoneNET uses PhoneNET connectors, using regular telephone lines for the cable that connects all the networked devices.

LocalTalk connectors and cabling were made by Apple; PhoneNET connectors are made by a company called Farallon. PhoneNET is now the primary means for connecting all Macs. It has proven so popular that even Apple has licensed PhoneNET technology from Farallon, and Apple sells PhoneNET connectors with the Apple logo.

Network connection　A combination of hardware and software that lets you set up a particular implementation of the AppleTalk network system, such as LocalTalk or EtherTalk.

Ethernet is another wiring standard that, unlike PhoneNET and LocalTalk, is an industry standard for all computers—not just Macs. It is a bit more complicated than PhoneNET, and if you work in an office where Ethernet is employed, your company probably has someone who sets up and maintains the network. It is very unlikely that you are expected to know how to hook your Mac into an Ethernet network.

PhoneNET and LocalTalk are low-speed networks, but Ethernet is a high-speed network. For now, it is enough to know what type of network cabling you use (you'll sound like a genius).

Cabling Mechanics

This section discusses how to physically connect your Macs with PhoneNET (or LocalTalk). The term *topology* describes the physical layout of networking cables. In this section, we look only at setting up a PhoneNET network using a daisy-chain topology. Although this sounds complicated, it is nothing more than connecting Macs with phone wire. Figure 13.2 illustrates a daisy-chain network.

Daisy chain (n.)　A colloquial term for a group of devices connected to a host device, where the first device in the *chain* is connected to the host, the second device is connected to the first, the third device is connected to the second, and so on.

There is nothing complicated about using PhoneNET connectors for networking your Macs. Basically, all you need are connector boxes like the ones shown in Figure 13.3 and enough phone wire to go from one Mac to the next. Two types of

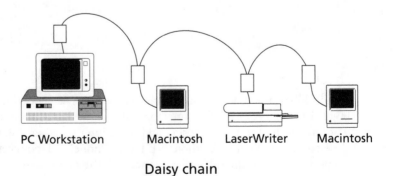

PC Workstation　　Macintosh　LaserWriter　Macintosh

Daisy chain

Figure 13.2　*A daisy-chain network.*

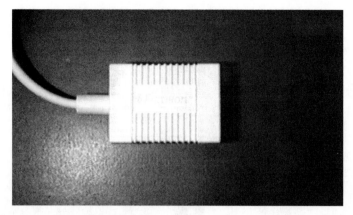

Figure 13.3 *PhoneNET connectors.*

PhoneNET connectors are shown in Figure 13.3. The PhoneNET connector is the most common connector used. The Star connectors are used only at each end of a network or to connect two Macs or a Mac and a printer. If you are buying connectors, your job is easier if you purchase the standard PhoneNET connectors. You need one PhoneNET connector for each Macintosh or printer on your network (you must make sure your printers are AppleTalk-compatible to use them in a network). The connector is plugged into the Mac's printer port, and then each Macintosh is linked to the next with telephone wire. Figure 13.4 shows how the phone wire is connected from one Mac to the next. At each end of the network (daisy chain), there is a small plug called a *terminator* in the open hole of the connector. The terminator is an electrical resistor that completes the connections for the network. The terminator is not always essential, but you should install one regardless—you don't want to have to troubleshoot your network as soon as it is set up. A terminator is included with every Farallon PhoneNET connector. Once all of your AppleTalk devices are linked, your network is complete.

PhoneNET Connector Clones

As mentioned earlier, Apple makes a connector just like Farallon's. Other companies also make PhoneNET-like connectors as well. All the connectors that use telephone wire use the same technology and can be interchanged.

So many companies use the same technology because Farallon has a patent for its PhoneNET connector technology, and it licenses to other companies, Apple included, the right to make and sell similar products. Because everyone uses the same technology, all these connectors are interchangeable.

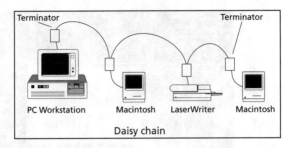

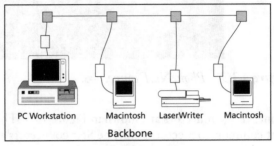

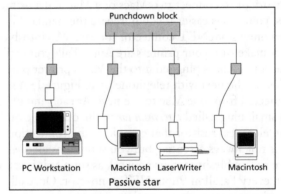

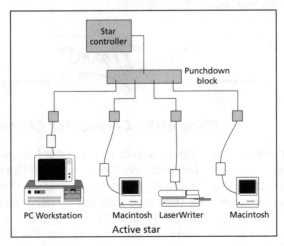

Figure 13.4 How the network is wired.

Troubleshoot   To locate and correct an error or the cause of a problem or malfunction in hardware or software.

Using the Network

The previous sections provided some information on connecting your hardware to form a network. Now, let's look at using the Mac's networking capabilities and some more networking concepts. Unless you use your network just for printer access, your network will have a file server. The *file server* is a shared hard drive that holds files that can be shared with other Mac users on the network—one of the primary reasons for having a network. It is usually easier to put data to be shared on a file server that others can access than it is to put the data on a floppy disk and pass the disk around the office. If sharing data is something done regularly, a network enables everyone to work more efficiently.

File server   (1) A specially equipped computer that allows network users to store and share information; (2) a combination of controller software and a mass-storage device that allows computer users to share common files and applications through a network. AppleShare software, Macintosh computers, and one or more hard disks make up a file server on an AppleTalk network system.

There are two basic types of file servers: One type is called *peer-to-peer* and the other is a *dedicated server*. A peer-to-peer network is one where any machine on the network can be a file server and a client at the same time, while a dedicated file server is a Macintosh that is set up to function as a file server only. Finally, you can have a mixture, where your network has a dedicated file server, plus users who are sharing files with Mac OS 8. Figure 13.5 illustrates both peer-to-peer file sharing and a dedicated file server.

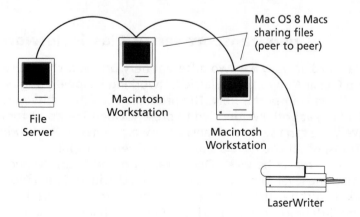

Figure 13.5   *Three networks.*

Client   A computer that has access to services on a network. The computers that provide services are called servers. A user at a client may request file access, remote logon, file transfer, printing, or other available services from servers.

Apple has provided every Mac OS 8 user with peer-to-peer file sharing software, based on Apple's dedicated file server software, AppleShare. Whether you use Mac OS 8's personal file sharing or a dedicated AppleShare file server doesn't matter; your interaction with the server is the same. If your Mac is going to be a file server, then you need to learn some things—namely, how to configure your system so that you can share files with other Macs.

Mac OS 8 allows you to use your Mac as a file server and to use the shared volumes from hard drives others have made available. (Using Mac OS 8's file sharing as a client or accessing an AppleShare file server employs the same procedures.) To use this capability, you need file sharing software installed (if it was not installed with Mac OS 8, you need to install it now). If your Mac is new, file sharing was installed at the factory. Read the installation section in any case; then you'll know how to install file sharing in the future should the need arise.

Volume   A general term referring to a storage device or to part of a storage medium formatted to contain files; a source of or a destination for information. A volume can be an entire disk or part of a disk. A volume has a name and a volume directory with the same name. Its information is organized into files.

If this is your first time using the Mac OS 8's file sharing, you might find it all a bit confusing; you have to become familiar with several control panels, the Chooser, and some special functions of the Finder. All file sharing controls are interconnected,

Open Transport versus Classic Networking

Mac OS 8 actually has two different networking architectures, Open Transport (OT) and Classic Networking. Classic Networking is Apple's original networking architecture. Open Transport is new. The problem is which architecture do I write about? After looking at both I've decided to present Open Transport for a couple of reasons. One, everyone can use Open Transport. Two, the newer PCI Power Macs can run only Open Transport. If you have a choice, use Open Transport.

The differences between Open Transport and Classic Networking are extreme at the machine level. Operationally, little has changed. Even if you use the Classic Networking architecture the information presented is usable. In cases where there are profound differences between OT and Classic Networking I'll try to point them out.

and the order in which they are presented here is not necessarily the order in which you might encounter them. Like most things Macintosh, there are usually several ways to accomplish file sharing.

This section covers all the steps to use Mac OS 8's file-sharing capability or to access an AppleShare file server. The topics covered are as follows:

❖ Installation

❖ Setup

❖ Sharing

❖ Mounting a shared volume

❖ Program linking

❖ Security and performance

Installation

Before any computer can connect to a network, it must have networking software. The Mac is no different from any other computer in this respect. If you need network access only to print, then all you need to install are the printer drivers. Instructions for installing the printer driver are included in this section.

To install Mac OS 8's file sharing, you need the Mac OS 8 CD-ROM. Insert it into your Mac (you do not need to boot from the CD-ROM) and double-click on the Installer. When the Installer starts, select the Mac OS 8 installation option. The Installer's main window appears (Figure 13.6).

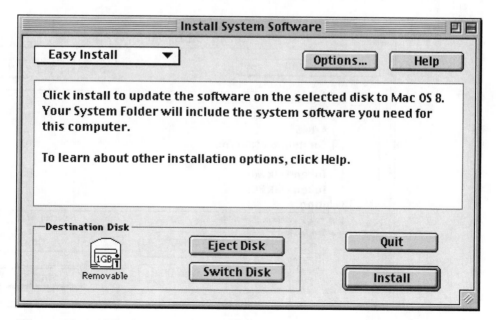

Figure 13.6 *The Installer's main window.*

Once the main window appears:

1. Select *Customize* from the pop-up menu.
2. A window that looks like Figure 13.7 appears.
3. From the list of installable options, click on the triangle next to *Networking Software* to expand a list of options, as shown in Figure 13.7.
4. Click in the check box next to File Sharing, Open Transport, and any other networking option that you need, such as Token Talk PCI (install only the software that you know you need; you gain nothing from installing software you can't or won't use).
5. Make sure the selected hard drive is the one you want to use. You can change disks by clicking on the disk selection section of the Installer's window.
6. Click on the Install button.
7. After the installation is complete, a message appears asking you to restart your Macintosh.

   Once you've clicked on the Install button, the Installer installs the software you need to share files, both as a server and as a client. To install printer software, follow the preceding steps, but replace steps 3 and 4 with the following:

8. From the list of installable options, click on the triangle next to *Printing* to expand a list of options, as shown in Figure 13.8.
9. Click in the check box next to LaserWriter 8 and any other printer option that you might need.

Once you've installed the software and rebooted your Mac, you're ready to use the network. If you use System 6.0.X, your Mac cannot act as a file-server, only as a

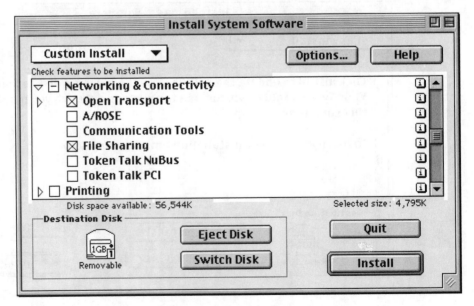

Figure 13.7   The Installer's Networking Software options.

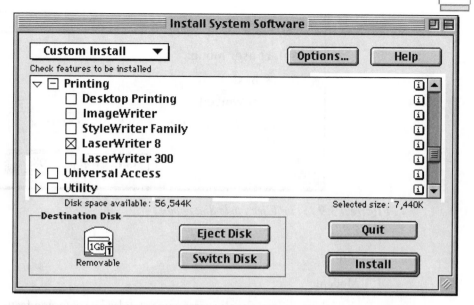

Figure 13.8 *The Installer's Printing options.*

client. The steps for mounting a file server volume on your Mac have been the same for years. Mac OS 8 will be used for the rest of the networking section.

The Open Transport Control Panels

For people who play with networks, Open Transport brings many welcome enhancements. Apple has finally provided some advanced features to networking that make networking easier to configure and control. One of the most welcome features of Open Transport is the ability to save network configurations. And if you're a network administrator, how would you like to lock a Mac's network configuration so that the person using it can't accidentally change the configuration?

These are some of the things you can do with Open Transport. This section looks at the Open Transport control panels. First I discuss common features of all OT control panels. Then I cover the AppleTalk control panel and, finally, TCP/IP issues.

Those of you not using OT should still read this section because the principles at work when discussing the control panels are the same whether you use OT or Classic Networking.

Common Features

Several Open Transport control panels come with Mac OS 8:

AppleTalk

TCP/IP

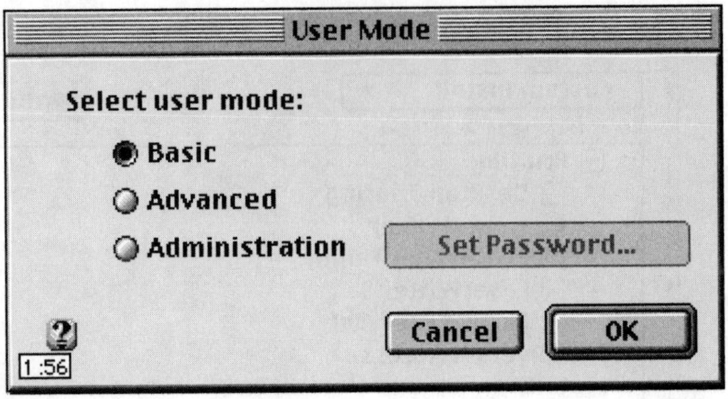

Figure 13.9   *The User mode dialog box.*

PPP

Modem

Each of these control panels shares some standard or common features. For each of these control panels you can have multiple configurations, and you have added control over the control panel's capabilities through a feature called User mode. To discuss these common features I will use the AppleTalk control panel as the example.

The first time an OT control panel is opened it is in the default User mode, which is called Basic. Two additional user modes are called Advanced and Administration. The user mode is accessed from the Edit menu or with the command-U keyboard shortcut. Figure 13.9 shows the User mode window. This window is the same for every OT control panel.

The following list describes each of the User modes.

Basic—Shows the minimum information needed to operate the control panel. This mode also has only the most basic configuration options. Figure 13.10 shows the AppleTalk control panel in the Basic User mode.

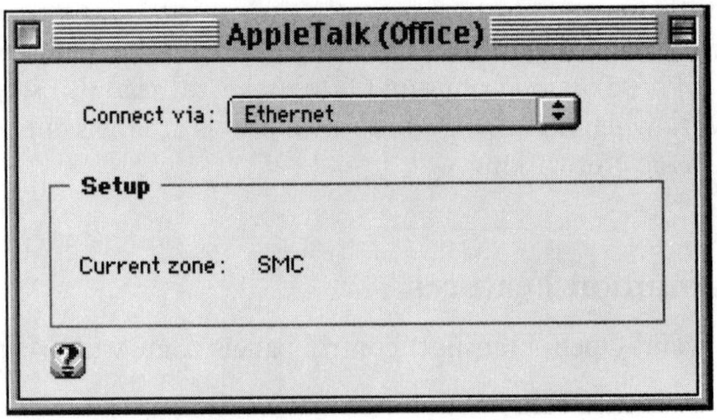

Figure 13.10   *The Basic User mode.*

Advanced—Shows all the information an administrator needs. Depending on the control panel, you can manually assign values to options not normally available. (Warning: If you do not know why you are changing some value, don't.) Figure 13.11 shows a control panel in the Advanced mode.

Administration—This mode has all the features found in the Advanced mode plus the ability to lock the settings. The Administration mode can also be password-protected to protect the settings. Figure 13.12 shows a control panel in Administration mode.

In the Advanced and Administration modes you see an Options button. The options for an OT control panel vary depending on the control panel's function. Figure 13.13 shows the options for the AppleTalk control panel. In the AppleTalk control panel, you can make AppleTalk active or inactive. This function can also be performed from the Chooser.

All OT control panels also share the ability to have multiple configurations. When OT is first installed, all the control panels have a default configuration, and in most environments, you won't want to change the default settings. There are occasions, though, when multiple configurations would be useful. One example is if you want to change System settings using the Location Manager.

One example I can think of occurs when you have multiple Internet accounts and need to change your TCP/IP settings quickly and easily. If you need one TCP/IP setup when connected to a LAN and another when accessing a dial-up IP account (see Chapter 14 for more information about the Internet), you can create a configuration for each purpose and use the Location Manager to switch between them.

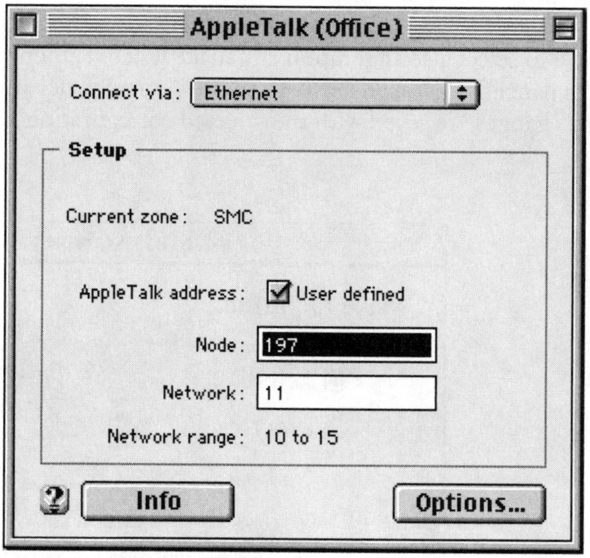

Figure 13.11   The Advanced User mode.

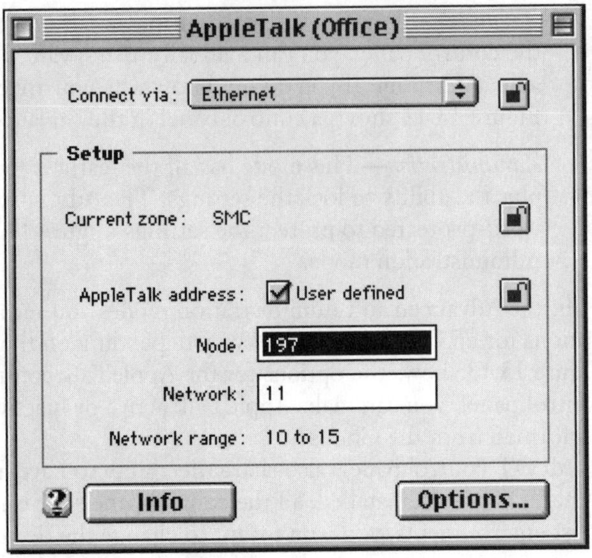

Figure 13.12 *The Administration User mode.*

The configurations feature is accessed by selecting *Configurations* from the File menu or with the ⌘-K keyboard shortcut. Figure 13.14 shows a Configurations window. This window is the same for all OT control panels.

You can do several things with the configurations. You can export a configuration and then use the exported configuration on other Macs by using the import function. To make a new configuration, duplicate an existing configuration, name it, and then set the configuration after making it active.

When working with different configurations the order of events is important. You have to select a configuration and make it active; then you are returned to the control panel. If you make changes to the control panel after switching configurations, the changes are saved with the selected configuration.

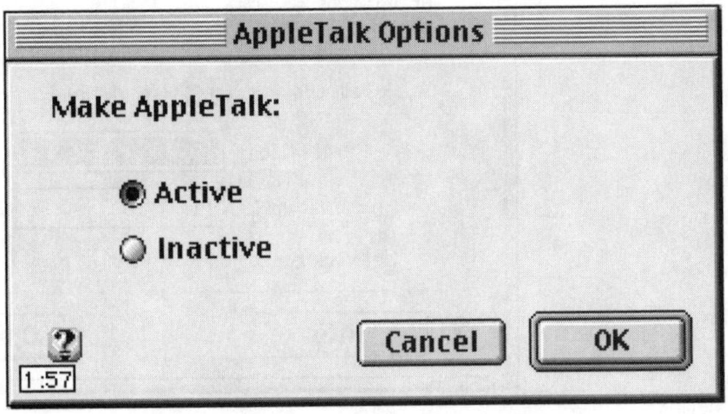

Figure 13.13 *The options for the AppleTalk control panel.*

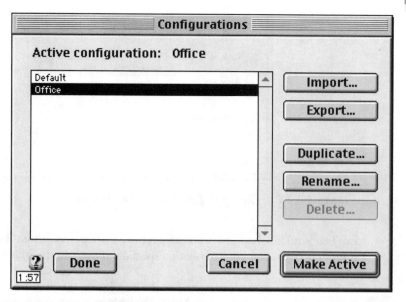

Figure 13.14 *The Configurations window.*

It is best to use names that make sense for your configurations, especially if you use the Location Manager for different configurations. I use names like "Office LAN," "Dial-up IP," and "Home." This way I can set up locations that correspond to reality and so not get confused.

When you change network configurations, network connections can be interrupted. Be careful; you could cause data damage if, while changing a configuration, you cause your Mac to unmount a server volume while it is being accessed.

The AppleTalk Control Panel

Once you have installed your networking software, you need to tell your Macintosh what type of network you're using. You do this from the AppleTalk control panel. (If you use Classic Networking, look for the Network control panel.) The AppleTalk control panel is used to tell your Mac what type of cabling you're using for your network.

Make the selection from the pop-up menu at the top of the control panel. Figure 13.15 shows the selections available for my PowerBook.

You could have different options. All desktop Power Macs can use both serial ports for AppleTalk and usually have an Ethernet option as well. One word of caution: If you have a modem or serial printer, do not select the peripheral's port and turn on AppleTalk. If you do so, your peripheral will not work.

TCP/IP Issues

The TCP/IP control panel is similar to the AppleTalk control panel, but you have to provide a lot more information. Most of the configuration information for TCP/IP

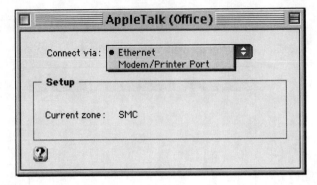

Figure 13.15 *The AppleTalk control panel's options.*

can be found in Chapter 14. In this section, I briefly talk about TCP/IP issues you might encounter on your network, especially if you use the Mac OS 8's Personal Web Sharing.

First, if you are not connected to the real Internet you need a set of IP numbers before anyone can access your Mac's Web pages or use the Personal NetFinder function. A set of network numbers has been set aside for use with private networks. These network numbers do not work on the Internet; that is why you should use them. If your network were to become connected to the Internet, no one could access your private network. The network numbers that you should use are these:

192.168.0.0 to 192.168.255.255 with a subnet mask of 255.255.255.0

This range of numbers gives you a lot of versatility. Just remember that the network number (the third set of numbers 192.168.210.0) must be the same on each of your machines. Otherwise, your network will suddenly be more complex than you wished. And, of course, the last set of numbers must be different for each machine. If you accidentally assign two computers the same machine number, neither will be able to use TCP/IP.

Configuring Your Mac for File Sharing

Now that your Mac has the software it needs for networking, you have to configure the software before you can use it. These steps are usually a one-time procedure, but there will be times when you might have to alter your File Sharing configuration. As such, you must be familiar with the configuration process.

Once you have installed your file-sharing software and restarted, turn on AppleTalk from the Chooser, found in the Apple menu. Figure 13.16 shows the Chooser; turning on AppleTalk is just a matter of clicking on the button. If the title next to the button says "AppleTalk active after restart" instead of "Active," restart your Mac before you use the network.

Chooser   A desk accessory that lets you configure your computer system to print on any printer for which there's a printing resource on the current

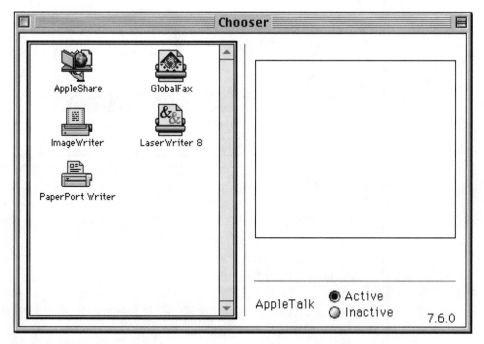

Figure 13.16 *The Chooser.*

startup disk. If you are part of an AppleTalk network system, use the Chooser to connect and disconnect from the network and choose among devices connected to the network.

Once AppleTalk is turned on, use the File Sharing control panel to control File Sharing. From the File Sharing control panel, give yourself and your Macintosh a name and set a password. Remember, all the control panels are accessed from the *Control Panels* menu item in the Apple menu.

Figure 13.17 shows the File Sharing control panel. The Owner name is the name that your Macintosh uses when you access file servers; the Macintosh name is the name that others see when your Mac performs any networking function. The File Sharing control panel is also used to turn on your Mac's server function. Regardless of whether your Mac will be a file server, you need to perform the following steps. Complete step 5 to function as a file server.

To share files using the File Sharing control panel:

1. Open the File Sharing control panel.
2. Give your Mac an Owner name. This can be your name, the name your network administrator tells you to use, or any name you want to use. This is the name you use when accessing other file servers.
3. Enter an Owner password. Use this password to access your Mac from another Mac on the network.

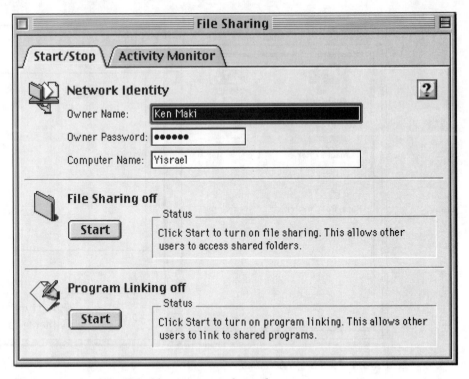

Figure 13.17 *The File Sharing control panel.*

4. Enter a Macintosh name, which is the name others see when your Mac acts as a file server and they access its volumes.

5. Click on the Start button in the File Sharing section of the window. This turns on your Mac's file-sharing functions. When the Status box says that file sharing is turned on, your Mac broadcasts your Macintosh's name, and other Mac users see your Mac on the network.

Next, tell your Macintosh who you will let access your shared files. To do this, use the Users & Groups control panel (Figure 13.18). Do four tasks from the Users & Groups control panel: Define new users, define a group, configure your access, and set up guest access to your Mac. This is where file sharing begins to get complicated—the Users & Groups control panel is deceptively simple in its appearance, but it is not simple.

To use the Users & Groups control panel:

1. Open the Users & Groups control panel.

2. Notice that a user is already defined as the Owner. Double-click on the Owner's icon.

3. A window opens, as shown in Figure 13.19; the default view is Identity; here you can change the name and password. If you change the Owner's name or password it is automatically changed in the File Sharing control panel. The

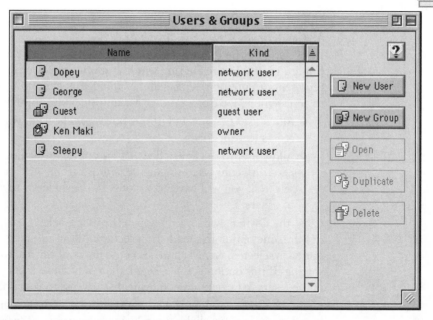

Figure 13.18 *The Users & Groups control panel.*

Figure 13.19 *The Owner's window.*

"Allow user to change password" checkbox option lets you change your Mac's password from someone else's Mac.

4. By clicking on the Identity pop-up menu you switch to the Sharing view (Figure 13.20). In the Sharing window are two check boxes. Each check box represents an option that specifies a connection condition, should you want to access your Mac from another Macintosh. Your options are two:

❖ Allow user to connect—If this box is *not* checked, you will *not* have access to your Mac.

❖ Allow user to see entire disk—This option lets you see and mount any hard disk connected to your Macintosh from another Mac. If it is *not* selected, you will have access only to the folders you've made available to others.

5. Close the Owner's window and open the user labeled Guest. The Guest window has one option in the Sharing section: Allow guests to connect. If this option is selected, any Macintosh on the network can access the files you're sharing. If this option is *not* selected, then only those users you have defined in the Users & Groups control panel have access to your shared files.

6. Close the Guest window and create a new user with the command-N keyboard equivalent, by clicking the New User button, or by selecting the *New User* menu item from the File menu.

7. In the window's Identity section give the new user a name and password (Figure 13.21). The names you choose should be descriptive enough so that

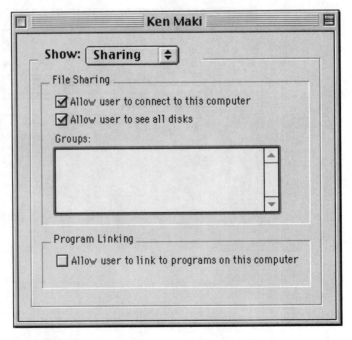

Figure 13.20   *The Sharing section.*

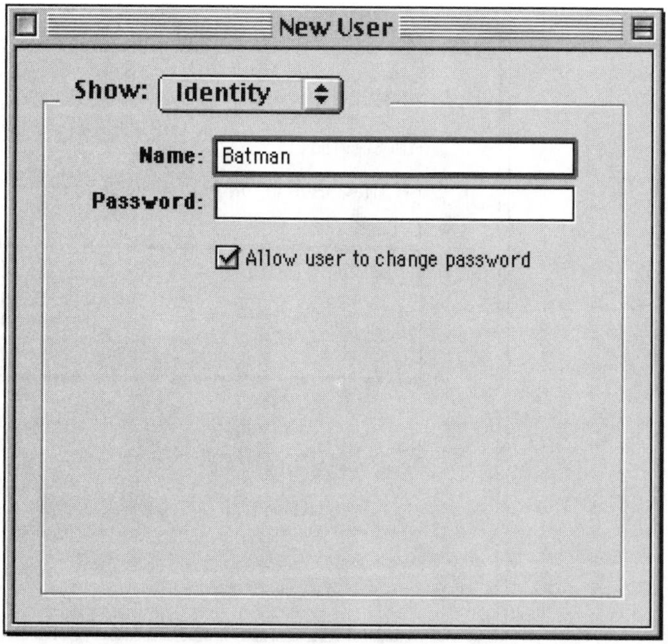

Figure 13.21 *The New User's window.*

the people who log in can do so easily. In the "User Password" box you can assign a password that will be required before the user can access your Mac. Passwords are case-sensitive. The "Allow user to change password" option allows a user to change the password when he or she connects to your Mac. Any changes made in a New User's window take effect immediately.

Case-sensitive Able to distinguish between uppercase and lowercase characters.

8. Switch to Sharing by clicking on the pop-up menu (Figure 13.22). There is only one option in the Sharing section; "Allow user to connect to this computer." When this check box is checked anyone who knows the user name and password can connect to your Mac.

   You determine who can access your Mac by the name and password you give the new user. Before others can access your Mac, they need to know their user name (whatever you named the user) and their password. At this point, you've just become the system administrator for your Mac. Although you can create up to 100 different users, it is highly recommended that you have no more than 50 users. And only 10 different users can connect to your Mac at the same time.

9. From the File menu, select the *New Group* item. The purpose of a group is to control access to the volumes you create. When it comes time to set up a volume for sharing, you can grant access by assigning a group instead of a user.

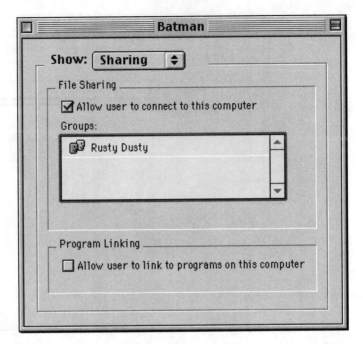

Figure 13.22   *The User's Sharing section.*

10. Drag a user or two to the group you just created. Groups are like folders; they hold users. You add a user to a group by dragging the user into the group. You also name a group just as you would a user or a folder in the Finder. Once a group has been named, it is called a *registered group*. Figure 13.23 shows a group with two users.

In Figure 13.22, a section in the User window is called Groups. Any groups to which the user belongs are displayed in this section. A user can be included in several groups. This method is necessary because you cannot assign multiple users or groups to a shared volume. You must choose a single user or a specific group, or you must give everyone access to your files. Think about how you will configure your groups and users; it may take some experimentation to set it up the way you want it.

All this information is stored in a Users & Groups Data File, stored in the System's Preferences folder. Make a copy of this file; if something happens to the Users & Groups Data File, file sharing will not work and you will have to set up everything again. Replacing the file with the copy is easier than making a new one. Make your copy immediately after setting up and after making any changes to your users and groups.

Sharing Your Data

Now that you have your users and groups set up, you are ready to share the data on your hard drive. You can share an entire hard drive, a single folder, or several fold-

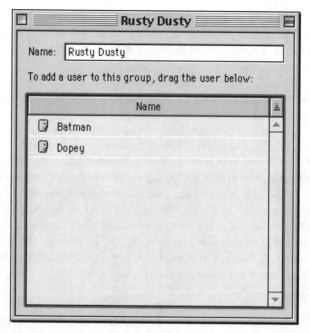

Figure 13.23 *The New Group window.*

ers. When sharing files, you need to think about your sharing strategy. Sharing affects your Macintosh's overall performance, so you need to make sure you do not cause problems. Performance issues are discussed here, along with security.

Before you can share a volume, sharing needs to be turned on from the File Sharing control panel. You do not need to open the control panel to turn on sharing—your Mac does that for you when you assign the first folder to be shared. Just highlight the folder you want to share and select the *Sharing* menu item from the Finder's File menu. If sharing has not been turned on, your Mac presents a dialog box like the one shown in Figure 13.24. After you turn on file sharing, it will take a couple of minutes to start.

Once sharing is turned on, it remains on until you turn it off. Every time you start your Mac, the first thing it does is start up file sharing. Also, if you share anything on

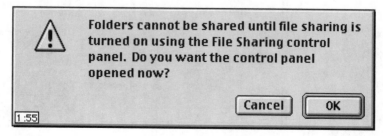

Figure 13.24 *Auto-starting the File Sharing control panel.*

a removable disk—whether a floppy, SyQuest, hard drive, or optical disk—you will not be able to unmount the disk until you turn off sharing for that disk. If, after you unshare a removable disk, it will not unmount, turn sharing off from the File Sharing control panel.

Once Sharing has started, reselect the folder you want to share and select *Sharing* from the File menu. At this point, your Mac asks you to assign its access privileges. A window like the one shown in Figure 13.25 appears.

In this window, you have the option of assigning an Owner and a user or group to the folder. The Owner field is automatically assigned as the Mac's owner, and the User/Group field is set to None. If you click on the name of the Owner, you have the option to assign any group or user as the owner, as shown in Figure 13.26.

Who you assign as the owner is important, especially if you do not allow everyone to have access to the shared folder. If you make yourself the owner and if you have several users who create folders within the shared folder, the folders created by one user are not accessible by other users. To prevent this problem, make a group the owner. A folder is inaccessible when someone drags a folder to the shared volume from his or her Macintosh or creates a new folder using the *New Folder* item from the File menu.

Next, assign the user or group. In Figure 13.27, you can see that the options for this selection are the same as those for the owner. Once you have assigned a user, the next step is to set access privileges. If you leave the User/Group set to none, and if you give read and write access to everyone, you are giving every assigned user access

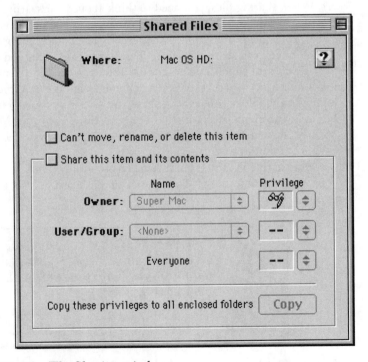

Figure 13.25   The Sharing window.

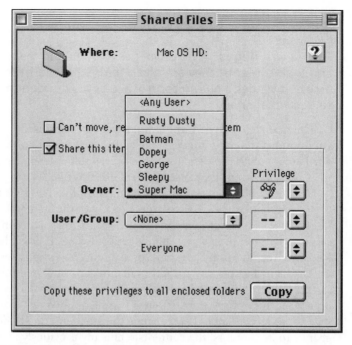

Figure 13.26 *Assigning an Owner.*

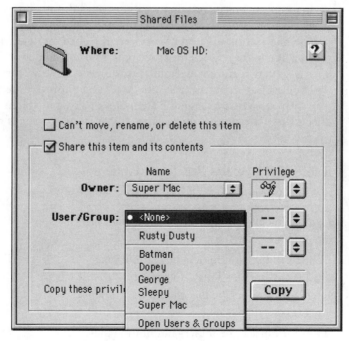

Figure 13.27 *Assigning a user or group.*

to the folder you are sharing. And if you have enabled guest access, everyone on the network can access the folder.

Access privileges   The privileges to open and make changes to folders and their contents; they are given to or withheld from users. By setting access privileges, you can control access to confidential information stored in folders on a server.

The next step is to determine what type of access users can have. Table 13.1 lists your options and their effects. This table assumes that you will assign the same attributes to all the folders inside the shared folder by clicking the Copy button next to "Copy all currently enclosed folders like this one."

Of course, all the preceding is meaningless if you give everyone Read & Write privileges. The privileges listed apply to any of the assignment groups: Owner, User/Group, and Everyone. As you can see, because you can set up three different sets of privileges, things can rapidly get confusing. If possible, follow the KISS philosophy (Keep It Simple, Stupid) for assigning access privileges.

The Copy button next to "Copy all currently enclosed folders like this one" assigns the attributes you set to all the folders in the folder you plan to share. If you do not set this option, the attributes you set apply only to the folder you are sharing, not to its contents. If you change the attributes of a folder and do not apply the change to its contents, the contents retain any previously assigned attributes. If you are going to change the attributes, force the change to all the folders. Otherwise, you will have different sets of attributes working all at once, which could be very confusing. If any folder that has set attributes is moved into another folder with different attributes, it retains its original attributes until the attributes for the enclosing folder are changed.

The final option of "Can't be moved, renamed, or deleted" prevents clients from moving, renaming, or deleting the contents of the folder or folders being shared. This is a safety feature you should probably always leave turned on.

The best way to get all these attributes straight is to experiment. Sit down and play with two Macs; change the attributes of a shared volume and then see what effects they have on the other. Move folders into and out of the mounted volume to

Table 13.1   Access Privileges Table

ACCESS ATTRIBUTES

Can see folders and files and make changes to any folder or file.	Read & Write
Can see all files and folders but cannot make changes to any file. This is like creating a template for a specific file; the user cannot add any files or folders.	Read Only
The user can see the folders but not the files. Files and folders can be added to the volume.	Write Only

see what happens. If you are methodical, you will quickly get a handle on what the attributes do.

Accessing a Shared Volume

The process of accessing a folder someone else has shared is called *mounting a shared volume*.

This process is done through the Chooser:

1. Open the Chooser.
2. Select the AppleShare icon.
3. The available file servers appear on the right side, as shown in Figure 13.28.
4. Select the file server you want to log onto by clicking on its name and then clicking on the OK button, or you can double-click the file server's name. When you select a file server, you get a dialog box like the one shown in Figure 13.29.
5. Enter your user password; this is the registration dialog box. In this box, you must enter the user name assigned to you by the person sharing their files or by the system administrator. At this point, you can change your password if you have been given the ability to do so. To protect your data and prevent others from logging in as you, you might want to set your own password

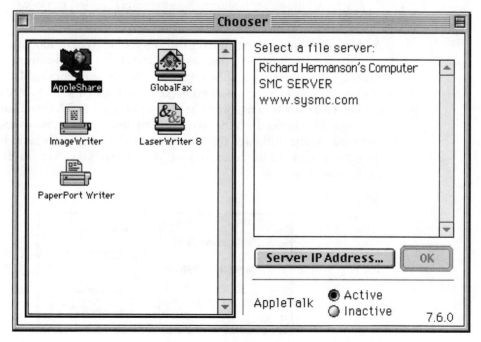

Figure 13.28 *Selecting AppleShare in the Chooser.*

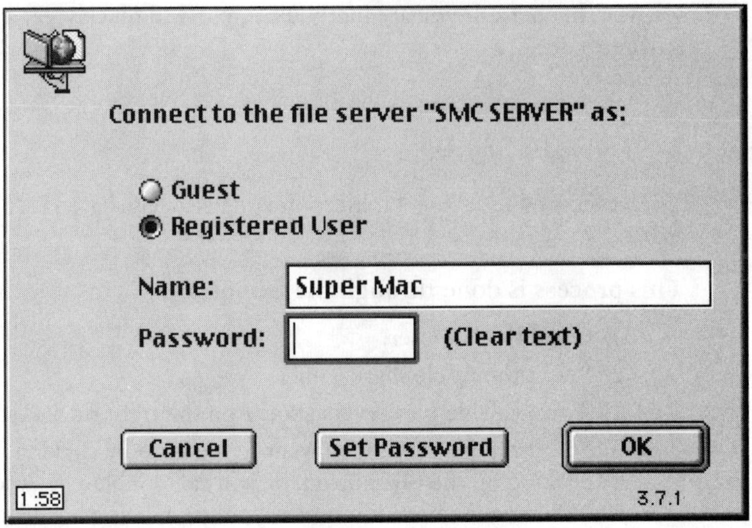

Figure 13.29   *The file server registration dialog box.*

(Figure 13.30). Also, if the attributes have been set for guest access, you could log on as a Guest.

6. Select the volume you want to mount; a dialog box like the one shown in Figure 13.31 appears. In this dialog box, every available volume on the selected file server is shown. Because several folders can be assigned, a server can have several volumes.

At this point, you have the option to set the volume(s) to be mounted at startup. This is useful if you work off a dedicated file server or a shared volume that you use all the time. If you select this option, you are asked if you want the Mac to remember your name (Figure 13.32). Some servers can be configured so that you can't have your Mac remember your password, as shown in Figure 13.32. If you have the option to have your Mac remember your password, anytime your Mac boots up, it mounts the selected volume. Although this may be convenient, it also obviates the need for a password unless no one has access to your Mac or unless you don't care if someone else can access your data.

Figure 13.30   *Setting your password.*

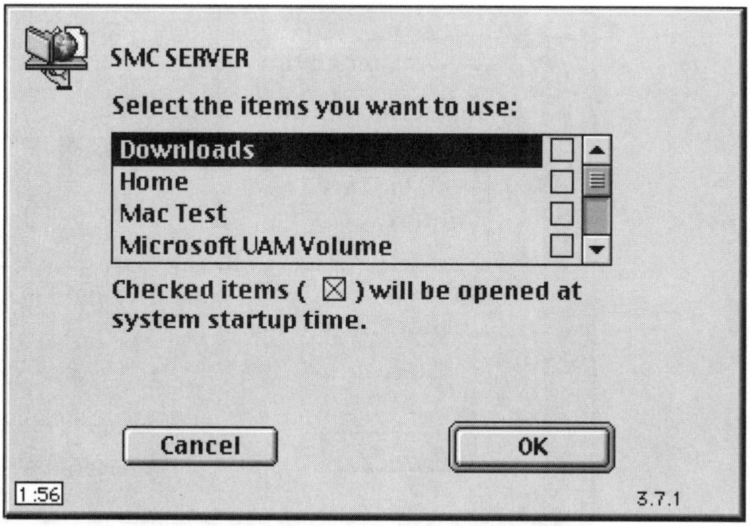

Figure 13.31 *Selecting the volume.*

Once you click on the OK button, your Mac mounts the volume and you are able to use it like any other disk drive connected to your Mac. Your only restrictions are those set up by the person who made the files available. If you want access to your Mac from another Mac on the network and sharing is turned on, you can log onto your Mac with your Owner name and password. Doing so gives you access to every drive and disk on your system (see Figure 13.33). For this reason, you should set the

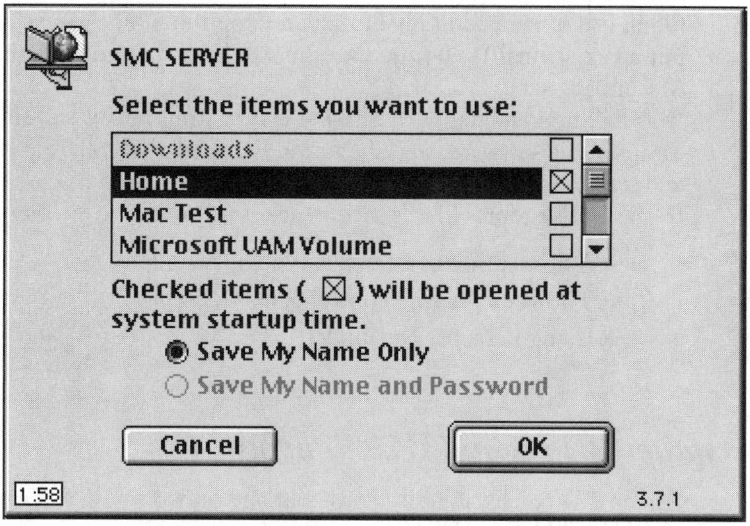

Figure 13.32 *Remembering your password.*

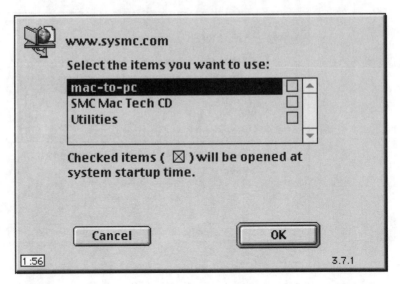

Figure 13.33   Disks and drives made available when sharing is turned on.

password—it is one thing to let other people have access to a folder as a volume; it is quite another to let them have access to your whole drive.

Personal Web Sharing

One of the neatest new networking features in Mac OS 8 is called Personal Web Sharing (PWS). Personal Web Sharing is installed if you do an Easy Install of Mac OS 8. It is also an additional installation option. Once you've installed PWS you can put up a personal Web page for others to look at or you can share files with non-Macintosh users.

Installing Personal Web Sharing is very straightforward. If you need instructions for installing software, see Chapter 9. Personal Web Sharing has several capabilities and setup options. Let's go through these options and discuss those things you need to know. The topics in this section are as follows:

❖ A description of Personal Web Sharing

❖ The Web Sharing control panel

❖ Using Personal NetFinder

A Description of Personal Web Sharing

Personal Web Sharing can be used in one of two ways. You can make your Mac a small World Wide Web (WWW) server and publish your own home page, or you can use the Personal NetFinder feature and make files available to people who do not have Macintoshes. Personal Web Server is just like its big brothers (Internet Web servers) in that it is an Internet Web server.

Your Web site can be configured to let everyone see your Web site, or you can use the security features provided through Mac OS 8's Personal File Sharing. As a Web site, your Web pages can use Common Gateway Interfaces, or CGIs as they are commonly called. The CGIs supported by Personal Web Sharing are those compatible with MacHTTP 2.2 and WebStar 1.3.1. One ideal use for PWS is Web page development. You can use your Mac to write and test your Web pages, complete with CGIs. Figure 13.34 shows Netscape accessing a Macintosh PWS.

As mentioned earlier, Personal Web Sharing can be used to give others access to files you want to share. This is done by telling Personal Web Sharing to share a folder without assigning a Web page. When a client accesses your Mac with its browser it will see the files and folders in your shared folder. Figure 13.35 shows a shared directory being accessed with Netscape. If you need instructions for using Netscape Navigator, see Chapter 14.

The Web Sharing Control Panel

Personal Web Sharing is controlled by your Mac's TCP/IP and the Web Sharing control panel. First, you have to configure Mac TCP/IP for use over your network.

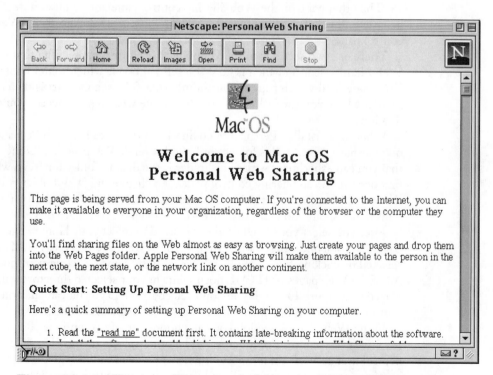

Figure 13.34 *Viewing a Web page on a Mac using Personal Web Sharing.*

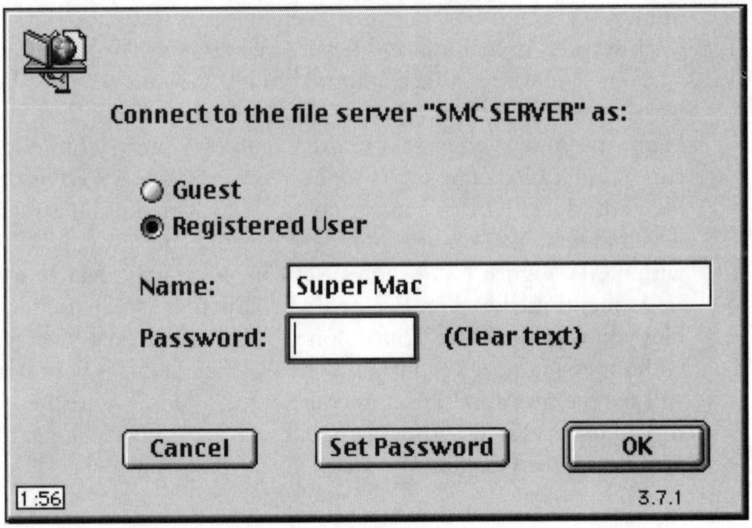

Connect to the file server "SMC SERVER" as:

○ Guest
◉ Registered User

Name: Super Mac

Password: ☐   (Clear text)

Cancel   Set Password   OK

1 :56   3.7.1

Figure 13.35   The Web Sharing control panel.

This information can be found it two places, earlier in this chapter and in Chapter 14. The other control, the Web Sharing control panel, determines how PWS behaves and who has access to your Web site. Figure 13.35 shows the Web Sharing control panel.

There are two sections to the Web Sharing control panel. The first part is the Web Identity section which is how you tell your Mac which folder contains your Web pages and which page is your home page. The second part is the control section where you turn PWS on and determine what type of access you're going to allow.

When you installed Personal Web Sharing a folder called Web Pages was placed on your hard drive. In this folder you'll find several Web pages and some samples that you can experiment with. This folder is the default folder for PWS when your first open the Web Sharing control panel. To change the Web Folder you click on the Select button next to the Web Folder label and select the folder you wish to use. This folder should no more than five folders deep on your hard drive.

After you select your Web Folder you need to select your Home Page. This is the page that someone will see when they log onto your Web server. Your Home page is selected by clicking the Home Page's Select button and selecting your home page. All of the Web pages or HTML documents in your selected directory will be displayed (see Figure 13.36). If you don't select a Web page you can click on the None button. Clicking on the none button turns on Personal NetFinder.

In the Web Sharing section you can choose one of two options. The first option is to "Give everyone read-only access." The other selection is to "Use File Sharing to control user access." Under most circumstances, you can use the first option, giving everyone access. The option to use File Sharing to control access is used only if you

Figure 13.36 *Selecting your home page.*

have sensitive information and need to restrict access. When you use the File Sharing option you have to turn File Sharing on and share the folder where your Web files are located. There is no advantage in using the File Sharing option other than security. Personal NetFinder cannot be used by a browsing client to place files into the shared directory.

Using Personal NetFinder

In the last section you learned how to turn on Personal NetFinder as well as a couple facts about it. NetFinder gets its name because your shared files are displayed in a Finder-like list view when someone browses your site. Using Personal NetFinder, your guests can download the files on your site just as if they were on the real (?) Internet.

Figure 13.37 shows Netscape being used to browse some shared files. There are two folders and one file in the figure, and everything is sorted by Name. If you click on the Size or Date Modified label, NetFinder creates a new view and sorts the files according to your selection. NetFinder creates a new page in which the sort order is changed (see Figure 13.38).

To get back to the original view, click Netscape's Back button. If you played with the sort order a couple of time you can revisit each of those pages using the Back button. So, you are better off using the Go menu and selecting the first page.

To download a file, all you have to do is click on the document's icon. It is automatically downloaded and stored in Netscape's download folder. If you need instructions for using Netscape, see Chapter 14. The only feature that NetFinder lacks is the ability to upload files. Maybe we'll see that in a later edition.

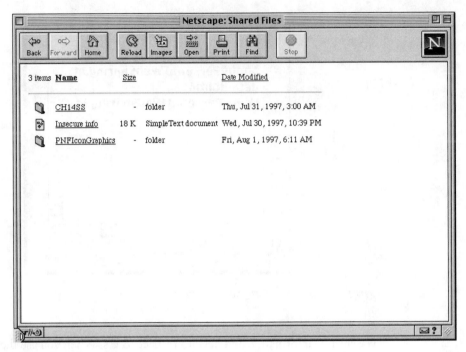

Figure 13.37 *Personal NetFinder in action.*

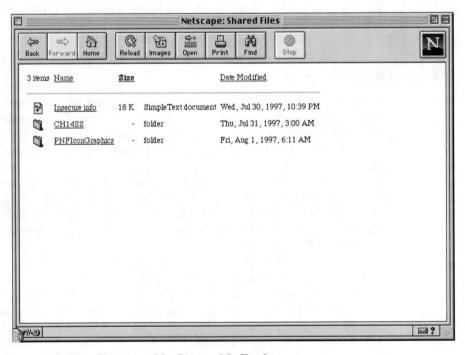

Figure 13.38 *Files sorted by Size in NetFinder.*

An Advanced Network Primer

This section is about the nuts and bolts of Macintosh networking. Here you encounter even more terminology that may be unfamiliar and even confusing. Just like the language used with data communications, the language used with networks can be a problem because it rapidly exceeds the boundaries of the Macintosh. This section attempts to clarify the concepts essential to understanding networking.

Apple has gone to great lengths to make Macintosh networking as simple as possible. After you read this section, pick up a book on networking DOS machines and glance through it. Networks have the capacity to span computer platforms, and once you reach beyond the Macintosh, a network becomes much more complicated and more difficult to use and manage. This section looks at what a network is and defines networking-specific terms.

Basically, to have a network, you need three components: the physical connection between the computers, the hardware in the computers that utilize the connection, and the software that makes the connection operate. Your Mac has the software for operating on a network built into its ROM or the System. Built into the logic board is the basic hardware for communicating via a network accessed through the printer port so that all you need to provide is the cabling. Figure 13.39 shows a basic network.

The term LAN, for local area network, describes a single network and all the devices it contains for one physical location, hence the word "local." It does not have to consist of only Macintoshes; it can include DOS, UNIX, mainframes, and other machines. It is the connection of all these different devices, in such a way that they can send data between the different machines and share common *network services* (any device that is provided for common use by the networked computers), that constitutes a network.

You can extend your network to include computers that are not connected directly to your LAN. You can even connect several LANs to create a networking environment called an *intranet*. An example of an intranet is two LANs on different floors of the same building connected to each other. To connect them, you have a

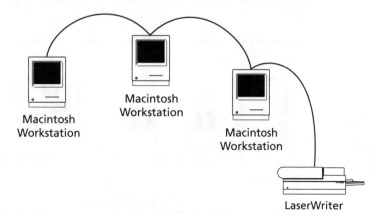

Figure 13.39   *Diagram of a basic network.*

hardware device called a *router* or a *local gateway* that makes the network services of the two networks available to all users. Figure 13.40 shows how two networks are connected.

The next extension of the networking concept is two networks in different geographic locations that are connected by modems that act as routers (see Figure 13.41). This configuration is called a *wide area network* or *WAN*. (This acronym is used primarily in writing, not in conversation.)

With a Macintosh network, whenever a router or a gateway is used, each of the different networks is called a *zone*. The difference between a router (sometimes called a *bridge*) and a gateway is that a router is used to connect two networks that use the same network protocol, and a gateway connects two networks that use different protocols and translates the protocols so that each network can communicate with the other. In this chapter, a router and gateway are used very specifically. Often, you find that all three of these terms—router, bridge, and gateway—are used interchangeably.

Networks are often labeled by the name of their protocol or the type of cabling used. As such, you hear Macintosh networks referred to as AppleTalk, LocalTalk, or PhoneNET networks, unless they are operating on an Ethernet or another type of network.

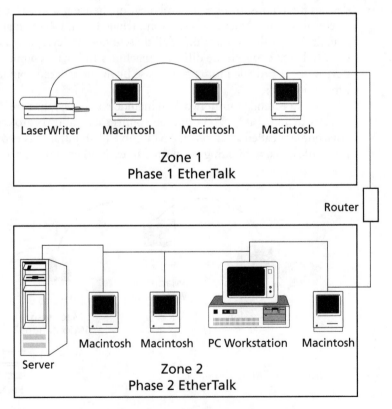

Figure 13.40 *Two networks connected via a router or a gateway.*

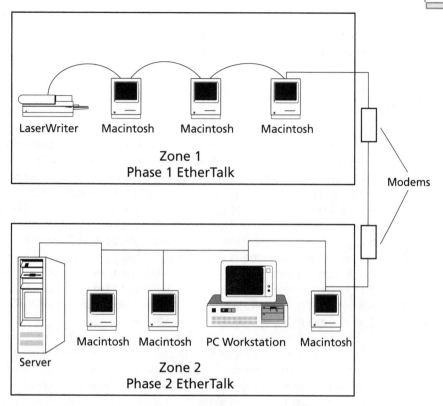

Figure 13.41 *Using modems to connect two networks.*

Ever since the advent of the Internet, which is different from an intranet mentioned here, the distinctions in networking terminology have become confusing. In most instances you'll be using an Ethernet network with AppleTalk as the networking protocol and there is also a strong chance that you'll also be using the TCP/IP protocol.

Networking Protocols

There are several different types of networks. Each type is usually described by the type of protocol— the set of rules under which the network operates—is used. In most cases, the protocol is an established standard that is recognized within the industry. Sometimes, a company establishes its own protocol. When it does, it also has to provide gateways so that other networks can operate in conjunction with theirs.

This happened with a DOS network manufacturer named Artisoft, which produces a very popular network called Lantastic—one of the best-selling networks for DOS machines. The Macintosh finally became so popular that it could no longer be ignored. As a result, there now is a gateway that connects an AppleTalk network with a Lantastic network. The gateway provides the translation between the Lantastic network operating system (or NOS, as it is called in the DOS world) and AppleTalk, which is the native protocol of the Macintosh. The Mac is capable of using other protocols, but every Mac has AppleTalk built into it. If you need to use a different protocol, you need the appropriate hardware and software.

AppleTalk

AppleTalk is Apple's protocol for the Mac; it has been a part of the Mac since the Macintosh 128K. It has also gone through a couple of evolutionary cycles. There are two versions of AppleTalk: Phase 1 and Phase 2. AppleTalk Phase 1 is the version used anytime you set up a LocalTalk or PhoneNET network. Regardless of the type of cabling, if you just plug cable connectors into the printer port of your Macintosh, you are using Phase 1 AppleTalk. System 7 includes AppleTalk Phase 2, but it is used only if you are on an Ethernet. If the version of AppleTalk is equal to or greater than 53, then it supports the basic elements of AppleTalk Phase 2.

Determining this number not difficult. Open the AppleTalk control panel, go to the Advanced mode and click on the Info button. As you can see from Figure 13.42, the current version of AppleTalk for the tested Mac is version 60.2; it is Phase 2-compatible. Remember, just because the version of AppleTalk is Phase 2-compatible does not mean that it operates in a Phase 2 mode.

Phase 2 differs from Phase 1 in how it handles network identification. A Phase 2 network uses a *network range number* rather than a single network number. This extends the ability of the network to address a theoretical maximum of 16 million devices, rather than the maximum of 255 under Phase 1. The network range number is a 16-bit number (2^{16}), selected from a possible range of numbers, such as 1,456:1,600. If the full range of possible numbers were used in a network (possible in theory only), each of the numbers in the range could then address up to 255 network devices. This

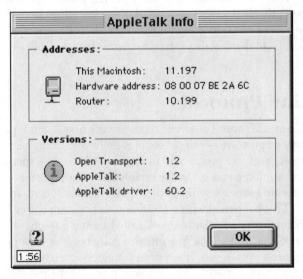

Figure 13.42 Checking the AppleTalk version.

would make the possible number of addressable devices represented by a 24-bit number 2^{24}, or 16 million.

A standard LocalTalk or PhoneNET network cannot take advantage of Phase 2 addressing because it would take forever to find a device on a network so large, even if it were possible to put so many devices on a network. The speed at which LocalTalk or PhoneNET networks operate is 230.4 kbps (kilobits per second), which equals about 235,969 bps (bits per second). This is not blindingly fast. In theory, you should be able to send a 1,728K file over the network in one minute. Because real life and theory do not coincide, the actual real-world rate will be about half the theoretical limit.

It takes 103 seconds to send a 1,440K file from a local machine to an AppleShare server—when there is no other network traffic and when the network is small. The speed rate for this transfer is about 114 kbps. The speed degradation is due to the error-checking that has to take place, the types of Macs involved, and other network activity. There is definitely a relationship between the CPU's speed and how fast a data transfer takes place. If you send data from a Mac Plus to a Quadra, the Quadra has to slow down to a speed that the Plus can handle.

Two cabling types are used with AppleTalk networks when connecting to any Mac through the printer port. You can use LocalTalk cabling or *twisted pair*, which is standard telephone wire.

LocalTalk

LocalTalk is Apple's old system for connecting Macs and their networked devices. A LocalTalk connection consists of a LocalTalk adapter and cabling. There is nothing special about LocalTalk and, in some ways, it is more difficult and expensive to use than twisted pair.

The one advantage that LocalTalk has over twisted pair is that LocalTalk cabling is more heavily shielded, which means you have fewer interference problems. On the other hand, the cable is more difficult to use, and it has a maximum length of 1000 feet for the network, with a recommended 32 nodes or networked devices.

PhoneNET

PhoneNET is the implementation of an AppleTalk network, using PhoneNET connectors from Farallon Computing and telephone wire, also called twisted pair. The wire itself is the same as the wire used to connect your telephone to the wall plug; the type of connector used is called an RJ-11.

The advantages of a PhoneNET network is that it can support lengths of 1800 to 4500 feet, depending on the *topology*, or wiring configuration. It is easier to install cabling with a choice of different topologies, and you can get additional technical support from Farallon. All of this makes PhoneNET the cabling system of preference for most installations. In addition, Farallon has received a patent on its connectors and has licensed the technology to other manufacturers who make PhoneNET-like connectors.

As far as its disadvantages are concerned, a standard PhoneNET network is still constrained to approximately 32 nodes. If you have more than 32 network devices, you have to set up two networks and a router to connect them. And, of course, there is the speed issue: If the speed of the network is an issue, you need to install an Ethernet network.

Topologies

When setting up an AppleTalk network, you need to be concerned with the network topology. First, there is the overall length of the network, measured in terms of actual cable length. The physical distance between the different devices to be networked may be only a few feet. But if you run the cable through a false ceiling that traverses the entire office, you could bump up against the limitations quite quickly.

The four possible topologies are these:

❖ Daisy chain
❖ Backbone
❖ Passive star
❖ Active star

This is where your network layout becomes a serious consideration. Before you run off to get cable and connectors, think about how you will hook everything up. If you use LocalTalk, you have only one choice for a topology—a daisy chain. A *daisy chain* allow the cable to run from one networked device to another, as shown in Figure 13.43. The daisy chain can also be used with PhoneNET.

The remaining topologies are possible only using PhoneNET, and two of them require additional PhoneNET hardware. The first is called a *backbone*, a single twisted-pair wire used to span the entire length of the network. Attached to this wire is a series of RJ-11 jacks into which you plug a Macintosh. The maximum length of the backbone is 4500 feet. Figure 13.44 shows how a backbone might look. The backbone offers the ability to easily install or remove a Mac from any spot on the network. Using a backbone, you can set up a network connection in every office, even though only some offices are used. This approach allows you to set up and

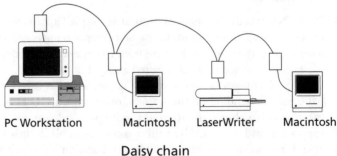

PC Workstation   Macintosh   LaserWriter   Macintosh

Daisy chain

Figure 13.43   *A daisy chain topology.*

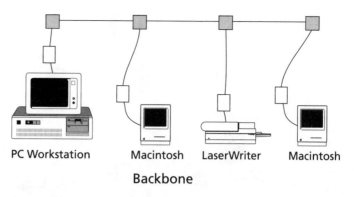

Figure 13.44 *A backbone topology.*

remove a Mac or other network device without affecting other people on the network. If you have to reconfigure a daisy chain, the network goes down and is unusable until all connections have been reestablished.

Another option is a *passive star*, which is created by running telephone lines to a *punchdown block*, a device used to interconnect phone wires. Figure 13.45 shows a punchdown block. With a passive star, you need a special punchdown block from Farallon. It enables you connect as many as four 1125-foot branches of wiring, for a total distance of 5000 feet. Each branch comes from the punchdown block and terminates at a phone-type jack in an office.

This is usually set up in the same place as the rest of your phone equipment because there will probably be at least two unused wires coming from each location to which you want to network. From the terminus of each branch, you can then attach a daisy chain or backbone to service your network devices. Figure 13.46 shows a passive star topology. The number of devices on a passive star is limited by the amount of network

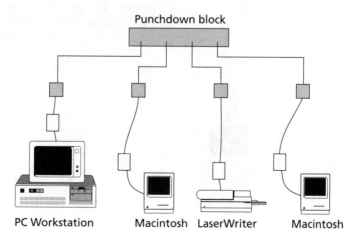

Figure 13.45 *A punchdown block.*

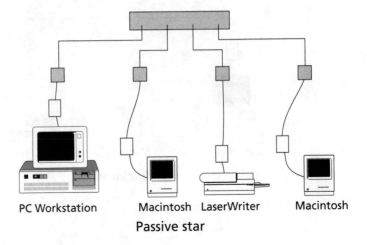

Passive star

Figure 13.46   A passive star topology.

traffic, but you are probably looking at about 32, Apple's recommendation for a straight AppleTalk network.

The other topology you can set up is called an *active star*, basically the same as a passive star, except you can have up to 48 branches (although this number exceeds the recommended limits for an AppleTalk network). The active star configuration works by having what is called a *star controller*, which has 12 ports. Each port can support four branches of up to 750 feet each, three branches of 1000 feet each, two

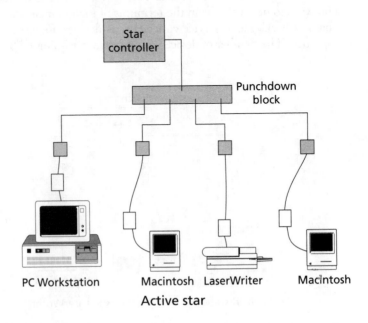

Active star

Figure 13.47   An active star topology.

of 1500 feet each, or one of 3000 feet. Figure 13.47 shows an active star configuration. Like the passive star, each branch of an active star can have a daisy chain or backbone topology as well. The primary concern here, once again, is the number of network devices that can be attached to the star. The active star can improve network performance because the controller manages data signals and helps prevent data collisions.

The other advantage of a star controller is that it can also act as a hardware router. You can connect several star controllers and create an intranet that spans different floors of the same building or even connects several buildings.

Zones

As mentioned previously, there is a recommended 32-device limit for an AppleTalk network. What truly determines how many devices you can have on a single network is not the number of devices, but rather the amount of network traffic you have. If you have a multiuser database, and if 10 people are using it all the time, you might find that you have reached the limits of your network. If, on the other hand, there is very little activity, you could have 40 devices on a network with very little speed degradation.

If your network is slow or if you have more devices than recommended, you might consider making two networks out of the one and connecting them via a router. This will create two zones, where each zone represents one network. The resources from each zone are available to the other users on the network. Figure 13.48 shows two networks connected with a router; the two zones are outlined.

If you need data from a file server in another zone, just log into the zone and then onto the server. The use of zones adds extensibility to your network. You are constrained by the limits of AppleTalk, but you can still have a network that connects everyone through a series of networks.

Termination

Whenever you use a PhoneNET network, make sure that each end of the network is terminated. The terminator is a 120-ohm resistor installed in an RJ-11 plug. This is inserted into the open port of the PhoneNET connector at each end of the network. All LocalTalk connectors are internally terminated, so you do not need to worry about them. Termination prevents the signals on the network from being reflected or echoed back down the network. On small networks, look at termination first thing if you have problems.

With a backbone or star topology, your termination configurations can be done a bit differently. With the backbone topology, you must terminate each end of the backbone itself. At the same time, put a terminator in the last device attached to the wall plug as well—especially if you happen to run a daisy chain from one of the plugs. If you have just a single device attached to the wall plug, you do not need to put a terminator in the PhoneNET connector. Figure 13.49 shows how to terminate a backbone topology.

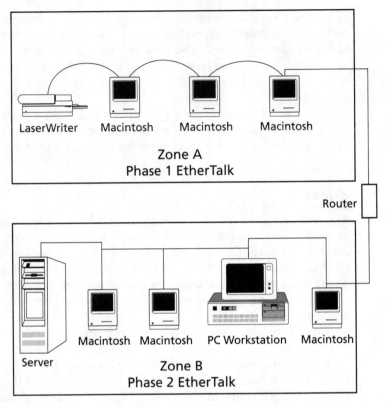

Figure 13.48   *The two networks as zones.*

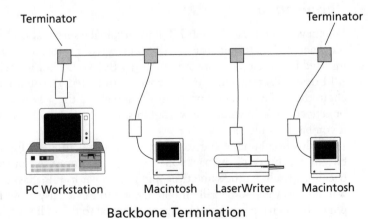

Figure 13.49   *Termination with a backbone topology.*

Star configurations should be terminated at the terminus of each wire in the wall jack. This means that you do not have to worry about termination for the device attached to the jack. This is similar to the backbone except that each wall jack should have a terminator, which is true for both an active or passive star.

Security and Performance

Whenever you work with a network, you need to be concerned about its performance and security. This section looks at things you can do to get the best performance while protecting your data.

Security

Although no one likes passwords, they are a necessary evil. There are few people who want anyone to have access to all their data; so you might consider some of the following as possible guidelines.

- ❖ Always give your Mac a password from the File Sharing control panel so that you can access it if you are on another Mac, and no one can log in using your Macintosh name without your password.
- ❖ If you want only specific people to access the folders you share, do not let them change the password. If the user can change the password, he or she can remove it altogether.
- ❖ Do not turn on program linking unless you have a specific reason for doing so. If someone has access to linking, it is possible, with the proper Apple Events, to use an application to access data on your Mac.
- ❖ Learn to use the file-sharing attributes, and never give "Everyone" complete access to a shared volume. Always set up your users in groups and give access to a group.
- ❖ Never share your entire drive.

Performance Considerations

Using Personal File Sharing, you can assign up to 100 users and groups. You can also make available as many folders for sharing as you wish. The more you share, the more work your Mac has to do to service network requests.

If your work requires that a lot of people have access to large quantities of shared data, look into a dedicated file server and something like AppleShare. Otherwise, consider the following suggestions. Some of these are also good security options as well as performance enhancing suggestions.

- ❖ When using Personal File Sharing, do not set up more than 50 users and groups. Even though 100 is the limit, more than 50 has adverse performance effects.

❖ Share only a couple of folders, never your entire hard drive.

❖ Restrict access to those people who need it. The fewer users logged into your system, the better. Each additional user slows down your Mac, especially if the users all access data.

❖ Distribute the shared data over the network, rather than keeping it all on one machine, unless you use it as a file server.

❖ Use small networks for groups of people who consistently share data. Install a router to connect the different networks as zones and create an intranet.

❖ If you find that your network is too slow, consider using Ethernet.

❖ Do not mount more than a couple of volumes at the same time, and try not to transfer data from one networked volume to another. Rather, perform file transfers (especially large files) from a networked volume to a local drive. If you go from networked volume to networked volume, you might have to take the afternoon off, and all network functions for everyone on the network will slow to a crawl.

Miscellaneous Thoughts

Networks are a complex subject; theory and real life do not coincide. What's worse, everyone you talk to has a different story. In researching this chapter, I asked a few people about how much faster Ethernet is over LocalTalk. I received answers that ranged from twice as fast to 20 times as fast, and no one was being dishonest.

Your network will be like no other, and the factors that affect it will be unique to how you work and how data flows through your office. What you really need to be concerned with is being able to modify your network as your needs change. If you have a few machines that cause the rest of the network to slow down, then you want to isolate them and put them on their own network so that they do not affect everyone else.

As you add computers, be prepared to make them part of the network; compromise between what you want to do and what is possible. To save time and money, think out your network. Plan it, map it, and make sure you know where you are going now and in the future. It is hard to predict where the technology is going and what your computing needs will be, but you can develop something that works in conjunction with your business plan.

Network Software

All kinds of network software are available. The most important, in addition to file-sharing software, is probably e-mail. You can also get different network software that works with other vendors' file servers, such as Novell's Netware and Banyan Vines. There are also utilities for mapping, checking network traffic, and troubleshooting. Networking is much more extensive than what can be covered in one chapter.

The remainder of this chapter lists and briefly describes some additional network software you can get for your Mac. The purpose of this list is to give you an idea of what is available and to include comments about some of the products. As always, a product's inclusion for the list does not mean that it is recommended. There is just too much software available to include everything; only you can be the judge of a product's suitability for your needs.

Apple's Networking Software

Apple has published a lot of networking software. This section looks at some of Apple's software and explores what you can do with it. Although Apple is not the only publisher of Macintosh networking software, it does provide excellent tools.

AppleShare IP

AppleShare IP is Apple's software for creating a dedicated file server. It works on the same principles as Personal File Sharing, and it is also an intranet server. An intranet is a small network that uses Internet technology. Anyone who has file sharing installed can access an AppleShare server.

Using a server has several advantages: First, all your organization's data can be kept in one location for easy retrieval. This also makes it easier to back up your data and keep it safe. Second, it has more powerful security features than Personal File Sharing, and you can have more users and groups. Finally, it is about 200 percent faster than Personal File Sharing, which will still be slow on a LocalTalk or PhoneNET network. Figure 13.50 shows some of the preferences you can set with an AppleShare file server.

Because the file server works on the same basic principles as Personal File Sharing, there is no reason to go into all its particulars. Some of its advantages have already been mentioned; some of the others are as follows:

❖ Improved remote access—By installing AppleTalk Remote Access on your server, people who work outside—clients or anyone you designate—can access and use your network via a modem.

❖ AppleShare print server—AppleShare now has a print server included with it. This is a *spooler* that uses the server rather than individual Macs. Using a network spooler means that you can spool data to the server drive and free your Mac to improve its performance. Figure 13.51 shows how the spooler appears in your Chooser's window. Although it takes longer to print because a document goes from your Mac to the file server and then to the printer, you can free your Mac and not have it slowed down by background printing.

Here is another trick you can use if you have a noisy printer and you want to turn off your printer but continue to print. Start the print spooler and, after it is up and running, turn off the printer itself. The spooler remains active so that it can be used as a printer by other Macs, but you can wait and turn on the printer later. You can print everything while you go to lunch.

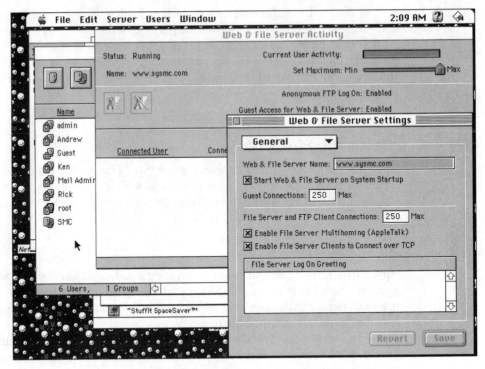

Figure 13.50 *File server preferences.*

AppleShare IP moves Apple's Networking software into the 1990s. With its intranet capabilities AppleShare becomes cross-platform-compatible, and it ships with client software for Windows 95 machines. Add to this WWW, FTP, e-mail, and Domain Name Services, and you have a machine that can be put onto the Internet. Not only that, but a Mac Internet server is the most secure Internet server available.

AppleSearch

AppleSearch is Apple's network document-retrieval system. AppleSearch indexes all contents of selected documents on an AppleSearch server and makes them available to others via the network. If you are a client and know that you have a document with a specific phrase but you don't know which document, you can search for the document from your Mac.

When AppleSearch finds the document, you can view it, retrieve the entire document, or just select part of it. This tool is great for environments where lots of documents are created and need to be frequently accessed. It can greatly speed the process of document retrieval by eliminating the trial and error of getting one document and then another, repeatedly, until you've found the right one.

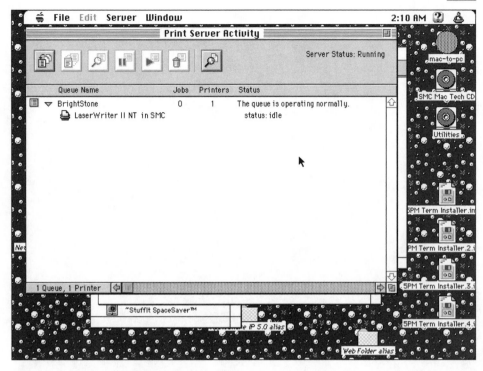

Figure 13.51 *AppleShare's print server.*

Summary

Well, that's it: your introduction to file sharing and networks. In this chapter, you
learned how to set up a basic Mac network, configure your Macintosh for file sharing, and mount volumes from other Macs. Not to mention Person Web Sharing. All
you got here were the basics. If you're saying to yourself, "If those were the basics,
I'd hate to see the real stuff," you're not alone. Networking is a complicated subject,
and the casual user generally does not need to know much about networking.

Surfing the Net

Introduction

The Internet has become an immense subject. I think the intense hype surrounding the Internet diminishes the subject's seriousness by making jokes. As such, the real title of this chapter is: "How to Avoid Pot Holes While Driving Up the On Ramp of the 'Misinformation Stupid Byway.'"

Even though I trivialize the Internet, it is one of the most exciting areas of computing today. To do the Internet justice I would have to write another book, but I have only one chapter to discuss the Internet.

Connecting to the Internet can be one of the most frustrating things you'll ever do with your Macintosh. The objective of this chapter is to provide you with the knowledge you need to connect to and use the Internet with your Macintosh. Thankfully, Mac OS 8 has made this process a lot easier. The following is the list of topics covered in this chapter:

❖ What Is the Internet?—This is a brief review of the Internet. In this section I discuss the acronyms and terms you need to know.

❖ Getting Connected—In this section I configure the TCP/IP control panel and discuss how to set up your Macintosh at home to connect to the Internet after you've selected and subscribed to an Internet service provider (ISP).

❖ Exploring the World Wide Web with Netscape—Although the World Wide Web (WWW) is what you hear the most talk about, it is also the easiest part of the Internet to explore and use once you are connected.

❖ Using Electronic Mail—One of the programs included with Mac OS 8 is Claris eM@iler Lite, an Internet electronic mail program. I discuss using this program to send and receive electronic mail. The principles you learn here are the same as those you'd use with any other Internet e-mail package.

❖ Other Interesting Things You Can Do on the Internet—This last section briefly looks at some of the things you can do on the Internet not covered in the other sections.

By the time you finish this chapter you should have enough information to get connected to the Internet, figure out why you might be having problems, and know how to use some of the services available on the Internet.

What Is the Internet?

The best way to describe the Internet is by looking at what the Internet can do for you and what you can do on the Internet. The Internet is a huge computer network that consists of hundreds of smaller networks. The Internet spans the world. Recently I was in Haiti, the poorest country in the Western hemisphere, and although connecting to the Internet had some challenges, it was possible.

A Very Brief History

The Internet originally started in 1969 as ARPANET (Advanced Research Projects Agency of the U.S. Department of Defense) for connecting university, military, and defense contractors.

ARPANET changed, and by 1973 more mainframe computers were being used to as part of the network. The agency changed, too, to become DARPA (Defense Advanced Research Projects Agency) at the same time that a program called the Internetting Projects was started to study how to link packet networks together. This project was the start of the Internet. Think about the state highway system, which was created in the 1950s, compared to the interstate freeway system. And you can get an idea of how the Information Superhighway is developing.

To maintain order in the budding Internet, classifications were needed for the various networks. At this point the networks started fragmenting into smaller networks that were connected using TCP/IP (the networking protocol; see Chapter 13) and ARPANET split into the following components:

❖ MILNET—For military communications

❖ ARPANET—For continuing research into networking

❖ CSNET—A network for linking computer science departments at universities and the first autonomous interconnecting network allowed to connect to ARPANET (1980)

❖ BITNET—The product of a merger with CSNET in 1989

Today the process started by the government continues. The continued growth is not fueled by businesses and the telephone communications infrastructure (read companies). Although the original ARPANET exists in a different form, the real backbone of the Internet is provided and maintained by all the major long distance telephone service providers like AT&T, MCI, US West, and Sprint in the United

States. And, likewise, the telecommunications industries in other countries cooperate in the process.

The networks created by the telecommunications industry can be called the major networks. Connected to the major networks are minor networks (even though some of them can be quite large). The minor networks are as follows:

❖ Internet service providers (ISP)—It is likely that you will connect to the Internet via an Internet service provider. Every Internet service provider is a minor network, and sometimes they are not connected directly to a major network but through another minor network that is also an ISP. When you use an ISP your computer becomes part of the Internet by being one of the computers on your ISP's network.

❖ Businesses, universities, and other organizations—Many businesses, universities, and other organizations are part of the Internet, too. How they are connected really doesn't matter; some connect through major networks, and others use minor networks. They are all considered to be part of the Internet. How everyone is classified is discussed later in this chapter. Different networks are classified by using domain names.

So, What Can You Do?

With an Internet connection (account) you can send electronic mail, find information about any subject that might interest you, take college classes, get technical support, or advertise your company. This short list does not begin to do justice to what you can do with the Internet. These are just a few examples of what you can do.

The amount and types of information you can get from the Internet are mind-boggling. Whenever I need an answer to a technical question I look on the Internet first, using the World Wide Web. The other day someone asked me what "cyber" meant. Because I didn't know and my dictionary was new in 1973 I turned to the Web and found an online dictionary. Then I looked up "cyber"; it isn't a word.

Do you have a special interest or hobby? If you do, you will probably find that there is more information about your interest or hobby in cyberspace (cyberspace is a word) than you can effectively use. I could spend everyday, all day, cruising the Web, reading e-mail, and playing on the Internet. The only drawback is that I'd soon starve to death. The implication is that you too could spend a lot of time on the Web if you were so inclined.

Cyberspace   A word used to describe the online world. It can be applied to the Internet, online services, or your small computer network. Usually cyberspace is used to describe the Internet.

The following list is a brief description of what you can get from the Internet. It is not an exhaustive list; it just covers the basics.

❖ Software—You can get software and data from around the world. One of the largest collections of Macintosh software is located at the University of Michigan.

❖ Newsgroups—A newsgroup is a discussion forum for obtaining information and expressing yourself. What you read and write is available to millions of people. At the moment, there are about 25,000 newsgroups. You can find a newsgroup for any interest. They range from alternative lifestyles to advanced technical subjects—and everything in-between. Are you interested in photography? There is a newsgroup that discusses photography. The same applies to religion, graphics, and Macintosh computers.

❖ Subscriptions—Do you want to know what and when the latest group of Macintosh files were put on the computers at the University of Michigan? You can be kept informed by subscribing to its list server and receive a list of files via e-mail whenever the information is updated. *Tidbits*, a biweekly electronic Macintosh magazine, is distributed through a subscription service.

You subscribe to an e-mail list by sending an e-mail message to the server. You will automatically be put on the mailing list. To get off a list server you usually have to unsubscribe.

❖ Special Requests for Information—This is an extension of the subscription services, only instead of being put on a mailing list you can request specific pieces of information via e-mail. You can receive press releases from the U.S. government and most major companies, articles from *Wired* magazine, or the latest NBA standings.

❖ Books—Project Guttenberg transcribes, electronically publishes, and makes available the text of entire books. They are free and yours for the asking.

❖ Electronic Journals—It is possible to receive journal articles from universities, some of which have gone through a peer review process.

All the services listed here are in addition to the World Wide Web. In some cases, the services described are being replaced by the WWW. But, change is the nature of emerging and dynamic technologies such as the Internet. By now you have a good idea about what is available. How is all of this wonder stuff done? And do you really care? One reason why you should care is that if you know what the Internet is, it will be easier to use and figure out.

How Do I Get onto the Internet?

Now that you know what the Internet is, how do you get onto it? First you need an Internet service provider (ISP). Service providers are companies or institutions that provide you with the means for connecting to the Internet. An ISP does this by providing a server (a computer specifically configured for the Internet) and the means for you to connect to the server, usually some type of modem connection.

Major long distance telephone providers provide a connection to the ISP, which then, in turn, provides one to you. The connection or feed from the long distance provider is expensive, and it charges based on how much data the connection can transport. The fees charged by the telephone companies are expensive.

The ISP essentially breaks up the bandwidth (the amount of data that can be moved onto the network) capabilities it gets from its primary service provider into smaller parts and parcels those parts out to you. There can be several service providers between the long distance provider and you.

Service Providers

The following is a list of the most common service providers you will encounter.

❖ Commercial online services—A commercial online service is a company such as America Online, Prodigy, or CompuServe that provides communications services for a fee and also allows you to access the Internet using its service. Connections via online services are not the same as using an Internet service provider. Although your computer is directly connected to the Internet, you do not have the speed that you would get from a local ISP because you are using the online services' computer to access the Internet. This means that you must use the tools provided by the online service rather than programs on your computer.

❖ An Internet service provider—An ISP is a local company you contract with that gives you an account and password so your computer can use its computer to connect to the Internet. The ISP gives you a link to the Internet so that your computer, after connecting to the ISP's computer, connects directly to the Internet.

❖ Your Employer—More employers are getting onto the Internet. As a result, one of the company perks, or even necessities, is your own Internet account. How you can use an employer-provided account is up to your employer.

❖ Your School—Most universities and now many schools in general give students Internet accounts. As with employer-provided accounts, how you can use the account depends on the institution.

In most cases you will probably want to get your own Internet account through a local ISP. If you are shopping for an ISP, talk to people you know who are on the Internet. Not all ISPs are equal, nor do they all offer the same services (even though the services are usually similar). Some ISPs charge extra for your Web page (yes, you can have your own if you can make it); some have poor tech support. Shop carefully.

Types of Accounts

There are two basic types of accounts. One is called a dial-in account; the other is called an IP account. *Dial-in accounts* are special-purpose accounts; except for the description that follows, we do not discuss them in this chapter. The remainder of this chapter focuses on IP accounts, specifically dial-in IP accounts.

❖ Dial-in account—A dial-in account is one in which you connect to the Internet via a modem and a communications package. You operate the ISP's UNIX computer to which you are connected by means of a terminal emulator. Think of this as playing with a radio-controlled car.

❖ IP account—An IP account is actually a special dial-in account or a connection you have over your local area network. The host computer (the service provider's) provides you with an Internet address and a connection that sort of bypasses its computer, instead linking you directly to the Internet.

The IP account gets its name from the networking protocol used on the Internet. This protocol is called TCP/IP, which stands for Transmission Control Protocol/Internet Protocol. Your computer must be able to communicate using TCP/IP before it can connect to the Internet. A control panel called TCP/IP (if you use Open Transport) or MacTCP (for Classic Networking) enables your Mac to use TCP/IP. You also need a special program that lets your Mac use TCP/IP with a modem; the software for your modem is called PPP (Point to Point Protocol).

Later on, I will show you how to use both the TCP/IP and PPP control panels for Open Transport networking. If you do not use Open Transport, this information is still valuable because TCP/IP configurations are basically the same regardless of the software or computer in use.

Cost

Somewhere, someone pays for your Internet access. If it is not you, then it is your employer, your school, the government, or someone. There is no free lunch, and there is no free Internet access. Just how much will it cost to get onto the Information Superhighway?

Dial-in IP accounts cost from $15 to $35 per month. Some service providers have staggered rates based on the amount of time you're online; others have a single fee for unlimited access. Rates also differ according to how you are connected. If you use an ISDN modem, the cost is more. And network connections can get very expensive. For most people, though, the basic dial-in IP account will be fine.

Equipment

To gain access to the Internet you need a computer, a modem, and a telephone line. You should have a high-speed modem. I recommend that you have a 28.8 kbps modem or higher. Modems are now up to 56 kbps, and most service providers support the 56K Flex technology. Check with your ISP if you plan to use a modem that is faster than 33.6 kbps.

Software Needed for a Dial-In IP Account Using PPP

Whether you're connecting to the Internet with a modem or over a network, all the software you need to connect to and use the Internet is included with Mac OS 8. You already have the TCP/IP and PPP control panels and all the essential applications you need to get going. The programs that come with Mac OS 8 are these:

❖ The Internet setup assistants
❖ Claris eM@iler Lite

❖ Netscape Navigator 3.1
❖ Internet Explorer
❖ Internet Config
❖ The Macintosh Runtime for Java
❖ Castanet Tuner
❖ The PointCast Network
❖ Cyberdog

In addition to what comes on the Mac OS 8 CD-ROM, the Revelations CD-ROM included with this book also has a bunch of Internet utilities. You could spend the rest of this week and next exploring all the programs on the CDs. And once you're connected to the Internet, well, you could disappear for days on end.

Getting Connected

Setting up your Macintosh so that you can connect to the Internet can be frustrating. You need to know several things before you start. Also, your Macintosh's hard drive must be in good condition. If there are problems with your hard drive, the PPP programs required for an IP connection can have difficulty.

For our purposes here I will show you how to manually configure your Mac's software. True, Mac OS 8 has an Internet setup assistant, but you need the same information to manually configure TCP/IP and PPP. And if you manually configure everything, you will learn how the software works and you will be in control rather than at the mercy of a consultant.

Collecting the Nuts and Bolts

You have to do a couple of things before you can connect to your ISP. First make sure your hardware is set up properly. And be sure you have the specific information you'll need before you can set up the software. Both of these topics are discussed in the next section.

Your Hardware Setup

Setting up your hardware will probably be nothing more than attaching a modem to your Macintosh. The time will come, however, when you might connect your Mac to a cable TV converter box, an ISDN modem, or even a local area network. All of these can be used to connect to the Internet as long as you have a service provider who supports the transport technology.

Each of these different connections are transport technologies because they represent the means for connecting to the Internet. In a sense, each of the different ways to connect represents on-ramps to the Information Superhighway. As such, you have to know how you connect with the Internet and how to connect the proper devices to your Mac.

Unfortunately, there is not enough time nor pages to cover the mechanics for all of these technologies. For the remainder of this chapter I assume that you are connecting to the Internet via PPP and that you are using a modem. If you need to know how to connect a modem to your Mac read Chapter 12, "Connecting to the Outside World."

Basically you need the following equipment:

❖ A Macintosh with a 68030 processor or better.

❖ A minimum of 16MB of RAM

❖ A minimum of 50MB of hard disk space

❖ A modem—The faster the better

❖ A printer Not required, but you'll probably want to print some of the information you get.

Once you have this equipment, perform some basic maintenance on your Mac. If it is not running properly, setting up your Internet connection could cause great distress. The software that lets you connect to the Internet is low-level system software, and your Mac needs to be running well before you start.

The rest of our discussions are about setting up the software you need for connecting to and using the Internet.

Required Information

Because the Internet is designed to accommodate almost any type of computer, configuring your Mac to work on the Internet is not very Macintosh-ish. You may be typing in numbers and names that don't make a lot of sense. Regardless of whether they make sense, these numbers and names are required if you ever trip on the Internet. The following table (Table 14.1) contains the technical names for the information you'll need. The terms used below are specific and technical. One term that is not explained is the IP address; it will be covered later in this section.

Now before you start thinking that nothing short of a miracle will get you onto the Internet, calm down. In most circumstances you need to know only the items with the * next to them. Usually all other items listed are taken care of automatically.

If you have to configure your Internet setup manually you need all the information shown in Table 14.1. Usually the Server Type is BootP or DHCP. With these servers you need just the information with the *.

Make a list of your required information. Now you are ready to configure your Mac to use the Internet.

Configuring Your Software

As mentioned earlier, Mac OS 8 has an Internet assistant that can walk you through the steps of configuring your Mac for the Internet. Even though the assistant can make installation easier I'd rather show you how to configure your Mac manually. When you manually configure your Mac to access the Internet, you learn which software components you need and how they work.

Table 14.1 Essential Configuration Information

INFORMATION NAME	EXAMPLE	EXPLANATION
ISP's phone number	(503) 555-1212	This is the phone number you use when you connect to the Internet.
*Server type for obtaining your IP address	Manually BootP Server DHCP Server RARP Server	If you do not have the correct server type you may never get connected. The server is how you obtain your IP address. You cannot get onto the Internet without an IP address.
IP address	192.168.210.45 This is a sample number.	You need an IP address if you are using Manually.
Subnet mask	255.255.255.0	The subnet mask is almost always the IP number at the left. The subnet mask is part of your network's numeric definition.
Router address	192.168.210.254 This is a sample number.	The router address is used only if you are connecting to the Internet via a network and if your network has a router.
Name server address	192.168.210.2 This is a sample number.	The name server is a computer that translates clear text names into IP addresses, and vice versa. You will probably have more than one name server address.
*Search domains	sysmc.com This is a sample name.	The search domain is the name of the network that contains your domain name server.
*POP3 (E-mail server—incoming)	mail.sysmc.com This is a sample name.	The name of your ISP's incoming e-mail server.
*SMTP (E-mail server—outgoing)	mail.sysmc.com This is a sample name.	The name of your ISP's outgoing e-mail server.
*News server	news.sysmc.com This is a sample name.	The name of your ISP's news server.
Proxy server	safe.sysmc.com This is a sample name.	The name of your proxy server. Proxy servers are rare; you'll probably never need this.
Your user name	Kmaki This is a sample name.	Your user name is your logon ID. It is possible to have one ID as a logon name and another for accessing e-mail.
Your password		Your password is a special identifier that you need to get access to your account. Like the user name, you could have multiple passwords.

On your Mac OS 8 CD-ROM, there is a folder called Software Installers; inside that folder is the Internet Access folder. The Internet Access Installer in this folder places everything you need for connecting to the Internet onto your Mac; "everything you need" is the software listed in the section, "Software Needed for a Dial-in IP Account Using PPP."

Let's assume that you've run this installer and that the software you need is already on your Macintosh. The TCP/IP and PPP control panels need to be installed and made active. If you need instructions for installing software, see Chapter 9. After you've installed the Internet Access software you'll have a folder on your Mac called Internet; it should look something like Figure 14.1.

The rest of this section will look at the following topics:

- ❖ Configuring TCP/IP
- ❖ Setting up PPP
- ❖ Using the Internet Config extension
- ❖ Once you've completed the steps in this section you will be able to connect to the Internet.

The TCP/IP Control Panel

The TCP/IP control panel enables your Mac to use the TCP/IP network protocol. TCP/IP is the acronym for Transmission Control Protocol/Internet Protocol. TCP/IP was created to let various machines communicate with each other over a very large network.

TCP/IP uses numbers to identify computers and networks. The number used by TCP/IP is called an IP number. These are the numbers shown in Table 14.1 above. All IP numbers look like this: 192.168.123.123. All the IP numbers used in this chap-

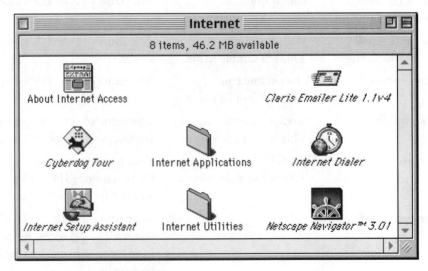

Figure 14.1   *The Internet folder.*

If You're Not Using Mac OS 8

Before you can connect to the Internet, the MacTCP or TCP/IP control panel must be installed on your Macintosh. MacTCP is part of Apple's System. If you use System 7.5 you need to install Apple's System 7.5.1 Update. The 7.5.1 update installs version 2.0.6 of MacTCP. MacTCP 2.0.6 is more stable than version 2.0.4, which comes with System 7.5.

If you are not using System 7.5, you have to purchase MacTCP from APDA, the Apple Programmers and Developers Association, or a commercial product that includes MacTCP, such as a telecommunications package like MicroPhone or a book like Adam Angst's the Internet Starter Kit.

Versions of the Mac OS prior to Mac OS 7.6 do not contain a PPP control panel. If you don't have the PPP control panel you can use MacPPP 2.5 or FreePPP 2.5, which are on the BMUG Revelations CD-ROM. The PPP control panels can be found in the Internet:PPP Tools folder. I recommend that you use FreePPP 2.5.

Finally, if you run System 7.5.3 or later, you can use Open Transport (Apple's new networking technology). Open Transport 1.2.2 includes the TCP/IP and PPP control panels, which you can use instead of MacTCP and FreePPP.

ter come from a special set of IP numbers that do not work on the Internet; therefore, do not use the example numbers. If you want to know more about IP numbers, pick up a book about the Internet.

Figure 14.2 shows the TCP/IP control panel. The sections of the TCP/IP control panel correspond to several of the items in Table 14.1. The TCP/IP control panel can have multiple configurations if you have more than one Internet account.

If you need to set up multiple TCP/IP accounts, open the TCP/IP control panel and follow these steps:

1. Select *Configurations* from the File menu.
2. Select the configuration labeled Default (see Figure 14.3).
3. Click on the Duplicate... button.
4. You are asked to name the new configuration. Give it a name and click on the OK button.
5. Make sure the new configuration is selected.
6. Click on the Make Active button.

Now you have to configure the TCP/IP control panel. Normally you do not have to do too much with the TCP/IP control panel because the Internet servers used by ISPs are configured to make logging in as easy as possible. And the less you (their

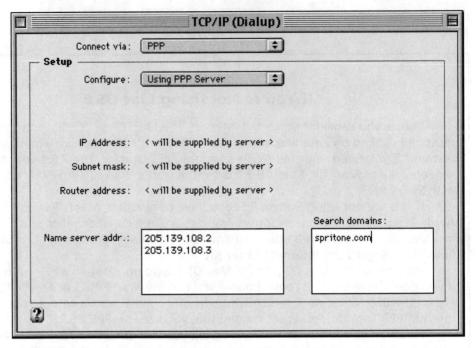

Figure 14.2 *The TCP/IP control panel.*

customer) have to do, the easier their (the ISPs') job. The determining factor is the type of server that your ISP uses. Usually it will be a PPP Server.

Let's briefly discuss each of the setting options in the TCP/IP control panel:

- ❖ Connect via—Your options for this selection are usually Ethernet, AppleTalk, or PPP. Select PPP.
- ❖ Configure—This is where you select your server. In most circumstances, you use the "Using PPP Server" option.
- ❖ IP Address—This section is usually automatic. If it isn't, enter an IP number into a field. (See Figure 14.4 for a manual configuration example.)
- ❖ Subnet mask—This section is usually automatic. If it isn't, enter an IP number into a field. (See Figure 14.4 for a manual configuration example.)
- ❖ Router address—This section is usually automatic. If it isn't, enter an IP number into a field. (See Figure 14.4 for a manual configuration example.)
- ❖ Name server addr.—You always have to enter an IP number here. Actually you should have at least two IP numbers to enter. The second and subsequent IP numbers are for backup domain name servers. These are necessary only if the primary domain name server is unavailable for some reason. If you do not have the address of a working domain name server in this field you cannot use the Internet.
- ❖ Search domains—The search domains correspond to the domain names for the domain name servers entered in the name server addr. field. A domain

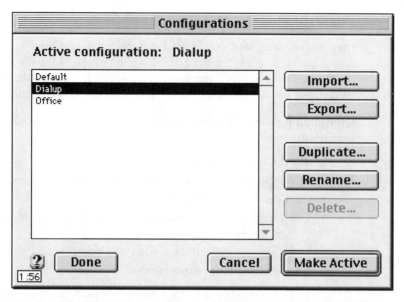

Figure 14.3 *The TCP/IP control panel Configurations selection window.*

name is a network name; each ISP has its own network name, just as most companies have a network or domain name.

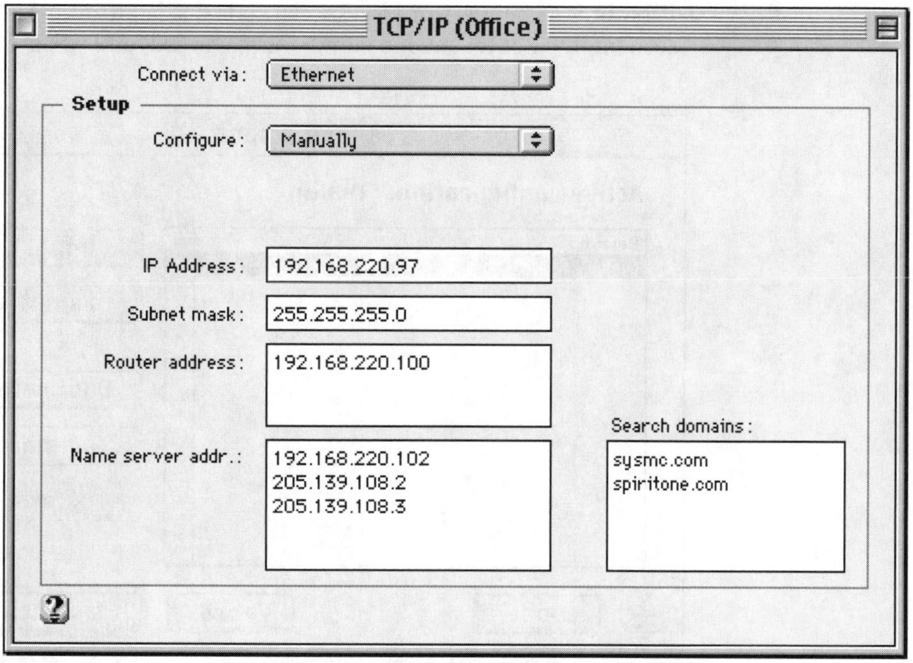

Figure 14.4 *A manually configured TCP/IP control panel.*

The PPP Control Panel

After you've configured the TCP/IP control panel you need to configure the PPP control panel. The PPP control panel is quite simple. Like the TCP/IP control panel, it can have multiple configurations. If you have multiple PPP accounts, name the configurations to match their TCP/IP configuration counterparts.

After opening the PPP control panel, follow these steps to set up a PPP configuration:

1. Select *Configurations* from the File menu.
2. Select the configuration labeled Default (see Figure 14.5).
3. Click on the Duplicate… button.
4. You are asked to name the new configuration. Give it a name and click on the OK button.
5. Make sure the new configuration is selected.
6. Click on the Make Active button.

Once you've created your configuration and made it active you can fill out the PPP control panel. Figure 14.6 shows a configured PPP control panel. The following are your configuration options:

❖ Registered User or Guest—In most cases, select Registered user. If you need to select Guest, you'll know.

❖ Name—This is your user name, assigned to you by your ISP.

❖ Password—The password is a special code needed to access your Internet account. Do not let anyone know your password; otherwise, he or she could

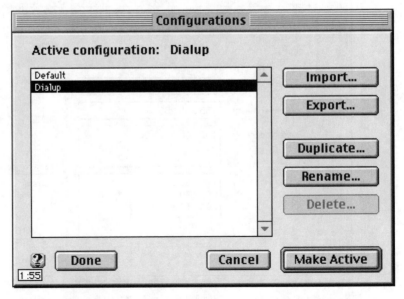

Figure 14.5 *The PPP control panel Configurations selection window.*

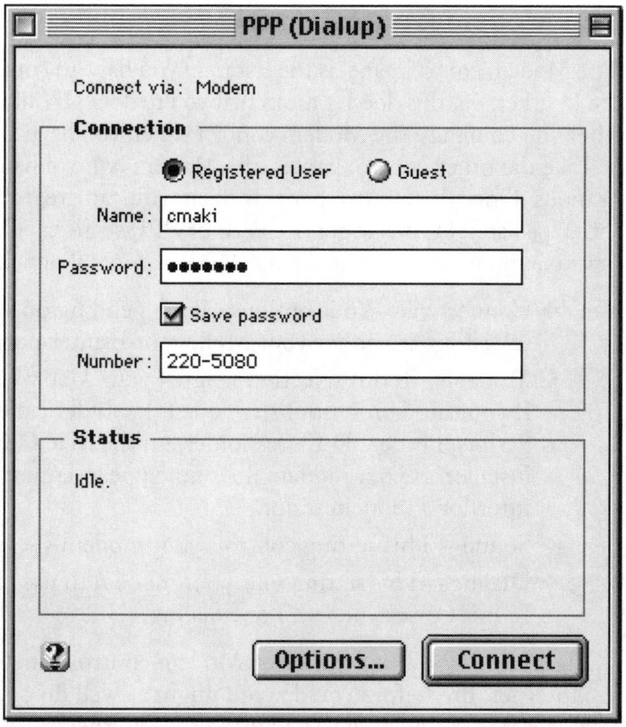

Figure 14.6 *A configured PPP control panel.*

imitate you on the Internet. If no one but you uses your computer you can tell PPP to remember your password. Otherwise, enter your password each time you connect to the Internet.

❖ Number—This is your ISP's network phone number. Each ISP has one main number that it gives out for accessing its network. Sometimes it gives you an alternate phone number. The PPP control panel dials the phone number exactly as you've entered it in this field. If you need to disable call waiting or get an outside line you have to enter those codes before you can connect. If you need help with the phone number, see Chapter 12, "Reaching the Outside World."

An Options… button appears in the PPP control panel. The Options… button allows you to fine-tune your PPP configuration. Under most circumstances, you won't need to change any default settings that you find here. If you are concerned about what settings to select, ask the tech support people who work for your ISP. If the support people cannot answer your questions, you might consider getting a different ISP. ISPs that do not know the Macintosh can provide you with Internet access, but they can't offer you any help when you need it.

When the PPP control panel is open, a PPP menu appears. From the PPP menu you can select TCP/IP and Modem. The TCP/IP selection opens the TCP/IP control panel, and Modem opens the Modem control panel.

The Modem Control Panel

The Modem control panel is the last item you have to configure before connecting to the Internet, but this doesn't mean that you're done. It only means that you can connect. After you configure the Modem control panel, you have a little more setup work to do.

Like the other control panels, the Modem control panel can have multiple configurations. Once the control panel is open, you can create configurations by following the steps listed in the earlier TCP/IP or PPP sections. Once you create your configuration, you need to configure the Modem control panel. Your options are four:

❖ Connect via—Your options vary depending on your Macintosh. Usually the selections are either your Modem or Printer ports.

❖ Modem—In this selection you tell your Mac what type of modem you have. If your modem is not listed, open the folder called Additional Modem Scripts, in the CD Extras folder, on the Mac OS 8 CD-ROM. Run the installer. If your modem does not appear, contact your modem's manufacturer for a modem script.

❖ Sound—This setting controls your modem's sound.

❖ Dialing—This setting tells your modem to use either Tone or Pulse dialing. In most cases you use Tone dialing.

Figure 14.7 shows a configured Modem control panel. Now, you can connect to the Internet. But before you do, you might as well do one more configuration. Then I will get into connecting to and using the Internet.

The Internet Config Utility

Inside the Internet Utilities folder (which is inside the Internet folder) is a folder called Internet Config, which contains a utility also called Internet Config. Internet

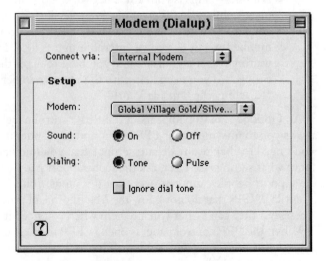

Figure 14.7 *A configured Modem control panel.*

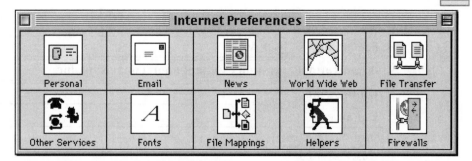

Figure 14.8 *Internet Config utility.*

Config creates a system extension that contains all your Internet preferences. Figure 14.8 shows the Internet Config utility's primary window.

The Internet Config utility is used by other Internet programs. If the Internet program (such as Netscape) is aware of Internet Config, it gets all the information it needs from the settings in Internet Config. This means that you don't have to worry about setting up an Internet program that you might want to use.

As you can see from Figure 14.8, there are several Internet preferences to be set. Let's look at only a few of these; explore preferences not covered on your own. The preferences I look at here are these:

- ❖ Personal
- ❖ Email
- ❖ News
- ❖ Home page

To fully utilize Internet Config, read its documentation. The documentation file is an HTML document, which means that it is a WWW document. To read the documentation, open it with Netscape or some other Web browser.

Each of the following sections talks about configuring the four items listed.

Personal

Figure 14.9 shows the Personal section for the Internet Config utility. This section tells any program, and in a sense the world, who you are, the name of your company, and any other information you might want to provide.

The primary sections you fill in are as follows:

- ❖ Real Name—This is the name that appears on each e-mail message that you send. If you want to call yourself Bozo the Clown, make that entry here. I advise you to use your real name. Some people don't, though, and you need to be aware of this, especially when you receive e-mail from someone you don't know.
- ❖ Organization—The organization field is where you might put your company name or the name of any other organization you want others to know about.

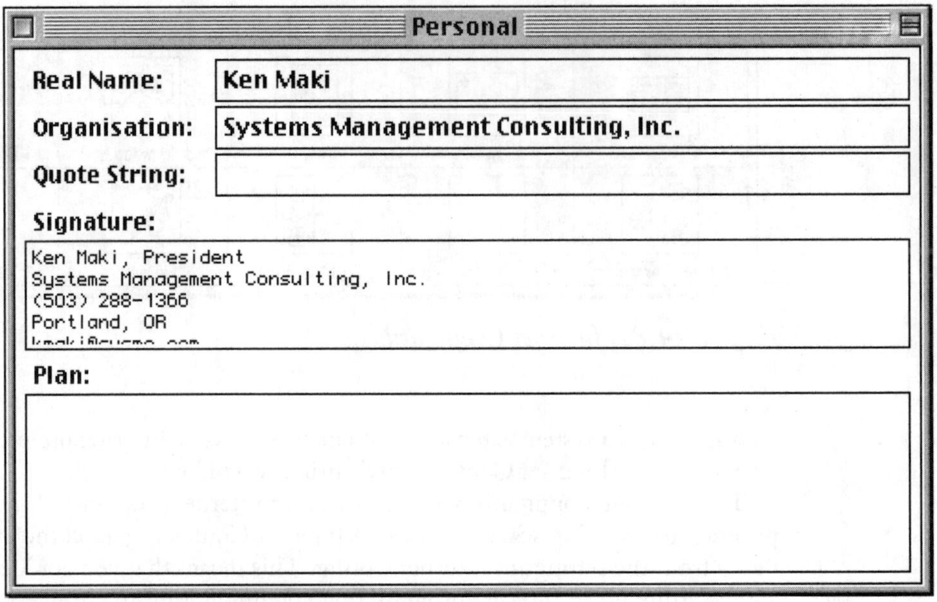

Figure 14.9   Internet Config's Personal settings.

Usually, you are affiliated with the name that you enter in the organization field.

❖ Signature—A signature is a message or information that you want attached to every e-mail message that you send. I usually put my name, title, company name, phone number, and my e-mail address in my signature.

❖ Quote String—The Quote String is a section where you can place some pithy quote that you like and want to share with everyone. The Quote String, like your signature, is attached to every e-mail message that you send. To use the Plan section, check out the documentation. A Plan is a file that can tell people an awful lot about you.

Email

The Email section is used to tell e-mail programs your e-mail address, the name of your e-mail servers, and your password. Your e-mail program uses this information, thereby making life just a bit easier for you.

Figure 14.10 shows a configured Email section. You should have gathered all the information that goes in this section earlier, using Table 14.1 as a guide. An explanation for each field is listed below.

❖ Email Address—This is the e-mail address where you receive e-mail. This information is placed in the return address field of your e-mail messages. When someone replies to a message you sent, his or her e-mail program uses this address as your e-mail address.

```
┌──────────────────────────────────────────────────────────────────┐
│ □ ═══════════════════════ Email ════════════════════════════ ▤ │
│                                                                    │
│ Email Address:   ┌──────────────────────────────────────────────┐ │
│                  │ cmaki@spirtone.com                           │ │
│                  └──────────────────────────────────────────────┘ │
│ Email Account:   ┌──────────────────────────────────────────────┐ │
│                  │ cmaki@mail.spirtone.com                      │ │
│                  └──────────────────────────────────────────────┘ │
│ Email Password:  ┌──────────────────────────────────────────────┐ │
│                  │ •••••••                                      │ │
│                  └──────────────────────────────────────────────┘ │
│ SMTP Host:       ┌──────────────────────────────────────────────┐ │
│                  │ mail.spiritone.com                           │ │
│                  └──────────────────────────────────────────────┘ │
│ Email Headers:                                                     │
│                  ┌──────────────────────────────────────────────┐ │
│                  │                                              │ │
│                  │                                              │ │
│                  │                                              │ │
│                  └──────────────────────────────────────────────┘ │
│                                                                    │
│ On New Mail:      ☐ Flash Icon                                     │
│                   ☐ Display Dialog                                 │
│                   ☐ Play Sound      ┌─────────────────┐           │
│                                     │ Droplet       ▼ │           │
│                                     └─────────────────┘           │
└──────────────────────────────────────────────────────────────────┘
```

Figure 14.10 *Internet Config's Email settings.*

❖ Email Account—This is the e-mail account from which you receive your e-mail. The name after the @ is the POP or POP3 mail server's name.

❖ Email Password—Enter your e-mail password here. Under most circumstances, it is the same as your login password. There are times, however, when it is different. Remember, if your password is incorrect, you won't get your mail.

❖ SMTP Host—The SMTP host is the server that sends your e-mail to other people. The SMTP host can be different from the machine name in the Email Account field.

❖ Email Headers—You will have to read the documentation for using this field.

❖ On New Mail—The settings you select here control what your Mac does when you receive e-mail. You can select all three options or none. The choice is yours.

News

The News section tells your Mac the name of the news server from which you receive your Internet newsgroups. Figure 14.11 shows a configured News section.
  The News settings consist of the following:

❖ NNTP Host—This is another name for the news server you'll be using. Put the news server's name in this field.

❖ News Username—Usually, you don't have to fill in this field. If you do, it is probably the same as your e-mail or User name. Check with your service provider.

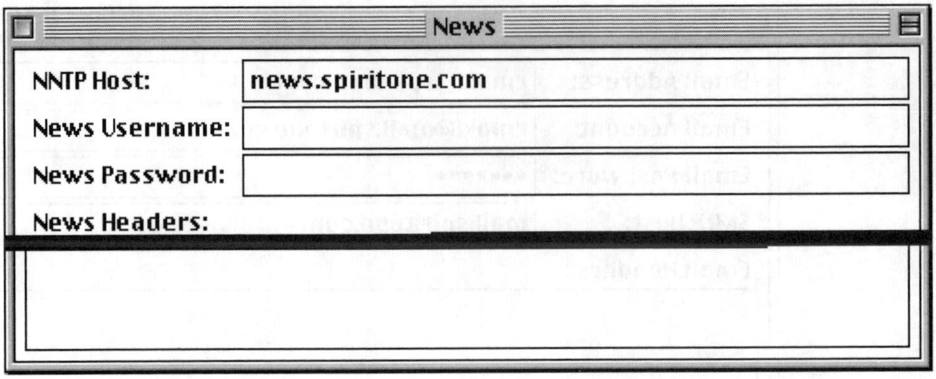

Figure 14.11   Internet Config's News settings.

❖ News Password—Usually, you don't have to fill in this field. If you do, it is probably the same as your e-mail or User password. Check with your service provider.

❖ News Headers—You'll have to read the documentation for instructions about this section.

World Wide Web

The World Wide Web section is very simple. There is just one field, as shown in Figure 14.12. This field is the page that your Web browser opens to whenever it starts. Think of this page as your starting or entry point into the World Wide Web. I usually set my default home page to one of the Web's search pages. I do this because I'm usually looking for something when I go onto the WWW, and a search page seems to be a good place to start.

The Rest of the Settings

The rest of the settings in the Internet Config utility are nice but not critical for using the Internet. Read the documentation for the Internet Config utility, then play with these settings. The more time you spend learning about how your Mac works on the Internet, the more useful it becomes. Keep in mind that this is only an introductory chapter about the Internet. You are responsible for continuing your education.

Figure 14.12   Internet Config's World Wide Web settings.

Saving the Internet Config Extension

After you've finished setting up Internet Config, save your settings and install the Internet Config extension. You have to install the extension before your Internet applications can use the settings. And you should save your settings as a backup.

To save your settings, follow these steps:

1. Select the *Save as...* command from the File menu
2. Give the settings a name and save the settings as you would any other document.
3. Select the *Save Extension...* command from the Extension menu.
4. Use the default name for the extension and save the extension.
5. Select the *Install Extension...* command from the Extension menu.

The extension is now installed, and the information it contains is available to your Internet applications.

Connecting to the Internet

Now that everything is configured, you're ready to connect to the Internet. The process of connecting is very simple. Just open the PPP control panel and click on

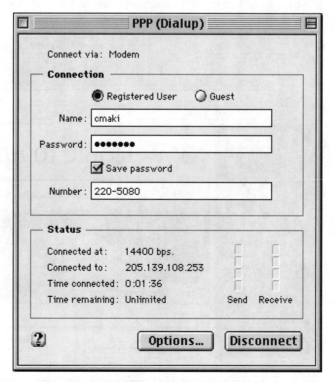

Figure 14.13 *The PPP control panel once you are connected.*

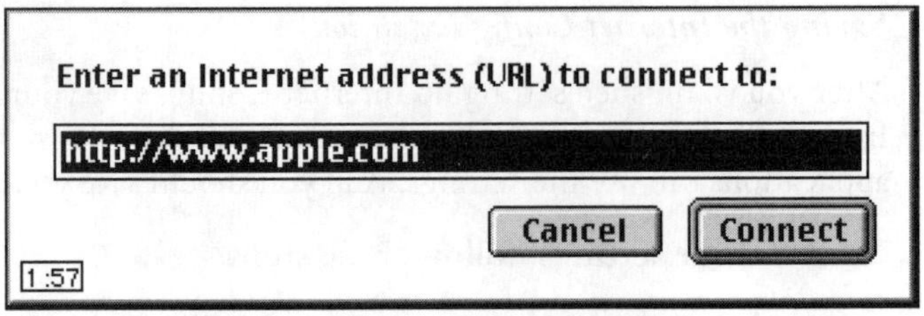

Enter an Internet address (URL) to connect to:

http://www.apple.com

[Cancel] [Connect]

1:57

Figure 14.14   *The Connect to... dialog box.*

the Connect button. Your Mac calls your ISP; once you're connected, the PPP control panel looks like Figure 14.13.

Once you are connected, test the connection. The easy way to do this is to use the *Connect to...* Desk Accessory from the Apple menu. The *Connect to...* Desk accessory brings up a window like the one in Figure 14.14. The default address in the dialog box is http://www.apple.com, the WWW address for Apple's home page.

Once you click on the Connect button, Netscape Navigator starts and your Mac connects to Apple's World Wide Web site. Figure 14.15 is an example of what you might see after you've connected to the Apple home page.

If everything was set up properly, you are now browsing Apple's Web site. If it wasn't, then you see a message that says you could not connect, like the one in Figure 14.16. The error message says that the "server does not have a DNS entry."

Figure 14.15   *Netscape after connecting to Apple.*

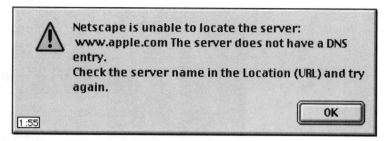

Figure 14.16 *Netscape when it can't connect.*

This means that your Mac is not communicating with the name server. Usually, this means that there is a problem with your Mac's TCP/IP configuration.

If you see a message like the one in Figure 14.16 after you have successfully connected to Apple's Web site, your Mac is configured properly and the problem is with the site you're trying to contact. If you have a problem connecting to the Apple site, review your TCP/IP settings. There is no easy fix when you can't connect. All you can do is carefully review all of the steps you have taken. The Internet Config settings do not need to be checked because they are not essential to connecting to the Internet. The Internet Config settings can affect how other programs operate, but even if they are incorrect they do not stop your Mac from browsing the Web.

I hope you got connected. The rest of this chapter discusses using various Internet applications.

The Internet and You

Here is the final section of this chapter. Before you begin, let me warn you: Each topic covered here could be at least a chapter in another book. This means that the information presented here is very basic. You will learn essential information for using the following applications:

- ❖ Claris eM@iler Lite
- ❖ Netscape Navigator

These programs are either on the Mac OS 8 CD-ROM or installed when you run the Internet Access Installer. This section concludes with general suggestions for using the Internet.

Electronic Mail

The Mail program installed with Mac OS 8 is the Claris eM@iler Lite program. eM@iler is an excellent e-mail program. If you need more than what is available with eM@iler Lite, you might want to get eM@iler 2.0.

When you launch eM@iler Lite for the first time, it looks at the Internet Config extension and presents you with a dialog box (Figure 14.17) that contains all your

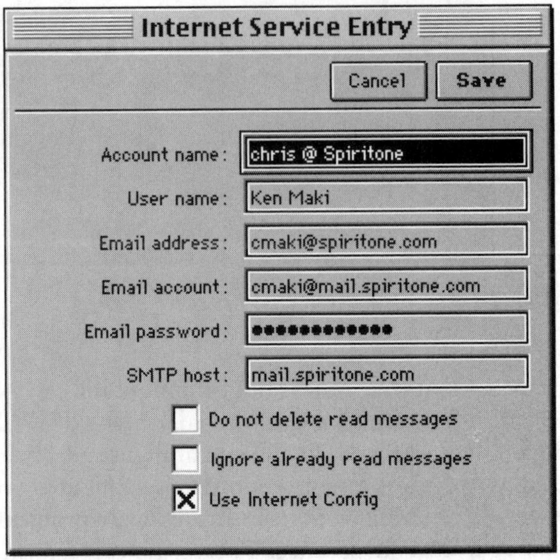

Figure 14.17   Internet setup dialog box.

Internet e-mail information. All you have to do is give the configuration a name and click on the Save button. Now you're ready to send and receive e-mail.

Now, if life were only that simple. To effectively use e-mail, you should know a few more things. What happens when you send and receive e-mail? What does the e-mail address mean? Where does undeliverable mail go? And so on. E-mail in and of itself can be a complicated subject, yet using e-mail isn't that difficult once you're connected.

If your Internet Config setup was done properly, you should be ready to send and receive e-mail. In Figure 14.17, the option to "Use Internet Config" is checked. When this option is used, the only field you can access is the Account name, which is your name for this setup. (If you use 2.0 you can have multiple accounts.) If you want, you can choose not to use the Internet Config information and manually enter the required information. If you do, though, you're on your own to figure it out. All I say is that the information is the same as that entered into Internet Config; you have to review that section to fill in the account setup.

The rest of this section will look at these topics:

❖ E-mail addresses
❖ E-mail services
❖ Basic functions

E-mail Addresses

Just as you need an address to receive mail from the U.S. Post Office, you need an address to receive Internet e-mail. I mentioned addresses earlier, but I did not explain them. This is where you get an explanation.

Internet addresses consist of three parts:

- ❖ The account name
- ❖ The network name
- ❖ The network type

When all these components are put together, you have an Internet address. Let's look at an address's parts and put one together.

If you were going to send me an e-mail message you'd send it to kmaki@sysmc.com. The first part of the address is my account name. The @ symbol tells any mail server that this is an e-mail address and everything after the @ sign is the network where the user account resides.

The network sysmc.com has two parts, each of which has meaning. As a whole, sysmc.com is called a domain name. You see domain names with various organizational names; the organizational or type name is the ".com" part of the domain name. Table 14.2 describes different domain types.

Any one can get a domain name, and almost any ISP will let you use your own domain name with its system. You just have to be willing to pay for the pleasure. The advantage to having your own domain name is that you will never have to change your e-mail address because you can take your domain name from one ISP to another. If you move from California to New York, for example, and you have your own domain name, you can take it with you and no one in your e-mail world will know that you moved.

If you want your own domain name, talk to your ISP. It should happily help you get your own domain name. Having your own domain name is one of the advantages of having an ISP instead of subscribing to an online commercial service.

When you send someone an e-mail you need to remember that an Internet e-mail address cannot have any spaces or punctuation marks, other than the @ symbol and a period [.]. The addresses mentioned in Table 14.1 that looked like "mail.sysmc.com" and "192.168.220.101" are machine addresses and will not work as an e-mail address. These addresses, however, can be used when working with the WWW, as will be discussed later.

Table 14.2 Domain Types

TYPE	DESCRIPTION
com	Commercial
edu	Educational
gov	U.S. government
mil	U.S. military
net	Administrative organization for the network
org	Organizations that don't fit in above categories. These are usually private.
us (the United States) or au (Australia)	Country domain names

The only other concern you may have regarding e-mail addresses is sending someone an e-mail who is not really on the Internet. Usually, to send mail to a commercial service the form is:

```
username@servicename.com
```

My CompuServe address is 76120,2755. If you were to send me a message at CompuServe you would address the message as:

```
76120.2755@compuserve.com
```

Notice that the comma is changed into a period. (Don't send an e-mail to me at CompuServe—you won't get a reply.)

If you need to communicate with someone on a commercial service and he or she can't tell you the Internet address, have him or her send you a message. When you get the message, look at the "From: " line in the message's header; it contains the sender's return address.

E-mail Services

E-mail can be used for more than just sending and receiving messages from friends and colleagues. Some of the services that are available by Email are as follows:

- ❖ Mailing lists
- ❖ Autobots
- ❖ File retrieval

The most important services are the mailing lists and autobots. File retrieval via e-mail is still possible, but it is usually easier to get files by using the WWW.

Mailing lists are subscription services that work in one of two ways. One type of mailing list is used when someone sends an e-mail message that goes to a whole bunch of people who've subscribed to a mailing list. Other types of mailing lists are a bit more interactive. A mail message sent to the mailing list could be redistributed to everyone who has subscribed to the list. Mailing lists have many flavors; some are private, requiring that you know someone who can get you onto the list, but others are public, which means you can subscribe by sending an e-mail message. The following is an example for subscribing to a public mail list.

Format for subscribing to a mailing list:

```
To: risks-request@csl.sri.com
From: yourname@yourdomain.com
Subject: Comp.risk subscription
Cc:
Bcc:
X-Attachments:
Request subscription to the comp.risk mailing list.
```

This example is a real mail list. If you subscribe you will receive at least one message every day or two. If you don't like getting this type of mail, then unsubscribe using the instructions contained in your confirmation e-mail.

An autobot is a program that acts on the contents of a mail message. The receiving computer looks at the incoming mail message and runs a program that returns information to you via e-mail. The following is an example whereby you can retrieve *Wired*'s guidelines for writers.

An autobot example:

```
To: infobot@wired.com
From: yourname@yourdomain.com
Subject: Requests
Cc:
Bcc:
X-Attachments:
send/writers.guidelines
send 1.1/features/virtwar
```

The example above results in your receiving *Wired*'s guidelines for writers. Although Autobots also are being replaced by the WWW, they are still used and you might find this useful.

Other things can be done via e-mail, but they are more complicated and go beyond the scope of this section. If you're interested, go to your local technical book store and look through the books in the Internet section.

Using eM@iler

eM@iler is an offline mail reader. This means that you can create and read e-mail without being connected to the Internet. Then when you log onto the Internet eM@iler sends and receives all your e-mail. The rest of this section deals with processing your e-mail. Processing your e-mail includes, but is not limited to, creating, reading, sending and receiving, and filing.

The instructions for sending and receiving mail are based on the assumption that you're using a dial-in IP account. If you are connected to the Internet via a local area network, you would probably use a slightly different setup. eM@iler has the ability to schedule e-mail retrieval, but if you're connected to the Internet all the time or don't want your Mac automatically dialing into the Internet without supervision, do not use the schedule feature.

It is almost as easy to connect to the Internet, launch eM@iler , and select the *Connect Now…* command from the Mail menu as it is to schedule mail retrieval. When you activate the *Connect Now…* command, a dialog box like the one in Figure 14.18 appears.

All you have to do is click on the Connect button and eM@iler connects, retrieves, and sends your e-mail. If you leave eM@iler open while you're connected to the Internet, selecting the *Connect Again* command from the Mail menu checks your e-mail without prompting you.

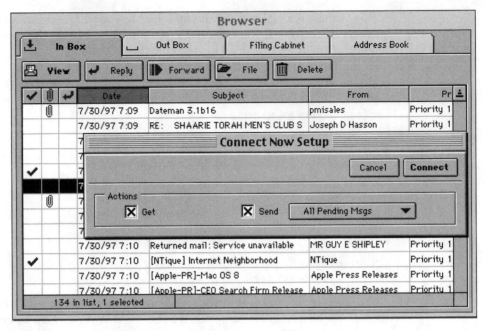

Figure 14.18 *The Connect Now Setup dialog box.*

While eM@iler is connecting and receiving messages, a dialog box like the one in Figure 14.19 appears.

Once you've received e-mail you can see your incoming mail in eM@iler's Browser window when the In Box tab is selected, as shown in Figure 14.20. Any mail that has a check mark next to it has been read. A paper clip signifies that a data file is attached to the e-mail; the return arrow means that you've replied to the message. All these indicators can be seen in Figure 14.20.

The buttons across the top of the browser window are actions you can perform on a selected message. The buttons have the following functions:

- ❖ The View button opens the message so you can read it.
- ❖ The Reply button creates a new outgoing message addressed to the selected message's sender.
- ❖ The Forward button copies the selected message to a new outgoing message. Then you add the address and forward the message.
- ❖ The File button moves the selected e-mail message(s) to the Read Mail folder, which can be viewed by clicking on the Filing Cabinet tab.
- ❖ The Delete button does what it says; clicking on it deletes all selected messages.

When you open an e-mail message, notice that you have the same options as those listed above. Figure 14.21 shows a received e-mail message. The message window has several additional buttons:

- ❖ The Left or Previous button—This button opens the previous message in your in box.

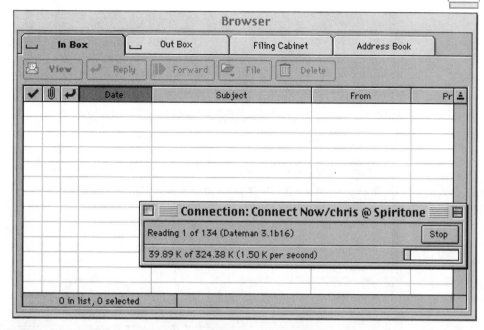

Figure 14.19   *The Connection/Connect Now dialog box.*

Figure 14.20   *eM@iler's browser window.*

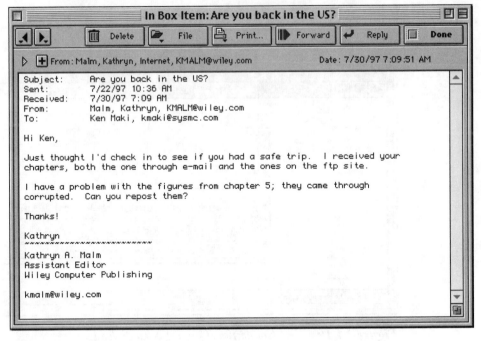

Figure 14.21 *An open e-mail message.*

> ❖ The Right or Next button—This button shows the next message in your in box.
>
> ❖ The Done button—This button closes the mail message window.
>
> ❖ The + button—This button lets you add the message sender's address to your address book.

When you select the *New* command from the Mail menu you create a blank e-mail. After you fill it out, it looks like Figure 14.22. Again, a series of buttons and options appears. By now, some of them should be familiar. The new ones are as follows:

> ❖ Send Now—This button sends the message immediately.
>
> ❖ Cancel—This button causes the window to disappear and cancels the message.
>
> ❖ Save—The Save button saves the e-mail message. The next time you connect the message is sent.
>
> ❖ Do not schedule—If this button is checked, the message is not sent. You must uncheck this box before the message can be sent.
>
> ❖ Use Signature—This button attaches your signature to the end of the message.

In the Recipient section, either select the message's recipient from your address book with the Add Recipient button or manually fill in the recipient's information. Use Figure 14.22 as an example for filling out this information. The Tab with the paper clip switches to the Attachments window from the Recipients window. In the Attachments window you can attach a file or enclosure that will be sent with your e-mail message. Clicking on the Add Enclosure button presents a standard Open dialog box from which you select the file you're going to send.

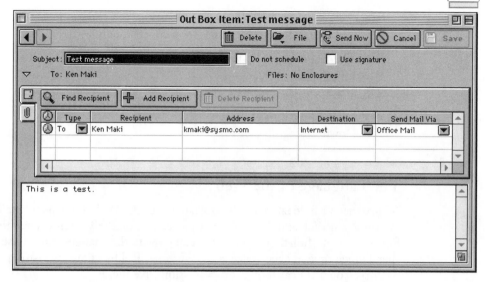

Figure 14.22   *An outgoing e-mail message.*

With what you've learned from this section, I'm sure you can figure out how the Filing Cabinet and Address Book sections work. With the eM@iler application, which can be found in the Claris eM@iler folder in the Internet Applications folder, you find some Read Me files and a FAQ (Frequently Asked Questions) document. You should read these documents.

Exploring the World Wide Web

When people talk about the Internet, invariably they mean the World Wide Web (WWW or the Web). The problem is that the WWW defies an easy explanation. I think the best way to describe the Web is to tell you some of the things you can do on the WWW:

- ❖ Visit the White House
- ❖ Get technical support
- ❖ Read the latest news
- ❖ Get up-to-the-minute stock quotes
- ❖ Download more software than you can put on your hard disk
- ❖ Tell the world about yourself, your family, and your dog
- ❖ Read about anything that interests you—I mean anything

At the beginning of this chapter, I mentioned trying to find the definition for "cyber." This was done on the WWW, where I found an online dictionary. Actually I found about a dozen dictionaries—regular dictionaries and a technical dictionary. And all of them could be accessed from the same location on the Web.

Now the question is, how do you do this? I'm sure you can't wait to start "surfing the Web." To get you started, this section covers the following topics:

- ❖ The language of the Web
- ❖ Introduction to Netscape
- ❖ Getting around the Web
- ❖ Performing searches
- ❖ Downloading files

The Language of the Web

Notice that a whole language is associated with the Web. How people talk about the World Wide Web and describe what you can do on the Web is constantly changing. For some, it is a full-time job just to keep up with the changes. And those who don't spend much time in cyberspace could, at times, feel like they are visiting a foreign country. You will hear terms and expressions like these:

- ❖ Surfing the Web—Going from one Web Site to another.
- ❖ What is the URL?—A URL is a Uniform Resource Location.
- ❖ http://www.apple.com—This is the URL for Apple Computer, Inc.
- ❖ Lost in cyberspace—Being confused about your location or where you're going.
- ❖ Home—The first or primary Web page for a WWW Site.
- ❖ Web browser—The program you use to do your Web Surfing.

I often wonder what our language will be like after being influenced by the Web for 50 years. Today I hear people talking about not having enough bandwidth (time or resources) to accomplish a task or participate in an activity. I'm sure you've heard people say that they were interfacing with someone, meaning that they had a meeting or were communicating with another person. As more people use the Internet and the Web, more of its language will infiltrate popular culture.

More important, you will have to deal with the language as you use the Internet. There isn't enough space in this chapter to talk about all terms specific to the Web and the Internet. You've had to learn some new language to deal with your Macintosh; now you must learn some more. If you're really concerned about the language of the Web, think about reading a book on the Internet and the Web.

As you learn about the Web, be aware of the language. I don't want you to be overly concerned about the language, just aware. The best way to figure out what something means is to examine the context of the word.

Introduction to Netscape

Mac OS 8 comes with three different Web browsers:

- ❖ Netscape Navigator 3.1

❖ Microsoft's Internet Explorer

❖ Cyberdog

There is no way I can tell you about all three, so I will concentrate on Netscape Navigator. Netscape can probably be credited with starting the Web craze, and it did it by creating Netscape Navigator. Its product seems to be the logical one to discuss. Besides, I like it better than the others.

Although Apple includes Navigator 3.1 with Mac OS 8, the current version of the Navigator is 4.0. You should think about upgrading because the new version is a bit faster and uses less memory.

Yes, Netscape is a memory hog. On a Power PC Mac, with virtual memory turned on, Netscape uses 9MB of RAM.

To use Netscape, you must be connected to the Internet. Once you're connected, double-click on the "Browse the Internet" icon that was placed on your Desktop during the Mac OS 8 installation. When you do, your Mac launches Netscape and you are transported to a Web page that looks similar to the one shown in Figure 14.23.

This page, called "My Channel," is a Web site provided by the Excite company that you can personalize and use as your own home page. You can think about this page as your entry point into the Web. You need to know several things about this page and how it works. It serves as a good example for learning about how the Web operates. We discuss the specifics of this page in the next section.

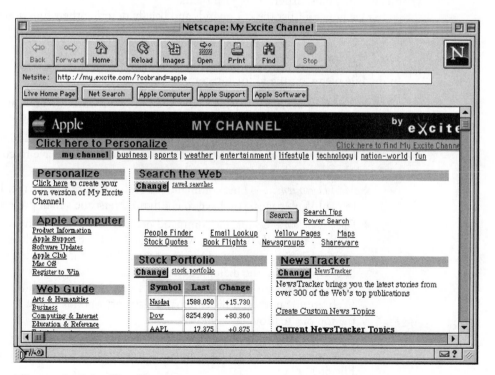

Figure 14.23 *Your first stop on the Web.*

For now, we will concentrate on Netscape Navigator itself. Netscape is a Web browser, but you can also use it as your e-mail program and newsgroup reader. How to use Netscape is a decision you must make after you've done some experimenting. The principles for using Netscape as your -mail program are similar to those discussed above in the eM@iler section.

The best way to look at Netscape is to examine its different menus; let's discuss just the most important menu command, as well as those that do not correspond to general Macintosh functions. The menus are as follows:

- ❖ File
- ❖ Edit
- ❖ View
- ❖ Go
- ❖ Bookmarks
- ❖ Options
- ❖ Directory
- ❖ Window
- ❖ Help

Of these menus I do not cover Edit or Help because they are self-explanatory. All of the others include items you'll want to understand. After you have read about the menu commands, experiment with them.

For each menu I list the commands and briefly describe their functions.

The File Menu

In the File menu are the following commands:

- ❖ *New Web Browser*—Opens a new Web browser window. You can have multiple browser windows open simultaneously.
- ❖ *New Mail Message*—This command uses the Netscape e-mail function to create a new e-mail message. To use this function you have to configure Netscape to handle your e-mail.
- ❖ *Mail Document...*—This command mails the current Web page. If you plan to mail Web pages, you have to configure Netscape's mail preferences.
- ❖ *Open Location*—Using this command presents a dialog box into which you can type the URL (http://www.apple.com) or Web page address for the location you want to visit. One way to use this feature is to just type a name like "Apple" into the dialog box that appears. Netscape adds the remaining URL elements for the address. This is a very quick way to jump from one Web site to another. This command also corresponds to the Open button at the top of the browser window.
- ❖ *Open File*—If you have saved, created, or received a Web page you can view it by opening the file. This command presents you with the standard Open File dialog box.

The View Menu

In the View menu you find the following commands:

❖ *Reload*—The Reload command tells Netscape to reconnect to the current Web page and download the page again. This is helpful if a page does not completely load. This command corresponds to the Reload button at the top of the browser window.

❖ *Reload Frame*—Some Web pages are divided into parts called frames. The Reload Frame acts on a frame just as the Reload command works on a page.

❖ *Load Images*—If you've told Netscape not to download images so that you can move about a little more quickly, the Load Images menu item downloads a page's images and displays them. This command corresponds to the Images button at the top of the browser window.

❖ *Document Source*—This command displays the HTML (Hypertext Markup Language) code for the page you're viewing. This is useful if you want to create your own Web pages. You can look at the pages that you like and see how they are constructed.

❖ *Document Info*—Use this command on different pages to display the technical info about a Web page.

❖ *Frame Source* and *Frame Info*—These two commands are the same as their document counterparts except that they work on frames.

The Go Menu

In the Go menu are the following commands:

❖ *Back*—This command corresponds to the Back button at the top of the browser window. The command takes you back to the last page you viewed.

❖ *Forward*—This command corresponds to the Forward button at the top of the Browser window. The command returns you to the last page you were viewing when you used the Back command or button.

❖ *Home*—This command corresponds to the Home button at the top of the Browser window. Using the Home command returns you to the Home location defined in the General Preferences.

❖ *Stop Loading*—This command stops the loading process for the current page.

❖ *List of places you've visited during this session*—As you cruise the Net, Netscape lists the locations you have visited in the Go menu. This listing is good for only the current program session. If you quit and reopen Netscape, the list is cleared.

The Bookmark Menu

Bookmarks are saved location addresses. As you cruise the Web you will find sites that want to visit again. The easiest way to revisit a site is to add it to your bookmark list. The Bookmark Menu has one command, *Add Bookmark*. When you select this command, the current page's address is added to your bookmark list. To revisit the site, all you have to do is select it from the Bookmark menu. You can keep your bookmark list manageable with the *Bookmarks* command in the Window menu.

The Options Menu

In the Options menu are the following commands:

- ❖ *General Preferences…*—The General preferences menu item lets you control Netscape's basic appearance and its interaction with other programs. Figure 14.24 shows the General Preferences' Appearance page.
- ❖ *Mail and News Preferences…*—This is the command you use to access Netscape's controls for handling e-mail and newsgroups. Figure 14.25 shows the Servers page where you set your basic e-mail configuration.
- ❖ *Network Preferences…*—The Network Preferences are where you fine-tune how Netscape behaves. One of the most important settings is the size of Netscape's cache. Netscape keeps copies of each page and image that you download so that it can more quickly display them when you return to pages you've already visited. The larger the cache, the faster Netscape runs. The drawback is that you lose disk space to the cache. The cache is one just one of the settings you adjust in this section. Figure 14.26 shows the Cache settings page.

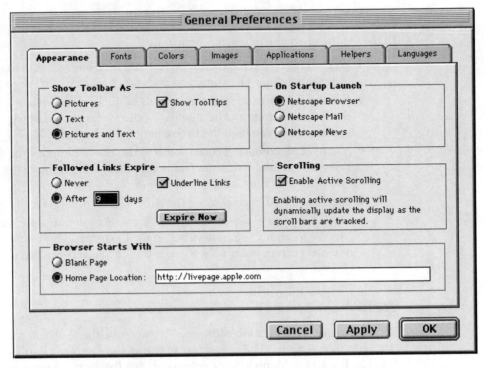

Figure 14.24 *Netscape's Appearance preferences.*

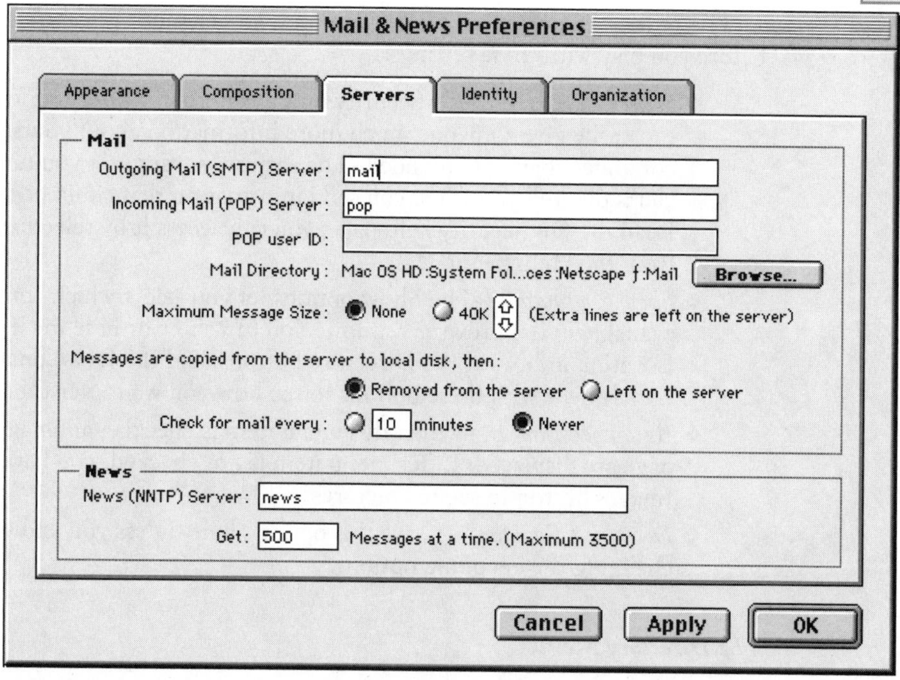

Mail & News Preferences

| Appearance | Composition | **Servers** | Identity | Organization |

Mail

Outgoing Mail (SMTP) Server: `mail`

Incoming Mail (POP) Server: `pop`

POP user ID:

Mail Directory: Mac OS HD:System Fol...ces:Netscape ƒ:Mail   **Browse...**

Maximum Message Size: ⦿ None   ○ 40K ⇕ (Extra lines are left on the server)

Messages are copied from the server to local disk, then:

⦿ Removed from the server   ○ Left on the server

Check for mail every: ○ `10` minutes   ⦿ Never

News

News (NNTP) Server: `news`

Get: `500`   Messages at a time. (Maximum 3500)

Cancel   **Apply**   **OK**

Figure 14.25 Netscape's e-mail configuration.

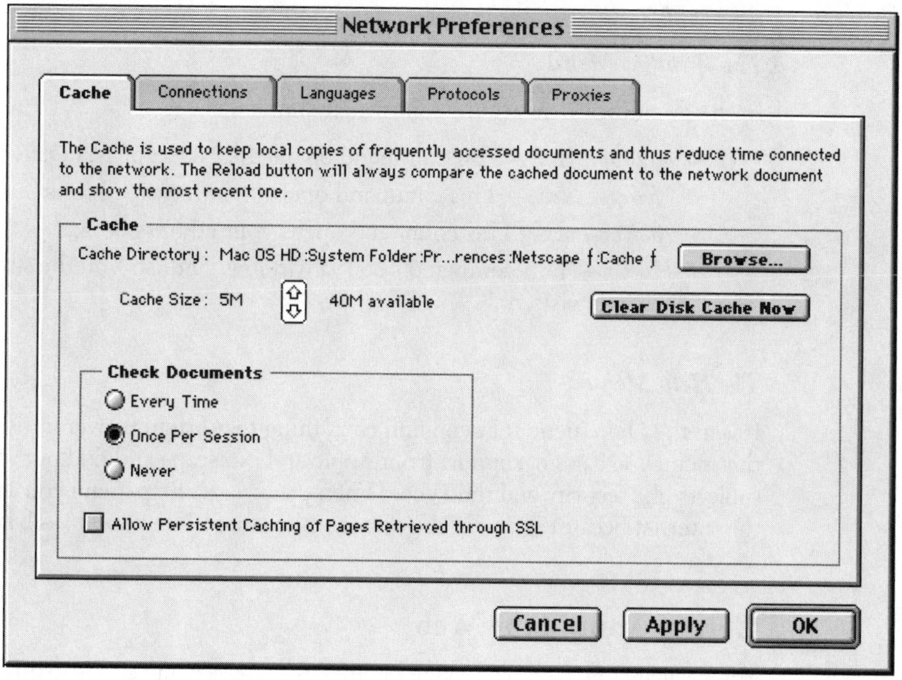

Network Preferences

| **Cache** | Connections | Languages | Protocols | Proxies |

The Cache is used to keep local copies of frequently accessed documents and thus reduce time connected to the network. The Reload button will always compare the cached document to the network document and show the most recent one.

Cache

Cache Directory: Mac OS HD:System Folder:Pr...rences:Netscape ƒ:Cache ƒ   **Browse...**

Cache Size: 5M ⇕   40M available   **Clear Disk Cache Now**

Check Documents

○ Every Time

⦿ Once Per Session

○ Never

☐ Allow Persistent Caching of Pages Retrieved through SSL

Cancel   **Apply**   **OK**

Figure 14.26 Netscape's cache settings.

The other settings are a bit more complex. Check out Netscape's help feature before you play with these settings:

❖ *Security Preferences...*—Security on the Internet is a very serious subject. You can easily give someone much more information about yourself or your computer than you intended. The security settings let you turn on (or off) alerts that tell you when you send information that could be compromised. Read the On Security help page; you can access it by selecting *On Security* from the Help menu.

❖ *Show Commands*—The Show options let you select which control buttons are available in the browser window. You can show or hide the Toolbar, Location indicator, the Directory buttons, and the Java Console. Experiment with these options to see how you want Netscape to look.

❖ *Auto Load Images*—When this menu item is checked, all images in a Web page are displayed. If this menu item is not checked, you have to click on the Images button to see the pictures.

❖ *Document Encoding*—Leave this option alone unless you know why you are changing the encoding options.

The Directory Menu

The commands in this menu correspond to the Directory buttons displayed in the browser. These buttons are customized by Netscape and Apple. Select the menu commands to see where you end up. Each command or button takes you to a different location.

The Window Menu

In the Window menu are the following commands:

❖ *Netscape Mail*—This command opens the Netscape Mail program.
❖ *Netscape News*—This command opens the Netscape News program.
❖ *Address Book*—This command opens your address book.
❖ *History*—This command opens a window that lists you the sites you've recently visited.

The Help Menu

It is in the Help menu that you find everything that I didn't cover in this chapter. From this menu you can get support from Apple and Netscape and find out about all kinds of subjects like security and the Web. When you use the help menu you are connected to the Internet because many of the options take you to Netscape's Web site.

Getting around the Web

You navigate the Web by clicking on links, which are connections to other Web pages. A link can be embedded in an image or connected to text. If you click on your Home button

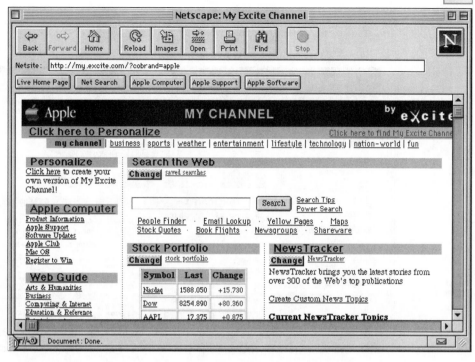

Figure 14.27 *Netscape's default home page for Mac OS 8.*

an image like the one in Figure 14.27 appears (assuming that you haven't changed the default home location). On this page words and phrases are underlined in several places.

To navigate to a new place all you have to do is click on one of the underlined phrases. Once you've done that, click on the Back button to return to this page. You've just gone from one page to another or maybe from one site to another and back. The difference between going from one page to another and going to another site is not great, but it is significant. When you go from page to page, you are still at the site where you started. When you go from one site to another, it is like going from one building to another.

Spend time playing with your default home page. This particular page offers a lot of options. You can even personalize your own page, customizing it with information sources that appeal to your tastes. Figure 14.28 shows how I've customized my page.

The only way to learn the Web is to use it. If you spend some time experimenting it will pay off later when you want to use the Web to do something serious. Yes, I said serious. The Web does not have to be all play. I use the Web all the time to help me do my work. I'm always looking up companies to get information about their products, download files, and keep on top of the news.

Performing Searches

If you need to find information or Web sites that address a specific topic, you can usually find what you want by performing a search. Searches are done by special

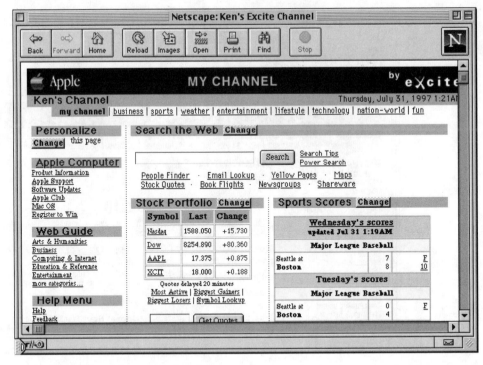

Figure 14.28   *My personalized channel page.*

Web sites that have collected information about thousands of sites. The default home page I've been using for examples in this section includes a search section.

To use this search function, all you have to do is type a word or phrase in the field. In Figure 14.29 note that I've typed "Macintosh" in the search field.

Once you have entered the topic you want to search for, click the Search button. Figure 14.30 shows the results of my search. As you can imagine, "Macintosh" is a rather broad subject—I received 566,800 hits. In this example, a *hit* is a Web site that contains the word Macintosh.

For a search to be effective the topic needs to be narrow. I don't want to look through 566 thousand Web sites. The next time I perform this search I might look for Macintosh error codes. To get the best results, click on the "Search Tips Power Search" link to get a page that looks like Figure 14.31. With this page you can fine-tune your search and avoid wading through thousands of results.

When I performed the search for "Macintosh error codes" shown in Figure 14.31, I received nine hits. Now there's a big difference. Another thing to keep in mind is that almost all large sites have their own search feature. When you search a site you are not searching the whole Web.

I'll say it again: Play around. Experiment with your searches. You'll find that you can get more information than you ever imagined.

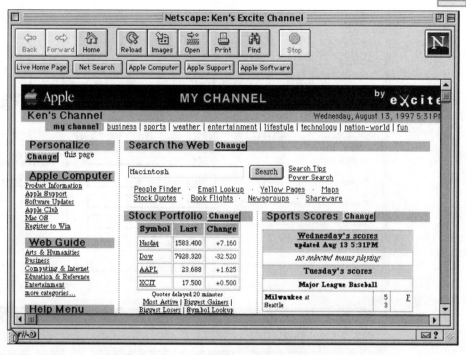

Figure 14.29 *Using Netscape's default home page for a search.*

Figure 14.30 *The search results.*

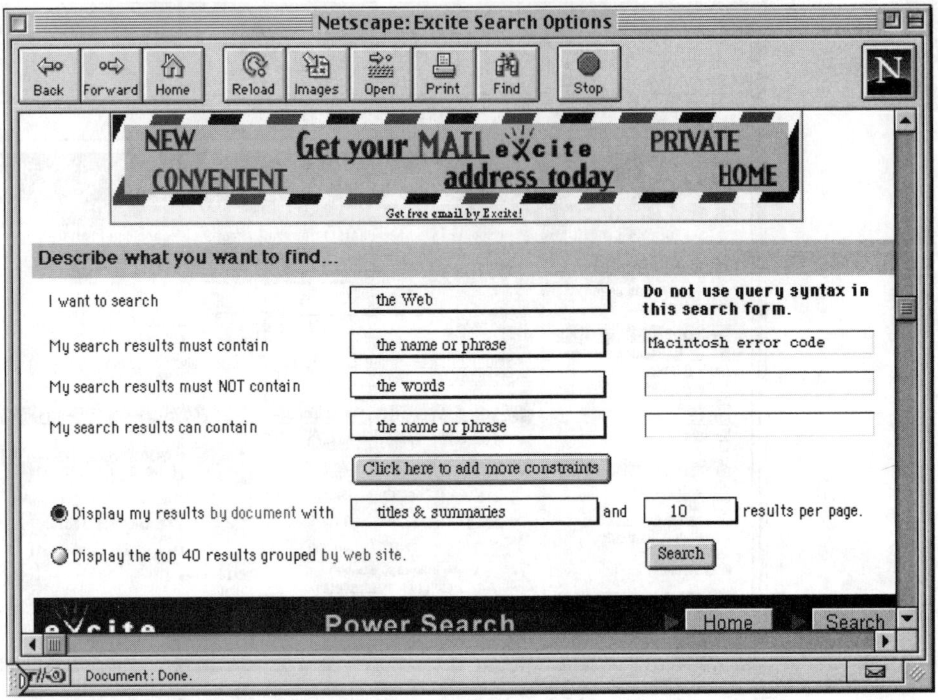

Figure 14.31   Excite's Power Search page.

Downloading Files

The final topic to cover is downloading files and software using Netscape. With the whole world at your disposal, you shouldn't have any problem finding things to download.

Go back to the Excite Channel page that we've been using as an example and find the link called "Shareware." When you click on the link you are taken to a search page where you can narrow your search. Figure 14.32 shows the Shareware search page.

Let's look for Macintosh communications utility shareware. Figure 14.33 shows the results.

If you see a program you want, all you have to do is click on the link. You are taken to a description page for the program; from there you can click on the Download button. Next you are taken to a page that lists the sites that have the file, as shown in Figure 14.34. When you click on one of the linked sites the file is downloaded and saved on your Mac.

One of the preferences you can set within Netscape is the location for downloaded files. The default location is your Mac's Desktop. If you want your downloaded files saved to a folder, use the *General Preferences* menu item and set the location in the Applications section. The next section about Stuffit Expander discusses what happens when you download files.

Figure 14.32   *The Shareware search page.*

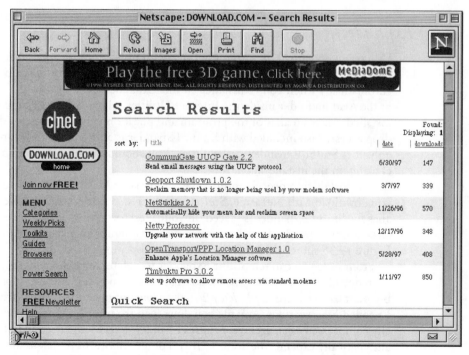

Figure 14.33   *The result of the Shareware search.*

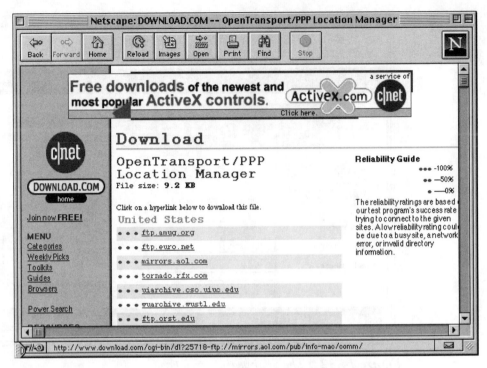

Figure 14.34   *Locations from which you can download the file.*

Stuffit Expander

When you download files from the Internet they are sent to you as text files. These files then have to be converted before they can be used. Thankfully, this happens automatically when you've installed Stuffit Expander. Stuffit Expander can be found in the Aladdin folder inside the Internet Utilities folder. Stuffit Expander is already installed. Make an alias of the program and put it on your Desktop for drag-and-drop access. Also included with Stuffit Expander is a program called DropStuff that enhances Stuffit Expander's capabilities. You should install this program by double-clicking on the installer icon.

The installation process installs everything your Mac needs to convert the files you download with Netscape. Stuffit Expander also works with eM@iler. Also, an alias for Stuffit Expander is placed on your Desktop. When you double-click on the alias Stuffit Expander launches, and you can configure how the program operates. Figure 14.35 shows the Preferences window for Stuffit Expander.

From here you can tell Stuffit Expander to delete the archive files after they've been downloaded and, in general, control how it operates. Two options you probably want to check are the *Delete after expanding* options for both the Archive and Encoded Files sections. Any file you download from the Internet is encoded and usually compressed as an archive. Stuffit Expander decodes the encoded file and then automatically expands the archive. If you don't tell Stuffit to delete the source files you will clutter your hard drive with these extra files.

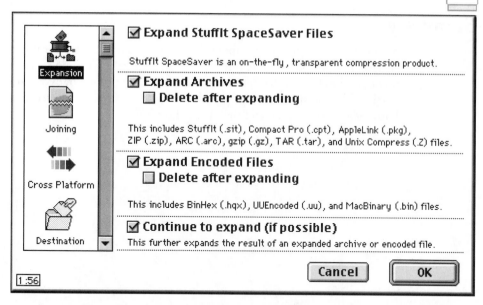

Figure 14.35 *Stuffit Expander's Preferences window.*

Setting a specific location for downloaded files is also a good idea. Doing so will ensure that you know where to find the files you have downloaded. You can set download locations in both Stuffit Expander and Netscape.

With Stuffit Expander installed you're truly ready to take on the Internet. Have fun.

General Suggestions

The following comments are just some suggestions you might want to keep in mind as you play and/or work on the Internet:

❖ When you play on the Internet you need to keep in mind that people use it to work. It is best to access other computers during nonwork hours. Be sure to keep time zone changes in mind. When it is midnight here, it is the middle of the day in other parts of the world.

❖ Keep mail messages brief. It is everyone's responsibility to be as efficient as possible. New users are joining the Internet community every day, and electronic traffic jams do occur. Be courteous.

❖ Because your mail messages can be sent around the world, they are not secure; any number of people could read them. And if you participate in newsgroups hundreds to millions of people see what you write. Don't say anything that you don't what to come back and haunt you.

❖ People will tell you when your comments are inappropriate or in the wrong location. Mail can be forwarded. And you can get *flamed* (a *flame* is a nasty message sent to you) for inappropriate behavior. Not everyone on the Internet is nice. It is real life, electronically.

Summary

So much more could be said about the Internet. This chapter barely scratches the surface. I hope you've got enough information to take a running jump into the digital ocean. I'm not too concerned because you can't drown, but you can be overwhelmed by the amount of information out there. At least, you are armed with some knowledge about e-mail and the Web. Have fun.

CHAPTER 15

Avoiding Problems

V ery few people are lucky enough to never have a problem with their Mac. And not being prepared to deal with a problem is a lot like tempting fate. If you are not prepared, you can almost bet that you will have problems. So as doctors (actually, it's mothers) have said for generations, an ounce of prevention is worth a pound of cure; this chapter is your ounce of prevention.

Macintosh problems are more than inconvenient; they always seem to happen at the worst possible time—when you have a deadline on a report or a term paper, or right before that big presentation is due. If you are not prepared, your problem will be a crisis—just like this true story of the tax preparer who), on April 15 at 5:00 P.M., had his hard disk crash. Although he did recover his data and get back to work by 9:00 P.M., he suffered, he aged, he became a bit grayer. The purpose of this chapter is to keep you from doing the same.

There are two things you can do to prevent a similar situation: One is to have tools for solving most Macintosh problems, and the other is to have a regular maintenance program that keeps your Mac in top-notch condition. Although you will never have a guarantee of trouble-free operation, you can use your Mac with a minimum of problems. And if you do have problems, you'll have the knowledge and tools for correcting the most common problems.

This chapter covers the following topics:

❖ What you need
❖ Maintaining your system
❖ Determining if you have a problem
❖ Getting help (when to call tech support)

What You Need

Just as you have a screwdriver, hammer, and pair of pliers around the house for taking care of pesky household problems and emergencies, you need some basic Macintosh tools. To be equipped for any emergency, you should have both software and hardware tools. What you need depends on your equipment configuration, so if a tool discussed here does not apply to your setup, don't buy it.

Software Essentials

The software tools you need are a clean System disk and various types of software utilities. You should have one of each of the following types of utilities:

- ❖ Antiviral
- ❖ Disk and file utilities
- ❖ Hardware profiler
- ❖ File manager

To begin, you don't have to buy any software. Between what's on the CD included with this book and the utilities you get with Mac OS 8, you have all the tools you need for doing maintenance checks. You can purchase commercial software for each category listed above, but before you go buy anything, use the tools you already have at your disposal.

The tools you already have are these:

- ❖ Disk First Aid—Disk diagnosis and repair utility
- ❖ Disinfectant 3.6—Antiviral utility
- ❖ TechTool—Hardware and System profiler, tester, and utility
- ❖ DiskTools on the CD—File Manager
- ❖ SCSIProbe on the CD—Utility for checking SCSI devices and IDs

All of these tools are on the Revelations CD-ROM included with the book, except Disk First Aid. Disk First Aid can be found on your Mac OS 8 CD.

After you are familiar with performing Mac maintenance and troubleshooting basics, you should purchase a commercial virus checker and Norton Utilities for the Macintosh. You will learn more about Norton Utilities as you progress through the troubleshooting topics in this book. The other software listed here is be discussed in this chapter and throughout this part of the book.

Hardware Essentials

Hardware problems cannot be cured with software tools; this is an unfortunate fact of life. Some hardware problems will be beyond your ability to repair. All kinds of bits and pieces can have problems or fail, such as SCSI cables, LocalTalk boxes, and terminators, not to mention hard drives and other peripherals. You can fix some of these when they have problems.

Which hardware essentials you need depends on your equipment. The following is a list of the most common accessories you should keep handy:

❖ SCSI cables

❖ An extra SCSI terminator

❖ Printer cable

❖ Network cables and connectors

Having extra hardware is important. The real issue, besides the cost, is how critical is your ability to continue working if a piece of hardware should fail. In extreme cases, you should have duplicate systems so that, no matter what, you can continue to be productive. The decision to have extra hardware is a bottom-line decision. But before you buy an extra Mac, remember that renting a computer is another option. Even more important than extra hardware is always having a backup. If you don't have a backup of your data, renting a system may not accomplish much.

Happiness Is a Clean System Disk

When things go awry, the most important software tool you can have is a clean System disk. A clean System disk is a floppy with a System and Finder that will operate your model of Macintosh. You may have got one with your Mac when it was new, but you might want to make one if your original disks have been lost. It is also possible that you didn't receive a System disk with your Mac; instead, you received a CD-ROM that you used to start your Mac.

Most people find themselves in a predicament when their Mac will not boot from their hard drive and they cannot find their current System disk. If you do not have a System floppy containing the same System you are currently running on your hard drive, then make one now.

An Installer disk is useless as a troubleshooting tool; it is good only for installing your System. The floppy disk you need is called either Disk Tools 1 or Disk Tools 2. These disks have a minimum install System that boots your Mac. When you deal with several Macs, make sure that each Mac has its own startup floppy.

Should you need to make one of these disks you can do so by following these steps:

1. Find the disk image for Disk Tools 1 or 2 on your Mac OS 8 CD-ROM.

2. Double-click on the disk image icon to start a program called Disk Copy.

3. Insert a floppy into your Mac when Disk Copy asks. The disk you insert is formatted, and the contents of the disk image are written to the floppy.

4. The disk is ejected when the copy is made. Disk Copy asks if you want to make another disk.

5. Make as many Disk Tools disks as you wish.

6. Quit the program when finished.

After you have made your disk use it to start your Mac. If it doesn't work, make another disk. Disk Tools 1 usually works on older Macs through the Quadra and some of the early Power Macs; Disk Tools 2 is made for Power Macs with PCI slots.

If and when you start having problems, reach for your startup disk. As a matter of fact, make a couple of them; it never hurts to have a backup. For your startup disk to be useful, make sure that it has the same version of the System that you currently use and that it is virus-free. To troubleshoot your System, you *must* have a clean startup disk.

After you make or find your startup disk, check it with a virus checker. This is a critical step because a computer virus could be your problem, and it can very easily be passed from your hard disk to your floppy disk, and vice versa. The method for checking your disk depends on the antiviral program you are using, and here, you can run into a real Catch-22.

The Viral Catch-22

Computer viruses are small programs written by programmers who have a sick sense of humor and no regard for others. These programs are designed to be self-replicating: They make copies of themselves and hide in your System and on your disks. One way a virus gets transmitted is by inserting a floppy disk in a System that has been infected, then inserting the same disk into a noninfected System, thus passing the infection along. The Catch-22 is that these highly virulent programs cause all kinds of problems; you must make sure you are not the victim of a virus. If your hard disk is infected with a virus and your *clean startup disk* is in the same condition, you cannot effectively troubleshoot your System.

The only protection you have from viruses (they have even been inadvertently distributed with brand new, shrink-wrapped software) is a virus checker. Viruses can cause any number of problems, from random System errors to erasing your hard drive. If your Mac is acting erratically, a virus may be causing the problem—especially if you share disks with other people and do not consistently use a virus checker.

The only way to be sure your Macintosh is not infected is to check it with an antiviral program. Usually, an antiviral program comes with an emergency disk that is locked and, therefore, cannot be infected. First, check your hard drive with the antivirus program on the disk to make sure it is clean (virus-free). After checking your hard drive, you can install the program and use it to check your floppy disks, including your emergency System startup disk.

If you do not check your System startup disk, you run the risk that it could be infected and that using it with your Mac could infect the hard drive. If this is the case, you will never be able to determine whether a virus is causing your problems. Once you are sure your System startup floppy is virus-free, unmount it from your Mac and lock it. This disk should be forever locked. If you upgrade from one System version to another, make a new startup disk at the same time.

Booting with the Disk

The sole purpose of the clean System disk is to have a System disk with only the essential files necessary to run your Mac. The clean startup disk is the only way to determine if the problem you are trying to solve is System-related, caused by something in your System folder, or a problem with your hard drive. The clean startup disk can also be used to isolate some hardware problems.

System Installation Disks

Just as you need a special disk for troubleshooting your Mac, you need quick access to your System installation disks. Most of your troubleshooting ends by installing a new System on your hard drive.

Not having your System installation disks or CD-ROM greatly hinders both your maintenance and troubleshooting efforts. All too often, Mac users can't locate or don't have their System disks. These are the most important disks you have, so make copies if you received Mac OS 8 on floppy disk and always have the disks or the CD-ROM close by.

General Maintenance

Finding a problem before it becomes a disaster is your best line of defense after making a backup of all your data. Just as your car needs periodic oil changes and tune-ups, your Mac should have both hardware and software inspections from time to time. Although there are never any guarantees that your drive will not crash, you can probably catch a potential problem before it becomes serious if you check your equipment monthly or bimonthly.

This section provides a thorough maintenance plan that, if followed, will keep your Macintosh in tip-top condition. Whatever you do, take the time to check your system.

The basic drill is to do the following:

1. Physically check your Mac and all of its connections.
2. Check it for viruses.
3. Make sure your hard drive is fine; periodically reformat your drive (at least once every year).
4. Check your drives for fragmentation.
5. Reinstall your system to keep it healthy.

If you do all of these steps regularly, you may never need to use any of the troubleshooting procedures outlined in this part of the book.

Periodic Inspections

When you get ready to do the software maintenance that follows, check your Mac for excessive dust in its air vents; clean the screen, case, and keyboard; and check all your connections. If your Mac is excessively dusty, with dust bunnies crawling out of the air vents in either your external hard drive or your Mac, you might want to take it to the shop for a cleaning. And, if you haven't cleaned the monitor screen in a while, you will be surprised by the detail you can see once it is cleaned.

To clean the monitor and the case, spray a mild cleaner onto a lint-free cloth and wipe down your Mac. Do turn it off before you start, and never spray a cleaner or any liquid directly on any component of your computer. Besides providing the potential for a shocking experience, spraying a cleaner directly on your Mac can discolor your equipment. After you have moved the Mac about to check for dust and cleaned it, reconnect all your cables. By checking your cables periodically, you will become familiar with your equipment's configuration.

Viruses

Begin your software maintenance with a virus check. But, before you do, contact the company that made your antiviral software to make sure that you have the latest version. It does not make a lot of sense to check for viruses that your software cannot detect. If your software is out of date, and if you need to add virus definitions, do so. After you are sure your software is current, check all your hard drives for infection. If you are conscientious in performing this task, you may never get infected with something that will cause grief and require hours to repair.

File Maintenance

A periodic check of your hard drive's data structures is the best thing you can do to avoid trouble. Hard drives develop problems over time, and Macintosh hard drives are particularly sensitive. Conduct the checks in this section monthly for Macs that are heavily used.

Getting Rid of Bad and In-Use Sectors

As time goes on, your hard drive will develop bad sectors. If you do not check for them and render them harmless, you will end up storing an important file in a sector that has gone bad, and it will take your file with it. Although Norton Utilities for the Macintosh is particularly good for this type of maintenance, Disk First Aid also performs these functions. Either program finds any bad and in-use sectors and verifies the integrity of your directory in a single scan of your drive. Then, the program maps out any bad sectors, frees all in-use sectors, and repairs any minor directory damage.

Of all the periodic checks you can perform, this one is the most important. All hard drives deteriorate over time. This is something that can and will happen; unless you check your drive regularly, you are courting disaster.

Checking for Fragmentation

As you remove and add files to your hard drive, it has a nasty tendency to become fragmented. *Fragmentation* occurs when a file is split up and placed in noncontiguous sectors, thereby slowing down data access. If your Mac does not access your data as fast as it did when you first set it up, then the hard drive is probably fragmented. The more fragmented it gets, the slower it goes; and the slower it goes, the more unhappy you become.

To check your Mac for fragmentation, use Norton Utilities for the Macintosh. Disk First Aid checks only your hard disk's integrity. By checking for fragmentation when you do your periodic maintenance, you will know how badly your drive is fragmented. In Figure 15.1, note that the drive is more than 5 percent fragmented, with only 1.3 megabytes as the largest contiguous block of free space. The remainder of the free space is represented by the white spaces in the figure, and each is smaller than 1.3 megabytes. A good guideline for judging if your drive is too fragmented is the 10 percent threshold: When your hard drive is 10 percent fragments, you might want to do something about it.

If your drive is fragmented, you have two options: Use an optimizer, or back up your data, reformat your drive, and restore the data. The second choice is the safest way to defragment your drive, and it also creates a good backup. If you use a backup utility, you more than likely have a couple of options for the type of backup you perform. One is an image backup, the other is a file-by-file backup.

With an image backup, your data is backed up sector by sector, which means that, when you restore your data, it is still fragmented and you have achieved nothing. Use the file-by-file method if you have a choice so that, when your data is restored, each file is placed back on your drive contiguously.

If you choose to use an optimizer, back up all your data and archive the backup (store it away and do not use the disks). The optimization process lifts your files from the drive and rewrites them to contiguous sectors. The optimizer could accidentally place data in a bad sector (even though the manufacturer would vehemently deny

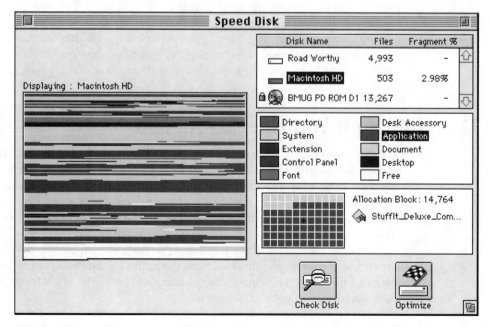

Figure 15.1 *Norton's Speed Disk window with statistics.*

this), and you could risk your data. This is especially true if you have not accessed some files for a long time. Not only will your file be corrupted, but also the next time you back up your drive, you will be backing up a corrupted file. By the time you discover the damage, you may not have a good copy of the file unless you archived one prior to the optimization.

Another warning about optimization software is the possibility of losing all your data. If your Mac should crash while the software is optimizing your drive, you will probably lose all your data, and, worse, it may not be recoverable. You could use Norton's Speed Disk (part of Norton Utilities) 100 times and have no problems, but it is for that *one time* that you have to be vigilant. Reformatting is the safer method of optimizing your drive.

When using Norton Utilities to defragment (optimize) your hard drive, make a special startup disk. It is not possible to optimize the hard disk that runs your Mac or the disk from which you run Speed Disk, Norton's defragmenting utility. Norton provides a special program to create the Speed Disk startup disk.

Keeping Your System Working

Over time, your System (the System file and track zero of your hard drive) can sustain damage. Random and infrequent System errors and improper restarts all have an effect on the System. Part of your regular maintenance should include reinstalling your System after performing the other maintenance checks. Reinstalling your System makes sure all the necessary resources are in their proper places and repairs minor damage. The installation process rewrites your boot blocks, installs most of your System file's resources, and replaces the Finder plus all of your printing resources. All in all, it makes sure everything is as it should be. Because your System files are used more than any other files on your computer, they are more easily corrupted. Reinstalling ensures their integrity. If you have any questions about this process, read Chapter 6 for a more complete description of this process.

Determining If You Have a Problem

You might assume that you are having a problem because your Mac has an occasional System error. Occasional System errors can be expected and are not, generally, a cause for concern. Something momentarily goes wrong, and restarting your Mac corrects the problem. A random System error is the computer equivalent of a hiccup, not really a problem. "Random" means the computer very occasionally crashes.

Your main concern with the occasional, random System error is data loss. If you are working on an important document, performing a database sort, or saving your work to a file when this occurs, you can lose data. Save your work frequently and make backups of all your important files.

If you get frequent or consistent System errors, then you have a real problem. Only after the problem becomes consistent are you able to fix it. If you cannot duplicate the problem or if it occurs infrequently, there isn't anything you can really fix. You will have to live with it until the problem gets worse. If your problem does not get worse, performing a general maintenance check might clear it up.

Determining that you have a problem is usually fairly easy. Either your Mac works properly or it doesn't. Diagnosing the problem is another story. The information you need to diagnose different types problems appears in the other chapters of the Troubleshooting section. Chapter 16, "Common Macintosh Problems," delves into some of the most common problems you'll have with your Mac, while Chapter 17, "Macintosh Hardware Problems," will look at how to fix your hardware difficulties. And Chapter 18 will look at System and Application Troubleshooting. Finally, to graduate, you'll learn how to recover hard drives in Chapter 19, "Disk Crashes and Data Recovery."

If, after you've performed a general maintenance check, you still have problems and don't want to fix the problem yourself, you may want to seek professional help or call the program's technical support line.

Before You Call Tech Support

The purpose of this section is to give you an extra edge so that you can get the most from your call to tech support. If you know what information the people at the other end of the phone need, you can make their job easier and your experience more satisfying by having your questions ready in advance.

Over the last two years almost all software companies have started charging for technical support after an initial period of free support. The period of free tech support is usually one to three months, and most companies start the countdown after your first tech support call. Other companies start the clock when they receive your software registration. I would recommend that you wait until you need help before you register your software (both electronic and mail-in registrations). Register your software, just wait a bit before you do. Also, if you do have problems you can always register over the phone when you call for support.

Almost every hardware and software manufacturer provides telephone technical support for their products. When you have problems with your computer, they can be very helpful and, at the same time, frustrating. Helpful because they often know what is wrong. Frustrating because you may have to wait a long time on hold to speak to someone and may get lost in a voice-mail system, and once you do get through, you may not get the answer you need. But, when you're stumped, give them a call.

What to Prepare for Tech Support

The following itemizes the information most tech-support departments want. Making notes as the problems occur definitely helps. Keep a record of things, such as what programs were running, whether you can duplicate the problem, if it is random, what error codes you are receiving, and so on. By keeping a good record of what happens, you have a much better chance of getting the help you need. The other information a technical-support person needs is discussed here. If you compile a list of all this information as you work on the problem, you won't need to scramble for it when you really need it.

Machine Configuration

Put together a complete description of your Macintosh's configuration. Include the Macintosh model, the type and size of the hard drive, the amount of RAM, and a list of the peripherals attached to your Mac. If your Mac is networked, don't forget to include what type of network you use.

For each piece of equipment, include the serial number on your list. If you call the manufacturer about a peripheral device, it may want your serial number. Trying to untangle your drive or modem so that you can look at the back or bottom of it while you are on the phone is inconvenient. For all SCSI devices, write down their SCSI ID numbers and whether they are terminated.

System Configuration

In addition to your hardware configuration, you also need the details of your System configuration. In this list, include all your extensions and control panels and the System software version in use. Include the version numbers of each of these System devices as well so that, if your problem occurred because one of your extensions is old, the version number can alert the technician.

Registration Numbers

If you are calling about a software package, chances are that tech support will want your registration or serial number before they help you. If it is a package you just purchased, they may want to register it while you are on the phone. They may even want you to fax the registration card to them. After you have decided that you will keep the package, send in your registration card.

Software licenses are becoming more of an issue all the time. Some companies are very particular about registration and their licenses, so be sure to read the license agreement with each software package and send in the registration cards as soon as possible.

Detail the Problem

Make a record of what is happening at the time it happens. Do not rely on your memory because you will forget the error code or exactly what you were doing when the error occurred. The more information you have, the easier it will be to fix the problem.

It is best if you can duplicate the problem. If not, still call tech support. Random errors are more frustrating than consistent errors, but, given enough information, the technician might have an answer—it never hurts to try.

Tools That Make This Easier

A system profiler like Tech Tool, which can be found on the Revelations CD-ROM, can make the information gathering task easier. Tech Tool looks at your system and makes a complete record of what type of Mac you are using and what extensions, control panels, and software you have installed.

Tech Tool is not the only software tool available for this task. Now Utilities comes with a program called Profiler, and Apple's Personal Diagnostics will also make a System record for you. Once again, if your system is unstable, you might not be able to check it when you have a problem, so run the Profiler before you need the information and keep your system profile handy.

Apple's Personal Diagnostics, in addition to compiling information about your System, is a hardware diagnostic utility. It checks your Mac's disk drives, memory, logic board, and video subsystems for problems. It can be a handy tool, especially if you take care of several Macs.

Calling the Doctor

When all else fails, you may need to get professional help from a consultant experienced in troubleshooting. If you are in this position, find someone you can trust who has references you can check. When you have problems with your Macintosh proper, your options for tech support are a bit limited. Apple relies on its dealers to be the source for user information and support, but dealers are not always as informed as you might wish. If your dealer can't help you, Apple has another avenue for providing support that is not as well publicized: a group of consultants who are part of Apple's Consultant Relations program.

For consultants to become members of this program, they must apply to Apple. Apple then checks their applications and references. If you don't know a consultant and need to find one, check with your dealer. If that doesn't work, call Apple and see if it has any consultants listed for your area who have an expertise with your particular problem or industry. Consultants usually specialize in areas like graphics, networking, small businesses, and so on.

The other thing to keep in mind about consultants is that they will have full access to all of your data. If the data on your drive is sensitive, have the consultant sign a nondisclosure agreement that states that he or she will not tell anyone, including his or her significant other, about your data. Be sure to protect yourself.

Summary

As the opening chapter of Part V, "Troubleshooting," this chapter provides you with the preliminary information you need when it comes time to fix your System. If you follow the advice in this chapter and perform the maintenance checks discussed here, you will have an easier time dealing with problems later. Consider the procedures in this section as computer exercise; they keep your Mac in top-notch condition so that it will be there when you need it.

CHAPTER 16

Common Macintosh Problems

I f you rarely or never have problems with your Mac, you will be amazed at the myriad problems that can occur; the list is almost endless. Troubleshooting your Mac can be a lot like putting together a jigsaw puzzle. First, you need a piece or place to start. When you are looking for a problem with your Mac, the best place to start is with some knowledge about what can go wrong, which, in turn, will give you a starting point for troubleshooting your system. The symptom that you perceive to be the problem is usually just the starting point. Often, the error code or crash is just a manifestation of a problem that is somewhere else, and you have to proceed backward from the symptom to the actual problem.

In addition to knowing about the specific problems you can encounter, you need to develop a strategy for determining what is causing the problem. After you find the offending software or hardware component, you can then fix it. Sounds simple, doesn't it? In principle, it is; in practice, it can be one of the most frustrating experiences of your life. It is like looking for something you have misplaced—you always find the thing you are looking for in the last place you look. Troubleshooting is no different. The last thing you try will fix your problem.

In addition to specifics on fixing a number of problems, this chapter endeavors to provide you with a technique for fixing problems that are not listed. The following are the most common sources of software and hardware problems you will encounter:

❖ Macintosh system crashes
❖ Desktop problems
❖ Viruses
❖ Extension and control panel conflicts
❖ A corrupted system file
❖ Application problems
❖ Hardware problems

503

Sometimes, these problems can be distinguished by their basic symptoms, and fixing them is relatively easy. This section deals with the simple problems. You are given a description of the Mac's behavior when these problems occur and of any quick fixes that may apply. If the problem is more complex, you can find more comprehensive help in the next three chapters.

This chapter contains preliminary information about troubleshooting. To use this information effectively, read this chapter plus Chapters 17 and 18. For some problems, the information in this chapter is all you need, but the entire subject of troubleshooting is like a four-course dinner—this chapter is the soup.

Macintosh System Crashes

A Macintosh system crash is a software malfunction that causes your computer to stop functioning. A crash can manifest itself as a frozen system—the computer stops functioning with no notification or other overt announcement. Another manifestation is a Mac that quits operating with a rather dramatic announcement; you are informed of the event by the dreaded bomb dialog box. Usually, when your computer freezes or you get a bomb, you have no choice but to restart your computer.

When the Mac freezes you usually have to figure out what has happened. The bomb usually displays an error code, a number (shown in Figure 16.1) that appears with a system error and sometimes with a bomb; the number is a code for a particular malfunction. Sometimes, a description in addition to the error code number appears in the dialog box. In most instances, the error code is close to meaningless, except to a programmer or a systems engineer. On occasion the error code can offer a bit of light.

By becoming familiar with the different error codes and their meanings, you might get some insight into what has gone awry and have a better idea of where to look for the problem. For example, anyone who is having consistent errors with ID 11 should know that ID 11 errors can be memory related and can often be fixed by reinstalling the System.

There are three types of error codes: System error codes generated by the Macintosh operating System; hardware error codes that occur when a hardware malfunction has occurred (these are also called Sad Mac codes); and error codes gener-

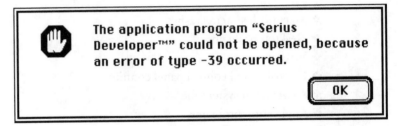

The application program "Serius Developer™" could not be opened, because an error of type -39 occurred.

OK

Figure 16.1 *System Error dialog box.*

ated by application software. Software errors codes usually have meaning only for the software manufacturer.

Apple's System Error Codes

Because the list of error codes that the System can generate is so large, only a few of the most common are listed here. Some of the descriptions are almost self-explanatory. The error code can provide an idea of what happened in some cases, but be careful in assuming they have real meaning by the time you see them. As the Mac crashes, a cascading effect very much like an avalanche occurs. The error code you receive could be one of the rocks from the top or the bottom of the pile. The cause of the avalanche may have long been lost in the noise and destruction of all the falling rocks.

Table 16.1 is provided for general information and to give you a better idea of all the things that can go wrong.

If your Mac is crashing and you are consistently getting one or two error codes, you can be pretty sure that you are experiencing a System-level error. The error code in this case may be meaningful and may provide a clue about your problem. This is a possibility that you will need to investigate. Your next task is to try to determine the cause of the problem.

Software Error Codes

Error codes generated by a program are fairly rare. When they do grace you with their presence they can come in one of two varieties. You either see a standard System bomb with a notice that program XYZ has caused a System Error, or you see an odd-looking error code number in a dialog box. Manufacturers can use their own numbers in place of the numbers generated by the Macintosh operating system. If you have an error code that is not included in Table 16.1, it may be a manufacturer's error code, and you should contact the technical-support department of the company that wrote the package you are using.

Hardware Error Codes

When a hardware malfunction occurs during bootup you can get an error code called a Sad Mac (see Figure 16.2). The numbers under the Sad Mac icon are the error code; they can be used to isolate what part of the startup diagnostic procedure failed and thus can locate the specific problem.

Two types of hardware faults can cause a Sad Mac: bad memory chips and hard-disk driver problems. Even though a problem with your hard-disk driver is really software-related, the Macintosh generates a hardware error code if your drive's driver is corrupted. Sad Mac error codes can be generated by software when the software causing the error is required to run the Mac at a pre-operating system level.

Table 16.1 Common Error Codes

ERROR CODE	DESCRIPTION
1	Bus error
2	Address error
3	Illegal instruction error
4	Zero divide error
5	Check trap error
6	Overflow trap error
7	Privilege violation error
11	Miscellaneous hardware exception error
12	Core routine error
13	Uninstalled interrupt error
14	I/O core error
15	Segment loader error
16	Floating point error
25	Out of memory
26	Can't launch file
27	File System map has been trashed
28	Stack has moved into application heap
30	Request user to reinsert offline volume
40	Welcome to Macintosh greeting
41	Can't load the Finder error
51	Unserviceable slot interrupt
81	Bad opcode given to SANE Pack4
85	SysErr—Cannot find MBDF
87	Could not load WDEF
88	Could not load CDEF
89	Could not load MDEF
90	FPU instruction executed, but machine has no FPU
98	Can't patch for particular model Mac
99	Can't load patch resource
101	Memory parity error
102	System is too old for this ROM

Table 16.1   Common Error Codes   *(continued)*

ERROR CODE	DESCRIPTION
103	Booting in 32-bit on a 24-bit system
104	Need to write new boot blocks
105	Need at least 1.5MB of RAM to boot 7.0
20000	User choice between Shut Down and Restart
20001	User choice between Switch Off or Restart
20002	Allow the user to Exit To Shell, return if Cancel
32767	General System error (catch-all used in DSAT)

Error Code General System

–1	Queue element not found during deletion
–2	Invalid queue element
–3	Core routine number out of range
–4	Unimplemented core routine
–5	Invalid queue element
–8	No debugger installed to handle debugger command

Error Code I/O System

–17	Driver can't respond to Control call
–18	Driver can't respond to Status call
–19	Driver can't respond to Read call
–20	Driver can't respond to Write call
–21	Driver reference number doesn't match unit table
–22	Driver reference number specifies NIL handle in unit table
–23	Requested read/write permission doesn't match driver's open permission
–24	Close failed
–25	Tried to remove an open driver

Error Code File System

–33	Directory full
–34	Disk full
–35	No such volume
–36	I/O error (bummers)
–37	There may be no bad names in the final System
–38	File not open

(continues)

Table 16.1 Common Error Codes *(continued)*

ERROR CODE	DESCRIPTION
–39	End of file
–40	Tried to position to before start of file (r/w)
–41	Memory full (open) or file won't fit (load)
–42	Too many files open
–43	File not found
–44	Diskette is write-protected
–45	File is locked
–46	Volume is locked
–47	File is busy (delete)
–48	Duplicate filename (rename)
–49	File already open with write permission
–50	Error in user parameter list
–51	Reference number error
–52	Get file position error
–53	Volume not on-line error (was ejected)
–54	Permissions error (on file open)
–55	Drive volume already on-line at MountVol
–56	No such drive (tried to mount a bad drive number)
–57	Not a Mac diskette (sig bytes are wrong)
–58	Volume in question belongs to an external file server
–59	File system internal error: during rename, the old entry was deleted
–60	Bad master directory block
–61	Write permissions error

Error Code Disk

–64	Drive not installed
–65	R/W requested for an offline drive
–67	Couldn't find valid address mark
–68	Read verify compare failed
–69	Address mark checksum didn't check
–71	Couldn't find a data mark header
–72	Bad data mark checksum
–75	Step handshake failed

Table 16.1 Common Error Codes *(continued)*

ERROR CODE	DESCRIPTION
–76	Track 0 detect doesn't change
–77	Unable to initialize IWM
–78	Tried to read second side on a one-sided drive
–79	Unable to correctly adjust disk speed
–80	Track number wrong on address mark
–81	Sector number never found on a track
–82	Can't find sector 0 after track format
–83	Can't get enough sync
–84	Track failed to verify

Error Code Memory Manager

–108	Not enough room in heap zone
–110	Address was odd or out of range
–113	Address in zone check failed

Error Code Resource Manager

–185	Extended resource has a bad format
–192	Resource not found

Figure 16.2   *A Sad Mac (very sad).*

This happens with hard-drive drivers when they are corrupted. The booting process is interrupted before the Mac looks at the boot blocks of your disk for its necessary startup information. Because the System is not yet loaded, it cannot generate a normal System error.

Anytime you have a startup hardware problem the Sad Mac icon shown in Figure 16.2 appears, with an error code. In addition to showing the Sad Mac, your Mac makes a chiming noise. Even though the chimes have a specific meaning, you only need to know about the Sad Mac codes.

Interpreting a Sad Mac Code

The type of Sad Mac you might get depends on the type of Mac you have. The older Macs have a Sad Mac with one line of digits under the image. The digits are six characters, hexadecimal numbers used to identify the problem. The format for the numbers is *XX XXXX*, where the *XX* is the Class Code and the *XXXX* is the Sub Code. The Sub Code corresponds to System error codes, while the Class Code specifies whether it is software or a hardware problem. Table 16.2 details the old-style codes; they apply only to Macs with 128K ROM or smaller:

This is not a complete list; however, it should give you an idea of what the codes mean. On all newer Macs, those with 256K ROM or larger, the format for the Sad Mac code occupies two lines; the top line is the Class Code, and the bottom line the Sub Code, both with the format *XXXXXXXX*. Other than having more Class and Sub Codes, the meanings are the same as the old Sad Mac codes. The numbers just have more zeros in front of them. For example, the old Class Code for a software error is 0F, but the new one is 0000000F; the same applies to the Sub Code.

Desktop Problems

Your Desktop files can become corrupted and fail to operate properly. If you add and remove a lot of applications and files from your hard disk, corruption can be a persistent problem, causing your drive to slow down and your icons to be improperly displayed. The Desktop file holds all the information about your files, which is displayed in the Finder, including icons and Finder comments displayed in the Get Info window (see Figure 16.3).

Desktop Issues

On your hard drive are two invisible files—the Desktop DB and Desktop DF (see Figure 16.4). These files are created by System 7.X and later and are more reliable than their System 6.0.X counterpart, the Desktop file. The Desktop files are critical to your Mac's operation and contain information about your files, including their Get Info comments and a file's icon.

When the Desktop files become corrupted, some strange symptoms that vary from files losing their icons to your Mac crashing as the Finder starts can occur. If

Table 16.2 Sad Mac Code

CLASS CODE	REFERENCE	CLASS CODE MEANING	SUB CODE	SUB CODE MEANING
01	ROM	ROM test failed	Varying Hexadecimal Number	Identifies the ROM chip that failed; usually meaningless
02	RAM	Bus test failed	Same as above	Identifies the RAM chip that failed
03	RAM	Write test failed	Same as above	Identifies the RAM chip that failed
04	RAM	Pattern test failed	Same as above	Identifies the RAM chip that failed
05	RAM	Address uniqueness test failed	Same as above	Identifies the RAM chip that failed

		SYSTEM ERROR NUMBER	SUB CODE	ERROR MEANING
0F	Software	01	0001	Bus error
		02	0002	Address error (odd address)
		03	0003	Illegal instruction
		04	0004	Zero divide
		05	0005	Check trap (CHK instruction)
		06	0006	Overflow trap (TRAPV)
		07	0007	Privilege violation
		08	0008	Trace trap
		09	0009	Trap dispatcher error
		10	000A	Line 1111 trap
		11	000B	Miscellaneous hardware trap
		12	000C	Unimplemented trap executed
		13	000D	Interrupt button pressed

you think your Desktop file is damaged, then rebuild it. Also, rebuilding the Desktop file, covered in Chapter 18, is a good maintenance procedure.

Another Desktop issue has to do with your Mac's performance. If you find that your drive is slowing down and not performing as fast as it used to, rebuild the Desktop. Rebuilding the Desktop will also reassociate your files with their related icons and programs, eliminating any excess baggage held in the Desktop files.

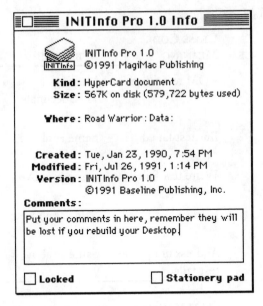

Figure 16.3   Get Info window with comments.

Repositioning Your Windows

Another function of the Desktop file is to keep track of where the windows from your disks were last positioned. If you have used your drive on a Mac with a large

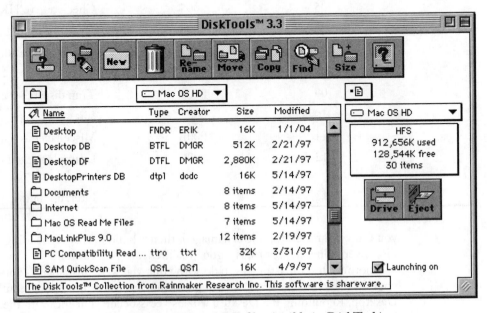

Figure 16.4   The Desktop DB and DF files (visible in DiskTools).

monitor and then returned it to your Mac, which has a smaller display, you could have moved a folder window to a position that you cannot see on your monitor. If you have done this, rebuilding the Desktop will make all your folder windows visible.

Extensions and Control Panels

Anytime you install a new piece of software, especially utility software, that puts an application or file in your Extensions or Control Panels folders, there is potential for a conflict. Extensions are not programs because you cannot run one by double-clicking on it. Extensions must be loaded as part of the System at startup.

Other types of software that often behave like extension are control panel devices. Control panels also load during startup, after your extensions. Some control panels do not load into RAM; instead, they are programs used to configure some aspect of your Mac and so are disguised as Control panels. Unless you want to test every control panel to see if needs to be loaded into RAM, keep all control panels in your Control Panels folder inside your System folder.

Control panels or extensions can conflict with each other or with the System. A conflict happens when the extension or control panel tries to use a memory location in use by another extension or control panel. Every extension stakes out its own special section of memory in an area created by the System, called the *System heap*.

Extension and Control Panel Conflicts

As the Macintosh boots up, it places all the System extensions in the Extensions folder (inside the System folder) into memory. Sometimes, an extension tells the System where it needs to reside within the System heap. If an extension must reside in a specific place in memory, and if another extension wants that same memory address, you will have a conflict. When this happens, your Mac crashes as it tries to start up. The control panels that load after your Extensions can cause the same types of problems, but with a slight difference. Sometimes, a control loads but it won't cause your System to crash until you access the control panel after the computer starts.

Not all the files in either the Extensions or Control Panels folder get loaded. Programs, such as the Map and Startup Device, do not load into memory. The way to test if a control panel loads into memory is to remove it from the Control Panels folder, place it outside your System folder, and reboot your Mac. After you've restarted, double-click on the control panel. If it runs, it does load into memory and can be stored anywhere on your Mac.

Extensions, on the other hand, must remain in the Extensions folder, regardless of whether they load into memory because they are all memory-resident programs, device drivers, or other tools that do not function outside of the System folder. The items that get placed in the Extensions folder are there for a reason—either they load into RAM at startup, or other programs need the files to be located in the Extensions folder. For example, printer drivers are not loaded into memory until you print a document. But, if the driver is not in the Extensions folder, the Chooser will not find it and your Mac won't print.

Unless you use an extensions manager that reorders the loading order of your extensions and control panels, they load in the following alphabetical order as your Mac boots:

❖ All System extensions in the Extensions folder

❖ All memory-resident control panels in the Control Panels folder

❖ All extensions or control panels that are loose in the System folder

A Quick Extension and Control Panel Fix

If you install a new extension or control panel, and if your System starts to crash on startup, you can be reasonably sure that the new addition to your System is part of the problem.

To find out for sure, follow these steps:

1. Turn off your Mac.
2. Turn it back on and hold down the Shift key as soon as you see the Smiling Mac.
3. When the "Welcome to Macintosh" screen appears, it should also display "Extensions Off."

If your Mac starts without a problem, you can be pretty sure that the problem was due to an extension or control panel. Open the Extensions Manager Control panel (instructions for using the Extensions Manager Control panel are in the next section), disable the new extension or control panel, and restart your Mac. When your Mac restarts, you have only partially solved the problem. The next step is to determine which extension or control panel the new one was conflicting with or if it was conflicting with the System in general. This is a more complicated process and is covered in Chapter 18.

A Corrupted System File

Any file can become corrupted. If you have frequent yet random System errors, one cause could be a corrupted System file. To determine whether your System is causing the problem, start your Mac with all the extensions turned off, as described previously.

Run the application that seems to be causing problems, and remember that the Finder is an application. If the Mac continues to crash, you have a problem with the System file, Finder, or the application. Any one of these files could be damaged, or you could have a problem related to your hard disk's directory.

To make the final determination, you need your clean startup disk. Boot from it, then run your application(s). If your Macintosh still crashes, you can assume it is your application that is corrupted and needs to be replaced. If your Mac runs without problems when booted from the floppy, then your System file is probably corrupted. Perform a clean System install and see if the problem goes away. Otherwise, if your Mac still crashes, replace your application and try again. If you still have no joy, refer to Chapter 18 for more System and application troubleshooting techniques.

Application Problems

In the last section, a quick reference was made about problems with applications. Just as System software can be the source of your misery, your programs can cause problems also. The following are possible problems you could have with your programs:

❖ A corrupted or incompatible application

❖ A corrupted data file

❖ A conflict between an application and a System element

When you have a problem with a specific application, it usually crashes or behaves strangely when it is run. The range of symptoms can be very diverse, from slow or inadequate performance to crashing your Mac.

Hunting down application problems can be very frustrating because you also have to troubleshoot your System in the process. There is no way to rule out a System problem unless you are running a stock Apple system. Only after you have a clean System can you troubleshoot an application.

Incompatible Applications

When you have an application that is bad, it usually crashes regardless of what you do. This is especially true of incompatible applications. If you install a new program and every time you try to run it, it crashes, you can be fairly sure that the program is incompatible with your System.

Remember that just because a program crashes it does not mean that anything is wrong with your Mac or System; it just means that the program does not work with your System. Be aware that repeated attempts to run an incompatible program can cause problems.

To determine if a program is truly incompatible, follow these steps after the program has crashed with your regular System configuration:

1. Boot with your extensions off, from a clean system, or with the Mac OS 8-only extension set (see Chapter 18).

2. Reinstall the program.

3. Run the program.

If your Mac crashes, call the program publisher's technical-support department. If the program is shareware or public domain software, you may have to write it off.

Corrupted Applications

Usually, when a specific application you've been using starts giving you trouble, it is because the program itself has suffered a mishap—a Preference file could be corrupted, or you might have been fortunate enough to have found a minor bug. Also, if you have installed a new utility, extension, or control panel, the new arrival could cause a problem with the application.

Many applications have support files, such as dictionaries and file translators, and sometimes they use extensions or other types of files. If any of these files or the application file gets damaged, your program will cease to work properly. The procedures for troubleshooting an application can be found in Chapter 18.

Corrupted Data Files

Some application problems are very easy to figure out. If your Mac crashes every time you attempt to open a specific file, there is a very good chance that the file is your problem, not your System or even the application. Try opening a different file or creating a new one. If you don't have any problems with another file, you can be fairly sure that the file itself is the cause of the problem. Replacing the file, from your backup, could fix the problem.

To double-check a problem with a file, copy the file onto another disk and try using the file again. If, while you are copying the file to another disk, you receive an error dialog saying that the file could not be read, it means that the CRC check failed as your Mac was reading the file. The problem could be a temporary hiccup; try copying it again. If the copy doesn't work a second time, its failure to copy could indicate more serious problems, such as a bad sector, a corrupted directory, or a damaged file. At this point, leave the file alone. Don't trash it and don't use it. Go to your backup, get a copy of the file, and try using the copy. It is possible that your copy is damaged as well, especially if it is an old file.

Files can go bad in several ways. Often, a file is damaged during an application crash, especially if the file is open or in use. Old files are also susceptible to damage due to disk deterioration. Usually file problems are indicative of a problem with your hard drive. If you suspect that the problem is more than just a bad file, perform a maintenance check on your hard drive.

Hardware Problems

As a rule, hardware problems are straightforward and easy to diagnose. You know you have a hardware problem when your Mac doesn't start, the monitor makes funny noises and flickers, a key does not work on the keyboard, or smoke comes from one of your peripherals. These are all immediate and obvious problems.

Hardware problems become a bit more obscure when you have a Sad Mac only when the computer is first turned on every morning. Or, you can work for several hours, and suddenly your Mac or the video goes out; yet when you come back after a couple of hours, it is fine. Another type of problem occurs when your Mac worked perfectly yesterday, but today it will not turn on. All of these consistent and intermittent problems can be hardware-related.

The Mac is a well-made machine, but there are times when it will break. Because the Mac is usually a reliable machine, hardware problems are not usually suspected, which therefore makes them harder to detect. Chapter 17 goes through detailed steps for troubleshooting your hardware. The rest of this section looks at some problems that could be hardware- or software-related. Because it is software that drives your Mac, sometimes what appears to be a hardware malfunction is really a software problem.

This section offers some specific suggestions, but the real intent here is to alert you to some of the problems and to get you to think about what might be going on. As some of these problems are discussed, think about possible solutions.

When Hardware Is Most Likely to Fail

Your Mac is particularly vulnerable to hardware problems at two times. The first is when it is newly unpacked. All new components are more likely to fail than those that have been in service for several months. The other problem time comes after you upgrade your system in some way, such as adding memory or installing a new hard drive.

When your Mac has been operating with a specific configuration for a period of time, changing the configuration can result in failures with the power supply or other components. New additions put an additional strain on the power supply. Although this is not a common occurrence, it does happen. If you just had an upgrade and your Mac goes on the fritz, you can bet the culprit is your upgrade.

Intermittent Failures and Memory

One hardware problem you are likely to encounter is a bad memory module. Sometimes, a memory problem is an intermittent failing, occurring after your Mac has been on for a couple of hours or when you first start it up. The components (memory chips) expand as they warm up and contract when they cool down. The result is that a component fails to make a good connection, causing the Mac to register an error.

If the problem happens after the Mac has been on for a while, it crashes with a System error and then registers a Sad Mac when you try to restart it. After it has had a chance to cool down, it will start as if nothing had happened. The opposite is true if the component is not connecting when your Mac is cold. It registers an error on the first few startup attempts; then, either after you have left the power turned on for a few minutes or after a couple of startup attempts, the Mac boots and all the problems disappear.

In either instance, take your Mac into an Apple Authorized Service Center and have a technician check out the problem. One way to minimize the chance of this problem developing is to leave your Mac on all the time. Leaving it on minimizes the wear and tear on the internal components caused by repeated heating and cooling. The risks in leaving your Mac on are about the same as leaving a television on. I have left my Mac turned on for about three years, turning it off only when I'm out of town for a week or more.

If you choose to do this, you need a good surge protector that will shut off your Mac if your power drops below a safe operating level. This safeguard is used to prevent your Mac from being struck by a power surge while you are away, or even while you are there working on it. Usually, a power surge (an extra high amount of power coming through your lines) occurs after there has been a drop in power.

Power Supply Failures

The power supply is the component in your Mac that converts your household current to a voltage that your Mac can use; it is a *step-down transformer* that takes the power down from 110 volts to 12 volts. When the power supply burns out, your Mac will not work. It can also fail intermittently, as previously described.

Logic Board Problems

If you try to start your Mac and you do not hear the startup *boing*, you could have a logic-board problem that can be fixed only by an Authorized Apple Technician or an independent computer repair technician. If your Mac is under warranty, go to your Apple Dealer; otherwise, it will probably cost less to find an independent repair technician to fix your problem.

Hard-Drive Problems

Next to problems with your System, hard-drive problems are the most common. The hard drive or, rather, the software on your hard drive controls everything your Mac does. If you have an unreliable hard drive, your Mac will be unreliable. Anything serious that goes wrong with your hard drive has an immediate effect. If your hard drive crashes and asks to be reinitialized, you know that you have problems; if you reinitialize the drive, you have worse problems.

These things happen more frequently than you might imagine. For this reason, your first line of defense against hard-drive problems is a current backup of your data. If you do not maintain a regular backup schedule, you are begging for a time-consuming and possibly expensive data recovery attempt—all data recovery procedures are attempts; it is not a successful data recovery until you've gotten all your data back intact.

The problem with data recovery is that you never know if it works until the data is actually retrieved. If you hire someone to perform the recovery, you have to rely on his or her judgment, and even if the technician cannot get your data back, you still have to pay for the time—$60 to $100 per hour can result in a very hefty bill.

Otherwise, hard drives are not suspected of being the cause of problems as often as they should be. Any problem your Mac has that appears to be System-related can actually be a hard-drive problem. What is worse is that you can check a hard drive using the best software utilities around and still not detect a problem; this is the reason why you should reformat your drive at least once a year, preferably once every six months.

Usually, to find a hard-drive problem not detected by your hard-disk utility (Norton Utilities or Central Points MacTools), you have to go through the entire System and application troubleshooting process. Only after you have eliminated all other possibilities do you suspect your drive—which means you could spend a lot of time trying to fix a problem.

If your drive boots and your System runs, these two conditions do not mean that you don't have a hard-drive problem. The obvious problems are a total crash, as described at the beginning of this section. Drives that do not start your System at all are always immediately suspect, but beyond the obvious, you must carefully consider all of your Mac's symptoms before deciding what's going on.

The more subtle things that can happen to a hard drive are corrupted directories, damaged drivers, and data errors caused by bad sectors. All the low-level data structures, as mentioned in Chapter 10, can sustain damage. And, just because they are damaged, it does not mean that your Mac does not work. People have run their Macs with drives that have problems for months and have never known. These same drives will one day crash unless the trouble is detected during a maintenance check.

If you have any of the following symptoms, check your hard drive immediately:

❖ Files or folders that cannot be found

❖ Files or folders that cannot be trashed, even though they are not locked

❖ Files or folders that disappear

❖ Files or folders that do not open

❖ Frequent System errors while in the Finder, especially after you've reinstalled your System

❖ Requests to repair a hard disk at startup

When you experience any of these problems, troubleshoot your SCSI bus as described in Chapter 17, "Macintosh Hardware Problems." Then perform a complete maintenance check as described in Chapter 15, "Avoiding Problems." After the maintenance check, go through the procedures outlined in Chapter 19, "Disk Crashes and Data Recovery."

Hard-Drive Failures

Most hard-drive problems are software- or System-related; even though this is not always the case, it should be your first assumption. If you use computers with any regularity, however, you will probably experience a hard-drive hardware failure. Hard drives, on a hardware level, can have a variety of problems. External hard drives have been known to have power-supply failures, head crashes, logic-board failures, and *stiction* problems (stiction is a computer term for sticky platters in a drive; see Chapter

19 for more details). An internal drive can also suffer from all these ills, except for the power supply because it is powered by the Macintosh power supply. Sometimes, it is not easy to tell what has happened, other than that the drive suddenly no longer works.

Most of the hardware-level problems you could experience are detailed in Chapter 17. Here, it is enough to say that hard drives are electromechanical devices and that they can and do fail. There are only a couple of things you can do to determine the hard drive's condition without removing it from its case or from the Mac and checking it out. If the drive is under warranty, removing it will void your manufacturer's warranty, so checking it at this level is not covered here.

Basically, if you cannot access your drive with your formatting software, it is in serious trouble. If your cables are properly attached and you cannot access your drive with its formatter, you probably have a dead drive. Exercise caution before you pronounce any drive dead. If it has a stiction problem, it is still possible to make it work and get your data. Also, if you get the Sad Mac, your drive is not dead—it has just lost its driver.

Internal Hard Drives

It is harder to tell if your internal hard drive has died rather than your external drive because there is no fan to listen to and you cannot hear the drive power up. You must rely on software or a technician to make a final determination.

Forcing the Mac to Ignore the SCSI Bus

If your hard-drive driver (or drivers) is bad, you will find yourself in a Catch-22. You cannot turn on your Mac without a Sad Mac, and, if the drive with the bad driver is external, the only way your Mac can start is to remove the drive. Apple anticipated this problem, however, and provided a means to access your drive.

If you have a bad driver, you can boot your Mac by using a clean startup disk. Make sure your formatter is on it, and hold down the Command + Option + Shift + Delete or Backspace keys simultaneously as you start your Mac. You have to be manually dexterous to accomplish this procedure, but the effort is worth the trouble: The Mac will ignore the SCSI bus as it starts. Your Mac will boot off the floppy, and none of your hard drives will be mounted.

At this point, use your formatter to reinstall your driver. Of course, you have to know which drive ID has the bad driver. Follow the instructions that came with your drive, and be careful—the process of reinstalling your driver can cause you to lose all your data. If you need to perform this procedure, be sure to recover your data first (see Chapter 19 for more on data recovery).

Printer Problems

You have finished your report, and you have to present it in 10 minutes. You select Print from the File menu and nothing happens. Now, you're in trouble. What do you do?

Most printer problems result in the inability to print. It is very easy to know that you have a problem, but figuring out why is another story. You could have printing difficulty for several reasons—they range from being out of toner or ink to a bad cable connection to improper system configurations. Chapter 17 includes a section on printer troubleshooting.

Network Difficulties

Like printing problems, network problems are immediately manifest: You are unable to connect to any of your network resources. If you work in a collaborative environment, network problems can be serious because they prevent access to data that people need.

Networks are a combination of wires, connectors, your Mac's System software, and configuration settings. All of these elements make networks difficult to troubleshoot. Once again, you will find network troubleshooting discussed in Chapter 17.

Summary

This chapter lightly touched on some of the problems your Mac can have. Sometimes, Macintosh problems are like a flat tire on a car. You go out one day to drive somewhere, get in the car, and it is only after you've started down the road that you hear and feel the flat tire. And, even then, you may go a block or two before you realize that something is wrong.

You don't think much about car problems because you're usually so familiar with your car that you know when something is not right, even when you don't know what the trouble might be. With your Mac, you may not know when things are wrong. From the information in this chapter, you will have a better idea of what can go wrong and what to look for. Think about what you've read in this chapter. Try to figure out some of the principles at work, and think about what your Mac is doing or not doing when these problems occur. This information will help as you set forth to fix any problem.

Macintosh Hardware Problems

I n this chapter I discuss some of the most common hardware problems and their solutions. This section briefly looks at how to distinguish hardware malfunctions from software errors. Usually, when you have a hardware failure, there is no question that something is very wrong. The only question is—what? This chapter helps you through the process of figuring out what is wrong and determining how to fix it in the following sections:

- ❖ First Steps (Hardware Troubleshooting)
- ❖ Peripheral Troubleshooting
- ❖ Troubleshooting the SCSI Bus
- ❖ Printers
- ❖ Troubleshooting Your Network
- ❖ Special Considerations (or Odds and Ends)

Because your Mac is a combination of hardware and software, some of these sections discuss software and configuration problems.

First Steps (Hardware Troubleshooting)

Hardware problems are either very obvious or very subtle. There are times when the Mac just dies, and you have no doubt that the machine has suffered some type of mishap. If you plug in or turn on your Mac and it begins to smoke, you know immediately that something is broken. The jargon used by technicians for this type of occurrence is "The Mac smoked" or "The Mac is toast."

If your Mac isn't smoking but it's not working either, you have to determine what's wrong. If your Mac does not completely boot, review the entire startup sequence described later in this chapter. By carefully watching your machine boot, you can determine at what stage of the startup process the error occurs. If you accurately pinpoint when your Mac crashes, you may know what caused the crash.

The next section outlines the basic troubleshooting steps to go through when dealing with hardware problems; then, it details the actual steps for fixing some of the problems.

Basic Troubleshooting Steps

As elementary as this may sound, the first things to check when something does not work properly are each of your hardware connections. Say that you have a Macintosh of any type and a couple of hard drives, all connected to a master switch so that you can turn on one switch and go to work. One morning, you sit down and turn on your master switch, your Mac goes *boing*, and all you get is the blinking disk icon with a question mark.

If you assume that everything is as you left it, you might not discover that your external hard drive had somehow had its power cord disconnected during the night. As a result, you could spend several hours trying to get your system working and conclude that something was broken; you would probably end up calling someone in to fix it. Always make sure that everything is connected properly; check each of the following:

- ❖ Power switches
- ❖ Power cables
- ❖ Printer cables
- ❖ Modem cables
- ❖ Network cables
- ❖ Monitor cables
- ❖ SCSI cables

Turn off, disconnect, and reconnect the cable for each device; then, turn it back on. Work methodically, going from left to right or right to left, and check each cable. Do this yourself, or you will have no way of knowing if everything is connected. This step is so critical that if you call a good consultant because your system will not start, the first question he or she will (or should) ask is, "Is the power turned on?" followed by "Is the Mac plugged in or the (generic) device connected?" The consultant will probably ask you to physically check these items while you're still on the phone. Check your cables and power sources; only after these are eliminated as potential problems can you go to the next step.

Troubleshooting Sequences

In this section, you find a set of troubleshooting sequences. The sequences contain steps and are designed to help you either fix the problem or identify what is wrong; this process is usually quick and simple. Four troubleshooting sequences are presented; each sequence is a starting point. Pick the one you need; you may have to work through a couple of the sequences.

When Connecting and Disconnecting Cables

Whenever you connect or disconnect cables from your Macintosh or any peripheral, shut down your Mac and turn off the power. Failure to do so could result in damage to your Mac and possible injury to you. *Never* connect a cable to any device that is turned on.

The only time these sequences can't be used is when your Mac has a monitor problem. If you have no visual display, take your Mac to an Apple Authorized Service Center unless you have a second monitor you can use to test your Mac.

To troubleshoot your Mac, start with Sequence One and follow the instructions.

Sequence One

If your Mac does not start at all, with no light(s) and no sound, the first part of the troubleshooting process involves these steps:

1. Disconnect and reconnect all cables and connections. If your Mac has an internal NuBus or PDS card that you can easily access, open your Mac and make sure the card is firmly seated. (Instructions for installing a card are in your Macintosh's manual.) When your Mac does not respond in any way, check the power outlet by plugging in a lamp.

2. After checking all cables and your power source, try starting your Mac again.

3. If it doesn't start, there is only one more question: Were you trying to start the Mac using your keyboard's Power On switch? If you were, try to start the Mac with its power switch.

4. If the Mac starts, your problem is either your keyboard or the keyboard's cable.

5. If the Mac does not start, with no noise of any kind or no video image, take it to an Apple Authorized Service Center.

Sequence Two

If your Mac displays some sign of life, such as a Sad Mac icon, musical chimes, video flickering, or some other noise (anything other than the blinking disk icon), follow these steps:

1. Complete step 1 from Sequence One.

2. Did you get a Sad Mac?

3. If the answer is yes, did musical chimes accompany the Sad Mac?

4. If the answer is yes, is the Sad Mac's class code 0F?

5. If the answer is yes, then go to Chapter 19, "Disk Crashes and Data Recovery."

6. If the answer to any of the questions in steps 3, 4, or 5 is *no*, disconnect any external SCSI devices and start over.

7. On your second pass through this process, one of the following conditions will occur:

    ❖ Your Mac starts. If your Mac starts, go to the section "Troubleshooting the SCSI Bus," later in this chapter.

    ❖ Your Mac did not start, and the Sad Mac code was the same as the first time. You probably have a memory SIMM or DIMM that has gone bad, or there is a problem with your logic board. Take your Mac to an Authorized Service technician.

    ❖ Your Mac did not start and the Sad Mac code is different, but it does not have the class code 0F. This means that the Mac's internal diagnostics have found more than one problem. This could also indicate an intermittent problem that is heat-related; take your Mac to an Authorized Service technician.

    ❖ The Mac starts to display the Smiling Mac icon and then crashes. This means that the driver for the internal hard drive is probably damaged; go to Chapter 19, "Disk Crashes and Data Recovery."

Sequence Three

Your Mac displays the Question Mark icon, or it repeatedly displays the Smiling Mac icon. The Question Mark icon means that the Mac's internal diagnostics all passed, but the Mac does not recognize the internal hard disk. The repeating Smiling Mac icon means that your Mac recognizes the hard drive, but the System file is missing or damaged.

You should follow these steps:

1. Perform step 1 from Sequence One.

2. Insert your clean System floppy disk and start your Mac. Any one of the following events could occur:

    ❖ Your Mac starts and your hard drive is visible on the Desktop. Your System file and/or your boot blocks are corrupted; go to Chapter 18, "System and Application Troubleshooting."

    ❖ Your Mac starts and, as it starts, it crashes and you receive the Sad Mac icon. This means that your hard disk's driver is damaged; go to Chapter 19, "Disk Crashes and Data Recovery."

    ❖ Your Mac boots and everything appears to be fine. If you disconnected any SCSI devices, you probably have a SCSI problem; go to the section "Troubleshooting the SCSI Bus," later in this chapter.

Sequence Four

If, when you boot with a clean System floppy, your Mac does not start or rejects your clean System floppy, try these steps again with another floppy disk:

1. If your Mac rejects the floppy disk, either it does not have a System file or the floppy disk is damaged.

2. Listen to the floppy drive to see if it is reading the disk; you can hear the drive make noise as it reads the floppy disk.

3. If you hear the Mac finish reading the floppy—this process could take several minutes—and you do not see anything on your monitor or your Mac still doesn't boot, you either have a video/monitor problem or some other problem that exceeds the scope of this book. Take your Mac to an Apple Authorized Service Center.

   During this last sequence, if you need to eject your floppy disk, hold down the mouse button as you turn on the Mac. The first thing your Mac should do is eject the floppy disk.

4. If your Mac starts, the first floppy you were using is bad.

Peripheral Troubleshooting

When you have only one Mac and one of your peripherals decides not to work, you can have a real problem; it is very difficult to test a peripheral without a second Mac. If your Mac is the problem, you can't completely test the peripheral. Consider the situation when a modem that suddenly fails to work: You don't know whether the problem is the serial port on your Mac, the modem, the cable that connects your Mac to the modem, or the software you're using. You have to check four things before you have an answer.

When you have a problem with a peripheral device, the cause is usually a poor connection or a bad cable, which is why you should always have at least one extra cable for each of your peripherals. If you have a peripheral that isn't working, test it with a different cable and, if possible, on a different Mac. It is advantageous if you have another peripheral that you can test with the Mac.

The following sequences can be used to test a peripheral device. Start with Sequence One and follow the instructions. If you are testing a serial device and have a PowerBook with only one serial port, or a Power Macintosh, make sure AppleTalk is turned off. Open the Chooser desk accessory and turn AppleTalk off before starting these sequences.

Sequence One

Check your cable and power connections as follows:

1. Disconnect and reconnect all cables and connections. If your peripheral does not respond in any way, check the power outlet by plugging in a lamp. All peripherals have an indicator light so that you can tell if they are receiving power.

2. If the peripheral is receiving power, make sure it is turned on.

   ❖ If your peripheral does not indicate that it is receiving power, call the manufacturer's technical support department or take the peripheral back to the computer store.

3. Some peripherals can perform a self-test; all printers and some scanners have this ability. If your device has this ability, perform a self-test (check its manual for instructions).

4. Double-check all of your peripheral's software settings.

5. Try to use the device.

Sequence Two

If the device does not work, suspect the cable:

1. Use a different cable with the peripheral.

2. Repeat steps 2 through 4 in Sequence One.

Sequence Three

If the device does not work, try using it on a different Mac if you have access to one:

1. Repeat all the steps in Sequence One using a different Mac.

2. If the peripheral does not work on a second Mac, it is a fair bet that the device is broken.

3. If the device works on the other Mac, then your problem is either your Mac or your software.

Sequence Four

If the peripheral is a serial device, try using it on your Mac's Printer port:

1. If you are connected to a network through your Printer port, open the Chooser and turn off AppleTalk.

2. Connect the peripheral to your Printer port.

3. Set the peripheral's software so that it uses the Printer port.

4. Try using the device.

Sequence Five

If your device still doesn't work, the problem could be its software; follow these steps:

1. Reinstall the peripheral's software.

2. Repeat steps 2 through 5 in Sequence One.

3. If you were able to test the peripheral on another Mac and it worked, the problem is either your Mac's logic board or your System software.

If your System has not been crashing and works properly for everything else, it is fair to assume that the problem lies in your Mac. Before you can even be sure that the Mac is the problem, you have to test it with another similar peripheral. If the second peripheral doesn't work, then the problem most likely is your Mac. It is time to call an expert or take your Mac to the service center.

Troubleshooting the SCSI Bus

Your SCSI bus will probably cause you more grief than any other aspect of your Macintosh because the SCSI bus, although a standard, does not always work according to the rules. Some manufacturers do not adhere to the standards, and Apple implements its own modifications as well.

Problems with the SCSI bus range from devices not being accessed to shutting down your entire system. Because you can have as many as eight devices on the SCSI bus, you could have a problem with the bus itself, any of the devices on it, or any of the cables connecting the devices.

Some of the information that follows has been covered in Chapter 10 in relation to hard drives. SCSI principles are the same for hard drives as well as other SCSI devices, so the following is a brief review, with the addition of a section on bad SCSI chips.

SCSI Cable Problems

If you are lucky, your problem is only a bad SCSI cable. If you do not have a good or new SCSI cable to use in the troubleshooting process, though, you could spend hours trying to find the problem. I urge you to keep a new or known good one on hand.

A known good SCSI cable is one that has been used on your system or another system without problems. If you know your cable is good, the problem is somewhere else.

SCSI Termination

Technically, your Macintosh SCSI bus should be terminated at the beginning and end of the SCSI chain, with the first and last physical devices. Your Macintosh is not considered a part of this equation unless you use a Quadra or a PowerBook. In the case of the Quadra, your Mac is the first device on the chain and is already terminated; this means that your internal hard drive is not terminated. The only device that should be terminated is the last one in the chain. Also, the Macintosh IIfx

PowerBooks and the SCSI Bus

If you use a PowerBook, you may have to experiment with SCSI termination. The internal hard drive in a PowerBook is only partially terminated, and PowerBooks do not provide termination power to the SCSI bus. When you connect external SCSI devices to your PowerBook, the rules say that the first and last external devices must be terminated, and it is likely that one of your external devices will have to supply termination power.

Also, some SCSI devices are incompatible with your PowerBook. In a sense, all bets are off. If you try the recommended termination scheme (the first external device and the last) and your Mac won't boot or you can't see all the drives, you have to experiment by removing termination and maybe even using a third terminator in the middle of the chain.

Because PowerBooks can be a problem, before you start experimenting back up your PowerBook. SCSI problems can cause hard-disk directory damage on any Macintosh, and you stand a chance of damaging your hard drive's directory and other low-level data structures. Be careful.

requires a special terminator, which can be obtained from your Apple Dealer, on the last device in your chain.

Any internally terminated device on your SCSI bus must be turned on, or none of your SCSI devices will be visible to the Macintosh. On too many occasions, someone turns on the Mac, has no hard drives, and thinks all the drives are dead. The only problem is that an internally terminated drive is not turned on or that the power cord has slipped out. Always check for this if you have a problem.

At times an external SCSI device will act as if it is terminated, even though it is not. Two devices that act this way are the NEC CDR 35 and CDR 36 portable CD ROM drives. Both of these drives have caused people to lose hair, along with their patience, because these drives do not work in the middle of the chain, with an external terminator attached, or with an internally terminated drive between the drive and the Mac if the Mac has an internal drive.

Microtech scanners can also act in a similar manner. Even though Microtech says the scanners are unterminated, in most circumstances, the scanner acts as if it is terminated. Therefore, it, too, has to go on the end of the SCSI chain without an external terminator.

Finally, a cable can sometimes act as a terminator. The cables most likely to do this are long cables, six feet or more. If you find a cable that causes this problem, take it back to the manufacturer and get a new one. All in all, if you have trouble and you arrive at a solution that works, even though it does not conform to the standard rules, adopt this philosophy: If it works, don't fix it.

SCSI ID Numbers

The rule governing SCSI ID numbers is very simple: You can have any SCSI ID number from 0 to 6, with no two numbers being duplicated on your SCSI bus. If you duplicate SCSI ID numbers on your SCSI bus, none of your devices will work, and you might even get the Sad Mac on bootup. If you need to determine what your ID numbers are, follow the instructions in your manual for setting the ID number, use a software utility such as SCSIProbe, or contact the manufacturer of the device and have it help you.

A Bad SCSI Chip

The hardest problem to troubleshoot is a SCSI chip that has gone bad on your logic board. In most instances, if the chip that controls all SCSI communication fails, no SCSI device will work on your machine.

The SCSI chip can also fail when the only SCSI device that works is your internal drive; all external devices fail to operate but are fine when attached to another Mac. In either of these instances, you need to find a technician who can repair your logic board. If you elect to take your Mac to an Apple Dealer, it will tell you that you need a new logic board because dealers do not perform component- or board-level repairs. Some companies provide or exchange logic boards at prices lower than an Authorized Service Center. One such company is Pre-Owned Electronics in Bedford, Massachusetts.

The Troubleshooting Steps

You have found your way here if your Mac is not booting properly or if you are having problems with a SCSI device. In principle, troubleshooting the SCSI bus follows steps similar to those for troubleshooting peripheral devices. Where the steps differ is in the number of devices you have to troubleshoot. To troubleshoot SCSI devices and the SCSI bus, use the following sequences. If you are testing multiple SCSI devices, write down the SCSI ID number and whether the device is internally terminated for each device you test.

Sequence One

To run your Mac without any external SCSI devices, follow these steps:

1. Disconnect all SCSI devices from your Mac.
2. Start your Mac and confirm that it and the internal hard drive(s) are working properly.
3. If the Mac is fine, check the SCSI ID number of your internal drive(s) and go to the next sequence. Otherwise, go back to "First Steps (Hardware Troubleshooting)" or to Chapter 19, "System and Application Troubleshooting."

Sequence Two

To test a device for internal SCSI termination, follow these steps:

1. Check the SCSI ID of the external device. Change the number if it has the same ID as one of your internal drives. Usually, your internal hard drive has SCSI ID 0, and the CD-ROM has SCSI ID 3.
2. Check the SCSI termination of the external device. If it is not terminated, put an external terminator on it.
3. Attach the device to your Mac.
4. If you do not know whether the device is internally terminated, turn it off.
5. Turn on your Mac; if you see the Blinking Disk icon, the drive is internally terminated.

Sequence Three

To test the device, follow these steps:

1. Turn on the external device.
2. Turn on your Mac.
3. If your Mac boots and the device mounts or works, it is fine.
4. If your Mac does not boot, there is a problem with the SCSI device, your cable, or its driver.

Sequence Four

To change the cable, follow these steps:

1. Put a different cable on the SCSI device.
2. Repeat Sequence Three.
3. If your Mac does not boot, there is still some problem with the SCSI device, your cable, or its driver:
   ❖ If you know the cable is good because it works on other SCSI devices, you can eliminate the cable as the problem. It is possible to have more than one bad SCSI cable.
   ❖ If you are trying to connect a hard drive, you probably have a bad driver. Perform the steps in Sequence Five.
   ❖ If you are using a SCSI scanner or printer, reinstall the device's driver software on your Mac and repeat Sequence Four. If the device fails to work after a second try, it probably has a problem and needs to go in for repair. Before sending the device off for repair, test your Mac with another SCSI device.
   ❖ If this is the only SCSI device you use, your SCSI chip could be bad and unable to work with external devices. Take both your Mac and the device into the shop.

Sequence Five

To test an externally terminated hard drive's driver, follow these steps:

1. Connect your hard drive after double-checking the SCSI ID number; do not turn on the drive.
2. Turn on your Mac.
3. After the Mac boots, turn on the external hard drive.
4. Run the formatting software for the external hard drive.
5. You can use the formatter to mount the disk or reinstall the drive's driver; reinstalling the driver is recommended.
6. If you mount the drive *before* reinstalling the driver and the Mac crashes, then the driver is bad. Repeat this sequence and reinstall the driver.
7. If you mount the drive *after* reinstalling the driver and the Mac crashes, then the drive needs to be reformatted. To recover data from the drive, go to Chapter 19, "Disk Crashes and Data Recovery."

Sequence Six

To test an internal terminated hard drive's driver, follow these steps:

1. Connect your hard drive after double-checking the SCSI ID number. Turn on the drive.
2. Insert your clean System disk into the Mac.
3. Turn on your Mac and hold down the Option + Command + Shift + Backspace or Delete keys simultaneously. You should be holding down the keys when the Mac sounds its startup chime; this is difficult to do, and you may have to repeat these first three steps several times before you can start.
4. After the Mac boots, release the keys.
5. Run the formatting software for the external hard drive.
6. You can use the formatter to mount the disk or reinstall the drive's driver; reinstalling the driver is recommended.
7. If you mount the drive *before* reinstalling the driver and the Mac crashes; then the driver is bad. Repeat this sequence and reinstall the driver.
8. If you mount the drive *after* reinstalling the driver and the Mac crashes; then the drive needs to be reformatted. To recover data from the drive, go to Chapter 19, "Disk Crashes and Data Recovery."

This is a very difficult sequence to perform. The command key sequence forces the Mac to ignore the SCSI bus during the boot sequence, but your drives will mount when the Mac boots. It is possible, even likely, that the external drive will try to mount as well. If the external drive's driver is damaged, it is likely to crash your Mac as it mounts. There is a way around this, but it is a "try at your own risk" procedure. If you try this and fry your Mac or your hard drive, you are 100 percent responsible for the damage: Repeat the steps in Sequence Six, but start with step 2 and, in between steps 4 and 5, perform these steps:

❖ Turn on the hard drive.

❖ Connect the hard drive to the Mac.

Then, proceed with the rest of the steps; reinstall only the driver—do not try to mount the hard drive.

Sequence Seven

After reinstalling the driver, do the following:

1. Turn on the external drive.
2. Boot your Mac.
3. If everything works, the drive is working.
4. If the Mac crashes as the external drive mounts, it has to be reformatted. To recover data from the drive, go to Chapter 19, "Disk Crashes and Data Recovery."

Sequence Eight

To test additional devices, do the following:

1. If you have several drives or SCSI devices, test each one individually before you put your SCSI chain back together.
2. Perform Sequences Two through Seven for each device you have.

Sequence Nine

After you have tested each device, you can put your SCSI chain back together. Repeat this sequence for each SCSI device that you use. As you add devices to your SCSI chain, make sure your total cable length does not exceed 18 feet.

To rebuild your SCSI chain, follow these steps:

1. Check the device's SCSI ID number against those of the other devices on your SCSI chain. Make sure each device has its own number.
2. If the device is not the last one on the chain (please note the exceptions in the earlier "Termination" section), make sure it is not terminated.
3. Make sure the last device on the chain is terminated externally or internally.
4. Insert the device into your SCSI chain.
5. Turn on all external SCSI devices.
6. Turn on your Mac.
7. If your Mac crashes as it starts up, double-check steps 1 through 6; then, try again.

8. If your Mac crashes again, or if a device is not visible on the Desktop, through its software, or in a SCSI checking utility, you probably have a bad cable.

9. Repeat steps 1 through 6 while using a different cable.

If your Mac still fails, start Sequence Nine over, using the last device added as the first device. At some point, you will find the other conflicting device. It is likely that you have the rare pleasure of having two SCSI devices that do not like each other and are incompatible. At that point, talk to their manufacturers to see if they are indeed incompatible or if one of them is defective.

If you go through these sequences in the order in which they are presented to troubleshoot your SCSI bus and still have trouble, take your entire System to the shop or have a technician come to you. There is little else you can do at this point, except for one more trick. You can try experimenting with the order of SCSI devices on the chain. Sometimes one drive has to physically precede another before it will work. This, too, is a rare occurrence, but it does happen.

Printers

When you have problems printing, you can go through a few quick steps to find the problem. Usually, this is not a difficult process, but you must start with a plan. This section covers troubleshooting problems for a Macintosh printer.

Defining and Fixing the Problem

Before you can fix anything, you have to figure out the problem. With printing, the problems are fairly straightforward. Use the following to plot your troubleshooting strategy.

If you can't print at all, your problem can be either software or hardware. Unless you know your problem is software-related, you must rule out hardware as a problem first.

To check the hardware:

1. First, check whether the printer is turned on.

2. If the printer is turned on, turn it off and then turn it back on.

3. If it still doesn't print, check the cables. Is everything attached properly? If you use an AppleTalk printer, you must be able to see the printer in the Chooser, as shown in Figure 17.1.

4. Open the Chooser and highlight the type of printer you want to use.

When you open the Chooser, if you do not see your printer icons, then your Mac has started from a System other than the one you normally use. This means that you either started from a disk drive you normally do not use or that you have a second System somewhere on your hard disk. If this is the case, restart from the

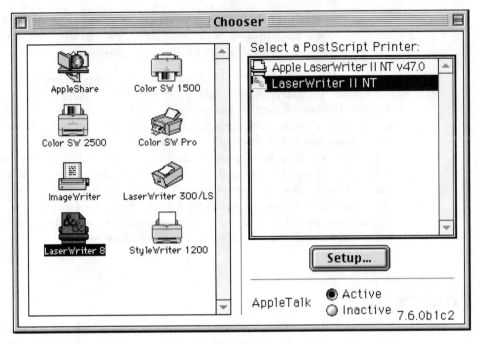

Figure 17.1   *Locating your printer in the Chooser.*

Disk Tools disk included with your System disk and trash the second System folder. After you do that, reinstall your System just in case any damage was done in the process.

If you can see the networked printer in the Chooser, then you know that the Mac and the printer are connected and communicating; your problem is probably software-related, not hardware.

If you are using an ImageWriter or a printer that is not an AppleTalk device, do the following to determine if you have a hardware problem:

1. Is the printer online? Almost all printers can be taken offline, which means that they are turned on but not communicating with the Macintosh. A printer that is offline talks only to itself. If you do not know how to tell if your printer is online, check your manual.

2. Force the printer to run a self-test. Every printer has the ability to test itself. If you do not know how to do this, follow the instructions in the printer's manual; if it completes the self-test, the printer is probably working. If the printer fails the self-test, then it is probably broken. Proceed with the next step. If the next step is not the problem, you probably have to take the printer to the shop for repairs.

3. Check the ribbon, toner cartridge, or ink cartridge. Several models of printers do not work if they sense that they are out of their imaging media. This

is not the case with the ImageWriter; it will happily print even if the ribbon is dry.

By this point, you will know if you have a hardware problem with your printer.

Software Problems

The first rule for troubleshooting a printer software problem is to start from the Finder. Because you probably have a problem printing from a specific application, you are actually several layers away from knowing where the breakdown is taking place.

Follow these steps to pinpoint the area where the trouble is occurring:

1. Turn off any print spooler in use. If you have a print spooler installed, it is possible to print all day long and have the output disappear on its way to the printer. Turn off the spooler; if you use a StyleWriter or a laser printer, turn off the background printing in the Chooser (see Figure 17.2). If you can't turn off the spooler, remove the spooler's extension or control panel from your System folder, then reboot your Mac. When you use Macintosh Desktop printers, the Start Print Queue menu option must be checked; see Figure 17.3. If the Stop Print Queue menu option is checked, your Mac will not print.

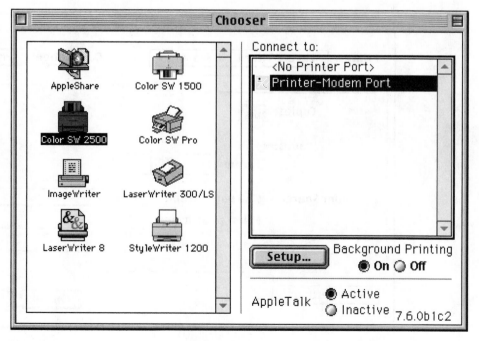

Figure 17.2 *The background printing option.*

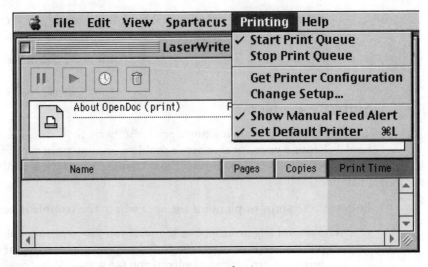

Figure 17.3 *The Desktop printer menu selection.*

2. Go to the Chooser and select the printer. Your Mac may have forgotten which printer to use. When you use the *Print* command, the Print dialog box always contains the name of the device to which you are trying to print. Figure 17.4 shows a Print dialog box.

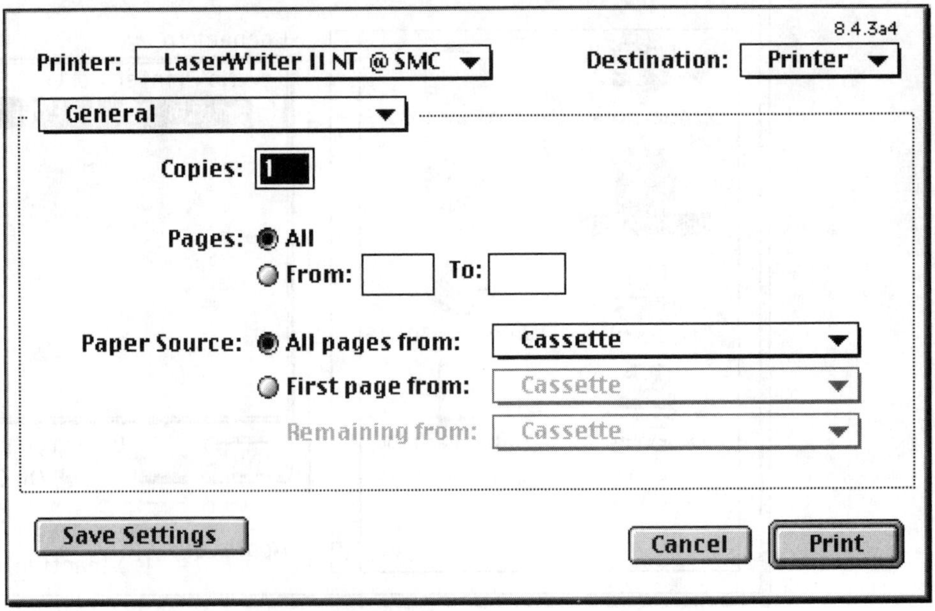

Figure 17.4 *The Print dialog box; notice the printer type and name.*

3. Print a window from the Finder. For the moment, forget the problem you are having with any application that will not print. Go to the Finder, open a folder or disk window, and use the *Print Window...* command from the File menu in the Finder (Figure 17.5).

If your printer prints at this point, either you have fixed your problem or the problem is within the program you were using. The other possibility is that everything you were printing is queued up in your print spooler. If this is the case, turn on the spooler and use it to check the queue; maybe all you have to do is instruct it to print.

If, on the other hand, you cannot print from the Finder, your problem is with either your hardware or your System. If you are absolutely sure that everything is connected properly and that the printer is turned on and online, then reinstall your printer drivers. The best way to do this is to open your Extensions folder, view the contents by type, find your Chooser extensions, and trash your printer drivers. After you have put them in the trash and emptied it, reinstall your System. When you reinstall your System, be sure to install the printers you want. After you have installed the System, repeat the preceding steps. If the printer still does not print, perform a Clean Install of your System, as described in Chapter 6.

Once you have a clean System, if you still can't print, you probably have a hardware problem. Try printing from the modem port (ImageWriter or StyleWriter only). Make sure you change the port setting in the Chooser. If you can print from the modem port but not from the printer port, you need to check your modem software. There is a good chance that your fax software is using the same port you've selected for your printer.

Figure 17.5   *The Print Window... command.*

At this point, if you still can't print, you may want to take your Mac and printer to a local service shop. The problem could be a bad cable; if you have an extra cable or can get one from another Mac, try swapping cables. Most home users have only one cable, printer, and Mac. You have to go to the computer store to get another cable, so you might as well take your System with you. The dealer can help you troubleshoot the problem and check the cable at the same time. You might save yourself a second trip if it turns out there is some obscure problem with your Mac or printer.

For those of you who have a second Mac, hook it up to the printer and see if the printer works. The likelihood of two Macs not working with a printer is very slim. If both Macs fail to print, then your printer has (or is) the problem. Likewise, if your printer works with the second Mac, the problem is the original computer.

Once you can print from the Finder, see if the problem still exists with your application. Start the program you had trouble with and try to print. If you cannot, the problem is with the program—a program setting is incorrect, or the application is corrupted and should be reinstalled.

After you reinstall the program, if your printer does not print, make sure that you installed the program properly. Check the instructions in the manual for printing. If you are sure that everything is correct, call the application's technical-support department. As long as your Mac can print from the Finder, there is nothing wrong with it. Do not let a tech-support representative convince you that your computer, rather than the program, is the problem.

If you have printed successfully, pack up the works and take it to the shop or call in your repair guru to fix things. Remember that there are no guarantees; you could have done all of the preceding things and still have a problem. The author is not responsible for the success or failure of any of these steps because of all the possible variables involved. However, experience infers that following the given procedures remedies 98 percent of all printing problems when the printer will not print.

Getting the Printing Output You Want

If you are printing but not getting the output you want, what the printer is or is not doing can almost always determine the problem. Before we start, assume that you can print and that the output is recognizable. If you keep getting total garbage from the printer, go to the previous section before starting here. Your problem is quite likely to be hardware- or System-related.

Most of the time, poor output can be remedied by replacing the toner, ink cartridge, or ribbon if the output is too light, splotchy, or otherwise inconsistent. A dirty printer often causes poor output problems—this is especially true with laser printers. This section assumes that your printer is not dirty. With that assumption, some common output problems are discussed according to printer type.

ImageWriters

You will run across one problem with your ImageWriter II: It consistently has a lot of paper jams. You can be merrily printing along and, all of a sudden, the paper twists and everything becomes a mess. There is no sure fix for this, but you can minimize the problem by loosening the tractor lock on the right side (as you face the front of the printer). When you load your paper and adjust the tractors, don't lock the one on the right; let it float freely. This change alone will prevent 80 to 90 percent of the jams.

Another problem you may run across occurs when every line you print has a thin, straight, white line through it. Should this occur, a pin in your printer head has died. The pin is no longer functioning, and as a result, it is not moving in and out as your printer prints. Using a head cleaner fixes this if the head is dirty and the pin just got jammed. After you get a head cleaner from your local dealer and clean the printer head, if the problem persists, the pin is probably broken. In this case, you need a new print head. A printer head is not cheap, but it costs less than a new printer.

Another problem people sometimes have is not making the proper selections in the Page Setup window. If you do not get the results you want, double-check the settings. Be sure to check the paper size and page orientation, then check your Print Window options. The one setting that could drive you crazy is the Draft mode setting. If you use draft, the printer does not print with the fonts you have selected, nor does your page formatting mean anything. In draft mode, the printer just prints the text of the document using its internal font.

Another tip: Do not try to save paper when your print job is done. After you have printed your document, click on the Select button to take the printer offline, then click on the form-feed button. This will advance one page through the printer. Now, rip off the pages you have printed and put the printer back online. Do not roll the page backward to try to save it; this puts strain on your printer and only rips the tractor's feed strips.

Laser Printers

Laser printers are great, but they, too, can have problems. Once again, most problems are due to a dirty printer, but there can be other problems.

The most common print-quality problems are due to an empty or almost empty toner cartridge. Blotchy or inconsistent toner coverage can be temporarily fixed by removing the cartridge and gently rocking it. Hold it on each end and rock it vertically (do not tip it!) to distribute the toner more evenly. Remember that the toner is also a lubricant, so don't run the cartridge when it is too dry.

Here are some common print-quality problems:

❖ Printing too dark or too light—Every laser printer has an adjustment that determines how much toner is used when you print a page. Use this adjustment if your output is consistently too light or too dark. The adjustment is in different places on different laser printers, so you will have to look at your manual.

Low-quality solid black coverage—If your printer has a Canon CX engine (check your manual), it will not do a good job of printing large areas of black. Unfortunately, there is nothing you can do about this limitation; it is just a fact of life with these printers.

❖ Thin vertical lines—A vertical black line can be caused by a scratch on the drum, lint on the corona wires (the very thin wires that horizontally cross the paper path), a dirty fuser cleaning pad, or a scratched fuser roller. One way to try to get rid of the problem is to clean the inside of the printer. Follow the instructions in your printer manual or those that came with your toner cartridge. If that does not work, change your toner cartridge and cleaning pad. Also, check your fuser rollers for damage, and get them repaired if necessary. Should none of these suggestions work, have your printer serviced.

❖ Thin horizontal line—A thin horizontal line can be caused by some of your printer's memory having died. If the line is in the same spot on each page, have it checked in the shop. If the line is in random locations, it could be a scratch on your toner drum.

❖ Consistent paper jams—The most common reason for consistent paper jams is dirty rollers inside the printer. Dirt on the rollers is caused by wear and tear over time, and a good cleaning can take care of it.

Something else you should be aware of is that, on many custom-printed letterheads, the paper is coated with a fine dust to keep the sheets from sticking together as they are printed. This dust then coats all the rollers inside your printer. Check with the printer about your letterhead paper; you might be able to use a paper with less powder. Otherwise, maintain a fairly rigorous cleaning schedule.

Maintenance

Your printer is the most abused piece of equipment you have. Everyone has a tendency to ignore printers until they are hungry and clamoring for toner, ribbons, or paper. It is only when printers start to act up that we pay any attention to them.

Set up a maintenance program for cleaning your printer. If you have a laser printer, have someone come in regularly and clean it. Whenever you change the cartridge, follow its instructions and do a mini-cleaning of your printer. Some companies deliver a new or reconditioned toner cartridge, install it, and perform a quick cleaning of your printer for the cost of the toner cartridge. Check with some of the local printer repair companies to see if anyone performs this service in your area.

An ImageWriter is not as difficult to care for. Pick up a head cleaner and use it regularly. Keep all large paper particles out of the bottom of the printer, and take it in for a professional cleaning once a year. With a little maintenance, any printer will serve you better and longer.

Troubleshooting Your Network

Network troubleshooting is a complicated task and, except for a brief introduction to the subject, exceeds the scope of this book. The more complex the network, the harder it is to troubleshoot. This section provides you with just a cursory look at network troubleshooting. If your networking troubles go beyond the information included in this section, you'll want to hire a professional or read a book about networks.

Before you troubleshoot your network, you need some network tools to make your job easier. In addition to tools, you should have a plan of action. To help you on the way, this section first looks at strategy and then discusses some tools that might be useful.

Your Strategy

Finding out what is wrong with a network can drive you crazy. You can have problems with System software, cabling, network software, or just clogged traffic patterns. Finding out what is wrong with your network can be an all-day task. The strategy you use for troubleshooting depends on your network's configuration. Most businesses today use Ethernet networks, with the majority using 10BaseT cabling. In addition to 10BaseT Ethernet networks, there are coax (10Base2) and LocalTalk networks.

Each type of network requires different troubleshooting steps. Some basic steps, though, apply to any network. The following list represents various starting points for your troubleshooting efforts and can be applied to most network configurations.

❖ Determine how many Macs are communicating on the network.

❖ Check the network software configuration on any disconnected Macs. A Mac will refuse to switch to Ethernet if the computer does not detect an active Ethernet connection.

❖ Check the physical network connections.

❖ If you use 10BaseT and all of the computers are offline, check the hub.

❖ If you use a daisy-chain configuration (LocalTalk or 10Base2), your entire network probably goes down if you have a break in a cable connection.

The two basic types of networks can be categorized as a daisy chain network and a hubbed network. Ethernet 10Base2 and LocalTalk networks are daisy chained; Ethernet 10baseT networks are hubbed. Both types of networks are discussed below.

Troubleshooting a Daisy Chained Network

For any daisy chain network configuration, the process described here works when and if the entire network goes down. To find the problem, start by segmenting the network, breaking it in half to see if either half operates. If you can isolate the section where the problem exists, you can fix the problem through a process of elimination. This process is one of dismantling and rebuilding the network by checking each cable in the segment that doesn't work.

As you check the cable segments, it helps to have a cable tester, to check the integrity of your cables, and a utility such as NetCheck, to see which machines are actually on the network. When troubleshooting a PhoneNET, LocalTalk, or a 10Base2 network, check the individual cables. If one of the cables has been pulled, the stress could cause the connector to become loose.

Here are some general guidelines to follow when tracking down a network problem:

❖ First, see which machines can connect to the networked laser printer or file server. If none of your Macs can access these from the Chooser, check the termination at each end of the daisy chain.

❖ Next, check your cabling; make sure all connectors and terminators have tight fits. Also, check how close your cabling is to any other electrical equipment. Power lines, outlets, and other electrical devices can interfere with the network. Always use shielded cable for your network.

❖ Start breaking the network apart. Try splitting it in half and then quarters until you find the section that has the problem.

❖ If you have problems transferring files, but you can access all networked devices, you probably have a System problem. Isolate the Macintosh that is having the problem and reinstall its System. Do not forget that the server could be the machine that is messing up.

Troubleshooting a Hubbed Network

Troubleshooting a hub configuration is usually easier than troubleshooting a daisy chain. Usually, the problems affect only one or two Macs. If all the computers fail to connect to the network, the hub is the problem. When the problem affects an individual machine, you can bet the problem is with the Mac or the cable that connects the Mac to the hub. The following list contains some suggestions for troubleshooting hubbed networks:

❖ If the entire network is down, reset the hub by turning its power off and on.

❖ The likelihood of there being a problem with all your cabling is highly unlikely. Once you're sure your hub is functioning properly, you need to look at the Macs.

❖ Any Mac that cannot connect to the hub during startup automatically switches to LocalTalk. If the Mac will not switch to Ethernet, it is not communicating with the hub.

❖ After checking a recalcitrant Mac's cabling, you may have to reinstall the Mac OS.

Network Troubleshooting Tools

Before you start out on any network troubleshooting endeavor, you should have a network map. If you know how the cables are laid out and which cable is connected to which Mac, you will be many steps ahead in the process.

You should also have a line tester for the type of network cable you use. AESP makes an inexpensive but good cable tester for phone line with RJ-11 plugs and LocalTalk cable. Using this, you can quickly tell if you have a bad or improperly made cable. Ethernet cable testers are more expensive, especially for coax cable. If you do not have a cable tester, you can always use a volt meter with a continuity checker, which is good for testing all twisted-pair cabling. A continuity checker sends a small electric current down one of the wires. If the current makes it to the other end, the volt meter beeps, letting you know the wire is good. By checking each wire, you can tell if your cable is good.

A software tool that makes life easier is a utility, such as NetCheck (there are other, similar tools that will also work). By using a software utility that shows you the name of every Mac or other device on the network, you can quickly see which Macs do not show up, thereby saving you hours of searching.

If your intent is to optimize your network, you need a utility that can analyze your network's traffic flow. If you have two machines at opposite ends of the network (in a daisy chain) that keep exchanging lots of data, they will slow the network functions for every device in between. If you determine that this is the case, you can reconfigure the network so that these two machines are more directly connected, thereby breaking up the bottleneck.

Installing an Ethernet backbone can also work wonders on slow networks, but optimization is almost more experimentation than anything else. You need a history of the network's traffic to identify where the problems occur. Once you know where the problems are, you can fix them. Otherwise, you can proceed by guesswork, which takes a lot of time and luck.

Special Considerations (or Odds and Ends)

There are a few odds and ends of which you should be aware. Because the heart of this chapter primarily covers the CPU, hard drives, and the SCSI bus, miscellaneous problems with monitors and other special problems are covered here.

Monitors and Displays

If your monitor should suddenly fail to display, examine the cables and connectors. If, after checking the power and cables, your monitor still does not work, turn off the power and let it cool down. After an hour or so, turn it back on. If it works, your monitor's power supply or logic board has a loose component; have it repaired by a dealer. If your monitor does not come back to life, the same solution applies.

With a color monitor, if you lose one of your colors, only two things are likely to cause the problem: One is that a cable has broken and needs to be replaced; the other is a malfunctioning color gun in the picture tube. The cable is easy to replace; a malfunctioning gun requires more professional care.

PowerBook Nicad Batteries

Most Macintosh PowerBooks are powered by nickel cadmium batteries, which keep it running and rechargeable. The problem with nicad batteries is that they can suffer from what is called a *memoring* effect. The memoring effect happens when you consistently use your PowerBook for an hour and then recharge the battery. After this has happened enough times, your battery will operate only for an hour before it needs to be recharged, even though it should last for two to three hours.

To prevent this from happening, use your PowerBook until the battery is dead, then recharge it. If you do this consistently, you can avoid the memoring effect of the nicad battery. Lind Electronic Design sells a recharger that performs a deep discharge on your PowerBook batteries prior to recharging them. This is really a necessity if you rely on your PowerBook and its full battery life, but don't use the full capacity of the battery regularly.

If you have extra batteries for your PowerBook, package them carefully when you travel. If you accidentally short the battery across the positive and negative leads, you could cause a fire. To prevent this, use a plastic carrying case for these batteries. If you need one, contact your Apple dealer.

Newer PowerBooks have nickel hydride or lithium ion batteries, which do not suffer from memoring problems. All batteries eventually wear out. If, after you've had your PowerBook for a couple of years, the batteries don't seem to be up to snuff, you probably need to replace them.

Dead Batteries

Every Macintosh has a battery that keeps the settings you select in Apple's control panels in the Macintosh's Parameter RAM. If the battery goes dead, any of the parameter RAM settings you have adjusted revert to their default factory setting. The best way to determine if your battery is dead is to check the internal clock on your Mac. If it does not keep time after you set it, turn off your Mac, then turn it on again; if it still does not keep time, then your battery is dead and needs to be replaced. On all Macs except the Macintosh Plus, the battery is inside the machine. On the Plus, it is behind a little panel on the back of the Mac.

Any Mac started by pressing the Power On switch on the keyboard can start only if the battery is working. If your Mac worked one day and won't start the next, you could very easily have a dead battery; but check the power cord first. The batteries in all Macs since the SE are long-life batteries that should last from three to five years, but they do not always last that long.

You can purchase a new battery from your dealer and install it yourself, or you can have your dealer install it. In several of the first models of the Mac II, the battery was soldered in place. If yours is soldered in place, have your dealer put in a battery socket so that the battery can be easily replaced. All Macintoshes that use the power switch have a battery holder, so replacing the battery is not as big a problem. If you are squeamish about opening your Mac even to replace a battery, let your dealer do it.

Fixing It Yourself

Fixing a hardware problem yourself can be a challenge. Unless you are comfortable with opening up your hard-drive case or your Macintosh, do not try to fix a hardware problem on your own. If you do decide to poke around inside your computer, observe these cautions:

- ❖ If you are unsure of what you are doing, stop.
- ❖ Discharge any static electricity you may be carrying by touching something metal before putting your hands into the computer.
- ❖ Never force anything when you are installing or removing a component.
- ❖ Do not leave any metal, such as screws or tools, on the logic board when you finish.
- ❖ If you turn on the Mac while it is open (not recommended), be very careful not to short out something.
- ❖ If opening a compact Mac, be careful of the CRT; it is easy to break the nipple and ruin your monitor. Also, do not discharge the CRT unless you know what you are doing and why. The CRT stores enough power to destroy your Mac and cause you serious harm, so be attentive.
- ❖ If your computer is under warranty, opening it voids the warranty—you will have to pay for any repairs.

These cautions, I hope, are enough to keep you out of your machine; if you decide to open it, you have been warned.

Fire and Smoke

If your Macintosh suddenly takes up the bad habit of smoking, it needs serious surgery. Should it ever make a loud buzzing sound, emit smoke, or catch on fire, turn it off and take it to the repair shop. Your problems are beyond the purview of this book.

Summary

I hope that you won't have to use this part of the book much. But if you do, you now have the information you need. Many problems have not been covered in this chapter—troubleshooting could easily be a book of its own; be aware that there are other problems you could face. From the information in this chapter and this part of *Macintosh Revelations, Second Edition*, however, you should be learning how to deal with even some unexpected and unexplained problems.

CHAPTER 18

System and Application Troubleshooting

Troubleshooting your Mac is work, and when it comes to troubleshooting your System or an application, it is a lot of work. This chapter takes some of the tedium out of troubleshooting your System. Because troubleshooting the System is more difficult than troubleshooting applications, this chapter concentrates more on System troubleshooting. If you pay attention to the techniques used for System troubleshooting and apply them to applications troubleshooting, you will have all the knowledge you need to correct most problems you'll encounter.

The sections of this chapter are as follows:

❖ First Principles (Troubleshooting Theory)
❖ Troubleshooting Techniques
❖ Understanding the Startup Process
❖ Bootup Problems (When Bits Collide)
❖ Using a StartUp Manager
❖ System Troubleshooting
❖ Applications Troubleshooting

If you've turned to this chapter because you have problems now, read the entire chapter before you start your troubleshooting adventure. There are several ways to troubleshoot your System, and everyone approaches troubleshooting from a different angle. You need an overview before you dive in. If you jump without looking, you could start a process that will take hours when you could have accomplished the task in minutes.

First Principles (Troubleshooting Theory)

If you watch someone who has lots of experience with Macs, the troubleshooting process he or she goes through can appear to be mystical. Often, you only need to describe your problem, and your expert knows what is wrong and how to fix it; don't let this scare you. Everyone starts in the same place with the same knowledge—little to none. It is only through experience and patience that Mac experts learn their craft. If you have the patience and take the time, you, too, can become expert enough to solve your own problems.

In addition to patience and experience, a Macintosh expert also has an arsenal of software tools to make the job easier. You should have some basic tools to remove some of the guesswork involved with troubleshooting. With these tools, you are able to find and correct common problems while eliminating other possible problems. (These tools were discussed in Chapter 15, "Avoiding Problems.")

In this section I describe a method for finding and isolating Macintosh problems. As you become experienced, you will develop your own technique for correcting Macintosh difficulties. There is no *correct* method, only methods that work. In developing your own techniques, remember one basic principle: If you tried it once and it didn't work, don't try it again—you'll get the same result. Remember that you are working on a *dumb* computer.

Finally, you want to know why your computer malfunctioned; everyone asks why this or that problem occurred. There is an answer to this question, but you would have to ask a programmer or a systems engineer to get an answer, and even then you may not get one. Quite often, your satisfaction will have to come from fixing the problem without learning the cause.

Remembering Where You Have Been

When troubleshooting your System, especially if you are new to the process, make a map, a list of the steps you've tried, so that you don't repeat yourself. Troubleshooting can be like getting lost in the woods; you need to take precautions to ensure that you are always going in a specific direction and not around in circles. If you do not use a checklist (like the one shown in Figure 18.1) or another tool to track your progress, you will end up lost and frustrated. The troubleshooting process will be more than frustrating, and it will take more time—time that you do not have because your problem probably occurred at the worst possible time.

Try It Once

If you know that you have tried something to solve a problem (for example, your drive won't start) that didn't work (such as switching a SCSI cable), why do it again? There is a natural and human tendency to assume that X must be the problem, and, as a result, you keep trying the same thing over and over again. Resist this temptation.

If whatever you try does not work the first time, the only reason to try it again is to ensure that you performed the procedure correctly the first time. If you tried it once and you know that you did it properly, try something else. This rule of thumb will also stop you from going in circles.

Troubleshooting Checklist Equipment Configuration	Description	Serial Number
Type of Macintosh		
Amount of Memory		
SCSI Device ID #0		
SCSI Device ID #1		
SCSI Device ID #2		
SCSI Device ID #3		
SCSI Device ID #4		
SCSI Device ID #5		
SCSI Device ID #6		
Type of Printer		
Type of Network		
Additional Equipment		

Enviroment

System Verision		
Problem Program Version		

Problem Description (include all error codes)

Actions Taken (Can You/Have You...)	Y/N	Add any additional steps you try
Backed up your data?		
Duplicate the problem?		
Checked for viruses?		
Reconnected Cables?		
Boot from clean floppy?		
Run program from a clean system?		
Turned off or removed extesions?		
Turned off or removed Cdevs?		
Reinstalled system?		
Replaced your system?		
Isolate the problem hardware device?		
Attempted a data recovery?		
Checked the recovered data?		

Figure 18.1 *Troubleshooting checklist.*

Troubleshooting Techniques

This section sets forth the actual steps for troubleshooting your system. First of all, you should know the following about your system.

Your troubleshooting starts with the following steps, in the order presented:

1. Which System version you are using?
2. Have all cables and connections been checked and reattached?

   Only when you are sure that your cables and connections are secure should you attempt to troubleshoot your system. If you skip this step, you might spend hours looking for your problem, only to realize that you have wasted your time chasing phantoms.

3. Is your System virus-free?

   You can proceed only if your system is virus-free. It is very hard to detect and fix a problem caused by a virus. The problems caused by viruses are very erratic, and there are enough viruses in the Mac world to add extra and unnecessary confusion to the troubleshooting process.

4. Is your hard drive's directory uncorrupted?

   The only way to know for sure that your directory is not corrupted is to check it. If you have directory problems on your hard drive, use a disk-drive utility and fix it before proceeding. After fixing your directory, back up your drive, reformat it, restore the data, and see if your problem persists.

5. Is your clean System disk ready for use?

   The first step in finding a system software problem is to use your clean System disk. Without one, isolating a System problem is impossible.

Isolating the Problem

The hunt for your problems must follow some form of logic. Begin with the symptom and work your way back to the cure. As stated above, you may not always know what caused the problem; you may only be able to fix it. After you are sure about the items listed above, and after they have been eliminated as potential problems, you need to ask if your Mac is doing any of the following:

- ❖ Does it start?
- ❖ Does it completely boot up?
- ❖ Does it crash after startup?
- ❖ Does it crash when an application is started?
- ❖ Does it have random System errors?

Of all these, the random System errors are often the most frustrating and difficult. If, after you go through the "Maintenance" section at the end of this chapter and your random system errors still persist, follow the steps for troubleshooting your applications.

When you have trouble with your Mac, it means that processing gets interrupted at some point. Your troubleshooting begins at the point where the error occurs. If the Mac fails to start, then that is where you have to begin. If it crashes as you launch an application, that is your beginning. Chapter 16, "Common Macintosh Problems," details several troubleshooting processes; you should review Chapter 16 before continuing.

Understanding the Startup Process

This section describes the procedures your Mac completes when it starts up. This information is important for troubleshooting because you can use it to diagnose a problem as your Mac starts. This checklist is very technical, and the language won't be explained. By now, you should know enough about the Mac to make some sense of this list. All you are looking at, at this point, is a sequence of events.

When you start your Mac, it performs a series of diagnostic checks called *Initialization procedures*, and it goes through the following internal checklist:

❖ Test of critical hardware—The Macintosh initially tests critical components such as the SCSI chip and other hardware circuits. When your Mac completes this procedure, you hear the familiar startup *boing*.

❖ Two stages of RAM testing—These stages depend on whether you are performing a software restart (choosing *Restart* from the Special menu) or a cold start (turning on the Mac). Your Mac tests all installed RAM during a cold start, but it tests only 1K during a software restart.

❖ Determination of the type and speed of the CPU.

❖ Initialization of global variables—This process sets aside memory for use by the computer and system during the entire computing session.

❖ Setting up the System heap—The System heap is a section of reserved memory (RAM) used for system functions and all memory-resident control panels and extensions.

❖ Initialization of ROM resources—During this step, the Mac prepares the different Toolbox Managers necessary for the computer to run.

❖ Initialization of the Apple Desktop bus—This step makes your keyboard and mouse available.

❖ Initialization of your video card—The Mac scans the NuBus or PDS slots looking for the primary video card.

❖ Initialization of the SCSI, Disk, and Sound Managers—The Mac begins looking for your hard drive.

When the computer is finished running these tests, the pointer appears on-screen. The preceding list represents the first half of the entire startup sequence. If the screen displays a blinking Mac with a question mark or a Smiling Mac, the computer has successfully passed its internal diagnostics. After the hardware initialization, the Mac performs the following system startup procedures. The Start Manager controls the functions in this list.

❖ The Mac obtains the SCSI ID number for the startup drive, which is stored in its parameter RAM (PRAM). After it finds the drive, the Mac waits 15 to 31 seconds for the drive to power up.

❖ The Mac then scans for a startup disk. If a System disk is inserted in your floppy drive, the Mac uses the floppy disk to boot; otherwise, it looks for the hard drive found in the last step. During this step, the Mac also ejects any floppy disk that is not a startup disk.

❖ If the Mac does not find a default startup disk, it tries to start from the installed internal hard drive. Then, it scans the SCSI bus looking for a bootable hard drive, starting with SCSI ID number 6 and working backward to SCSI ID 0.

❖ In the case of any Mac with a NuBus slot, it checks the NuBus slot for a startup device before checking the drives. If there is a device, such as an accelerator that starts the Mac, the startup procedure gets transferred to the NuBus device.

❖ After the Mac selects the startup disk (either a floppy or a hard disk), it checks the SCSI bus for additional hard drives. As the Mac finds the driver for each drive, it reads the driver into memory.

❖ The Mac reads the startup information off the startup disk and finishes its startup procedure. After the Mac has found a startup device and has read the drivers for all hard drives into memory, it begins the final stage of the booting process by reading the startup information contained in the boot blocks of the disk selected to boot the Mac. Your Mac will always boot from a floppy disk if the floppy has a System and Finder.

The remainder of the startup process begins at this point with the System startup. The following is the sequence of events that the Mac goes through to start:

1. At this point, your Mac displays the Smiling Mac as it boots, which means that it has found a disk that has valid startup information in its boot blocks. This does not mean that the System is intact or even present.

2. From the information in the boot blocks, the Mac gets the location of the System file, which initializes the Resource Manager, the System Error Handler, and the Font Manager. If an error should occur prior to the System Error Handler being initialized, you get a Sad Mac error code rather than a System error. If you get a System error or a Bomb dialog box, then your Mac successfully booted past this point.

3. When the Welcome to Macintosh or StartUp screen is displayed, your Mac loads its debugger if you are using one. (A debugger is a programmer's tool for finding problems in programs.) After this, it makes any adjustments for the ROM in your Mac by installing software patches.

4. At this point, the ADB bus is activated, and your mouse begins to track. (In English: You can move the pointer.)

5. If your Mac has slots in use, the drivers for the cards are read into memory and initialized.

6. The RAM cache is initialized, and the System heap is installed.
7. Your Mac then loads all its extensions, control panels, and Chooser devices into memory.
8. Finally, the Mac loads the Finder, and you are off and running.

Bootup Problems (When Bits Collide)

Bootup troubleshooting is actually part of System troubleshooting, but it is easier to discuss bootup problems as a separate topic. In this section, you learn how to determine what is interrupting the startup process and how to fix the problem. If you have trouble starting your Mac, this is the section you want to read. This section assumes that you are *not* having a hardware problem and that your System is virus-free.

The problems presented here are all software-related and concentrate on conflicts in System software, a damaged System, and damaged System components. When your Mac crashes on bootup, it does so because two extensions or a control panel and an extension are competing for the same location in memory, or one of them is trying to use a memory location needed by the System. When the bits collide, they shut down the Mac.

As your Mac loads its memory-resident extensions and control panels, most of them are displayed as icons across the bottom of your screen. They are displayed in the order in which they are loaded into the System heap. If one particular icon appears and immediately afterward your Mac crashes, the problem is with the extension or control panel that loads after the one whose icon was last visible.

To correct this, disable the piece of software that caused the crash. To accomplish this, you can boot with your clean startup disk and remove the offending software

Your First Quick Check

One of the quickest ways to determine if a non-Apple extension or control panel is causing you grief is to use the Extensions Manager control panel. You should start your Mac while holding the Shift key down. Once the Mac has started, open the Control Panels folder and start the Extensions Manager. From the Selected Set: menu you can select the Mac OS 8 base set of extensions (as shown in Figure 18.2) or the base set of extensions for the Macintosh OS from 7.5 on.

After selecting the base set of extensions, restart your Mac. If the problem goes away, you have narrowed the problem to some extension or control panel that is not part of the standard Macintosh System. Now you are at a very good starting point for continuing your hunt for the offending software device.

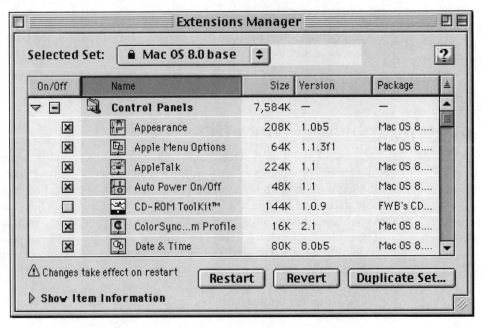

Figure 18.2   *The Extensions Manager with the Mac OS 8.*

from the Extensions or Control Panels folders, placing it in a folder other than the System folder. Or, you can reboot while holding down the Shift key, which disables all extensions and memory-dependent control panels.

Finding the Source of Your Misery

This section details how to find an extension or control panel conflict manually. Although Mac OS 8 comes with the Extensions Manager control panel that can help and expedite this process, you need to know how to do this by hand if you use a version of the Macintosh OS that is older than System 7.6. The Extensions Manager for the Macintosh OS prior to System 7.6 does not show all the extensions and control panels in your System. And if the offending software is one of those not displayed, you must find the extension or control panel manually to fix the problem.

When your Mac fails to boot, the problem is almost always a control panel or extension conflict. If you do not know what control panel or extension caused the crash, you have to do a bit of detective work to find it. Otherwise, if you know which file is the culprit, identify it by its icon or name and remove it from the Control Panels or Extensions folder.

As described above, if you use System 7.X or later, you can hold down the Shift key as soon as you hear the startup chime. Release the Shift key when you see the words "Extensions Off" on the startup splash screen. At this point, your Mac should boot without a problem. If it still crashes, your System file or Finder is broken and needs to be replaced (see the following section "Replacing the System").

If, after you've replaced your System, you still have problems, you must find the cause of your misery. Remove all system extensions and control panels (except the standard Apple ones) and place them in a folder on your Desktop that is easy to access (keep the extensions and control panels separate).

Now, put them back into the System methodically. The number of extensions and control panels you have determines how you go about this process. If you have just a few, it is a simple task to put one or two at a time into the System folder, reboot, and see what happens. When your Mac crashes on bootup, you know that one of the last two devices installed caused the crash; remove one of them and try it again.

However, you could have 100 or more of these devices installed. Now the task is more like looking for a needle in a haystack. Restoring them to the System folder two at a time would be very tedious. A better method is to work on your extensions first and then your control panels; of course, you can do it the other way around if you wish. For this example, let's start with the extensions.

Open the folder with your extensions, set the view to View By Name, and select about half of the extensions and put them back into the System. Viewing them by name makes it easier to know which group you just installed. Now, restart your Mac. If it boots without a problem, repeat the process with another group of your extensions and continue until all the extensions are installed. If you haven't crashed yet, do the same thing with your control panel devices.

At some point, your Mac will crash. When this happens, reboot while holding down the Shift key to disable the extensions and control panels that require System memory. Open either the Extensions or Control Panel folder and remove half of the last group of devices you just installed. Then, reboot again. Repeat this process, each time removing half of the remaining devices from the last group installed. You should have to reboot no more than four times before your Mac starts without crashing. Once it starts without crashing, you know that the offending device is in the last group of items removed from your System. At this point, select half of the last group removed, put them into the System, and repeat the drill. If it crashes, you know it is one of the devices you just installed; remove half of the group you just installed and try again. (See, it really is a tedious process.) By now, you should be able to identify a couple of suspects. Keep repeating this process until you have identified the source of your misery.

Remove the offending device and reboot. If everything starts, replace the rest of your extensions or control panels, using the 50-percent method just in case you had more than one problem. Once you have all devices back in your System, you are ready to get back to work. If during this process, however, you had lots of System errors, reinstall your System software just in case all of the crashes caused a problem.

Is It the One You Found?

By now, you should have found the problem System element. Now, your task is to determine whether that System element is the culprit or the victim. If the element is a shareware or freeware product, it could be that the device is just buggy and not working as intended. To find out, try using it by itself to see if it crashes your Mac without help from another control panel or extension. Chances are, however, that the device causing the crash did so only because it conflicted with another device and that the two together are a toxic combination. Another possibility is that the element that caused the crash did so only because of the loading order, and if it is loaded earlier or later in the startup process, it will not crash your Mac.

This is where the process of troubleshooting gets more sophisticated. The usefulness of the offending System element that determines whether you want to spend another hour or so trying to get it to work. If you want to continue from this point, use a StartUp Manager. Without one, you have difficulty setting the order of your extensions and control panels during startup. To conduct this type of troubleshooting, do the following:

❖ Determine if the extension or control panel works by itself.

❖ Change the name of the extension or control panel to alter its loading order; put a space before the name. Changing the name affects the loading order because extensions and control panels load alphabetically. (Some extensions and control panels do not work if you change their names.) The Mac always loads the contents of the Extensions folder first.

❖ Search out the conflicting device by leaving the device that "apparently" caused the crash in the System. Then, repeat the process previously described in "Finding the Source of Your Misery," until you find the other conflicting extension or control panel.

❖ After you have done all this, you may have to choose between two different devices and use only one of them, or use your Extensions Manager to create two startup sets, allowing you to use the device you need during different operating sessions.

Other Techniques

Rearranging the loading order of your extensions or control panels by changing their locations or names is one troubleshooting technique. Reordering how these System components load is a two-edged sword. You might solve a problem, or you might create one. If an extension or control panel needs to load at a specific time, before or after another System element, changing the loading order or location will make your Mac crash. This type of troubleshooting should be done as a last resort—and very carefully.

Using an Extension or StartUp Manager

The tedium of the process should convince you that the Extensions Manager is a necessity. Third-party software publishers make startup managers that have more features than Apple's. You might want to consider either Conflict Catcher by Cassidy and Green or StartUp Manager, a part of Now Utilities by Now Software. Either of these products makes your troubleshooting work easier. With both of these products, you can turn on or off your extensions or control panels at will and at startup. Each disables an element that interrupted (crashed) the startup process; this feature alone could save you a couple of hours. And both do conflict resolution, eliminating the tedium described previously.

Replacing the System

Replacing the System can seem like a drastic step, but really, it isn't. The Macintosh System has a way of deteriorating over time, and it needs to be replaced periodically. Remember that Chapter 15, "Avoiding Problems," recommends periodic reinstallation of the Macintosh OS. If you have reached this point in your troubleshooting effort, chances are that you haven't been performing maintenance on your System. And if you have been performing maintenance on your System, check out the note "The Biggest Tip in the Book."

When you have System problems that you know are not caused by an extension or control panel conflict, you have to replace your System. Before you embark on this adventure, check your hard drive with a hard-disk utility. Checking the hard drive is important because your Mac can act as if it is having System problems when the real problem is your hard drive's low-level data structures. If your hard-disk utility says that you have serious or major problems with your hard drive, reformat your drive.

Once you have decided to reinstall your System, you have two choices. You can perform a reinstall or a Clean Install of your System. A reinstall is always preferable

The Biggest Tip in the Book

In my consulting practice, I have reached the point where I routinely, after performing a few diagnostic steps, copy a client's data to another hard drive and reformat the drive(s). I have found that this approach is quicker and costs the client less if I immediately perform this step rather than take a series of steps to check the hard drive, check for conflicts, and then reinstall the System. The above procedures rarely work, usually because little to no maintenance has been done on the hard drive, and the problems go away only after the drive is reformatted and the Mac OS is reinstalled.

In short, it costs the client less and I look like a hero. I take care of the client's problems with minimal fuss and mess, and the client has an optimized and functioning Mac when I am done. I recommend that you also consider this tactic. You can spend days trying to find the source of a problem. You could repeatedly install the System, only to have the Mac malfunction again in a couple of days. I call this procedure the "shotgun approach" to troubleshooting. It is so effective that I use it most of the time.

to a Clean Install because you don't have to reinstall all your other software afterward. When you do a Clean Install you have to spend several hours or days rebuilding your System. Many applications have to be reinstalled, such as Microsoft Office. All your utility software needs to be reinstalled and configured. And it takes days or weeks for your Mac to work as it did before. Try reinstalling the Mac OS before you do a Clean Install. The instructions for performing both procedures are covered next.

Reinstalling the System

At this point, you need to make a couple of decisions. You can reinstall your System in different ways. You can perform a "Hot Install," where you reinstall the System while running your Mac from the System you're going to replace. You can reinstall your System while booting from another hard drive or your CD-ROM drive. In most circumstances a "Hot Install" is not recommended.

The only reason to do a "Hot Install" is if you don't have any means for booting your Mac other than the hard drive you are trying to fix. And, if this is the case, my question to you is "How have you backed up your hard drive?" If you have not backed up your hard drive and you are trying to reinstall the System, you are flirting with disaster. Actually, this is a disaster waiting to happen. *You should proceed only if you are willing to lose everything on your hard drive.*

There is a safer method for reinstalling your system. I call this method a "Standard Reinstall." The Standard Reinstall occurs when you reinstall your System and, when you are done, your Mac looks and works as it did before. It can be done with or without reformatting your hard drive, and your Mac should look as it did before you started surgery. The steps for both the Hot Install and the Standard Reinstall are discussed below.

Performing a Hot Install

I want to warn you again before you perform a Hot Install: *You must back up your hard drive before performing this installation.* There is always a chance that reinstalling your System will result in a hard disk crash. If your drive is not backed up, you might have to learn disk recovery in a hurry.

If you have any problems during the installation, you will have a real challenge before you because your Mac will not boot properly. The first thing to do is to make a startup disk from your installation CD-ROM. If you need instructions for making a startup disk, look in Chapter 15, "Avoiding Problems."

The steps for performing a Hot Reinstall of the System are as follows:

1. Using the Extensions Manager, select the *Mac OS 8 all* extension set.
2. Restart your computer.
3. Once the computer is started, open the System folder and drag the System and Finder files to the Trash. *Do not empty the Trash!* If your machine crashes at this point it will not boot from your hard drive.
4. Insert your Macintosh System CD-ROM.

5. Launch the Mac OS Install application.

6. Install the System as described in Chapter 7.

7. Restart your computer.

8. Empty the Trash after your Mac restarts.

Performing a Standard System Reinstall

A Standard Reinstall is similar to the Hot Reinstall except that you boot from a disk other than the one on which you are installing the System. As with the Hot Install, you should have a backup of your data when performing a Standard Reinstall. If anything goes wrong during the installation, you could lose the contents of your hard drive.

The following steps help you perform a "Standard Reinstall":

1. Boot from the hard drive you wish to repair. With the Extensions Manager, select the *Mac OS 8 all* extension set.

2. Select the Startup drive you want to use with the Startup Disk control panel. Restart your computer.

3. Once the computer is started, open the System folder into which you want to reinstall the system and drag the System and Finder files to the Trash. *Do not empty the Trash!*

4. Insert your Macintosh System CD-ROM.

5. Launch the Mac OS Install application.

6. Install the System, as described in Chapter 7.

7. Restart your computer.

8. Empty the Trash after your Mac restarts.

Performing a Clean Install

You need to perform a Clean Install of your System if the reinstall was unsuccessful or if you want to rebuild your System from scratch. The Clean Install option installs a fresh System folder onto your Mac. The installation process disables your old System folder but leaves it intact. Having your old System folder makes it possible to move items from the old System folder to the new System folder. If you do move items from the old System to the new one, be careful that you don't move the problem into your new System folder.

The following steps result in a Clean Install of your System:

1. Boot your Mac from your Startup floppy or the Mac OS 8 CD-ROM.

2. Double-click on the Mac OS Install program.

3. In the Install program's Select Destination window, select your hard drive.

4. Check the Perform Clean Installation check box (Figure 18.3).

5. Click on the Select button.

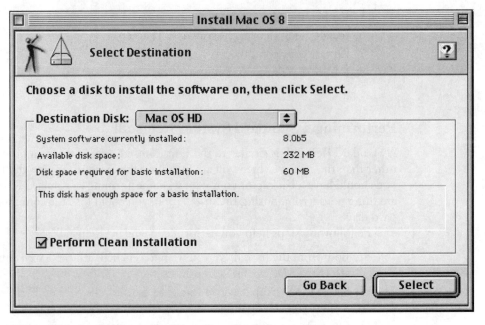

Figure 18.3   *Selecting the Clean Install option.*

6. Continue with the installation.
7. If you need additional instructions, see Chapter 7.

System Installation Notes

You should keep a couple of points in mind when you perform a System install. Whenever possible, a freshly formatted hard disk offers the best environment for a System installation. If you're doing a reinstall, copy the System folder onto the freshly formatted hard drive and perform a Standard Reinstall. Do not copy your applications or data back onto the hard drive until you have completed the System installation.

If you cannot format your hard drive before installing the System, make sure you have a backup. I know I've said this in every other paragraph, but it is the most important thing you can do besides fixing your Mac. It doesn't matter if your computer works if you do not have data to use.

System Troubleshooting

This section covers the problems that can occur once your System has booted up and you are in the Finder. At this point, determining where the difficulty lies becomes more difficult because anything from a bad hard-drive driver to a software incompatibility problem could cause the problem. To limit the search, there are a few prerequisites for this section:

❖ Does your Mac boot without a problem? Do you get to the point that you are in the Finder and have some functionality? This means that you can move your mouse, select menus, open drives, and so on.

❖ Have you checked all cables, power sources, and so on? You need to ascertain that you are not experiencing a hardware problem.

❖ Is your System virus-free? If you have a virus, all the troubleshooting in the world will not fix your problem.

❖ Intermittent problems can be impossible to fix. Sometimes, you just have to live with them. If you have a random problem that is intolerable, fixing it could take several days to several weeks. If your problem is intermittent, you back up your drive, reformat the drive, and perform one of the System installations discussed above. This type of shotgun approach almost always works.

Any operating problem could be caused by the problems just described. Therefore, the steps covered there are not repeated in this section.

Determining Your System Problems

How do you know if you have a System problem? Basically, if your Mac can find its way to the Finder, you do not have a hardware problem unless it is a hard-disk directory problem. But, if once in the Finder, your mouse freezes, you crash while selecting a menu, your fonts do not display properly, or you experience any other operating anomaly, you have a System problem. In this case, the troubleshooting procedures include one additional step. As part of the investigation process, you may have to make a Sherlock Holmes-like deduction. After exhausting all likely possibilities, whatever is left is your problem, regardless of how unlikely it may seem.

Your troubleshooting process should be dictated by what is wrong and should follow a logical path for eliminating possibilities. Start with the manifestation of the problem: What is your Mac doing? Does the error have any connection with some piece of hardware, such as a trackball or alternative pointing device, a printer, or a SCSI device?

Try the following steps to see if the problem goes away:

1. Boot from your clean startup disk.
2. If the problem seems to be peripheral-related, disconnect or replace the peripheral.
3. Zap your PRAM.
4. Rebuild your Desktop.
5. Replace your Preference files.
6. Replace your System.
7. Troubleshoot your extensions and control panels.

8. Reinstall your hard-disk driver.

9. Reformat your hard drive.

These steps are not cast in stone, nor do they have to be done in the order listed. As you gain experience in troubleshooting your System, you will learn what steps to skip or reorder. To begin, though, start with step 1 and work through each step.

Booting with a Clean System

You should always boot with a clean System disk first. Booting with a clean System disk tells you if everything is working properly at the hardware level. If you boot from your clean System disk and your trackball is still acting up, there is a good probability that the problem is hardware related. Is the trackball dirty? Similarly, if you boot from a clean System and everything works as it should, you have eliminated obvious hardware problems.

Zapping the PRAM (Restoring All Default Parameters)

From time to time, your Mac's parameter RAM gets confused, and your Mac will not boot from the disk you specify, or your mouse starts acting up, or you have problems connecting to the network. Anything set by your General Controls control panel or other standard Apple control panels can be stored in your parameter RAM. When the PRAM gets corrupted, any number of odd things can happen. By resetting the PRAM to the Mac's default settings, zapping the PRAM, you eliminate any problems associated with corrupted PRAM settings. There are two ways to zap your PRAM with Mac OS 8:

❖ Hold down the Command + Option + P + R keys as you turn on the power and reboot.

❖ Use a freeware utility called TechTool, which is on the BMUG Revelations CD-ROM included with this book.

If you use the command key sequence, your Mac starts to boot, *boing*, and reboot. If you continue to hold down the keys, it continues to cycle through the zapping process. Once is not enough; let the Mac cycle through four or five *boings* before releasing the keys.

The TechTool application actually does a better job of zapping the PRAM than the command key sequence. TechTool can be found in the Utilities:Diagnostics folder. Figure 18.4 shows TechTool and its options. Zapping the PRAM is as simple as clicking on the Zap PRAM button. Once you click on the Zap PRAM button, your Mac automatically restarts. If you wish, you can also save your PRAM settings and restore them if something goes wrong with the zapping process. I've always wondered why I would want to save PRAM settings if I believe that my current settings are corrupted, so I've never used this option. I have zapped a lot of PRAM settings, though, without saving them.

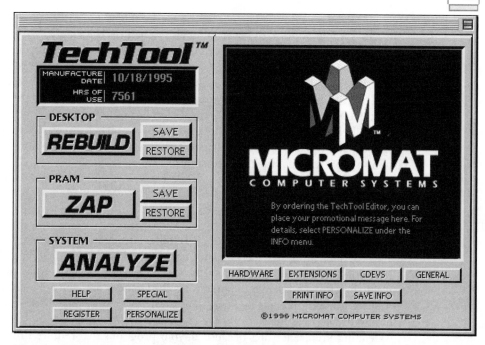

Figure 18.4 *Zapping the PRAM with TechTool.*

Rebuilding the Desktop

The next step is to rebuild your Desktop file. Although this probably will not solve your problem, do not skip this step. It is primarily a general maintenance step. If your problem was the result of a corrupted Desktop file, this step corrects it.

To rebuild the Desktop, hold down the Command + Option keys while your Mac boots. As the Mac finishes booting, it asks if you really want to rebuild the Desktop (see Figure 18.5). After you click on OK, your Mac rebuilds your Desktop file. The Desktop files are not re-created; rebuilding the Desktop relinks all your data files with their applications and removes any icons that no longer have files associated with them.

You may have noticed in Figure 18.4 that TechTool has an option to Rebuild the Desktop. Once again, using TechTool rather than Apple's built-in option is pre-

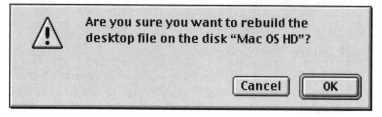

Figure 18.5 *Request to rebuild the Desktop.*

ferred. TechTool completely deletes the Desktop files and forces the Mac to recreate them; Apple's option only verifies and restructures the files.

The only danger you face when replacing your Desktop files is if your hard disk has directory damage and cannot re-create the Desktop files. If the Desktop files cannot be re-created, you must recover the data on your drive, as described in Chapter 19, "Disk Crashes and Data Recovery," and then reformat your hard drive.

If this should happen, the only consolation I can offer you is that your data recovery should be easy and that your drive would have crashed anyway. You just forced the issue, and you are probably better off discovering the problem now, rather than having a more serious situation arise later.

Replace Your Preferences

Inside the System folder is a Preferences folder. Inside the Preferences folder are all your program and System settings not held in the PRAM. If one of your Preferences files is corrupted, your Mac could act erratically. If you can isolate the problem to a specific function and delete the function's Preferences file, you may just solve your problem. For example, if File Sharing was not working, you could trash the File Sharing Preferences file.

Deleting Preference files because all your programs that require Preferences files are supposed to store their files in the Preferences folder and re-create them if the file is missing. You don't want to trash the Preferences folder because some programs do not work according to Apple's specifications, and because they do not re-create their preferences. Also, some programs store more than their preferences inside the Preferences folder.

The best thing to do is to remove the Preferences folder from your System folder and rename it. After doing this, reboot your Mac. It will re-create a new Preferences folder on bootup. Next, re-create your File Sharing Users and Groups. Some of your extensions and control panels also want to re-create their Preferences. Some programs no longer have the settings you selected. If a corrupted Preferences file caused your problem, the problem should go away. Each program and utility you use is supposed to re-create its Preferences file if it is missing when the program or utility is used. If one of your programs doesn't re-create its Preferences file, you still have the old folder, so you won't have go hunting for the master disk. You can move the Preference file from the old folder to the new folder.

This is a quick way to eliminate a potential problem source without replacing your entire System. If you want to skip this step, fine—but it could save you some time.

Replace Your System

To save time and eliminate the possibility of a corrupt System file, replace the System as previously described. Although reinstalling the System may seem like shooting a fly with an elephant gun, this is the only way to be sure your problem is not with the System.

Extension and Control Panel Conflicts

Just as these wonderful and useful utilities can be a source of grief by interrupting your Mac's startup, they can also cause problems in general. Once your System has started, control panel devices are more likely to be a problem than extensions. Either one can become corrupted.

Corrupted control panels or extensions are a real problem when they are only partially broken, meaning that they do not interrupt the startup process. They generally work properly except for some small distinctions. For example, the driver for your fax software may go through the process of printing your fax, but all you get is a blank page. You trust that the fax software is working correctly, and you send a bunch of blank faxes without knowing it. The driver is broken, but you don't find out until one of your fax recipients calls you.

In this case, figuring out what is wrong is fairly easy. It's not as simple if your System keeps crashing after you perform a few Finder functions, such as opening a window or getting information on a file. Follow the procedure in "Bootup Problems (When Bits Collide)," or install a new System.

System Problems and Your Hard Drive

If you have tried all the suggestions listed above and your Macintosh continues to crash, then your problem is at a level below the System. This is especially true if you can boot from your clean startup floppy without trouble, but even after you have installed a clean System, you continue to crash. You could have a problem with your hard drive that the best disk utilities cannot find. If you have such symptoms, reinstall your hard-drive driver.

Reinstalling your driver can result in the loss of your data, so be sure to back your data up before you reinstall the driver. Follow the instructions in your hard-drive manual. Afterward, if your Mac still acts up, reformat your disk. You can at least take heart in having backed up your data. After you have reformatted your drive, be sure to reinstall the System or do a Clean Install. If, at this point, your Mac still does not work properly, take it to your dealer or call in a service professional.

Applications Troubleshooting

Usually, when a specific application starts giving you trouble, it means that the program itself has suffered a mishap, a Preferences file is corrupted, or you have been fortunate enough to find a minor bug. Also, if you have installed a new utility, extension, or control panel, the new arrival could be causing a problem with the application.

Application troubleshooting is not as complex as System troubleshooting, but it can be frustrating nevertheless. In principle, the steps are the same except that you start with the application and work backward. Use the following steps as a guide for correcting the problem; try to duplicate the problem in between each step:

❖ Remove the application's Preferences file from the Preferences folder.

❖ Check the application's folder for other subsidiary files that could cause the problem, and replace all subsidiary files.
❖ Reinstall the application.

Should these steps fail, start the troubleshooting process by booting from your clean startup disk. Then run the program to see if the program and your Mac work properly. After you have started your Mac, run your application. It should work without a problem. If it does, you know that the application is fine and that your problem is related to the System on your hard disk.

At this point, replace your System. If the problem is particularly sticky, go through the procedures outlined in the "System Troubleshooting" section. Remember that very intermittent problems, although frustrating, may not be curable. Also, try starting with your extensions disabled (boot while holding the Shift key down) before you get too far into the process. This can quickly determine whether your problem is due to one of your extensions or control panels. If one of them does turn out to be a problem, call the technical support department for the software manufacturer, to see if it knows what is causing your problem. If your luck is as good as mine, though, you will have discovered something with which the tech support representative is completely unfamiliar, and he or she will be of little help.

Summary

Does your head hurt? Well, sometimes headaches are part of troubleshooting. I hope that your headache is not too bad—just think about what you've gained. You now know how to troubleshoot your Mac.

You can fix System problems, reinstall your System, and isolate hardware problems—you can be Mac self-sufficient. If you practice these techniques, you will have the skills when you need them. Remember, your Mac will probably act up when you're in a time crunch. At that time, you might not have time to learn how to fix the problem. Learn it now, and you'll have what you need when . . .

CHAPTER 19

Disk Crashes and Data Recovery

I n Chapters 10 and 11 disk drives are covered in detail, and most of the evils that can afflict your drive are mentioned there. The evils missed in those chapters are covered in Chapter 17, "Macintosh Hardware Problems." This chapter is about recovering from those demons. The cause of a hard disk problem is secondary to getting your data back. Therefore, this chapter contains procedures for recovering deleted files, mounting drives, and recovering crashed drives.

Before you read this chapter you need to have read:

❖ Chapter 10, "Macintosh Disk Drives"
❖ Chapter 11, "Essential File, Disk, and Data Information"
❖ All of the preceding chapters in Part V

If you haven't read these chapters, your success with this chapter will be limited unless you already have extensive knowledge about your Mac. In a sense, this entire book has been building up to this chapter because dealing with disk problems is one of the most complicated and difficult things you can do with your Mac, and the procedures assume that you have most of this knowledge. Not only that, but if you do not properly recover a disk or if you make a mistake, you can lose all of your data.

Data recovery is not a substitute for backing up your hard drive; it is what you do as a last resort. Disk-drive problems are the most nerve-racking problems you can have. If you have to use the information in this chapter, you are already at a disadvantage because you're scared and nervous. Both of these conditions increase the risk of your making a mistake. Read this chapter before you have to. Make backups of your data so that you know it is safe. Be familiar with your hard-disk utility, and if you're at all unsure about what you're doing and your data is important, hire a professional to recover your data or fix your hard drive.

The best way to learn to troubleshoot your Mac is to think about what your Mac is doing or trying to do. Everything your Mac does follows a specific logic. It has to perform specific steps to accomplish any task, and if you understand what it is supposed to be doing, when it doesn't work you can figure out how to fix it.

Read This Before You Touch Your Drive

Any time you have a hard-drive problem, keep in mind all the other things that could be wrong. Your best indication of trouble occurs when you experience errors reading or writing data or, worse yet, when your hard drive asks to be initialized. Regardless of what error you are experiencing, start with the first principles mentioned in Chapter 15, "Avoiding Problems." Check your cables and review the section on SCSI bus troubleshooting in Chapter 17 before continuing.

Any symptom that appears to be a hard-drive problem can have other causes. Although the other causes may be hard-drive-related, you may not have a problem with the drive itself. Problems with SCSI cables, improper termination, and System software can all appear as hard-drive problems. Even read and write errors could have other causes.

At the other end of the spectrum, your entire System can be functioning properly with the exception of a pesky, totally random yet consistent System error that can actually be a hard-disk problem. Your disk utilities that check the drive reveal no anomalies, but you've checked everything and nothing other than your drive could be the problem. In that case, it probably is a hard-drive problem. You know something is wrong, but you don't know what. The process of troubleshooting hard-disk problems becomes a combination of factual knowledge and intuition. The hardest part is trusting your intuition; sometimes, that is all you have to go on.

I hope that you are beginning to see the magnitude of the issue. If you go off half-cocked you stand the danger of losing your data at one extreme or, at the other extreme, doing a lot of work for no reason because your drive was not damaged.

The final warning is that the author, publisher, or anyone else associated with this book is not responsible if you lose your data by following the steps, procedures, or recommendations in this book. If you try to recover your drive and lose all your data, none of us can be held responsible. Data recovery is a *"perform at your own risk"* venture.

Determining the Problem

When you have Macintosh problems, determining their cause can be difficult. Ninety percent of the time, your problem will be hard-drive-related. This does not mean that your physical hard drive is broken, only that the problem is one with your hard drive or the data it contains.

Before you can determine what the problem is, you have to know what problems you could possibly have. Unfortunately, this list is quite long, and determining the problem can be a trial-and-error process. The solution may be obvious, even though you can't define the exact problem.

This section provides some basic steps for determining the problem and, failing that, outlines what steps to follow, given a specific set of symptoms. When you suspect that you have a hard-drive problem, you can follow a specific set of steps to help you determine the problem and/or which procedures you should use to correct the problem and save your data.

This section describes the most common hard-drive problems you may encounter. Knowing the problem before you begin can greatly expedite the troubleshooting process. After the descriptions, I present a series of steps that you can perform to help you determine the problem and your next step. The sections are as follows:

- ❖ Hard-Disk Hardware Problems
- ❖ Disk-Drive Software Problems
- ❖ Figuring It Out

Hard-Disk Hardware Problems

Hard drives are complex electromechanical devices that can and do malfunction. When a hard drive malfunctions, the result can be equated to a heart attack—a hard-disk hardware problem stops your computer cold. This section looks at the most common hard-disk hardware problems you might encounter.

When a hard drive has a hardware problem, there is little that you can do. Recovering data from a malfunctioning hard drive is sometimes possible, but even the attempt is very expensive and carries no guarantees. You have to ship your drive to a drive recovery specialist, and the attempt takes several days. You can easily spend several hundred dollars and still not get your data back.

The hard-drive problems you could have are these:

- ❖ Crashes
- ❖ Stiction
- ❖ A dead drive

Drives Fail

When manufacturers test hard drives, they create a number for mean time between failures (MTBF), which represents how long your drive can run before it fails. The number they use is based on a drive being left on for 20,000, 50,000, or 100,000+ hours. Manufacturers continually increase this number, although the number couldn't *really* have been tested—50,000 hours equals 5.71 years. No manufacturer has tested a drive for 5.71 years before releasing it for sale. Don't be fooled by the MTBF rating; it is an extrapolated number using statistical averages and has a nominal bearing on reality.

What does this number have to do with dead drives? It is an admission by disk-drive manufacturers that drives fail. Because a drive is an electromechanical device, it is more susceptible to problems than any other component of your system.

Sometimes, when a drive fails, you have difficulty determining whether the drive is dead or just suffering from a software crash. The section on crashes makes a very important distinction between a software and a hardware crash, a distinction that you should understand.

Crashes

Two types of hard-drive crashes occur on the Macintosh:

❖ A *software crash* occurs when your program has a bug or a conflict with your system software; a software crash is indicated by an on-screen bomb. These crashes are distressing, but they are more inconvenient than detrimental. Sometimes, they can cause damage of a software nature, but they are almost never the cause of a hardware problem.

❖ A *hardware crash* can affect your hard drive. Remember, your drive's heads float on a cushion of air above the platters, not touching the platters while they are spinning. Abrupt jarring, sudden movement, or a power loss to the drive while it is reading or writing data can cause the heads to come in contact with the media. When this happens, you have experienced a hardware crash.

The damage caused by a hardware crash can be minor—lost data—or fairly extensive—media damage that requires you to reformat or replace the drive. If the heads *are* damaged along with the media, the problem can be serious. As long as your drive can map out the bad sectors, all is fine. If the media has many damaged sectors or damaged heads, your drive becomes an expensive paperweight. If your drive is under warranty, you may be able to get it replaced.

Head crashes are rare. The drives manufactured today have high tolerances, and generally crashes are caused only by serious mishaps. Do not be careless with your hard-disk drive—should a crash occur, you will inevitably lose data that is not backed up. To stay on the safe side, follow a regular backup routine so that you do not lose data in a crash.

Stiction

Another problem, one more common than it should be, is *stiction*. Your drive has a stiction problem when the platters in the hard drive do not spin and when your drive does not power up. When your drive has a stiction problem, the platters inside the drive do not spin. If you have an external drive, the power light comes on, but your drive does not boot, and you are not able to access it with your formatter. If one day you do not hear your drive's platters spinning, you may be experiencing a stiction problem. A failure of your drive's logic board can have the same symptoms. When you have a drive with a stiction problem, it is usable if you get it running again—as long as you never turn it off. A drive with a stiction problem is not dependable (you never know when it will freeze for good).

When a drive first starts to experience stiction, the problem is usually intermittent. The drive starts one time but does not start the next. If you turn on your Mac and the disk that was fine yesterday doesn't start today, try turning the power on and off a couple of times. If the drive finally starts after a few tries, it is suffering from a stiction problem. Like most progressive diseases, the stiction problem gets increasingly worse. One day, the hard drive will not start no matter how many times you turn the power on and off. To extend the life of a drive that you know has a stiction problem, leave the drive or your Macintosh turned on all the time.

When a hard drive has a stiction problem, a dealer says that the drives are no good. You also may be told that you cannot recover data from one of these drives after they begin to fail. The former assertion—that the drive needs to be replaced—is true. The latter—that the data cannot be recovered from the drive—is false. If you need to recover the data, call different repair shops and consultants to find a technician who can start your drive. Usually, a drive with a stiction problem can be started and its data recovered. If the drive cannot be started, it no longer has a stiction problem—it is dead.

A Dead Drive

A dead drive is one that no longer functions. Pronouncing a drive dead is a very delicate process because many problems can appear to be drive problems when they are not. A dead drive can refuse to power up, run but not format, or cause your Mac to exhibit the Sad Mac. Usually, you can determine that a drive is definitely dead only after an extensive troubleshooting process, described in the upcoming section "Figuring It Out."

This section discusses some symptoms that could indicated a dead hard drive:

❖ Not holding a format—One type of failure occurs when a drive will run, format, work for a week, and then suddenly fail, telling you that it needs to be initialized. This failure is due to the drive's not holding a format; a drive that cannot hold a format is useless and cannot be fixed except by sending the drive to its manufacturer to be rebuilt.

When this problem first occurs, your drive appears to have suffered a software crash. It asks to be initialized, and only after you've recovered your data, reformatted the drive, restored the data, and run it for a few days to a week do you know that this is a problem—because the drive will ask to be initialized *again*.

When a drive loses the ability to hold a format, the drive's condition deteriorates. It will get to the point where you format the drive, and either it will not format or it will work only for a few minutes to a few hours before wanting to be initialized. If you suspect this is the problem, run the drive with a plain system, install your system, and don't add any non-Apple extensions or control panels while you are troubleshooting it.

❖ Hard disk controller failures—Every hard drive has a logic board called a *controller*. Sometimes, a component on the controller fails. When this happens, the hard drive does not format or, if it formats, it does not initialize. And, in some cases, it is impossible to see the drive with your formatting software; it appears as if the drive just disappeared.

❖ Noises made by the drive—Some drives, over time, get noisier and noisier. A noisy drive does not mean that your drive is dead or dying. The noise, though, can be a warning sign. If, all of a sudden, your drive starts making noises, immediately back it up.

Usually, a drive will not die suddenly. A drive's total failure often occurs over a period of time. Grinding, shrieking, or other odd noises coming from your drive are warning signs; if you ignore them, you will try to start your Mac one day and the drive will be gone.

❖ Sudden failures—Every once in awhile, a hard drive will be fine one day and will not work the next. There will be no warning signs or indicators of any type. Basically, the drive is here today and gone tomorrow. The protection you have against this type of failure is a backup of your data.

Disk-Drive Software Problems

The most common disk-drive problems, in addition to the Desktop problem described in Chapter 16, "Common Macintosh Problems," are listed below. Each has its own symptoms and different cures. If you have a disk-repair and recovery utility, such as Norton Utilities for the Macintosh, you can correct most of these conditions.

In-Use Sectors

In-use sectors occur when you have trashed a file and the Mac fails to make all of the freed space available. The sectors are still marked as being used. Sometimes, there can be just a few in-use sectors, and you do not notice any loss of space. At other times, you can have thousands of sectors marked as being in use, depriving you of a lot of hard disk space as a result. This is not a serious problem; you will probably run across it in the course of performing a maintenance check or while correcting another problem. Unless you notice that a lot of disk space is missing, as in Figure 19.1, where more than half of the space on the floppy disk is missing, you should not be concerned about this as a problem.

To correct this problem, use Norton Utilities for the Macintosh by Symantec, Apple's Disk First Aid, or Central Point Software's MacTools Deluxe. Any of these packages is more than adequate for freeing your in-use sectors and making them available for use again. The actual steps for freeing your in-use sectors depend on the utility you're using, so check your utility's manual before attempting this procedure.

Bad Sectors

Bad sectors are areas on your hard disk that have deteriorated or been damaged; they can no longer hold data. All hard drives develop bad sectors over time (if yours does not, consider yourself blessed). When sectors go bad, you can have problems reading or writing data to your disks. Most often, you get a dialog box like the one shown in Figure 19.2.

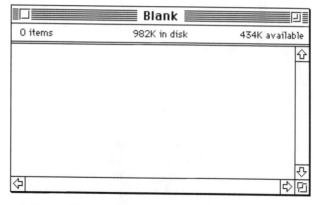

Figure 19.1 *A floppy disk with missing space.*

Sometimes, this error is just a glitch in the reading and writing process, and recopying the file corrects it. If you have this problem consistently, your hard drive needs to be reformatted or you have to use a utility, such as Norton Utilities for the Macintosh, to map out the bad sectors. Norton Utilities is the only utilities available that maps out a bad sector without requiring you to reformat your hard drive. All other programs that check for bad sectors just notify you of the problem.

Norton fixes the problem by creating an invisible file that occupies the bad sector(s). By doing this, Norton prevents data from being written to the sector that has died. If you get more than a few bad sectors, the safest course of action is to reformat your drive.

A Corrupted Directory

Because the hard disk's directory contains all the information about where your files are stored, a corrupted directory is one of the most serious problems you can have with your hard drive. And, at times, it is one of the most difficult to detect. If you have difficulty with your drive, check if a corrupted directory is a possibility. There are no specific rules to guide you in determining that this is the problem, other than Norton Utilities, Disk First Aid, and general difficulty with your drive's reliability.

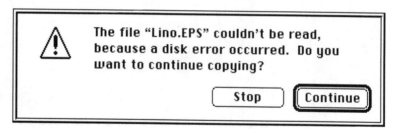

Figure 19.2 *Error message while writing or reading disk.*

If you have had a series of system errors, or if your Mac crashes while reading or writing to the hard drive, check for directory damage. A system error usually does not cause damage, but if it does, it corrupts either a file or your hard-drive directory.

Problems involving the saving, copying, moving, or deleting of files can all indicate directory damage. Often, this type of damage is not discovered until it is too late, when you receive the dialog box that says "This disk is damaged. Do you want to initialize?" Even this dialog box can occur for reasons other than a damaged directory, so the only way to know is to check your drive with one of the software tools previously listed. The best tool for determining whether your directory is damaged is Norton Utilities or Disk First Aid. Disk First Aid does not have the overall capabilities of Norton Utilities for the Macintosh.

Using either Disk First Aid or Norton Utilities is a straightforward process. Figure 19.3 shows the progress of Disk First Aid as it checks a hard-disk directory.

As you can see in Figure 19.4, Norton checks more than just the directory. If Norton finds directory damage, it offers to fix it. Figures 19.5 and 19.6 show the progress of Norton Utilities as it checks your drive.

If your directory is damaged and you repair it using any of the utilities mentioned here, immediately back up your data and reformat your drive. The directory structure of a Macintosh hard drive is complicated, and no utility can guarantee that it has completely fixed your directory. The only way to know that the directory and other low-level disk structures are working is to format the drive; any other action courts disaster. If you use a utility to fix your directory, think of it as a temporary repair for the purpose of retrieving your data.

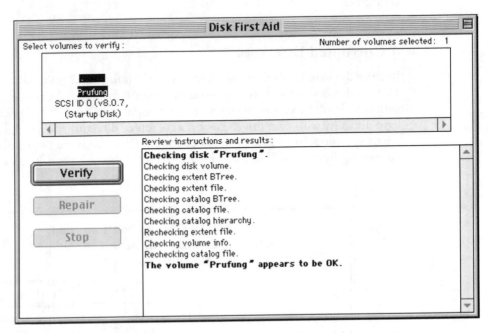

Figure 19.3   Disk First Aid as it checks a hard disk.

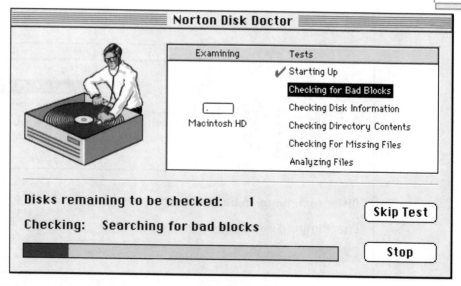

Figure 19.4 *Display of Norton's Disk Doctor startup.*

Insufficient Disk Space

It is very easy to run out of disk space. Even when the Finder tells you that you have disk space available, you may not have enough. Most programs write temporary files to the disk while they run, which means you really need more space than you might

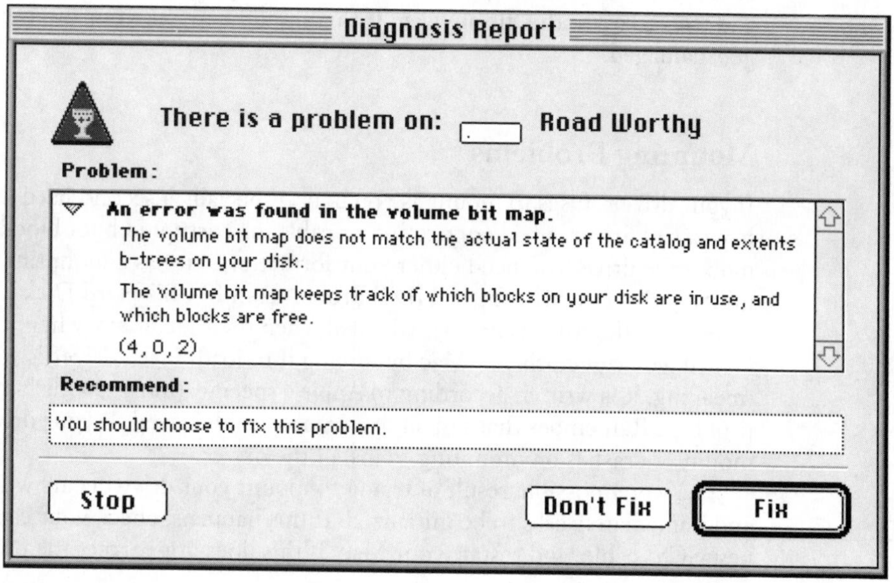

Figure 19.5 *Norton's offer to repair directory damage.*

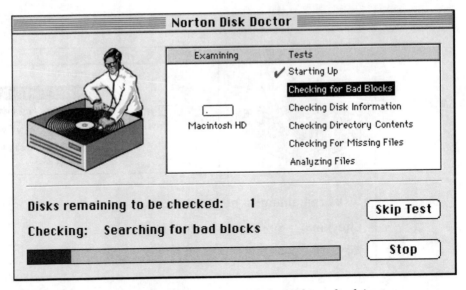

Figure 19.6 *Display of Norton's progress while checking the drive.*

think. A good rule of thumb is to keep 10MB or 10 percent of your hard drive free. This approach ensures that you have enough disk space for temporary files and that your Desktop file has room to grow.

Letting your drive get too full and then writing a file when you do not have enough room can also result in directory damage. The Macintosh is very good about not letting this happen, but sometimes a program may not be well behaved and tries to write the file anyway. If this should happen, your directory probably gets damaged.

Mounting Problems

If your drive refuses to mount as you boot, especially a second hard drive, you can have a bad driver, a bad connection or cable, or corrupted boot blocks. To force-mount the drive, you need either your formatter, if it has a mounting feature, or a utility such as SCSIProbe or HDT Prober from FWB's Hard Disk ToolKit.

Because the drive is normally loaded when the Mac boots, when it does not get loaded, you can crash you Mac by forcing it to load. If the driver is well behaved (meaning, it is written according to Apple's specifications), the disk mounts without a problem. Remember that not all drivers are well behaved. If your drive does not mount or crashes on mounting, reinstall the driver.

The worst possible result of trying to mount your drive occurs when it mounts and immediately asks to be initialized. If this happens, check your cables again, try a new SCSI cable, and restart your Mac. If this does not correct the problem, go to the section on disk recovery.

Corrupted Drivers

In Chapter 10, "Macintosh Disk Drives," a brief section discussed corrupted drivers. Every once in awhile, the driver on your hard drive can become corrupted; when this happens, your Mac can exhibit a wide range of symptoms.

Driver problems can be manifested as random system errors, a request to reinitialize the drive, or display of the Sad Mac. Instructions for determining if you have this problem are in the later section, "Figuring It Out."

Low-Level Data Structure Problems

One of the worst situations you can encounter is one that involves problems not detected by any hard-disk utility. These problems involve your directory, boot blocks, or other low-level elements on your drive. When this problem occurs, the only fix is to reformat your hard drive; determining that you have this problem takes some work.

The symptoms for low-level structure problems are random System errors. You can reinstall your System and disk-drive drivers, run a very clean System folder, and still have these errors. The only indicators that you see are the random System errors, but you won't know for sure that your problems are due to low-level data structural damage until you reformat your drive and the problems go away.

This is the last problem you suspect, and you do not get to this point until you've performed every troubleshooting technique in this book. After you fix the problem, you'll wonder why you waited so long to reformat your drive.

Figuring It Out

Before you can determine if your hard drive is the problem, you have to perform all the techniques for System troubleshooting found in Chapter 18, "System and Application Troubleshooting." Once you've determined that your Mac is not suffering from System software problems, follow the steps for driver troubleshooting and then read the section about determining if your drive is dead.

Driver Troubleshooting

If your Mac does not work when booting from your clean startup disk, even when forcing it to ignore the SCSI bus (see Chapter 17), you have a serious problem.

To determine if you have a bad driver, try the following:

1. Turn off the power for your Mac and any equipment connected to it.
2. Find your Macintosh Disk Tools disk or your Mac OS 8 CD.
3. If you do not have an internal hard-disk drive, disconnect all external drives and boot from the System Tools or the Disk Tools disk. If your Mac

starts without the Sad Mac, reconnect your drive and reinstall your hard-disk driver.

If your Mac has an internal hard drive, follow the remaining steps:

4. Disconnect any SCSI devices attached to your Mac and try to boot the computer. If it starts properly, check all cable connections and reconnect your hard drives one at a time until you find the one that is causing problems. When your Mac displays the Sad Mac, you have found the offending device.

5. If your internal drive is causing the problem, turn off the power and insert your Disk Tools disk. Press and hold down the Command, Option, Shift, and Delete keys as you turn on the Mac.

   Forcing the Mac to boot while ignoring the internal drive may require several attempts. It is difficult to start the Mac and press the proper keys. If you still get a Sad Mac, disconnect all hard drives, including the internal drive, and start your Mac from a floppy. Disconnecting the drives is the only way to determine if your problem is hard-drive-related or hardware-related. If you get the Sad Mac with all hard disks disconnected, you have a hardware problem unrelated to your hard drive. If your Mac starts from the floppy, you need to reinstall the hard disk-drive drivers. The instructions for reinstalling your hard disk's driver are in Chapter 10, "Macintosh Disk Drives."

Danger is involved when you reinstall your hard disk's driver. The driver may not install properly. If there is a problem with the driver installation, your disk asks to be initialized and you have to reformat your drive. Do not attempt to reinstall your driver more than once. Repeated attempts to re-install a driver result in your drive's needing to be formatted. If the driver re-installation is successful, back up your data and reformat your drive. If it is unsuccessful, recover your data and then reformat your drive.

Another way to determine if an external drive's driver is corrupted is to follow these steps, which work only on a drive that is not internally terminated:

1. Turn off the drive.
2. Start your Mac.
3. After the drive has started, turn on the hard drive.
4. Use a disk-mounting utility to mount the drive. If your Mac crashes when you try to mount the drive, the driver is probably corrupted.

Determining If Your Drive Is Dead

When you are deciding whether you should pronounce your drive as dead, use the following guidelines:

❖ Always check the cabling and power connections in case they have become loose. Also, make sure the SCSI ID has not been inadvertently changed.

❖ Whenever possible, test the suspect drive on another Mac.

Service Technicians

Take your drive to someone you trust. Too many times, an Apple dealer tells you that your drive is dead and the data cannot be retrieved. As a rule, dealers do not keep the best people as technicians because they can't pay them enough and the training Apple provides is limited to how to determine the problem and how to swap parts. Therefore, an Apple dealer technician is more apt to want to swap a part than try to find the problem and really fix it. In every metropolitan area you can find people who work on Macs who resort to swapping a part as a last resort. You might want to find one of these technicians.

❖ If more than one drive is attached to your system, remove the other drives and test the suspect drive by itself. A SCSI ID conflict, improper termination, or a bad cable can make any drive feign death.

❖ Make sure your drive is getting power, then turn it on. If your drive does not power up, you could have a stiction problem. Find a hard disk drive expert who understands stiction problems, and maybe he or she can recover your data.

❖ A drive requesting to be reinitialized shortly after it is formatted could be a symptom of a software problem, but it is more likely a problem with the drive. Run the drive with a clean system for the same length of time as the drive ran before crashing, or longer. If the drive fails again with a clean system, test the drive on a different Macintosh. The problem could be with the Mac, not with the drive. If the results are the same on another Mac, the problem is the drive.

❖ Try formatting the drive with the best formatting software you can find. Dead drives often won't format. If you can't format your drive, there is a very good chance it is dead.

Now That My Disk Has Crashed...

There is nothing more distressing than having your drive display the message shown in Figure 19.7.

"What do I do now?" is the first question you ask after crying "Oh, no!" Of course, you want your data back, which means you want to perform a recovery. The cause of your crash could be any number of things, but the real concern is to get your data back. Before you try to recover your drive's data, make sure the request to initialize your disk is the result of a drive problem, not a bad SCSI connection. For this reason,

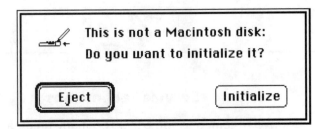

Figure 19.7   *A hard disk requesting to be initialized.*

double-check your cables and all connections after you dismiss the request to initialize. Once you're sure your drive has crashed, you can perform your data recovery.

In general, your drive probably has one or more of the following problems:

- ❖ A corrupted directory
- ❖ An invalid bitmap partition
- ❖ Corrupted volume information
- ❖ A corrupted hard-disk driver
- ❖ Incorrect initialization from the Finder or other utility

In the case of an initialized disk, your directory is completely rewritten so that it displays a blank disk. Of the listed problems, the most serious ones are an initialized disk and an invalid bitmap partition. The other problems can often be repaired by a utility such as Norton Utilities for the Macintosh.

There are three types of disk recoveries: One is actually a repair, the second is a directory recovery, and the last is a file-by-file recovery. With a repair recovery, all you have to do is run your utility package and it will automatically repair your disk's damage, giving you access to all your data. Doing a repair recovery makes modifications directly to the disk that has crashed. It makes correcting changes to the file allocation table, the directories, and the files themselves. If a repair recovery does not work—it is not always successful—the chances of a directory recovery being successful are greatly diminished. You will probably not get any more than you got with the easy recovery, provided you can repair and mount the hard drive.

If you think the damage to your disk is serious, do a directory recovery instead of a repair. The directory recovery allows you to recover files on the crashed disk by copying them to another drive, leaving the crashed disk drive untouched. The directory recovery uses the information in your directory to recover your drive. If the directory is too damaged, the directory recovery does not work and you must resort to the file-by-file recovery method.

Your drive has serious damage when it does not mount or asks to be initialized. With serious damage, your bitmap partition is usually corrupted, and the Mac sees the disk as being unformatted. Sometimes the drive does not ask to be initialized. With serious damage, your disk does not mount, and using a mounting utility does not work either. Your drive is displayed by a SCSI utility, and you can hear it spinning. The SyQuest disk at SCSI ID 6 shown in Figure 19.8 is an example of a disk that is damaged and not mounting. Notice that the name of the disk does not appear in HDT Prober.

Figure 19.8 *A nonmounting disk.*

The third type of recovery, file-by-file recovery, is the same as the procedure used to restore deleted files. The recovery utility scans the hard disk, looking for file-recognizable patterns. When it finds a file pattern it recognizes, the utility copies the file to another drive. The file-by-file recovery can recover files, but it rarely recovers the file's name and never recovers the directory structure. With the large drives in use today, this type of recovery results in thousands of recovered files. All recovered files are without names, and they are all in a single directory.

I'm sure you've figured out that the file-by-file recovery method is the least desirable. To hunt through several thousand files, opening each one, trying to find the few to few hundred you need, is as tedious a task as you will ever do. Often, people give up at this point and try to use their latest backup; they may even re-create their data.

The following sections demonstrate how to recover deleted files and your disk using Norton Utilities for the Macintosh. Norton is not the only utility available, but it is one of the best.

The Basic Disk Recovery Process (Directory Recovery)

Use a directory disk recovery either after you've done a directory recovery (if you think your drive has serious trouble) or if you are willing to live with a partial recovery. The basic recovery steps are similar to what you should do when performing periodic maintenance checks on your drive; this is not just a procedure to recover lost data.

These steps pose potential dangers because Norton's Disk Doctor makes modifications to a drive's directory, allocation blocks, and B-tree when it is run. If you modify these disk structures with Norton Utilities or any other recovery program,

Norton and Disk Recovery Utilities

The instructions in this chapter for recovering a disk are for Norton Utilities 3.5. Two major disk utility programs are on the market: Norton and Central Point's MacTools. These programs are similar in both their features and how they work. If you use MacTools and don't have Norton, read your manual and then follow the steps given in the next section. The procedures are basically the same regardless of which package or version you use.

and don't get your data back, recovering your data is ten times harder, if you get your data back.

Always try these preliminary steps before doing a recovery; it just might be possible to get your drive back without doing a recovery:

1. Check all cables and go through the SCSI Bus troubleshooting procedures previously detailed.
2. Run Apple's Disk First Aid.
3. If the drive does not mount, try to mount it using a mounting utility. If your Mac crashes when mounting the disk, try reinstalling the driver.

Once you've done the preliminary steps, go on with these steps for an easy recovery:

1. Run Norton Utilities, and select Norton Disk Doctor (Figure 19.9).
2. Select the crashed drive from the disk selection window (Figure 19.10). If the drive is not visible, choose the *Show Missing Disks* menu item from the Disks menu. Any disks that weren't mounted but are accessible by Norton appear in the Norton Disk Doctor window. Select the disk you want to recover.
3. Click on the Examine button after selecting your disk (Figure 19.11).
4. Your Mac starts scanning the disk to look for problems. The first problem with the disk in the example is shown in Figure 19.12. As Norton scans your disk, it pops up various messages asking if it should correct the problem. Unless you have a reason for not fixing a specific problem, answer "Yes" to all correction requests.
5. During the repair process, if you see *link, leaf, or catalog b-tree* errors (Figure 19.12), fix them. Reformat the disk after you've recovered and copied all your data from the disk. The disk will not be reliable. After the recovery is

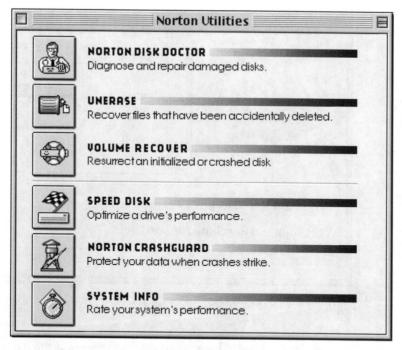

Figure 19.9 *Norton's opening window.*

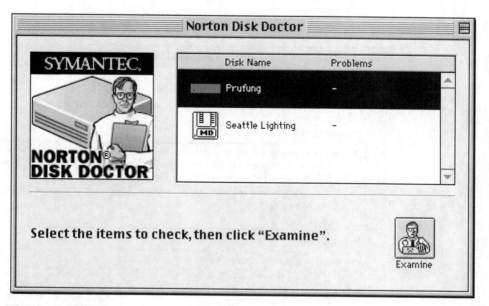

Figure 19.10 *Norton's selection window.*

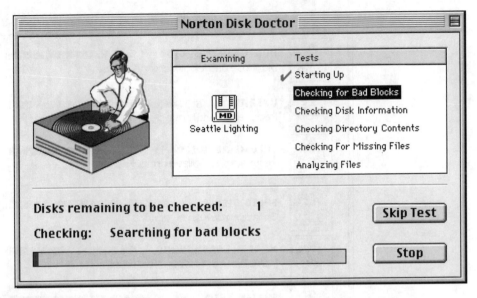

Figure 19.11   *Starting the Norton recovery process.*

complete, your disk appears on the Desktop. If the recovery was not success-ful; perform a directory recovery.

6. A recovery is not successful if filenames are garbled or the disk shows other anomalies like those shown in Figure 19.13, where 38 megabytes are used,

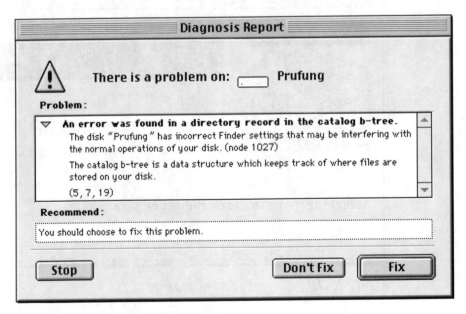

Figure 19.12   *Request to fix a directory error.*

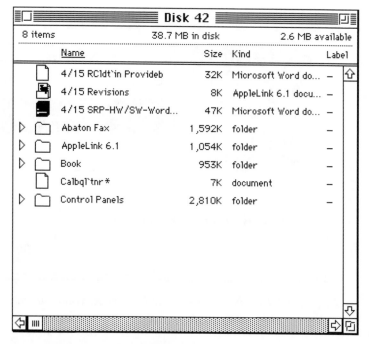

Figure 19.13 *Disk window after recovery.*

but the totals of the displayed files do not equal 38 megabytes. The next step is to see what you can get with a directory recovery.

An Advanced Disk Recovery Procedures (Directory and File-by-File Recoveries)

The first steps for doing a directory recovery are the same as for the easy recovery: Check your cables, do the SCSI troubleshooting, and so on. Where the steps change is in the option you select. Rather than using the Norton Disk Doctor, use the Volume Recover program, as seen in Figure 19.14. The drive selection process is also the same.

If your drive does not appear or if you are trying to recover a disk partition, you need to use the *Add Custom Disks...* menu item from the Disk menu. Figure 19.15 shows the window that appears when you select the *Add Custom Disk...* option.

When your disk does not appear, Norton may need some help. Usually your drive has lost its defining parameters. Unfortunately, you need to get this information before your drive crashes. When you install Norton on your hard drive, you have the option of creating a Volume Information File; you should always create one of these files and then store it on a floppy disk.

If you don't have a VIF file, Norton can guess, but guessing is not always successful. When Norton guesses, it scans your disk for bitmap volumes, ignoring the volume information stored on the disk. Use this option if your directory and/or your volume information blocks are damaged.

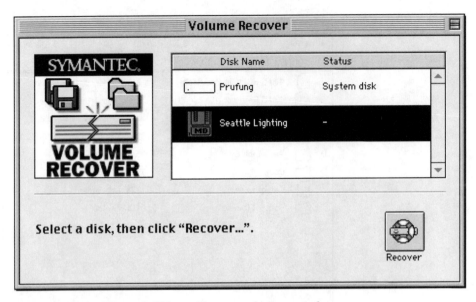

Figure 19.14   *Norton's Volume Recover selection window.*

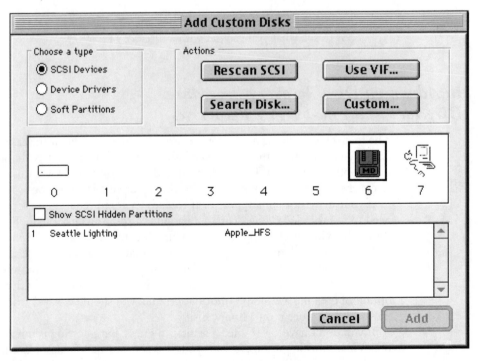

Figure 19.15   *Norton's Add Custom Disks window.*

Norton's FileSaver

FileSaver is a special backup directory that Norton creates and updates periodically. The FileSaver data is created and maintained by the FileSaver control panel. If you add a drive to your system after you have installed Norton, use FileSaver to create a FileSaver data file on the new drive. If you consistently use FileSaver, your data recovery attempt will more than likely be successful. The only time a recovery fails when you've used the FileSaver properly is if the drive is dead. So, the moral is to always use Norton's FileSaver.

The best way to get this information after the fact is to find a disk of the same type as the one that crashed, format it with the same formatter, and use Norton to make a VIF file. Then, use the VIF file with Norton for your drive. Guessing at the values can sometimes work—but not always—and you may have to scan your disk several times, using different parameters until you get the correct ones. If you guess and are partially correct, and if Norton detects what it believes to be the correct parameters, it will ask to change them. To manually enter values use the Custom button. Figure 19.16 shows the parameters Norton asks for when you use the Custom button to define your disk.

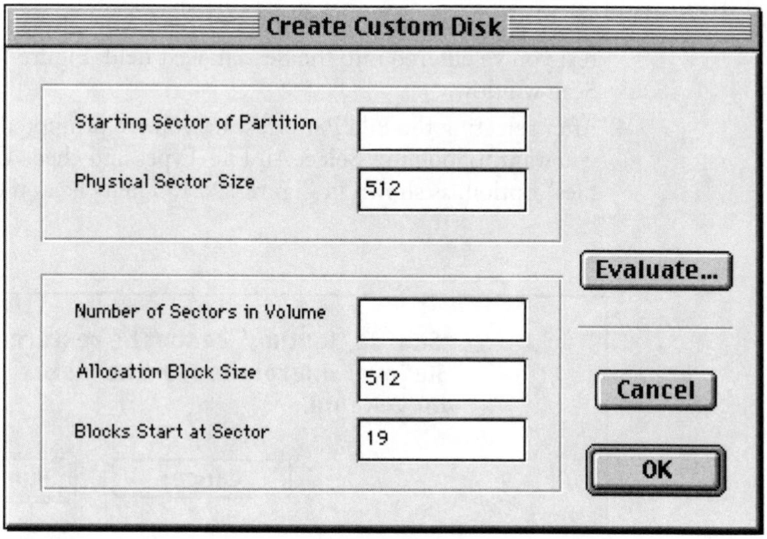

Create Custom Disk	
Starting Sector of Partition	
Physical Sector Size	512
	Evaluate...
Number of Sectors in Volume	
Allocation Block Size	512
	Cancel
Blocks Start at Sector	19
	OK

Figure 19.16   *Norton's Custom Drive Information window.*

The disk type you're recovering is placed into the Volume Recover window. When you click on the Recover button Norton scans the disk for FileSaver data.

After you click the Recover button, go through the following steps:

1. Norton scans the disk for a FileSaver data file. If you were not using FileSaver or if the drive does not contain FileSaver information, Norton asks if you want to run the UnErase program (Figure 19.17).

2. If you were using FileSaver, Norton asks if you want to use the FileSaver data. Say yes. Norton then replaces the disk's directory with the FileSaver data. You have to reboot your Mac and rebuild the Desktop.

3. Norton then replaces the disk's directory with the FileSaver data. You have to reboot your Mac and rebuild the Desktop.

Follow these steps if you do not have FileSaver data on your drive to perform a file-by-file recovery:

1. When UnErase is started, it automatically performs a directory scan. The directory scan offers you the best chance of recovering your files. Figure 19.18 shows the results of a directory scan.

2. If the directory scan is unsuccessful, you do not see the files you want to recover. At this point, select the Search Again button. A dialog box like the one in Figure 19.19 appears.

3. You can do a FileSaver, Directory, a File Pattern, or a Text scan. If you are at this point, then you probably should do the File Pattern scan, which scans the entire drive looking for files that match Norton's predefined file patterns. These file patterns are hard-coded into Norton and updated only when Norton gets updated. Make sure that you always use the latest version of Norton.

   If you use the Text Scan, Norton searches your drive for files containing the text you've entered into the Search Text field. Figure 19.20 shows the Text Scan window.

4. After selecting the File Pattern scan, you are prompted for the types of files you want to look for. Select All File Types and check the Search for "erased files" option, as shown in Figure 19.21. Then click on the Search button.

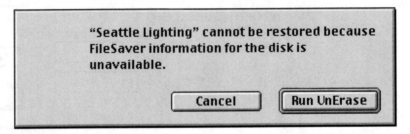

Figure 19.17   The request to run UnErase.

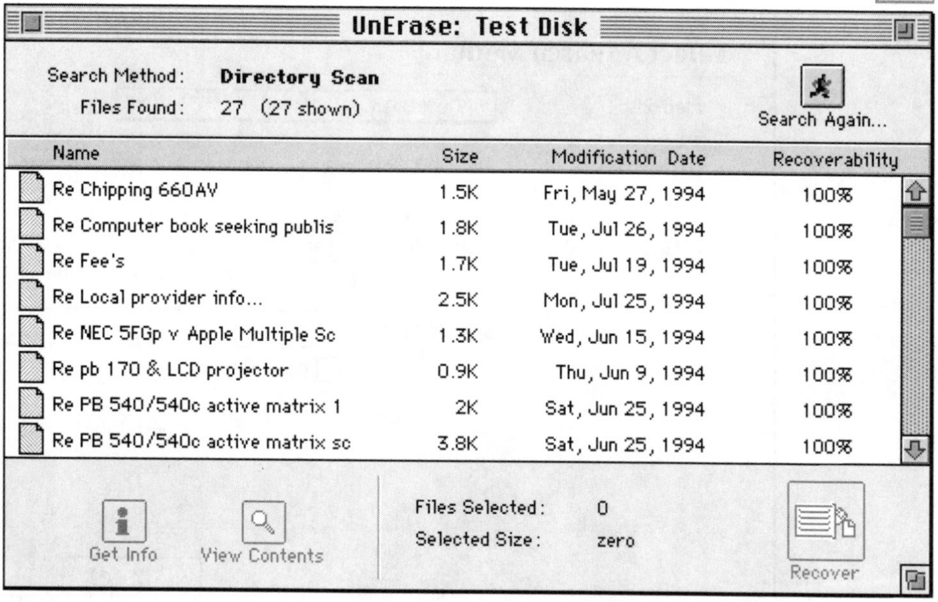

Figure 19.18   *The results of the UnErase directory scan.*

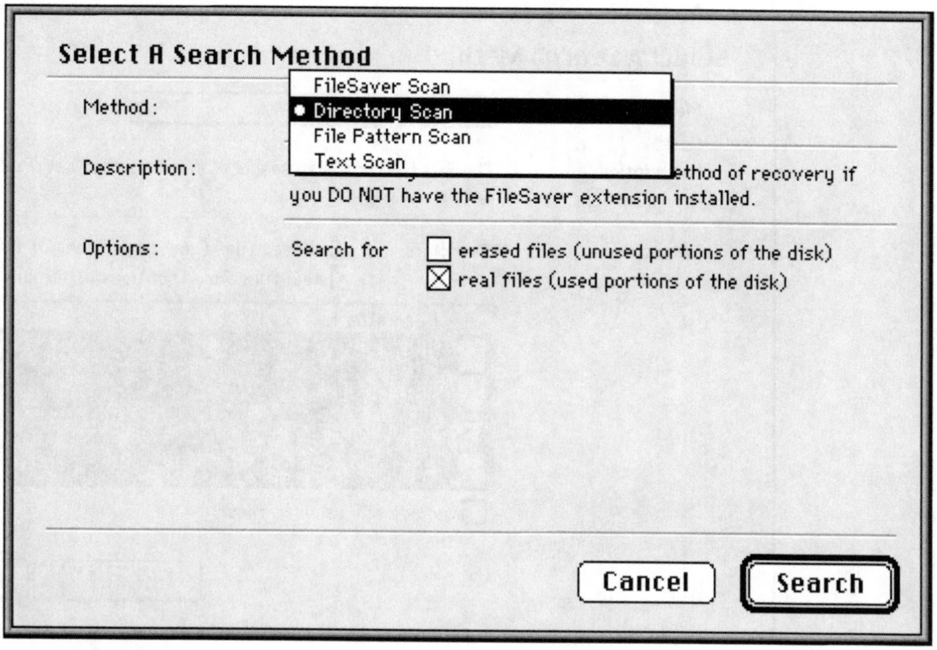

Figure 19.19   *The Select a Search Method dialog box.*

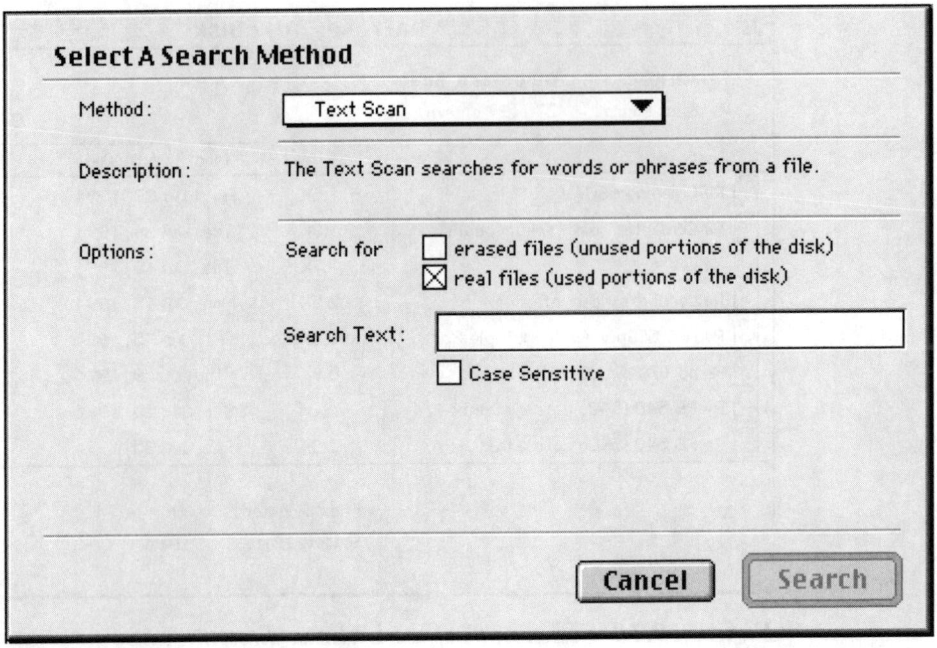

Figure 19.20   *The Text Scan dialog box.*

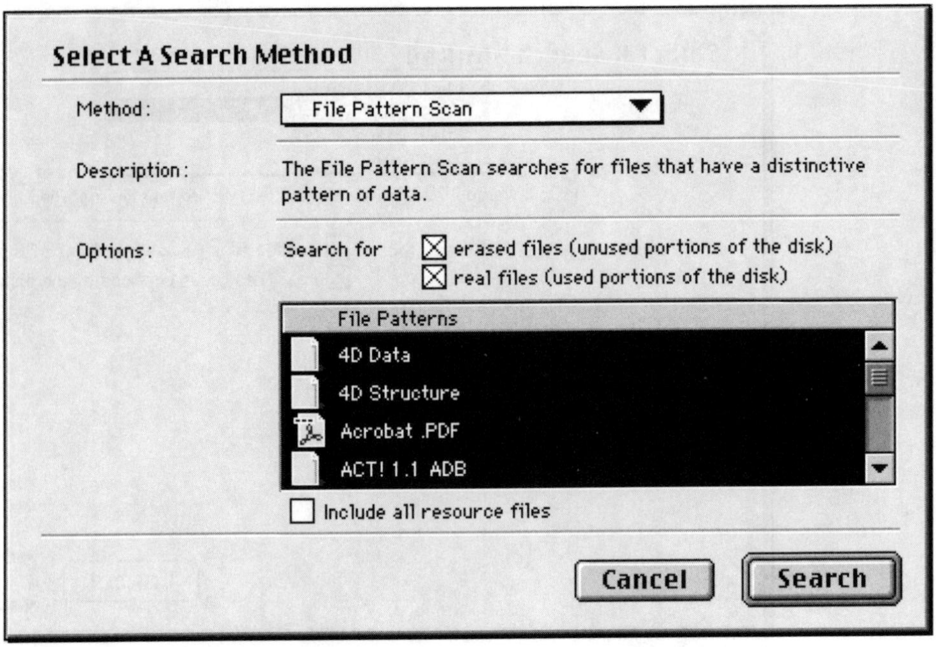

Figure 19.21   *The File Pattern Scan options.*

5. As soon as you have selected your search criteria, Norton searches your drive. This process can take awhile, about 10 to 15 minutes per 150 megabytes.
6. After Norton has finished scanning your drive, a list of files appears. Figure 19.22 shows the results of a File Pattern scan.
7. From this window, select the files to recover. You do not need to recover the entire drive, just the files you want. You have to recover your files to another drive.

After the Recovery

Whenever you recover data, regardless of the method, you should verify its integrity. That you had to recover your data indicates that you had a crisis. There is no sense in compounding the problem by performing a recovery only to discover, after you have reformatted the disk, that the recovery was no good.

Whenever you recover or undelete a file, check it out. Often, your recovered data has icons that can lull you into a false security; the icon means only that the Finder recognized it as a file associated with a specific program. Open the file(s) with the program that created it, double-click on the icons, and check every piece of critical data. At the very least, perform a thorough, random sampling of your files.

If you recover files using the Directory Scan, you get complete file names and the files are recovered in their entirety. The results from the Pattern Matching scan are bit more difficult. The Pattern Matching files do not always have file names, and the

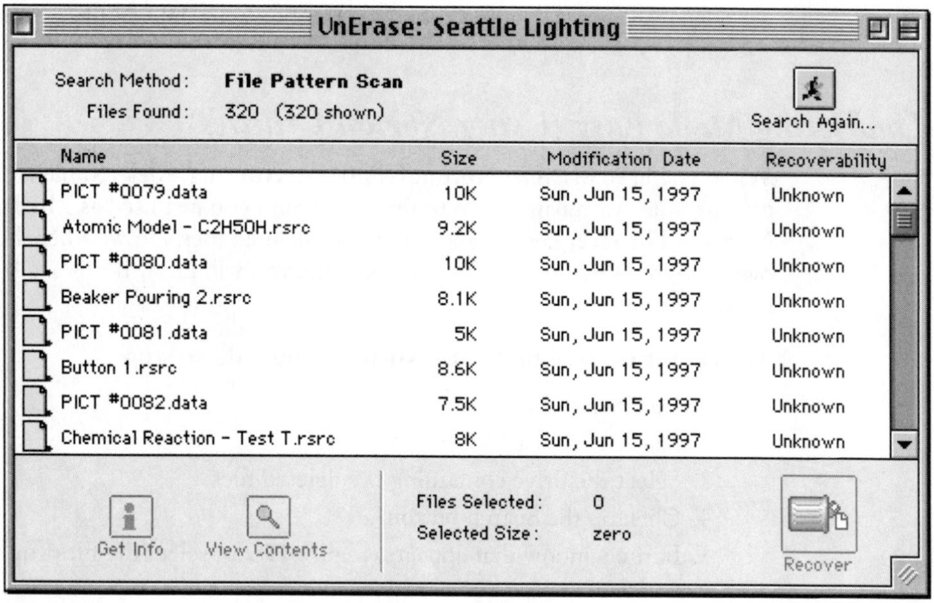
UnErase: Seattle Lighting
Search Method: File Pattern Scan
Files Found: 320 (320 shown)
Search Again...
Name
Size
Modification Date
Recoverability
PICT #0079.data 10K Sun, Jun 15, 1997 Unknown
Atomic Model - C2H5OH.rsrc 9.2K Sun, Jun 15, 1997 Unknown
PICT #0080.data 10K Sun, Jun 15, 1997 Unknown
Beaker Pouring 2.rsrc 8.1K Sun, Jun 15, 1997 Unknown
PICT #0081.data 5K Sun, Jun 15, 1997 Unknown
Button 1.rsrc 8.6K Sun, Jun 15, 1997 Unknown
PICT #0082.data 7.5K Sun, Jun 15, 1997 Unknown
Chemical Reaction - Test T.rsrc 8K Sun, Jun 15, 1997 Unknown
Get Info
View Contents
Files Selected: 0
Selected Size: zero
Recover

Figure 19.22 *The results of the File Pattern Scan.*

files Resource and Data forks are separated. It is not possible to put these files back together, so complex files like page layout files can be recovered only in bits and pieces. To look at the data you've recovered, use your word processor and graphics programs to open the Data forks.

After your data is recovered and before you format your hard drive, back up your data. Back up your data. Back up your data. Once you format your hard drive, all of its data is gone—*no one can get data from a formatted hard drive.*

Recovering Deleted Files

It will happen: Some day, you will place a file into the Trash and empty it. When this happens, you will either wail and gnash your teeth or rejoice because you have a utility installed that lets you dig in the Trash and get back your file. If you don't have such a utility, your chances of recovering the file are the same as those for recovering a disk using the File Pattern scan discussed in the last section.

When a file is deleted, it is not erased from your hard drive; initially it is just removed from your directory. If you do not write anything to your disk after the file is trashed, it is still there. If, however, you copy files onto your disk or save new documents, you stand a chance of overwriting the file. And, if you optimize your drive, the file is overwritten and gone forever. As soon as you know that you have deleted a file that you really need, do not run any programs, copy any files, or use your Mac until you have gotten back the file.

The reason for not running any programs is that many programs create temporary files while they run. Just running some programs can cause data to be written to your drive. And, if your drive is almost full, the temporary file will be written wherever there is space, including the space freed by your deleted file.

Undeleting Made Easy (Using Norton Utilities)

When you have installed Norton Utilities, recovering a deleted file is easier than turning your wastepaper over to find the memo you just used as a basketball. Norton's FileSaver keeps a record of your deleted files and whether they have been overwritten. When you try to undelete one, you will know if it is available in its entirety or only in part.

To recover deleted files with Norton, follow these steps:

1. Run Norton Utilities.
2. Select UnErase.
3. Select the drive containing the deleted files.
4. Click on the Search button.
5. In the window that appears (Figure 19.23), select the files you wish to undelete.
6. Click on the Recover button.

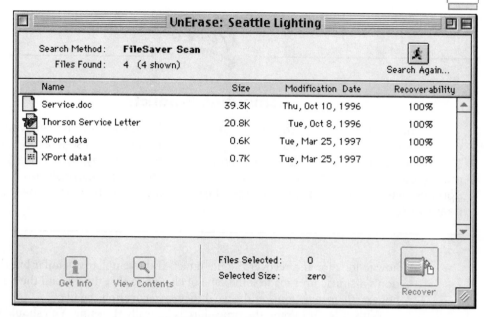

Figure 19.23 *Norton's UnErase window with files.*

The files are restored to a folder called Recovered files on your selected destination disk. It is best not to recover deleted files to their original disk because you could be overwriting files you want to recover.

Norton can be a lifesaver when you accidentally trash the quarterly report or another important document; you can recover it in minutes. If you get a recovery utility other than Norton, and even if you get Norton, read the manual and make sure it is installed properly. Then, practice by deleting a couple of files and recovering them so that you are prepared if and when a crisis occurs.

Oh, No, I Haven't Installed My Disk Utilities!

This is what you say when you trash that file before you purchased or installed your undelete utility. Think back to Chapter 11, where Macintosh files are described: Files can be quite complicated, containing many different attributes or other files even though they appear on the Desktop as a single file. Because of this, more complicated files are harder to recover (for example, files made by QuarkXPress, Excel, and PageMaker).

To recover any file that has been deleted or one that has no directory reference (one of those unfortunate times when your directory gets damaged), use a disk utility that scans your hard drive for files and file fragments. Both MacTools by Central Point Software and Norton Utilities' For the Mac by Symantec scan your hard drive for deleted files . Also, each of these packages has templates for different file types so that when it finds a file, if its structure is similar to a template, the package knows

Competing Products

Although I mention both Norton Utilities and MacTools as disk recovery tools, if you're shopping for a disk recovery program you should purchase Norton Utilities. This is because both products are owned by the same company, Symantec. Symantec purchased Central Point (the original publisher). Since then MacTools has not been updated even though it is still available. I expect to see MacTools disappear in the near future.

how to look for and recover the file intact. If the template is similar but the application's manufacturer made some type of change so that the file and the template do not exactly match, you could have difficulty recovering the file.

With either program, the procedure is basically the same. You should have a second hard disk, or at least a floppy to hold your recovered data and, if possible, to run the program. If the program is installed on your hard disk, you can run it off your drive (do not install either program if you want to recover your deleted files). Otherwise, run the disk utility from another hard drive or a floppy disk. Norton Utilities comes with an emergency disk just for this purpose. The procedure for recovering deleted files using Norton is detailed in the previous section.

Whenever you go after a deleted file, you have to determine whether the time to recover it is worth as much as the file. Sometimes, you could spend more time trying to recover a file than it would take to re-create it. If you have to scan a large drive, it takes about 10 to 15 minutes for every 150 megabytes. And, to perform the operation, you have to scan the entire drive, so a 2 Gig drive could take an hour to scan.

Disk Utility Packages

In this chapter, several disk utilities were mentioned. Each utility has different features, and ideally, you should have at least two different packages: Microcom's 911 utilities and Norton Utilities. But, if you have to choose one, then it probably should be Norton Utilities.

Norton Utilities

Norton Utilities is published by Symantec and delivers more for your money than any other package. It has a complete set of recovery tools, plus a series of disk maintenance utilities that will make your life easier. The extra utilities include backup, disk copy, encryption, and a security disk eraser.

MacTools

Central Point Software has a lot of experience in making disk recovery tools—it has been doing it for years. As a suite of utilities, the package is almost identical to Symantec's. It has recovery tools, an undelete utility, an encryption program, plus a backup package, and don't forget the optimizer. Because Central Point is always running promotions, you can usually get its software at a good price. Even though its tools are not quite as efficient as Norton's, it is still a perfectly adequate package.

Other Utilities

Do not forget to use Apple's Disk First Aid. It does not do a whole lot, but it can save your disk and repair minor directory damage. In addition, remember the antivirus utilities made by Symantec (Anti-Virus Utilities for the Mac) and Microcom (Virex). You should have one of them installed and running.

Summary

Well, that's it. You now have the basic information you need to recover your drive and diagnose almost any other Macintosh problem. To get the most from this chapter, read your utility's manual. The intent of this chapter is to provide you with information about what has gone wrong, not necessarily to walk you through every procedure. If you learn what has happened and the principles for fixing a problem, you can use any utility on the market to recover your data.

One final word of warning: Disk drive problems are complex. I can't emphasize enough how *many* different problems are possible. Most problems you will encounter are discussed in this chapter, but I, of course, cannot describe every one of them. You should, however, have a good foundation on which you can figure out any unusual problems.

Do not forget to back up your data. A backup is always your best recovery tool.

Finder Shortcuts

The following lists all the keyboard shortcuts for performing Finder actions and special startup procedures. This list does not include contextual menu information. To activate a contextual menu, hold the Control key down while clicking on a Finder object.

Actions	Shortcut
Open an icon	Double-click on the icon, press ⌘+Down Arrow, or highlight the icon and press ⌘+O.
Copy an icon into another folder	Hold down the Option key and drag the icon.
Clean up selected icons	Hold down the Shift key and select *Clean Up* from the Special menu.
Clean up and sorting icons	Hold down the Option key and select *Clean Up* from the Special menu.
Select an icon by name	Start typing the name.
Select the next icon in alphabetical order	Press the Tab key.
Select the previous icon in alphabetical order	Hold down the Shift key and press Tab.
Select an icon to the left or right in icon views	Press the Left Arrow or Right Arrow.
Select an icon above or below in icon views	Press the Up Arrow or Down Arrow.

Actions	Shortcut
Select more than one icon	Hold down the Shift key and click on the icons, or drag to enclose them with the marquee.
Make the Desktop active	Hold down the ⌘+Shift keys while pressing the Up Arrow.
Close all windows	Hold down the Option key and select *Close* from the File menu, click the Close box, or press ⌘+W.
Collapse and expand all windows	Hold down the Option key and click in the Collapse box.
Move a window without making it active	Hold down the ⌘ key and drag the window by the title bar.
Display a pop-up menu of the enclosing folders and disk	Hold down the ⌘ key and click on the window title.
Open the window that encloses the active window	Hold down the ⌘ key and press the Up Arrow.
Close a window after opening one of its icons	Hold down the Option key while selecting Open from the File menu, double-click the icon, or press ⌘+W.
Zoom a window to the full size of the screen	Hold down the Option key and click the zoom box.
Change the view	Click a view title in the window header, such as Size or Date.
Expand the outline of the selected folder	Hold down the ⌘ key and press the Right Arrow.
Collapse the outline of the selected folder	Hold down the ⌘ key and press the Left Arrow.
Expand the entire outline of the selected folder	Hold down the ⌘ and Option keys while pressing the Right Arrow.
Collapse the entire outline of the selected folder	Hold down the ⌘ and Option keys while pressing the Left Arrow.
Take a snapshot of the screen	Press the ⌘, Shift, and 3 keys simultaneously.
Delete locked files	Hold down the Option key while selecting *Empty Trash* from the Special menu.

Actions	Shortcut
Avoid seeing a warning message	Hold down the Option key while selecting *Empty Trash* from the Special menu, or Get Info on the Trash and turn off the warning.
Reverse the current setting of "Always snap to grid" while moving an icon	Hold down the ⌘ key and drag the icon.
Rebuild the Desktop file	Hold down the ⌘ and Option keys during startup.
Turn off all system extensions when starting up	Hold down Shift during startup.
Invoke the Location Manager during startup	Hold down the space bar during startup.
Zap the PRAM (Parameter RAM)	On startup, before you see the Smiling Mac, hold down the ⌘, Option, P, and R keys simultaneously. When your Mac restarts, release the keys.
Create a new folder	Press ⌘+N.
Batch-print selected documents	Press ⌘+P.
Eject a floppy disk from Drive 1	Press the ⌘, Shift, and 1 keys simultaneously, or select disk icon and select *Eject* from the Special Menu, or press the ⌘ and E keys.
Eject a floppy disk from Drive 2	Press the ⌘, Shift, and 2 keys simultaneously, or select disk icon and select *Eject* from the Special Menu, or press the ⌘ and E keys.
Get Info on a selected item	Select *Get Info* from the File menu, or press ⌘+I.
Make a copy of a file or folder	Select *Duplicate* from the File menu, or press ⌘+D.
Make an alias	Select *Make Alias* from the File menu, or press ⌘+M.
Put away a file folder or unmount a disk that is on the Desktop	Select *Put Away* from the File menu, or press ⌘+Y.
Find a file or folder by name	Select *Find* from the File menu, or press ⌘+F.

Actions	Shortcut
Search again with the same criteria used with the last find	Select *Find Again* from the File menu, or press ⌘+G.
Close an open window	Select *Close* from the File menu, or press ⌘+W.

BMUG's
Macintosh Revelations
CD-ROM

I ncluded with this book is the BMUG *Revelations* CD-ROM. The CD-ROM contains more than 600MB of software. All the software is shareware, freeware, or demonstration software.

There are 17 categories of software on the BMUG CD-ROM:

Business—This is a collection of utilities, templates, and programs related to business or personal activities. Some of the items are information managers, spreadsheets, and calendar programs as well as templates and macros for Microsoft Excel and Claris's FileMaker Pro.

Demos—This collection is a bunch of demonstration software for commercial products. It contains five categories of software: Business, Education, Games, Graphics, and Utility. This is an opportunity to test-drive some software you might not otherwise see.

What's Shareware?

Shareware is software that is distributed through bulletin board services (BBSs), user groups, and other public distribution methods so that you can try it before you buy. The concept behind shareware is honor-based. If you try the software and like it and use it, then you are bound by honor to pay the prescribed fee to the software's author. Each of the shareware programs has a notice that specifies the software's cost and how to make payment.

Education—Don't think that this is a category for teachers only. It contains the works of Shakespeare, programs that demonstrate computer artificial intelligence, and aids for teachers and students. There's lots of information about a wide variety of subjects.

Fonts—Do you need a special font for that flyer you're putting together? Here, you have more than 16MB of fonts and font utilities that you can use with your publications. The collection of fonts includes both Type 1 PostScript and TrueType fonts.

Games—Games, games, and more games. In this category, you find strategy, adventure, and card and word games, just to name a few. There are enough games here to keep you from ever getting any work done. Be careful—some of them are addictive.

Graphics—This is a collection of graphics programs and utilities. You find banner makers, paint programs, and graphic converters. Check here before you buy another graphics program or utility; you might find what you're looking for.

Information—Do you want to read the Free Trade Agreement (NAFTA)? Well, you can if you wish. It is here. This category is an eclectic collection of miscellaneous information, including some of our country's founding documents.

Internet—This bunch of Internet tools should keep you busy for a few weeks, if not months. Consider this folder to be your advanced Internet education after you read Chapter 14.

Multimedia—Multimedia is a catch-all term for sound, movies, video processing, and electronic publishing. What you find in this category are some tools, movies, and maybe a few ideas.

Newton—Now here is something that is not mentioned in the book anywhere—the Apple MessagePad. If you have one, here are some goodies for you. You have 31 demos and/or shareware programs to explore.

Programming—If you want to tame your Macintosh, you might want to start with this collection of programming utilities and languages. Maybe you will create the next killer application and get rich.

Screen Savers—Here are a few options. If you're tired of looking at the same screen saver or if you need some new After Dark modules, look in this folder. Although it hasn't been updated in a while, I still like Dark Side of the Mac. Actually, I think it is the program's name that I like.

System Enhancements—Here you will find cool control panels, extensions, control strip modules, and other wonderful ways to enhance and (if you're not careful) screw up your system. Read the readme files for anything from this category. If the software modifies how the Finder behaves, be careful. Mac OS 8's Finder doesn't like some of the older programs that make modifications to the Finder. Otherwise, you should have a lot of fun with this stuff.

Telecom—Connect your Mac to the world. In the Telecom folder, you find terminal programs, BBS listings, and First Class BBS settings files. If you use AOL, check out the ArtValve control panel.

Text—Are you tired of SimpleText? Do you want a text editor that does more? Do you want a find function in your text editor? Well, look here and sample the wonderful text tools. You'll find something you like, I'm sure.

Updaters—Do you have the latest version? Maybe we can help. This folder contains updates for 24 different programs. Maybe you can update one of your utilities. You know you've been meaning to, but . . .

Utilities—There are more utilities here than you can use, one for every purpose. It will take you months to explore all of them. If you want extensions or control panels to enhance and streamline the way you work, you find them here. Do you need to change a file's type or creator code, want a different text editor, or some drag-and-drop utilities? They're all here, just waiting to be used.

It would take a book the size of this one to describe everything on the CD-ROM, so you just have to explore the disk. There is an extra benefit with the CD: It gives you an opportunity to really learn about your Mac. As you experiment and use the software on the CD-ROM, you learn how to use different programs, fonts, and other utilities. The CD-ROM has already saved you some money—you'd pay more for the CD-ROM by itself than you did for the book and the CD. Enjoy.

Index